AF183298

Bolivia

Public Policy Options for the Well-Being of All

Edited by

Vicente Fretes-Cibils

Marcelo Giugale

Connie Luff

THE WORLD BANK

WASHINGTON, DC

Copyright © 2006 The International Bank for Reconstruction
and Development / THE WORLD BANK
1818 H Street, N.W.
Washington, D.C. 20433, U.S.A.

All rights reserved
Manufactured in the United States of America
1 2 3 4 09 08 07 06

The findings, interpretations, and conclusions expressed in this paper are entirely those of the authors and should not be attributed in any manner to the World Bank, to its affiliated organizations, or to members of its Board of Executive Directors or the countries they represent. The World Bank does not guarantee the accuracy of the data included in this publication and accepts no responsibility whatsoever for any consequence of their use. The boundaries, colors, denominations, and other information shown on any map in this volume do not imply on the part of the World Bank Group any judgment on the legal status of any territory or the endorsement or acceptance of such boundaries.

The material in this publication is copyrighted. The World Bank encourages dissemination of its work and will normally give permission to reproduce portions of the work promptly.

Permission to *photocopy* items for internal or personal use, for the internal or personal use of specific clients, or for educational classroom use is granted by the World Bank, provided that the appropriate fee is paid directly to the Copyright Clearance Center, Inc., 222 Rosewood Drive, Danvers, Massachusetts 01923, USA; telephone 978-750-8400, fax 978-750-4470. Please contact the Copyright Clearance Center before photocopying items.

For permission to *reprint* individual articles or chapters, please fax a request with complete information to the Republication Department, Copyright Clearance Center, fax 978-750-4470.

All other queries on rights and licenses should be addressed to the Office of the Publisher, World Bank, at the address above or faxed to 202-522-2422.

Library of Congress Cataloging-in-Publication Data has been applied for.

Contents

Part II
With Benefits for All

Part III
Without Corruption and with Civic Participation

Preface

After many years of severe institutional crisis, Bolivia is reorienting its development strategy and closing the gap between the country's problems and effective solutions. The recent elections brought Bolivia its first indigenous President, whose party is supported by the majority of the population. This support provides the government with an opportunity to strengthen the country's political stability and move forward in its development.

The new government is confronting the challenge of building a state that is more inclusive and effective. Its initiatives to achieve that objective include the Constituent Assembly, the introduction of public policies that modify obligations and rights, and efforts designed to revitalize the participation of the state in the national economy. This is a turning point from which a new Bolivia will emerge. Nevertheless, a variety of risks may prevent positive results, even when intentions are good. Bolivia can take a step forward to proactively integrate itself within the global market, or it can prolong, or even exacerbate, the stagnation that has hindered its economic and social development for many years.

The purpose of this book is to contribute to the debate on how to confront the challenges that Bolivia faces today. It is composed of a series of studies on the current reality of Bolivia and has been developed in conjunction with national and international public policy experts. The studies present a diagnostic by sector, a summary of the main challenges, and public policy recommendations aimed at meeting these challenges.

We seek to contribute ideas about what can be done to help the country grow equitably, with a transparent and efficient government that provides improved social services to its population. We are all committed to this goal, and we are confident that Bolivia has the ability to achieve it.

Pamela Cox
Vice-president
Latin America and Caribbean Office
Washington, D.C.
May 19th, 2006

Acknowledgments

This publication is the result of a team effort, and because of this, it benefits from many valuable contributions. Our acknowledgements are directed to a great number of people. First of all, to the main authors—Sara Calvo, Carlos Mollinedo, Julio Velasco, Steven Webb, Yira Mascaró, Javier Bolzico, Alberto Didoni, Paola Granata, M. Goldberg and W. Tyler, Eleodoro Mayorga and Alejandro Tapia, Marcelo Olarreaga, Omar Arias, Raja Bentaouet, José Pablo Gómez, Ian Walter, Rafael Rofman, Franz Drees and Alejandro Tapia, Ernesto Sánchez Triana, Carolina Urrutia and Abel Mejía, David Tuchschneider, Malcom Childress, Ruth Llanos, Marcela Silva, Edgardo Mosqueira, Azul del Villar, Marco Scuriatti, Lisa L. Bhansali, Jonas Frank and Christopher Humphrey. Their commitment to Bolivia is highly appreciated.

Even though this book is the compilation of the authors' points of view (and not necessarily those of the World Bank, its Executive Board, or its Countries Members), its production has been institutionalized at the World Bank. We want to express thanks, particularly, for the suggestions of Guillermo Perry (Chief Economist for Latin American and the Caribbean) and of Dan Biller, Pablo Gottret, Aurelio Menéndez, Richard Newfarmer, and Augusto de la Torre. It is also important to aknowledge the support of the World Bank Sector Leaders who carefully reviewed this document: Maria Donoso Clark, Daniel Cotlear, Franz Dress-Gross ,and Vicente Fretes-Cibils.

Likewise, as interested counterparts, it is essential to thank the President of Bolivia, Mr. Evo Morales; the Minister of Planning and Development, Mr. Carlos Villegas; the Minister of Micro Enterprise and Productivity, Mrs. Celinda Sossa; and Hernando Larrazabal, Viceminister of Public Investment, who were committed to the idea of producing this book.

We acknowledge, as well, the great contributions of the participants in the Discussion Notes Workshop, which was held on March 17, 2006, in La Paz, Bolivia. This workshop not only gathered many of the authors, but moreover included government authorities and technical staff of the new administration. A special mention to those who helped with the organization of this event from the government side, Claudia Cardenas, Ivonne Cuba, and Glenda Brozovic; and from the World Bank, essential efforts and constant support were provided by Carmen Romero, Claudia Encinas, Rocío Recalde, Fernanda Padrón, Elma Rossel, Jose Francisco Irias, Rosario Pinto, Monica Claros, Gonzalo Klein, and Gabriela Carrasco.

Finally, were are most grateful to Juan Luis Guillén of Global Communications, who reviewed and improved the style and argumentation of this book, and to Martin Sanchez and Rubén Salinas, in charge of the design and publishing. The English language volume has come into existence thanks to Randy B. Hecht and Carol Levie of Grammarians under the direction of Mellen Candage. Thanks are also extended to Nancy Lammers, Santiago Pombo-Bejarano, and Stuart Tucker in the World Bank's Office of the Publisher for their various roles. As well, it is important to recognize that the production of the following document is a reality thanks to the contributions and efforts of Rafael Archondo and Michael Geller.

Editor Biographies

Vicente Fretes-Cibils, a native of Argentina, completed his undergraduate work at Argentina's Universidad Nacional Del Nordeste and subsequently pursued postgraduate studies at the university of Pennsylvania and North Carolina State University, where he received, respectively, a master's degree in business administration and a PhD in economics. Following his university studies, he joined the World Bank in 1987 through the Young Professionals Program. Following stints in the bank's Office of the Vice-President for Europe and the Middle East and its Treasury Department, he served from 1988 to 1992 as Economist in the Office of the Vice-President for West Africa operations. Later, from 1992 to 1996, he served as Chief Economist in the Department of Operations for Andean countries, supervising adjustment programs and heading up economic and analytical missions to Bolivia. From 1996 to 2002, Mr. Fretes-Cibils served as Senior Economist for Venezuela, and subsequently for Colombia and Mexico. Currently, he is Lead Economist in the Poverty Reduction and Economic Management sector for the subregion of countries that includes Bolivia, Ecuador, Peru, and Venezuela. Additionally, he has taught at Argentina's Universidad Nacional del Nordeste and at North Carolina State University; and he has published numerous works addressing topics in the areas of finance, applied econometrics, public finance, international economics, and economic development.

Marcelo Giugale, an Argentine/Italian national, holds a PhD and MSc in Economics from London School of Economics and a B. A. in Economics from Universidad Catolica Argentina. After a spell in academia, he joined the World Bank's Young Professionals Program in 1989 as an economist in the financial research department. From 1990 to 1994, he was a Senior Economist in the Middle East Operations Vice-Presidency, supervising Egypt's structural adjustment program and leading the Bank's reconstruction work in post-war Lebanon. From 1994 to 1998, Mr. Giugale was Principal Economist in the Eastern Europe and Central Asia Region, responsible for the Bank's lending and analytical economic work in Lithuania and Kazakhstan. In September 1998, he became the Lead Economist for the Colombia-Mexico-Venezuela Department. He is currently the Director of the Bank's Andean countries Department (Peru, Ecuador, Bolivia, and Venezuela). He has held teaching positions at London School of Economics and American University in Cairo and has many publication credits in the areas of applied econometrics, finance, business economics, and economic development.

CONNIE LUFF, an American native, completed her master's degree, with honors, in Business Administration from the Escuela de Negocios (ESADE) in Spain. She joined the World Bank in 1988. Since then, she has worked with several countries in different regions from the Headquarters Office in Washington, D.C. In addition, she served in Africa and Latin America in countries such as Cameroun, Congo, Chad, Gabon, Mexico, Colombia, Ecuador, Venezuela, and Bolivia. She worked and lived for two years in Mexico, and in July 2004 was assigned as Country Manager for the World Bank in Bolivia.

Acronyms

AASANA	*Administración de Aeropuertos y Servicios a la Navegación Aérea (*Airports and Air Navigation Services Administration)
AFP	*Administradoras de Fondos de Pensiones* (Pension Funds Administrators)
AIN-C	*Atención Integral a la Niñez Comunitario* (Integral Attention to Community Childhood)
AMP	Aid Management Platform
ASOFIN	*Asociación de Entidades Financieras Especializadas en Micro Finanzas de Bolivia* (Association of Bolivian Financial Entities Specializing in Micro-Finance)
ATPDEA	*Ley de Promoción Comercial Andina y de Erradicación de Drogas* (Andean Trade Promotion and Drug Eradication Act)
BCB	Central Bank of Bolivia
BIAPE	*Banco Interamericano de Ahorro y Préstamo* (Inter-American Savings and Loan Bank).
BONOSOL	*Bono Solidario* (Solidarity Bond)
BUN	*Banco Unión*
CAF	*Corporación Andina de Fomento* (Andean Development Corporation)
CAP	*Coeficiente de Adecuación Patrimonial* (Capital Adequacy Ratio)
CAPYS	*Comités de Agua Potable y Saneamiento* (Potable Water and Sanitation Committees)
CDF	Comprehensive Development Framework
CECAC	*Comisión Especial de Constitución de la Asamblea Constituyente* (Special Commission for Convening the Constitutional Reform Assembly)
CEDEIM	*Certificado de Devolución Impositivo* (Tax Refund Certificate)
CELADE	*Centro Latinoamericano y Caribeño de Demografía*
CEMLA	*Centro de Estudios Monetarios Latinoamericanos* (Latin American Monetary Studies Center)
CEPO	Educational Councils of Original Peoples
CEPROBOL	*Centro de Promoción Bolivia* (confederation of private businesspeople)

CG	Consultative Group
CIDA	Canadian International Development Agency
CIM/GTZ	German Agency for Technical Cooperation - Center for International Migration and Development
CISE	*Consejo Interinstitucional de Seguimiento y Evaluación* (Inter-Institutional Follow-up and Evaluation Council)
CJ	*Consejo de la Judicatura* (Judicial Council)
CNCV	*Cuenta Nacional de Conservación Vial* (National Roads Maintenance Fund)
CNPV	*Censo Nacional de Población y Vivienda* (National Population and Housing Census)
COA	*Control Operativo de Aduanas* (Customs Operating Control unit)
COFOG	Classification of Functions of Governments
CONACAL	*Consejo Nacional para el Control de Calidad* (National Quality Control Council)
CONAPES	*Consejo Nacional de Política Económica y Social* (National Economic and Social Policy Council)
CPI	Corruption Perceptions Index (by Transparency International)
CSJ	*Corte Suprema de Justicia* (Supreme Court of Justice)
DAC	Development Assistance Committee (of the OECD)
DEA	Drug Enforcement Agency (US)
DEL	*Esquemas de Desarrollo Local* (Local Development Endeavors)
DFID	Department for International Development (UK)
DGAC	*Dirección General de Aviación Civil* (General Directorate of Civil Aviation)
DGAG	*Dirección General de Asuntos de Género* (General Directorate on Gender Affaire)
DGCP	*Dirección General de Crédito Público* (General Directorate of Public Credit)
DILOS	*Directorios Locales de Salud* (Local Health Boards)
DMI	*Distritos Municipales Indígenas* (Indigenous Municipal Districts)
DNBP	*Diálogo Nacional Bolivia Productiva* (Productive Bolivia National Dialogue)
DUF	*Directorio Único de Fondos* (Unified Funding Board)
EBRP	*Estrategia Boliviana por la Reducción de la Pobreza* (Bolivian Poverty Reduction Strategy)
ECLAC	Economic Commission for Latin America and the Caribbean (of the UN)
EFP	*Estatuto del Funcionario Público* (Civil Service Rules)
EIB	*Educación Intercultural Bilingüe* (Intercultural Bilingual Education)

EIH	*Encuesta Integrada de Hogares* (Integrated Household Survey)
ENDSA	*Encuesta Nacional de Demografía y Salud* (National Demography and Health Survey)
ENE	*Encuesta Nacional de Empleo* (National Employment Survey)
ENFE	*Empresa Nacional de Ferrocarriles del Estado* (government-owned railroad company)
EPSAs	*Entidades Prestadoras de Servicios de Agua Potable y Alcantarillado Sanitario* (Potable Water and Sewage Systems Service Provider Entibies)
EPZs	Export processing zones
EXTENSA	*Programa Nacional de Extensión de Coberturas de Salud* (National Health Coverage Extension Program)
FASF	*Fondo de Apoyo al Sistema Financiero* (Financial System Support Fund)
FCA	*Ferrocarril Andina*
FCC	*Fondos de Capitalización Colectivo* (Collective Capitalization Funds)
FCO	*Ferrocarril Oriental*
FDC	*Fondo de Desarrollo Campesino* (Peasant Development Fund)
FERE	*Fondo Especial de Reactivación Económica* (Special Economic Reactivation Fund)
FINRURAL	*Asociación de Instituciones Financieras para el Desarrollo Rural* (Association of Financial Institutions for Rural Development)
FNDR	*Fondo Nacional de Desarrollo Regional* (National Fund for Regional Development)
FONAMA	*Fondo Nacional para el Medio Ambiente* (National Fund for the Environment)
FONDESIF	*Fondo de Desarrollo del Sistema Financiero y de Apoyo al Sector Productivo* (Fund for the Development of the Financial Sector and for Support to the Productive Sector)
FONPLATA	*Fondo Financiero para el Desarrollo de la Cuenca del Plata* (Financial Fund for the Development of the El Plata Basin)
FORADE	*Fondo para la Reducción de Riesgos y Atención de Desastres* (Risk Reduction and Disaster Response Fund)
FPS	*Fondo de Inversión Productivo y Social* (Productive and Social Investment Fund)
FRF	*Fondo de Recapitalización Financiera* (Financial Recapitalization Fund)
FSN	*Fondo de Solidaridad Nacional* (National Solidarity Fund)
FUNDASAB	*Fundación de Apoyo a la Sostenibilidad en Saneamiento Básico* (Foundation in Support of Sustainability in Basic Sanitation)

FUNDESNAP	*Fundación para el Desarrollo de Sistema Áreas Naturales Protegidas* (Foundation for the Development of Natural Protected Area Systems)
GA	*Gravamen Arancelario* (Duties)
GDP	Gross domestic product
GFS	Government Finance Statistics
GTL	Gas-to-liquid
HDI	Human Development Index
HPIC	Heavily Indebted Poor Countries
IACC	Inter-American Convention against Corruption
IALS	International Adult Literacy Survey
IBTA	*Instituto Boliviano de Tecnología Agropecuaria* (Bolivian Agricultural Technology Institute)
ICE	*Impuesto a los Consumos Específicos* (Specific Consumption Tax)
IDA	International Development Association
IDB	Inter-American Development Bank
IDH	*Impuesto Directo sobre los Hidrocarburos* (Direct Tax on Hydrocarbons)
IEHD	*Impuesto Especial sobre los Hidrocarburos y sus Derivados* (Special Tax on Hydrocarbons and Derivatives)
ILO	Internacional Labour Organisation
IMF	International Monetary Fund (of the World Bank)
INE	*Instituto National de Estadísticas* (National Statistics Institute)
INRA	*Instituto Nacional de Reforma Agraria* (National Agrarian Reform Institute)
IOPS	International Organization of Pension Supervisors
IPBIVA	*Impuesto sobre la Propiedad de Bienes Inmuebles y Vehículos Automotores* (Real Property and Motor Vehicles Tax)
IRP	*Impuesto a la Renta de Personas Naturales* (personal income tax)
IRPE	*Impuesto a la Renta Presunta de Empresas* (Presumed Corporate Income Tax)
IT	*Impuesto a las Transacciones* (transaction tax)
ITC	International Trade Center
ITF	*Impuesto a las Transacciones Financieras* (Financial Transactions Tax)
IUE	*Impuesto a las Utilidades de las Empresas* (Corporate Earnings Tax)
IUM	*Impuesto a las Utilidades Mineras* (Tax on Mining Income)
JMP	United Nations Joint Monitoring Programme for Water Supply and Sanitation
LAIA	Latin American Integration Association

LDA	*Ley de Descentralización Administrativa* (Administrative Decentralization Act)
LDN	*Ley del Diálogo Nacional* (National Dialogue Act)
LGA	*Ley General de Aduanas* (General Customs Act)
LLECE	*Laboratorio Latinoamericano de Evaluación de la Calidad de la Educación* (Latin American Laboratory for Assessment of Quality in Education)
LNG	Liquid natural gas
LPG	Liquid propane gas
LPP	*Ley de Participación Popular* (Popular Participation Act)
MAS	*Movimiento al Socialismo* (Movement to Socialism)
MDGs	Millennium Development Goals
MDRI	Multilateral Debt Relief Initiative
MECOSUR	*Mercado Común del Sur* (Common Market of the Southern Cone)
MECOVI	*Encuesta de Mejoramiento de Condiciones de Vida* (Survey on Improvement in Living Conditions)
MEFs	Microfinance entities
MINEDU	*Ministerio de Educación* (Ministry of Education)
MSD	*Ministerio de Salud y Deportes* (Ministry of Health and Sports)
NAFIBO	*Nacional Financiera Boliviana* (Bolivian National Financier)
NDF	Nordic Development Fund
NGO	Non-governmental organization
NIT	Enrollment number
ODA	Official development assistance
OECD	Organisation for Economic Co-operation and Development
OTB	*Organizaciones Territoriales de Base* (Territorial Base Organizations)
PAHO	Pan American Health Organization
PAI	*Plan de Acciones Inmediatas* (Immediate Action Plan)
PAN	*Programa Nacional de Atención al Niño y a la Niña*
PEI	*Proyectos Educativos Indígenas* (Indigenous Educational Projects)
PEN	*Proyectos Educativos de Núcleo* (Cluster Educational Projects)
PER	*Proyectos Educativos de Red* (School System Educational Projects)
PEU	*Proyectos Educativos de Unidad Educativa* (Instructional Unit Educational Projects)
PFFs	Private financial funds
PHRD	Policy and Human Resources Development Fund (Japan)
PIA	*Plan Integral Anticorrupción* (Integral Anticorruption Plan)
PISA	Programme for International Student Achievement

PLANE	*Plan Nacional de Empleo de Emergencia* (National Emergency Employment Plan)
PMAP	*Programa Multidonante de Apoyo Presupuestario* (Multi-Donor Budget Support Program)
PNC	*Política Nacional de Compensación* (National Compensation Policy)
PNN	*Programa Nacional de Nutrición* (National Nutrition Program)
POMA	*Plan Operacional Multi Annual* (Multi-Annual Operating Plan)
PRI	*Proyecto de Reforma Institucional* (Institutional Reform Project)
PROFOP	*Programa de Fortalecimiento Patrimonial* (Capital Strengthening Program)
PROMA	*Programa de Reforma y Modernización de la Administración de Aduanas* (Customs Administration Reform and Modernization Program)
PROME	*Proyectos Educativos Municipales* (Municipal Educational Projects)
PROPAIS	*Programa contra la Pobreza y Apoyo a la Inversión Solidaria* (Program Against Poverty and in Support of Investments in Solidarity)
PROSABAR	*Programa de Saneamiento Básico Rural* (Basic Rural Sanitation Program)
PROSIN	*Programa Integral de Salud* (Integral Health Program)
PRSP	Poverty Reduction Strategy Paper
PTC	*Política de Transferencia Condicionales*
RAU	*Regimen Agropecuario Unificado* (Unified Agricultural System)
RC-VAT	Tax on the Supplementary Regime to the VAT
RDA	*Registro Docente Administrativo* (Administrative Teaching Staff Registry)
RIPS	*Red Integral de Protección Social* (Comprehensive Social Welfare Network)
RITEX	*Régimen de Internación Temporal para Exportación* (Temporary Importation Regime for Exports Development)
RPS	*Red de Protección Social* (Integrated Social Protection Network)
RTS	*Regimen Tributario Simplificado* (Simplified Tax System)
SAFCO	*Ley del Sistema de Administración Financiera y Control Gubernamental* (Financial Administration System and Governmental Control Law)
SAFIS	*Sociedades Administradoras de Fondos de Inversió* (investment companies)
SAG	*Subsecretaría de Asuntos de Género* (Vice Secretariat on Gender Affairs)

SBEF	*Superintendencia de Bancos y Entidades Financieras* (Superintendency of Banks and Financial Entities of Bolivia)
SBPC	*Sistema Boliviano de Productividad y Competitividad* (Bolivian Productivity and Competitiveness System)
SBS	*Seguro Básico de Salud* (Basic Health Insurance)
SEDES	*Servicio Departamental de Salud* (Departmental Health Service)
SEDUCA	*Servicio Departamental de Educación* (Departmental Education Service)
SENASAG	*Servicio Nacional de Sanidad Agropecuaria e Inocuidad Alimentaria* (National Agricultural Health and Food Safety Service)
SENASIR	*Servicio Nacional del Sistema de Reparto* (National Apportionment System Service)
SEPCAMs	*Servicios Prefecturales de Caminos* (Prefecture Roads Services)
SERNAP	*Servicio Nacional de Áreas Protegidas* (National Protected Areas Service)
SIAS	*Sistema de Información Sectorial en Agua y Saneamiento* (Water and Sanitation Information System)
SIBTA	*Sistema Boliviano de Tecnología Agropecuaria* (Bolivian Agricultural Technology System)
SICOES	*Sistema de Información de Contrataciones Estatales* (Government Procurements Information System)
SIDUNEA	*Sistema Aduanero Automatizado* (Automated Customs System)
SIG	Geographic information system
SIGADE	*Sistema de Gestión y de Análisis de la Deuda* (Debt Management and Analysis System)
SIGMA	*Sistema de Información y Administración Financiera* (Information and Financial Administration System)
SIMECAL	*Sistema de Medición y Evaluación de Calidad de la Educación* (Educational Quality Measurement and Evaluation System)
SIN	*Servicio de Impuestos Nacionales* (National Tax Service)
SIP	*Sociedad de Instrucción Primaria* (Primary Instruction Society)
SIRESE	*Sistema de Regulación Sectoral* (Central Bank and the Sector Regulation System)
SISAB	*Superintendencia de Saneamiento Básico* (Superintendency of Basic Sanitation)
SISE-ODM	*Sistema para el Seguimiento y Evaluación de los Objetivos de Desarrollo del Mileni* (Follow-up and Evaluation System for Implementing the Millennium Development Goals)
SISFIN	*Sistema de Seguimiento Financiero* (Financial Follow-up System)
SISPLAN	*Sistema Nacional de Planificación* (National Planning System)

SITE	*Sistema de Transferencias Electrónicas* (Electronic Transfers System)
SLIM	*Servicios Legales Integrales* (Integral Legal Services)
SMEs	Small and medium enterprises
SNAP	*Sistema Nacional de Áreas Protegidas* (National Protected Areas Service)
SNC	*Servicio Nacional de Caminos* (National Roads Service)
SNII	*Servicio Nacional de Impuestos Internos* (old Internal Revenue Service)
SNIS	National Health Information System
SNMAC	*Sistema de Normalización, Metrología, Acreditación y Certificación* (Standards, Measurements, Accreditation and Certification System)
SOAT	*Seguro Obligatorio de Accidentes Personales* (Mandatory Personal Accident Insurance)
SPVS	*Superintendencia de Pensiones, Valores y Seguros* (Superintendency of Pensions, Securities and Insurance)
STI	*Sistema Tributario Integrado* (Integrated Tax System)
SUMI	*Seguro Universal Materno-Infantil* (Universal Mother/Child Insurance)
SWAp	Sector Wide Approaches
TA	*Tribunal Agrario Nacional* (National Agrarian Court)
TC	*Tribunal Constitucional* (Constitutional Court)
TCF	Trillion cubic feet
TCO	*Tierras Comunitarias de Origen* (Original Community Lands)
TIMSS	Trends in International Mathematics and Science Study
UCAELR	*Unidad de Control de Activos de Entidades en Liquidación y/o Reestructuración* (Control Unit for Assets of Entities in Liquidation and/or Undergoing Restructuring)
UDAPE	*Unidad de Análisis de Políticas Económicas y Sociales* (Economic and Social Policies Analysis Unit)
UFL	*Unidad Fondos en Liquidación* (Funds in Liquidation)
UFV	*Unidades de Fomento a la Vivienda* (Housing Development Units)
UNASBVI	*Unidades de Servicios Básicos y Vivienda* (Basic Services and Housing Units)
UNDAF	United Nations Development Assistance Framework
UNDP	United Nations Development Programme
UNFPA	United Nations Population Fund
UNICEF	United Nations Children's Fund
UPEPP	*Unidad de Planificación Estratégica y Participación Popular* (Strategic Planning and Popular Participation Unit)
USAID	United States Agency for International Development

UTIM	*Unidades Técnicas Internas del Municipio* (Internal Technical Units of the Municipality)
VAT	Value-added tax
VIPFE	*Viceministerio de Presupuesto y Financiamiento Externo* (Vice-Ministry on the Budget and External Financing)
VMT	*Viceministerio de Transporte* (Vice Ministry of Transportation)
WEF	World Economic Forum
WHO	World Health Organization
YPFB	*Yacimientos Petrolíferos Fiscales Bolivianos* (Bolivian oil company)

Overview

Vicente Fretes-Cibils

I. Context

Bolivia has a historic opportunity to reduce poverty and social exclusion through (i) sustained high economic growth that creates jobs; (ii) public services that benefit all; and (iii) public administration that is transparent and participatory. Two factors support this opportunity, one socio-political and the other economic. On the social-political side, the Bolivian people have elected representatives from groups historically excluded from political and economic power. Moreover, for the first time in recent years, an absolute majority of the voters elected the President of the Republic. This is the first administration of the current democratic period directly elected by the people, rather than through a second-round congressional vote. The popular mandate also extends to the Congress, as the party in office holds more than half of the 157 congressional seats. This new political panorama allows for an institutional solution to one of the most unstable periods in the democratic history of the country.

A relatively good economic context accompanies the favorable political and social conditions. The economy is experiencing a notable recovery following the slowdown period at the start of the decade. Due to good economic and financial management and a benign international context, the gross domestic product (GDP) is expanding at an annual real rate of 4 percent, and exports have reached the record level of about US$2.7 billion. The fiscal deficit, which amounted to 9 percent of the GDP in 2003, dropped to 1.6 percent of the GDP in 2005, the lowest level in the last 15 years. International reserves are at record levels (equivalent to almost nine months of imports of goods) and the financial system, though reduced to two-thirds of its size with respect to the year 2000, has remained stable and has gradually recovered bank deposits. In addition, Bolivia will reap the benefits of external debt forgiveness on the order of approximately US$1.7 billion. Moreover, the Hydrocarbons

Law has generated an annual increase of about US$600 million in fiscal revenue (23 percent of tax revenue in 2005), even though this law could harm the development of the gas industry in the mid term. Thus, the new administration enjoys initial conditions favorable to promoting the economic and social development that the country demands.

Despite these favorable conditions, the challenges facing the government are significant, and there is limited time and opportunity to address them. Poverty is high, with two out of every three Bolivians poor and one in four indigent. There is a large gap in the distribution of wealth (the richest 20 percent of the population controls almost half of total wealth), and nine out of every ten Bolivians (poor and non-poor alike) believe that this distribution is unjust. Economic and financial stability is fragile and vulnerable to internal (especially, political and social) and external (especially, economic and financial) changes. Recent economic growth, although positive, is insufficient to reverse poverty and inequality, and investment is insufficient to sustain economic growth. In addition, the basic public services of education, health, social welfare, pensions, water, sanitation, and transportation are still deficient and barely accessible for the poor, rural, and indigenous population, even though their coverage has notably improved over the past fifteen years. In addition to all this, the country depends heavily on financial transfers from the international community (approximately 7.5 percent of GDP on average annually during the past decade). The institutional framework is weak, with corruption and distrust toward the judicial system and a perception of impunity in the face of crimes. Looking toward the immediate future, expectations are high for the Constitutional Assembly to change the Constitution and a referendum on autonomy that would widen the redistribution of natural resources and increase decentralization, which may affect political stability.

The challenge to live better, with less poverty and greater inclusion, is multifaceted, profound and urgent. The World Bank would like to contribute to the discussion on how best to respond to these challenges. Accordingly, the World Bank makes this book available for consideration by the Bolivian people and their new government. In addition to this synthesis chapter, the book contains twenty-three chapters that reflect the national and international experience of World Bank staff and experts contracted especially to conduct this study. The chapters include a diagnosis of issues that cover the full spectrum of economic and social development—among others, macroeconomic management, the financial sector, rural development, health, education, the environment, transportation, the public sector, the justice system, and decentralization. To obtain the best results for all Bolivians, each chapter presents a series of public policy options for policy makers' considerations.

II. Reflections on the Past

Analysis of economic and social trends in Bolivia and comparisons with other countries in the region and around the world provide three important lessons. These lessons are (i) per capita economic growth has been very low (even negative) and sporadic, accentuating economic inequality; (ii) access to basic public services has increased and social indicators have improved, but major social inequality persists; and (iii) institutional stability and transparency have weakened.

Low Economic Growth ... High Poverty

The second half of the twentieth century witnessed intermittent episodes of growth generated by export booms and waves of capital inflow, followed by collapses and crisis. The economy grew, on an average, at a rate far below the rest of Latin America and other developing countries, and incomes fell slightly in real terms. At the start of 2000, an average Bolivian earned one percent less than his/her grandparents earned in 1950. By contrast, in that same period, the real income of Chileans doubled, that of Brazilians more than tripled, and that of South Koreans grew by a factor of twelve.

The slow growth of the economy is due to low rates of investment and low productivity. During the past 35 years, total average annual investment (private and public) in Bolivia represented approximately 16 percent of GDP, compared to an average of 20 percent in the countries of Latin America, 21 percent in other developing countries—Turkey, Hungary, and Romania, to name a few—and more than 30 percent in South Korea. At the same time, the contribution of productivity to economic growth in Bolivia was approximately 0.2 percentage points of GDP, compared with an average of 0.6 percentage points in Latin America and 1.0 percentage point in other developing countries. In addition, there are large disparities in the productivity of different sectors, although since 1999 they have all experienced slow growth. These disparities are even greater when viewed at the level of individual businesses. For example, the productivity of workers in large companies (especially capital-intensive companies) is 25 times greater than that of workers in micro-enterprises. Large companies produce 65 percent of GDP but employ less than 9 percent of the economically active population. A good part of the productivity differential is due to the predominance of informal firms. The degree of informality is the highest in Latin America (two-thirds of the economy functions outside of the formal sector), and is among the highest in the world.

The importance of economic growth to the well-being of the population cannot be underestimated. Even with a moderate growth rate, over a long period, people can be better off. If Bolivia had grown over the past 50 years at a rate similar to the median for Latin America, average income would be more than double current levels and the poverty rate would have been cut in half (Table 1).

Bolivia's economy improved in the 1990s, with an average economic growth rate of 4 percent, in part because of the economic reforms implemented. The general upturn in the economy stimulated job growth and poverty reduction, although income inequality did not improve. However, after 1998, a series of shocks decelerated economic growth and investment and lowered productivity. Some of these

Table 1. If Bolivia Had Matched the Pace of Economic Growth in Latin America, 1950–2000 ...

If Bolivia had grown at:	*Bolivia's Average Income (decade of 2000)*	*Bolivia's Poverty Rate (decade of 2000)*
–0.02% per year (Actual rate of growth)	$900	65%
+1.5% per year (Median for Latin America)	$1888	30%

shocks were external (for example, the financial crises in Asia and Russia, which raised international interest rates and reduced the flow of capital to Bolivia, and the devaluations in Brazil and Argentina, which affected Bolivia's terms of trade). Others were internal, induced by public policies (for example, the eradication of the coca crop and the high cost of pension reform). During that same period, the economy benefited from favorable shocks (for example, the boom in exports of gas and soybeans and the pardoning of some bilateral creditors' debt). However, these shocks were insufficient to offset the economic slowdown and mitigate political and social unrest. Public policies have been erratic, with administrations reacting to events more than anticipating them. The results of these policies have negatively affected the business climate, creating uncertainty and reducing private investment from 18 percent of GDP in 1998 to 6.5 percent in 2004. Policy reversals and changes have discouraged investors, both foreign and domestic, in the recent past. Policies reversals and changes include the new Hydrocarbons Law and uncertainties with respect to the future of the gas industry, the recision of contractual agreements, and trade policies. Under these circumstances, Bolivia is at a disadvantage to compete and prosper in the twenty-first century.

The impact of low economic growth in the rural sector, where the worst poverty is concentrated, is even more notable. Despite the fact that Bolivian society has urbanized during the past 50 years (the percentage of the population living in rural zones has dropped from almost 75 percent to approximately 40 percent), the mean monetary income in the rural area is approximately US$0.60 a day, one-third of the average urban income. At the same time, the agricultural sector underwent a change while its overall contribution to GDP remained constant (15-16 percent) during the past 15 years. Commercial agriculture in the lowlands expanded significantly; the share of industrial agricultural production (mainly soybeans) in the agricultural sector rose from 10 percent in the late 1980s to 20 percent in 2004. This growth offset the losses associated with eradication of the coca crop, whose size, in the same period, dropped from 8 to 4.5 percent of the agricultural sector. The participation of the rest of the sub-sectors in the agricultural sector, including traditional agricultural products, forestry, and fishing, remained stagnant.

The agricultural sector thus exhibits a dual character. One sub-sector devoted to the export of agricultural products (soybeans) is highly dynamic and generates most of the sector's growth. On the other hand, another sub-sector with low productivity is devoted to the production of food for the domestic market. This second sub-sector is principally concentrated in the Andean zone, with farmers caught in a vicious cycle that perpetuates poverty, environmental degradation, loss of soil fertility, and decreasing yields (and, therefore, diminishing self-consumption or income from sales). Nonetheless, not all peasants in the Andean zone correspond to these characteristics; an estimated 20 percent have increased their productivity and income through improved penetration of the product markets. These farmers provide most of the food consumed in the cities, and some are increasingly linked to international markets (worth mention are mountain-grown coffee, quinoa, and other high-Andean crops, as well as llama ranching). This shows that Andean agro-ecological conditions do not set absolute limits on competitiveness. It is essential that support to high-Andean agriculture focuses on products that allow the development of territorial competitiveness based on entry into dynamic product markets.

Improvement of Services ... with Inequalities

In addition to slow economic growth and low levels of investment and productivity, deep-rooted economic and social inequalities mark the history of Bolivia. The wealth of the richest 10 percent of the population is 140 times greater than that of the poorest 10 percent, the educational gap between the richest and the poorest is approximately 8.5 years of education (compared to approximately five years in Venezuela and Colombia) and 10 percent of the agricultural units control 90 percent of the arable land. Differences in income, access to public goods and services, and political power are marked by differences of ethnicity, race, region, and gender; that is, factors beyond the control of the individual. History and public policies have not reversed social exclusion. Nonetheless, Bolivia over the past decade has significantly extended coverage of basic public services, including social programs, which has translated to an improvement in the various indicators of social well-being.

For example, in education (especially primary education) coverage indicators have improved: approximately 95 percent of children between the ages of seven and 14 are currently in school, a figure that places the country in the same position as wealthier neighbors, such as Brazil or Peru. In addition, the dropout rate from primary schools is down, especially in rural areas (30 percent), the repetition rate has decreased, and the rate of completion of studies has increased. This puts Bolivia on the path to attain the Millennium Development Goal (MDG) of universal completion of primary school by the year 2010. Despite these achievements, universal coverage continues to be a pending goal, especially among the less privileged groups (the rural and indigenous populations). In addition, Bolivia needs to overcome limited and unequal access to middle and secondary schools. Academic performance is still deficient, and shortcomings persist in an inefficient educational system. The low enrollment rate in secondary schools has resulted in a shortfall in the capacity of the Bolivian workforce and a shortage of trained personnel.

In health, the improvements attained during the preceding decade in terms of coverage, reduction of maternal mortality (by almost 60 percent as compared to 1990) and of infant mortality (by almost 40 percent with respect to 1990), among other accomplishments, were significant. If sustained, this progress will make it possible to attain the 2015 MDGs for the sector. However, Bolivia's health situation continues to be one of the most worrisome in Latin America. The results on indicators such as the maternal and infant mortality rates place Bolivia among the worst in the region, after Haiti. Indicators for transmissible and recurring diseases are also worrisome—Chagas disease is endemic, malaria and yellow fever have waned but are still present, and dengue fever has reappeared. Bolivia ranks 113 on the Human Development Index, on a par with Honduras (116) and Guatemala (117), although the health indicators of those two countries are better than in Bolivia.

Inequality compounds this critical health situation. There are marked differences in access to health services among those who are poor and those who are not, and among the population of indigenous origin and the non-indigenous population. For example, approximately 25 percent of the population from the bottom income quintile receives medical care for childbirth, as compared with 90 percent of the top income quintile. Inequality also exists among regions: the highlands (La Paz, Potosí, and Oruro), valleys (Cochabamba, Chuquisaca, and Tarija) and lowlands (Santa Cruz, Beni, and Pando). The maternal mortality rate, for example, is twice as high in the highlands as in the lowlands, and the rate of chronic malnutrition among children age of five or younger in the highlands is twice that of the valleys. The weak performance of the health sector is cause for concern, especially in recent years. Certain activities essential for improving health indicators have held constant or cut back, which threatens to halt the progress of previous years toward reaching the MDGs. The reasons for the low performance of the sector are essentially threefold. First, the political crisis has hindered the development of stable policies, proper coordination, and follow-up. Second, the decentralization of the sector has not always been beneficial and has resulted in high transaction costs. Third, misallocation of funding resulting from the decentralization has prevented closing of inequality gaps.

Bolivia has made significant efforts to increase coverage of pensions, non-contributive programs (such as the BONOSOL) and social programs targeting the most vulnerable population segments (children, the elderly, the unemployed, and those without social security healthcare). Over the past six years, the country earmarked an annual average of approximately 4.5 percent of GDP to cover the deficit of the pension system and doubled the amount earmarked for the various social welfare programs, to almost 23 percent of social expenditures (higher than the average for the rest of Latin America). Several programs have helped mitigate the negative impact of economic deceleration in the first five years of this decade. These programs include universal health insurance for mothers and children, comprehensive healthcare, vaccinations, job creation, cash transfers to citizens age of 65 and older, housing improvements, social funds, and land tenancy to improve rural economic competitiveness. Despite these efforts, the pension system suffers from low coverage, especially for the rural and indigenous population, and a high fiscal cost. Similarly, the system for social welfare programs requires better targeting (that is, greater emphasis on children, the indigenous population, and adults most vulnerable to economic instability) and a strengthening of its institutional framework.

In the 1990s and the beginning of the new century, coverage of basic infrastructure services (water, sanitation, and transportation) increased considerably. Access to better sources of water increased nationwide by 18 percent (reaching 72 percent of the population) and access to sanitation increased by 24 percent (reaching 67 percent of the population). Movement of cargo and passengers through the transportation system doubled (highways, which are the preferred mode of transportation, accounted for more than 90 percent of the total movement of passengers and 60 percent of the volume of cargo). The transportation system has been essential to the country's economic progress, contributing almost 9 percent of GDP per year on average. Transportation has absorbed more than 30 percent of public investment, and activities related to the sector have generated 7 percent of the jobs in the cities.

Despite these achievements, the coverage of sewage systems and potable water, along with improved sanitation, continues to be below average for Latin America. Operating costs are high, especially in the rural zones. In addition, there are major inequalities in coverage—in some cases more than double—between the relatively rich departments (for example, Santa Cruz and Tarija) and the relatively poor ones (such as Beni, Pando, and Potosí). Inequalities also exist between urban and rural areas—for example, 86 percent of the water supply in the cities is running water, as opposed to 28 percent in the rural area, and maintenance of local rural roads is deficient. The basic sanitation sector faces a series of structural challenges, including low labor and operating efficiency, a low level of investment, institutional deficiencies, and a lack of sustainability of services in the rural areas. In addition, the government needs to define the model for the provision of water services in the cities of La Paz and El Alto. With regard to transportation, the institutional framework on the national and sub-national level is weak, which reduces transparency in decision making. In addition, high costs and the risk of arbitrary changes in the legal and institutional framework jeopardize investment and the development of the sector.

The provision of public services includes not only social services and basic infrastructure, but also the preservation of the environment for the benefit of present and future generations. Good environmental management in Bolivia has had positive results in conserving biodiversity and reducing deforestation. Nonetheless, numerous environmental problems aggravate the quality of life of the population, particularly the poor. These problems, resulting mainly from inadequate public policies, include air and residential pollution, waterborne diseases, natural disasters, and soil degradation. The transportation sector's excessive consumption of fuels, at subsidized prices, generates high levels of air pollution. Residential pollution results from the use of firewood and other fossil and liquid fuels in homes. Lack of access to water and sanitation and of programs focused on the basic hygiene of the most vulnerable population produces waterborne diseases. These problems worsen the health of the population and hinder the development of the most vulnerable population (especially children). Their annual cost is equivalent to almost 5 percent of GDP, more than in the majority of countries in the region.

Environmental and social sustainability, along with efforts to promote economic growth with more inclusion and equity, demand concerted and sustained attention to policies on coca leaf production and the management of natural resources, especially land and forests. Approximately 40 percent of the population inhabits rural areas; the rural sector contributes approximately 15 percent of GDP and employs more than 40 percent of the active population. Over the past ten years, authorities have made efforts, legal and otherwise, to improve land distribution, although implementation has been inconsistent and frequently ineffective. For example, implementation of Law 1715 has not fulfilled expectations (only 15 percent of the total land to be regularized actually was). Efforts to better utilize underused lands and make their distribution more equitable also failed. Land taxation has not created a structure of incentives that improves productivity and foments market transactions: 51 percent of municipal taxes come from tax on lands, but 90 percent of this revenue is collected in only ten municipalities (out of 327), which reflects the existing difficulties in this tax's design and administration, especially in small, rural municipalities. There is progress in registration of indigenous lands, but the process is negatively affected by conflicts and claims, including calls for land grants, that are not adjudicated. The system for protected areas and forestry management is functioning, but some areas are being illegally exploited or are being cleared for cattle raising, soybean farming, and small agriculture.

Institutions and Transparency ... Weak

The enactment of the Financial Administration System and Governmental Control Law (*Ley del Sistema de Administración Financiera y Control Gubernamental*—SAFCO) in the early 1990s provided the framework for public administration reforms. Based on this law, Bolivia has promoted various reforms, principally at the central level in administrative, financial, and control processes, the civil service, and tax collection, which have increased the efficiency of public expenditures and reduced corruption. However, the country's political and social instability since the late 1990s limited the results of these reforms. The functionality of the budget process, planning, and procurements continues to be deficient. The information technology system is incomplete, and the government is advised to reevaluate its efficiency and usefulness. Civil service reform made progress, with the creation of a legal and institutional framework, the institution of competitive selection processes and the implementation of a biographical data registration on officials, retirees, and awardees that covers 25 percent of the civil service. This registration contributes to the professionalization and transparency of the public sector. The modernization of the National Tax Service (*Servicio de Impuestos Nacionales*—SIN) and the Customs Service has improved management and reduced corruption, which has translated into improved tax collections. Tax revenue increased by 50 percent in real terms over the past five years (excluding the impact of the recent tax increase on the oil industry), reaching 13.5 percent of GDP, similar to the average for Latin America, but less than that of Brazil (28 percent) and Colombia (18 percent). The strengthening of the Comptroller General and the obligation for officials to submit an affidavit of their financial situation have contributed to the fight against corruption. Nonetheless, the reform process has been incomplete and has not extended to all parts of the public sector. Public sector management remains deficient and management information is not transparent.

The judicial system, and with it legal security for the citizens, suffers from a lack of access for the majority of Bolivians, especially the poor. This not only makes it difficult for the population to enforce their rights through the courts, but also generates a lack of confidence in the judicial system and a perception that criminals enjoy impunity. In response to a justice system that is too slow (for example, it takes an average of almost 600 days to resolve and execute judgment on contractual commercial conflicts, as opposed to 300 days in Chile), the population avoids taking recourse in the courts and takes justice into its own hands. Protests and land takeovers, among other extreme actions, reflect this lack of confidence in the justice system.

A general weakening of institutions occurred in parallel to the first phase of the decentralization process, which, as in other countries of the region (for example, Colombia, Peru, and Venezuela), was strictly municipal and driven by political considerations. In Bolivia, decentralization began in the mid-1990s with the Popular Participation Law, which created the current municipal governments. While far from perfect, municipalities are now playing an increasingly significant economic, social, and political role. Municipal expenditures now represent close to 18 percent of total public expenditures; this could increase further as a result of the Hydrocarbons Law. Shortly after municipal decentralization began, the departmental governments were reformed. As deconcentrated units of the central government, departments are governed by prefects (designated by the President) together with departmental councils (with members locally elected through indirect suffrage by the provincial municipalities). The prefects prepare budgets, which are approved by the council. Prior to the enactment of the Hydrocarbons Law, departments disbursed approximately 9 percent of total public expenditures. Yet the departments, in general, were unable to strengthen themselves and faced limitations in providing public services. Efforts to bring those in charge of providing public services (supply) close to the citizens (demand) were delayed. For example, in 1999, responsibility for the main roads system was handed back from the departments to the central government due to deterioration in service quality.

In this first phase, Bolivia became a relatively decentralized country in terms of expenditures, but the sub-national governments continued to depend almost exclusively on transfers from the central government for their financing: tax collection efforts at the sub-national level represent less than 6 percent of their total financing. The fiscal management of the sub-national governments has been relatively prudent, with a certain degree of control over indebtedness. This has prevented vertical fiscal imbalances that could affect overall macroeconomic equilibrium, as occurred in Argentina and Brazil. Nonetheless, horizontal imbalances—that is, inequalities among transfers to (and expenditures of) the various departments—persists. For example, Tarija and Pando receive, respectively, 20 and 13 times greater funding per inhabitant than does La Paz. The distribution foreseen in the Hydrocarbons Law, through the effect of equal, additional payments for producing departments, could increase this horizontal imbalance. In addition, a series of institutional weaknesses marked the decentralization process. These weaknesses include (i) limited capacity and autonomy to manage funds (for example, the prefectures can spend only 8 percent of their resources in accordance with their own priorities); and (ii) deficient information technology and record-keeping systems (municipal and departmental debt is under-declared by an estimated 5 percent of GDP). In addition, the fragmentation of responsibilities diminishes effectiveness and efficiency of the decentralization process. For example, the central government is responsible for paying teachers, departments are in charge of managing them, municipalities are responsible for monitoring them, and districts have the authority to hire and fire.

Deficiencies in the provision of public services are reflected in a lack of confidence in public institutions. Accordingly, the Corruption Perceptions Index (CPI) by Transparency International for last year indicates that Bolivia ranks 117 among 159 countries, roughly the same position it has occupied for several years. As well, the country continues to suffer from excess regulation. Starting a business requires an average of 15 applications and 50 days, almost double what occurs in Chile, and the cost (in percentage of per capita income) is ten times higher than in South Korea, 15 times higher than in Chile and almost 25 times higher than in Taiwan. Basic institutions needed for developing markets and attracting investment are deficient, including an independent and functional judicial system, protection of intellectual and physical property rights and the overall legal and regulatory framework for businesses. Bolivia, for example, ranks 116 from among 155 countries in cross-border trade (among the countries of Latin America, only Haiti and Honduras rank lower). Exports require nine different documents and 15 different signatures, which take an average of 43 days to obtain. For imports, the process is even more complicated, raising transaction costs and encouraging informality, contraband, and corruption.

III. Opportunities and suggestions for the Future

The favorable initial social, political and economic context; lessons learned from the review of the trends in Bolivia's economic and social development; and the experience of other countries provide a solid analytical platform from which to propose suggested goals to respond to the challenges of reducing poverty and achieving social inclusion. The goals are (i) sustained high growth that creates jobs; (ii) public services that benefit all; and (iii) government that is transparent and participatory.

Sustained High Growth that Creates Jobs

The implementation of sound economic policies could allow Bolivia to grow once again at an annual real rate of 4.5 to 5 percent per year. Such economic growth would increase income and reduce poverty. In just one generation, the poverty rate could be almost half of today's rate (Table 2). However, this would demand more investment and greater productivity than in the recent past. In order to achieve and maintain such growth, total annual investment would have to average between 18 and 22 percent of GDP. In addition, total productivity would have to increase and contribute to economic growth by an average of 2 percentage points per year.

Given the public sector's fiscal limitations and the need to respond to a growing demand for public services, attaining this level of investment will require efforts from the public sector and, especially, participation of the private sector. Average public investment has been 5.5 percent of GDP (between 2001 and 2004), and due to fiscal restrictions, the outlook for a significant increase in public investment is limited. Therefore, in order to attain investments amounting to 20 percent of GDP, private investment would have to increase from 8.3 percent (the average between 2001 and 2004) to 15 percent of GDP. Without a growing and dynamic private sector, it will be very difficult to accelerate and maintain economic growth. If the authorities wish to establish the conditions needed for private sector growth and investment in Bolivia, two issues require immediate and ongoing attention.

First, minimize uncertainty. Political and social instability and an environment of uncertainty in the legal and regulatory framework are the restrictions that most jeopardize investment and growth. Strong political leadership, capable of maintaining a certain consensus among the various economic and social interests, is needed to resolve this uncertainty. Instituting fair and binding processes to resolve investment disputes related to the oil industry and to the water and sanitation sector will also be critical.

Second, maintain macroeconomic and financial stability. In order to create a framework favorable to economic growth, price stability is a must. This, in turn, demands

Table. 2. How Sustained Growth of 4.5 to 5% Could Increase Income and Reduce Poverty

	Average Income in Real Terms	*Poverty Rate*
Bolivia today	$900	65%
... in 10 years	$1134–$1188	55 %
... in 20 years	$1395–$1539	35 %

sound management to maintain fiscal equilibrium. Alternatives are available to the authorities to control the growth of public expenditures; increase public sector revenue (through a progressive tax system on a wide tax base that is equitable and easy to administer); improve the administration and management of transfers from international cooperation; and exercise sound and sustainable management of public sector debt. We strongly recommend that the authorities continue preserving the independence of monetary and financial institutions. It is advisable that in addition, the authorities focus on three areas, starting in the short term by (i) defining and implementing policies that increase the public's confidence in financial stability; (ii) resolving the problems of banks that are in distress; and (iii) expanding access to financial services through alternative instruments to bank loans. Nonetheless, both in Bolivia and in other countries of the region, this long and difficult process demands legislative and institutional changes as well as a redefinition of the strategies of existing public institutions. It would be prudent to bear in mind international and Bolivian experiences, which illustrate the shortcomings of public banks.

These conditions are necessary but not sufficient in and of themselves to reach the levels of investment and productivity—and, therefore, of broad-based economic growth, job creation, and reduction of poverty and inequality—that Bolivia hopes to attain. For that, the country must once again take up the reform agenda. The authorities could concentrate on (a) improving the investment environment, in order to increase investment and productivity; (b) reinforcing trade policies and further integrating into world markets to maximize opportunities for job-creating growth; and (c) promoting rural development, to have the largest impact on reducing poverty.

Improving the Environment to Increase Investment and Productivity

The government has progressed in several areas but, in general, the investment environment has deteriorated. The government could reverse this situation through several public policies. These policies could include (i) defining the legal and institutional investment framework, with the aim of promoting investment and the development of natural resources (especially of hydrocarbons); (ii) introducing a legal framework that encourages a modern business environment; (iii) reinforcing property rights, the rule of law, and institutions, and improvement of the regulatory framework; and (iv) monitoring indicators on the investment environment.

The development of natural resources and exports of minerals and hydrocarbons will continue to be central to promoting Bolivia's economic growth. The authorities will have to specify the terms for obtaining the necessary investments (including strategic partners) to continue developing natural resources and expanding export markets. They will also have to define the criteria for sharing the benefits of this development among the various regions and sectors of the population. Some of the more relevant decisions pertain to negotiations for the migration of operators to new contracting models, transparency in collecting and allocating revenue, and a definition of the industrial operations to be carried out by *Yacimientos Petrolíferos Fiscales Bolivianos* (YPFB, Bolivian oil company). In addition, the government will need to make decisions regarding adjustment of fuel prices in the internal market and the opening of new markets for gas within the region and elsewhere.

With respect to defining the legal framework for a modern business environment, given the current social and political stability, a legislative agenda could include the following laws:

- *Bankruptcy*—The Bankruptcy Law should allow unsuccessful companies to depart more quickly and allow creditors to take effective possession of assets placed as security.
- *Labor*—The Labor Law discourages the creation of formal jobs, provides incentives for informality, and keeps Bolivia from being competitive with other countries. By modernizing the law based on international criteria, the governments could achieve the aim of encouraging job creation and, at the same time, protecting the legitimate rights of workers.
- *Intellectual Property*—As a basis for negotiating international trade agreements and expanding markets, and to encourage domestic innovation, Bolivia ought to have a law adapting good international practices related to the enforcement of patents and copyrights.

The enforcement of property rights and a predictable legal system would eliminate one of the restrictions to investment and growth. The initial step is making a commitment to and exercising the political will to attain a supportive environment so that the legal framework will function properly. At the same time, companies have to deal with a very heavy regulatory burden, while a lack of regulatory independence also creates problems such as high staff turnover and political interference. The government could take measures to reduce this burden and ensure the professionalism and independence of regulatory agencies through transparent, non-political contracting of their personnel.

The government's economic team could monitor key indicators associated with the investment environment in comparison with other countries. Some relevant indicators include the size of the informal sector; the time needed to start up a business and to hire or fire a worker; property registration; access to credit; and performance of contracts. After compiling a list of indicators, the government could assign responsibilities and concrete improvement objectives among the cabinet. These efforts, like the measures taken to improve indicators, must be transparent and public.

Strengthen Trade Policies and Integrate into World Markets

Given that Bolivia's internal market is very small, economic growth will depend upon the capacity to expand exports and integrate into the global economy. The country has a great export potential based on its natural resources, the agricultural sector, and an abundance of labor. Some policy options are to (i) develop a broad strategy for opening export markets to Bolivian products; (ii) strengthen business institutions and trade instruments; and (iii) fight contraband and corruption.

Current policies should focus on obtaining and maintaining access to key markets for Bolivian products. Measures to achieve this goal could include entering into negotiations with the United States and other countries for a Free Trade Agreement that guarantees continual access to these markets even after the current trade preferences under the Andean Trade Promotion and Drug Eradication Act (ATPDEA) expire. In addition, the government would find it productive to negotiate lower non-tariff barriers with preferential trading partners in the Andean region, MERCOSUR, Chile, and Mexico, and join the promotional activities of MERCOSUR which already has a joint mechanism for this purpose. Furthermore, the government could realize important benefits by bringing the Bolivian Promotion Center (*Centro de Promoción Boliviano*—CEPROBOL) up to date and consider turning its management over to the private sector, with clear objectives and accountability.

In order to improve business institutions and trade instruments, the authorities could consider promoting the temporary importation regime (*Régimen de Internación Temporal para Exportación*—RITEX) among exporters, reducing costly and burdensome procedures, and simplifying the refund of VAT and Specific Consumption Tax (*Impuesto a los Consumos Específicos*—ICE) for exporters. The government could complement these measures by reducing delays for issuing the Tax Refund Certificate (*Certificado de Devolución Impositivo*—CEDEIM) and strengthening the basic infrastructure and institutions for the control of standards and quality. To accomplish this last goal, the government needs to improve the regulation of the Standards, Measurements, Accreditation, and Certification System (*Sistema de Normalización, Metrología, Acreditación y Certificación*—SNMAC). It could also reactivate the National Quality Control Council (*Consejo Nacional para el Control de Calidad*—CONACAL), presided over by the Minister of Economic Development, to improve export product quality.

To fight contraband and corruption, the authorities need to define and implement a national policy created with the participation of all relevant public and private sectors institutions. This policy could include key elements such as continuing the program to strengthen the Customs Operating Control unit (*Control Operativo de Aduanas*—COA) by providing more personnel, appropriate training, and upgraded communications and tracking technology. The reforms in the Customs Administration and the National Tax System to facilitate trade and control contraband should continue, as should studying the feasibility of merging these two institutions. It is also advisable for the government to eliminate the legal restriction that prohibits Customs from prosecuting retailers of contraband items and promote cooperation with customs administrations in neighboring countries—initially to exchange official information on imports and exports, and later to establish a joint border infrastructure.

Promote Rural Development

The experience of the last half century at the global level has confirmed that there are fundamentally three ways to promote rural growth and development in order to create jobs and reduce poverty. These are (i) support the competitive entry of rural producers (agricultural and non-agricultural) in dynamic markets; (ii) facilitate labor integration through migration; and (iii) improve the income of the poorest and most vulnerable groups through direct cash transfers. The suggestions here focus on improving the efficiency of financing for rural development and targeting poverty programs, taking into account territorial factors and the lives of the poor.

To improve the efficiency of financing for rural development, the government could consider two groups of interventions. The first would involve the government's making a clear differentiation between the financing of public assets and that of subsidies. One way to eliminate the confusion resulting from the mixed objectives of efficiency and equity in municipal transfers could be to differentiate the sources and modes of financing. To achieve this, the government could agree with the various financers on an explicit, transparent policy that defines eligibility criteria for potential beneficiaries, as well as competitive rules for filtering access to funding, the various financing modes, and the types of eligible initiatives. Furthermore, the government could bring the various existing projects in line with that policy and restrict the use of municipal transfers for financing public infrastructure and strengthening civil society organizations. The intervention would involve the government's readjusting co-financing mechanisms for municipal and community infrastructure. The reformulation of mechanisms for co-financing infrastructure projects would be most effective if they were to include subcontracting of Productive and Social Investment Fund (*Fondo de Inversión Productivo y Social*—FPS) operations to the private sector, and reinforcing its supervision and control capacity. Moreover, the FPS could co-finance a limited number of priority sectors to ensure compliance with guidelines and the institutional strengthening necessary for its success. Finally, in some sectors (for example, rural roads), the government and FPS could design performance-based program transfers rather than financing individual investments.

Measures to better target programs for the fight against poverty should work to improve existing programs to strengthen life-promoting strategies or to eliminate barriers that restrict the opportunities and capacity of peasants in the highlands and Andean valleys, rather than funding new programs. The focus should be on three priorities. The first is for the government to formulate and implement a natural resource management program linked to generating income for the country's highlands, including community and family competitions for the management of natural resources and productive technologies. The second is for the government to facilitate job-seeking support for migrants, reducing the costs of entry into their destinations by providing information on housing and job references. The third is for the government to develop and implement conditional transfers that focus on the country's poorest inhabitants and seek in particular to reduce the incidence of malnutrition among children under the age of two, which is essential to give children the opportunity to develop to their full potential.

Public Services That Benefit All

Bolivia can reduce inequality and social exclusion by formulating and implementing sound social policies to improve coverage and quality in the provision of public services. In meeting these challenges, the various levels of government and the public sector will play a crucial role, from the strategic definition of objectives and priorities to the actual provision of the services. Below are suggestions for the various sectors, based on progress already made, lessons learned in Bolivia, and the experiences of other countries as well as on the more detailed analyses of specific sectors and/or issues presented in the different chapters of this work.

In order to meet the three principal education challenges of access, quality, and coverage, the authorities could consider the following overall priority goals: (i) facilitate access and continued attendance for middle school and high school education; (ii) improve educational results; and (iii) promote decentralization to improve efficiency and effectiveness.

By expanding the supply of education, the authorities could improve access and continued attendance in middle and high school. This process implies investing in existing systems, including bilingual education, and exploring alternative methods for the provision of services (for example, education by radio and/or combinations of home tutoring and schools, as well as high-school tele-education in areas with electricity). In addition, it would be beneficial to implement cash transfers to female heads of poor households, conditional on having their children enroll in school and maintain high attendance rates, and contract the services of alternative schooling models such as *Fe y Alegría* (Faith and Joy).

To improve education results, it is important for the government to consider: (i) implementing national evaluations, such as the Educational Quality Measurement and Evaluation System (*Sistema de Medición y Evaluación de Calidad de la Educación*—SIMECAL) to establish results standards, and use these results to inform teacher training and curriculum; and (ii) facilitating the provision of quality instructional materials, especially in low-income areas. The efficiency and effectiveness of the educational system could improve through greater community and parent participation along with greater decentralization and autonomy in each school. In light of the country's social and political reality, the best education solution in the autonomous areas of Bolivia might consist of changing the rules so that the funds "follow" the students.

In health, the priorities are to reduce inequality and expand coverage. The reasons behind the sector's poor results are fundamentally institutional in nature. Accordingly, to resolve the institutional problems, the government could adopt performance-based guidelines that use incentives to support orderly decentralization, encourage accountability, and link financing to performance.

The government would realize significant benefits by strengthening the Ministry of Health, both in terms of its regulations and technically. This should ensure that the sector is run effectively and efficiently. It also will improve the information technology systems and vital statistics, which must be made compatible with other systems, such as Universal Mother/Child Insurance (*Seguro Universal Materno-Infantil*—SUMI). The Ministry of Health would also find it valuable to set access and care standards for the population, especially for the poorest population—the experience of the SUMI, in this regard, would be highly useful.

Decentralization in the health sector should clarify responsibilities for service provision and financing. The poor management capacity of most municipalities, coupled with costs associated with supervising and monitoring the performance of a greater number of municipalities (compared with departments), could tip the scales toward assigning responsibility for the provision of health services to the new departments. This measure, which is consistent with the need to ensure efficient service networks, would involve transferring human resources management and the organization of the networks to the departments, with accountability for the operations of the health networks entrusted to them. Under this alternative, within a gradual decentralization process with well-defined stages, the institutional capacity of the departments would be reinforced through training and instruction on the rules for accrediting health establishments. In addition, the Ministry of Health must strengthen the management agreements and the allocation of funds to the departments, in recognition of the need to achieve equity and compensating the departments in accordance with their healthcare objectives or their results in the area of health. It is recommended that the Ministry of Finance publicly announce the availability of funds for each of the departments in order to verify that the funds allocated to the sector are spent on activities in line with priorities. Finally, the population can support performance-monitoring efforts by participating in the election of departmental authorities.

The government could realize significant achievements by linking financing to performance through incentives. In this regard, the SUMI has incentives and accountability mechanisms for monitoring both equity and efficiency of healthcare providers. Nonetheless, it is necessary to expand the SUMI to cover the entire population in need (especially the poor and indigenous population) and to provide access to the same comprehensive package of services. A user identification system is needed to supervise the number, type, frequency, and quality of the services received by each user. With this, it will be possible to correlate health expenditures with specific results outcomes (such as maternal or infant mortality), the provision of health services (for example, the coverage of vaccination campaigns or campaigns for hospital births), or equity (access to SUMI's services for those previously excluded). In order to reinforce SUMI, it would be advisable to consider institutional strategies that combine the current transfers through co-participation in tax revenue and other funding sources (remunerations or the insurance for the elderly, for example). Finally, the Ministry of Finance must allocate the necessary funding for the operations of the Ministry of Health and for implementation of national programs such as vaccination campaigns and programs for the control and monitoring of vector-transmitted diseases.

The safety net comprises pensions, the non-contributive BONOSOL program to protect the elderly, and social assistance programs. With respect to the system of protection for the elderly, the most relevant issues are (i) cost and fiscal deficit for traditional pensions and (ii) the management of the BONOSOL program.

In order to ensure the financial consolidation and long-term sustainability of the traditional pension system, a strategy needs to consider both design issues and policy implementation. The government would find it advisable to review the statistics on pension expenditures. The tradition of including items such as benefits guaranteed to the retired staff of the Armed Forces, or the cost of compensation granted to government employees due to the 1996 changes in the contributions, have exaggerated the magnitude of the pension system's fiscal cost. The debate would be more transparent if these and other expenditures were correctly assigned. In addition, the measures defined in the Supreme Decree (January 2005) are well suited for controlling future expenditures. It is recommended that the government ensure their application and, to the extent appropriate, further extend them.

The government strategy to address the problem of financing the current and future pension deficit will be most productive if it is focused on obtaining additional contributions from those who participate in the system. The government can achieve this either by creating a "solidarity contribution" for active workers (under a model similar to the one developed in Colombia) or by explicitly or implicitly reducing the benefits of retirees (in this latter case, by applying a contribution from the retirees), following the example of the Peruvian retirement system for government employees.

The BONOSOL is an innovative program without current fiscal cost and with a significant impact on the quality of life of its beneficiaries. Nonetheless, problems of access, fraud, management, and sustainability are in need of attention and correction. With respect to access and fraud, the authorities need to conduct a survey, either independently or as part of the program of activities of the National Statistics Institute (*Instituto Nacional de Estadísticas*—INE) to assess the magnitude of these problems. Based on the results of this survey, the government could define a strategy of progressive correction that seeks to rectify the lists of beneficiaries in order to eliminate those groups that have wrongfully obtained the benefit and, at the same time, incorporate those persons who meet the requirements but who, for myriad reasons, are not receiving the program's benefits. With respect to the financial management and sustainability of the system, a review of the valuation criteria of the assets currently registered in the Collective Capitalization Funds (*Fondos de Capitalización Colectivo*—FCC) is needed in order to determine mid- and long-term strategies aimed at safely maximizing the return on those assets. The analysis should include a review of the rules of corporate governance and their application in Bolivia to ensure that the interests of the FCC are properly protected. A demographic and actuarial analysis is also needed in order to project the flow of benefits to be paid in the coming years and adjust investments strategies and the availability of liquid assets accordingly.

The government originally conceived the BONOSOL as a mechanism to "return" ownership of part of the companies that were previously government-owned to Bolivians. The authorities could now readjust some aspects of the program. In particular, the government could seek to make it more inclusive in terms of time (that is, by eliminating the requirement of having to be born prior to 1974), while streamlining its distribution (for example, by integrating it into the contributive system, turning it into a minimum universal benefit that would not be paid to those who receive regular pensions). The government's decisions regarding the ownership of the shares of capitalized oil companies will be central in the debate on the BONOSOL and its future. If the assets of the FCC are transferred to the state, an alternative funding source will have to be defined, or else the program would have to be reformulated (by better targeting the benefits or reducing their amount) to keep the program financially sustainable.

Regarding social welfare programs, it is necessary to improve targeting objectives (that is, greater emphasis on children, the indigenous population, and adults most vulnerable to economic instability) and to strengthen the institutional framework. The government could make significant strides in improving children's human development by strengthening the provision of primary healthcare. To achieve this, it could establish a gatekeeper system, mandating that SUMI services be accessed via primary care clinics, and institutionalizing the links between the mobile brigades, EXTENSA (the National Health Coverage Extension Program—*Programa Nacional de Extensión de Coberturas de Salud*), and the healthcare posts. Furthermore, the government would realize important improvements by emphasizing social welfare health measures in the first years of life (greater pregnancy monitoring and the provision of integrated primary healthcare support and nutrition throughout the first two years), and grant conditional cash transfers to the poorest households provided they utilize basic health and education services.

Measures to improve the indigenous population's access to healthcare services could include (i) implementation of an outreach strategy to promote awareness among indigenous women of the Accord on the Rights of Pregnant Women; (ii) cash incentives to increase the use of hospital childbirths among indigenous women; and (ii) the involvement of indigenous organizations in healthcare planning.

Policy options to support adults most vulnerable to economic instability include (i) making the counter-cyclical National Emergency Employment Plan (*Plan Nacional de Empleo de Emergencia*—PLANE) temporary, and not continuing it if the economy recovers; and (ii) reforming labor legislation, for example reducing the private sector burden of social expenditures to encourage investment in labor-intensive products and technologies.

The institutional framework for the social welfare strategy requires effective leadership. The National Economic and Social Policy Council (*Consejo Nacional de Política Económica y Social*—CONAPES) could assume such a leadership. The authorities will need to discuss the budget for the principal programs, considering the costs of the various results sought. Greater coordination and consistency is needed between national and municipal priorities to improve the use of funds, including grants. Finally, a review the criteria for the National Compensation Policy is needed, with the aim of increasing the percentage of funds earmarked for poor communities to improve equity.

Regarding basic services (water, sanitation, and transportation), coverage continues to be low, especially for the poor and rural population. The water and sanitation sector is facing a temporary crisis regarding the best model for providing water services in the cities of La Paz and El Alto, and a series of more structural challenges, such as poor labor and operating efficiency, insufficient financing, regulatory deficiencies, and the unsustainability of services in the rural areas. These challenges need to be resolved in the short and medium term to ensure a sustainable increase in coverage and better-quality services. Under the current conditions, an efficient, proven model is needed to guarantee the continuity of supplies in a context of high demographic growth in La Paz and El Alto. At the same time, operator efficiency must be maintained, the coverage of the sewage system in El Alto must be increased substantially, and avenues of participation must be opened for municipalities and civil society. In order to accomplish this, an option could be a mixed private-public water and sanitation company, created through a capital increase of the Aguas del Illimani company, earmarked for the necessary expansion works, with participation from the municipalities of both urban centers. To address more structural challenges facing the sector, the government could consider (i) increasing public financing for the water and sanitation sector; and (ii) implementing the financial policy for the sector and establishing the Foundation in Support of Sustainability in Basic Sanitation (*Fundación de Apoyo a la Sostenibilidad en Saneamiento Básico*— FUNDASAB)—Supreme Decrees 27486 and 27487 of May 2004. In addition, the government is advised to strengthen and delineate the scope of regulation of the Superintendency of Basic Sanitation (*Superintendencia de Saneamiento Básico*—SISAB).

The transportation sector is facing a series of institutional and financial restrictions and weaknesses that adversely affect public and private investment and the provision and quality of services, especially in the rural zones. The government could overcome these limitations by establishing a planning system (led by the Ministry of Transportation, with additional technical and financial support) reviewing the principal public and private investments to economically unprofitable and/or socially costly projects. It would be equally productive to define sound financing strategies to ensure the sustainability of the roads sector and strengthen institutional coordination (to integrate the roads system in all jurisdictions, which could reduce transportation costs and increase the productivity and competitiveness of local products). Another priority for the government would be to strengthen the National Roads Service (*Servicio Nacional de Caminos*—SNC) with emphasis on professional development and the management of contracts; support the rationalization of expenditures on roads and work programs at the deparmental and municipal levels, based on appropriate design and maintenance standards; and design and implement a rural community roads program. The government would also find it advisable to review the new proposed transportation law to more clearly define roles for the sector and ensure the independence of regulators.

In order to improve the quality of life of all Bolivians, and especially of the poor, the government could focus its environmental policy on essential areas such as (i) air, water, and residential pollution control; and (ii) reduction of vulnerability to natural disasters. In order to reduce air pollution, it would be advisable to substitute liquid and solid fuels with natural gas. The most efficient mechanism to encourage this substitution would be to tax fuels according to how much they pollute, with taxes on "cleaner" fuels (natural gas) at a minimum level. Eventually, the government should consider programs for substituting solid and liquid fuels with natural gas (depending on a cost/benefit analysis). To control residential pollution, in addition to increasing gas use, the government could introduce incentives for the use of efficient stoves and improving ventilation in homes. Measures such as educational campaigns on hygiene, home disinfection of water for consumption, and the development of sewage systems are effective in reducing the incidence of waterborne diseases. The government could reduce vulnerability to natural disasters by focusing on structural measures (for example, flood and erosion control works and slope stability works) as well as on non-structural measures (for example, zoning of land use and design of emergency response programs).

To sustain economic and social development, the government must address the challenges in managing natural resources, especially lands and forests. One key to this process is for the government to complete the regularization of land ownership and restore confidence in the National Agrarian Reform Institute (*Instituto Nacional de Reforma Agraria*—INRA). Another essential element of this process is to adopt land distribution mechanisms that are prioritized by objective and use multiple instruments; improve taxation on land; regularize land tenancy for indigenous peoples; and maintain the integrity of protected areas and forest reserves. Land redistribution goals should be established using a pragmatic approach, including mechanisms such as hectare-purchase programs. Land tax reform should focus on updating the land registries and their assessment rates as the cornerstone of fiscal decentralization. Indigenous peoples' land claims should involve user-friendly procedures, and the basis for indigenous territorial administration must improve. Finally, the National System for Protected Areas and forest areas must be reinforced with more professional management and investment in the communities located in and around these areas.

Government Without Corruption and With Participation of the Citizenry

Sound economic and social policies can help increase the level and quality of growth and reduce inequality and social exclusion. To help attain and maintain these objectives, Bolivia needs an efficient and transparent public sector and the active participation of the citizenry. The lack of results, an inability to provide services for all (and in particular, for the poorest and the excluded), and a perception of high corruption of public servants leads to a lack of citizen confidence in the public sector. The policies suggested below could help turn this trend around, and improve the effectiveness and efficiency of the public sector and extend access to public services, especially the justice system.

The government could focus, in the first place, on consolidating reforms in the administrative, financial, and oversight processes regulated by the Financial Administration System and Governmental Control Act (*Ley del Sistema de Administración Financiera y Control Gubernamental*—SAFCO). This includes budgeting, planning, and procurements processes, among others. In addition, the government would benefit from a program to modernize the Information and Financial Administration System (*Sistema de Información y Administración Financiera*—SIGMA), which is a central tool in administrative processes. With respect to budgeting and planning, the government is advised to prepare estimates of the budget over a period of three years, restrict itself and Congress from exceeding limits without a supplementary budget, and ensure that the budget covers all agencies of the public sector and all liabilities. The central government would promote higher levels of improvement by providing timely estimates of transfers to the subnational governments. At the same time, the National Planning System should establish processes and methodologies for prioritizing investments and public expenditures to be reflected in the general budget, which would make it possible to turn the Economic and Social Development Plan into a tool for management, supervision, and evaluation. With respect to procurements, the government would find it beneficial to introduce a new institutional framework through a Purchases and Contracting Act. This framework should have a central office in charge of supervising the purchasing system, with specialized personnel. In addition, the framework should include an Electronic Goods and Services Procurements System integrated into the SIGMA system, a consolidated database of providers, and an information system for the citizenry regarding state purchases. Finally, the institutional framework should include an auditing and special investigations plan to ensure quality of results, and a corporate purchasing plan to generate savings.

The government could make great progress in modernizing SIGMA by focusing on measures such as (i) expediting system and transaction operations and generating reports for the principal users; and (ii) developing a web page that provides public access to SIGMA, with data that is easy to use and understand. Moreover, the government would do well to improve following up on results in those sectors that have solid program-based classifications, linking intermediate indicators to the respective areas of public intervention, clarifying the information on the underlying budget rules, and designing pilot programs to involve the public in the budget process. It is not advisable for the government to extend SIGMA to subnational levels beyond the extent allowed by its processing capabilities or to establish a committee of SIGMA users whose principal purpose is to discuss and define the features that the system should have.

The government could also consider continuing with civil service, tax administration, and Customs reforms. With respect to the civil service, the principal policy recommendations include updating the registration of government employees, extending it to the entire public administration, and controlling the hiring and termination of personnel. The registry should be integrated with the individual service record of each government employee to make available all the information regarding the services the employee provides to the state. The government also needs to establish incentives and penalties in the registration program to ensure compliance and to extend competitive, transparent hiring of public employees to other entities or sectors (for example, education and health). Furthermore, the government needs to implement a new salary and human resources policy to rationalize the civil service, reorder its human resources, harmonize public functions and wages across the public sector, and establish performance-based promotion mechanisms.

Pending tasks with respect to tax administration and Customs include, in the first place, reaching a political and social consensus that keeps these services from being co-opted by interested sectors, reinforcing the technical nature of the National Tax Service (*Servicio de Impuestos Nacionales*—SIN), the Customs Service, and the Superintendency of Taxation, and doing away with interim mandates. Second, in the case of the SIN, the government's priorities include (i) completing taxpayer enrollment; (ii) improving information technology control processes and auditing; and (iii) establishing specialized units for the various economic sectors. In the case of the Customs Service, the government needs to devise a means to (i) consolidate the strategic plan; (ii) redefine the organization, role, and positions of the directors; (iii) improve auditing; (iv) define a strategy for the fight against contraband; and (v) incorporate management techniques and teamwork and coordinate with other auditing bodies.

These government policies, designed to improve the effectiveness and efficiency of the public administration, must be combined with others aimed at increasing transparency and eliminating corruption. Among these, the government could consider (i) simplifying processes and adopting e-government; (ii) defining and implementing mechanisms to allow citizens to participate in and evaluate public management; and (iii) approving rules for access to public information.

With respect to the justice system, in order for the services to be accessible to all citizens (especially the poorest population), the scope and quality of the service should be extended, and efficiency should be improved to reduce implicit and explicit costs. This would require (i) allocating more funds and logistic resources to the operators of the sector so that they can efficiently respond to the demands of the population; and (ii) increasing professional and administrative training for the personnel of the justice system. In addition, the government is advised to improve the selection and evaluation processes for judges, with the aim of ensuring the independence of the judiciary and reducing corruption; create new courts; and locate them to cover the more than 40 percent deficit at the local level. The design of the system should respond to the needs for justice of the different population groups, recognize cultural differences, consolidate community justice, and train operators in the correct application of justice (including gender issues and family violence). By promoting the participation of civil society as an external oversight agent, the government can encourage anticorruption practices, universal access to the justice system, and the proper management of the justice system. In addition, the authorities could consider measures to improve the security of the citizenry, including prevention (which is the most efficient measure in terms of costs and benefits), implementation of the national security plan (contemplated in Law 2494, with modifications if necessary), and reinforcement of the connection between the plan and the justice system, with coordination for its implementation.

The political and institutional framework of a more decentralized system in Bolivia will have a significant impact on the management and provision of public services. The government could anticipate this by defining a strategy for the second stage of decentralization, which will involve departmental governments. This strategy should focus, in the short term, on stabilizing the intergovernmental system. This would involve the application of public policies that should (i) improve regional equity in the distribution of transfers, with a priority on reducing inequality; (ii) promote the exchange of information among the various levels of government to increase transparency and create basic institutional capacities; and (iii) protect and improve the quality of the provision of services of the various subnational governments. In the medium and long term, the government could strengthen the intergovernmental system and decide what additional functions and responsibilities should be transferred to subnational governments. In this second phase, a possible alternative would be to proceed with decentralization by sectors (for example, rural roads, health, or education) through the various national, regional, and municipal levels, in an integrated manner. This process will involve negotiations and framework agreements. Progress will be gradual, and responsibilities for the provision of the least complex services should be transferred first. Equally important will be for the government to address vertical fiscal imbalance to reduce dependency on transfers as much as possible and reinforce the subnational governments' own revenue base. The experience of other countries shows that it is preferable to transfer expenditures, responsibilities, and functions before transferring revenue. At the same time, in order to address the challenge of fiscal responsibility, Bolivia could adopt fiscal responsibility rules that include the subnational governments, with explicit and transparent fiscal indicators, and defined penalties in the event of violations. Finally, so that the second phase of the decentralization will progress satisfactorily, the central government needs to ensure institutional strengthening of subnational governments (especially of the departments), in terms of both human resources and management systems.

IV. Some Suggestions on Areas of Priority and Schedule

The initial favorable social, political, and economic context allows for a certain margin in the design and implementation of public policies to promote the economic and social development of the country. It is, however, evident that the challenges are multiple and deep, and therefore call for comprehensive, immediate proposals. The preceding section attempts to address these challenges in their various dimensions and presents public policy options to increase growth and raise its quality, to create public services that benefit all, and to promote a transparent government, without corruption, and with civil society participation. It is not feasible to design and implement all these options simultaneously or in the short or medium term. We present a succinct suggested set of priority policy goals and schedules that represent a sub-set of the options described in detail in the preceding section (Table 3). Based on the lessons learned from Bolivia and the experience of other countries, achieving these goals would likely have the greatest impact on the challenges in the three areas—growth, public services, and good governance—with the fundamental objective of reducing poverty and exclusion.

Table 3. Suggested Areas of Priority and Schedule

	THE FIRST STAGE—2 YEARS	
Higher, better growth	***Public services that benefit all***	***Eliminate corruption and increase participation***
Strengthen the legal framework and improve the regulatory environment for business. Develop the oil industry. Negotiate free trade agreements. Improve the efficiency of financing for rural development.	Education—Facilitate access and continued attendance in school at the primary and secondary levels. Health—Link financing to performance incentives. Water—Resolve the current crisis and implement a financial policy. Social Program—Focus on the human development of children.	Public Administration—Consolidate reforms in administrative, financial, and oversight areas. Justice—Strengthen administration and management.

Part I

Growing More and Better

1

Socially Responsible Macroeconomic Management

Sara Calvo
in collaboration with Julio Velasco

Summary

Macroeconomic management in Bolivia has been adequate but remains vulnerable to political and social pressures. Though a favorable external environment has contributed to stabilization, the economy is still fragile. Investor and business confidence must be strengthened through clear signals in order to stimulate investment and allow the public sector to offer quality services to all Bolivians. One priority is to avoid increasing the fiscal imbalance while improving the efficiency of public sector spending. This will make room for increased public investment. Another priority is to to continue strengthening the financial sector. An adverse external or internal shock could jeopardize economic stability if the financial system were to weaken.

I. Introduction

Economic growth in Bolivia started to slow in 1999. Although this surprised many, given the strength of the reforms implemented, from a regional perspective the economic results were very good. Starting in 1998, Latin America suffered several adverse shocks, but Bolivia did not stop growing and did not suffer a financial crisis such as occurred in Argentina or Uruguay. Sound monetary and foreign exchange policy, a strengthened financial sector, and a strong expansion of gas exports contributed to this performance. The results could have been even better had there been a fiscal policy free from political and social pressures, which would have allowed a quicker adjustment to the external shocks. The immediate challenge facing the new government is to create conditions that will raise the level of investment and increase productivity throughout the economy. To accomplish this, it is necessary to maintain the current macroeconomic framework, continue eliminating obstacles that impede growth, and improve public services. This, in turn, will generate growth, reduce poverty, and help attain the Millennium Development Goals.

Bolivia currently enjoys a favorable economic climate, both externally and internally. Thanks to high international prices on gas exports, mining products, and soybeans, gross domestic product (GDP) grew by 4 percent in 2005; the fiscal deficit fell from approximately 9 percent of GDP in 2003 to 2 percent in 2005; inflation is single-digit; the exchange rate remains stable; and gross international reserves cover a third of the liabilities of the financial sector. In addition, the external debt has dropped to 50 percent of GDP and domestic debt has stabilized at approximately 25 percent of GDP (Figure 1). Imminent debt relief from the World Bank and the International Monetary Fund (IMF) highlights Bolivia's progress in macroeconomic management, public sector financial management, and implementation of its poverty reduction strategy.

Nonetheless, the current macroeconomic framework could easily deteriorate. The economy faces significant risks, which, if they were to materialize, would cause economic instability and, even in the best of cases, insufficient growth rates to reduce poverty. The risks in question include a possible fall in prices on export products and/or an increase in international interest rates. There is also a risk of major political and/or social pressure that could undermine the recent fiscal performance, which would inhibit growth if the economic program were to become unpredictable. If the economy were to decelerate or contract, deposits and credit would diminish, which would create problems in the financial and business sectors, as occurred in the late 1990s. Economic fragility would be exacerbated if this situation led to a devaluation of the currency, which would have a disproportionately strong impact on the real income of the poor.

The priority for the new government is to give clear signals on how it intends to apply its economic program and to continue strengthening its fiscal, financial, and institutional situation. Only macroeconomic stability would create an environment ripe for improving the public sector and increasing the productivity and growth rate of the economy. Section II of this chapter provides some background to the reforms of the late 1980s and early 1990s and assesses the principal risks facing the economy. Section III gives an overview of macroeconomic management and public expenditure from the late 1990s to the present, and Section IV presents specific recommendations.

II. Background and Diagnosis of Economic Risks

Bolivia has implemented major reforms, but its growth has been insufficient to reduce poverty. Social pressures and policies that interfere with fiscal management and threaten private property, along with regulations that make it costly for businesses to enter and exit from the economy, have hindered growth in the private sector.[1] Despite the reforms starting in the mid 1980s, only the primary export sectors have grown rapidly. (Box 1).

Figure 1. Trends in the Macroeconomic Situation

GDP is growing more . . .

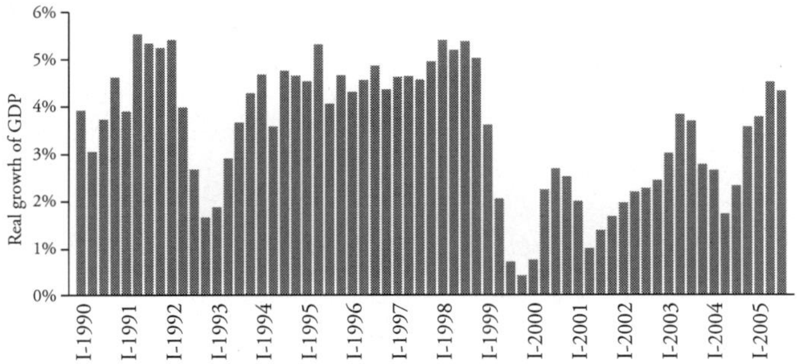

. . . thanks to record gas exports

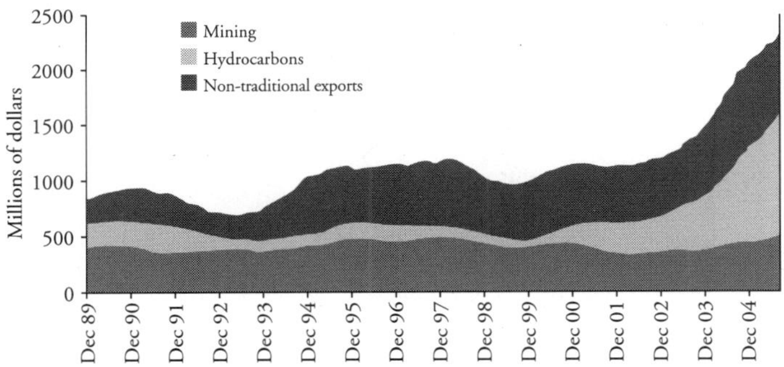

Single-digit inflation continues, devaluation is almost null,

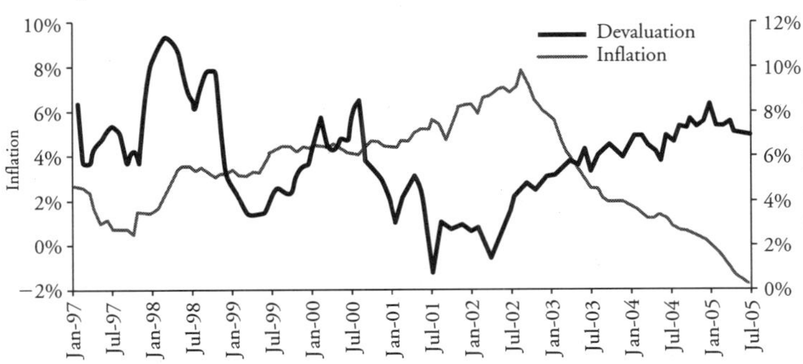

(*Figure continues on the following page.*)

Figure 1. Trends in the Macroeconomic Situation *(continued)*

and international reserves have risen

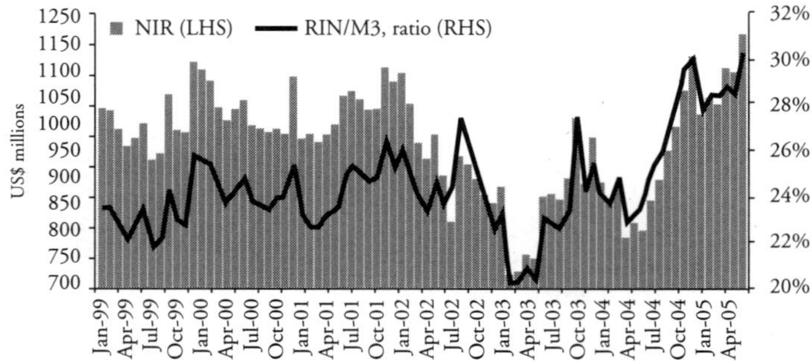

Public revenue has increased considerably . . .

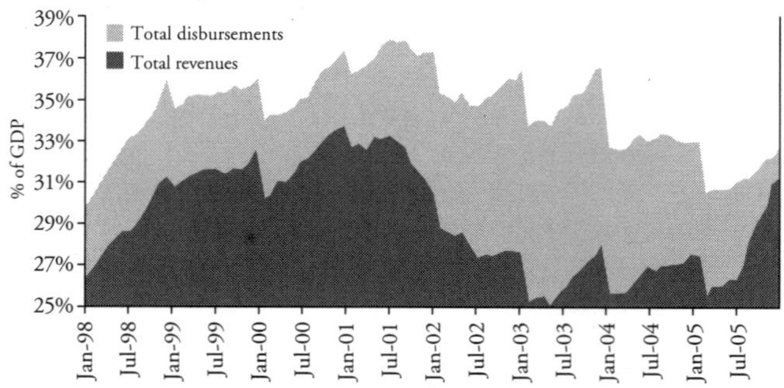

. . . reducing the fiscal deficit. Public debt has fallen.

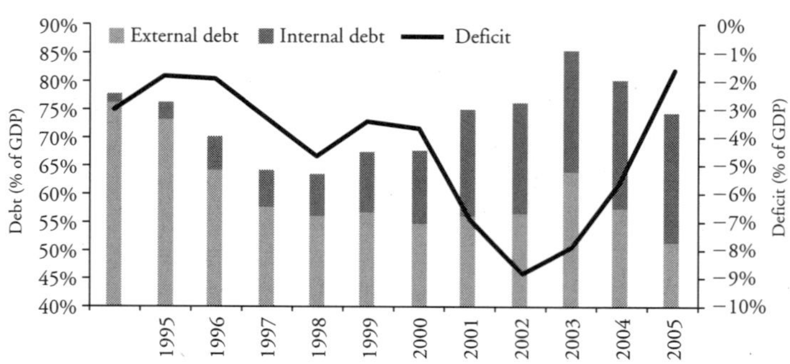

Sources: Central Bank of Bolivia (BCB), Ministry of Finance and the IMF.

Box 1. Macroeconomic Fragility and Growth in the 1990s

Beginning in the mid 1980s, Bolivia implemented a series of reforms intended to do away with inflation and improve economic efficiency. GDP growth, up until 1998, was significant (though not spectacular) and averaged 4.5 percent per year. Between 1985 and 1998, exports grew by 55 percent, while other countries of Latin America that also implemented reforms were able to increase their exports by 250 percent, and other developing countries had tripled their exports.

The reforms of the 1980s succeeded in stabilizing the economy but did not overcome the fragility of the fiscal and financial sectors. Political and social pressure led to greater expenditures (for example, on pensions) and therefore weakened the supervision and prudent regulation needed to maintain a strong financial system. The result was that the problems of the financial system remained, and in 1996, the bolstering of banks raised public expenditures by 4 percent of GDP. In this deficient business climate, foreign firms could develop only in sectors that offered a secure return on investment, such as exported products (in particular gas and soybeans). This sector prospered under the benefits of a favorable exchange rate and regional trade agreements.

The rest of the economy also grew, though at a slower rate, driven by the greater availability of bank credit (thanks to external financing received by local banks)—but productivity remained weak. In 2002, domestic private investment failed to surpass US$54 million (less than 1 percent of GDP), and it has since remained at low levels. The unfavorable situation of the Bolivian private sector can be explained by the high risk of appropriation on investment returns (as is reflected by financial capital flight starting in the late 1990s), constant changes in the "rules of play," and brain drain (that is, human capital flight).

Source: World Bank (2005a).

The Bolivian economy has faced a number of important risks, both external and domestic, that have affected its performance:

- *Nearly 90 percent of exports are primary products—namely hydrocarbons, mining products, and soybeans.* As a result, international price variations for these exports have had a negative impact on economic activity and have affected the influence of pressure groups in society.[2]
- *The percentage of exports destined for Latin American countries is high.* These exports represent approximately 48 percent of total Bolivian sales abroad—a

high amount compared with a ratio of approximately 20-30 percent for the rest of the region (Table1).[3] Therefore, if an external crisis were to strike the region, Bolivia would suffer from both the direct and indirect impact of the crisis on its trading partners.

- *The country depends on funds from the international community.* Nearly 2.5 percentage points of the budget deficit (in terms of GDP) are covered by grants, and approximately 5 percentage points (in terms of GDP) of public investment is financed through official external grants and loans. Any change in attitude toward Bolivia by donors and lending institutions would have a major effect on its financing sources for public expenditures.
- *The high degree of dollarization leaves little margin for an active monetary and foreign exchange policy.* The economy has the highest level of dollar liabilities in the region (approximately 90 percent of total bank loans at the end of 2005) and, after Uruguay, Bolivia is the country with the largest currency mismatch of all highly dollarized economies. Approximately 50 percent of the firms in the non-export sector have debts denominated in dollars.[4] This means that a devaluation would have a major impact on the liabilities of the public and private sectors, particularly on those with income from the non-traded sector, which operates in bolivianos.
- *Macroeconomic management in Bolivia is highly vulnerable to political and social pressure.* Bolivia is a poor country with multiple social demands and weak institutions vulnerable to fraud and corruption. This explains in part why Bolivians prefer to hold their deposits in dollars and not in national currency. It is also the reason why Bolivia is considered by international surveys to have one of the worst business climates in the world in terms of the effectiveness of the judicial system, respect for property rights, and bureaucracy (Figure 2). The drop in direct foreign investment from nearly 8.5 percent of GDP in 2002 to 1.3 percent in 2004, in the context of the debates on the new Hydrocarbons Act (characterized by its anti-private sector bias), is a recent example of the impact of this situation. Political and social pressures have interfered considerably with efforts to build a more resilient economy adaptable to economic shocks. For example, the government has not been able to implement a general tax reform due to opposition from Congress and the business community.
- *Institutional weakness makes political and social pressures effective.* Bolivia's institutional fragility is reflected in a deficient budget process and increased expenditures that have led to large fiscal deficits and to a rapid increase in the public debt. This brought the public debt stock back to levels predating the relief plan for Heavily Indebted Poor Countries (HPIC). The Bolivian budget, as compared with the level of its primary deficit, is the worst among many countries in the region (Figure 3).[5]
- *The expectation of economic instability also exposes the vulnerability of a possible flight in bank deposits.* Since 2002, there have been frequent withdrawals of

Table 1. Destination of Trade, 2003

Country	Regional Exports	USA	European Union	Rest of the World	Total	Regional Exports, by Region: Andean Community	Mercosur	Chile	Central America
Bolivia	48	22	27	3	100	23	18	5	0.1
Colombia	31	41	19	9	100	20	2	2	5
Ecuador	26	38	19	17	100	12	2	4	5
Peru	20	28	24	28	100	7	5	2	2
Venezuela	27	54	6	13	100	9	4	1	8
Andean Countries	27	45	13	15	100	12	4	2	6

Source: Rojas (2005). Differences in the totals are due to an approximation of the figures.

Figure 2. The Business Climate—Regional and Global Context

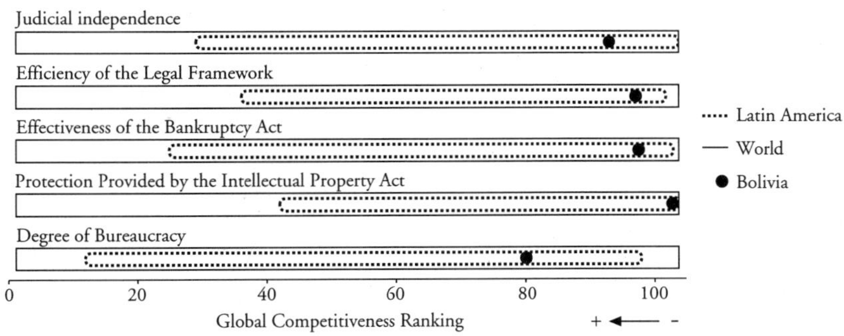

Source: World Economic Forum, 2004.

Figure 3. The Business Climate—International Comparison

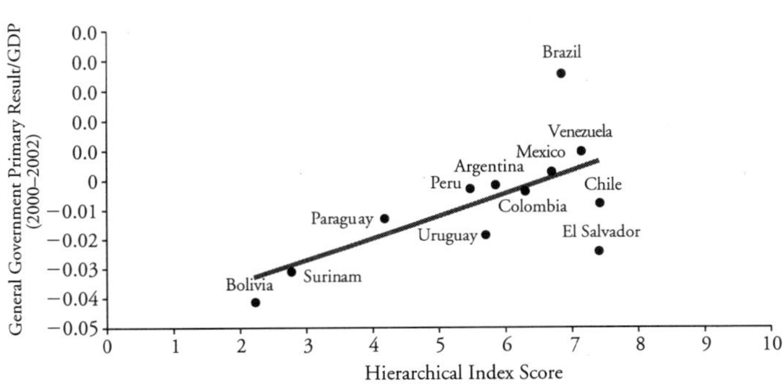

Source: Filc and Scartascini, 2004

bank deposits and interest rate hikes to prevent the collapse of the banking system (Figure 4). The country has also suffered from a loss of reserves. All of this illustrates the economy's sensitivity to social and political unrest. The runs on deposits are based on fears that the government will cave in to pressures for increased expenditures that would destabilize the economy, particularly if there were no additional income to back such spending.

III. Macroeconomic Management Since 1998

Bolivia has suffered intense external and domestic shocks since 1998.[6] These include the international capital market crisis of 1998 (which affected all of Latin America and provoked an abrupt fall in private capital inflows to the region) and the devaluations that occurred in Brazil in 1999 and Argentina in 2001. In Bolivia, public and private international capital flows (not including foreign direct investment) represented an average of less than 3.5 percent of GDP from 1999 to 2003 and reached their low point in 2002 (Box 2 and Figure 5).[7] These shocks were accompanied by an intense acceleration in coca leaf crop eradication and efforts aimed at reducing contraband through customs reform. Later, the pre-electoral uncertainty of 2002 also contributed to intensifying the effects of the external crisis.

Unlike Argentina and Uruguay, Bolivia did not experience a sizeable depreciation in the real exchange rate or a financial crisis as a result of this turbulence. Between 1998 and mid 2002, a gradual depreciation of the currency helped to sustain the competitiveness of the economy and had a limited impact on inflation. Nonetheless, while the Central Bank's monetary and foreign exchange policies were sound and contributed to stability, fiscal policy aggra-

Figure 4. Social Instability and Interest Rates

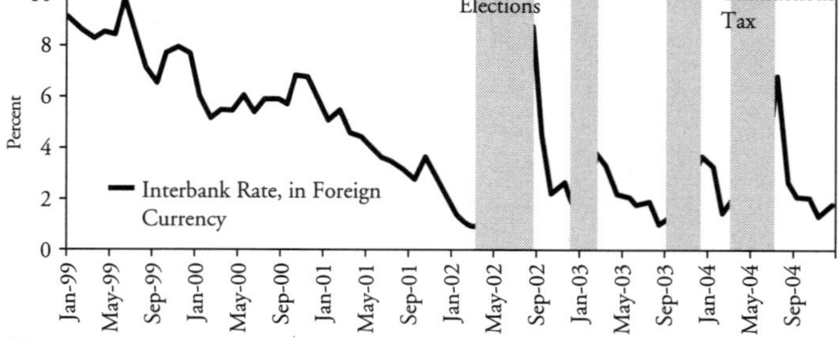

Source: BCB.

vated existing fiscal vulnerabilities. During the first half of 2000, tax incentives for creating jobs, pressures for wage increases from strong trade unions (such as the teachers' union), and a freezing of fuel prices increased the fiscal deficit. The increase in the fiscal gap was covered by domestic debt denominated in dollars at market interest rates, which placed even more pressure on public finances. Increased debt, slow growth, and a growing deficit threatened the solvency of the public sector in those years. In 2002/2003, Bolivia was on the brink of a financial collapse.

Bolivia's annual growth rate during the period of 1998 to 2003 averaged 2.4 percent. Though this is less than remarkable, it surpassed the rate of other economies in the region that faced similar shocks (including Argentina, Brazil, Ecuador, Peru, and Uruguay). The factors that contributed to this were: (i) sound monetary and foreign exchange policies; (ii) efforts that began in 1995 to strengthen the financial system; (iii) a major expansion of the oil and gas industry in 2001-2002, which resulted in the establishment of a new gas pipeline to transport gas to Brazil; and (iv) major transfers from the international community starting in 1999 (see Figure 1).[8] Chile also faced the same turbulence, but good macroeconomic management of the economy allowed it to keep growing, albeit at a slower pace.[9]

Box 2. How Have the Shocks Affected the Economy?

Economic turbulence decelerated the economy in Bolivia starting in the late 1990s. A sudden increase in the cost of external credit and a subsequent decline in internal credit, which, in particular, affected the non-traded sector, was the most direct blow. Indirect blows included a decreased demand for exports by Bolivia's Latin American trading partners, who also faced the same increase in the cost of credit. On the other hand, Brazil's devaluation in 1999 and Argentina's in 2001 also took their toll, since Bolivia lost competitiveness vis-à-vis those trading partners. These adverse factors caused deposits and bank credit to stagnate, increased the non-performing loan portfolio, and weakened the financial sector. The productive sector also suffered, in particular those enterprises with debt in dollars and income in bolivianos, that is, the non-traded sector (World Bank, 2002). The burden was particularly felt (as throughout the region) by the small and medium enterprise sector, which typically only receives short-term loans.

Source: BCB, Ministry of Finance, and the IMF.

Figure 5. Public and Private International Capital Flows

Private capital (without foreign direct investment) reversed, and . . .

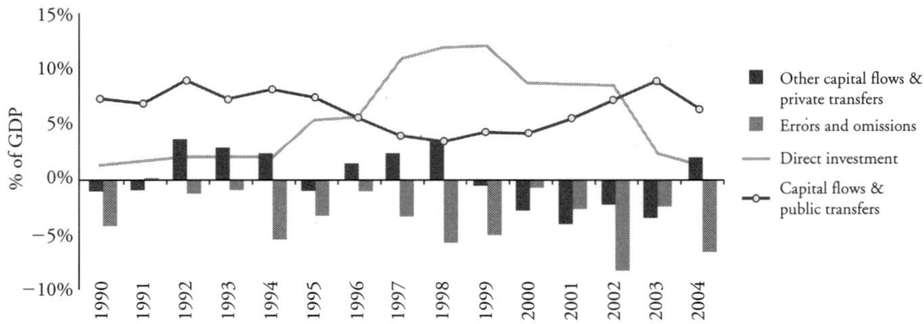

. . . a loss of competitiveness began

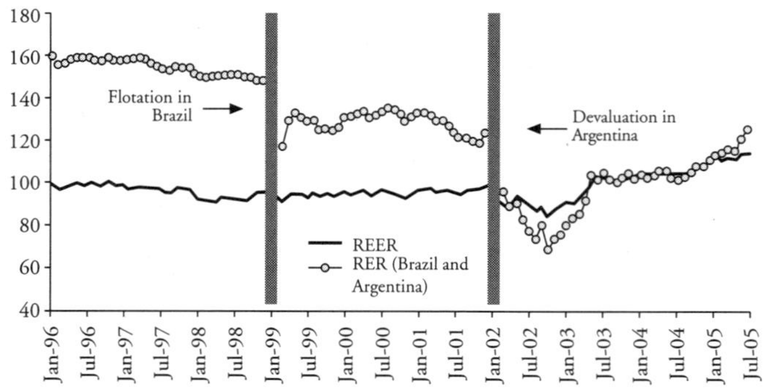

The banks' external financing diminished, and The financial sector's operations diminished, loans to the non-traded sector fell

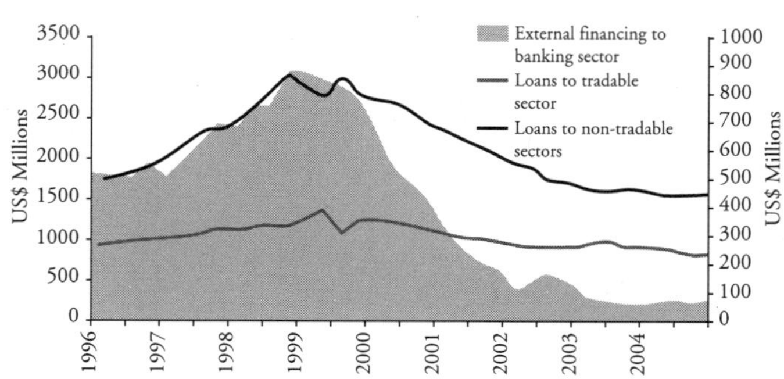

Figure 5. Public and Private International Capital Flows *(continued)*

and the default portfolio grew

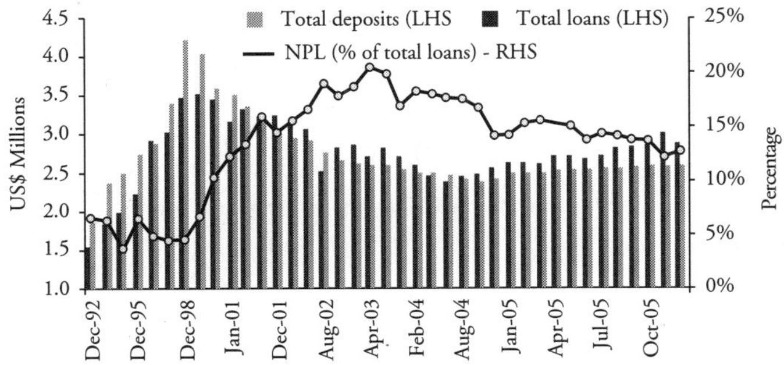

Source: BCB, Ministry of Finance, and the IMF.

Macroeconomic Management Today

Bolivia's monetary and foreign exchange policies merit credibility.

The monetary and foreign exchange policies ("crawling peg") of recent years have served the economy well given the country's high dollarization. Since mid-2002, the appreciation of the real exchange rate of its trading partners has helped maintain the real exchange rate in Bolivia without Central Bank intervention. This has limited the volatility of the real exchange rate, thereby limiting risks for exporters. As in the rest of the region, rising exports (and rising external revenue) have strengthened the boliviano. Until recently, unlike Brazil, Uruguay, and Chile (and perhaps wisely so, given significant uncertainties over future policies that could influence the exchange rate), the Central Bank maintained the nominal exchange rate through market interventions, but prices also rose, which limited the impact of this practice.[10]

A *high degree of liability dollarization*, that is, of public and private debt denominated in dollars, has limited the Central Bank's ability to use monetary or foreign exchange policy to absorb the impact of external shocks without threatening the stability of the business, financial, and public sectors. Dollarization of assets helps prevent an erosion in the value of capital in the event of increased inflation or a drastic devaluation. Yet holders of debt denominated in dollars (and, in particular, producers from the non-traded sector) run the risk of insolvency in the event of a devaluation. High dollarization requires low levels of debt and high levels of exports to absorb the impact of external shocks; this is something that Bolivia lacks.[11] The recent increase in open market operations with instruments indexed at long-term maturity price levels has contributed to de-dollarizing the economy without increasing refinancing risk. Other measures that have also considerably reduced the incentive to dollarize are: (i) increased international reserves, (ii) a financial transactions tax on deposits in dollars and (iii) changes in prudent regulations to internalize the credit risk of currency shortfalls on the balance sheets of lending companies. Although these measures help control the increase in liabilities denominated in dollars, it will be difficult to significantly reduce them unless there is confidence in the local currency's stability.

The Central Bank of Bolivia is independent and is one of the few institutions that enjoys credibility in Bolivia. This is clearly reflected in the surveys taken of companies— they indicate that inflation is not a concern, but the public deficit is.[12] Currently, there is still uncertainty regarding a possible major withdrawal of bank deposits. In such a case, if the Central Bank were to inject liquidity to support the financial sector, pressure would be exerted on the exchange rate that would require an exchange rate adjustment, as occurred in Mexico in 1994 and Argentina in 2001. The Argentine crisis had two characteristics that could be instructive for Bolivia: a fragile productive and financial sector and strong political pressure. In response to the flight of deposits from the Argentine financial system, and under instructions from the Ministry of Finance, the Central Bank injected liquidity to prevent a collapse of the payments system. This put pressure on the exchange rate, leading to the corresponding exchange rate adjustment, which increased public and private debt (denominated in dollars) in nominal terms. The result was a serious currency mismatch problem, especially for the non-traded sectors, whose income was in Argentine pesos and whose debt was denominated in dollars. A cessation of payments ensued for the public sector, along with serious problems of business solvency, with significant repercussions for growth and jobs. Bolivia could be vulnerable to something similar and should learn from the lessons of the Argentine case to avoid traumatic adjustments.

Fiscal policy, though improved, continues to be subject to social and political pressures.

The deficit of the consolidated non-financial public sector has fallen to 1.6 percent of GDP. Efforts to reduce the deficit have also affected pensions, the deficit on which fell from 4.4 percent of GDP in 2003 to 4.1 percent in 2005. The improved economic situation in recent years has facilitated implementation of sound measures to raise tax revenue, including the introduction of a new financial transactions tax in 2004. The application of the New Hydrocarbons Act in 2005 has also significantly increased revenue. Given the growing importance of taxes collected from the hydrocarbons sector, public revenue has become vulnerable to fluctuations in prices for hydrocarbons (see the chapter on taxes). On the expenditures side, payroll expenses have to some extent been contained and other cutbacks have been made. Unfortunately, investments have also been cut back, though in non-priority areas.

The public debt remains at 72 percent of GDP. Subnational debt has increased in recent years and is estimated at close to 5 percent of GDP.[13] Contingent liabilities remain high (World Bank, 2004). In recent years, as occurred in other countries that benefited from HIPC relief, domestic debt negotiated at market interest rates has become a significant source of financing. Almost all of the total public debt is domestic debt indexed at price levels or to the dollar. This raises concern over the country's long-term solvency should the current level of public debt, moderate growth rate, and fiscal deficit remain constant. In view of this situation, efforts have intensified to improve public debt management. A first step in this direction has been to issue debt with a longer maturity, indexed at price levels. Fiscal sustainability will also improve to the extent that debt relief is effective (for more details, see the chapter on debt).

Weak institutions lead to fiscal imbalance.

Institutions are weak in Bolivia. The most notable case is that of the entities managing the pension system, since they have contributed to fraudulent benefits and to inflating expenses. In addition, the budget process has not been used as an instrument to reflect the preferences of all Bolivians. This process, extensively discussed in the Public Expenditure Review,[14] is deficient and creates budget overruns. Until recently, the government was aggressively addressing the weaknesses of the pension institutions, and these efforts should continue.

Lessons and Diagnosis

The economic problems of the late 1990s and the social conflicts that commenced in 2000 were very costly for Bolivia. The growth rate of approximately 5 percent per year since the early 1990s was cut in half. Unemployment doubled, reaching 9 percent in 2003, and poverty increased from 62 percent of the population in 1999 to 65 percent in 2002.[15] Although the monetary and foreign exchange policies of these years were sound, a deficient fiscal policy and slow institutional reform prevented a quicker adjustment. This, in turn, caused social protests to intensify. Fiscal policy caved in to political and social pressures, which magnified economic instability and radicalized the protests. This slowed growth until 2004, despite the reforms (Figure 1).

Today, Bolivia is benefiting from a positive external environment. Its strongest growth in 2005 was based on record exports of primary products, such as gas, minerals, and soybeans. Other sectors of the economy, including non-primary exports, continue to experience modest growth. The priority for Bolivia is to continue addressing the vulnerability of the fiscal and financial sector and to strengthen its institutions, thereby protecting the economy in the event of an adverse external shock that would be particularly costly for the poor. It is also important to create conditions for other sectors to grow by, for example, improving the efficiency of the legal framework and effective enforcement of contracts to make it easier to access long-term loans.[16]

INCREASE THE EFFICIENCY OF THE PUBLIC SECTOR

Bolivia's social indicators have improved substantially. There are more rural households with access to electricity, coverage of healthcare services for the poor has increased, as has coverage for water and sanitation services in all the departments. Advances in education have also been admirable. Decentralization and the HIPC relief plan have contributed to improve the coverage of public services and to reduce inequality in public spending. Nonetheless, serious problems remain. In education, for example, the students who benefit the most from public spending are university students of the highest income level. Table 2 illustrates that the wealthiest students benefit from 52 percent of total expenditures at universities, while those with the lowest income receive only 2 percent. The distribution is more equitable at other levels of education.

In other sectors the distribution is more equitable. In the case of health, public per capita expenditures increasingly reach the poorest families. In the case of infrastructure, while the richest families benefited the most until 1997, after 2000, the gap in municipal budget allocations narrowed. With respect to access to services, there is a strong positive correlation between levels of access to services and per capita income. For example, the percentage of households with access to electricity among the richest households is more than twice the percentage among the poorest households with access to the same service. These results do not indicate that the municipal governments favor those who are not poor. They merely suggest that efforts need to be channeled toward policies that increase the speed at which the poor benefit from infrastructure services.[17] In the rural areas, access to infrastructure services is even more limited, which calls for greater efforts to reach that population.[18] Finally, the need to address fiscal imbalance has mandated cutbacks in public investment. Counterpart funds for investments in projects financed by multilateral institutions were not always available, in particular during episodes of adjustment; therefore, public investment fell.[19]

LESSONS AND DIAGNOSIS

Bolivia has advanced considerably in terms of the coverage and equity of social services. Nonetheless, fiscal imbalance and institutional weaknesses have hindered rapid progress in the fight against poverty and jeopardized the sustainability of the the past decade's achievements. Although public investment has been decentralized, the

Table 2. Public Spending by Level of Education in Total Expenditures on Education, by Quintiles (Percentages)

	Quintile 1 (poorest)	*Quintile 2*	*Quintile 3*	*Quintile 4*	*Quintile 5 (richest)*	*TOTAL*
Primary education	24	23	21	18	14	100
Secondary education	12	20	21	22	25	100
University education	2	4	14	28	52	100
Other higher education	6	9	19	29	37	100

Source: Bolivia Public Expenditure Review, 2004.

transfers received by the municipalities have been volatile, which has affected the quality of public services. The low technical capacity of some municipalities and prefectures has also been a hindrance, as has the absence of coordination among them. Recent government efforts have limited fiscal imbalance, but that imbalance must continue to diminish. Unfortunately, the need to maintain fiscal discipline comes at a time when social demands are high and when Bolivia needs to make investments to ensure growth, with special emphasis on improving the income-generating capacity of the poor. This means that corrections cannot be made merely through spending cuts, but rather by applying reforms to improve the efficiency and equity of expenditures and promoting private sector participation. In that way, the government will be able to continue providing public services and investments within a sustainable fiscal framework.

IV. Conclusions and Recommendations

The growth of the Bolivian economy during the past 20 years has not been sufficient to significantly reduce poverty. The root of the problem lies in political and social pressures, due to which Bolivians have had to face changing and unclear economic measures that increase the risk of a drop in expected yields and therefore inhibit investment. Only with reliable management that sustains macroeconomic stability, contributes to maintaining a solid financial sector, and allocates public funds efficiently and equitably will private investment increase, which in turn will contribute to creating new job opportunities. Macroeconomic stability is a necessary but insufficient condition to attain this objective. Legal, institutional, and regulatory reforms are also needed to improve the business environment, topics that are addressed in other policy notes. This note limits itself to public policy proposals related to sound macroeconomic management.

Priorities in Macroeconomic Management

One of the major challenges of macroeconomic management is to minimize risks that could interfere with growth and job creation. These obstacles are the adverse domestic events and government responses that lead to an unsustainable fiscal expansion or to capital flight and problems in the financial sector. There is a wealth of knowledge gathered from the experiences of different countries on how poor management of these risks affects the economy. Bolivia itself provides several examples. Increased international interest rates in a context of high public and private debt denominated in dollars led to the debt crisis of the 1980s. Failure to reduce public expenditures on time led to financing them by creating money, which, in turn, led to hyperinflation in 1985. The result was an unstable and highly dollarized economy. The deceleration of the late 1990s was associated with external shocks that led to a tightening of credit in the region, including credit for Bolivia. It also intensified public and private fragilities given that private activity and, with it, tax collections, slowed down. Unfortunately, domestic problems further aggravated these fragilities.

Monetary and foreign exchange policies, though limited by extensive dollarization, have served Bolivia well, kept inflation under control and helped keep Bolivian products competitive on the international market. The foreign exchange policy has served as the anchor of economic and financial policy. It is helping to maintain Bolivia's competitiveness through small adjustments in the exchange rate while also limiting the negative effects of exchange adjustments on the balances of the non-traded sector. The less positive aspect of this foreign exchange policy is that it cannot respond rapidly to external changes. It would be wise to proceed with caution in moving to policies more strictly anchored to monetary aggregates while maintaining strict fiscal discipline and prudent fiscal management. In addition, to best protect the country from adverse events, given Bolivia's high degree of dollarization, it is important to:

- maintain current bank reserve levels, in case liquidity is needed to protect the banks against deposit withdrawals;
- maintain a high level of international reserves; and
- keep the economy open to international trade in order to increase and intensify the diversification of exports and thus better mitigate external shocks.

In the fiscal arena, equilibrium depends upon containing public expenditures and increasing tax collections. The fiscal deficit has fallen significantly, but tax revenue is volatile and total public debt is now higher than prior to implementation of the HIPC relief plan. The Public Expenditure Review and other policy notes provide an exhaustive analysis of public sector expenditures, with concrete recommendations regarding fiscal stability, the budget process, and reform of the civil service and payroll, along with suggestions for specific sectors. The analysis emphasizes the benefits of fiscal rules, which have given some countries the tools needed to develop credibility. Brazil, Chile, and Peru have successfully implemented these rules. As the economy becomes less dependent upon external financing, the Chilean approach, where budget allocations are contingent upon the growth cycle, could be the correct one for Bolivia.[20] Similarly, maintaining a fund to reduce the volatility of fiscal revenue, given its high dependence upon the price of gas, could help maintain fiscal stability. The current fiscal position is a good opportunity to start designing such an approach.

Another major challenge is to increase *the efficiency of public spending*. Bolivia's high debt suggests that the government sector is too large in relation to the revenue it collects.[21] Because cutting spending in the face of pressing social needs is difficult, the government must make every effort to maximize the impact of scarce public resources. It is important to remember this in light of the country's next stage of decentralization—bearing in mind that the subnational debt is already high. An increase in the fiscal gap, with public expenditures that remain volatile, would not be good for maintaining quality public services. Issues involving tax revenue, debt, and decentralization, as well as the challenges they pose, go beyond the scope of this chapter. As for government spending, the Public Expenditure Review provides an exhaustive list of measures that could be implemented to increase efficiency and equity. Implementation of the following measures is still pending, in whole or in part:

a. **Prioritize public investment**. In Chile and Colombia, the office in charge of evaluations is also responsible for protecting budget allocations for the projects selected.
b. **Contain the payroll.** In this area, it will be useful to extend administrative reforms, make the wage policy more transparent, and continue to improve the registration of public sector employees.
c. **Strengthen the budget formulation process**. This entails implementing the framework law on the budget, aimed at improving the budget formulation process at all levels of government. This law would lay the foundation for implementing a system based on initial estimates of three or four years using available and projected funds.
d. **Strengthen execution and supervision of the budget**. To accomplish that, it would be necessary to:
   i. Implement a plan of action to reduce delays in payments and improve compliance with informational requirements on the budget's implementation.
   ii. Implement the recent recommendations of the General Comptroller of the Republic to strengthen and support implementation of the internal control system using performance indicators.
   iii. Continue implementing the plan of action to train members of the oversight committees on issues such as control and social auditing, the budget process, and systems administration.
   iv. Complete implementation of the Comptroller's recommendations on the central government's financial reports in order to facilitate external auditing.
   v. Implement the plan of action developed to harmonize rules and regulations for public procurement.
   vi. Enact a public procurement act.
e. **Improve the administration of tax revenue**. Here, it is suggested that Bolivia start with fiscally neutral measures.
f. **Strengthen national and subnational debt management**. Improve the domestic debt's currency composition and term and strengthen institutional support for debt management.
g. **Contain the subnational debt**. Continue to implement the subnational debt registration system for the prefectures and municipalities.

Bibliography

Ajwad, Mohamed Ihsan and Quentin Wodon. 2002. "Who Benefits from Increased Access to Public Services at the Local Level?" *World Bank Economist Forum*, vol. 2.

Antelo Callisperis, Eduardo. 2002. "*El balance fiscal cíclicamente ajustado.*" Prepared for the Andean Development Corporation.

Calvo, Guillermo, Alejandro Izquierdo, and Ernesto Talvi. 2002. "Sudden Stops, the Exchange Rate and Fiscal Sustainability: Argentina's Lessons." Inter-American Development Bank, Washington DC.

Filc, Gabriel and Carlos Scartascini. 2004. "Fiscal Deficits and Disenchantment in Latin America. A New Look at the Role of Fiscal Rules and Budget Procedures on Determining Fiscal Outcomes." Office of Evaluation and Oversight. Inter-American Development Bank. Washington, DC. September.

Galindo, Arturo and Alejandro Micco. 2005. "Bank Credit to Small and Medium Sized Enterprises: the Role of Creditor Protection." *Working Document No. 347*, December. Central Bank of Chile.

Inter-American Development Bank (IADB). 2003. "Good Jobs Wanted. Economic and Social Progress in Latin America." Inter-American Development Bank. Washington, DC.

———. 2004. "Unlocking Credit. Economic and Social Progress in Latin America." Inter-American Development Bank. Washington, DC.

Klein, Herbert. 1992. *Bolivia. The Evolution of a Multi-Ethnic Society.* New York: Oxford University Press.

Morales, Juan Antonio. 1990. "Bolivia's Economic Crisis," in Jeffrey D. Sachs (*ed.*), *Developing Country Debt and Economic Performance.* National Bureau of Economic Research. The University of Chicago Press, Chicago.

———. 2004a. "The National Revolution and its Legacy, in Merilee S. Grindle and Pilar Domingo (*eds.*), *Proclaiming Revolution: Bolivia in Comparative Perspective.* Cambridge, MA: Harvard University Press.

Perry, Guillermo and Luis Servén. 2003. "Anatomy of a Multiple Crisis: Why was Argentina Special and What Can We Learn from It?," in George M. Von Furstenberg, Volbert Alexander, and Jacques Melitz (*eds.*), *Monetary Union and Hard Peg: Effects on Trade, Financial Development, and Stability.* New York: Oxford University Press.

Reinhart, Carmen, Kenneth Rogoff, and Miguel Savastano. 2003. "Addicted to Dollars." NBER Working Paper 10015, National Bureau of Economic Research, Cambridge, MA.

Reinnhack, Robert and Masahiro Nozaki. 2006. "Financial Dollarization in Latin America." IMF Working Paper WP/06/7. International Monetary Fund. Washington, DC. January.

Rojas, Laura. 2005. "The Challenge of the Regional Trade Agenda for the Andean Countries." Presentation prepared for Johns Hopkins University SAIS Course, April 19.

Talvi, Ernesto. 2002. "*Frenazos, endeudamientos y dolarización.*" Presentation at the Central Bank of Bolivia.

World Bank. 1994a. "Bolivia: Structural Reforms, Fiscal Impacts, and Economic Growth." Country Economic Memorandum. Washington, DC.

———. 2000a. "Securing Our Future in a Global Economy," in David De Ferranti, Guillermo Perry, Indermit Gill, and Luis Servén (*eds.*). World Bank Latin American and Caribbean Studies. Washington, DC.

———. 2000b. "Bolivia. From Patronage to a Professional State. Bolivia. Institutional and Governance Review." Washington, DC.

———. 2002. "Bolivia. Financial Sector Assessment Program." Washington, DC.

———. 2004. "Bolivia. Public Expenditure Review." Washington, DC.

———. 2005a. "Bolivia. Country Economic Memorandum." Washington, DC.

———. 2005b. "Chile. Development Policy Review." Washington, DC.

World Economic Forum. 2004. *The Global Competitiveness Report.* New York: Oxford University Press.

Endnotes

1. World Bank (2005a).
2. The fall of prices on minerals and the increased price and demand for coca leaves in the 1980s gave the coca leaf growers a prominent role, to the detriment of trade unions in the mining industry (Klein, 2004).
3. Rojas (2005).
4. Reinnhack and Nozaki (2006).
5. World Bank (2004).
6. See World Bank (2005a, Annex 2.1) for a detailed list of these shocks.
7. Includes official transfers, money remittances, foreign direct investment, portfolio flows and errors and omissions. This item of the balance of payments typically reflects capital flight. The reversal of the inflow of private capital (excluding foreign direct investment) starting in 1999 occurred following a virtually constant inflow of capital since 1992, principally in the form of debt assumed by local private banks.
8. Since 1995, the government has taken measures to strengthen the financial sector by enacting a new banking law and a series of regulations and statutory requirements that have improved the solvency and efficiency of Bolivian banks. In general, the reforms have significantly improved the capacity of banks to withstand potential withdrawals of deposits and have strengthened the monetary authorities' ability to manage such situations.
9. World Bank (2005b).
10. During an economic expansion, the Central Bank can decide to allow the nominal exchange rate to appreciate, or may keep it relatively fixed at the cost of a certain degree of inflation (since the increased liquidity is not accompanied by an increase in the demand for local currency).
11. Calvo, Izquierdo, and Talvi (2005).

12. World Economic Forum (2004).
13. World Bank (2000b).
14. World Bank (2004).
15. Bolivia was also hit by shocks in the mid 1990s, but major capital inflows attracted by high yields prevented a deceleration of the economy.
16. Galindo and Micco (2005).
17. Ajwad and Wodon (2002).
18. World Bank (2004).
19. Wage control also contributed to a slower growth in public spending from 2004 to 2005.
20. Central Bank of Chile, from World Bank (2000a) and Antelo (2002).
21. Given that different countries have different strategies for the public sector, international comparisons of the size of the public sector based on spending data can lead to distortions (for example, Peru has fewer expenditures, but higher levels of tax exemptions and fiscal expenses, which are not taken into account).

2

Taxes, Collection Capabilities, and Distribution

Carlos Mollinedo and Julio Velasco
with contributions from Steven Webb and Enrique Fanta

Summary

Bolivia has made significant progress in improving the tax system and modernizing tax administration. Nonetheless, the tax system still has limitations, including a lack of progressiveness, deterioration of the tax base, and administrative weakness. Recent developments related to the gas and oil industry are also posing new challenges in terms of taxation. The latest change in the tax rules for the gas and oil industry has significant consequences and deserves careful analysis. At the same time, that sector's accelerated growth is distorting the current tax allocation system and intensifying existing imbalance among the different regions and levels of government.

I. Background

Until 1985, Bolivia collected a large number of taxes—more than 150—yet tax revenue continually declined, bottoming out at 2 percent of GDP that year. After the tax reform of 1986, the current system went into effect it mainly consists of taxes on consumption, particularly the Value-Added Tax (VAT). This new system reduced the number of taxes and simplified the tax structure. As a result, tax revenue rose to 15 percent of GDP by 1990.

This system continued without major changes until the mid 1990s, when the Presumed Corporate Income Tax (*Impuesto a la Renta Presunta de Empresas*—IRPE), based on the net equity of the taxpayers, was replaced by the Corporate Earnings Tax (*Impuesto a las Utilidades de las Empresas*—IUE). The IRPE was replaced because it failed to encourage investment, since the tax was independent of a company's financial results and was not eligible for tax credits abroad. The tax system was also changed for the gas and oil industry to make it competitive with international standards. On the other hand, intensified decentralization was accompanied by the creation of the Special Tax on Hydrocarbons and Derivatives (*Impuesto Especial sobre los Hidrocarburos y sus Derivados*—IEHD), introduced to cover the jurisdiction granted to the department and the transfer of the Real Property and Motor Vehicles Tax (*Impuesto sobre la Propiedad de Bienes Inmuebles y Vehículos Automotores*—IPBIVA) to the municipalities.

Thanks to these changes, tax revenue increased from 15 percent of GDP in 1990 to 21 percent in 1998 (see Figure 1). This rise in revenue helped absorb the decline in royalties, which fell from 7 percent of GDP in 1990 to only 2 percent in 1998 due to stagnation in the mining sector and a temporary suspension of gas exports to the Argentina. Meanwhile, revenue from customs duties and municipal taxes, introduced in 1995, held steady at 2 percent of GDP.

Starting in late 1998, tax revenue fell due to diminished economic growth, with national tax revenue falling by 2 percentage points of GDP between 1998 and 2003. In response, the government introduced several tax amnesties and added the Financial Transactions Tax (*Impuesto a las Transacciones Financieras*—ITF), intended to be interim measures to increase revenue. These measures were taken despite the adverse effects they might have in the medium term, given that tax regularization programs tend to encourage tax evasion, create expectations of future amnesties, and involve a partial sacrifice of revenue. In July 2004, the government temporarily introduced the ITF, which, since it taxes bank debits as well as bank credits, has a potentially negative effect on financial intermediation. In addition, as of 2000, IEHD revenue diminished due to a price freeze on hydrocarbons in the domestic market. This freeze was applied by the government as an anti-cyclical policy in response to intense social resistance to price increases on hydrocarbon derivatives.

Figure 1. Trends and Structure of Tax Revenue in Bolivia, 1990-2004
(Percentages of GDP)

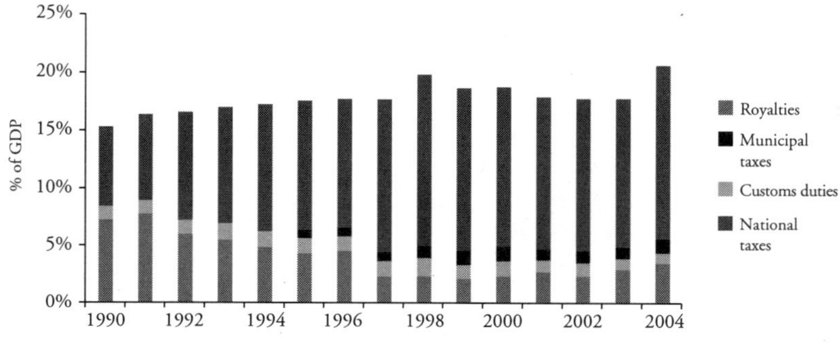

Source: Ministry of Finance, Fiscal Programming Unit.

These measures prevented a greater fall in revenue but did not overcome structural problems in the national tax system. Indeed, they introduced distortions limiting the tax system's efficiency and in some cases created adverse incentives for private activity. On the other hand, the simplicity of the current tax system, a trait lauded in the past, has compounded inequities in revenue collection. This problem is particularly important considering that Bolivia has one of the most regressive tax collection structures in the region. Table 1 illustrates that the national tax system is regressive, since tax pressure on the income of households in the wealthiest quintile is only 14 percent, while it represents 25 percent for the poorest quintile. Though certain taxes are progressive, such as the IPBIVA, their impact on the system is limited, since their amount is so low.

Despite this unfavorable framework, several measures have been introduced to improve the efficiency of the tax administration. Of note are the institutional reforms to the National Tax Service (*Servicio de Impuestos Nacionales*—SIN) and to the National Customs Service. Begun in the late 1990s, these measures are significantly improving revenue. In 2004, a new tax code went into effect that further empowers the authorities in charge of controlling and reducing tax evasion, and a Tax Superintendency was created as a mechanism to expedite hearings on disputes. These reforms have improved efficiency, but need to be better targeted and intensified.

The development of the gas and oil industry and last year's amendment to the Hydrocarbons Act have created new tax challenges. Starting in the mid 1990s, the gas and oil industry grew rapidly. This increased natural gas reserves and, due to a strong injection of foreign capital resulting from a favorable legal framework for private activity, raised gas exports to Brazil and Argentina. Nonetheless, government revenue did not increase proportionally. The Hydrocarbons Act was reformed in 2005, introducing the Direct Tax on Hydrocarbons (*Impuesto Directo sobre los Hidrocarburos*—IDH). Though this new tax has considerably increased tax revenue in the short term, it could also inhibit the future growth of the sector. The new law is also intensifying imbalance in the allocation of tax revenue among the different levels of government (central government, departments, and municipalities) and the regions, not only increasing inequity among the regions, but also compromising fiscal sustainability.

Table 1. Tax Burden as a Percentage, by Household Income Quintiles

	Quintile				
	1	*2*	*3*	*4*	*5*
Percentage of household income	25%	20%	21%	19%	14%

Source: Cossio (2001).
Note: The following taxes are included: VAT, IT, ICE, and IEHD*
(*) Value Added Tax (VAT); Tax on Transactions *(Impuesto a las Transacciones*—IT); Specific Consumption Tax (*Impuesto a los Consumos Específicos*—ICE); and the Special Tax on Hydrocarbons and their Derivatives (*Impuesto Especial sobre los Hidrocarburos y sus Derivados*—IEHD)

II. Evaluation of National Taxes and Policy Options

The current tax system in Bolivia consists primarily of consumption taxes, which represent more than 70 percent of total tax revenue, or 11 percent of GDP (Table 2). The Value-Added Tax (VAT) and the transactions tax, which are taxes on general consumption, represent 6.3 percent and 2.2 percent of GDP respectively. The Specific Consumption Tax, on the sale of beverages, tobacco, and automobiles, and the IEHD, on hydrocarbons consumption, both raise about 2 percent of GDP. Among non-consumption taxes, the Corporate Income Tax and the Supplementary System to the VAT together amount to approximately 2.5 percent of GDP. Interim taxes and the ITF raised the equivalent of 1.6 percent of GDP in 2004. However, this revenue is not sustainable as it is generated by interim measures designed to overcome specific financial problems of the public sector. The remaining taxes, including an array of special taxes for small businesses, transportation companies, and agricultural producers, account for only 0.1 percent of total tax revenue (see Annex 1 for details).

General Taxes on Consumption (VAT and IT)

The VAT, with its broad tax base, raises the most revenue, about 42 percent of tax collections, or more than 6 percent of GDP. The VAT rate in Bolivia is close to the region's average, though much lower than the rates in Uruguay, Argentina, Brazil,

Table 2. Structure of National Tax Revenue, 1990-2004

	% of the Total				*% of GDP*			
	1990	*1995*	*2000*	*2004*	*1990*	*1995*	*2000*	*2004*
VAT	52.3	54.7	40.5	41.8	3.6	6.4	5.6	6.3
IT	16.4	19.3	13.9	14.8	1.1	2.3	1.9	2.2
ICE	11.2	9.8	9.1	5.4	0.8	1.1	1.3	0.8
IEHD	0.0	0.3	19.2	10.9	0.0	0.0	2.7	1.6
IUE*	0.0	1.6	13.8	13.9	0.0	0.2	1.9	2.1
RC-VAT	6.4	4.5	3.0	1.8	0.4	0.5	0.4	0.3
ITF	0.0	0.0	0.0	3.0	0.0	0.0	0.0	0.5
Interim Programs **	0.0	0.0	0.0	7.5	0.0	0.0	0.0	1.1
Special Regimes	0.4	0.1	0.1	0.1	0.0	0.0	0.0	0.0
Others ***	13.3	9.7	0.4	0.8	0.9	1.1	0.1	0.1
Total	**100.0**	**100.0**	**100.0**	**100.0**	**6.8**	**11.7**	**13.9**	**15.1**

Source: SIN.

Note: (*) Includes the Presumed Corporate Income Tax (*Impuesto a la Renta Presunta de Empresas—*IRPE), which, as of 1994, was replaced by the Corporate Earnings Tax (*Impuesto a las Utilidades de las Empresas*—IUE). (**) Interim programs prior to 2004 are not explicitly included. (***) Includes the Real Property and Motor Vehicles Tax (*Impuesto sobre la Propiedad de Bienes Inmuebles y Vehículos Automotores*—IPBIVA), which was transferred to the municipalities with the Popular Participation Act, as well as other taxes of less importance.

Table 3. The VAT in Latin America, 2001

	*Standard Rate**	*Productivity***
Argentina	21.0	0.30
Bolivia	**14.9**	**0.43**
Brazil	20.5	..
Chile	18.0	0.58
Colombia	16.0	0.32
Costa Rica	13.0	0.45
Dominican Republic	12.0	0.31
Ecuador	12.0	0.42
El Salvador	13.0	0.49
Guatemala	12.0	0.42
Honduras	12.0	0.55
Mexico	15.0	0.28
Nicaragua	15.0	0.60
Panama	5.0	0.52
Paraguay	10.0	0.51
Peru	18.0	0.42
Uruguay	23.0	0.31
Venezuela	14.5	0.31

Source: Stotsky and WoldeMariam (2002).
Note: (*) The effective rate, calculated as rates on price net of tax. (**) Efficiency C: VAT collections, as a percentage of consumption divided by the effective rate.

Chile, and Peru (Table 3). VAT productivity is relatively high, though there is still room for improvement. The experience of Nicaragua demonstrates that it is possible to be more efficient with rates similar to those of Bolivia. Chile and Peru demonstrate that higher effective rates can result in the same or greater productivity levels.

The VAT falls short of its collection potential because many sectors are exempt from paying it, notably the special regimes, which in 2004 covered nearly 30 percent of taxpayers. There are also exemptions that benefit specific departments and municipalities.

Collection of the transaction tax (*Impuesto a las Transacciones*—IT) has held steady at approximately 2 percent of GDP. However, this is a cumulative tax that distorts relative prices, inhibits the economy's vertical integration, and hinders the competitiveness of domestic production. Due to this tax, goods produced in Bolivia can be more expensive than their imported counterparts. In addition, though exports are not taxed by the IT, exporters cannot recover the IT included in the inputs used, which reduces their international competitiveness. On the other hand, the IT paid by companies is deducted from net earnings taxed by the Corporate Income Tax (*Impuesto a las Utilidades de las Empresas*—IUE), which reduces the combined collection of the two taxes.

Policy Options

Based on the preceding diagnosis, the government could:

- Expand the VAT tax base, reduce exemptions and the existing special regimes and special zones.
- Substitute the collection of the IT with an increase in the VAT rate and/or an expansion of the VAT tax base. The VAT rate should increase by a few percentage points, depending upon the expansion of the tax base.

Selective Taxes on Consumption (ICE and IEHD)

The ICE taxes only the production or importation stage of beverages, tobacco, and vehicles. Rates of 10 to 18 percent apply on most vehicles, and the rate on tobacco is 50 percent. The ICE also sets fixed rates in bolivianos per liter, adjusted each year to the exchange rate, on alcoholic and non-alcoholic beverages. ICE revenue is quite modest; it accounts for less than 1 percent of total revenue, due to contraband and tax evasion. Nearly two-thirds of the revenue raised from this tax is on beer consumption, while imports add only another 20 percent. On the other hand, tax amnesties applied in recent years on vehicle imports have significantly reduced revenue from this tax.

The IEHD taxes domestic consumption of oil and natural gas derivatives through fixed rates in bolivianos. Since 2000, its revenue has sharply diminished because the government froze prices on hydrocarbons in the domestic market. This policy has created a *de facto* subsidy on hydrocarbon derivatives (the subsidy on imported diesel oil alone would be equivalent to 0.8 percent of GDP in 2005). A continual increase in international prices on hydrocarbons and the constant devaluation of the boliviano have resulted in a fall in IEHD revenue from 3 percent of GDP in 2000 to less than 2 percent in 2004. Revenue from this tax was expected to be 2.5 percent of GDP for 2005, since the government reduced the margins of earnings of the refineries. Price differences compared to neighboring countries have led to illegal exports of LPG and diesel to some border areas, which has created supply shortages on the domestic market.

Policy Options

Based on the above, the government could:

- Adjust the proportion of the ICE on beverages so that the combined weight of the VAT and the ICE represent a uniform percentage of prices. Based on international experience, these taxes could represent approximately 25 percent of the final consumer price.
- Aggressively combat contraband to reduce evasion of the ICE tax. Tax amnesties should be avoided, since they erode revenue and encourage tax evasion.
- Do away with the use of the IEHD as a tool to subsidize hydrocarbons on the domestic market, gradually free domestic prices and allow them to adjust to international price variations and to the exchange rate, particularly gasoline and diesel prices.

Taxes on Earnings (RC-VAT and IUE)

The three taxes on earnings are i) Corporate Income Tax (IUE), ii) Supplementary System to the VAT (RC-VAT), and iii) Tax on Mining Income (*Impuesto a las Utilidades Mineras*—IUM). Of these, only the IUE generates significant revenue of approximately 2.1 percent of GDP. In contrast, the contribution of the RC-VAT is only 0.3 percent of GDP and that of the IUM is insignificant.

Originally, the RC-VAT was created to monitor the VAT, since the system for providing proof of its payment encourages consumers to request invoices. Nonetheless, implementation of the RC-VAT is weak because: (i) there is an informal market for selling and falsifying invoices, which has destroyed the base of this tax, making it useless for controlling the VAT; (ii) the RC-VAT most closely emulates an income tax, though its structure makes it more similar to a tax on savings; (iii) its contribution to tax revenue is marginal; and (iv) it does not add progressivity to the tax system, since it has a fixed rate.

The IUE has several positive features. Unlike taxes with a presumed tax base, it promotes private activity as it keeps taxation from being too lenient on companies during expansive cycles, or from being too aggressive during cycles of contraction. It also favors foreign investment, since foreign companies are allowed to credit it in their countries of origin.

The IUE's 25 percent share of tax revenue is close to average for the region (Table 4). However, in the absence of a personal income tax, the IUE taxes independent professionals, assuming that net taxable earnings are equal to 50 percent of gross revenue for the tax period, after deducting VAT that has been declared and paid. This discriminates between individuals subject to the IUE and those subject to the RC-VAT, making it difficult to administer this tax. Earnings kept in the country are taxed at 25 percent; those

Table 4. Taxes on Corporate Income in Latin America

	Minimum	*Maximum*
Argentina	35	35
Bolivia	**25**	**25**
Brazil	15	34
Chile	17	17
Colombia	35	35
Costa Rica	30	30
Dominican Republic	25	25
El Salvador	25	25
Guatemala	31	31
Mexico	32	32
Panama	30	30
Uruguay	30	30
Venezuela	15	34

Source: KPMG (2004) and Stotsky and WoldeMariam (2002).

sent abroad are taxed at a combined rate of close to 35 percent, that is, 25 percent on taxable income, plus the tax on remitted earnings, established on a presumed basis.

The design of the IUE makes it susceptible to tax evasion. Special systems greatly reduce the number of its taxpayers, particularly in agriculture, whose contribution to revenue from this tax is a mere 2 percent. Moreover, since the IUE is based on the principle of source or territoriality, it is not tailored to tax the operations of multinational corporations.[1] This problem is amplified since this tax is now being introduced on an international level. Finally, ever since passage of the Securities Act, the exemption on capital gains from stock market transactions provides a fast track for evading this tax.

Policy Options

Based on this diagnosis, the government could:

- Transform the RC-VAT into a new personal income tax (*Impuesto a la Renta de Personas Naturales*—IRP) with the aim of eliminating distortions and introducing progressivity into the tax system. A simple design is suggested, with progressive rates ranging from 5 to 25 percent on wages, with a lower exemption limit to ensure that Bolivia's low-income population will be exempt from its payment. A fixed rate without deductions could be placed on revenue from interest earnings, capital gains from stock-market transactions, and other types of intermittent earnings.
- If the above-mentioned policy option is applied, the IUE should be limited to legal entities and individual businesses that keep accounting records. For that purpose, the incomes of independent professionals and other individuals currently paying the IUE could be transferred to the IRP. This would reduce discrimination among taxpaying individuals and would substantially simplify the administration of the IUE.
- Prevent IUE taxpayers from evading payment. Strategies that could help to accomplish this include: (i) better incorporate agriculture into the taxed universe, by modifying simplified systems such as the Unified Agricultural System (*Regimen Agropecuario Unificado*—RAU); (ii) limit the excessive deduction of interest, which disguises equity as debt; (iii) prevent disguised distributions of earnings, by establishing penalties for transactions between a company and its partners, shareholders, administrators, and other associated persons, under conditions other than those of the market; (iv) introduce pricing rules on transfers for transactions between associated companies, following international practices; and (v) eliminate exemptions on capital gains from stock market transactions, to prevent financial maneuvers that reduce the IUE tax base.

Special Regimes and Tax Zones

At present, there are three special systems designed to support specific activities and simplified to integrate small taxpayers. These include the Simplified Tax System

(*Regimen Tributario Simplificado*—RTS), created for small businessmen and craftsmen, the Integrated Tax System (*Sistema Tributario Integrado*—STI) for transportation companies, and the Unified Agricultural System (*Regimen Agropecuario Unificado*—RAU) for the agricultural sector. In practice, these systems have created distortions that harm the tax base of other taxes. Allowing for a single payment replacing the IUE, IT, and the VAT has resulted in a considerable loss of tax revenue and provides a shelter for economic units that could be covered by the general system. An estimated 30 percent of taxpayers are enrolled under one or more of these special systems, which together generate a mere 0.1 percent of national tax revenue.

These systems also make the tax system inefficient, because they create obstacles for controlling tax evasion and are an incentive to sell contraband on the domestic market. Moreover, they are very difficult to audit, given the large number of taxpayers enrolled and the myriad eligible categories (the RTS has seven categories and the STI has five). Similarly, limits to qualify under these systems are too liberal: in the case of the RAU, there are eligible taxpayers with 10,000 hectares; while almost all modes of transportation are enrolled under the STI.

Together with these exemption systems, there are special zones. At present, there are 14 exempt zones where the following taxes are not applied: VAT, IT, GA (*Gravamen Arancelario*—Duties), ICE, and IEHD. In addition, it is legally unclear whether the exemption extends to the IUE, since it did extend to the IUE's predecessor, the Presumed Corporate Income Tax (*Impuesto a la Renta Presunta de Empresas*—IRPE). These special areas have not succeeded in becoming industrial zones and are mainly limited to promoting trade activities. This hinders control over the movement of goods and creates opportunities for tax evasion.

These special tax regimes not only affect tax efficiency, but also undermine equality among taxpayers. Such a situation encourages informality, since those enrolled under the general system are at a disadvantage vis-à-vis those enrolled under the special regimes. This also hinders the development of a better chain of production, because large companies prefer to use imported inputs rather than buy from domestic small businesses, which do not provide tax credits when enrolled under special regimes.

Policy Options

Given this situation, the government could:

- Reduce the number of beneficiaries of the RTS and incorporate some of the economic units enrolled in the RTS into the general system and establishing a fixed annual contribution for the smallest taxpayers.
- Integrate the two highest categories of the STI into the general system, leave the three lower ones exempt from taxes, and charge them a small annual fee that benefits the municipalities.
- Substantially reduce the scope of the RAU by introducing a tax system for rural activities based on the VAT and the IUE.

- Stop the proliferation of special tax-exempt zones and better supervise existing ones, making sure that they are fulfilling the objectives for which they were created.
- In the medium term, replace the current simplified regimes with a new, consolidated, universally applicable system with three categories of taxpayers, in accordance with the amount of their sales or assets: (i) the very small, who would be exempt; (ii) small taxpayers, who would pay a fixed percentage of their annual sales; and (iii) all others, who would be incorporated into the general tax system. This should be accompanied by a comprehensive effort to reduce startup costs for companies in order to lower transition costs.

Financial Transactions Tax

Designed to be in effect for two years, the ITF was introduced in July 2004 to address the difficult fiscal situation that the country was facing. The ITF taxes financial credit and debit operations; the only exemptions are on checking account movements in national currency or Housing Development Units (*Unidades de Fomento a la Vivienda*—UFV) and savings accounts in foreign currency of less than US$1000. During the first year of its application, the rate was 0.03 percent, but it was reduced to 0.025 percent in July 2005. This rate is lower than that of Colombia and other countries in the region, though in Bolivia, unlike other countries, it is applied on both credit and debit transactions. The ITF was scheduled to be eliminated in July 2006.

Recently, it has been recommended that the ITF be maintained, given its success in reducing the dollarization of the financial system and the significant revenue it has raised (revenue was 0.5 percent of GDP in 2004, and it was expected to raise significant revenue in 2005). However, international experience shows that in the end, such a tax harms the financial intermediation sector.

Policy Options

Based on the above, the government could achieve its goals by phasing out the ITF, as initially proposed.

III. Tax Administration and Customs

The index on the efficiency of the system reflects the perceptions of those surveyed regarding the system's simplicity and transparency. Bolivia's relatively good position (58 out of 104 countries) reflects the fruits of the reforms implemented (Table 5). Accordingly, Bolivia has a better performance than many developed countries, such as Australia, the United States, or Germany. Despite this, regarding the degree to which the tax system encourages work or investments, Bolivia ranks poorly (80th), though higher than Argentina, Brazil, Peru, and Ecuador. On the other hand, views on corruption, reflected in the responses to the survey question on irregular pay-

Table 5. Comparisons between Tax Systems, Positions of Selected Countries, 2004

Country/Region	*Scope and effect of Taxation*	*Efficiency of the Tax System*	*Irregular Payments in the Collection of Taxes*
Argentina	90	100	60
Australia	66	91	10
Bolivia	**80**	**58**	**88**
Botswana	15	6	45
Brazil	103	102	55
Chile	28	21	19
Colombia	70	76	46
El Salvador	12	11	43
Hong Kong (China)	1	1	4
Korea, Republic of	48	69	63
Malaysia	11	10	39
Mexico	71	99	53
Nicaragua	93	59	67
Paraguay	32	36	90
Peru	86	77	42
Singapore	4	4	11
Taiwan (China)	9	16	25
United States	17	89	20
Venezuela	42	64	82

Source: Based on information from the World Economic Forum (WEF), 2004. The indices are based on survey data from 104 countries. See the Policy Note on Macroeconomic aspects for comparative data regarding the effectiveness of tax collections based on information from 2001.

ments to tax collectors, continue to cast doubt on the Bolivian authorities. Interviews with several companies corroborate these results, though several survey participants underscored recent improvements.

In the late 1990s Bolivia started to reform the SIN and the Customs Service. Despite political and social instability and resistance from those opposed to the modernization of these entities, the reforms have continued to gain ground, with technical development similar to those of more advanced administrations. However, these reforms are facing hard times, particularly in Customs Service. For example, the repeat interim terms of the presidents and of several board members of both organizations is contrary to what was contemplated in the laws that established them.

Today, these two institutions are backed by modern legislation that gives them flexibility to address change and use state-of-the-art technologies in their management and contact with taxpayers and users. Both institutions have incorporated systems that, in the case of the SIN, allow taxpayers to e-file their tax returns; and in the case of Customs, file their returns through the Automated Customs System (*Sistema Aduanero Automatizado*—SIDUNEA). Likewise, the Tax Code, in effect since 2004, consolidated the auditing powers of the two institutions; created fair, expedited processes in the event of a dispute; and set harsh penalties for tax evasion, fraud, and contraband. However, the slowness of the judiciary and weak enforcement prevent some penalties from being effectively applied.

The SIN has undergone sustained improvements in increasing the taxpayer base and controlling tax evasion. Between 2000 and 2004 the number of taxpayers enrolled has more than doubled. Tax evasion has systematically diminished. In the case of VAT, it dropped from 43 percent in 2000 to an estimated 29 percent in 2004 (Figure 2). At the same time, despite modest economic growth, the SIN revenue almost doubled between 2000 and 2004. The cost of collections for 2005 is estimated at less than 2 percent—1.57 bolivianos for every 100 collected, which is less than average for the region. (In Peru and Chile this figure is nearly 3 percent).

The Customs Service has experienced operational improvements. The amount of merchandise that undergoes a physical assessment is 20 percent, which is lower than in most countries in the region, with the exception of Chile. On the other hand, customs clearance times are less than three days, and in the case of unassessed merchandise, the process takes but a few minutes (this takes longer in most countries in the region). Results of audits prior to 2003 were less than one percent of revenue, while in 2005 adjustments to values through Customs Service audits alone surpassed three percent. The Customs Service has a high degree of efficiency in terms of the number of operations processed per customs official, which in turn is reflected in lower costs, amounting to only 2 percent of revenue (Table 6). In the region, only Chile and Uruguay have lower costs.

There are many pending tasks. For SIN, several measures to consolidate its reform are still outstanding, including completion of taxpayer enrollment, further reinforcement of the auditing process, establishing specialized units for the various economic sectors, and improvement of computerized controls, especially in relation to omissions and tax refunds. For Customs Service, the reforms include defining the

Figure 2. VAT Tax Evasion, 2000–2004
(% of Expected Revenue)

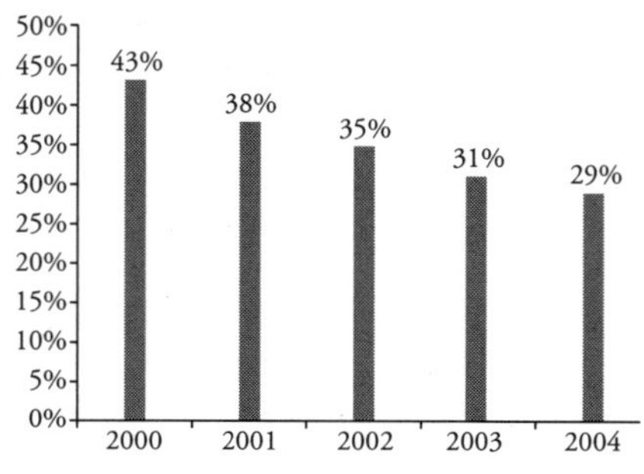

Source: Tax Statistics, SIN.

Table 6. Imports Processed Annually by Customs Employees

	Year	*Number of Employees*	*Number of Import Declarations*	*Declarations Processed per Employee*
Argentina	2002	4,226	306,372	72
	2001	4,226	554,708	131
Philippines	1998	5,400	795,000	147
Thailand	1998	7,000	1,467,243	210
Chile	2001	1,250	621,874	497
Ecuador	2002	750	193,353	258
Bolivia	2004	750	200,000	267

Source: World Bank.

organizational structure, role, and positions of the Board of Directors; using information to improve auditing; establishing an integral strategy to combat contraband; incorporating management techniques and teamwork; and coordinating with other auditing entities, as well as institution-wide implementtaion of a strategic plan. All these tasks call for an end to interim positions, which need to be replaced by a management team with a long-term vision. They also require that the reforms become financially sustainable by reducing their dependency on international cooperation.

Though the Customs Service has made significant progress, contraband is still a major issue, equivalent to US$700 million per year. However, no strategy has been developed to contain it. Bolivia's Customs Administration Reform and Modernization Program (*Programa de Reforma y Modernización de la Administración de Aduanas*—PROMA) pursued an institutional modernization, facilitated trade, and reduced corruption within the entity. The fight against contraband needs to involve other institutions and not just the Customs Service. Here, coordination between the Customs Service and the SIN is vital, but it is not occurring at present.

Tax amnesties have counteracted the efforts of the Customs Service and SIN, particularly in the regularization of vehicles during 2004 and 2005. Both institutions had to use funds initially earmarked for control activities to finance this task. In addition, these measures have generated more demands for new tax amnesties.

Policy Options

Based on the above, the authorities could:

- Create a political and social consensus that keeps the SIN and the Customs Service from being coopted by special interests, reinforcing its technical character.
- Do away with the interim terms of presidents and board members, which create obstacles for cultivating management with long-term vision and cause institutional development to stagnate.

- Evaluate the current financial sustainability of the institutions, which calls for reducing their dependency on international cooperation. In this regard, it is important to have a system of budget and salary incentives for the institutions and their officers, which would make it possible to attract and maintain competent professionals. These incentives should be tied to achievements in reduction of tax evasion, tax fraud, and contraband and in service to taxpayers.
- Develop a government strategy with the participation of the formal private sector, to serve as a guideline for the fight against contraband and strengthen the operating units involved.
- Establish formal coordination mechanisms between the Customs Service, SIN, and other entities of the Ministry of Finance, without merging them, to strengthen auditing and control functions. A first task in this regard could be the creation of a specialized group, formed by auditors from Customs Service and SIN, to audit major operators and users of foreign trade.
- End tax amnesties.

IV. Tax System on Upstream Hydrocarbons

Tax collections on oil companies have been the subject of hot debate in recent years. This sector is one of the major sources of tax revenue because it involves the exploitation of a non-renewable natural resource (see the Gas Era chapter). Since 1990, the regulations on hydrocarbons have been modified on three occasions in Bolivia (see Annex 2).

The first change took place in 1990, through Law 1194, which was an attempt to open the industry to private operations in association with the government oil company (Yacimientos Petrolíferos Fiscales Bolivianos—YPFB). The tax regime established by this law was based on the collection of royalties, since the sector was under a special tax regime that exempted it from the payment of other taxes. Under this law, all operations of the sector, including those of the YPFB, had to pay a 31 percent royalty on the price of production. At the same time, private companies were paying close to 19 percent of production operations in favor of the YPFB. This first attempt to develop the industry was unsuccessful, due to the limited investment capacity of the public sector, which led to a stagnation of investments and reserves (see Figure 3).

The second change took place in the mid 1990s, starting with what was called the capitalization of the YPFB's operations. To accompany this process, Law 1689 was enacted in 1996; it changed the tax regime for the sector in a second attempt to make it more flexible and internationally competitive. This time, a distinction was made between new and existing fields (those that were in production in 1996). While taxation on new fields was based on an 18 percent royalty, plus taxes on earnings, a surtax, and a foreign remissions tax; taxation on existing fields came under a 50 percent royalty.

Figure 3. Investment in Gas Exploration, Exploitation, and Reserves, 1990–2004

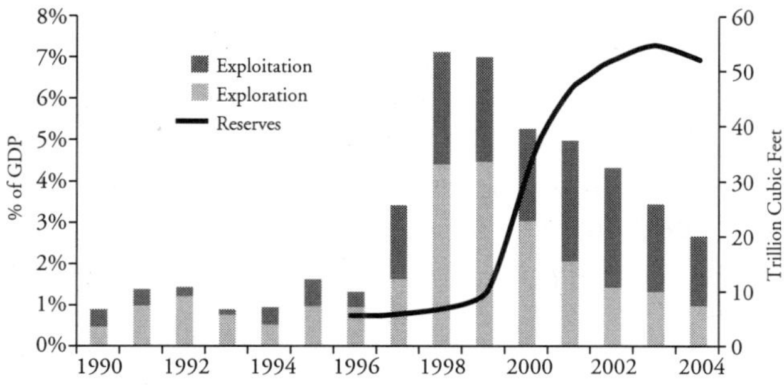

Source: Ministry of Oil and Gas.

Together with capitalizing YPFB's operations and opening the Brazilian market for gas exports, this new tax regime allowed investment in the sector to increase from 1 percent of GDP in 1995 to 7 percent in 1999. This also helped potential and proven reserves to increase from less than 6 TCF (trillion cubic feet) in 1997 to 52 TCF in 2004, giving Bolivia some of the largest reserves of gas in the region (see Figure 4).

Financial earnings were lower than expected due to poor performance in collections under the general system, to which the new fields were subject. This was because investments could be depreciated very rapidly, which reduced earnings-based tax collections (IEU, surtax, and remittances). At the same time, the surtax, intended to offset fallen royalties, allowed many deductions, which once again affected revenue. These losses were aggravated by the administrations' institutional weaknesses, especially in the case of the SIN, which failed to apply the new law rapidly, falling behind with respect to oil companies.

Figure 4: Reserves of Gas in Latin American Countries (TCF of Gas)

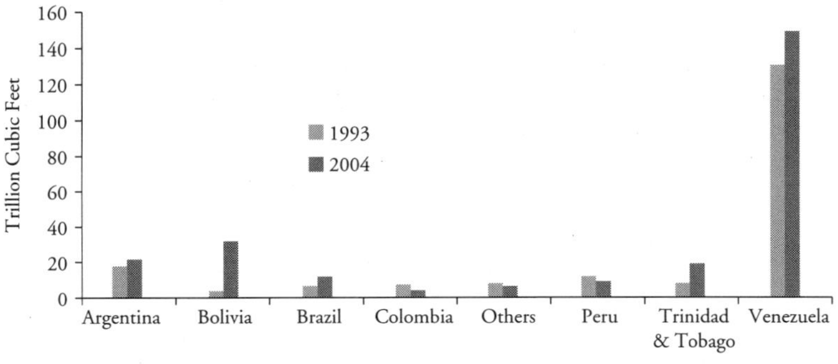

Source: Ministry of Oil and Gas.

The huge gas reserves discovered have led to endeavors to create new projects above and beyond increasing exports to Brazil and Argentina. The most ambitious of them was one seeking to export liquid natural gas (LNG) to Mexico and the United States. However, at the same time, social and political opposition was growing against the Hydrocarbons Act and capitalization of the sector, based on a perception that the companies were not paying taxes and were interested only in exporting natural resources without contributing added value. The resistance intensified in October 2003, with public demonstrations against the use of a Chilean port for gas exports. The protests culminated with the indefinite suspension of the LNG project. This set of events was aggravated by lack of transparent, detailed public information on the taxes charged on upstream activities.

As the protests intensified and became more violent, the demand to nationalize the oil industry became widespread, creating a major political crisis. In response, the new Hydrocarbons Act was enacted in May 2005. The new law changes the approach to taxes on the sector, returning to a system consisting of taxes on production. This law eliminated the distinction between new and existing fields and introduced the Direct Tax on Hydrocarbons (*Impuesto Directo a los Hidrocarburos*—IDH), equivalent to 32 percent of prices on production (technically this tax is equivalent to a royalty). Since this tax is in addition to royalties, companies pay 50 percent of production prices, as determined by the referendum held in July 2004. The companies are also subject to taxes under the general system, and the IDH cannot be credited either domestically or internationally. Accordingly, taxes on the sector are somewhat greater than 50 percent. The law also obliges companies to move their contracts toward these new regulations—an aspect that is being negotiated at present.

In the short term, the new tax regime is helping to increase tax revenue. However, the fact that the taxation on production is 50 percent and that additional taxes also have to be paid through the general tax system makes Bolivia's one of the most burdensome tax systems in the world, which affects possibilities for developing the industry (see Figure 5). In the medium term, this could exert greater pressure on the sector while simultaneously producing less revenue, which would have a negative impact on the sustainability of public finances and the provision of public services. A sign of this adverse effect has been the launch of initiatives to unilaterally modify contracts, which have reduced investment in the sector and stagnated the exploitation of reserves. Legal instability and a lack of regulations have reinforced the idea that Bolivia is still a high-risk country for new hydrocarbons projects, especially for major ones, such as projects for exporting natural gas. In that context, it is highly probable that over the next two to three years, Bolivia will be able to attract investments only to maintain production at current levels, and will not be able to monetize proven reserves in keeping with their true magnitude.

Policy Options

In this framework, these needs merit the government's consideration :

Figure 5. Royalties on Natural Gas Production Worldwide

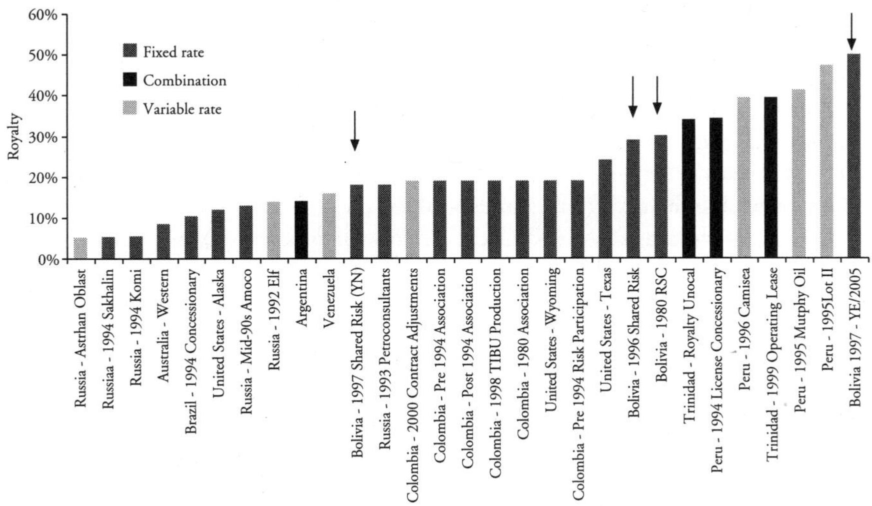

Source: Target Consulting Group (2004).
Note: Since it is a tax on production, the IDH is considered to be a royalty.

- Complete the regulations for the current Hydrocarbons Act in order to eliminate legal gaps in tax matters and allow the industry to operate on a solid legal basis. The critical legal gaps encompass: a definition of marginal fields and of gas industrialization projects, including the differentiated treatment they would receive.
- Strengthen the government units in charge of tax collections and audits. In particular, strengthen the recently created gas and oil industry unit in the SIN. Provide transparent informational reports that are simple and available to the public regarding tax revenue from upstream activities.
- Modify the current tax regime established in the new Hydrocarbons Act so that the tax burden and lack of flexibility do not continue to compromise the sector's development.

V. Distribution of Tax revenue

Despite Bolivia's advances in decentralization, the tax system continues to be administered by the central government. The only tax over which the subnational governments are in charge is the Real Property and Motor Vehicles Tax (IPBIVA), which was transferred to the municipalities through the Popular Participation Act in 1994 and represents only 1 percent of GDP. Even in this case, the municipalities cannot change the rates or the tax base of this tax.

Tax revenue is delivered to the subnational governments through a system of allocations by formula (see Annex 3). This system remained practically unchanged from its consolidation in the mid 1990s until the recent enactment of the Hydrocarbons Act in mid 2005, which establishes the manner of distribution of the IDH.

The current allocation mechanisms are not an integrated, flexible system adapted to Bolivia's new economic situation. In recent years, these failed criteria have exacerbated the existing imbalance between different levels of government and regions, attributable to the economic crisis of the late 1990s and expansion of the gas and oil industry. Such imbalance could intensify as the energy sector expands.[2] The current system of distribution of the IDH has the following problems:

- *Insufficient funds for the national Treasury.* The allocations system allows the Treasury to keep 72 percent of the funds. Yet this allocation has been insufficient to respond to the economic crisis. The fall in growth has reduced the funding of the Treasury, leading to a budget deficit that has jeopardized fiscal sustainability. This is because the Treasury has assumed the pension reform cost and has a more rigid expenditure structure than the departments and municipalities: close to 90 percent of the expenditures of the Treasury cannot be eliminated.
- *High dependency of the subnational governments.* Even though the departments receive only 12 percent of tax revenue and the universities and municipalities receive the remaining 16 percent, these transfers are fundamental for those levels of government. Departmental governments have no funding source of their own. Municipalities, despite having such funding sources, are dependent on these transfers, because their institutional weaknesses and reduced scale often limit their ability to collect taxes. About 80 percent of the revenue of small municipalities comes from shared national tax revenue, and the majority of the remaining 20 percent comes from other transfers, such as HIPC.
- *Large, growing differences among the regions.* In recent years, imbalances in allocations among the regions have worsened, though to the benefit of Tarija and Pando which receive a much higher allocation than the rest of the departments (Figure 6). Most of the departmental royalties, which amount to 11 percent of production, are appropriated by the producing department. Since most of the hydrocarbon production is concentrated in Santa Cruz, Cochabamba, and Tarija (more than 86 percent of the gas reserves are in Tarija), royalties are also concentrated in these departments, which also have the lowest poverty rates in the country. Despite this, since Cochabamba and Santa Cruz have large populations, the per capita allocation is not high. The opposite occurs with Tarija, which has a mere 5 percent of the population and receives 50 percent of the departmental royalties, making its per capita allocation three times the national average. Since the 1970s, Pando, together with Beni, since they are the least developed departments, have been favored with a share in the royalties equivalent to 0.33 and 0.66 percent of national production of hydrocar-

Figure 6. Distribution of Taxes among Departments, 2000–2004
(Constant bolivianos for the year 2000, per capita)

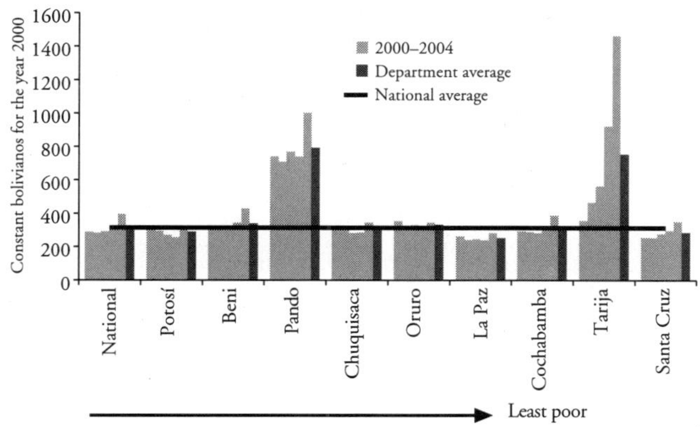

Source: Ministry of Finance.
Note: Includes allocations to departments, municipalities, and universities, but does not include the municipalities' own revenue.

bons, respectively. This share may seem insignificant, but it makes Pando's per capita allocation twice the national average, since it has a mere 0.65 percent of the total population. Figure 6 also illustrates that the least favored departments in per capita terms are the non-producers. Within them, La Paz is the most dramatic case, since it does not participate in the revenue generated by the hydrocarbons sector and also has the largest population in the country (close to 30 percent).

- *The departmental compensation mechanism is exhausted.* Recognizing that royalties could provoke imbalance among the regions, the regulations include a mechanism known as the Departmental Compensation Fund, which transfers funds to prefectures whose per capita allocation of royalties is less than the national average, until they reach that average or until the amount transferred by the fund is 10 percent of the IEHD tax revenue. Due to the magnitude of the regional imbalance, this Fund is not meeting its objective, even though it is using all the resources available to it. In fact, the increase in per capita royalties in Tarija and Pando has caused the national average to rise, on account of which more departments are benefiting from the Fund's transfers. Departments such as Oruro, Santa Cruz and Cochabamba, which have significant amounts of royalties, are starting to receive these transfers. The situation has been aggravated because the IEHD funds, on which the compensation depends, tend to grow more slowly than royalties, since royalties are linked only to the performance of the domestic market. Moreover, since 2000, IEHD revenue has been limited because prices on hydrocarbon derivatives have been frozen.

- *Imbalance between departments and municipalities.* Since allocations to departments depend on royalties, while allocations to municipalities depend on national taxes, the municipalities' share in the departmental allocation is quite low in Tarija and Pando, and quite high in La Paz and Potosí (see Figure 7). This situation is creating an imbalance in the provision of public services, because the jurisdictions of these two levels of government are totally different. As a result, efficient use of the funds is adversely affected.

In June 2005, a distribution of the IDH was established, which notably modified the intergovernmental transfer system. This new mechanism suffers from the same problems that plague the rest of the allocations, because political and social pressures had an impact on its design criteria; this crowded out considerations of equity and efficiency. Moreover, the municipalities and universities also exerted pressure for their share in this revenue (see Annex 3). As a result, the IDH is being distributed through a rigid series of allocations and is determined in an isolated manner. The existing imbalance, rather than diminishing, is intensifying.

The IDH reduces the Treasury's share in tax revenue from 72 percent to 65 percent, aggravating the imbalance among the Treasury, the departments, and the municipalities (Figure 8). This reduction is due to the new Hydrocarbons Act which: (i) eliminates the 32 percent share of the Treasury in the production of existing fields and replaces it with the IDH, which is distributed among the various levels of government; (ii) establishes that the Treasury must make transfers to any departments that

Figure 7. Participation of the Municipalities in Departmental Allocations, 2004

(Percentage of the Total)

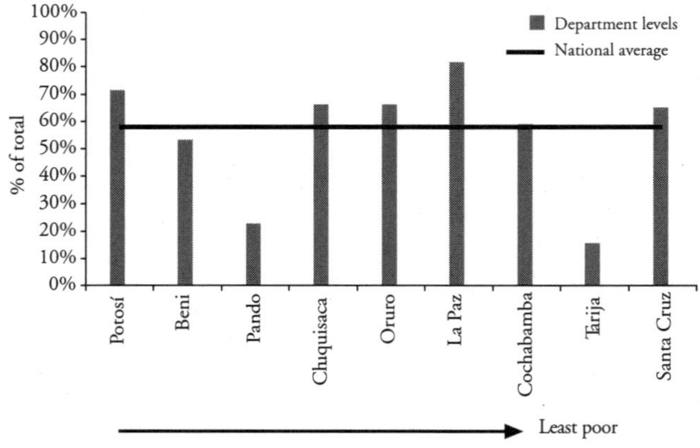

Source: Ministry of Finance.

Note: Includes allocations to departments, municipalities and universities, but does not include the municipalities' own revenue.

Figure 8. Effect of the IDH on the Vertical Distribution of Taxes, 2004*
(Percentages of the Total)

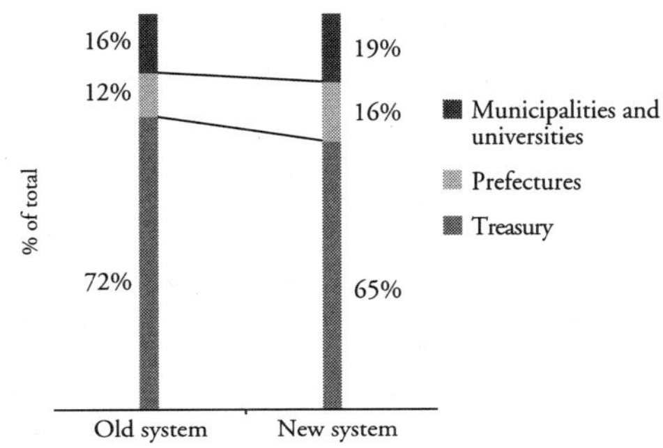

Source: Ministry of Finance.
Note: (*) The results for 2004 under the new system are based on a hypothetical assumption.

do not receive a minimum allocation from the IDH, and; (iii) establishes preset allocations of Treasury funds for several uses (for example, the Armed Forces and indigenous organizations) and reduces the flexibility of the funds received by the Treasury.

This approach to allocations could even cause the Treasury to have fewer funds in absolute terms than what it had under the prior legislation. In other words, the IHD is not likely to allow for a reduction of the fiscal deficit, though, in the short term, it could contribute to a drop in the public sector deficit due to a potential surplus for the subnational governments. In the medium term, this effect could dissipate, since both municipalities and departments could improve their capacities to use these funds and increase spending.

The IDH would exacerbate regional imbalance by favoring departments with low populations, especially Pando, which would receive a per capita allocation eight times greater than the national average (Figure 9). However, at least in the short term, it would allow all the regions to have a greater per capita allocation.

Based on the foregoing diagnosis, the government could find the following strategies useful toward making progress:

Short-Term Policy Options

- Avoid instituting new offsetting mechanisms that draw on the accounts of the Treasury, in order to preserve fiscal sustainability.
- Transfer part of the royalty revenue from the producer departments Pando and Beni to their respective municipalities, in order to better balance these two levels of government within those departments. Additionally, provide allocations to the municipalities from which production is extracted, to compensate for the outflows.

Figure 9. Effect of the IDH on the Distribution of Taxes to the Departments, 2004*
(Constant bolivianos for the year 2000, per capita)

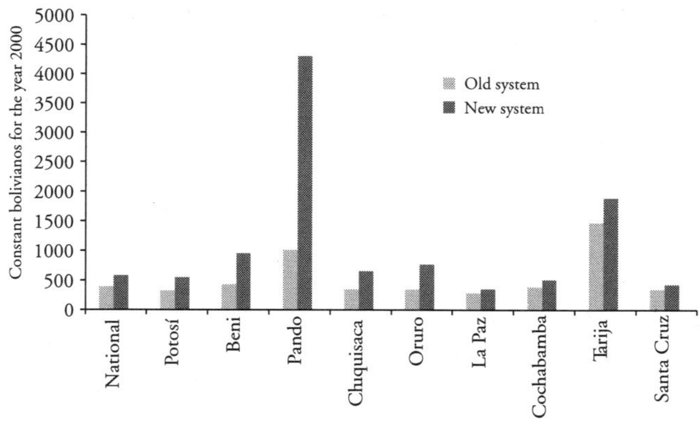

Source: Ministry of Finance.
Note: (*) The results for 2004 under the new system are based on a hypothetical assumption.

- Change the way that the IEHD is distributed, to strengthen the Departmental Compensation Fund without affecting the finances of the Treasury. The 25 percent of the IEHD currently allocated to the departments could be channeled through this Fund. Thus, departments with a high allocation of royalties would not also receive an allocation from the IEHD.
- Change the way in which the average national departmental royalty is calculated, so that it will not be influenced by extreme values that distort the functionality of the Departmental Compensation Fund.
- Increase counterpart requirements in regional investment projects to the departments that receive the largest allocations. This will free up funds to be allocated in other regions.

Medium-Term Policy Options

- Grant the Treasury greater leeway to prevent increased indebtedness and preserve fiscal sustainability. The Treasury should not be responsible for compensating differences among the regions and if preset allocations were avoided. In addition to reducing leeway for the Treasury, preset allocations make the spending structure more rigid, reducing the Treasury's efficiency.
- Allow subnational governments to take charge of administering more taxes and have more control over the taxes' characteristics, or at least work with the SIN to determine these characteristics. This only is advisable, however, in a more decentralized context, after the subnational governments have been institutionally strengthened (see the chapter on Decentralization).

- Create mechanisms to prevent distortions introduced by growing hydrocarbons revenue. The oil revenue itself could be used to reduce discrepancies in per capita departmental allocations or to reduce the maximum per capita royalty that a department receives.
- Modify both the allocation structure and jurisdictions so that they are better aligned. This process should go hand-in-hand with institutional strengthening that improves the use of funds by the subnational governments, with a view toward improving the provision of public services.
- Establish a technical commission that engages in continual follow-up on the fiscal transfers system and proposes periodic improvements and adjustments.

VI. Conclusions

The tax system is marked by certain limitations and problems associated principally with a lack of progressness. This, paradoxically, results from the tax system's simplicity; a continual deterioration and vulnerability of the tax base due in large measure by dysfunctional special tax regimes; and the fragility of the tax administration. To increase progressivity, a personal income tax should be introduced to replace the RC-VAT. In that way, the tax system could effectively mitigate inequalities in the distribution of tax collections. Reforming the special tax regimes would facilitate expansion of the tax base and allow tax exemptions for poor taxpayers only. Many taxpayers who should be included in the general tax system are registered under the special regimes. Likewise, to reduce the high prevalence of contraband and tax evasion, improvements in the tax administration attained through a reform of the SIN and the Customs Service could be expanded and consolidated. In particular, a political and social consensus must be created that provides greater political support to these two reforms.

Finally, recent developments related to the gas and oil industry as well as social and political conflicts are presenting new challenges for taxation. These events have led to changes in laws and regulations that could compromise the development of the oil industry, which therefore might need to be revised. At the same time, the accelerated growth of that sector is distorting the current tax allocation system and intensifying imbalance among the different regions and levels of government. In this regard, it is necessary to establish new compensation mechanisms that can help overcome such imbalance without compromising the financial situation of the central government.

Table 7 summarizes some of the main issues and recommendations for Bolivia's tax system.

Table 7. Principal Policy Options

Problem	*Objective*	*Policy Option*
Continual deterioration of the tax base and lack of progressivity.	Improve the tax system.	• Limit existing exemptions, special regimes, and special zones. • Transform the RC-VAT into a personal income tax. • Implement other specific recommendations for each tax presented in Section II.
Despite progress, the tax administration remains fragile.	Consolidate the tax administration.	• Create a political and social consensus that keeps the tax administration from being taken over by interested sectors, reinforcing the technical nature of the institutions involved. • Do away with interim terms. • Reduce dependency on international aid. • Establish a system of budget incentives for the amounts earmarked to the institutions (related to reducing tax evasion, tax fraud, and contraband) and offer competitive salaries. • Establish formal coordination mechanisms between Customs and the Tax Administration.
The new tax system is increasing tax revenue, but the tax burden is very heavy, compromising the development of the oil industry.	Devise a tax system on upstream hydrocarbon activities.	• Complete the regulations for the existing law to eliminate gaps and allow industry to operate on a solid legal basis. • Strengthen the government units in charge of tax collection and audits. • Modify the current system so that the tax burden will not compromise the development of the sector.
There are growing imbalances among the different levels of government and among the regions.	Correct the distribution of tax revenue.	• Give the central government more fiscal leeway. • Transfer part of the royalty revenue from the producer departments to their respective municipalities. • Change the way that the IEHD is distributed, in order to strengthen the Departmental Compensation Fund. • Modify the way that the national average departmental royalty is calculated, so that it will not be influenced by extreme values. • Allow subnational governments to take charge of administering more taxes.

Bibliography

Alborta, P., M. Montalvo, and M. Zapata. 2005. Bolivia: *Régimen de Transferencias Intergubernamentales para las Autonomías Regionales*. La Paz, Bolivia: USAID.

Antelo, E. 2000. *Políticas de Estabilización y de Reformas Estructurales en Bolivia a partir de 1985*. Santiago, Chile: UNDP.

Barja, G. 2003. *Distribución de la Renta Petrolera Generada en el Upstream: El Caso de Bolivia*. La Paz, Bolivia.

Coelho , I., J.C. Gómez-Sabaini, P. Medas, and P. Serra. 2004. *Hacia un Sistema Tributario más Eficiente y Justo*. La Paz, Bolivia: IMF.

Cossio, F. 2001. *El Sistema Tributario y sus Implicaciones en la Reducción de la Pobreza*. La Paz, Bolivia: IIDEE.

KPMG. 2004. Corporate Tax Rates Survey. Available at http://us.kpmg.com/microsite/Global_Tax/CTR_survey/2004CTRS.pdf

Medas, P. 2004. Fiscal Strategy Brief, Review Division: Fiscal Operations II. La Paz Bolivia: IMF.

Muller & Asoc. 2003. *El Regimen Impositivo en el Sector Hidrocarburifero Boliviano*. Confidential Report, Number 126. La Paz, Bolivia.

Perry, G. 2005. *Sistemas Tributarios, Mejores Prácticas Mundiales*. Cartagena, Colombia: World Bank.

Romera, D., Spindola, L. 2004. *Consolidación del Proceso de Modernización de La Administración Tributaria*. La Paz, Bolivia: IMF.

Shepherd. G., T. Waagstein, et al., 2005. *Bolivia: Proyecto de Reforma Institucional, Evaluación Independiente*. Mimeo. Institutional Reform Project.

Stotsky, J. and A. WoldeMariam. 2002. "Central American Tax Reform: Trends and Possibilities." IMF Working Paper. WP/02/227. Washington, DC.

Target Consulting Group. 2004. "International Hydrocarbons Fiscal Systems Benchmarking Review." Mimeo.

World Bank. 2004. Bolivia: Policy Note, *Manejo Fiscal de la Renta Petrolera: Diagnóstico y Opciones de Política*. La Paz, Bolivia: World Bank.

ANNEX 1. Principal National Taxes

Tax	*Subject*	*Amount*	*Exemptions, Deductions, and Refunds*
Value Added Tax, (VAT)	• All sales of personal property, service provision contracts, and all provisioning conducted in Bolivia.	• 13% on total sales - tax paid through purchases. • Effective rate: 14.94%.	• Exports, to prevent the export of taxes and preserve the competitiveness of exports. • Services associated with tourism, although it is not well specified when a service can be treated as an export. • Real property is exempt from payment, but not construction services and materials. This favors construction companies, which have an incentive to make purchases without invoices.
Transaction Tax, (IT) ***Impuesto a las Transacciones***	• Includes individuals and legal entities, public or private companies that receive payments from: trade, professional and business services, the leasing of goods and services, or any other activity, for profit or otherwise, that involves a transfer of real property and rights.	• 3% on gross revenue.	• Work performed in a dependency relationship, services provided by the central government, departments, and municipalities (with the exception of public companies), interest on savings account deposits and checking accounts and fixed-term deposits. Private educational establishments incorporated into official curriculums and the publishing and importing of books and informational publications in general.
Specific Consumption Tax, (ICE) ***Impuesto a los Consumos Específicos***	• Specific products and services when imported or sold by domestic producers. • Imports: on the C.I.F. price. • Domestic Sales: on the sales price, excluding VAT.	• Alcoholic beverages (local or imported) and bottled non-alcoholic beverages (between 0.18 and 6.00 bolivianos) • Tobacco: 50%. • Vehicles: 18%. • Electrical energy consumption higher than 200KW/hour/month: 20%.	• Exports, passenger motor vehicles, and high-capacity cargo motor vehicles. Electrical energy for industrial consumption not generated by hydraulic sources or gas, acquired through a foreign source.

Tax on the Supplementary Regime to the VAT (RC-VAT)	• Paid monthly by the withholding agents and quarterly by direct taxpayers on income from Bolivian sources.	• 13% on monthly gross revenue (deductible from the VAT).	• Christmas bonus and social benefits as specified by law, wages of foreign diplomats and official personnel accredited in Bolivia. Interest in favor of international entities and official foreign institutions and interest with a term of more than three years. • Annuity payments received from the Treasury. • Taxpayers in a dependency relationship are allowed an exemption equivalent to twice the minimum wage. Dividends and distributions of earnings from partnerships and sole proprietorships subject to the IUE. Interest is not taxed on deposits denominated in Housing Development Units (UFVs) with terms in excess of 30 days. The exemptions were introduced in 2002 through Law 2382.
Corporate Earnings Tax (IUE) ***Impuesto a las Utilidades de las Empresas***	• Paid annually by both public and private companies on earnings from Bolivian sources per financial statements. Remunerations, fees, and salaries; for services abroad, when the same are related to obtaining earnings from a Bolivian source.	• 25% on the net earnings of companies. In the case of professions, it is presumed that net earnings are equivalent to 50% of revenue. • 12.5% on payments of remittances abroad.	• Deductible: Depreciation, bad debts, fees of directors and trustees, moving expenses, per diems, and similar expenditures, Christmas bonuses, and other bonuses to personnel. • Exempt: Activities of the central government, prefectures, and public institutions. Earnings obtained by associations, foundations, institutions, and legally authorized non-profit organizations. • The Stock Market Act of 1998 and, afterwards, the Economic Reactivation Act, provide that capital gains on purchases and sales of listed securities conducted at the stock exchange are not subject to the IUE.
Special Tax on Hydrocarbons and their Derivatives, (IEHD) ***Impuesto Especial a los Hidrocarburos y Derivados***	• Individuals and legal entities that trade in hydrocarbons or their derivatives on the domestic market, whether produced domestically or imported.	• Maximum rate of 1.50 bolivianos per liter or equivalent unit of measurement in keeping with the nature of the product. This rate will be updated annually based on the exchange rate with the dollar.	• None.

(*Annex continues on the following page.*)

ANNEX 1. Principal National Taxes *(continued)*

Tax	*Subject*	*Amount*	*Exemptions, Deductions, and Refunds*
Financial Transactions Tax (ITF) ***Impuesto a las Transacciones Financieras***	• Applies to all credit and debit operations in checking accounts and on savings, payments, and transfers of funds, as well as the purchase of cashiers checks, travelers checks, or other similar financial instruments.	• 3 per thousand on banking transactions during the first year, and 2.5 per thousand during the second year.	• Accounts in Bolivian currency, savings deposits of less than US$1,000.
Simplified Tax System (RTS) ***Régimen Tributario Simplificado***	• Paid every two months by retailers, sellers of foodstuffs, and craftsmen. Consolidates the VAT, the RC-VAT, the IUE, and the IT into one tax payment.	• Payment corresponding to estimated capital, with fixed contributions every two months set by category with respect to the capital. Varies between 11 and 438 bolivianos.	• Sellers of electronics and home appliances.
Integrated Tax System, (STI) ***Sistema Tributario Integrado***	• Owners of up to two urban, inter-provincial, or inter-departmental transport vehicles, Consolidates the VAT, the RC- VAT, the IUE and the IT into one tax payment.	• Different categories to determine the amount of the tax, depending on the vehicle, service, or district of registration. • The tax ranges, depending on the category, from 100 to 700 bolivianos.	• Urban, inter-provincial, interdepartmental, and international transportation companies.

Sources: Coelho, Gómez-Sabaini, Medas, and Serra (2004); Cossio (2001).

Note: Does not include the Direct Tax on Hydrocarbons (*Impuesto Directo sobre los Hidrocarburos*—IDH) which is reviewed in Annex 2.

ANNEX 2. Tax Regime on the Upstream Hydrocarbon Activities

	Law 1194 (1990)		*Law 1689 (1996)*		*Law 3058 (2005)*	
	Rate	***Description***	***Rate***	***Description***	***Rate***	***Description***
Taxes on Production						
Departmental royalties	12%	• Includes the royalty of the producer department and of Pando and Beni.	12%	• No change	12%	• No change
National tax	19%	• This was received when the field was operated by a private company or YPFB.				
Participation of YPFB	19%	• This was received when the field was operated by a private company.				
Participation of the Treasury—YPFB			6%	• Applies both to new and existing fields. Existing fields are those that were in production in 1996.	6%	• No change
National Supplementary Royalty			13%	• Applies only to existing fields.		
National participation			19%	• Applies only to existing fields.		
Direct Tax on Hydrocarbons					32%	• Applies to all production, since the law eliminates the distinction between existing and new fields.
Other Taxes						
Tax on Earnings	40%	• This tax on earnings can be credited against departmental royalties and national taxes.	25%	• In effect in the sector since 1994 (Law 1606). • Not applicable to existing fields: The IUE can be credited against the National Supplementary Royalty. • The base is the earnings of companies, meaning revenue less depreciation, royalties, and amortization.	25%	• No change

(*Annex continues on the following page.*)

ANNEX 2. Tax Regime on the Upstream Hydrocarbon Activities *(continued)*

	Law 1194 (1990)		*Law 1689 (1996)*		*Law 3058 (2005)*	
	Rate	***Description***	***Rate***	***Description***	***Rate***	***Description***
				• Losses from prior years can be indefinitely discounted. • It is not allowable to deduct VAT paid or interest.		
Surtax			25%	• Applied to companies involved in extractive activities. • Applied on net earnings: Earnings used for payment of the IUE less 33% of total updated investments and 45% of the net income obtained, unless net income surpasses 55 million dollars.	25%	• No change
Remittances			12.5%	• A base equal to 50% of earnings is presumed, "without admitting proof to the contrary." • Does not apply to existing fields: The Tax on Earnings Remittances can be credited against the National Supplementary Royalty.	12.5%	• No change
VAT		• Until 1994, the sector was under a special regime and was not entitled to the VAT tax credit.	13%	• Applied to companies involved in extractive activities. • Not applicable to the export of hydrocarbons, on account of respect for the principle of tax neutrality	13%	• No change
IT		• Until 1994 the sector was under a special regime.	3%		3%	

Note: Excludes penalties and fees.

ANNEX 3. System for the Allocation of Tax Revenue

	Treasury	*Departments*	*Municipalities*	*Other*	*Comments*
National Taxes					
Revenue shared by municipalities	75%		20%	5%	• Includes the VAT, IT, RC-VAT, IUE, ICE, GAC, ISAE, ITGB. • This revenue sharing was introduced by the Popular Participation Act (1994) to allocate funds to the municipalities. • The 20% distributed to the municipalities is allocated in proportion to the municipalities' population. • The remaining 5% is allocated to the universities in proportion to the population of the department.
Direct Tax on Hydrocarbons (IDH) *Impuesto Directo sobre los Hidrocarburos*	Residual	43.75% + departmental compensation 53.9% of the departmental allocation	34.48% of the departmental allocation + municipal offsetting	8.62% of the departmental allocation + universities' offsetting + other allocations	• This tax was introduced by the new Hydrocarbons Act (2005) with the aim of increasing the government take on the industry. • 43.75% of the revenue from this tax is allocated to the departments. 29% of this allocation (12.5% of the IDH) is distributed among the producer departments (Tarija, Santa Cruz, Cochabamba, and Chuquisaca) based on their production. The remaining 71% (31.25% of the IDH) is distributed in equal parts to the non-producer departments. • If a producer department has an IDH allocation less than that of the non-producer departments, the Treasury must make a transfer to it so it will have the same allocation as the non-producer departments. • Once the departmental allocation has been determined (43.75% of the IDH plus the departmental offset), it is distributed among the departments, municipalities, and universities in a proportion of 54.9%, 34.48%, and 8.26%, respectively.

(*Annex continues on the following pages.*)

ANNEX 3. System for the Allocation of Tax Revenue *(continued)*

	Treasury	*Departments*	*Municipalities*	*Other*	*Comments*
					• 56.25% of the IDH is allocated to the Treasury. Nonetheless, part of these funds are committed. These commitments are: offsets to producer departments, offsets to universities and municipalities of specified departments, allocation to the Fund for the Development of Indigenous and Original Peoples and Peasant Communities, allocation to the Armed Forces and the Police, and Internal Aid Fund for National Development to massify the use of natural gas (see compensation mechanisms). • Introduction of the IDH eliminated the National Supplementary Royalty (32% of the production of existing fields), which were Treasury allocations.
Special Tax on Hydrocarbons and their Derivatives (IEHD) *Impuesto Especial sobre los Hidrocarburos y sus Derivados*	75% - Departmental Compensation Fund	25% + Departmental Compensation Fund			• The sharing of the IEHD was introduced by the Administrative Decentralization Act (1995) to allocate funds to the prefectures. • Half of the allocation to the prefectures (12.5% of the IEHD) is distributed in equal parts among the nine departments. The other half (the other 12.5%) is distributed in proportion to the population of the departments. • The Treasury must allocate a maximum of 10% of the IEHD to the Departmental Compensation Fund (FCD) as an offset for departments with reduced royalties (see Compensation Mechanisms).
Financial Transactions Tax (ITF) *Impuesto a las Transacciones Financieras,* and interim programs	100%				• Includes only ITF revenue (pursuant to the regulations in effect, the ITF is only applicable until July 2006), and revenue from the special tax regularization programs (which is also temporary in nature).

Real Property and Motor Vehicles Tax (IPBIVA) *Impuesto sobre la Propiedad de Bienes Inmuebles y Vehículos Automotores*				100%	• The Popular Participation Act transferred this tax to the municipalities so that they could generate their own funds. • This is the only tax administered on a subnational government level in Bolivia
Royalties and Fees on the Hydrocarbons Sector					
Departmental Royalties		100%			• Each producer department receives 11% of the price of the department's production as departmental royalties. • The departments of Pando and Beni, since they are considered to be the departments with the least relative development, receive a departmental royalty equivalent to 1% of national production of hydrocarbons. 1/3 of that amount is allocated to Pando and the remaining 2/3 to Beni.
Participation	100%				• This participation was part of the former Hydrocarbons Act, but was maintained in the new Law. • This participation is 6% of the national production of hydrocarbons, and is allocated to the Treasury.
Fees			50%	50%	• The municipalities in whose jurisdiction the concessions are located receive 50% of the fee collections. • The remaining 50% is allocated to the Ministry of Sustainable Development.
Royalties and Fees on the Mining Sector					
Royalties		100%			
Fees			30%	70%	
Royalties and Fees on the Forestry Sector					
Usage		35%	25%	40%	
Fees		25%	25%	50%	

(Annex continues on the following page.)

ANNEX 3. System for the Allocation of Tax Revenue *(continued)*

	Treasury	*Departments*	*Municipalities*	*Other*	*Comments*
Compensation Mechanism					
Departmental Compensation Fund	–100%	100%			• The Departmental Compensation Fund was created by the Popular Participation Act to provide an offset to departments with reduced royalties. • If there are sufficient funds, the fund makes transfers to departments that have a per capita royalty lower than the national average until they reach that average. But if there are insufficient funds for this purpose, the Fund's distribution is prorated among the beneficiary departments until exhausting the available Fund. • The Fund can use up to 10% of IEHD revenue, reducing the allocation corresponding to the Treasury. It is currently using this 10%.
Departmental IDH Offset	–100%	100%			• This mechanism was introduced by the new Hydrocarbons Act so that the Treasury could provide an offset to producer departments whose absolute allocation of the IDH is less than that of the non-producer departments.
Municipal and University IDH Offset	–100%		80%	20%	• This mechanism was introduced by the new Hydrocarbons Act so that the Treasury could provide an offset to the municipalities and universities of the departments crossed by the main highway (La Paz, Santa Cruz, and Cochabamba).

Sources: Alborta, Montalvo, and Zapata (2005); Barja (2003); and World Bank (2004).

Endnotes

1. According to this principle, the tax base is limited to earnings obtained in Bolivia, without taking into account the nationality or residence of the companies involved, or the place where the contract is signed.

2. An analysis of expenditure allocations is beyond the scope of this study. (See the chapter on decentralization.) Nonetheless, it is worth noting that there is a growing imbalance between revenue collection and jurisdiction, which is illustrated by the fact that, starting in 1994, revenue collection at subnational levels has slowly increased, while their subnational jurisdiction has remained unchanged.

3

Transaction Costs and Aid Effectiveness

Marco Scuriatti

Summary

Bolivia is highly dependent on international aid. Paying special attention to the donor harmonization and alignment agenda not only reduces the cost of international aid, but also increases its benefits. In fact, such an approach improves the quality and increases the impact of government spending. This policy note will first explain why harmonization and alignment are important and what is happening in the international arena in this regard. It will then give a brief summary of Bolivia's progress and describe pending challenges. Finally, three principal policies are recommended to provide a pragmatic map for reducing costs and increasing the effectiveness of these funds.

I. Background

The International Scenario—The Need for More Effective Assistance

Over the past decade, external Official Development Assistance (ODA) financing has been approximately US$35 billion per year throughout the world. International experience suggests that 15-25 percent of these flows are lost due to inefficiencies in the system. Though the aid has provided many benefits to the receiving countries, it has also created involuntary burdens. For example, donor policies and procedures differ from one donor to another and may also be different from the policies of the receiving country. This has led to choosing priorities misaligned with the needs of the country, poorly channeled efforts, inconsistent systems and programs, information gaps, avoidable duplications, and waste. Moreover, the enormous quantity of procedures, reports, and missions that the receiving countries have to manage involve high costs, particularly the opportunity cost of tying up the country's scarce political and management talent, which could be used to plan and implement development programs.[1] Those funds could be used to reduce poverty, educate children, save lives, and promote growth. Finally, due to the high volume of assistance, increasing its effectiveness is of timely importance.

Work to harmonize, align, and administer development aid in order to achieve better results is beginning to have a dynamic of its own, starting with the 2002 International Conference on Financing for Development in Monterrey, the 2003 Forum on Harmonization in Rome, and the Second International Roundtable on Managing for Development Results, held in Marrakech in 2004. More recently, at the Paris Forum on Aid Effectiveness, held in February 2005, 60 partner countries, 30 donor countries, and 30 development agencies again committed to increase donor-provided funds in order to achieve development results in the receiving countries.

The Declaration of the Paris Forum of 2005 contains 12 indicators to monitor progress related to ownership, alignment, harmonization, results, and mutual accountability (Annex I). The indicators and goals were designed to allow for follow-up and promote overall progress among the countries and agencies that signed this declaration.[2] For receiving countries, the agreed-upon indicators include national development strategies, reliable national systems for procurements and public financial management, development and use of results-oriented frameworks, and a joint analysis of the progress attained. For donors, the indicators contemplate aspects such as alignment with national strategies, joint analytical work, the use of common agreements and strengthened national systems, and harmonized support for capacity development and more predictable flows of assistance. Annex II presents some examples of activities carried out at the country level based on the Paris indicators.

The Bolivian Context—Highly Dependent on Aid

Bolivia is highly dependent on international aid. Between 1990 and 2004, external financing was approximately US$590 million, of which more than 80 percent was soft loans and grants. Disbursements of external financing represented an average of 8.5 percent of GDP, approximately 25 percent of the central government's expenditures, and 50 percent of total public investment (Box 1).

Due to the government's heavy dependency on external financing, all recent administrations have addressed the issue of how to improve aid effectiveness in their national agendas, and the country has piloted a series of coordination and harmonization initiatives.[3] In 1999, in an effort to bring together other coordination and harmonization initiatives, the "New Relationship Framework between the Government and the International Cooperation Community in the 21st Century" was developed in Bolivia, with technical and financial support from certain development assistance agencies.[4] This framework includes an analysis of experiences in the country regarding harmonization and alignment, institutional capacities of the different sectors, and an implementation plan with tasks and specific activities (Annex III).[5]

Box 1. Incidence of International Aid in Bolivia

	Percentage of Total			Percentage of External Financing				
	Commercial	*Soft Loans*	*Grants*	*Gross Domestic Product*	*Exports*	*Tax Revenue*	*Total Expenditures*	*Capital Outlays*
1990	7.9	73.6	22.3	11.0	63.5	72.2	43.0	133.4
1991	12.7	46.4	36.8	10.0	68.5	60.8	36.9	114.8
1992	21.9	25.3	56.1	11.3	99.6	68.0	39.5	112.3
1993	18.3	37.1	51.2	9.9	79.5	57.9	33.4	107.3
1994	28.1	39.3	52.8	9.0	54.8	52.4	31.4	100.8
1995	29.2	31.3	56.0	9.3	60.1	53.4	33.0	113.7
1996	11.6	28.4	49.7	7.3	47.7	41.3	26.1	89.6
1997	20.7	25.2	56.4	6.4	43.5	36.4	23.5	88.5
1998	12.4	20.5	51.3	5.7	44.2	29.1	19.3	81.9
1999	20.0	18.6	52.3	5.4	42.6	29.1	18.5	75.9
2000	19.6	33.9	54.5	6.2	41.8	33.3	21.2	87.7
2001	13.9	27.4	51.8	6.5	41.2	36.4	20.4	77.9
2002	33.9	36.6	51.0	8.8	53.4	49.4	26.3	104.3
2003	28.9	31.0	49.0	11.5	58.1	64.6	35.9	141.9
2004	29.4	35.9	44.5	8.8	35.9	42.7	27.2	96.4
Average	**20.6**	**34.0**	**49.1**	**8.5**	**55.6**	**48.5**	**29.0**	**101.8**

External financing as a percentage of GDP dropped from 11 percent in 1990 to 5.5 percent in 1999. Nonetheless, due to an economic crisis and a high fiscal deficit, disbursements increased to 11.5 percent of GDP in 2003 and 8.8 percent in 2004. Though this process was accompanied by an increase in soft loans and grants, trade loans grew the most. Trade sources increased from an average of 16.5 percent of external financing between 1998 and 2001 to 31 percent between 2002 and 2004. The incidence of international cooperation funds is even more prominent in the fiscal accounts, especially in public investment. In 2004, the ratio of aid/tax revenue was 30 percent and the ratio between aid and capital outlays was 96 percent. Moreover, in this same period, external financing represented more than 50 percent of public investment programs.

In late November 2005, on the initiative of the Vice-Ministry on the Budget and External Financing (*Viceministerio de Presupuesto y Financiamiento Externo*—VIPFE), a workshop was held to evaluate the relationship between the government and the international cooperation community. The workshop's purpose was to identify progress made, lessons learned, and the next steps in coordination efforts. A basis was also laid for follow-up indicators on the commitments of the Paris Forum, in order to leave behind an institutional record and a relationship proposal for the next government administration (Annex IV: executive summary).

In recent years, though at differing paces and with respect to different issues, the government and donors have made progress on this agenda. Some examples are:

- Bolivia has started to implement programs for specific sectors, and varying degrees of progress have been achieved in the three most important social sectors: education, health, and basic sanitation. The government has created interagency roundtables and has held national and international workshops. In addition, a study soon to be conducted will provide the government with a diagnosis of the rural and agricultural sector. The feasibility of implementing Sector Wide Approaches (SWAp) is closer to becoming a reality in the health sector and in education (see Box 2).
- Currently, work is being carried out to harmonize the procurement rules for domestic goods and services with the rules of the World Bank and the Inter-American Development Bank (IDB). Common points are being identified in this regard, and an analysis is being made of the potential for flexibility on some positions (see Box 3 in section III).
- Some co-financing is already underway, while other co-financing efforts are being developed in several governmental and social sectors (see Box 2).
- A harmonization and alignment gateway has been created with the goals of improving communications between the government and the cooperation community and providing information on the activities and products of the coordinating roundtables.

Box 2. Fiscal Roundtable And Sector Wide Approaches In The Education Sector: Two Concrete Examples Of Coordination And Harmonization

Fiscal Roundtable: The fiscal roundtable has made significant achievements. The government, together with the international cooperation community, created the Multi-Donor Budget Support Program (*Programa Multidonante de Apoyo Presupuestario*—PMAP). This program, designed to guarantee support for reducing the 2004 fiscal gap, was linked to a matrix of actions, which were satisfactorily performed. A new matrix, designed for 2005, included government commitments related to improving public administration management and transparency, distribution and equitability in public expenditures, and efficient implementation of the Poverty Reduction Strategy. This Memorandum of Understanding was signed by Germany (embassy and KFW), the IDB, the DFID (Department for International Development of the United Kingdom), Belgium, France, USAID, the Netherlands, Sweden, the European Union, Denmark, and Canada.

Box 2. *(continued)*

The quarterly review of the PMAP revealed that the government fulfilled approximately 90 percent of the commitments, except on the Development Strategy, four versions of which were written, but not implemented. Nonetheless, an inter-institutional government team drafted the Actions in the Fight Against Poverty document, which provides a good reflection of the country's orientation and commitment. This document includes a quantification and analysis of public expenditures and investments targeting the Millennium Development Goals (MDG), through programs related to the fight against poverty: The National Emergency Employment Plan, (*Plan Nacional de Empleo de Emergencia*—PLANE), PROPAIS, Investment Funds, the Follow-up and Evaluation System for Implementing the Millennium Development Goals (*Sistema para el Seguimiento y Evaluación de los Objetivos de Desarrollo del Milenio*—SISE-ODM), the Productive Bolivia National Dialogue (*Diálogo Nacional Bolivia Productiva*—DNBP), and the Comprehensive Social Welfare Network (*Red Integral de Protección Social*—RIPS).

Sector Wide Approaches in the Education Sector: Bolivia has a long history of donor participation in education. The Education Reform Program (*Programa de Reforma Educativa*—PRE) for primary education was financed by the World Bank and the IDB, and by other members of the community of donors (1992-2002). Its implementation led to a high degree of coordination among donors in the form of joint supervision missions, progress reports, individual auditing reports, and other coordinated activities. Since 2004, the community of donors (Sweden, Denmark, the Netherlands, France, Spain, and Japan, as well as the World Bank, the IDB, the United Nations Population Fund (UNFPA), and UNICEF have provided financial and technical aid to the Multi-Annual Operating Plan (*Plan Operacional Multi Anual*—POMA 2004-2008) for education in Bolivia.

Currently, the principal agreement between the government and the donor communites regarding education is an alignment of objectives and activities described in the POMA with the goal of applying a sector wide approach, regardless of the financing mechanism and technical support used by each of its components. Donors are using several different mechanisms and financing modes to support the sector (such as specific investment projects and financing pools). Donors are working together to strengthen the Ministry of Education's fiduciary capacity through various activities established in a specific action plan. For example, using this type of agreement, the World Bank supported the design and adjustment of financial and procurement procedures and for restructuring the administrative unit of the Ministry, with funds provided through the Grant Agreement of the Japan Policy and Human Resources Development Fund (PHRD).

II. Pending Challenges

Despite some progress, donors and Bolivia have yet to make significant changes in the provision and administration of aid. In Bolivia, as in the majority of receiving countries, challenges for reducing transaction costs and improving aid effectiveness fall into four major categories: (i) ownership; (ii) alignment; (iii) harmonization; and (iv) results-oriented management. Intensified efforts on the part of bilateral and multilateral donors to work closely with the government in these four areas will bring Bolivia closer to fulfilling the 12 Paris indicators listed in Annex I.

Ownership. The political turbulence in recent years has clearly affected the government's ability to maintain effective leadership in designing its development priorities in terms of specific results and in targeting donor contributions towards those priorities. The current situation of the Bolivian Poverty Reduction Strategy (*Estrategia Boliviana por la Reducción de la Pobreza*—EBRP) and the fact that the Consultative Group has not met in the past three years are illustrative of the absence of an established agenda. In addition, more and better national capabilities are needed to help build viable strategies and more firmly integrate them into national processes, for example, with respect to the budget, international aid management, and collaboration of the legislature and other stakeholders, such as the private sector.

Alignment. There have been several efforts in Bolivia to align international cooperation funds with government-defined priorities, from orderly investment matrices to alignment exercises for the existing portfolio based on efficiency criteria and prioritizations. Some interventions are still present, though with significantly less influence than in years past, that go beyond government-defined policies and programs. Such interventions are geared more towards addressing the priorities of financiers and the restrictions they face than towards the government's priorities. Part of the problem is that the government's most important programs have not been formally confirmed, which would improve funding allocations. In addition, the wide range of projects has not been grouped into a reduced set of major plans defined into pillars, which would make a comprehensive, multi-sector approach possible on the national, regional, or local level.

Even more important, for the reasons analyzed in the following table, donors have been reluctant to place their confidence in Bolivia's administrative system, which includes areas as diverse as provisioning, financial management, auditing, monitoring and evaluation, and environmental protection. This reluctance persists, despite recent efforts to develop common standards and systems using high-performance indicators to meet these challenges. In order to advance in this area it would be necessary to agree upon satisfactory common measures that encourage transparency and improved fiduciary agreements.

Strengthening alignment is key for increasing the use of Sector Wide Approaches (SWAps) and budget support mechanisms, which are perhaps the two most important tools available to facilitate harmonization and alignment among a broad spectrum of participants. As mentioned in the preceding section, Bolivia has progressed in developing SWAps. Nonetheless, until internationally accepted fiduciary requirements and effective internal control systems are developed, these two types of support will continue to be marginal.

Harmonization. Though progress has been made on activities such as joint analyses and donor co-financing, such activities have been *ad hoc* and disperse among the different sectors. Positive examples were generally the result of discussions among donors. A clear map led by the government and agreed upon by donors is still missing. For example, institutionalizing all harmonization activities, such as joint agreements to specify conditions and cooperation delegation agreements, would help wind down the policy debates. Too many donors are still imposing their own work agenda and are indifferent to the government's capacity and funds. There are still too many independent requirements regarding auditing, missions, and reports, and too much information remains unshared, which saturates the system, increases costs, and creates confusion.

Results-Oriented Management. Timely and accurate information is needed to make decisions on supervision, monitoring, and evaluation. However, in Bolivia, using information to improve the decision-making process for aid management and results-focused implementation has not yet matured into a full policy agenda. This is because widespread pressure for such an agenda has peaked only recently, and its implementation requires major efforts at the country level in multiple (and complex) areas, including strategy, planning, public expenditure management, results-based monitoring and evaluation systems, and statistical capacity.

For example, the Ministry of the Treasury has a very complete database on external financing, but it is not always up to date due to delays—sometimes considerable delays—in the provision of information from the implementation institutions of the government and the international cooperation community. Moreover, suitable information on the sector is frequently lacking for monitoring and evaluating results and the country's statistical capacity is still limited (see Box 4).

Equally important is the internal drive for results-based management within the donor agencies to link the aid programs more explicitly to Bolivia's priorities and desired results. So far, the government has made limited progress in agreeing with donors on central principles and results agendas that share common elements and approaches.

III. Policy Recommendations—An Opportunity

International experience shows that if the efficiency of aid flows to Bolivia were improved internally (for example, through government leadership and management to reduce transaction costs) and externally (for example, through better monitoring and evaluation systems to improve effectiveness), it would be possible to improve the performance of the system by 15 to 25 percent, or about 1 percent of GDP. This would result from gains in efficiency based on changes in government spending.

Box 3. Harmonization of Policies and Procedures for Procurements and Financial Management

Complicated, Unclear Procurement Procedures. National procurement systems are still complicated and unclear. A recent decree on procurements contemplates positive discrimination in support of Bolivian companies, but its status is under review. Bolivia's public procurement framework comprises rules and regulations that implement a set of principles and procedures for purchasing goods and non-consultant services, public works, and the selection of consultants. These regulations were established in January 2004 through a decree that does not have the status of a law. Due to the deficiencies of this legal framework, the decree was amended five times over the past 18 months, usually in response to pressures from contractors, vendors, and local consultants. Both the regulations and the documentation for local procurement incorporate practices and requirements that are not compatible with good international practices and lead to deficient management of purchasing, reduced transparency in tender processes, a low level of competition, and higher contract prices. Constant changes in the decree without any type of prior consultation have led to significant setbacks with respect to internationally accepted practices and procedures.

The replacement of that decree by a Procurement Act that is consistent with internationally accepted standards seems difficult given the current political context. In order to advance in harmonizing procurement procedures, the World Bank and other donors (for example, the IDB, Denmark, the Danish and Dutch cooperation agencies), have agreed to use common procurement guidelines to support the Ministry of Education in the implementation of its recent development strategy for the sector. These guidelines include detailed procedures for competitive bidding on a national level, as well as standardized bidding competition documents that will be part of an Operating Manual, which could be a pilot for future operations of SWAps. The procedures will be based on current national procurement procedures and practices but will incorporate internationally accepted standards. These common guidelines could serve as a basis for a future Procurement Act. Until that law is passed, all bidding processes financed by the World Bank will use its own purchasing guidelines.

SIGMA. Government public investments are made through the Follow-up and Evaluation System (*Sistema de Seguimiento y Evaluación*—SIGMA), which is integrated into a broader governmental information management system that is still under development. SIGMA is coordinated through government institutions, though to date it is operational only at the central level and serves a limited number of ministries. The goal is to expand SIGMA in the Executive branch, incorporate regions and municipalities, harmonize the monitoring and evaluation of associated external partners, and have those partners align their systems with SIGMA.

Box 4. Inter-Institutional Follow-Up and Evaluation Council

The traditional system for monitoring of public expenditures (a large part of which is still financed through external assistance), the Financial Follow-up System (*Sistema de Seguimiento Financiero*—SISFIN) remains weak. There is a growing recognition by the government that a results-based management system needs to be introduced to monitor public expenditures. The national public expenditures reporting system currently focuses on monitoring implementation rates but does not evaluate the impact of expenditures. The government took a major step towards results-based management in December 2001 with the creation of a new system to measure the impact of the national poverty reduction strategy, known as the Inter-Institutional Follow-up and Evaluation Council (*Consejo Interinstitucional de Seguimiento y Evaluación*—CISE).

The CISE is composed of three entities: a reporting and monitoring unit, the Economic and Social Policies Analysis Unit (*Unidad de Análisis de Políticas Económicas y Sociales*—UDAPE), which belongs to the Ministry of Finance; the National Statistics Institute (*Instituto Nacional de Estadística*—INE); and the Strategic Planning and Popular Participation Unit (*Unidad de Planificación Estratégica y Participación Popular*—UPEPP), which belongs to the Ministry of Sustainable Development and Planning. The INE is the technical implementation agency of the CISE. The UDAPE is responsible for designing indicators to monitor progress on a national level, including five impact indicators, seven of which are results based, and 40 intermediate indicators. The UPEPP is currently negotiating with the municipalities to agree upon and define 40 indicators to monitor progress at the municipal level. Given the municipalities' lack of capacity to measure results, the UDAPE is planning to use substitute poverty reduction indicators. Nonetheless, more coordination is still needed among actors at the central and municipal levels. CISE is present at the central level, and public oversight mechanisms are present at the municipal level, but the two are not adequately linked.

Moreover, a focus on developing national systems and institutions that make more effective use of international funds could be crucial for providing the necessary financial support to implement the new administration's social, institutional, and administrative agenda.

As a result, sustained attention at the highest level continues to be essential to overcoming persistent limitations and ensure that the current window of opportunity is not lost. The legitimacy of the new government, together with the country's focus on an aid effectiveness agenda in recent years, should provide an opportunity to consolidate these pending challenges. The new government should capitalize on the progress made and at the same time clear away the obstacles created by the recent political turbulence.

In this context, three actions could help reduce costs, improve aid effectiveness, and increase public confidence in the effectiveness of development cooperation: (i) political dialogue and strategic planning; (ii) impact measurement; and (iii) institutional training at the national government and local levels.

Planning—Formulating a Unified National Development Strategy

Several steps can be taken to create a national unified strategy that aligns internal and external funds with key development priorities agreed among different social sectors within the country. Development goals could be identified using existing participatory mechanisms, reinforced by the regular meetings of the Consultative Group. Discussion on and approval of a national development strategy by the Congress could also help ensure that priorities are in line with appropriate legislative actions and budget resources.

Bolivia's Vice Ministry of Budget and External Financing (*Viceministerio de Presupuesto y Financiamiento Externo*—VIPFE) is a highly respected public institution responsible for administering aid coordination. The VIPFE is in a privileged position to strengthen government ownership of this important issue. It is important that future administrations and the international cooperation community place their confidence in the skill and knowledge of the VIPFE to manage and direct available funds, in order to make sensible policy decisions and articulate a national development strategy.

The VIPFE can facilitate reaching this goal by continuing to manage the harmonization process without political interference. A technical secretariat could be established under its aegis specifically devoted to fulfilling the 12 Paris indicators, with financing from the government and donors. Special attention would be paid to identifying key actions needed to strengthen and make full use of national systems.

At the same time, it is crucial that the new government reform and administer the Consultative Group (CG) mechanism, which it has not done for the past two years due to a climate of political uncertainty. This first CG could provide an opportunity for the government to present its policy agenda and seek support from development partners and private investors.

This new CG would be in a position to assist the new administration in pursuing its interests in the "New Relationship Framework between the Government and the International Cooperation Community in the 21st Century." This process could be supervised by national meetings of the CG, conducted by actors familiar with the budget process, to ensure that development aid is synchronized with the country's internal goals. This would increase the CG's capacity to form government-led work teams, provide a mechanism to coordinate implementation of policies and programs at the sector/thematic level, and thus create conditions for more SWAp-type operations.

Impact Measurement—Strengthening the Inter-Institutional Follow-up and Evaluation Council and Investing in Communications and Information Technology to Better Manage Aid Flows

Results-based measurements are key to ensuring the effective use of aid flows and improving accountability and transparency. Bolivia could achieve progress in this area by undertaking the following actions:

- Continue to improve the country's results-based measurement and management capacity and intensify current efforts to strengthen statistical capacity, in particular by supporting the efforts of the Paris 21 Consortium and the World Bank Fund for Statistical Capacity Building. This would involve expanding and strengthening international partnerships on statistical work, including the preparation of new and prioritized methods of collecting comprehensive information, and expanding the International Household Surveys Network support to the CISE.
- In order to adopt a baseline and comparative information in key areas of donor aid, it is essential to use the current advances in information and communications technology (ICT), which offer a variety of tools to better manage the complexity of a country's portfolio. A small investment by the government in web-based software and in processes such as the Aid Management Platform, developed by the Development Gateway Foundation, could help governments and their donors share information. Some of the main advantages of this technology are: (i) standardized, validated access to information on ODA flows at any stage, and on their status and patterns of disbursement; (ii) strengthening of the VIPFE's capacity to monitor key performance and budget indicators; (iii) transparent access for stakeholders, including citizens, civil society, and the private sector, to policy documents and national development strategies, which contributes to achieving shared accountability; and (iv) strengthening of the government's internal administrative capacity to provide information systems that enhance public financial management, procurements, and other public sector areas.

Strengthen the Human Resource Capacity of the Public Sector in Relevant Areas for the Harmonization Agenda—Increasing Confidence in the Systems and Procedures for Managing and Coordinating the Aid

Implementation of the harmonization and alignment agenda calls for increasing donor confidence in the systems and procedures used to manage and coordinate the development aid of the partner countries. This requires solid administrative systems nationwide. Strengthening the public sector's human resource capacity continues to be a major challenge in Bolivia. In addition, in the decentralization process, the departments and municipalities still suffer from institutional weaknesses that keep them from being effective in implementing public investment programs aimed at overcoming poverty.

The introduction of a professional civil service is essential for attaining a genuine partnership with donors. Reforming the civil service would yield major dividends, because it substantially improves aid effectiveness. In this regard, if a second phase of the current institutional reform project is decided upon (see the policy note on institutional reform in this volume), it would be well advised to pay special attention to training the personnel in three relevant areas for the harmonization and alignment agenda: (i) public financial management; (ii) formulation of the budget; and (iii) financial management and provisioning systems.

Resource Guide

The New Relationship Framework for the Government and National Harmonization and Alignment Plan, prepared by the VIPFE in 2005 and 2003 respectively, are summarized in Annexes III and IV.

www.aida.developmentgateway.org. The **AiDA** website provides information on activities of the principal donors of international development aid as well as on civil organizations and foundations.

www.aidharmonization.org. A website on harmonization for professionals involved with development, located on the **Development Gateway**, which offers easy access to the growing series of works on harmonization, provides a space for discussion by professionals, and highlights implementation activities and useful tools from around the world.

www.countryanalyticwork.net. This website is a repository of analytical and diagnostic reports, methodologies, and information on best practices of more than 25 donors. Its purpose is to facilitate coordination and prevent duplication of efforts in this important area of development.

www.oecd.org/dac. The **OECD Development Assistance Committee** has published a series of documents on good practices entitled "Harmonising Donor Practices for Effective Aid Delivery."

www.worldbank.org/harmonization/romehlf. The website of the **High Level Forum** includes the Rome and Paris Declarations (which describe the commitments assumed regarding harmonization and alignment), a list of participants, background, harmonization implementation plans offered by donors and partner countries, as well as video clips that can be disseminated for instructional purposes.

Annex I. Paris Agenda: Goals Agreed Upon in Relation to the 12 Progress Indicators

	Indicators		*2010 Goals*
1	Partners have operational development strategies		**At least 75% of partner countries** have operational development strategies.
2a	Reliable Public Finance Management (PFM) Systems		**Half of partner countries** move up at least one measure (i.e., 0.5 points) on the PFM/CPIA (Country Policy and Institutional Assessment) scale of public finance management performance.
2b	Reliable Procurement Systems		**One-third of partner countries** move up at least one measure (i.e., from D
to			C, C to B, or B to A) on the four-point scale used to assess performance for this indicator.
3	Aid flows are aligned on national priorities		**Halve the gap** — halve the proportion of aid flows to the government sector not reported on government's budget(s) (with at least 85% reported on budget).
4	Strengthen capacity by coordinated support		**50% of technical cooperation flows** are implemented through coordinated programs consistent with national development strategies.
5a	Use of country public financial management systems	For countries with a **score of 5 or more** on the PFM/CPIA scale of performance (see Indicator 2a)	**All donors** use partner countries' PFM systems, and **A two-thirds reduction of the gap:** A two-thirds reduction in the percent of aid to the public sector not using partner countries' PFM systems.
		For countries with a **score of 3.5 to 4.5** on	**90% of donors** use partner countries' PFM systems, and **A one-third reduction of the gap:** A one-third reduction in the percent of
aid		the PFM/CPIA scale of performance (see Indicator 2a)	to the public sector not using partner countries' PFM systems.
5b	Use of country procurement systems	For countries with an **A score** on the procure-	**All donors** use partner countries' procurement systems, and **A two-thirds reduction of the gap:** A two-thirds reduction in the percent of

(*Annex continues on the following page.*)

		ments scale of performance (see Indicator 2b)	aid to the public sector not using partner countries' procurement systems.

Annex I. Paris Agenda: Goals Agreed Upon in Relation to the 12 Progress Indicators (*continued*)

	Indicators		*2010 Goals*
		For countries with a **B score** on the procurements scale of performance (see Indicator 2b)	**90% of donors** use partner countries' procurement systems, and **A one-third reduction of the gap:** A one-third reduction in the percent of aid to the public sector not using partner countries' procurement systems.
6	Avoid parallel Project Implementation Units (PIUs)	**Reduce by two-thirds** the stock of parallel project implementation units (PIUs).	
7	Aid is more predictable	**Halve the gap:** Halve the proportion of aid not disbursed within the fiscal year for which it was scheduled.	
8	Aid is untied	**Continued progress over time**	
9	Use of common arrangements or procedures	**66% of aid flows** are provided in the context of program-based approaches.	
10a	Field missions	**40% of donor missions to the field are joint.**	
10b	Country analytic work	**66% of country analytic work is joint.**	
11	Results-oriented frameworks	**Reduce the gap by one-third:** Reduce the proportion of countries without transparent and monitorable performance assessment frameworks by one-third.	
12	Mutual accountability	**All partner countries** have mutual assessment reviews in place.	

Source: Paris Declaration, 2005.

Note: This agreement is subject to reservations by one donor on (i) the methodology for assessing the quality of locally managed procurement systems (relating to targets 2b and 5b) and (ii) the acceptable quality of public financial management reform programs (relating to target 5a.ii). Further discussions are underway to address these issues. The targets, including the reservation, have been notified to the Chairs of the High-Level Plenary Meeting of the 59th General Assembly of the United Nations in a letter dated September 9, 2005, by Mr. Richard Manning, Chair of the OECD Development Assistance Committee (DAC).

Annex II. Examples of Activities at the Country Level

Ethiopia–As part of the Strategic Partnership between Africa and the pilot processes of the IMF, donors are focusing on harmonized budget support aligned with the Poverty Reduction Strategy Paper (PRSP) and government budget cycles. These are forumlated on a multi-donor approach of sector-based financing for capacity development. The donor states have completed a joint review of public expenditures and a diagnosis of procurements and financial management. Donors are working to develop common guidelines for presenting financial information, standardized bidding documents, and common thresholds for competitive bids both on a national and international level, and for their *ex ante* and *ex post* review. DFID and the World Bank are jointly conducting an environmental assessment of the country. Donors are supporting a government-led plan of action that includes a new Aid Management Platform (AMP). The AMP is an online information system that streamlines the way countries and donors monitor and report on international aid flows and programs. This system helps improve planning, targeting, disbursements, and general financial management. It also reduces the administrative burden on Ethiopia's Ministry of Finances.

Honduras–Under the government's leadership, donors have agreed to provide support aligned and coordinated with the PRSP, including SWAps in education, health, water and sanitation, security, and agro-forestry. This effort also includes alignment with governmental budget cycles, joint reviews, planning and evaluation activities, information sharing, and the use of national systems prior to the parallel systems of the donors.

Vietnam–The government has led the development of a plan of action for well-defined, comprehensive harmonization supported by: development banks (the Asian Development Bank, the French Development Agency, the Japan Bank for International Cooperation, the Kreditanstalt für Wiederaufbau, and the World Bank), a group of seven to nine bilateral donors with a shared vision on development, the European Commission and United Nations agencies. On a strategic level, the government and donors have agreed upon and continue working to achieve the desired results for increased effectiveness, including the use of a poverty reduction strategy for aid planning and the use of other mechanisms to ensure the consistency of sector-targeted policies. At the level of processes, donors have made considerable progress toward developing common guidelines for bidding documents; thresholds for competitive bids on a national and international level; *ex ante* and *ex post* reviews; financial report formats; acceptability criteria for audits, with a shared list of acceptable companies; and terms of reference for such purposes. Donors are also conducting joint performance portfolio reviews with collective follow-up on generic issues. The government and donors are using group consultation meetings as the principal forum of discussion for current harmonization and aid effectiveness initiatives.

Annex III. The New Relationship Framework between the Government and the International Cooperation Community in the 21st Century, a Proposal to the Consultative Group, 1999

Unquestionably, if the problems mentioned in this document were overcome and coordination between the government and the international community were strengthened, we could achieve the goal of significantly increasing the cooperation's effectiveness. Hand-in-hand with the local effort, poverty rates in Bolivia could diminish more quickly, and levels of growth and sustainable development could be consolidated in the twenty-first century.

Below, we briefly review the principal existing initiatives, which complement one another; the principles that will guide this new relationship framework; and the next actions that are recommended for the government and the international cooperation community to undertake jointly.

a) Certain Shared Initiatives

The search for new initiatives for the twenty-first century is a reflection of not very encouraging results in the fight against poverty in developing countries. Assessments made by financing entities and countries show that the development cooperation they have granted has not had the expected results. Three initiatives are most prominent in relation to the search for new mechanisms in the coming century:

- The initiative proposed by OECD/DAC countries through the document entitled, "*El Papel de la Cooperación Internacional para el Desarrollo en los Albores del Siglo XXI*" ["The Role of International Cooperation in Development at the Dawn of the Twenty-first Century"], which proposes a new strategy for the future based on defining the roles that the principal partners for development should play, contemplating strategies that incorporate economic, social, and political elements.
- The initiative proposed by the United Nations System, including the "United Nations Development Assistance Framework" (UNDAF), and the Joint Country Assistance Evaluation. These provide a planning framework for the system in the country as well as joint cooperation objectives and strategies, a common funds framework, and proposals for follow-up, monitoring, and evaluation. These initiatives use a program-based approach as a tool to attain specific results, which need to be integrally related to the country's own development strategies.
- The World Bank initiative known as the "Comprehensive Development Framework," which proposes to improve the efficiency of donor participation in development by including macroeconomic and structural considerations within a comprehensive strategy. It seeks specific results, with the countries leading the development work, while placing greater emphasis on the principal partners involved. This framework's objective is a results-based approach to poverty alleviation.

- Finally, the decentralization processes implemented some years ago through several bilateral cooperation efforts; the experience of the IDB, where local representatives accompany the entire cycle of operations very closely; and, above all, the management of the portfolio, are also convergent actions.
- These initiatives, in addition to the experience amassed in Bolivia in recent years, allow us to propose a "New Relationship Framework between the Government and the International Cooperation Community in the 21st Century," with the objective of providing Bolivia with sustainable development in the twenty-first century, with an accelerated reduction in current levels of poverty. This "New Framework" is based on principles and actions that should be jointly addressed by the government and the international cooperation community over the coming months.

b) Principles

The new relationship framework proposed by the government embodies fundamental principles that define the actions of the partners (government, the international cooperation community, civil society, the private sector) involved in the development of the country. These principles call for:

- Ensuring that governmental development plans are compatible and complementary, which means that investment initiatives should have a relationship to the plans, development strategies, and priorities established by the country. Development aid should be complementary in nature, and, as a result, national priorities and commitments assumed by the country at international summits should be the reference framework for scheduling International Cooperation funds. With respect to NGOs and civil society, a greater coordination with these partners in development would be of benefit to all.
- Recognizing that Bolivia sets the direction and the objectives, which means that the programs to be implemented have an absolute sense of "ownership" for the State, the implementing agency, and the beneficiaries, through a concertation process.
- Promoting effectiveness, which means that local and external funds should go to the best investment options, geared toward supporting the fight to overcome poverty.
- Expecting accountability, which includes clear accountability for meeting the programs' specific goals and for efficient use of the funds.
- Fostering sustainability, which means the need to have the basic conditions for sustainable development, in order to guarantee the continuity of the development process in the mid and long term. This also includes a strategy for the post-cooperation period.
- Strengthening institutional capacities, which means that the effective application of a program-based approach requires the improvement of national capacities.
- Assuring that efforts are complementary, which means the need for joint efforts and work in partnership, through dynamic coordination processes

and strengthening of strategic alliances between the government, the international community, civil society organizations, and the private sector.

- Increasing transparency, which means the need to make existing information on the various programs as available as possible to all development partners, and to have effective monitoring mechanisms.

c) Proposed Actions
To reach the proposed goal on the principles mentioned above, the government proposes to the Consultative Group that the following actions be implemented in the course of the coming months.

Defining the Strategic Framework

To strengthen the government's strategic framework, which brought together the initiatives of the municipalities, prefectures, and the principal stakeholders of civil society, it would be beneficial to institutionalize the National Dialog so that it becomes a mechanism for continual discussion with civil society.

Defining Priorities

Within the framework of the national consensus strategy, it is necessary to confirm the government's most important programs in order to improve the allocation of international cooperation funds.

Defining Programs

The wide range of projects should be grouped into a reduced set of principal programs, defined by pillars, which will permit a comprehensive, multi-sector approach to the 1997 - 2002 Plan of Action (POA 97-02), at the national, regional, or local level.

As one of the inputs for this work, use could be made of the Positioning Matrix. The expected result would be to develop a simple, ordered matrix for a program-based approach, structured around four pillars.

Results-Based Programming

The programs' conception will be oriented around the accomplishment of concrete results, with monitoring of the various implementation stages. The programming and follow-up on inputs and procedures will be adapted as necessary to ensure transparency, effectiveness, and efficiency in the programs' execution.

Accordingly, the governmental sectors, together with the international community, will continue to work toward establishing specific program-based indicators and goals as well as follow-up and evaluation mechanisms. Results-based programming requires suitable follow-up and evaluation mechanisms on the programs' execution. It further demands additional funds and capacities, such as timely, reliable information; continuity in management; and skilled human resources.

Supervision, Monitoring, and Evaluation

After deciding to formulate and finance programs, as opposed to projects, to the extent that the programs could be co-financed, it would be advisable for individual and joint mechanisms to be established for supervision, monitoring, and evaluation.[6] These measures will prevent a dispersion of efforts and contradictions when it comes time to supervise programs and evaluate their impact.

Achieve Greater Decentralization

Greater decentralization and delegation of authority to local representations would facilitate prompt, timely decision making. This, in turn, would facilitate improved execution of programs, and thereby contribute to obtaining the programmed results. Such a proposal must be accompanied by sufficient capacity for analysis, and therefore, where necessary, the local representations must be strengthened.

Reprogramming and Reallocation of Funds

Based on the results of the Positioning Matrix analysis, work should be done to allocate new funds or reprogram existing ones, in order to cover the financing deficit faced by some sectors under POA 97-02. This reallocation would be made on the basis of clear rules established jointly by the government and the international cooperation community. The objective of these reallocations would be to rationalize and complement efforts, search for synergies and improved efficiencies, and develop an optimal positioning matrix. In addition, it may eventually be necessary to reallocate funds toward those programs that have the greatest impact in the fight against poverty.

To carry out this work effectively, in many cases approval will be needed from the Home Offices and Boards of Directors of the international cooperation entities within the framework of their respective mandates, in order to reprogram or reallocate financing in effect in keeping with the country's current priorities.[7]

Development of Multi-Year Budgets

In order to turn projects into programs with a multi-year duration, it is critically important to ensure that the financiers commit funds for the full execution of the programs, thus helping to make sure that the programs will not suffer from interruptions that hinder the attainment of their goals.

For this to be possible, it will surely be necessary to approve changes in the budget programming procedures of certain friendly countries and multilateral institutions. To the extent possible, these budget programming cycles should take the government's term of office into account.

The Search for Joint Financing

In order to improve efficiency in the allocation of external funds, joint financing of programs will be sought from multilateral and bilateral institutions simultaneously, when that would lead to a better allocation of funds. A good illustration is the work that a number of donors have engaged in together for the institutionality pillar in support of the National Integrity Plan.

This will facilitate the government's and the international cooperation community's coordinating work in one and the same sector, with the resulting benefit of attaining goals with a greater impact. It will also simplify the administrative management of the government and of program implementation work.

Co-financing will continue to use the various existing modes, to best allow the members of the international cooperation community to fulfill their respective mandates.

Procurement of Goods and Services.

The country has rules for the procurement of goods and services under the Financial Administration System and Governmental Control Act (*Ley del Sistema de Administración Financiera y Control Gubernamental* - SAFCO) to ensure that institutions will have transparent, competitive, efficient processes. Nonetheless, to properly meet the fiduciary accountability standards of each financier, this system has to be updated, simplified, and better implemented. It will be important, as the current rules are updated, that the international community contemplate how these rules will be used, as is already being done by a series of financiers.

Implementation of the above, in many cases, will require approval from the Home Offices and Boards of Directors of the international cooperation entities.

Conclusions

The challenge of fighting poverty includes maintaining a proper political, economic, and social balance. In the case of Bolivia, the country has maintained a positive growth rate within a framework of political and economic stability. Yet this progress is still insufficient to position Bolivia at the average for social indicators in Latin America.

The current governmental administration, based on program proposals from the parties that comprise the coalition in office, and incorporating the suggestions of civil society through the National Dialogue, has established a program of government with clear goals around four pillars: Opportunity, Institutionality, Equitability, and Dignity.

Though foreign aid to the country has been gradually diminishing as a proportion of GDP over recent years, it continues to be significant, especially in the Public Investment Program, which is the main tool in the government's fight against poverty. With the aim of accelerating the fight against poverty, the government has prepared a "New Relationship Framework between the Government and the International Cooperation Community in the 21st Century," which it has submitted to the international community, and which sets forth a series of principles and actions.

The government, during the XII Meeting of the Consultative Group, expects to receive support from the international community to implement this "New Framework" over the coming months. If successful, this initiative could serve as an example to be followed by other developing countries.

Annex IV. Executive Summary: National Harmonization and Alignment Plan

Background

When asking whether development aid has had the expected impact, the answer is usually "no." This demonstrates a need to change the way that the cooperation agencies are currently working by allowing developing countries to assume the leadership (ownership) of their own development processes.

In 1999, in an effort to bring together other coordination and harmonization initiatives, the "New Relationship Framework between the Government and the International Cooperation Community" was developed in Bolivia. It sets forth principles and actions aimed at improving the intervention of donors and increasing the efficiency of development aid. Currently, the harmonization and alignment process is based on the commitments assumed at the Rome High-Level Forum.

Bolivia has piloted a series of coordination and harmonization initiatives (the Comprehensive Development Framework [CDF], the UNDAF, the OECD/DAC Task Force on Donor Practices, and currently the OECD/DAC Task Team on Harmonization and Alignment), which means that the country has extensive experience in this area.

This study explores some of the reasons for stagnation in the harmonization and alignment process and proposes actions that will concretely lead to the success of this initiative.

Coordination

We understand coordination to be the conduct of the government and the international cooperation community aimed at improving their relationship in all regards, and at reducing transaction costs in the management of development aid.

The coordination should take place on four levels: between the government and the international cooperation community, within the government, among donors, and among the cooperation agencies.

With the aim of coordinating actions and efforts, the government and the cooperation community have established formal coordination mechanisms.

Currently, the government is starting to execute its coordination proposal by holding five roundtables based on President Mesa's Plan of Government (National Dialogue, Constitutional Reform Assembly, Productivity and Competitiveness, Fiscal Measures, and Harmonization). A decision-making body, the "Management Group," has been established, with participation from representatives of the government and the international cooperation community.

The purpose of this study is to develop and reach a consensus on a proposal that facilitates the conditions needed for a successful implementation of the harmonization process in Bolivia. Political will in this regard is fundamental, and the degree of leadership that the government has assumed is notable, but the socialization of the agreements and actions is still weak, and there is little coordination.

For this study, the international cooperation community and the government have worked in a joint, coordinated manner. Worth noting is the establishment of an oversight team for the process, which has held meetings and has made significant contributions to accomplishing the objectives defined in this study.

The relationship between the government and the international cooperation community is based on two fundamental pillars:

- Alignment, which includes Development Strategy, Policy Definition, Prioritization of Actions, Use of Existing Capacities, and Reprogramming.
- Harmonization, which is related to the Budget, the National Public Investment System, Rules for the Procurement of Goods and Services, Delegated Cooperation, the Project Cycle, and Counterpart Analysis (Appropriation).

Alignment

There have been several efforts in Bolivia to align international cooperation funds with government-defined priorities. These have taken a variety of forms ranging from orderly investment matrices all the way up to alignment exercises for the existing portfolio based on efficiency criteria and prioritizations.

The study recognizes that alignment to the development strategies of the countries should be based on three important points: What is being aligned, to what is it being aligned, and how is it being aligned?

Currently, the alignment exercise suggests that funds should be reprogrammed by taking funds from programs and projects whose implementation has been insufficient and reallocating them to prioritized programs, in order to meet the goals set by the government. Another proposal calls for increased flexibility for the disbursement conditions of specific projects to turn them into program-based conditions with a results-based management approach, in accordance with the country's defined priorities.

Harmonization

The framework for harmonization efforts consists of an international agenda, based on the commitments assumed at the Rome High-Level Forum on Harmonization, as well as a national agenda, in which the government identifies actions needed to optimize the use of international cooperation funds in the context of the New Relationship Framework between the Government and the International Cooperation Community.

Harmonization refers to a unification of processes and procedures among donors, among government institutions, and between donors and government institutions, as part of a single initiative.

The areas identified in the study on which actions are proposed for simplifying and/or harmonizing procedures follow:

Phase One

Budget Modifications
Procurements and Contracting (Basic Rules, World Bank and IDB)
Statements of Expenditures (SOEs)

Phase Two

Number of accompaniment, follow-up, and evaluation missions (frequency and duration)
Financial Reports
Presentation of Audits

Cost/Benefit Analysis of Harmonization

This work seeks to estimate transaction costs, considering three aspects: (a) budget modifications, (b) contracting processes and (c) preparation of statements of expenditures (SOEs) under three scenarios: i) estimating "current" transaction costs ii) estimating transaction costs through "harmonizing" (a), (b) and (c), and iii) estimating transaction costs through separately "harmonizing" each of the processes.

The estimate of transaction costs uses the project cycle during the agreement implementation stage.

Three entities have been considered for the study: the Fund for Productive and Social Investment, the Ministry of Education, and the Bolivian Agricultural Technology System.

The average project execution delay in the three entities is 93 days. The average time resulting from harmonization of the project's execution in the three entities is 76.26 days, which represents an 18 percent reduction.

To estimate harmonization by processes we must:

- Reduce the budget modifications by 4.55 percent for all financiers.
- Reduce the procurement processes by 2.96 percent in all financing sources.
- Reduce the statements of expenditures, with respect to current transaction costs, by 2.49 percent for all financiers.

If we compare the current transaction cost with the harmonized transaction costs (a, b, and c), we see that they are reduced by an average of 19.28 percent. If we break the analysis down by financier, we have a reduction for the IDB of 25.19 percent, a reduction for the WB of 17.02 percent, and a reduction for bilateral agents of approximately 15.57 percent.

Based on an analysis of the two scenarios, we can conclude that we should seek harmonization in the three processes, given the overall impact on transaction costs. Otherwise, the risk is that the harmonization of any isolated process will be less effective, or that the overall impact will be marginal.

Counterparties

The study focuses on two aspects of Public Investment.

1) Analysis of the counterparties:
   One of the most important aspects of the reforms and of the structural adjustment of the state was a redefining of the State and of participation by the Treasury as a principal source for financing public investment projects. On the one hand, the Popular Participation Act, Administrative Decentralization, and the National Dialogue Act have defined, established, and instituted new mechanisms and procedures for funding transfers and allocations from the Treasury to departmental and municipal levels. On the other hand, these measures have created new management levels and jurisdictions for the state.
   This analysis has considered the national, departmental, and municipal jurisdictions in terms of the characteristics of the counterparties, current requirements, funds, entities, and types of projects. A proposal is made for each level.

2) Analysis of institutional capacities in public sector entities, including: planning capacity, capacity for developing rules, human resources, provision of public services, and management capacity.

Sector- and Program-Based Approach

An effective partnership at the sector level requires the establishment of administrative structures to ensure the international cooperation community that funds earmarked for development will be allocated in a coordinated manner, based on consensus, considering the government's priorities. Sector-based programs are one way to meet this challenge. They reconcile the priorities of the government with those of the international cooperation community.

Bolivia has commenced the process of implementing sector-based programs. In fact, the country has been laying the basis for this approach for some time. The sectors that have progressed the most on this initiative are basic sanitation and education. The health sector is undergoing a preliminary process. It had some interesting experiences in the past, but authorities in this sector have expressed their will and political determination to start preparing for the program in question.

For the basic sanitation sector, there is a financing agreement between the Bolivian government and the Cooperation of the European Union, named "Sector Support Program for the Supply of Water and Sanitation" (*Programa de Apoyo Sectorial para el Abastecimiento de Agua y Saneamiento* - PASAAS) whose objective is to support the government's policy for the sector by promoting the sustainability of the services, improving the financing system, and increasing investment funds.

This operation is the result of many years of coordinated work between the government and the international cooperation community, which first focused on strengthening the sector, institutionalization of public servants, and financial support.

In the education sector, a significant experience was the Education Reform Program (*Programa de Reforma Educativa*—PRE) carried out in 1995-2003. Negotiations with the international cooperation community commenced because the state was short of funds to finance implementation of educational reform in Bolivia.

The government decided to continue taking charge of educational policy-making decisions, without outside influence or pressure. It succeeded in implementing the educational reform through a sub-sector approach that channeled funds from the various international cooperation agencies to the objectives established by the national government.

The education sector has a financing agreement called the "Fund to Support the Education Sector" between the government of Bolivia and the Netherlands Ministry for Development Cooperation, using a sector-based approach for education in Bolivia, further extending the sub-sector-based approach of the first stage of the Education Reform Program. The amount of financing is US$ 75 million, and the implementing agency is the Ministry of Education.

The health sector is one of those most behind in preparing sector-based programs. Nonetheless, in late November of this year, the Ministry of Health and Sports organized the Sector-Based Approach in Health Workshop in the City of La Paz, where the following commitments were assumed:

- The Ministry of Health and Sports agreed to develop policy for the health sector.
- The strategy of the Ministry of Health and Sports will include sector-based approach principles.
- The national government and the international cooperation community will strengthen institutional capacities and respect the government mechanisms in effect.
- The Ministry of Health and Sports will formulate the plan of action.

The results of the above-mentioned workshop demonstrate that the Ministry has the will and political determination to start preparing the program for the sector.

Implementation Plan

Implementation of the Plan will make it possible to identify the steps to be carried out in the National Harmonization and Alignment Plan as well as the time frames, budget, and actions needed to progress on these efforts.

General Objective

To achieve greater development aid effectiveness, improve the way the the government and the international community work together, and reduce transaction costs, by implementing specific actions and initiatives within the harmonization and alignment process.

Requirements for implementing the National Harmonization and Alignment Plan:

Implementation of the National Plan has three important requirements: political will, strengthening of institutional capacities, and financial commitments.

POLITICAL WILL

One of the most fundamental requirements for implementing the National Harmonization and Alignment Plan is political will, which needs to be reflected in the government's express will to carry out a National Harmonization and Alignment Plan, which, among other things, would involve a simplification of procedures. The will of the international cooperation community is also needed to undertake a harmonization and alignment process, starting with decentralizing decisions, by moving them from the central offices to the resident missions, in order to avoid delays and increased transaction costs.

STRENGTHENING OF INSTITUTIONAL CAPACITIES

The need to strengthen institutional capacities at the level of the Sector Ministries, decentralized entities, and implementation entities was one of the most relevant conclusions in the diagnosis on obstacles to public investment and management of projects that have external financing.

A technical assistance program needs to be defined at the various levels of government to undertake an institutional reform program. The main suggestion is that the technical assistance program should be aligned with the need for institutional reforms, whose priority objective is to strengthen institutional capacities.

FINANCIAL COMMITMENTS

It is important to ensure a financing mechanism for implementation of the National Harmonization and Alignment Plan (*Plan Nacional de Armonización y Alineamiento*—PNAA), with a commitment from the international cooperation community and with financial and technical assistance funds, administered by the Technical Secretary for Harmonization and Alignment.

Implementation Schedule

The implementation schedule for the National Harmonization and Alignment Plan contemplates a timeline of approximately 16 months, broken down as follows.

- Achieving greater coordination: Operations are scheduled to start in March 2005 and continue through July 2006.
- Strategic alignment area: the tasks are scheduled to start in January 2005 and continue through April 2006, for a total of 16 months.

- Harmonization and simplification of the six processes identified has a duration of seven months, from April to October 2005.

Budget

The implementation time of the National Harmonization and Alignment Plan is approximately 16 months, and its total cost is US$497,000. External funds amount to US$267,000 and the national counterpart is US$230,000.

Critical Route

The National Harmonization and Alignment Plan has a short, medium, and long-term horizon, with specific actions and tasks for each of them.

The short term refers to the first 16 months of implementation, whose objective is to lay the basis for a process of coordination, harmonization, and alignment between the government and the international cooperation community. In the medium term, the objectives are to structure sector-based programs supported by harmonized procedures and processes and to design sector-based plans and policies.

Finally, in the long term, the goal is to develop a policy for the relationship between the international cooperation community and the government based on the principles of the new relationship framework, translated into an alignment with national development strategies. This should lead to strengthened institutions, efficient management of funds from external financing, and fully harmonized processes.

Endnotes

1. According to figures provided by the Organisation for Economic Co-operation and Development (OECD), over the past decade, multilateral and bilateral donors have financed more than 60,000 development assistance projects around the world. The demands on the capacity of the receiving party are overwhelming: some developing countries receive approximately 800 new projects each year, host more than 1,000 missions who monitor their work, and are required to submit 2,400 quarterly progress reports.
2. As a follow-up method, it was agreed to hold two monitoring rounds between now and 2008, when the Third High-Level Forum on Aid Effectiveness takes place. The first round will be held in 2006 and the second in 2008.
3. For example, the Comprehensive Development Framework, the United Nations Development Assistance Task Force, the OECD Task Force on Donor Practices, and currently the OECD Task Team on Harmonization and Alignment.
4. Canada, the Netherlands, Sweden, the Inter-American Development Bank, the United Nations Population Fund, the United States Agency for International Development (USAID), the World Bank, and the Bolivian Vice Ministry on Public Investment and External Financing.
5. This framework was presented at the Paris High-Level Forum and forms the basis for the relationship between the government and the international cooperation community. In addition, at a recent meeting of the Working Party on Aid Effectiveness, Bolivia expressed an interest in hosting the Regional Forum on Harmonization that will be taking place in 2006. This offer has been officially made to the IDB, the entity sponsoring that event.
6. This is contemplated in the guidelines of the UNDAF and the UN Joint Country Assistance Evaluation.
7. The World Bank portfolio, for example, was restructured in July 1999 to adapt it to the pillars and indicators, which will require approval from the board of directors.

4

Management and Sustainability of the Public Debt

Carlos Mollinedo and Julio Velasco

Summary

Between 1998 and 2005, Bolivia's total public debt increased rapidly in absolute terms and as a percentage of the Gross Domestic Product (GDP). Domestic debt more than doubled during this period, while external debt surpassed its levels prior to the debt relief initiatives. This trend is cause for concern. To limit the risk of a new debt crisis, the country needs to maintain a primary surplus greater than 1 percent of GDP. This will be possible if public sector income is increased through measures that are sustainable over time and if public expenditures are administered more efficiently without affecting public services. Equally important is for the government to improve its public debt management in order to properly manage risks and define a debt strategy that goes beyond the need to finance the public sector. The final component of this strategy would be to organize subnational (departmental and municipal) debt, because as decentralization expands, subnational debt could create fiscal vulnerability.

I. Background

Bolivia's public debt increased from 64 percent of GDP in 1998 to nearly 75 percent in 2005 (Figure 1). This was due to a rise in the fiscal deficit, which peaked at close to 9 percent of GDP in 2002. This lack of fiscal balance can be attributed to three causes: the cost of pension reform, which each year costs about 4.5 percent of GDP; deterioration of tax revenue due to the economic crisis that started in the late 1990s; and the sporadic application of expansive spending policies by the government. These factors do not have equal impact on public finances: while the scope of a drop in tax revenue and expansionary spending is limited to the economic cycle, the cost

Figure 1. Public Debt Trends
(as a percentage of GDP)

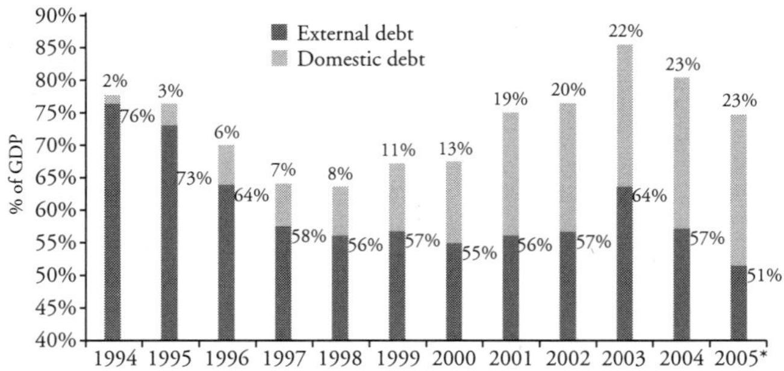

Source: Ministry of Finance and the Central Bank of Bolivia (BCB).
Note: (*) The information for 2005 is estimated using data from November 2005.

of pension reform will continue affecting public finances; according to recent estimates, this cost could represent 3 percent of GDP by 2020 (World Bank, 2004). Fiscal deterioration has led Bolivia to have one of the highest debt ratios in the region, surpassed only by Argentina and Uruguay, which have had payment moratoriums (Figure 2).

Figure 2. Public Debt in Latin America
(as a percentage of GDP)

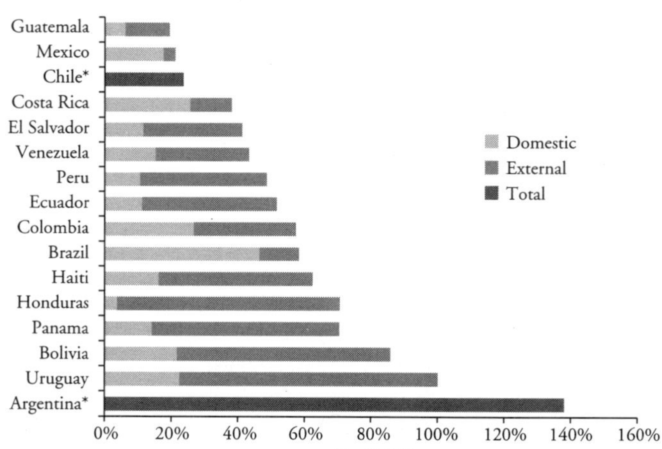

Source: Economic Commission for Latin America (ECLAC, 2004), Ministry of Finance, and the BCB.
Note: (*) No breakdown is available for Argentina or Chile.

Domestic debt went from insignificant amounts in the mid 1990s to a third of the total debt in 2005. The impact of this increase was partially mitigated after 1997, when the external debt leveled off at approximately 55 percent of GDP, due to the debt relief program for Highly Indebted Poor Countries (HIPC). This change will be deepened by the Multilateral Debt Relief Initiative (MDRI), which will allow for a cancellation of the debt contracted with the International Monetary Fund (IMF) and the World Bank (WB) (Box 1). On the other hand, the increase in domestic debt is making the public debt more costly. While the implicit interest rate on domestic debt is approximately 8.5 percent, that of external debt is approximately 2 percent (lower than that of Chile, Peru, and Ecuador, where it surpasses 5 percent, or that of Colombia and Mexico, where it is approximately 8 percent).

The low cost of the external debt reflects the fact that 90 percent of the external debt is multilateral: 38 percent with the WB, 36 percent with Inter-American Development Bank (IDB), and 16 percent with the Andean Development Corporation (*Corporación Andina de Fomento*—CAF) (See Figure 3.). The WB and the IDB grant loans under very favorable conditions due to Bolivia's low level of economic development. The concentration of external debt in three entities is due to the restructuring and relief programs conceived of in the mid 1980s, which made it possible to eliminate almost all the debt of private creditors and reduce the burden of bilateral and multilateral debt. Nonetheless, the cost of the external debt could increase in the future, for the following reasons: (i) the CAF, which loans money under more costly terms than the WB or the IDB, is increasing its loans, thereby raising the average cost of the external debt; and (ii) in the medium term, as Bolivia is now reaching a relatively high per capita income level, access to soft funds will be reduced.

Another problem associated with the growing domestic debt is its high degree of dollarization. In late 2004, 75 percent of the domestic debt was denominated in US dollars, which makes fiscal accounts vulnerable to fluctuations in the exchange rate. This fragility became evident in the late 1990s, when the Central Bank of Bolivia (*Banco Central de Bolivia*—BCB) had to accelerate Bolivia's currency devaluation in order to maintain the competitiveness of the real exchange rate. That, in turn, raised the cost of servicing domestic debt. Recently, the government has attempted to reduce dollar-denominated domestic debt by introducing debt instruments denominated in Housing Development Units (*Unidades de Fomento a la Vivienda*—UFV). This protects their holder from inflation but also makes it possible to reduce the debt's exposure to variations in the exchange rate.

The rapid growth of the domestic debt made efficient debt management difficult. Prior to the growth of the domestic debt, management of the public debt was relatively simple, since it was limited to debts concentrated among a small number of creditors, contracted under favorable financial conditions. This problem is not yet severe, since the Pension Funds Administrators (*Administradoras de Fondos de Pensiones*—AFP) hold more than 50 percent of the domestic debt, contracted under very rigid terms ranging from nine to 15 years (Figure 4). Nonetheless, as the domestic

Box 1. External Debt Restructuring and Relief

Since the mid 1980s, several initiatives have been launched in an effort to reduce the burden of external debt on public finances. Among them are the private debt buyback programs carried out until 1993, which made it possible to eliminate almost all private external debt, and the Paris Club negotiations conducted throughout the 1990s, which rescheduled bilateral debt. The most extensive efforts since 1997 have been within the framework of the HIPC initiatives.

The structural reforms applied in the 1990s allowed Bolivia to implement a relief plan through the first two HIPC initiatives in a relatively flexible manner as compared with other beneficiary countries. The first initiative went into effect as of September 1998 and eliminated debt worth US$476 million in current value. The second HIPC relief was implemented in June 2001 and was equivalent to US$1.2 billion in current value. The Cologne Initiative HIPC relief further allowed Bolivia to cancel the majority of its remaining bilateral debt. The first and third initiatives amounted to fiscal relief, since they do not demand that the funds be allocated for specific purposes. Under the National Dialogue Act, however, the funds from the second initiative must be used to increase spending on health and education.

In mid 2005, the G8 proposed the Multilateral Debt Relief Initiative (MDRI), which will make it possible to pardon the debt contracted with the IMF and with the International Development Association (IDA)—a soft-terms financing window of the WB. In December 2005, the IMF approved relief of the outstanding debt contracted by Bolivia prior to January 1, 2005, and this relief was to go into effect in early 2006. This represents nearly US$231 million, or US$222 million if the remainder of the HIPC relief granted by that entity is excluded. It is expected that in July 2006, the WB will cancel nearly US$1.5 billion of the debt contracted with IDA, or 100 percent of the outstanding debt contracted and disbursed through December 2003. Unlike HIPC II, the MDRI may result in a decrease of funds allocated to Bolivia by IDA. Any additional funds allocated by the WB for relief will not be automatically delivered to the beneficiary countries. Rather, those countries will have to compete with the rest of the IDA countries for a larger allocation, based on their performances and policies.

debt market develops and soft sources of external financing become exhausted, it will be indispensable to improve the debt management system.

Another key item associated with public debt is subnational debt, contracted by departmental governments and municipalities. The fiscal decentralization promoted

Figure 3. Composition of the External Debt, 2004
(Percent of Total)

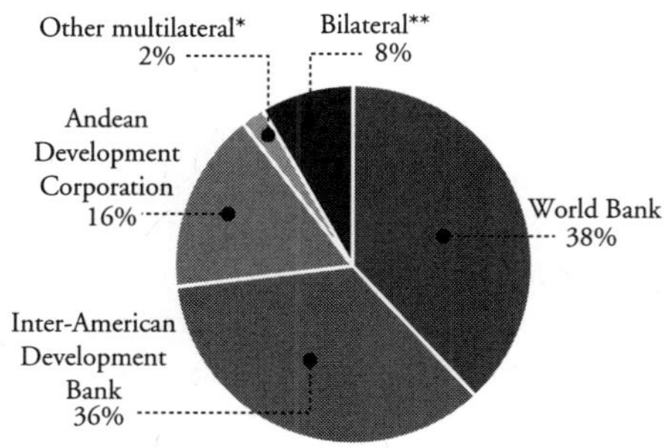

Source: BCB.
Note: (*) FONPLATA, NDF, OPEC, and BIAPE.
(**) Spain, Brazil, Japan, Germany, France, People's Republic of China, Italy, and Republic of Korea.

Figure 4. Composition of the Domestic Debt, 2004*
(Percent of Total)

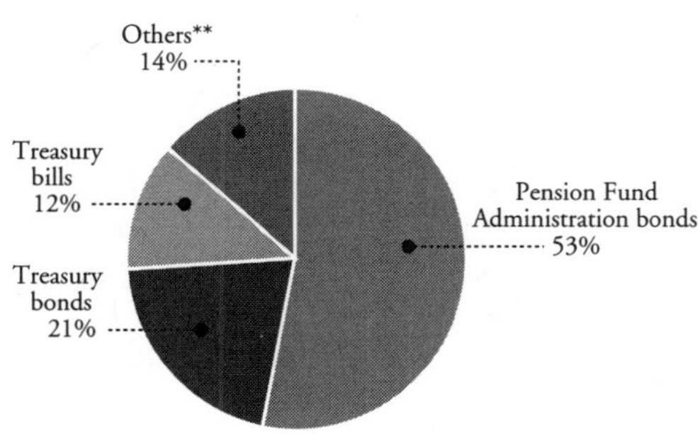

Source: Ministry of Finance and BCB.
Note: (*) Only domestic debt contracted with the private sector.
(**) Securities issued by the BCB, other bonds from the General Treasury of the Nation, floating debt, and fiscal certificates.

during the 1990s allowed departments and municipalities (especially large ones) to contract debt. The result has been a mass of contingent liabilities for the central government amounting to 5 percent of GDP. The sustainability of these obligations is fragile, since 90 percent of municipal debt is concentrated in 10 of the 327 municipalities. Moreover, if the proposal for regional autonomy progresses and decentralization deepens, the sustainability of the departmental debt could be compromised, unless oversight mechanisms are reinforced.

II. Sustainability of the Debt

The current structure of Bolivia's public debt makes it unsustainable in the medium term. According to an analysis conducted by Fitch Ratings in December 2005, Bolivia's credit rating was B-, with a negative outlook. As such, it is pertinent to ask how a fiscal adjustment should be made that would guarantee the sustainability of the debt. In order to address this problem, a model is presented that includes the amount of the consolidated debt. Due to a lack of information, contingent liabilities are excluded. (Annex I provides a detailed description of the characteristics of the model employed). Box 2 presents the assumptions used in this exercise.

If the primary deficit between 2006 and 2020 stays at around 1.7 percent of GDP, as occurred between 1990 and 2005, the debt will not be sustainable, notwithstanding a cancellation of the debt with the IMF and IDA (Figure 5). In this scenario, the debt would drop from 74 percent of GDP in 2005 to 60 percent in 2006 thanks to the cancellation, but would then continually rise, reaching more than 115 percent of GDP in 2020. This is because the deficit observed in the past was so great

Box 2. Assumptions of the Base Scenario

- Growth holds firm at 3.5 percent, which is equivalent to the average growth observed between 1990 and 2005. This assumption implies that Bolivian exports of natural gas will not increase considerably and that Bolivia will be supplying only the regional markets of Brazil and Argentina. But it also excludes the possibility that a social and/or financial crisis significantly affects growth in the medium term.
- Inflation and devaluation are 4.5 percent.
- Net external disbursements used to finance the fiscal deficit progressively diminish from 50 percent to 40 percent of the public deficit. Given its more flexible usage, the government might prefer internal financing as external soft credit becomes depleted.
- The cancellation of the debt with the IMF and IDA goes into effect in 2006 and amounts to approximately US$1.7 billion.
- The implicit interest rate of the external debt hovers around 2.3 percent during 2006 but increases to 2.8 percent in 2007 given that the cancellation of the debt results in a smaller—but more costly—external debt portfolio. Following 2007, the implicit rate would progressively increase, reaching 5.5 percent in 2020 due to a depletion of soft external financing sources.
- The implicit interest rate on domestic debt would remain close to 8.5 percent.

Figure 5. Debt Trends if the Primary Deficit Remains at Historic Levels
(As a Percentage of GDP)

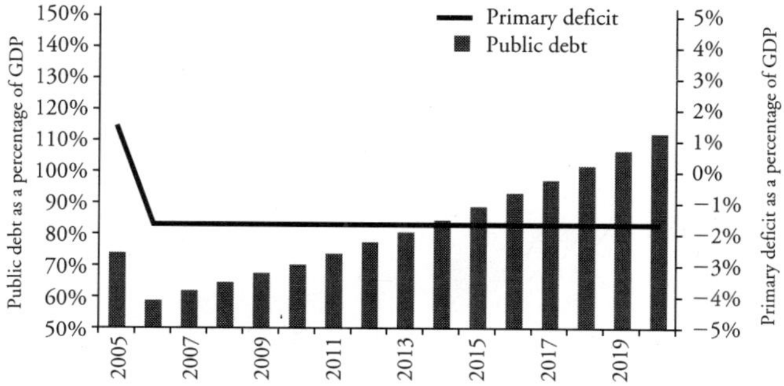

Source: Authors' own calculations.
Note: The information for 2005 is estimated using the November 2005 data. The reduction in the accrued debt observed in 2006 is due to the MDRI.

that it neutralized the various relief initiatives for the external debt. The process would be aggravated by the expected increase in the cost of the debt due to the exhaustion of soft financing sources and the growing trend toward internal financing. Without debt relief, the debt would increase to 140 percent of GDP in 2020.

In order for Bolivia not to undergo an exorbitant increase in its public debt, it must maintain a sustained and growing primary revenue surplus. Figure 6 illustrates that, in order to keep the debt close to 55 percent of GDP following the MDRI relief, a primary surplus of 1 percent of GDP is needed in 2007. But since the cost of the debt is expected to increase over time, it will be necessary for that surplus to increase to 1.8 percent of GDP in 2020. This result could be affected by variations in the GDP growth rate (Table 1). For example, if economic growth as of 2007 were 2.5 percent, the primary surplus should reach 2.3 percent of GDP in 2020, not 1.8 percent. These results demonstrate that a one percentage-point reduction in long-term growth implies an increase in the required fiscal effort of nearly 0.5 percentage points of GDP, while a one percentage-point increase in growth reduces the required primary deficit by nearly 0.5 percentage points of GDP.

According to the preliminary information, the primary surplus for 2005 may surpass 1.0 percent of GDP. That would be considerable progress in containing the growth of the public debt. Nonetheless, the sustainability of this accomplishment is as yet uncertain. The recent deterioration of the investment climate has affected the outlook for growth in the medium term and could hinder the implementation of long-range fiscal adjustment measures. Moreover, this result is principally due to a favorable external context and to the introduction of the Direct Hydrocarbons Tax (*Impuesto Directo a los Hidrocarburos*—IDH), which is increasing revenue in the short term, but could be compromising the development of the oil industry. In addi-

Figure 6. Primary Deficit Needed to Maintain Debt Levels following the Debt Cancellation
(As a Percentage of GDP)

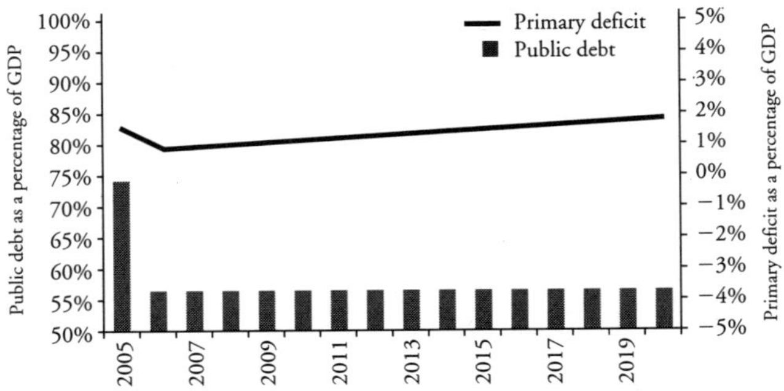

Source: Authors' own calculations.
Note: The information for 2005 is estimated using the November 2005 data. The reduction in the accrued debt observed in 2006 is due to the MDRI.

Table 1. Sensitivity of the Required Primary Deficit, Depending Upon Different Economic Growth Assumptions
(Percent of GDP)

Growth Rate of GDP	*2007*	*2010*	*2015*	*2020*
2.5	1.5	1.7	2.0	2.3
3.0	1.2	1.4	1.7	2.1
3.5 (base)	**0.9**	**1.1**	**1.5**	**1.8**
4.0	0.6	0.8	1.2	1.5
4.5	0.4	0.6	0.9	1.3

Source: Authors' own calculations.

tion, the distribution of revenue generated by the IDH leaves little room for containing public expenditures, since most revenue is currently funding subnational levels of government, which are harder to control. This places the Ministry of Finance in a delicate situation. On the other hand, public finances are vulnerable to changes in these flows of international assistance. An abrupt reduction in these funds could limit the possibility of containing the deficit and would affect public investment.

At the same time, an increase in the devaluation rate could also affect the sustainability of the debt, due to the debt's extensive dollarization. If the currency is continually devalued at one percentage point above inflation, amounting to an annual rate of 5.5 percent, the required fiscal effort would go up by 0.3 percentage points of GDP. Currently, this risk seems to be minor, given that the increase in the reserves of the BCB derived from exports of natural gas has made it possible to reduce the devaluation rate far below the inflation rate. Nonetheless, maintaining such low devaluation rates does not appear to be sustainable in the medium term, since that would imply a sustained real appreciation, which affects the competitiveness of the economy.

Policy Options

Based on the preceding diagnostic, we offer the following observations:

- Taking advantage of the current favorable external environment would facilitate consolidation of a primary surplus greater than 1 percent of GDP. This means that the increased revenue and the debt relief would not be used as an equivalent increase in expenditures. In the current favorable context, such an adjustment would reduce the social impact and also generate an extra fiscal margin to help weather future crises.
- For optimal impact, the fiscal adjustment attained is best consolidated in the medium term through policies that contain expenditures and increase tax revenue in order to reduce debt. More efficient public expenditure would prevent delays in public service provision, especially those directed toward reducing poverty. Furthermore, the structure and efficiency of the tax system could improve if revenues increase without a major impact on the poor (see the chapter on Taxes, Collection Capabilities, and Distribution).
- Improved management capacities would strengthen administration of the highly vulnerable, increasingly complex public debt.

III. Public Debt Management

Until the mid 1990s, debt management was relatively simple, because the debt was concentrated in a small number of creditors under very favorable financial conditions. Since then, a steady rise in domestic debt is making the portfolio ever more complex. This demands an improvement in management systems. In addition, the gradual exhaustion of soft external financing sources, which is expected in the medium term, will make public debt management increasingly relevant. Furthermore, the high degree of subnational debt demands improvements in the debt information and management systems (the issue of subnational debt is addressed in the following section).

The Ministry of Finance leads the debt management system and is responsible for formulating and implementing debt policy (Box 3). However, responsibilities are loosely defined and there is a lack of coordination that reduces the effectiveness of the management system. No entity has a clear mandate to manage all types of public sector liabilities with a unified strategy. As a result, there is no explicit debt policy that establishes clear objectives, which would allow for the setting of intermediate goals and the evaluation of results. Indebtedness responds to the need to finance the deficit, and the reduction of costs and risks is pushed to one side.

Box 3. Institutions Involved in Public Debt Management

The following institutions participate in public debt management:

- The Ministry of Finance heads up the Public Credit System and is therefore in charge of determining the debt strategy together with the National Council on Economic Policy, in a manner consistent with the rest of the policies of the state.
- The General Directorate of Public Credit (*Dirección General de Crédito Público*—DGCP) of the Ministry of Finance is the executive agency in charge of ensuring efficiency in public debt management. The DGCP takes charge of determining the modes of credit operations engaged in by the public sector and supervises compliance with debt servicing. The DGCP is also responsible for supervising subnational debt.
- Several operating units at the central, regional, and municipal levels, as well as other government agencies, are in charge of supervising and recording the debt operations of these levels of government. The central level's operating unit establishes the procedures to govern debt management at the national, regional, and municipal level.
- The BCB keeps the official record of the public external debt. In its role as the government's financial agent, it is responsible for carrying out external debt servicing and for providing services related to external credit contracting. It also participates in renegotiating external debt and in the issuance, placement, and administration of public debt instruments.

The debt information systems are not well integrated, which creates difficulties for their management. External debt is recorded by the BCB, while domestic debt administered by the DGCP is handled by the Debt Management and Analysis System (*Sistema de Gestión y de Análisis de la Deuda*—SIGADE). This system is well interfaced and allows for consolidation of the central government's debt. Nonetheless, there are still problems regarding the debt of subnational governments, and the total amount of the public sector debt is not fully known (this problem is addressed in the following section). In addition, the debt information systems are not linked with the Integrated Administrative Management System (*Sistema Integrado de Gestión Administrativa*—SIGMA), which creates financial management difficulties: in order to make and pay transactions, the DGCP needs to output data from the management system and then manually input debt service transactions into the SIGMA system.

The BCB has a team trained to analyze the sustainability of the total public debt, which allowed it to take the lead when the HIPC relief initiatives were negotiated.

Likewise, the DGCP has developed capacities to analyze the sustainability of the central government debt. Contingent liabilities, which could jeopardize the sustainability of the public debt, have yet to be identified or quantified. This is of special importance for the central government. For example, if a given municipality is unable to pay its debt, the central government reschedules the debt internally, thereby creating an implicit guaranty system (Annex I presents a preliminary valuation of the contingent liabilities).

Despite these limitations, the government has engaged in notable efforts to reduce the debt vulnerability, especially for domestic debt, for example by reducing the dollarization of the domestic debt. In 2003 it was decided that all new debt contracted with the Pension Funds Administrators (*Administradoras de Fondos de Pensiones*—AFP) must be denominated in Housing Development Units (*Unidades de Fomento a la Vivienda*—UFV). This made it possible to reduce the dollarization of AFP bonds, which represent more than 50 percent of the domestic debt. The UFVs are a mechanism for indexing the Consumer Price Index. Open market operations have been used to reduce the dollarization of the remaining domestic debt from nearly 95 percent in mid 2002 to levels of less than 60 percent in late 2005 (Figure 7).

Another relevant vulnerability related to the domestic debt is the high proportion of short-term maturities, which creates major refinancing risks. This problem continues despite the government's effort to extend the maturity of the domestic debt, which went from an average of 200 days in 2002 to 700 by late 2005 (Figure 8). The AFP bonds have long maturation periods that assuaged the public sector's liquidity needs. However, the maturing of AFP domestic debt could create liquidity problems in the medium term, because their debt servicing is expected to increase rapidly after 2008.

Figure 7. Composition of Treasury Instruments on the Open Market
(As a Percentage of the Total)

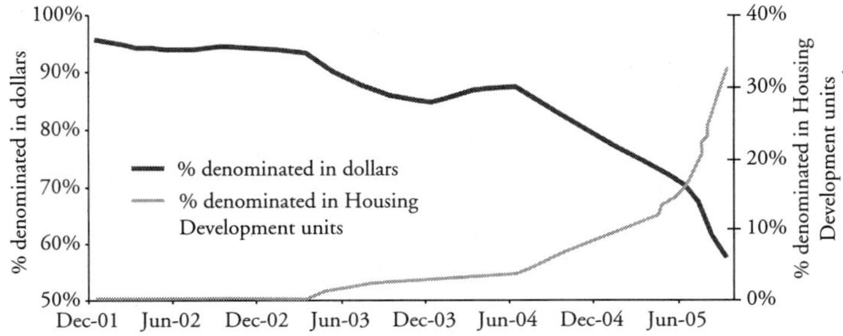

Source: BCB.

Figure 8. Average Maturation of Placements of Treasury Instruments
(Number of Days)

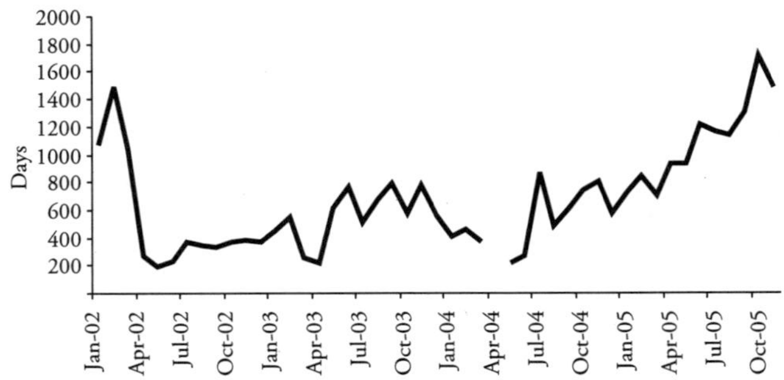

Source: BCB.

Policy Options for the Short Term

Based on the above, the following would be advisable:

- Extend the use of UFVs in public debt instruments.
- Continue restructuring the terms of the domestic debt to avoid liquidity problems in the future. This will be possible only if the current amount of the domestic debt can be maintained or reduced.
- Formulate an explicit debt strategy beyond responding only to the liquidity needs of the government. This process must be accompanied by more information, available on issues of public debt.

Policy Options for the Medium term

In the first year of the new administration, the following would be desirable:

- Improve the legal framework for debt management, making it more precise and strengthening its institutional framework. To optimize effectiveness, this effort would coordinate the activities involved in managing the external and domestic debt.
- Integrate the debt information systems into SIGMA. To do so, it is important to first overcome the problems of sustainability that still affect the SIGMA system.
- Strengthen capacities for analyzing contingent liabilities and the risks associated with the portfolio.
- Conduct annual public-debt management audits and publish their results.

IV. Efficient Control of Subnational Debt

The advance of fiscal decentralization during the 1990s allowed for an increase in municipal investment and improved the provision of public services. But it also brought about subnational debt, without the corresponding control and coordination tools. These measures have left the government with significant contingent liabilities, turning the national government into more of a guarantor for the subnational debt than a regulator. On an aggregated level, this problem might not seem so alarming as the subnational debt represents only 5 percent of GDP. Nonetheless, it has already provoked conflicts in large municipalities. In addition, this problem may increase in the medium term as the decentralization advances to the departmental level. Disorderly growth of the subnational debt could have negative effects on macroeconomic stability.

At present, the subnational governments can accrue debt from three principal financing sources. The first is debt owed to private agents, associated above all with delayed payments to contractors and to vendors of goods and services. The second source is external funds directly managed by the decentralized governments. This mode tends to be used by departments and the larger municipalities. The third is generated through the National Fund for Regional Development (*Fondo Nacional de Desarrollo Regional*—FNDR), which obtains funds from international creditors, guaranteed by the central government. Certain large municipalities have also started to explore the possibility of accessing the capital market.

In response to the uncontrolled increase of the subnational debt, an effort was made in 1999 to limit its growth through norms that set limits on debt and internally rescheduled the obligations of the most indebted subnational governments (Box 4). This initiative allowed five large municipalities, six small ones, and a department to sign Financial Restructuring Plans. Table 2 summarizes the indicators agreed to under this initiative. Unfortunately, the Financial Restructuring Plans have not succeeded in resolving the problems of many municipalities. On the contrary, a moral risk has been introduced that feeds expectations that the central government will bail out those in trouble, especially in the case of loans from the FNDR.

The scope of this initiative was limited by institutional weakness. Most of the municipalities do not have sufficient information to evaluate their debt. In fact, not all the subnational governments that signed Financial Restructuring Plans refer to them as often or as much as required. This is because there is no central risk entity. Similarly, the lack of adequate information on subnational debt thwarts evaluations of the contracting governments' debt risk, limiting those governments' access to the capital market. In order to correct these problems, the DGCP, as of October 2005, started to implement the Subnational Debt Administration and Information System (*Sistema de Administración e Información de Deuda Subnacional*—SAIDS) in the nine departments and 18 municipalities.

Box 4. Budget Administration Act and Control of the Subnational Debt

The Budget Administration Act, No. 2042 of 1999, states:

- *Limits on Indebtedness.* The present value of the debt of a decentralized, autonomous, or semi-independent government institution may not exceed 200 percent of the recurring current revenue of said institution, received in the prior management term, and the service of that debt may not exceed 20 percent of the recurring current revenue received in the prior management term.
- *Financial Restructuring Plan.* Institutions exceeding the established limits have the option of refinancing their liabilities in exchange for agreeing with the Ministry of Finance on a Financial Restructuring Plan that includes measures to reduce expenditures and increase revenue, to attain fiscal sustainability within five years.
- *Prohibition against Contracting Debt not Categorized as Soft.* Debt not characterized as soft may be contracted only in exceptional cases, with express authorization from the Ministry of Finance.

Table 2. Principal Debt Indicators of the Institutions in the Financial Restructuring Plan

		Accrued Debt/ Current Revenue (Percent)			*Debt Servicing/ Current Revenue (Percent)*		
			2003			*2003*	
Institution	*Date Signed*	*At Signing*	*Goal*	*Execution*	*At Signing*	*Goal*	*Execution*
Large Municipalities							
La Paz	10/05/00	181	150	182	24	10	11
Santa Cruz	11/08/00	152	175	189	39	44	32
Cochabamba	11/08/00	158	360	413	20	121	74
Tarija	12/05/00	126	121	14	20	8	6
Trinidad	03/16/01	314	234	227	141	27	22
Mid Sized Municipalities							
Quillacollo	10/09/01	169	114	254	21	36	35
Guayaramerín	08/01/01	136	212	196	27	54	5
Portachuelo	05/31/02	244	217	256	23	21	11
Villazón	07/10/02	511	238	no data	0	32	no data
Rurrenabaque	11/12/02	182	136	no data	37	34	no data
Cotoca	12/07/02	196	161	183	36	47	9
Departments							
Tarija	06/03/02	218	335	313	10	22	27

Source: Financial Restructuring Program.

Still, several subnational governments have managed to exceed the debt limits. Others contract debt directly from the providers and/or through decentralized agencies under their umbrella, such as municipal trash collection companies, taking advantage of the fact that these modes of contracting debt are not considered in calculating the restrictions. In addition, the municipalities are taking advantage of difficulties for detecting the floating debt, and it has not been possible to correct this phenomenon, despite the efforts of the Ministry of Finance to introduce provisional mechanisms to detect a part of that debt.

Debt limits also present problems that must be resolved in the medium term. If one bears in mind payroll, benefits, leases, and other regular obligations of the subnational governments, many of these institutions would have less than 20 percent of their funds available to cover debt servicing. Since debt ratios are static measurements, one cannot evaluate the sustainability of the obligations.

Given the above, in the first months of its administration, the government's options include considering these options:

Policy Options for the Short Term

- Consolidate the initiative of the DGCP aimed at improving the subnational debt information systems. It would be advisable for the DGCP to make these systems compatible with the SIGMA and the SIGADE.
- Establish a Central Information and Risks Agency to promote the transparency of municipal financial information and the subsequent risk rating of the subnational entities.
- Incorporate within the calculation of the debt ratios the debt directly contracted with vendors and the debt of the decentralized institutions subordinated to the subnational governments.

Policy Options for the Medium Term

- Give greater independence to the central government entity in charge of controlling the subnational debt, to protect it from political pressure. This initiative must be accompanied by strengthening its capacity for sanctioning failures to meet reporting obligations and/or the nonperformance of commitments.
- Review debt limits, bearing in mind the structure of primary expenditures of subnational governments and establishing mechanisms to evaluate whether the debt of these institutions is sustainable over time. This final measure will make it possible to establish early alert mechanisms to prevent the widespread use of Financial Restructuring Plans.
- Continue promoting risk rating performed by specialized private companies on subnational institutions capable of borrowing money on the capital market. Let market mechanisms independently define the instruments' price and risk rating.

- Establish explicit mechanisms, under the responsibility of the domestic debt management authority, to determine when a subnational government is prepared to issue debt instruments in the capital market.
- Avoid the subrogation of subnational liabilities by the Ministry of Finance, including any subrogation contracted with the FNDR.
- Reform the FNDR, granting it complete autonomy from the rest of the public sector, and promoting the private sector participation in its shareholdings. In that way, loans from the FNDR to subnational governments would depend upon market criteria and would not compromise the sustainability of the public sector.

Bibliography

Ahmad, E., Brosio, G., Díaz, A., Fainboim, I., Villela, R., and Parente, C. 2004. "Bolivia: Improving Budget and Decentralization Processes." IMF. La Paz, Bolivia.

Alborta, P., M. Montalvo, and M. Zapata. 2005. "Bolivia: *Régimen de transferencias intergubernamentales para las autonomías regionales.*" Mimeo. USAID. La Paz, Bolivia.

Comisión Episcopal de Pastoral Social Caritas [Episcopal Commission of the Caritas Social Ministry]. 2005a *"La deuda interna de Bolivia, ¿Un agujero negro?"* Magazine No. 3. La Paz, Bolivia.

———. 2005b. *"¿Es sostenible la deuda externa de Bolivia?"* Magazine No. 4. La Paz, Bolivia.

Economic Commission for Latin America and the Caribbean. 2004. "Economic Survey of Latin America and the Caribbean, 2003-2004." Santiago, Chile.

International Development Association and International Monetary Fund. 2002. "External Debt Management in Heavily Indebted Poor Countries." Washington, DC.

Mantel, A., Albino, M. and Jiménez, J. 2004. *"Bolivia: Evolución de la descentralización fiscal y el control de la deuda de los gobiernos municipales."* IMF. La Paz, Bolivia.

Navarro, O. 2005. *"Marco normativo; Sistema de crédito publico."* Ministry of Finance. La Paz, Bolivia.

Ruiz, J. 2005. *"CIR: Central de información y riesgo."* Ministry of Finance. La Paz, Bolivia.

Salcedo, L. 2004. *"Escenarios de departamentalización de la deuda pública en Bolivia."* Ministry of Finance. La Paz, Bolivia.

———. 2005. *"SAIDS: Análisis de deuda subnacional."* Ministry of Finance. La Paz, Bolivia.

Terán A. and J. Ruiz. 2003. *"Relaciones fiscales intergubernamentales: Lecciones aprendidas a la luz de la evidencia."* Mimeo. La Paz, Bolivia.

World Bank. 2001. "Bolivia's HIPC Initiative Completion Point." Washington, DC.

———. 2004. "Bolivia: Public Expenditure Management for Fiscal Sustainability and Equitable and Efficient Public Services." Report No. 28519-BO. Washington, DC.

World Bank and Inter-American Development Bank. 2004. "*Evaluación de la capacidad de gestión financiera del país.*" (Draft). La Paz, Bolivia.

World Bank and International Monetary Fund. 2001. "Guidelines for Public Debt Management." Washington, DC.

ANNEX I. Analytical Framework for Debt Sustainability

In order to evaluate the sustainability of Bolivia's debt, a model was developed to take into account the most relevant characteristics of the debt in the consolidated public sector. Unlike most static equilibrium approaches used to evaluate debt sustainability, this model is based on the debt dynamics over time, which makes it possible to include recurring changes in the parameters used. Concretely, the model distinguishes between domestic and external debt, making it possible to determine the effects of differences in the cost associated with these modes of debt. The model also makes it possible to progressively modify the cost associated with the external debt, in order to account for the eventual exhaustion of soft financing sources. Furthermore, the model makes it possible to assimilate the effects of dollarization, since all domestic debt is considered to be denominated in dollars. Finally, the model makes it possible to assimilate the effect of the MDRI, since it allows part of the external debt to be canceled.

The model starts with the accounting identity for the public sector that establishes that the financing of the public deficit (F_t) is equal to the interest paid on the domestic debt (I_t^E) plus the external debt (I_t^D) less the primary balance (X_t) all denominated in current bolivianos:

$$F_t = I_t^E + I_t^D - X_t$$

Since the model assumes that both the external debt (D_t^E) and the domestic debt (D_t^D) are denominated in dollars and that the implicit interest rates associated with them are different (R_t^E and R_t^D), the foregoing equation can be modified as follows:

$$F_t = S_t \cdot \left(R_t^E \cdot D_{t-1}^E\right) + S_t \cdot \left(R_t^D \cdot D_{t-1}^D\right) - X_t$$

where S_t is the average exchange rate.

Introducing an exogenous parameter (β_t) that defines the percentage of external financing with respect to the total and considering that the financing is the flow associated with the debt, one can establish the functions for the accrual of the external and domestic debt denominated in dollars as:

$$D_t^E = D_{t-1}^E + \beta_t \cdot \frac{F_t}{S_t} - C_t^E \quad \text{and} \quad D_t^D = D_{t-1}^D + \left(1 - \beta_t\right) \cdot \frac{F_t}{S_t}$$

where C_t^E is the cancellation of the external debt denominated in dollars.

Replacing the accounting identity in the debt accrual equations and dividing this result by the Gross Domestic Product (GDP), we obtain two equations that make it possible to determine that the external (d_t^E) and domestic (d_t^D) debt ratios with respect to GDP depend upon the past level of indebtedness and upon the ratio of the primary balance to GDP (x_t):

$$d_t^E = \left(1 + \beta_t \cdot R_t^E\right) \cdot Z_t \cdot d_{t-1}^E + \beta_t \cdot R_t^D \cdot Z_t \cdot d_{t-1}^D - \beta_t \cdot x_t - c_t^E$$

$$d_t^D = \left(1 + \left(1 - \beta_t\right) \cdot R_t^D\right) \cdot Z_t \cdot d_{t-1}^D + \left(1 - \beta_t\right) \cdot R_t^E \cdot Z_t \cdot d_{t-1}^E - \left(1 - \beta\right)_t \cdot x_t$$

where $Z_t = (1 + \dot{s}_t)/1 + \dot{y}_t + \dot{p}_t \cdot \dot{y}_t)$, the rates of devaluation, inflation and growth are given by $\dot{s}_t$, $\dot{p}_t$, and $\dot{y}_t$, respectively; and c_t^E, the equivalent of the cancellation of external debt with respect to GDP.

Summing these two equations, we obtain the ratio of total debt with respect to GDP, which depends on the external and domestic debt from the previous period, on the primary balance, and on the amount of debt cancellation, also expressed as a percentage of GDP:

$$d_t = \left(1 + R_t^D\right) \cdot Z_t \cdot d_{t-1}^D + \left(1 + R_t^E\right) \cdot Z_t \cdot d_{t-1}^E - x_t - c_t^E$$

Using assumptions, which are not necessarily static, on implicit interest rates, the proportion of the deficit covered by the external financing, and the rates of devaluation, inflation and growth, the last three equations presented establish a recurring relationship between indebtedness and the primary balance. This makes it possible to use the equation to define the dynamics of the debt with respect to GDP using a trend previously defined based on the trend of the primary balance with respect to GDP. On the other hand, the model can be modified to establish the required levels of the primary balance with respect to GDP in order to attain a pre-set indebtedness goal.

ANNEX II. Contingent Liabilities

Together with explicit liabilities, implicit or contingent liabilities increase the vulnerability of fiscal accounts and jeopardize public debt sustainability. This problem is even more serious considering that the current debt management system has problems with these types of liabilities, since they are not being adequately recorded and quantified. The government has recently deployed an explicit effort in this regard. According to a preliminary estimate made in the World Bank's Public Expenditures Review, these liabilities, given their magnitude, pose a possible risk for the sustainability of the public debt. In addition, most of these liabilities need to be clarified, because the government is identified as a guarantor of the operations of other public and even private agents. Moreover, another part of these liabilities appears to be associated with specific policies that make it possible to overcome social conflicts, but that further undermine the already fragile position of public finances. The table on the following page summarizes available information on contingent liabilities in Bolivia.

Direct and Contingent Liabilities

Contingent Liability	*Amount*	*Description*
Pension System		
Compensation of contributions: proposal to modify the Pensions Act of 1996, No. 1732	Single payment of US$260 million. US$160 million after one year	Proposal to change the nature of the government's obligations related to the former pension system.
Insurance and Special Systems	US$20 million	Transfer of amounts to several special systems and creation of temporary corporations.
Financial Sector		
Support to the banking sector	US$294 million	Costs associated with the rescue of banks and restructuring operations.
FONDESIF *Fondo de Desarrollo del Sistema Financiero y de Apoyo al Sector Productivo* Fund for the Development of the Financial Sector and for Support to the Productive Sector Peasant Loan Program	US$94 million, to be recovered in 2015	Expansion of the capital base of companies in the private financial intermediation sector, using funds loaned with a state guaranty from multilateral donors and the BCB. Government loan to the agricultural sector to buy 1,000 tractors.
FERE *Fondo Especial de Reactivación Económica* Special Economic Reactivation Fund PROFOP	US$80 million	Loans from NAFIBO [*Nacional Financiera Boliviana* – Bolivian National Financier]/FERE, guaranteed by the Government, to financial intermediaries for restructuring. Strengthening of the capital base of

Contingent Liability	*Amount*	*Description*
Programa de Fortalecimiento Patrimonial Capital Strengthening Fund		financial intermediaries, using public loans.
Public Debt		
External subnational debt and private sector debt guaranteed by the government	US$497 million	The Capitalization Act, No. 1554 of 1994, transferred external obligations guaranteed by the State to private companies and subnational entities.
Municipal Debt	US$280 million (2002)	The municipal debt is a Contingent Liability for the central government in the event of nonperformance of the municipal governments.
Debts of the National Roads Service (*Servicio Nacional de Caminos* - SNC)	US$42 million	In the event of nonperformance, the debt of the SNC is a liability for the government.
Public Universities	US$100 million (2003)	The public universities have social security obligations that could become a liability for the government
Institutional Reform / Bolivian Strategy for the Reduction of Poverty		
Institutional Reform Program	US$22 million (2003)	As of 2008, the government must assume the financing of the complete amount of $33 million to sustain the reform.
National Dialogue Act Municipal Solidarity Fund	US$27 million per year	Transfers from HIPC II funds for health and education.
Special Dialogue Account	US$60 million per year	For the Special Dialogue Account.
Tax Refunds and Subsidies		
Tax Refund Certificates (*Certificados de Devolución de Impuestos* - CEDEIM)	US$50 million per year	Tax refund to exporters for VAT and excise taxes as well as fees that depend on the level of exports.
Liquid Petroleum Gas (LPG) Subsidies	US$30 million (2003)	Government subsidies to set the price of LPG, which depend on the international price and on the exchange rate.
Natural Disasters		
Government assistance in case of natural disasters	US$46 million per year	Government support in excess of the capital in the FORADE trust (*Fondo para la Reducción de Riesgos y Atención de Desastres* – Risk Reduction and Disaster Response Fund).

5

Challenges and Opportunities for the Financial System

Yira Mascaró, Javier Bolzico, Alberto Didoni, and Paola Granata

Summary

The size, solvency, profitability, and quality of assets in Bolivia's financial sector all diminished in the wake of the financial crisis that began in the late 1990s. These problems were further aggravated by several runs on deposits, motivated to a large degree by political and social instability. Withdrawals of deposits and the small number of profitable businesses have required an increased liquidity that negatively affects the profitability and capitalization of the system. The authorities have adopted successful measures to solve these problems, including the improvement of prudent rules and of the financial security network, and have effectively resolved the problems of insolvent mutual savings and loan entities, the capitalization of Banco Unión (BUN), and the modernization of the payments system. Other policies have had incomplete results, because, despite progress, they have not succeeded in resolving existing weaknesses, while still others have directly harmed the system. Policy options are proposed in three areas. In the short term: (i) mitigate the risk of deposit withdrawals by defining and implementing policies that increase public confidence in financial, macroeconomic, and legal stability; (ii) resolve the problems of the Banco Unión, by selling the shares of Nacional Financiera Boliviana (NAFIBO) to the private sector; and in the medium-to-long term, (iii) extend access to financial services through alternative instruments to bank loans. In this regard, international (and Bolivian) experience must be borne in mind, which discourages the creation of public banks, particularly public retail banks.

I. Background

Recent Trends in the Financial System (1998–2005)

Smaller size. The Bolivian economic crisis significantly reduced the size of the financial system, though the total number of entities has been relatively constant.[1] The crisis greatly weakened the business sector and the economy in general, significantly affecting the solvency and size of the financial system, especially of banks. Between 1998 and 2005 bank portfolios diminished by 40 percent, while those of other financial entities increased by 27 percent (Figure A1). Foreign banks held on to their high share in the sector (50 percent) thanks to a consolidation in the early 1990s. Nonetheless, their portfolios also diminished due to of the difficult economic situation, which, in turn, discouraged foreign investment.

Among non-bank entities, microfinance entities (MFEs) better weathered the crisis and increased their portfolio (in addition to having lower interest rates), due to a greater relative share in the system's total assets. The portfolio of the regulated MFEs continued growing (by 23 percent in 2003 and 27 percent in 2004) and in 2004 reached US$415 million, which represents nearly 15 percent of the regulated financial system. Bolivian MFEs, pioneers in the world, continue to be a successful model, given their greater efficiency, prudence, and coverage of a large number of customers, coupled with reduced interest rates.[2] They also better withstood the crisis (which reduced debtor repayment capacity), the over-indebtedness caused by an increase in loans for consumption, diminished payment amenability (on account of massive debt-pardoning programs such as the FERE) and increased competition (due to the maturing of the subsector).

The good performance of the MFEs is explained in large measure by: (i) the nature of their loans, which had shorter terms than the banks and were more closely supervised, which made it possible to better and more quickly assess debtor repayment capacity; (ii) the adaptation of credit technology, with a greater proportion of individual loans (Box 1) and more supervision;[3] (iii) a smaller proportion of large depositors, who are more likely to withdraw their deposits; and (iv) access to information from the credit office, which contributes to avoiding over-indebtedness.

Nonetheless, the unregulated MFEs (non-governmental, non-profit organizations operating on a non-profit basis) continue to be a small subsector, and their recovery has been slow. The total assets of the Association of Financial Institutions for Rural Development (*Asociación de Instituciones Financieras para el Desarrollo Rural*—FINRURAL), which unites financial non-governmental organizations (NGOs), was US$109 million, one-sixth the total for the regulated MFEs, and equivalent to one-third of the amount for open cooperatives (FINRURAL, 2005). The credit granted by these entities grew, but at a lower rate than for the regulated MFEs (10 percent in 2003 and 1.5 percent in 2004). Despite that, this subsector requires attention, since it continues to be an important source of credit for a large number of microenterprises, especially those of women (78 percent of its total port-

Box 1. Credit Technologies of the MFEs

- The MFEs use individual or joint-and-several credit technologies to adapt to the particular characteristics of microenterprise and, above all, to the lack of a traditional guarantee (real property), which reduces access for microenterprise to formal credit. The joint-and-several technology utilizes the joint liability of the group as a guarantee and motivates the members to monitor one another. In the individual mode, loans are secured through property of the family group with a high consumption value for the debtor.
- The individual credit mode is generally more effective in times of crisis, since its selection of debtors is based on a stricter control, which increases the probability of obtaining a higher quality portfolio. It is more likely that an economic recession will have a greater impact on the portfolio quality of joint-and-several liability groups, since: (i) their members are not selected based on an evaluation of their productivity and risk; and (ii) the crisis can affect several members of the group simultaneously, thus reducing the effectiveness of the loan's joint and several guarantee (see Navajas et al., 2003).

folio) and the poorest population (with an average loan of US$386 dollars, one-quarter the average for regulated MFEs).

Frequent withdrawals of deposits. Since mid 2002, the system has experienced several runs on deposits, accompanied by capital flight; (Figures 1 and A1).[4] Runs on deposits have been closely linked to political and social instability. Though some entities have been affected more than others, the mass withdrawals have generally affected the entire system and therefore have not led to bank closures on account of a lack of liquidity.[5] Neither have they created a systemic problem, due to the system's high and growing liquidity and to the authorities' sound need-based management.[6] Nonetheless, bank deposits stabilize at a lower level with each such episode. As of June 2004, the amount of deposits in the banking system was 75 percent of the December 2001 level and represented 80 percent for the financial system (Figure 1).

Signs of recovery of deposits and total loans. In June 2004, the downward trend in bank deposits started to reverse, although the system continued to experience occasional runs on deposits (in mid 2005 with the resignation of President Mesa); the total portfolio also started to recover in 2005. Despite the recent increase in bank deposits, as of September 2005, bank deposits were still 12 percent below their 2001 levels. Recovery of deposits in the non-banking sector started sooner, in June 2002, above all in regulated MFEs, which received a significant portion of the banking system's deposits (resulting in a reduction of their funding costs). This led to an increase in the size and quality of the MFEs' portfolios despite the crisis. Banks,

Figure 1. Financial System Trends in Public Obligations

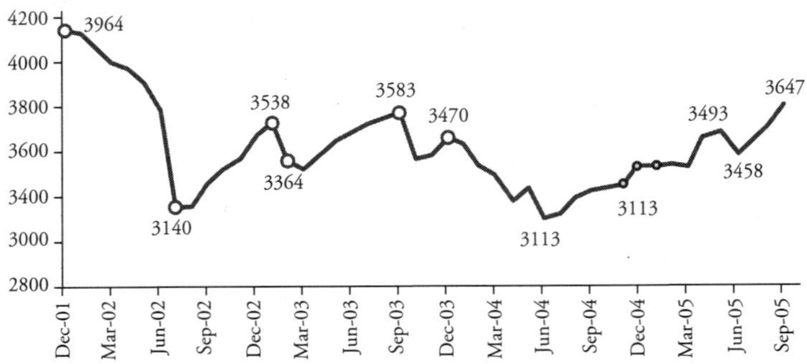

Source: SBEF Presentation, September 2005.

on the other hand, just started to resume their lending activities in 2005 with an incipient growth, still less than their volume in 2003 (Figure A1) and more skewed towards the corporate sector (BCB 2005e).

Dollarization, Quality of Assets, Solvency, Liquidity, and Profitability

High dollarization. Despite recent improvements and policies promoting the use of local currency, the Bolivian financial system is still characterized by a high degree of dollarization. In December 2004, approximately 88 percent of deposits and 95 percent of total loans were denominated in dollars. Dollarization exposes financial entities to a greater risk of insolvency of their debtors in the event of a devaluation, since a high percentage of the loans go to economic sectors that receive their income in national currency.[7] The high degree of dollarization, which started in the second half of the 1980s due to hyperinflation, reflects a lack of confidence in the local currency. In the past two years, the proportion of deposits denominated in dollars has diminished and, from January to November 2005, deposits in local currency increased by 53 percent, reducing the dollarization of the banking system to 80 percent. In addition, between March 2004 and September 2005 deposits in national currency, including fixed-term deposits, savings accounts, and checking accounts, have increased their relative share of total deposits (Figure A2). In the same period, only fixed-term deposits in foreign currency increased their relative proportion of total deposits, in part due to introduction of the Financial Transactions Tax (ITF) and other measures.

Low quality assets, greater capital at risk. The persistence of a high default rate and the non-performing loan portfolio is a fundamental weakness of the financial system. In general, the rise in the non-performing loan portfolio was due to decreased profitability of local companies owing to the economic recession of 1999-2002.[8]

This effect was particularly relevant in the banking sector due to its high exposure to the corporate sector, and even greater for those banks that granted higher-risk loans during the economic upswing of the early 1990s. At the same time, improved regulation and supervision of financial entities allowed for greater recognition of the portfolio in default. In September 2005, the default rate had fallen considerably but continued to be high (15 percent for banking entities and 6 percent for non-bank entities, Figure A3).[9] On the other hand, regulated MFEs continue to have the system's best quality portfolios. The MFEs' portfolio at risk (a measure equivalent to the default rate) is less than 3 percent, one-quarter for 2001 and half as much as during the crisis.[10]

Portfolio rescheduling made it possible to temporarily defer bad debts, but their default rate has been increasing as their terms mature; the coverage of provisions diminished, increasing capital at risk. The FERE portfolio restructuring program started in 2000 and reached its high point between 2002 and 2003 (in December 2002, 32 percent of bank portfolios and 6 percent of MFE portfolios were rescheduled).[11] In August 2005, the high and still growing rate of rescheduled portfolio default reached 27 percent for the banking sector and 6 percent for the MFEs.[12] On the other hand, as seen in Figure A3, provision coverage levels on bank portfolios in default dropped to 73 percent in September 2005 (from 84 percent in December 2004). This reflects an increase in the default rate of the rescheduled portfolio (from 19 to 26 percent in the same period, see Figure A4) which negatively offset the May 2005 increase in provisions resulting from a strengthening of the prudent rules of the Superintendency of Banks and Financial Entities of Bolivia (*Superintendencia de Bancos y Entidades Financieras*—SBEF). At the same time, capital at risk[13] rose from 15 percent in December 2004 to 23 percent in September 2005, though with marked improvements for some banks. The estimated solvency of the system, measured by the *Coeficiente de Adecuación Patrimonial*—CAP, which is the Bolivian equivalent of the Capital Adequacy Ratio (CAR—a solvency index), held steady at 14.5 percent as of September 2005 (one percentage point less than in December 2004). Nonetheless, the system's "CAP" and, in particular, that of certain banks, would be less if the provisions pending under the new rules were borne in mind[14] as well as those for the rescheduled portfolio not yet deemed to be in default.

High liquidity. Liquidity has continued to grow since 1998 (Figure A1), taking into account the withdrawal of deposits and the shortage of profitable businesses.[15] In September 2005, liquidity was 30 percent of total assets, 41 percent of total deposits, and 75.5 percent of short term deposits (demand deposits, savings accounts, and deposits with a term of less than one year). On the other hand, the degree of coverage of the deposits without affecting the legal reserve position was 32 percent.[16] An important part of this liquidity is invested in government bonds and in short-term deposits and investments abroad.[17] In addition, financial entities have maintained important surpluses in cash in the Banco Central de Bolivia (BCB), above the required legal reserve (even after the recent increase of the legal reserve requirement, see Section III). In December 2004 this amounted to a 58 percent surplus in foreign currency and a 321 percent surplus in national currency (BCB, December 2004). Nonetheless, the high concentration of the system's deposits (greater than in 2002) is still worrisome. As of November 2005, 518 accounts (representing less than 1 percent of the total number of accounts) represented more than 26.3 percent of the volume of deposits (see Table A1).

Low profitability. Despite slight recent improvements, the period of 1998-2005 has been characterized by low profitability of the banking sector, in a context of fewer businesses, low quality assets, and high risk of a run on deposits. The recent economic crisis generated losses for banks by lowering the quality of their assets and reducing the size of the banking business. Nonetheless, during 2005 the banks started to recover their profitability (with bank earnings of US$10 million from January to September 2005), which contrasts with the losses experienced up until 2004 (US$6 million during the same period in 2004). In September 2005, the banks' average returns on assets and equity (ROA and ROE, respectively) continued to be very low (0.4 and 4.2 percent, respectively). This suggests a need for mergers, since the system now has almost half the banking business as before, but the same number of banks, and faces a certain degree of competition from the non-banking sector for attracting deposits. In contrast, regulated MFEs recovered more rapidly in this regard, with an average ROA and ROE as of September 2005 of 1.3 and 11.4 percent, respectively.[18]

Insufficient access to financial services

Insufficient access to credit. Bolivian companies find that lack of access to credit notably limits their growth.[19] This observation is consistent with the fact that credit provided by the financial sector to the private sector has not succeeded in recovering its pre-crisis level (33 percent of the GDP), given the slow recovery of the business sector. The problem is even greater for SMEs, since banks have tended to concentrate their credit in large (or medium-to-large) companies, while the MFEs target microenterprise (though they have recently also started to serve medium-sized companies). For banks, the culture of credit is based on granting loans against real property guarantees, through overdrafts or trade loans, which limits credit for smaller-sized companies with little access to such collateral. Other alternatives to bank trade loans, such as factoring, financial leasing, or securitization, have not been fully exploited to date, but could facilitate credit access in the Bolivian context, above all for SMEs.

With respect to the number of branches, the non-bank entities (regulated MFEs) have the most coverage and the greatest increase since 1998, even in rural areas (Table 1). In the banking sector, Banco Unión (BUN) and Banco de Crédito (a Peruvian bank) have the most branches (44 and 43, respectively) with participation in the rural zones (20 and 16 respectively), but still number less than the MFEs.

Micro-credit. MFEs grant the most micro-credit, covering more customers than the banking sector as a whole. NGOs grant loans to 200,000 microenterprises (1.5

Table 1. Number of Branches in Rural and Urban Areas, by Type of Entity

Bolivia	*December 31, 1998*	*June 30, 2005*		
	Total	*Total*	*Urban Area (as a percentage)*	*Rural Area (as a percentage)*
PFFs + Banco Sol	83	180	67.2	32.8
S&LCs	93	71	53.5	46.5
MSLs	36	39	84.6	15.4
Total non-banks + Banco Sol	**212**	**290**	**66.2**	**33.8**
Total banking institutions	**278**	**279**	**78.6**	**21.4**

Source: SBEF Presentation, September 2005.
Note: PFF = Private Financial Funds (*Fondos Financieros Privados*); S&LCs = Savings and Loan Cooperatives (*Cooperativas de Ahorro y Crédito*); MSLs = Mutual Savings and Loan Entities (*Mutuales de Ahorros y Préstamos*).

times the total number of customers of the banking sector). Regulated MFEs grant an even greater volume of loans to microenterprise (250,000), though this figure has gone down since the crisis. In response to the crisis and intense competition, regulated MFEs have gradually shifted their target to larger businesses, and they have also reduced the interest rate they charge. Small loans (less than US$500) have gradually diminished as a percentage of total loans provided by the regulated MFEs, amounting to 5.6 percent in June 2005. This is partly due to small borrowers gradually taking on larger commitments, in accordance with the MFE practice of granting larger loans each time the customer pays. The percentage of large loans (over US$100,000) has doubled since the end of 2003. This change in the distribution of loans is also due to the recent specialization of certain MFEs in granting loans to SMEs, which demonstrates the capacity of these entities to fill the gap in credit access faced by that sector.

Rural credit. The lack of access to credit is a major problem in rural areas, which are generally serviced by non-regulated MFEs, but with a recent increase in the presence of regulated MFEs. Although the NGOs devote 60 percent of their portfolio to the rural sector, the average balance of US$572 is not sufficient to satisfy the medium-term needs of export-oriented farmers. Private Financial Funds (PFF), despite being predominantly urban,[20] have helped improve farmers' access to credit by offering them products adapted to their production cycles, in addition to credit for other rural activities.

Distortions introduced by public sector programs targeting this area and social unrest in recent years have affected regulated financial entities' ability to extend credit services in rural areas, while also restraining the growth of non-regulated MFEs. The rural expansion of regulated MFEs has been limited by: (i) the subsidized rates offered by the Fund for the Development of the Financial System and Support to the Productive Sector (*Fondo de Desarrollo del Sistema Financiero y de Apoyo al Sector Productivo*—FONDESIF); and (ii) increased difficulty in loan collections due to debt forgiveness proposals in the recent past. FONDESIF's lower interest rates and its relatively lax conditions for granting credit[21] have also limited the development of non-regulated MFEs. FONDESIF's disbursement criteria lack transparency and are exposed to political influences. This might discourage better financial performance and a truly corporate governance of the NGOs, which depend on subsidized funds administered by FONDESIF.[22] It has also provoked a low leverage rate (1.6x, insufficient to significantly increase their credit) and a greater exposure to exchange risks and volatility.[23] As well, road blocks and other social unrest have lessened the interest in investing in the rural sector, since such conflicts raise the price of loan collections and increase the volatility of rural businesses (especially of smaller ones).

Recent development of micro-deposit financial services and other financing modes. The number of depositors of the regulated MFEs has recently increased above the number of micro-borrowers, reflecting the relevance of deposit services for small customers. In December 2004, the regulated MFEs had 300,000 savings accounts (half the number of bank depositors), and 260,000 loans; the total volume of deposits was US$278 million. The average size of their deposits is small (US$178, or one-fifth of per capita income), which suggests that micro-deposit services are effectively oriented to the poor. This indicates that MFEs are having success in developing micro-deposit technology. The MFEs have been developing other important products to extend access to financial services for microenterprise, including micro-insurance, micro-leasing, and remittance payments.

II. Recent Policy Measures Relevant to the Financial Sector

Measures to reduce dollarization. Both the Ministry of Finance and the BCB have adopted measures to reduce preference for the dollar in the financial system. As part of its fiscal policy to reduce the deficit, in February 2004 the Ministry of Finance announced the creation of the Financial Transactions Tax (*Impuesto a las Transacciones Financieras*—ITF), applicable to deposits and withdrawals in dollars, which went into effect six months later.[24] Although the ITF has contributed to reducing the dollarization of deposits, it also has led to a decrease in financial intermediation and lower volumes of demand deposits and savings accounts during the second half of 2004 and early 2005. The BCB also introduced monetary and foreign exchange policy measures to reduce preference for the dollar.[25] In April 2005, the increase in the legal reserve in dollars contributed to a decrease in dollarization and an increase in the mandatory coverage of deposits.[26] In addition, the BCB increased the differential between the purchase and sale exchange rate, which raised the cost of exchanging local currency into dollars and then back into local currency at the time of a transaction. This contributed to raising the proportion of deposits in local currency maintained by depositors to conduct their transactions.[27]

Measures to increase the term of deposits. While the ITF does not tax fixed-term deposits, banks have accentuated the slope of the curve on the rates they pay on deposits. Both measures seek to increase the term of deposits. Although these policies have contributed to changing the structure of bank deposits, increasing the relative participation of fixed-term deposits, they also entail certain risks in terms of the irreversibility of the structure of deposits (in part due to the risk of runs on deposits). For example, the fact that rates paid on short-term deposits in dollars are far below international rates could foment a loss of deposits.[28] In addition, the recent confirmation of the ITF as a permanent tax is leading to a decrease in intermediation and excess legal reserves. These aspects are already cause for concern in the Bolivian system.

Recent strengthening of prudential rules and greater orientation of the SBEF towards risk-based supervision. In May 2005, more cautious rules went into effect for rating and granting loans,[29] while the prudential framework of non-regulated entities has been strengthening. In addition, in recent years the SBEF has endeavored to focus more on the measurement and supervision of risks, in anticipation of adopting the Basel II principles in 2009. As a result of the adjustment in the rules, the banking sector required US$57 million in additional provisions, of which some US$10 million were made in May 2005. According to SBEF rules, the pending provisions will be made gradually over the next three years. Some banks have started to make the pending provisions, reflecting their greater leeway in terms of solvency, which has significantly reduced their capital at risk. In early 2005, the non-regulated MFEs affiliated with FINRURAL established a system for self-regulation based on SBEF rules in order to facilitate the incorporation of the more successful NGOs into the regulated system within three years.[30] On the other hand, the SBEF started to orient its work more towards the measurement and supervision of risks, including the creation in 2005 of a unit specialized in Basel II.

Strengthening the security network. As of 2003, the SBEF and the BCB adopted measures to implement the bank resolution mechanisms set forth in Law 1488 and for the functioning of the Financial Recapitalization Fund (*Fondo de Recapitalización Financiera*—FRF).[31] The SBEF approved the regulations, manuals, and procedures needed to apply bank resolution processes in accordance with best international practices. The BCB started to collect contributions from financial institutions for the FRF, and the fund's legal nature was clarified. The authorities recently drafted a bill for the creation of an explicit security deposit fund with limited coverage, and the bill was sent to Congress in late 2005.

Effective resolution of insolvent mutual savings and loans. Between May 2003 and October 2004 the resolution procedure was applied to four mutual savings and loan entities (La Frontera, Manutata, Del Pueblo, and Tarija), reversing the "regulatory tolerance" that had prevailed for years. All first-order obligations were honored. The portfolios and deposits of these institutions were transferred to other institutions (for the equivalent of US$2 million), preserving their business and reinforcing a culture of payment.

Intensive Supervision and capitalization of Banco Unión (BUN). In late 2003, NAFIBO[32] capitalized the subordinated debt it had acquired in BUN and took control over the entity. Through capitalizing its subordinated debt,[33] NAFIBO acquired 75 percent of the shares of BUN, which, pursuant to Decree 27258, were to be sold in a term of two years from the date of issuance of the new shares (June 2004). At the time, the capitalization reversed BUN's deficit and allowed for its continuity. However, the institution continues to have a fragile equity situation and operating losses, and is engaged in litigation with NAFIBO and the private shareholders, which makes the lack of progress on the terms of sale worrying. The sale of Banco Unión has yet to take place, and there has not been any merger or solution, in part due to the difficult political and social context.[34]

Financial System Support Fund (*Fondo de Apoyo al Sistema Financiero*—FASF). Decree 27386 created the FASF with the aim of strengthening the equity position of institutions that participate in resolution or purchase procedures (as acquirers) and/or in the corporate restructuring program (according to Law 2495). FASF can also make subordinated loans to entities and/or loans to shareholders to capitalize entities. FASF was created as a $30 million trust (whose settler is the Ministry of Finance and whose trustee is NAFIBO). To date, FASF has not made any disbursement, because on the one hand no sales, mergers, or resolutions have occurred; and on the other hand, the corporate restructurings under Law 2495 (Box 2) have involved loans already 100 percent charged off.[35] Given that the solvency of the banks involved has not been affected, these processes have not given rise to FASF intervention.

The law on the corporate restructuring and the insolvency framework. Law 2495 is inadequate to improve the legal framework for restructuring companies. Furthermore, the framework for insolvency processes (set forth in the Commercial Code) continues to be antiquated and ineffective. This regulation has improved some deficiencies of Law 2495 (for example, the 50 percent limit on debt remissions that can be applied to debts with the state). Nonetheless, the more important unresolved aspects require a change in the law that would also include a reform of the Commercial Code, which has been difficult to accomplish in the political context of recent years. These problems principally affect the rights of creditors and, as such, affect the increase of corporate credit. In addition, the impossibility of reaching a restructuring agreement for a company is grounds for bankruptcy, which leaves the company with the stigma of a presumption of fraud. This, among other weaknesses, makes it obsolete and keeps it from being used. A short time ago, the authorities renewed their efforts to improve the insolvency processes, by drafting a bill that was recently sent to the Congress (included as a "goal" in the agreement with the IMF).

Modernization of the payments system. In recent years, the BCB has played a very important role in launching a new interbank electronic payments system, but it would be advisable to extend the scope of the reform. The reform process has

Box 2. Weaknesses of Law 2495

- The law does not contain objective eligibility criteria to be able to initiate the restructuring process. This means that restructuring can be unilaterally imposed upon creditors by any debtor, even if the debtor is not in a state of insolvency or of suspension of payments (or anything close). In practice, the system has attracted not viable, but rather insolvent, companies. It has attracted only entities with serious problems for other reasons.
- Both the legal regulation itself and practice demonstrate that insufficient consideration is given to the viability of the company being brought into the system. There is no strict, competent evaluation of the viability of the company placed under this legal regimen.[36] Accordingly, several companies had ceased their business activity prior to restructuring. Many players have encouraged the incorporation of a impartial third party diagnosis, in a reasonable time and with a reasonable cost, to determine the viability of all companies that wish to receive the benefits of the program.
- The voting system for reaching agreements does not take the hierarchy of the loans and the priority of secured creditors into account. This undermines the primary function of collateral guarantees to protect creditors in the event of a potential payment failure or the insolvency of the debtor. Secured creditors are not only prejudiced by having the same voting rights as unsecured creditors, but can also lose their collateral guarantees if the agreement made under Law 2495 so provides. This circumstance could be seen as a disincentive to the granting of credit, making access to credit difficult, and increasing its cost.
- The protection of property rights, the right to a defense through litigation, and due process for creditors has been weakened. The exercise of these rights is prohibited or limited in the restructuring process, by restricting recourse to the court system, conditioning the exercise of that right, and/or remitting the appeals process to an administrative entity, which is granted functions inherent to courts.

included: (i) implementation of an Electronic Transfers System (*Sistema de Transferencias Electrónicas*—SITE) for the high-value payments system, which enables real-time gross settlement; (ii) the Check Clearinghouse has obtained an operating license from the SBEF, after adapting to the rules of the BCB; (iii) approval of regulations for the High-Value Payments System; (iv) implementation of the regulations for electronic clearing and settlement houses; and (v) approval of e-signature regulations for the Payments System with the aim of validating e-transactions. It is important to support an extension of the reform program in order to integrate all clearing and settlement systems (for example, the systems for securities settlement and custody) and also incorporate improvements in the legal, regulatory, and oversight frameworks. Particularly important would be a solid legal framework; completing the reform of the high- and low-value systems; integrating the securities clearing and settlement systems; and establishing the oversight function of the BCB in cooperation with other supervising authorities.[37]

III. Selected Issues and Policy Recommendations

How to Mitigate and manage a Run on Deposits

Based on the country's recent history and institutional weakness, runs on deposits continue to be an significant risk. These episodes, even if the authorities can properly manage them, have a high cost for the economy and for the financial system. Therefore, the authorities are encouraged to take measures (summarized below) to reduce the risk of a run on deposits and, if that occurs, mitigate its effects.

■ Policy Options to Reduce the Probability of a Run on Deposits and Mitigate its Effects Should it Occur

A run on deposits can be triggered by the public's lack of confidence in the stability of the financial system or in macroeconomic, legal, and/or political or social stability. The recent episodes appear to be due to the second cause, since in the majority of the cases they have coincided with times of deep political and social uncertainty. *Nonetheless, it is crucial that the authorities work on both causes in order to prevent future runs on deposits.*

Improve confidence by the public in the stability of the financial system. In order to promote the stability of the financial system, the authorities would do well to ensure that the following conditions are always present:

- *High capitalization.* It is advisable to maintain high capitalization requirements and, at the same time, see to it that institutions make timely adjustments and set aside the necessary provisions so that their accounting statements reflect the real value of their assets.
- *Adequate liquidity.* The prudent rules (of the BCB and the SBEF) should seek to have banks maintain sufficient liquidity to handle situations of stress without affecting their operations. These margins discourage the withdrawal of deposits, although a very high degree of liquidity notably affects profitability. It is also important for the authorities to demand that banks limit their maturity mismatches.
- *Good executive teams.* Executives must have the technical and moral capacity to manage a banking business. The supervisors need to maintain technical stan-

dards and "fit and proper" criteria for those aspiring to the leadership positions. It's also advisable to demand that banks have a technical team and procedures in keeping with the volume, risk, and complexity of their operations.

- *BCB and SBEF that are autonomous.* The autonomy and technical capacity of the monetary and supervision authorities is key for creating confidence in the financial system. Autonomy requires that the authorities of the BCB and the SBEF be able to hold their ground in the face of political conflicts or differences over technical criteria with the executive branch, and that they have sufficient funds to fulfill their role. It also requires that the executive branch abstain from interfering in the financial system's regulatory and supervision activities.
- *System-wide liquidity mechanisms.* The financial system must have instruments that allow it to obtain more liquidity, under certain conditions, than what is present within the system. Sources of liquidity are the reserves maintained by banks, the capacity of the BCB to act as a LLR without generating inflation, funds of the banks or of the BCB located abroad, and foreign lines of credit to which the entities or the BCB can obtain access in case of a system-wide liquidity shortage. Although the system-wide liquidity mechanisms of the BCB are generally adequate and demonstrated their effectiveness during the recent run on deposits, it is important to continue reinforcing them. This includes adding new potential sources of liquidity in case of a systemic crisis.[38] In response to large withdrawals of deposits, the Central Bank of Bolivia recently increased its repurchase rates[39] (which are higher than market rates) in order to raise the liquidity premium in dollars and encourage the development of the interbank market and stock market activity. During May and June 2005 (the most recent run on deposits), when President Mesa resigned, the Central Bank of Bolivia temporarily increased repurchase rates by more than 100 points to restrain withdrawals following the political unrest of the times. Once the deposits withdrawn during that last episode were reintegrated, the liquidity that the Central Bank of Bolivia had lent to the banks was paid back and the repurchase rate dropped.[40]

Improve Confidence in Macroeconomic, Political/Social, and Legal Stability

- *Macroeconomic stability.* Macroeconomic policies have had a positive effect on economic growth and have helped improve the business environment, fiscal discipline, and price stability. This stability must be maintained in order to avoid creating a lack of confidence that could lead to a run on deposits. Maintaining the stability of the national currency, while taking care not to compromise competitiveness, is also essential for the financial sector due to the high degree of dollarization. Nonetheless, the objective of foreign exchange stability should remain secondary to the objective of making sure that the local currency is not over-valuated at unsustainable levels, since sudden adjustments to the exchange rate negatively affect the stability of the financial system.

- *Political and social stability.* Political and social stability is a prerequisite to the stability and growth of the financial system. Although political and social stability is achieved and maintained through instruments that are beyond the scope of the financial system, a system with well-capitalized banks that offer good financial services to the population (loans, deposits, and other banking services) can also contribute to creating a climate of stability. Nonetheless such stability fundamentally depends on political and macroeconomic factors beyond the scope of this policy note.
- *Respect for contracts.* Legal insecurity harms the stability of deposits in the financial system. When there is a risk that the government will modify the conditions of contracts between banks and their customers (for example, by changing interest rates, terms of maturity, and currencies), especially in a context of high dollarization, the normal reaction of economic agents will be to withdraw their deposits. Therefore, signs indicative of the government's determination to not interfere in private contracts and to ensure their performance are important for the stability of the economic and financial system. This also encourages foreign investment in the financial system, which has diminished in Bolivia in recent years.

The Case of Banco de la Unión (BUN)

The capitalization of the debts owed to NAFIBO (effective in June 2004) substantially improved the equity position of the BUN, although subsequent adjustments have been necessary and its profitability is still deficient. Its sale is still pending. Adjustments in the value of its assets subsequent to the capitalization agreement and the need for additional provisions cast doubt on the current solvency situation of the bank. In addition, the BUN continues to have a deficient balance in its results.[41] The BUN is in a stage of transition until the state's stake is sold. A resolution is urgent in order to prevent greater deterioration and negative effects on the behavior of other institutions.

In October 2005, NAFIBO and the private shareholders had disagreements over the capitalization of the BUN and the valuation of assets, which could jeopardize the bank. There are at least three main court cases pending between the parties. If they are not settled, these conflicts could threaten the sale of the NAFIBO shares and the administration of the BUN during the transition process.

■ **Policy Options with Respect to the BUN:** *Administering it efficiently, maintaining the value of its assets, managing litigation, and facilitating its timely resolution.*

Conduct an evaluation to understand the BUN's true current financial situation. The management, shareholders, and supervisors of the BUN have not agreed on a unified position regarding the financial situation of the bank. The differences are over pending adjustments and the valuation of contingencies. This task could be entrusted to NAFIBO, with external support from the management of the BUN and SBEF. The sale process has been held back by a lack of preparatory activities during 2004 and 2005.

Complete the analysis of the conflict with private shareholders, evaluate options, and adopt a sound strategy that verifies the following conditions:

- that neither the operations of the BUN nor the process of selling the shares in the possession of NAFIBO are affected and;
- that the private shareholders are not "salvaged" with public funds (either of the government or of the BUN). The private shareholders cannot collect more than NAFIBO or prior to NAFIBO on their shares. The authorities committed themselves to this objective during the negotiations of the BCRP I loan and the agreement with the IMF.

Seek a timely and definitive solution that normalizes the BUN. Capitalization by NAFIBO was a temporary measure aimed at preserving the bank and the credit NAFIBO had against it. The Ministry of Finance and NAFIBO have not significantly advanced in the transfer of shares to the private sector, as is ordered by Presi-

Box 3. NAFIBO Contribution and the Value of Holding Shares of the BUN

- In late 2003, NAFIBO capitalized debt owed to it valued at US$12 million, thereby obtaining a 75 percent shareholding majority, with a majority on the Board of Directors and control over the bank's management. At first glance, it seems that if the government sells the shares at a price lower than that amount, the capitalization could be a ruinous business for it. Nonetheless, this is not necessarily so, since the government did not capitalize the BUN with cash, but with *previously issued subordinated debt* whose recovery value would be very low or equivalent to zero if the entity were to be liquidated (to a certain extent, the cost has already been assumed). What are additional costs for the state, as the majority shareholder, are losses that continue to accrue.
- Therefore, although NAFIBO should maximize the value it can obtain on the shares, the former nominal value of the shares should not constitute a minimum price, only a reference price. A transparent, public sales mechanism is the best way to ensure that NAFIBO (and hence the government) receives the market price on its shares, which could be higher or lower than the value of the capitalized subordinated debt.

dential Decree 27258. One of the challenges for the new government is to transfer shares to the private sector (Box 3) in such a way that the private sector will capitalize the bank, take charge of its administration, and increase the offer of loans and services. To attain these objectives, the government must delineate and support a framework of action that allows for the transfer of shares to the private sector and that ensures the entity's adequate capitalization and management.

Increase Access to Credit and Other Financial Services

Lack of access to financial services is a general problem in both Bolivia and the region. In addition, increased access to credit, which is indispensable for economic development, takes time. Although immediate results should not be expected from the reforms proposed, it is crucial to advance in the short term in order to improve their effectiveness.

■ **Policy Options to Increase Access to Financial Services:** *Improve the conditions for access to credit and financial services and grant access to those who lack it, especially entrepreneurs and SMEs.*

Promote alternative financial instruments to bank loans, above all to improve access to credit for SMEs. One policy that could improve access to financing is the promotion of alternatives such as financial leasing, factoring, and securitization of assets. International experience indicates that these instruments can be effective if the problem of lack of collateral is solved, which typically affects SMEs. This could be accomplished by separating the credit quality of the financing (backed by invoices owed by large companies, leased equipment, or future assets/flows) from the credit quality of the SMEs, thereby allowing for the intermediation of other financial institutions (other than banks) and increasing financing sources. To develop such alternatives the following issues would need to be addressed: [42]

- The development of a local and international factoring industry would require: (i) an expansion of the legal definition of invoices that can be used—currently, they are limited to foreign exchange invoices—to include other valid local and international sales documents; (ii) power to enforce out-of-court collections on invoices; (iii) clarification of the definition of factoring as the sale/transfer of a credit and not the sale of goods or services; and (iv) facilitation of processes to authorize the issuance of bonds by non-bank financial companies.
- The leasing industry would benefit from: (i) a clear definition of accounting and fiscal rules and of the possibility of out-of-court enforcement of leased assets registered in the name of the financial intermediary; (ii) a review and expansion of the universe of goods that can be leased. It would be advisable for the proposed financial leasing act currently being developed to resolve these issues.

- Although the securitization process in Bolivia has certain precedents, it is perceived to be long and costly. Such a perception limits the assets and flows that can be securitized in an economically viable fashion. In this regard, the feasibility of securitization is much more limited in Bolivia in the short term, though it cannot be discarded in the future.[43]

Improve access to bank and non-bank credit by filling the gaps in the legal and institutional framework for enforcing and registering collateral, and by making financial products better meet the needs of companies. It is vital to carefully evaluate the financing needs of companies (including possible additional demands for restructuring) in order to develop financial products or other services best adapted to those needs (in the same way that the microfinance technology has advanced by adapting its products to the needs of its potential borrowers). Although improved access is also relevant for both mid-sized and large companies, it is especially important for mid-sized companies, because large companies have more ways to directly access financing abroad. A crucial element still in need of improvement is the legal framework for the enforcement and registration of collateral.[44]

With respect to MFEs, develop new products that will make it possible to extend access to financial services—savings, insurance, channeling of remittances—apart from the more traditional micro-credits. It is imperative that authorities do not diminish the payment *capacity* and *will* of current and potential debtors. Payment capacity increases when good macroeconomic policies are maintained and legal security is improved. Payment will is preserved by avoiding mass debt-forgiveness programs. Both international experience (for example, Mexico) and Bolivian experience (for example, FERE) reflect the damaging effects that debt-forgiveness efforts can have, since the benefits are relatively small compared to the persistent, major economic costs.

Make a critical analysis of the role played by public Apex institutions in Bolivia (FONDESIF, NAFIBO) and the fulfillment of their objectives, in order to redefine strategies regarding the future of these entities in light of relevant international experience. This is important to avoid unnecessary distortions in the affected market, and would be especially important in relation to the rural market, given its more limited access. Based on international experience, alternatives could be evaluated that would allow the two existing Apex banks to develop markets without generating large distortions. In all events, it is a good idea to avoid retail banks, which tend to be even more exposed to political influence, poor management, and a limited accomplishment of objectives, with very costly consequences (as has already been seen in Bolivia).

Bibliography

BCB. 2004a. "*Boletín Informativo No. 131.*" La Paz, Bolivia: BCB, April.
———. 2005a. "*Boletín Informativo No. 143.*" La Paz, Bolivia: BCB, April.

———. 2005b. "*Boletín Informativo No. 144.*" La Paz, Bolivia: BCB, May.

———. 2005c. "*Boletín Informativo No. 148.*" La Paz, Bolivia: BCB, September.

———. 2005d. "*Parte IV: Políticas del Banco Central de Bolivia.*" *Memoria de 2004.* La Paz, Bolivia: BCB.

———. 2005e. "*Evaluación de la economía en 2005.*" La Paz, Bolivia, BCB, December.

Cheikhrouhou, Hela. 2006 (publication pending). "Finanzas Estructuradas para Pymes." Chapter 6 in *Finanzas Estructuradas para Inversiones de los Ahorros de Vejez.* Washington, DC: World Bank.

FINRURAL. 2005. "*Autorregulación: Reporte de las Instituciones Financieras de Desarrollo.*" Monthly Bulletin. La Paz, Bolivia, Association of Financial Institutions for Rural Development (*Asociación de Instituciones Financieras para el Desarrollo Rural*), May.

González-Vega, C. 2002. "*Dilemas en la expansión de la frontera de las finanzas rurales: oportunidades, retos y peligros para la cooperación internacional y el FONDESIF en Bolivia,*" *Cuadernos de Sefir*, Development Alternatives, Inc., La Paz, Bolivia.

IMF. 2005a. "Bolivia: Fifth Review Under the Stand-By Arrangement, Request for Waiver of Nonobservance of Performance Criteria, Rephasing, Augmentation, and Extension of the Stand-By Arrangement – Staff Report; Staff Statement; Press Release on the Executive Board Discussion; and Statement by the Executive Director for Bolivia." *IMF Country Report No. 05/146.* Washington, DC: International Monetary Fund, April.

———. 2005b. "Bolivia: Sixth Review Under the Stand-By Arrangement, Requests for Modification and Waiver of Nonobservance and Applicability of Performance Criteria, Rephasing, and Reduction of Access – Staff Report; Staff Statement; Press Release on the Executive Board Discussion; and Statement by the Executive Director for Bolivia." *IMF Country Report No. 05/393.* Washington, DC: International Monetary Fund, November.

IMF and World Bank. 2003. "Selected Technical Annex: Microfinance." *Financial Sector Assessment Program: Bolivia.* Washington, DC: International Monetary Fund and the World Bank, August.

Navajas, Sergio, J. Conning, and Claudio González-Vega. 2003. "Lending Technologies, Competition and Consolidation in the Market for Microfinance in Bolivia," *Journal of International Development*, 15, 747-770.

Superintendency of Banks and Financial Entities [*Superintendencia de Bancos y Entidades Financieras*]. 2000. "*Editorial: Evaluación del sistema bancario al 31 de diciembre de 2000.*" La Paz, Bolivia: Bolivian Superintendency of Banks and Financial Entities.

———. 2001. Editorial: "*Evaluación del sistema bancario al 31 de diciembre de 2001.*" La Paz, Bolivia: Bolivian Superintendency of Banks and Financial Entities.

———. 2003. Editorial: "*Evaluación del sistema bancario y no bancario al 31 de diciembre de 2003.*" La Paz, Bolivia: Bolivian Superintendency of Banks and Financial Entities.

———. 2004. Editorial: "*Evaluación del sistema bancario y no bancario al 31 de diciembre de 2004.*" La Paz, Bolivia: Bolivian Superintendency of Banks and Financial Entities.

———. 2005a. Editorial: "*Evaluación del sistema bancario y no bancario al 30 de septiembre de 2005.*" La Paz, Bolivia: Bolivian Superintendency of Banks and Financial Entities.

———. 2005b. Editorial: "*Evaluación del sistema bancario y no bancario al 30 de junio de 2005.*" La Paz, Bolivia: Bolivian Superintendency of Banks and Financial Entities.

———. 2005c. Presentation: "*Seguimiento del sistema financiero.*" La Paz, Bolivia: Bolivian Superintendency of Banks and Financial Entities, September.

Superintendency of Companies [*Superintendencia de Empresas*]. 2005. "*Resultados, Programa de Reestructuración, tercer trimestre.*" Note prepared for the BCRP I mission, La Paz, Bolivia: Bolivian Superintendency of Banks and Financial Entities.

The Economist Intelligence Unit. 2005a. "Country Report: Bolivia." London, UK, November.

———. 2005b. "Country Profile 2005: Bolivia." London, UK.

Western Hemisphere Payments and Securities Settlement Forum, WB and Latin American Monetary Studies Center (*Centro de Estudios Monetarios Latinoamericanos*—CEMLA) (2004). "Assessment and Observations on the Payments and Securities Settlement Systems of Bolivia." The Centre for Latin American Monetary Studies, Mexico City. October.

World Bank. 2004. "Program Document for a First Programmatic Bank and Corporate Restructuring Program Adjustment Loan in the Amount of US$ 15 Million and Credit in the Amount of SDR 10.5 Million (US$ 15 Million Equivalent) to the Republic of Bolivia." Report No. 27495-BO. Washington, DC: The World Bank, January.

———. 2005. "Bolivia Country Economic Memorandum: Policies to Improve Growth and Employment." Report No. 32233-BO. Washington, DC: The World Bank, June.

World Bank and International Finance Corporation. 2001. "Pilot Investment Climate Assessment: Bolivia Microeconomic Constraints and Opportunities for Higher Growth." Washington, DC: The World Bank and International Finance Corporation. March.

Annex: Banking Trends

Figure A1. Trends in the Variables of the Bank and Non-Bank System (1998–September 2005)

Banking System (Excludes BLA and BSO)
(millions of US$)

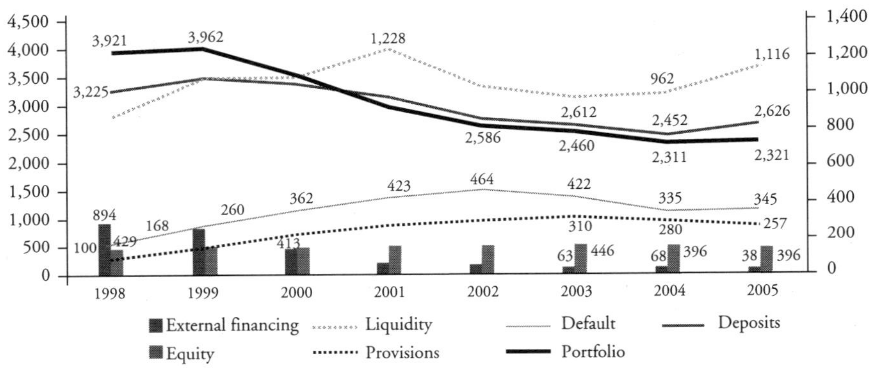

Non-Banking System (Includes BLA and BSO)
(millions of US$)

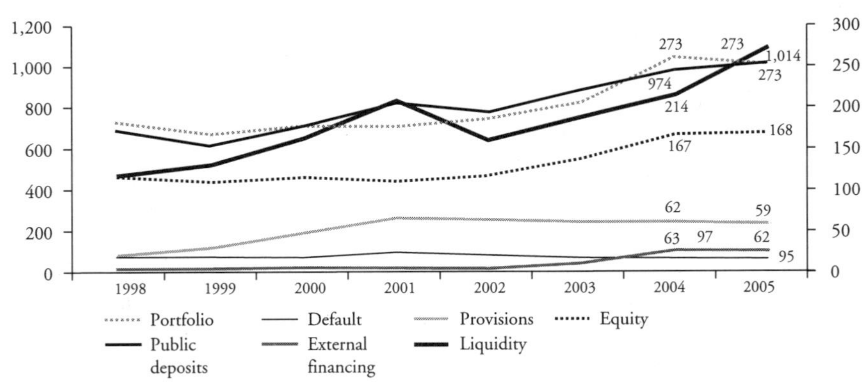

Source: SBEF Presentation, September 2005.

Figure A2. Trends in Bank Deposits Denominated in Local Currency and Dollars, by Term (March 2004–September 2005)
(Thousands of bolivianos)

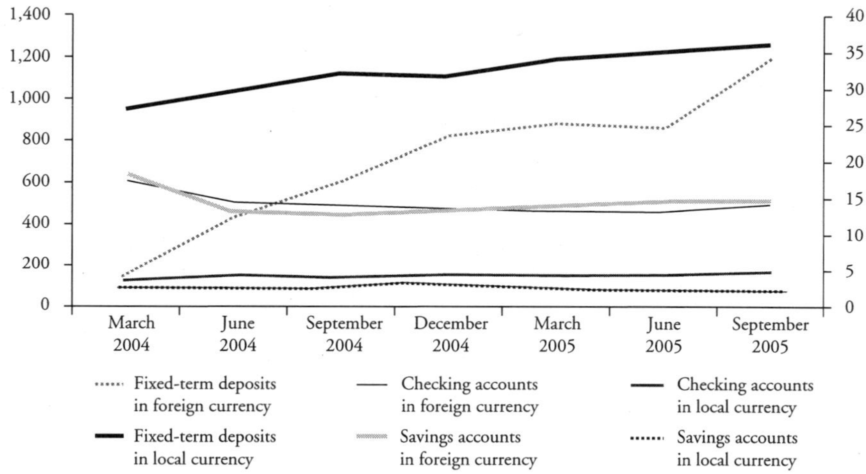

Figure A3a. Annual Trends in Default Rates by Group of Entities (2002–September 2005)

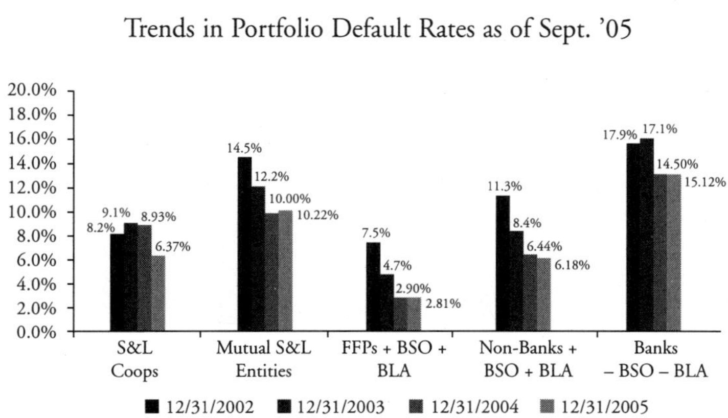

Source: SBEF Presentation, September 2005.

Figure A3b. Annual Trends in the Coverage of the Default Portfolio, by Group of Entities (2002–September 2005)

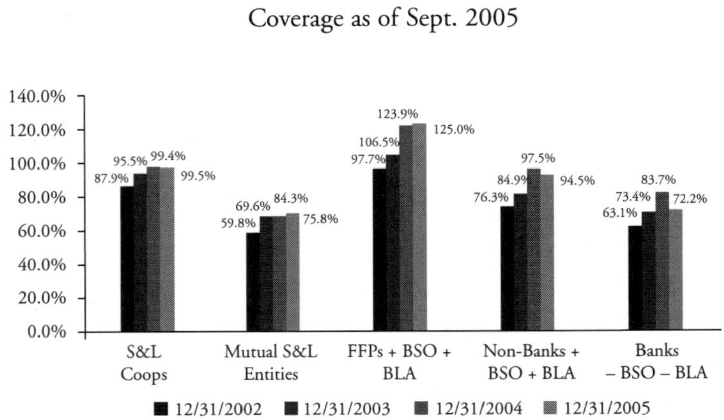

Source: SBEF Presentation, September 2005.

Figure A4. Trends in the Default Rate for the Rescheduled, Non-Rescheduled, and Total Portfolio of the Banking System (December 2003–September 2005)

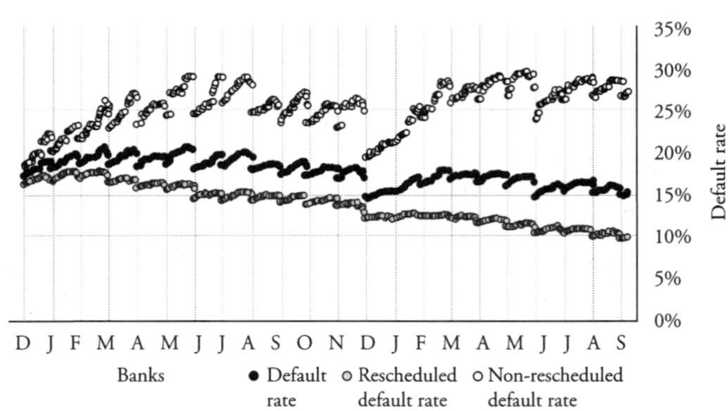

Source: SBEF Presentation, September 2005.

Table A1. Concentration of Bank Deposits, November 2005 and December 2002

Total Deposits-Categories	*Number of Accounts*		*% of Accounts*		*Value (US$ million)*		*% of Total Deposits*	
	2005	***2002***	***2005***	***2002***	***2005***	***2002***	***2005***	***2002***
> US$ 2,000,001	57	47	0.01	0.04	359	202	12.5	7
US$ 1,000.001 to 2,000,000	128	89	0.02	0.04	170	127	5.9	4
US$ 500,001 to 1,000,000	333	312	0.05	0.10	226	227	7.9	8
US$ 200,001 to 500,000	1,208	1,523	0.20	0.30	372	521	13.0	18
US$ 100,001 to 200,000	2,096	2,132	0.34	0.58	294	328	10.2	11
US$ 50,001 to 100,000	4,949	4,747	0.80	1.21	374	378	13.0	13
US$ 30,001 to 50,000	5,884	5,607	0.95	1.54	239	235	8.3	8
US$ 20,001 to 30,000	6,207	6,030	1.00	1.80	152	155	5.3	5
US$ 15,001 to 20,000	5,951	5,829	0.96	1.62	105	107	3.7	4
US$ 10,001 to 15,000	10,413	10,206	1.68	2.85	126	129	4.4	4
US$ 5,001 to 10,000	26,267	26,687	4.24	6.14	189	200	6.6	7
US$ 1,001 to 5,000	81,298	88,033	13.13	18.20	195	218	6.8	8
US$ 501 to 1,000	53,875	45,425	8.70	8.08	39	34	1.4	1
< US$ 500	420,325	377,250	67.90	57.50	32	31	1.1	1
TOTAL	**618,991**	**573,917**	**100.00**	**100,00**	**2,872**	**2,892**	**100**	**100**

Source: SBEF and FSAP.

Endnotes

1. At present, the regulated financial sector includes 11 banking entities (six foreign banks) and 40 non-bank entities (excluding deposit warehouses and other entities). The non-banks include the regulated MFEs, 24 mutual savings and loan entities, and 10 open savings and loan cooperatives. For their part, the regulated MFEs include six Private Financial Funds (PFFs) and two specialized banks, Bancosol (transformed from the NGO named PRODEM in 1992) and Banco Los Andes (which was an FFP named Caja Los Andes until January 2005).

2. Better funding of the MFEs and the strong competitiveness of this subsector reduced the average (nominal) interest rate of the MFEs, which was 21 percent in June 2005 (Association of Bolivian Financial Entities Specializing in Micro-Finance - *Asociación de Entidades Financieras Especializadas en Micro Finanzas de Bolivia*—ASOFIN)—as compared with 27 percent in Peru, whose portfolio was also dollarized. The rate is higher than the banks' rates, which reflects the increased transaction costs and risks borne by micro-finance activities. The effective differential of the FFPs dropped by 6 percentage points as of 1998 to 14.3 percent in December 2004 (Superintendency of Banks and Financial Entities of Bolivia - *Superintendencia de Bancos y Entidades Financieras*—SBEF).

3. In addition, the average amount of the MFEs' loans increased (see sub-section on rural credit on page 141) in order to provide a cushion so that the debtors could better handle the crisis.

4. The interest-rate reduction policy, started in late 2000 by the banking sector, also contributed to reducing the total volume of deposits. The banks hoped that the demand for loans would be stimulated with lower lending rates and that lower rates on deposits would reduce their financial costs by discouraging deposits from the public (given the lower demand for credit). As of December 31, 2001, the effective average lending rate and the average rate on deposits in foreign currency reached their lowest level in ten years (13.5 and 2.8 percent, respectively). Both rates continued to fall in subsequent years (though with slight temporary increases), exacerbated by international trends. By September 2005, the rates fell to 12.5 and 1.8 percent, respectively.

5. In fact, banks perceived at the time as the weakest suffered comparatively fewer withdrawals than other entities considered to be very strong (including certain foreign banks). It has been said that the allegedly stronger banks perhaps had more sophisticated depositors who could more easily withdraw their money, for example, over the Internet.

6. Fundamental was timely access to liquidity from the BCB, in its role as a lender of last resort, granting loans to banks with transitory liquidity problems (as opposed to solvency problems), at penalized rates, and with significant collateral.

7. According to the BCB (2005b), "approximately 67 percent of credit is granted to the non-traded sector."

8. The crisis was principally due to external shocks that hurt exports and investment, the two principal sources of growth from 1990 to 1998. These shocks included: (i) decreased capital flows to the region due to the Russian crisis; (ii) deteriorated competitiveness of Bolivian exports as a result of the crisis in Southeast Asia and devaluations in Brazil, Chile, and

Argentina; (iii) decreased demand for Bolivian products on account of the Argentine crisis and slower economic growth in Latin America; and (iv) the negative effects of natural disasters on production. For more information, see for example World Bank (2004).

9. Although the default rate of the non-bank entities is much lower (reflecting the better quality of their portfolio), of concern is the possible exposure of FFPs and of other non-bank entities with highly dollarized portfolios who lend, above all, to borrowers that do not generate foreign currency.

10. The non-regulated MFEs have a portfolio at risk greater than 5 percent; four have more than 10 percent.

11. The program of the Special Economic Reactivation Fund (*Fondo Especial de Reactivación Económica*—FERE) closed for new cases in 2004. For more information on the FERE and its effects on portfolio quality, see World Bank (2004).

12. If the total rescheduled portfolio is considered as potential portfolio in default, the combined default rate of the rescheduled portfolio and the portfolio in default would increase to 46 percent for banking entities and to 11 percent for non-bank entities.

13. Defined as (portfolio in default - provisions)/shareholders' equity.

14. If the complete adjustment had been made in 2005, three banks would have had a CAP of less than 10 percent.

15. Nonetheless, this also implies a decrease in the already low profitability of the financial entities. For more information on the opportunity costs of increased liquidity, see BCB (2005b).

16. This amount, equivalent to US$851 million, does not include restricted investments or the RAL Fund (US$301 million), but it does include negotiable investments accounted for as long-term investments. Nonetheless, this calculation of coverage does not include amounts from investment companies (*Sociedades Administradoras de Fondos de Inversión*—SAFIS). In the past such investment companies received huge demands for cash and covered them by borrowing from their related banks, which in turn borrowed from the BCB.

17. These latter two were induced by the recent rise in international interest rates and the fall in effective return on Bolivian assets.

18. Though these rates are much higher than those of the banks, they reflect in part the greater risk involved in the micro-finance business.

19. Apart from major restrictions resulting from the business climate.

20. Except PRODEM, which is completely rural, Bancosol, and more recently FIE, have started to target this segment.

21. The maximum loan term is 12 years, with a three-year grace period. See González-Vega (2002) regarding the effect that FONDESIF's directed policies have on competition.

22. Almost all the NGOs that belong to FINRURAL (except two), have sufficient capital to become PFF's (minimum required capital of approximately US$1 million) and thus be able to fund themselves with deposits, but none has expressed such an interest (except for Agrocapital, which is currently processing its license). This is due partly to a perception that the regulatory system is very rigid for NGOs and partly to the absence of a legal framework for some of their products (such as agricultural loans).

23. FONDESIF also provided technical assistance to the NGOs in the amount of US$6.5 billion from January to June 2005 (FONDESIF). Nonetheless, it is difficult to evaluate the effectiveness of these efforts, given the low quality of the NGOs' portfolios and to shortcomings in the effective management of risks (FINRURAL and ASOFIN).

24. The law in question was passed on April 1, but the decree that implements it was published in July, provoking an instability in deposits in anticipation of the ITF going into effect. Initially, the ITF was to be applied for two years, but recently the government has made it permanent. During its first year of existence, the proportion was 0.3 percent on each transaction; in its second year, that proportion dropped to 0.25 percent. Deposits in dollars of less than US$1,000 are exempt.

25. The International Monetary Fund (IMF) provided technical assistance as part of this effort.

26. The legal reserve (in securities) on deposits in foreign currency (except for fixed-term deposits whose maturity is more than 720 days) increased from 10 to 12 percent, which, added to the 2 percent in cash, amounts to a legal reserve of 14 percent (12 percent in local currency). A marginal legal reserve of 7.5 percent was also added for deposits in dollars (unless their term is more than 360 days), but it is only applicable to financial accounts above 80 percent of the deposits as of March 31, 2005 (BCB 2005b).

27. In particular, the BCB has sought to prevent the real appreciation of the local currency notwithstanding its nominal appreciation (see BCB 2005e). This measure not only attempts to prevent a decline in competitiveness, but also serves to prevent a run on deposits, since in a highly dollarized system, massive withdrawals can be set off by the public's fear that their deposits in foreign currency will be subjected to obligatory conversion into local currency at an official exchange rate that differs from the market rate (especially given the recent experiences in Argentina).

28. In this context, the banks are starting to increase their rates, which will put pressure on their margins and affect the profitability of the system.

29. This progress is very important, since the rules for rating and granting loans had become much more flexible in recent years in response to the crisis, distorting declared solvency and affecting banking incentives. The process of strengthening the rules was delayed because of this difficult situation, even though the authorities were aware of the essential need to reverse the effect of less prudent measures.

30. In general, the MFEs benefited from a flexible legal and regulatory framework that notably encouraged their growth. Nonetheless, favorable results have yet to be confirmed for the non-regulated MFEs.

31. The FRF (through the BCB on behalf of the Ministry of Finance, up until 2006) can now contribute up to 30 percent of covered deposits when financial entities undergo a resolution process through exclusion of assets and liabilities, down from 50 percent, which was applicable until January 1, 2005.

32. NAFIBO is a mixed-ownership Apex bank, with the government as the majority shareholder and the *Corporación Andina de Fomento* (CAF) as the minority shareholder. The presence of the CAF may have reduced the moral risk that tends to affect public banks.

33. This debt resulted from the Equity Strengthening Program (*Programa de Fortalecimiento Patrimonial*—PROFOP) for capitalizing financial entities with government funds. For more information on PROFOP and the capitalization process of BUN, see Document BCRP I.
34. Banco Bisa (a Bolivian Bank) recently announced an agreement with Banco Santa Cruz (a foreign bank) for purchasing Banco Santa Cruz's share. This agreement is now being evaluated by the SBEF.
35. Law 2495 creates a bad incentive for the restructuring of companies that have large debts with the State, since the State does not participate in the negotiations during the creditors meeting, but debt remission (reduction of the original amount of the debt) agreed upon by a majority of those who attend the meeting applies to it. In practice, debt remissions have been as high as 98 percent.
36. According to Law 2495, it is the receiver who should give an opinion on the "soundness of the agreement." Given that the receiver presides over the negotiations, it is difficult to ignore the difficulties he will have in maintaining his independent judgment and definitively indicating whether the company is not viable and whether the agreement makes it viable. Apart from this, in cases where financing is granted by NAFIBO, the law provides for the action of an international agent. In practice, such a measure has been subject to certain criticism, given the cost and time it involves.
37. See the report prepared by the Western Hemisphere Payments and Securities Settlement Forum, the World Bank, and the Latin American Monetary Studies Center (*Centro de Estudios Monetarios Latinoamericanos*—CEMLA) (2004), which includes details on how to proceed in reforming the aspects in question.
38. For example, by establishing agreements for contingent lines of liquidity between the BCB and foreign banks. It is also important to formulate an *ex ante* liquidity policy that prioritizes the different types of deposits when granting liquidity in the event of an extreme emergency (the experience of Uruguay, which prioritized deposits with the shortest maturity, could be considered).
39. In September 2005, the BUN reported a Capital Adequacy Ratio (CAR) of 12.1 (with a capital of US$16 million). This includes a US$4.1 million adjustment in May 2005, but if one bears in mind the pending adjustments estimated as of May 2005 (for additional provisions and an adjustment to the value of awarded assets), the capital position becomes a deficit. The cumulative result is negative by US$800 billion as of August 2005. Nonetheless, the sale of awarded assets has caused the results for some months in 2005 to be positive (US$ 900 million in August).
40. These are rates on securities of the Central Bank of Bolivia acquired through a resale or repurchase agreement.
41. In addition, there has been an increase in the liquidity of the financial system in the form of foreign assets, including a substantial strengthening of Net International Reserves. The authorities have recently limited the increase of the floor on Net International Reserves in the context of the agreement with the IMF, in order to have sufficient flexibility to react to a possible run on deposits during the elections.
42. This paragraph is based on the working note prepared by Hela Cheikhrouhou regarding alternative financing instruments to bank instruments in Bolivia. For more information on

international experience with these mechanisms and success stories in the LAC countries (Mexico, Brazil, Peru, Chile), see Cheikhrouhou, 2006, Chapter 2: "*Titularización y financiamiento de PYME*").

43. Ibid.
44. The law on personal property collateral is pending passage by the Congress.

6

The Gas Era

Eleodoro Mayorga and Alejandro Tapia

Summary

This chapter aims to help Bolivia make the most of its hydrocarbons resources to the benefit of its population, particularly the poor. In order to take advantage of this potential, Bolivia needs significant investments to develop its gas fields and build processing and transportation services. Due to the public sector's financial limitations, these investments must come from the private sector, above all from the foreign private sector and strategic partners. With a new law for the industry and as yet incomplete regulations for the sector, the government must define the terms under which it expects to obtain these investments and inform the population as to how earnings will be distributed. This study discusses recent developments in the sector and identifies areas where major decisions need to be adopted, such as the negotiation of new contract models, improved transparency in the collection and distribution of revenue, delineation of the operations to be conducted by Yacimientos Petrolíferos Fiscales Bolivianos (YPFB), fuel price adjustments on the domestic market, and the opening of new gas markets in the region and elsewhere. Errors and omissions in redefining policy for the sector could have a high cost—by preventing Bolivians from taking full advantage of their greatest source of income—and exacerbate social tensions.

I. Background

With 908 million barrels of proven and probable petroleum reserves, Bolivia is not a major oil country. Nonetheless, in the late 1990s and the start of this decade, significant natural gas deposits were discovered, amounting to 27.6 trillion cubic feet (TCF) of proven reserves—almost 52 TCF, if probable reserves are added to this figure—

which makes Bolivia holder of the third largest gas reserves in Latin America, surpassed only by Venezuela and Mexico. The development of this wealth could significantly change the country's economy, especially if export plans materialize (see Table 1).

Bolivian natural gas contains an appreciable volume of condensates (liquid hydrocarbons), which has allowed the country to also increase its oil reserves. Between 1999 and 2004, the discovery of natural gas fields in Bolivia increased reserves of oil/condensates from 240 to 908 million barrels.

Between 1995 and 2002, approximately US$2.8 billion was invested in the oil and gas industry,[1] that is, 25 percent of total investments made in Bolivia. Investment in the industry has increased since 1997 as the result of: (i) the reform and opening of the sector; (ii) invitations to bid on concessions for new areas, in a legal framework favorable to investment; and (iii) the construction of the gas pipeline from Santa Cruz to southern Brazil.

In this process, YPFB ceased production activities and became a government agency with a mandate to promote exploration and exploitation, administer contracts, and act as an aggregator of natural gas production earmarked for export to Brazil. Under this framework, private oil companies commenced exploration activities, and found very significant natural gas reserves.

The department of Santa Cruz, in the region of Pie de Monte, is the country's traditional gas-producing region. Historically, 75 percent of YPFB's gas, in terms of volume, was produced in this department. These deposits were turned over to private management in 1996 and are currently exploited by Andina S.A. and Chaco S.A. Following the opening of the oil and gas industry, several international oil companies, including British Gas, British Petroleum, and Total, Repsol—Yacimientos Petrolíferos Fiscales (YPF) of Spain, the Brazilian government-owned Petrobrás, and other smaller companies (Pluspetrol, Vintage), made major successful investments, particularly in the department of Tarija.

This favorable investment framework has changed considerably with the new Hydrocarbons Act, published in May 2005.[2] According to this new law, the Ministry

Table 1. Bolivia—Certified Natural Gas and Oil/Condensate Reserves

Reserves	*1999*	*2000*	*2001*	*2002*	*2003*	*2004*
Natural Gas (TCF)						
Proven	5.3	18.3	23.8	27.4	28.7	27.6
Probable	3.3	13.9	23.0	24.9	26.2	24.7
Total Proven + Probable	**8.6**	**32.2**	**46.8**	**52.3**	**54.9**	**52.4**
Oil/Condensates (million barrels)						
Proven	151.9	396.5	440.5	477.0	486.1	462.2
Probable	88.6	295.5	451.5	452.1	470.8	446.5
Total Proven + Probable	**240.5**	**692.0**	**892.0**	**929.1**	**956.9**	**908.8**

Source: YPFB.

of Oil and Gas is in charge of formulating, promoting, and supervising governmental policies on hydrocarbons. The government-owned YPFB, through its Office of the Vice President for Management and Oversight, is responsible for signing and administering oil and gas contracts, overseeing production, and acting as an aggregator,[3] while its Office of the Vice President for Operations is authorized to operate and/or participate in all activities of the chain of production. The Superintendency of Hydrocarbons continues to be the regulating agency for activities that involve petroleum by-product transportation, refining, and marketing as well as natural gas distribution through pipe systems. The new law notably expands the jurisdiction of the public sector and, in large measure, reintroduces a price control system.

At the end of 2004, there were twelve international companies in Bolivia involved in the exploration and exploitation of hydrocarbons, five working in pipeline transportation, three devoted to refining activities (particularly Petrobrás), five in charge of natural gas distribution pipe systems, and approximately 600 involved in marketing petroleum by-products.

Figure 1 illustrates investments in the sector, including transportation-related investments, while Figure 2 illustrates specific investments in exploration and the development of new oil and gas production.

II. Industry Features

Hydrocarbons Production and Energy Supplies

Hydrocarbons represent the core of Bolivia's energy matrix. They are used extensively in the transportation sector, industry, and the generation of electricity. Only in the residential sector, above all in rural zones, does biomass continue to play an important role.

Figure 1. Bolivia: Foreign Direct Investment
(Millions of US$)

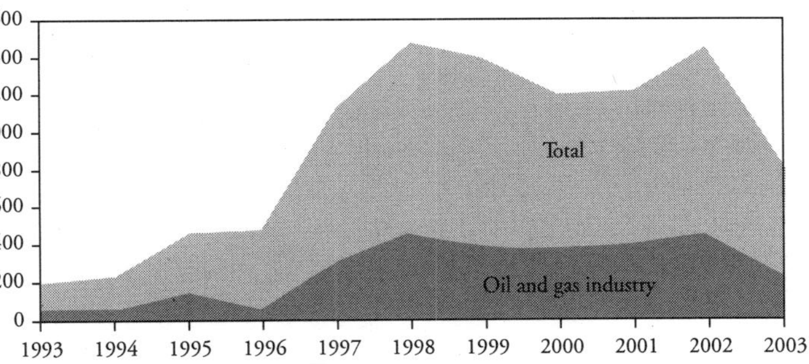

Source: ESMAP study on the Distribution of Revenue.

Figure 2. Investments in Exploration and Exploitation (1992–2005)

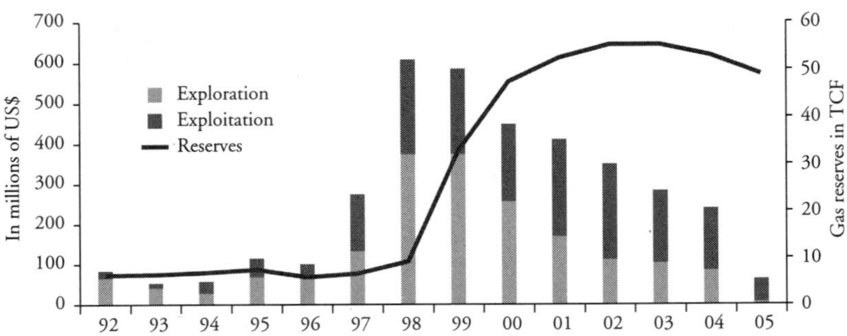

Source: YPFB Statistics and ESMAP study on the distribution of revenue.[4]
Note: Figures for 2005 correspond to the first half of the year.

In 2004, oil production in Bolivia was 46,400 barrels per day, while consumption was 40,000 barrels per day. As a result, Bolivia is presently an exporter of condensates and reconstituted crude oil. Despite this situation, given the quality of the oil, which is extremely light, the refineries are not satisfying fuel consumption patterns and the country has to import approximately 5,000 barrels of diesel oil a day.

The development of natural gas fields to supply the domestic market and especially for export to Brazil has led to the production of associated liquids (particularly condensates), which they have started to export. With the strong increase in international oil prices, these exports amounted to US$171 million in 2004 (see Table 2)—30 percent of natural gas exports in economic terms.

With respect to domestic energy consumption, it has not been possible to make full use of the gas reserves, largely due to the domestic pricing policy. Subsidies on liquid petroleum gas (LPG) and diesel oil hinder the development of natural gas demand on the domestic market and contribute to the fiscal deficit.

Since public sector funds are limited, much of the development of the sector depends on the policies and legal-contractual structure under which foreign invest-

Table 2. Oil Exports

Oil	*1998*	*1999*	*2000*	*2001*	*2002*	*2003*	*2004*
Volume (Barrels per day)	6,027	4,658	3,288	4,384	6,027	7,945	10,490
Price (US$/Barrel)	14	16	30	30	28	33	45
Total Oil Exports (US$ million)	30	26	36	47	62	96	171

Source: Central Bank of Bolivia.

ments are made. Nonetheless, political tensions, the new Hydrocarbons Act, and changes in pricing rules and other regulations have not contributed to creating the legal stability or the incentives needed for foreign investment. The Hydrocarbons Act gives greater responsibility to the public sector, in particular to the government-owned company.

Change in the Tax Regimen

Until the introduction of Law No. 3058 in 2005, the tax system on the oil and gas industry differentiated between existing fields and new ones. Law No. 1689 continued this classification and developed the following taxation table for existing hydrocarbons and those resulting from new exploration (Table 3):

It has been erroneously argued that YPFB was paying more taxes as a producing company. In practice, Bolivia did not have a fiscal policy regarding oil and gas applied to the public sector, because the treasury appropriated two-thirds of YPFB's total sales—a variable controlled by the price of fuels set by the Minister of Finance. At the time, gas exports to Argentina were lower in quantity. This practice cost YPFB its financial viability as it was unable to reinvest its earnings.

Figure 3 illustrates the situation of legislation regarding the oil and gas industry between 1999 and 2002. It shows how Bolivia's contractual framework offered favorable incentives to attract private investment as compared with the regimens for oil and gas exploration in neighboring countries.

The left side of the figure is based on a consultant study conducted by Wood Mackenzie on legislation related to the oil industry in the year 2002. It shows that at the time, the Bolivian tax model for natural gas offered the lowest governmental share in revenue from the projects, as compared with Colombia and Peru. Ecuador does not appear in this figure because it does not have natural gas projects. The right side of the figure is based on a study conducted by the ESMAP program on

Table 3. Taxes under Law 1689 (Exploration and Exploitation)

Type of Tax/Royalties (Rates as a Percentage)	*Existing Fields*	*New Fields*
Departmental Royalties	12	12
YPFB Participation – General Treasury of the Nation	6	6
National Supplementary Royalty (General Treasury)	13	-
National Participation (General Treasury)	19	-
Subtotal	**50**	**18**
Corporate Income Tax (25%)	No	Yes
Tax on Remittances sent Abroad (12.5%)	No	Yes
Surtax (25%)	No	Yes
Total Taxes	**50**	**18 + other taxes**

Source: Law No. 1689.

Figure 3. Comparison of Government Revenue on Exploration and Exploitation Contracts

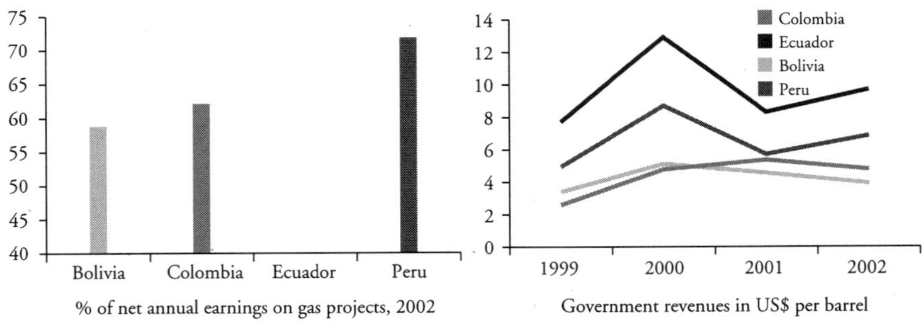

Source: Wood Mackenzie and ESMAP.

the distribution of revenue in those same countries; it shows that Bolivia (red line) was receiving the lowest amount per equivalent barrel of oil produced.

While increasing the government's revenue from the previously low level is a perfectly reasonable goal, under the new Hydrocarbons Act, Bolivia will have one of the harshest tax regimens in the region. This situation is aggravated by the new Direct Tax on Hydrocarbons (*Impuesto Directo sobre los Hidrocarburos*—IDH), which taxes production as opposed to earnings. Accordingly, the IDH cannot be credited against income taxes to be paid in the operating companies' country of origin (see Table 4).

The new tax regimen for the sector does not appear to be creating an environment conducive to investment, nor will it help reverse the falling trend in exploration and exploitation investments over recent years. Investments in exploration

Table 4. Royalties and Income Taxes
(Countries of Latin America – Situation in Mid 2004)

	Royalties		
Country	***Minimum***	***Maximum***	***Corporate Income Tax***
Argentina	N/A	12.0%	35.0%
Bolivia (under the new law)	**50.0%**	**50.0%**	**25.0%**
Brazil	N/A	10.0%	25%-35%
Chile	28.0%	45.0%	N/A
Colombia	5.0%	25.0%	35.0%
Ecuador	12.5%	18.5%	25.0%
Guatemala	5.0%	20.0%	N/A
Trinidad Tobago	N/A	12.5%	35.0%
Venezuela	N/A	16.7%	34.0%

Source: YPFB, based on data from the Capitalization Representative.

and exploitation have steadily diminished, from US$605 million in 1998 to only US$65 million during the first half of 2005.

The situation is even more worrisome in the case of investments in exploration, which, in this same period, diminished from US$375 million to only US$7.5 million (Figure 2). In the case of transportation, though major investments were made during 1997-2003 (approximately US$1.4 billion, principally for the construction of export-oriented gas pipelines), recent years have seen a considerable decline.

Projects for Exporting Natural Gas and Changes in the New Law on the Sector

The development of gas is intrinsically linked to investments for processing, transportation, and distribution infrastructures. Given that the domestic market is quite small, private investment in gas exports are indispensable for Bolivia.

The exploration efforts of the oil companies in the mid 1990s were principally aimed at satisfying export commitments for natural gas to Brazil. Nonetheless, the size of the new discoveries far exceeded the Brazilian market's absorption capacity, which opened new business opportunities for private companies and for the government.

The abundance of reserves created the need for a natural gas market diversification and industrialization strategy for the government. This strategy rested on two principal pillars. The first pillar targets the Southern Cone, where Bolivia hopes to maintain natural gas exports to Brazil and Argentina and, at the same time, become the center for energy integration projects related to natural gas in the sub-region (adding value to its exports—to the extent possible—through developing power plants and a petrochemicals industry). The second pillar targets North America but requires new infrastructure as well as access to a port on the Pacific Ocean. A difficult choice must be made between the port of Mejillones in northern Chile and the port of Ilo in southern Peru.

The enormous newly discovered volume of natural gas has encouraged private companies to pursue new projects. Beyond the increase in exports to Brazil and Argentina, companies have sought to develop several other projects. The most ambitious of them is a project to export gas to Mexico and California, which would require the building of a gas pipeline to the Pacific Coast, a liquification plant, and supplementary installations at the shipping port, as well as the corresponding marine fleet and the construction of a regasification facility at the port of destination. The project's total investment (including investments at the markets of destination) is estimated at US$6 billion, one-third of which would be used in Bolivia and in the selected port on the Pacific.

In July 2001, the Pacific LNG consortium was established to carry out this project. But the Bolivian population's resistance to exporting natural gas through Chile and uncertainty resulting from changes in the laws for the sector caused the project to be suspended.

In late 2003, a popular uprising in opposition to the gas exportation project led to a change of government. In April 2004, then-President Carlos Mesa proposed changes to the Hydrocarbons Act (increased taxes, renewed production and trade activities for YPFB, alternatives for industrializing natural gas, etc.), and also proposed a referendum through which the citizens could express their opinion on the advisability of the reform to the law and the conditions for exporting natural gas.

The referendum took place on July 18, 2004, with a majority voting in favor of the government's proposals. The results provide a very significant illustration of the people's expectations. Following the pattern for the region, where domestic oil companies have taken on a major role, Bolivians said "yes" to the proposal to "re-establish" YPFB. Table 5 provides the results of the referendum.

In institutional terms, the new Hydrocarbons Act, inspired by what was decided in the referendum, aims to have the public sector play a leading role in the industry's operations. In practice, the Hydrocarbons Act seeks to consolidate the current activities of YPFB in relation to administering contracts and supervising private companies that operate in the sector. It also seeks to strengthen YPFB's operating capacity, so that it will participate in all activities of the sector's chain of production.

Without public funds, the new YPFB will need to form alliances with companies willing to advance initial investment funds and guarantee the financing of gas development projects. Those would primarily be government-owned oil companies, above all Petrobrás, and companies with access to markets in the same region (such as Repsol-YPF in Argentina). It is up to the government to build these alliances, by providing conditions of legal and contractual stability.

With respect to exploration and production (upstream) activities, the law provides that YPFB will receive blocks both in traditional areas and in areas classified as border zones. According to Supreme Decree No. 28467, in a term of three years YPFB will start exploiting these areas, using its own resources, or will find a company with whom to contract their exploitation. As for refining and marketing (downstream) activities, in order to effectively implement a price control policy and at the same time make the necessary investments in refineries, the new YPFB will have to satisfactorily conclude the negotiations opened with Petrobrás.

From a fiscal point of view, the referendum was used as a basis for the new Hydrocarbons Act, whose objective is to increase the government's share in oil revenue

Table 5. Results of the June 2004 Referendum

1)	Revoke the existing Hydrocarbons Act (Law No. 1689).	**87%**
2)	Recover hydrocarbons at the wellhead.	**92%**
3)	Grant YPFB a more important role.	**87%**
4)	Use natural gas as a tool to obtain a sovereign outlet to the Pacific Ocean.	**55%**
5)	Export natural gas based on a policy that first covers the needs of the domestic market, industrialize natural gas, charge a tax/royalty of 50%, and principally allocate the funds to education, health, roads, and jobs.	**62%**

Source: Developed by the author.

through a combination of royalties and taxes. An important aspect of this new law is the introduction of the Direct Tax on Hydrocarbons, which uses gross production as its tax base.

The new law changes the tax regimen, reverting to a tax system on production. The law eliminates the distinction between new and existing fields and introduces the IDH, equal to 32 percent of the value of production (technically, this tax is a royalty). Adding the IDH to royalties, one arrives at the 50 percent tax rate on production established by the referendum. Nonetheless, since the companies are also subject to taxes under the general regimen and since the IDH cannot be credited against taxes in Bolivia or abroad, the impact on the sector is slightly higher than 50 percent (Table 6).

The fact that taxation on production amounts to 50 percent and that taxes also need to be paid under the general regimen makes Bolivia, a landlocked country with a very small domestic market, one of the world's most burdensome tax systems for hydrocarbons, which compromises the potential to develop the industry. As a result, even with increased taxation on the sector, revenue collections could diminish due to a fall in production. That would adversely affect the sustainability of public finances and possibilities for improving public services. This adverse effect has been felt over the past two years, given that the initiative to unilaterally modify contracts has created legal uncertainty, reduced investment in the sector, and caused reserves and production capacity to stagnate.

One of the elements of the new law that deserves greater attention is the introduction of greater transparency in the collection and distribution of revenue. From the point of view of social consensus, it is very important that both the payments made by companies on the various hydrocarbons taxes as well as the accounts of YPFB (and their distribution or pre-set allocation) be as transparent as possible. Bolivia could decide to join the Extractive Industries Transparency Initiative, which is based on the principle that public and private companies should declare their income and the payments they make to the central government, which, in turn, should report the distribution of revenue received, all of which should take place in an open process with the participation of civil society.

Table 6. Taxes under Law 3058 (Exploration and Exploitation)

Type of Tax/Royalties	*Existing Fields*	*New Fields*
Departmental Royalties	12%	12%
YPFB Participation – General Treasury	6%	6%
Direct Tax on Hydrocarbons	32%	32%
Subtotal	**50%**	**50%**
Corporate Income Tax (25%)	Yes	Yes
Tax on Remittances sent Abroad (12.5%)	Yes	Yes
Surtax (25%)	Yes	Yes
Total Taxes	**50% + other taxes**	**50%+ other taxes**

Source: Developed by the author based on Law No. 3058.

The new law also provides that companies must adapt their contracts to the models partially defined in the law itself. In addition, it increases YPFB's involvement in the sector's operations. In practice, the concessions system is being superceded by a system of contracts based on remunerations for services. It is worth noting that the law has little flexibility to respond to changes in international market conditions and does not include a clear treatment of minor and marginal fields (marginal fields are important for domestic supplies). There is only one clause of note in relation to these fields, which requires regulations.

Mandatory adaptation of contracts is not advisable as a way to proceed if the country wishes to attract investments, given the legal uncertainty it introduces. There are examples of countries in the region that have succeeded in modifying their tax regimens and in having companies migrate to new contractual formulas. This is the case in Peru, which created a framework of incentives to facilitate the voluntary migration of companies to the new contractual framework. Otherwise, companies would be tempted to resort to an international arbitration process, the cost of which would be high for Bolivia.

Given new oil prices and the growing concern of governments over the need to enhance their energy security, it is important that Bolivia negotiate access to the markets of neighboring countries where it can expand its exports, along with new terms and business alliances that respond to the new objectives for the sector. Until these negotiations are completed, uncertainty will continue delaying investments, which are important for maintaining production for the domestic market and for fulfilling export commitments, above all with Brazil. Exports of natural gas to Brazil commenced in 1999 and have increased from an average of 5.7 million cubic meters per day (million m^3/d) in 2000 to 24 million m^3/d in July 2005 (Figure 4).

Though the Brazilian gas market has not grown as expected, the payments received by Bolivia have been covered by the take-or-pay clauses of the export agree-

Figure 4. Gas Exports to Brazil – Mutún (in millions of m^3/d)

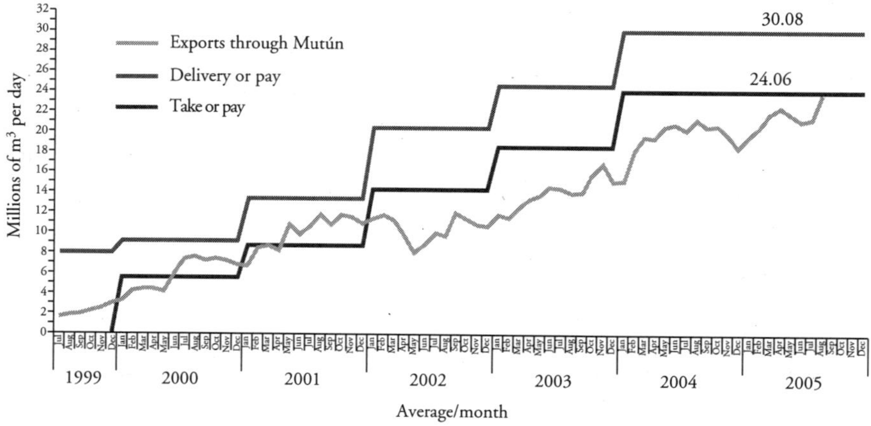

Source: Superintendencia de hidrocarburos, www.superhid.gov.bo.

ment. This situation should change this year, when the exported volume approximates the transportation capacity of the gas pipeline (30 million m^3/d).

The future growth of the Brazilian and Argentine markets and, in particular, the price that Bolivia will attain on future exports, is uncertain. In 2004, Argentina and Bolivia signed a preliminary agreement to build a 700-kilometer gas pipeline that will transport 20 million m^3/d to northern Argentina. The project has Repsol YPF as its principal interested party, but the prognosis is uncertain, since insecurity regarding prices and investments for exploration and production continues.

Legal instability and a lack of regulations have reinforced the idea that Bolivia is, for now, a high-risk country for undertaking hydrocarbons projects, (especially mega-projects, such as exports of natural gas). In this context, it is quite likely that for the next two or three years, Bolivia will manage to attract only enough investment to maintain production at current levels and will not be able to monetize the proven reserves in their true magnitude. It will be necessary to wait until the policies translate into an appropriate regulation of the law and until sufficient time has passed to regain the confidence of investors and gas purchasers.

One of the first projects the country would profit from considering is sub-regional integration, in particular interconnection of the sub-region's gas transportation pipe systems, which cover the reserves of Argentina, Peru, and Brazil. This project is of vital importance, since it would allow Bolivia to increase its exports and possibly obtain better gas prices than those prevailing on exports to markets outside of the region.

Increased Tax Collections and Ever More Frequent Pre-Set Allocations of Revenue

In the short term, the tax regimen introduced by the new law is increasing tax revenue. A significant part of the reduction in the fiscal deficit seen in 2005 is due to the introduction of this law. Nonetheless, these improvements need to be understood in the context of an intensified fiscal decentralization process. Without question, this process would be most productive if based on oil revenue. There is no disputing that. In this regard, it is very important to seek transparent, participatory mechanisms that ensure the payment and effective distribution of revenue to civil society and the people of the different regions.

Figure 5 presents the distribution in 2006 of expected revenue from the IDH and its possible allocation. It should be noted that a large part of the IDH is allocated by law to subnational governments and there is great pressure to use these funds on projects at that level. Under these conditions, an equivalent expansion of spending is most likely unavoidable; this undermines this tax's potential to correct the fiscal deficit in the medium term.

Fiscal decentralization in Bolivia is similar to what has taken place in other countries in the region and—as seen in those examples—creates serious administrative problems. In the Andean countries, there is a trend toward decentralizing the management of oil revenue and decreasing the central government's share in that rev-

Figure 5. Distribution of Revenue from the Direct Tax on Hydrocarbons (IDH), 2006

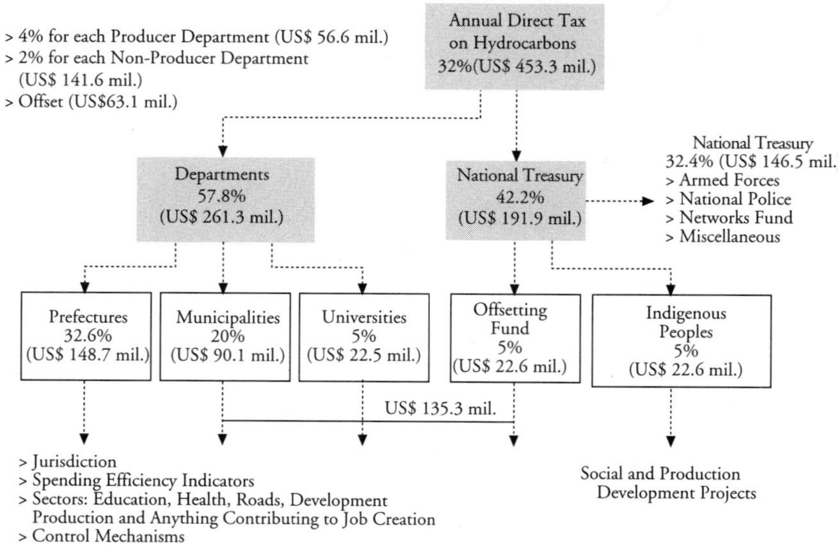

Source: Ministry of Finance

enue. In Bolivia, the central government's revenue decreased from 77 percent to 68 percent between 1998 and 2002, and this trend has accelerated in recent years.

The ESMAP study[5] on the distribution of oil revenue in the Andean countries was unable to establish the efficiency and effectiveness in Bolivia of the different subnational entities' use of funds generated by the refining and marketing of hydrocarbons. All it could conclude was that this revenue was probably administered in the same manner as the rest of the funds. In this regard, criticisms of the municipal administrations are, in general, equally applicable to this case. They are:

(i) Under-implementation of the budget (UDAPE estimates it at 50 percent).
(ii) Weak institutional development due to technical and administrative deficiencies, lack of compatibility of annual plans and programs with budgets, political interference on municipal councils, high turnover of personnel, and lack of transparency in administrative processes.
(iii) Inadequate design of instruments, manifested in laws, regulations, and procedures, and inflexible, complex administrative procedures.

The distribution of revenue favors the regions of Santa Cruz and Tarija, which are also the regions with the greatest per capita income. Legal measures are in place, however, to offset regional revenue. Among these are budget mechanisms designed to modulate transfers of additional funds to the departments, thereby increasing the funds received by regions not directly benefited by oil royalties. It is advisable to determine how the new government can moderate these tensions in coordination with the new regional governments.

Refining and Marketing (Downstream) Activities and Subsidies of LPG and Diesel

Although the natural gas reserves discovered are plentiful and are accompanied by reserves of condensates, the growing domestic demand for diesel oil and LPG makes it necessary to invest in the refining and marketing sector. Similarly, it is indispensable to correct the price distortions that affect the behavior of energy demand. The policy of subsidizing diesel has translated into an increased internal demand for this product, which is vital for transportation, the agricultural sector, and small industry. Since these sectors consume high volumes that are subject to contraband, they are forced to take recourse in costly imports.

Table 7 presents a comparison of gasoline and diesel prices in several different Latin American countries between December 2004 and January 2005.

In order to reduce fuel subsidies, the Mesa administration decided in late 2004 to increase prices, as follows:

(i) A 10 percent increase in the price of gasoline;
(ii) An initial 23 percent increase in the price of diesel, which, after the unrest in Santa Cruz, was reduced by 6 percent (the price of diesel, a fuel that Bolivia imports, went from 3.23 bolivianos/liter to 3.96 and, after the unrest, to 3.74); and
(iii) Prices on LPG, which covers almost 80 percent of domestic market needs, were unchanged. This level of subsidies keeps contraband from being eliminated and creates difficulties for building new networked distribution systems for natural gas.

Table 7. Gasoline and Diesel Oil Prices (December 2004–January 2005)

Dollars/Liter	*Gasoline*	*Diesel*
Argentina	0.57	0.54
Paraguay	0.57	0.52
Peru	0.81	0.73
Brazil	0.84	0.60
Chile	0.81	0.53
Uruguay	1.00	0.67
Bolivia – prior to the Dec. 2004 increase	0.43	0.42
Bolivia – following the Dec. 2004 increase	0.47	0.46

LPG prices in Bolivia were not affected by the change and are still much lower than the Mont-Belvieu import-export reference prices used throughout the region as of mid 2005 (Figure 6). These price differences have increased with the rise of the reference price on oil to current levels of more than US$60 a barrel. Such a difference has encouraged more contraband with neighboring countries. While the countries in the region have reduced differences between their domestic prices and import parity prices, the gap continues to widen in Bolivia.

Hydrocarbon producer countries have been discussing the possibility of bringing domestic prices in line with those of the external market and to redistribute the bonanza of price increases among the greatest possible number of their citizens in the most direct manner. Although revenue obtained in Bolivia does not yet correspond to the country's gas reserves potential, its fuel pricing policy and the social impact thereof has attracted the attention of many analysts. A 2005 article[6] discusses the potential incidence of policies promoting domestic consumption of natural gas. In general, such policies would benefit the population given the lower relative price of this product compared with other energy sources, its abundance and its compatibility with sustainable development (it is less polluting). Nonetheless, the social and economic characteristics of the population must be taken into account—a large rural population, low income levels, nearly free alternative energy sources (firewood and guano), and other fuels competing on the market (LPG, gasoline, etc.)—together with the substantial initial investment needed for natural gas distribution pipe systems. Accordingly, the impact of a policy to promote domestic natural gas consumption would be less than expected. Therefore, the benefits and costs of natural gas consumption should be weighed, along with its possible effect on the composition of the energy matrix. The principal conclusions of this article are:

Figure 6. Costs and Prices of LPG
(US$/million BTUs)

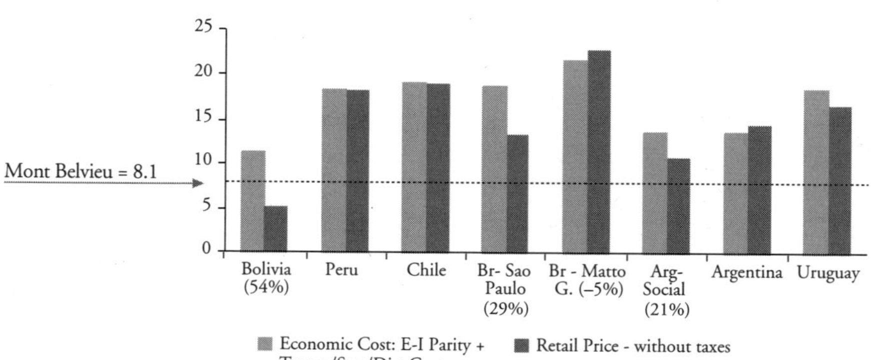

i) In the short term, a price-reduction policy on natural gas earmarked for residential consumption would be of greater benefit to high-income families, since they are the ones who consume that fuel. If such a policy is coupled with suppression of the subsidy on LPG, the effects would be even more regressive, since low natural gas prices benefit high-income families and high LPG prices negatively affect high-income, middle-income, and, in a lesser proportion, low-income families.
ii) In the medium term, when families are given an opportunity to change their portfolio of durable goods, many of them opt to acquire those that use natural gas. Nonetheless, a bias in favor of high-income families is still present, since they are the ones now using electrical home appliances.

It is evident that, given the average energy consumption in urban and rural households, subsidies provide a greater benefit to the rich in urban zones than to the poor in rural zones (Figure 7).

An adjustment to immediately align domestic prices with neighboring countries is not viable. Only strong governments have been capable of eliminating fuel subsidies through an immediate adjustment. But in Bolivia, these conditions do not appear to be present, despite the huge electoral support for the new president. For the people, "cheap gas" means "cheap LPG," because the natural gas distributed to households does not meet residential energy needs in the mid- to low-income strata.

The low degree of industrialization, coupled with fuel subsidies, in particular on LPG, are a serious limitation for developing natural gas distribution over pipe systems. Recent studies in Bolivia and Peru evaluating the penetration of natural gas pipe systems reveal the importance of gas and oil policies based on real economic prices. In Peru, where the price of this fuel is high, gas transportation and distribution pipe systems were successfully developed in certain regions with relatively small markets. In contrast, Bolivia maintains price subsidies. The installation of 260,000 residential connections (equivalent to 25 percent of the demand for LPG) within five years,

Figure 7. Incidence of Subsidies on the Population

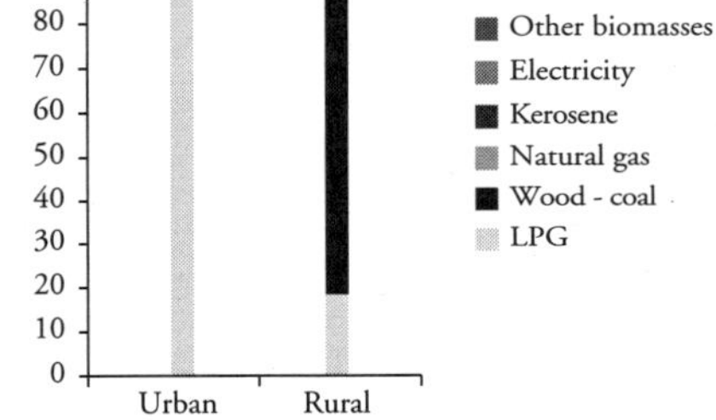

Source: Mayorga Alba, E. "Presentation on the Bolivia Hydrocarbon Sector to the World Bank 2005 Energy Week." Internal document.

announced by the former government, appears to be unattainable. In the past two years, YPFB increased the number of connections from 15,000 to 45,000. There is much left to do, and success depends in large measure on a reduction in the current subsidies.

The problems of the gas market are mirrored in the market for liquid hydrocarbons. Figures 8 and 9, based on information from YPFB, demonstrate projections for demand and production of oil and liquid petroleum gas (LPG).

The gap between crude oil needs and production volumes is growing. This gap has been handled through the production of condensates and the importation of petroleum by-products (particularly diesel). To avoid an accelerated growth of diesel imports, new investments are needed both for exploration and technological innovation at the refineries (installation of catalytic cracking plants), aimed at improving the output of the products demanded on the domestic market. As part of the reform, it would be advisable to target the YPFB refineries, already small and inefficient, for modernization investments, which could be obtained from the private strategic partners acquiring the refineries.

Figure 8. Supply and Demand for Oil

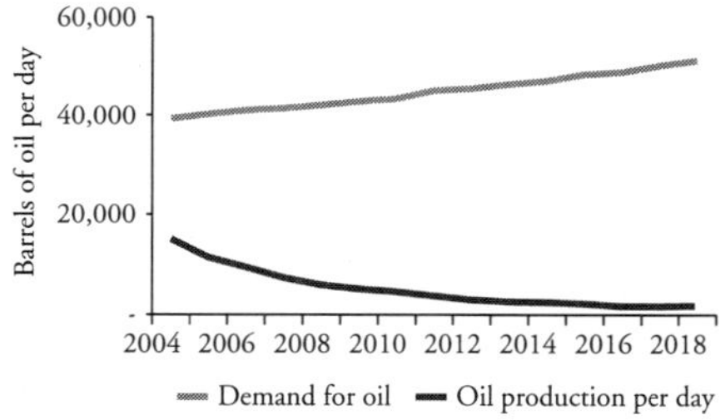

Source: YPFB.

Figure 9. Supply and Demand for LPG

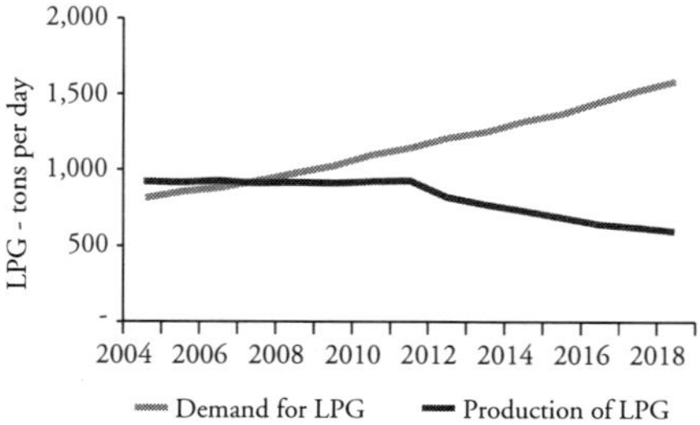

Source: YPFB.

In the late 1990s, Petrobrás signed agreements to assume control over these refineries, but for a various reasons, it has not yet modernized them. This needs to change. In a context of continued price controls, YPFB needs to control the sector and, at the same time, obtain financial investments that would allow diesel production to increase. YPFB also needs to regain a certain degree of balance between production and demand for middle distillates.

In the case of LPG, there is a certain balance at present between supply and demand, but future scheduled production is not expected to cover growth in demand. Accordingly, new investments are also needed for this product.

Furthermore, the sufficiency of domestic market supplies, whether of natural gas or liquids and LPG, depends on continual new investments in transportation, especially considering that many of the country's gas pipelines, oil pipelines, and logistic facilities are reaching their capacity.

A change in fuel pricing policies is clearly a difficult task for the new government. On the one hand, it is unacceptable to principally benefit the upper-income classes, continue allowing contraband, and compromise the investments needed to develop the future domestic market. On the other hand, it appears quite difficult to conceive of a one-step price adjustment that succeeds in bringing domestic prices closer to international parity values without buffer mechanisms for the poor.

One solution could be to drastically reduce fuel subsidies by adopting consumer prices close to those of neighboring countries (to eliminate contraband) while introducing a regimen of direct monetary transfers for poor families. Direct transfer mechanisms work well in other countries that have had to adopt similar drastic measures at some point, such as in Ecuador during dollarization. Another solution—although this presents logistic problems for the sector—consists of introducing small LPG cylinders, marketed with a subsidy at certain sites close to the homes of the targeted poor. Such a measure would be accompanied by an increase in fuel prices to realistic levels.

Industrialization Proposals

One of the most important aspirations in Bolivia is the industrialization of gas, defined as an increase of added value in the chain of production for this product. The first industrialization option proposed is an increase in the quantity of gas processed at the production field to obtain LPG and liquid hydrocarbons. The second option is gas phase polymerization to produce high-value products, such as middle distillates with a low sulfur content, in large demand on the markets of the OECD countries.

The possibility of raising the recovery rate of LPG and natural gasoline from output gas depends in large measure on the price received by the operator for these products. A second option, building gas-to-liquid (GTL) conversion plants, also opens the possibility of reducing dependency on imported diesel. This proposal to commence the domestic industrialization of natural gas has benefited from new technologies, made more economical by the high price of oil and new environmental standards. In order to facilitate these investments, it would be necessary to adjust the price of gas at the wellhead, perhaps in relation to the price of products obtained at the consumer (end) level. Successful implementation of this strategy also would require assurance of the necessary legal and fiscal stability. Although operating costs and yields are known for GTL plants being run on an experimental basis in different countries, it is important that YPFB estimate the risks that still exist for developing GTL plants on an industrial scale and evaluate existing conditions. That information should be shared with an investor capable of providing the necessary technology and willing to contribute the capital required.

For more than three years, companies with gas reserves have been studying the potential for GTL technologies in Bolivia. Along these lines, in 2002 Repsol-YPF Bolivia and Syntroleum signed two memoranda of understanding to carry out joint pre-engineering evaluations for the development of two GTL conversion plants: the first with a capacity of 13,500 bpd to produce diesel for the domestic market, and the second with a capacity of 90,000 bpd to manufacture exportable products. Both plants would use the process registered by Syntroleum. This assessment would analyze aspects of planning, construction, ownership, and operation of the plants. In late 2003, Ivanhoe Energy joined with Repsol and Syntroleum to contribute its experience in designing the GTL plant for the project. Ivanhoe would select the place, the transportation logistics, and the project's economic profile. According to projections, this work would take three years. It would be a good idea to identify under what conditions this project, which has benefited from the high price of oil, can be reconsidered, with participation from the new YPFB.

Another proposal comes from Rentech, a technology development company that, working with GTL Bolivia, has started working on plans that would use the gas from the Itau field managed by Total as their raw material. The proposed plant has a capacity of 10,000 bpd. In June 2003, Rentech reported that it was about to commence the FEED (Front End Engineering and Design).

Among the ideas proposed for industrializing gas in the medium and long term is the development of a petrochemical project. Different concepts have been proposed in association with Brazilian companies, but decisions will only be made after the government announces its energy policy. The decision to develop a petrochemical complex on the border between Bolivia and Brazil, fed with Bolivian natural gas, also needs to be made and is closely linked to decisions regarding upstream developments and the refining sector.

Recommendations

The new government is faced with the task of making important decisions to ensure the hydrocarbon sector operates smoothly, improves its efficiency and tries to maximize its contribution to the economy. Proposals to nationalize the industry could have harmful effects, delay investments and hold back the much needed development of the gas industry. By making commitments to obtaining the best advantages for the country, which requires preserving the interest of investors, the new government will be most strongly positioned to capture the increased revenue that gas can contribute and, in practice, start to reverse the status quo.

Law 3058 does not provide a legal framework conducive to attracting investments (both public and private) needed by the hydrocarbons sector that would enable Bolivia to receive greater benefits from this natural resource. The current law does not provide flexibility to facilitate investments in the sector's various projects. It lacks a clear plan and might place YPFB in charge of problems that are beyond its technical and financial capacity. It would be best to replace this law with another one that more clearly defines roles and provides flexibility for the sector's contractual and fiscal framework. Providing for a higher governmental share in hydrocarbons revenue than was provided by the former law (1689) is fully compatible with a modern law. Along these lines, it would be very reasonable if, for example, the additional collection were obtained through taxes directly or indirectly linked to earnings, through a combination of parameters such as the area of the field, production costs, and prices for gas and petroleum products in the various markets. If Law 3058 is not modified (which is very difficult politically), the second best option would be to develop regulations for the law that would improve its execution.

In summary, the decisions that this report recommends making are:

- Complete development of the legal and regulatory framework for the sector and, to the extent possible, uphold the mandate resulting from the referendum. In effect, this requires differentiating projects based on a calculation of the desired governmental share in revenue while showing signs of flexibility and realism.
- In preparing the new regulations and formulating the new contract model, it is advisable for the government to maintain a balanced position. Forced migration would have negative repercussions on legal stability and would discourage investments for a long time. There is always a risk of having to deal with litigations in international courts, which would seriously complicate the development of the sector in the short and medium term.
- To the extent possible, oversight of the gas and oil industry should be implemented with adequate instruments funded through net project income, after costs, to minimize the impact of high royalties.
- Maintain an open mindset that makes it possible to expand the use of natural gas both domestically and in new export markets, especially the markets closest to Bolivia, which could grow within the regional integration framework.
- Develop mechanisms to ensure transparency in the management of oil revenue and make information available on the different payments made by the companies, as well as the destination of these funds. Bolivia could join the Extractive Industries Transparency Initiative.[7]

- Establish a realistic business plan for YPFB, consistent with its technical and financial capacities, that includes only projects deemed to be priorities and proven to be feasible.
- The negotiations with Petrobrás and Repsol-YPF to access the markets of neighboring countries are of vital importance, since they deal with core projects (modernization of the refineries and GTL, in addition to upstream projects and the transportation of gas to Argentina) and provide a model for negotiations with other companies.
- In lieu of raising fuel subsidies, attempt to replace them with better targeted subsidies or transfers to the lowest-income sectors. Indiscriminate subsidies create costly distortions in the demand for energy (for example, importation of diesel and contraband) and are not the best way of redistributing revenue. To the extent possible, when prices are set, political intervention should be limited. Prices should be based on economic criteria that reorient demand and encourage investment in the necessary infrastructures.
- Redefine policy for allocating hydrocarbons revenue, as well as control mechanisms that ensure an efficient use of these funds at the subnational level.

Bibliography

Banco Central de Bolivia. 1998–2004. Estadísticas: Exportaciones de Petróleo.

Congreso Nacional de Bolivia. May 2005. Ley No. 3058. (Nueva) "Ley de Hidrocarbons."

Congreso Nacional de Bolivia. Abril 1996. Ley No. 1689. "Ley de Hidrocarbons."

ESMAP (Programa de Asistencia a la Gestión del Sector de la Energía). 2005. "Estudio compartivo sobre la distribución de la renta petrolera en Bolivia, Colombia, Ecuador y Perú," Documento 304/05. BIRF/World Bank. Washington, DC.

Iniciativa para La Transparencia en las Industrias Extractivas. Página de Internet <http://www.eitransparency.org

Medinaceli, Mauricio and Silvana Zeballos. 2005. "Consumo de gas natural en el mercado interno: ¿beneficia a los pobres? – Un Análisis de micro-simulación" en Estudios Económicos y Sociales: Estadísticas & Análisis. Instituto Nacional de Estadística (INE).

Ministerio de Hacienda. 2006. Distribución de la recaudación del IDH.

Wood Mackenzie. 2002. "Global Oil and Gas Risks and Rewards – Upstream Economics Benchmarking Study." – Estudio del periodo 2000-2001. Wood Mackenzie. Scotland.

Yacimiento Petrolíferos y Fiscales Bolivianos (YPFB). 1999-2004. Datos de Reservas Certificadas de Gas Natural y Petróleo/Condensado. YPFB.

Endnotes

1. Without including the investments made in pipeline transportation.
2. Law No. 3058.
3. Pursuant to Law 3058, YPFB is authorized, among other functions, to act as an aggregator, seller, and administrator in the natural gas export contracts it signs, where the Bolivian state is the agent.
4. See, ESMAP (2005).
5. Ibid.
6. Medinaceli and Zeballos (2005).
7. For more information on this initiative, see www.eitransparency.org.

7

Economic Growth through Productivity and Competitiveness

William Tyler and Michael Goldberg

Summary

Economic growth is vital to alleviate poverty, create a significant number of jobs, and improve Bolivians' standard of living. Given fiscal restrictions on the public sector and the limited size of the domestic market, a growth strategy would have to be based on private sector investment and on the expansion of exports. Under the current policies and circumstances, Bolivia is not likely to attain the levels of investment and productivity necessary for the economy to grow at a sustainable rate of 5 percent per year. The business environment is not attractive for investors, who, under different circumstances, would be in a position to continue introducing new technologies, training, and job opportunities. In order to develop public policy that would improve those conditions, the government could examine the following: (i) property rights, institutions, and the rule of law; (ii) the business regulation environment; and (iii) regulations for the labor market. This chapter analyzes those issues and provides suggestions on how the government can address them.

I. Background: The Problem is Slow Growth

Recent Economic Development. While most countries have seen economic progress and increased per capita income over the past 50 years, Bolivia's has declined. Per capita income levels were lower in 2000 than in 1950. The average Bolivian today is nearly 1 percent poorer in real terms than 50 years ago.[1] In contrast, real per capita income in Chile and Brazil increased by 200 and 350 percent, respectively. The challenge for the new Bolivian government is to break out of this prolonged stagnation. Growth is necessary in order to reduce poverty and improve standards of living, and only through greater investment can the economy grow.

The country's prolonged stagnation has been interrupted by spurts of intermittent growth (driven by export booms), followed by collapses and crisis, exacerbated, in turn, by poor economic management. Hyperinflation in the 1980s was followed by successful stabilization and structural reforms. The result was economic growth and greater total productivity in the 1990s. It appeared as if Bolivia was emerging from its prolonged economic stagnation. Nonetheless, in the late 1990s, a series of shocks decelerated economic growth, undermining enthusiasm for the reforms. Some of the reforms were even partially reverted, owing to a wave of social conflicts.

Informality. One of the most prominent characteristics of the Bolivian economy is its high degree of informality. Though it is impossible to precisely determine the exact percentage of the economy that is informal, the most commonly cited estimates agree that it is more than 67 percent of GDP. This places Bolivia among the economies with the highest levels of informality in the world. Figure 1 compares Bolivia to other Latin American countries. The average rate of informality in the region is approximately 40 percent. Out of 104 countries covered by the 2004 World Economic Forum (WEF) competitiveness survey, Bolivia placed 101 due to its high informality.[2] Among manufacturing companies, 90 percent are informal, and 72 percent of the manufacturing labor force is employed by the informal sector.[3]

One of the reasons for the prevalence of the informal economy is the cost of doing business. Frequently, companies fail to register, so that they can avoid paying

Figure 1. Informality

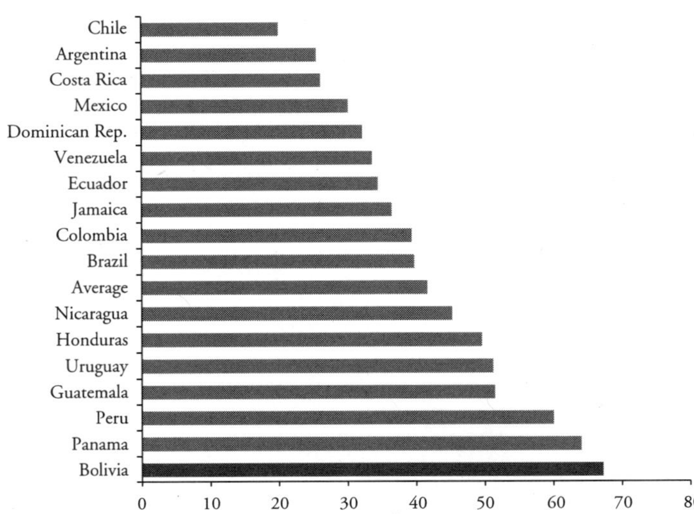

Source: Djankov and Mcliesh (2004).

taxes, get around business regulations and inspections, and minimize the effects of labor regulations. In addition, contraband is widespread. A recent investigation has concluded that growth of the informal sector is associated with lower growth overall.[4] The factors tending to exacerbate this situation are high taxes and social security contributions, labor market restrictions, burdensome regulations, and weak public institutions. Informal companies can avoid these obstacles, and that allows them to survive economically. The financial costs of formality can be substantial, while its benefits are much less clear.

Productivity is inversely proportional to the extent of informality. Informal companies are unable to receive credit on favorable terms or take advantage of institutions that facilitate business growth and allow for economies of scale. Informal companies generally, but not always, operate in non-tradable sectors such as services, transportation, and construction. The informal sector is competitive within Bolivia because it can avoid taxes, but it is incapable of competing in the global economy.

Company Size, Productivity, and Employment. In Bolivia and throughout the world, productivity is related to the size of a business. Large companies tend to be more productive than small ones (Table 1). Small companies have fewer fixed assets, use outdated technology, and are less efficient. Micro-enterprises provide 83 percent of jobs, but only produce 26 percent of GDP. This means that large companies have a labor productivity 25 times greater than micro-enterprise. Accordingly, for each one percent of the labor force that would be moved, through new investments, from micro-enterprise to large companies, there would be a 7 percent potential gain in productivity.

Micro and small companies are the great job creators in Bolivia. Large companies (those with 50 or more employees, which consist of approximately one thousand production units), for their part, produce 65 percent of GDP, though they only employ 9 percent of workers. Table 1 also includes informal companies, but their

Table 1. Contribution of Companies to the GDP and to Jobs, by Size, 1999

Company Size (number of employees)	*Product (% of the GDP)*	*Jobs (thousands)*	*Jobs (% of the total)*	*Productivity (in thousands of bolivianos)*
Micro (1–9)	25.5	2,984	83.1	4
Small (10–19)	2.7	170	4.7	8
Medium (20–49)	3.3	123	3.4	13
Large (>50)	65.3	312	8.7	101
Adjustment	3.2			
Total	100	3,589	100	13

Source: World Bank (2004), p. 23, based on data from the Assistant Ministry of Micro-enterprise. See also CONAPE (2005), p. 58.

Note: Productivity is measured as GDP per employee. The 1999 GDP was 48.156 billion bolivianos.

productivity may be under-represented, especially for small and micro production units. In 2002, the formal sector provided jobs for only 31 percent of urban employed labor, much of which was in government jobs. The rest of the jobs were in the informal sector, including domestic service[5].

Modernization and growth of small companies would increase productivity and competitiveness. Micro-enterprises share the same problems as the rest of the private sector, but most of those problems are more severe for them since they lack access to financial services and cannot achieve economies of scale. Addressing these problems would improve the investment environment and increase growth.

Preconditions for Economic Growth. Three preconditions should underpin a strategy to achieve significant growth. First, given the public sector's fiscal restrictions, the private sector holds the key to future growth. Private investment is the driving force behind the economy. Second, given the small size of Bolivia's domestic market, economic growth will be dictated by the country's success in expanding its exports and integrating into the global economy. Third, the informal sector cannot be expected to lead the country's growth, even though it does have a role to play. Since its productivity is low and profitability is often based on illegal activities, a transition is needed toward new practices that will reduce the size of the informal sector.

Improve the Investment Environment. Under present policies and circumstances, it is not likely that Bolivia will attract investment and achieve productivity in the amounts required to promote economic growth at an annual rate of 4.5 to 5 percent. The business environment is not attractive for investors, whether domestic or foreign. However, public policy can change this, and should be a high priority for the government.

Measured by international standards, Bolivia's competitiveness is very low (Table 2). Bolivia ranks 95 out of 104 countries in the survey, and is the least competitive economy in Latin America.[6]

Bolivia's low ratings in the category of institutions illustrate the difficulties faced by investors in exercising their property rights and dealing with the regulatory environment. Along similar lines, the low rating in efficiency of the labor market reflects the impact of the current Labor Act. The low score for physical infrastructure reflects not only problems with ground transportation (that is, a lack of paved roads) but also the organization of frequent roadblocks.

Two recent World Bank reports have analyzed Bolivia's competitiveness and investment environment.[7] In the four-year period between the two studies, several recommendations formulated in the first report were applied by the authorities. There were major improvements in areas such as customs and the tax administration, the registration of businesses and the roads system. Despite these achievements, Bolivia continues to be a difficult place for business. Difficulties persist with respect to property rights, application of the rule of law, and the regulatory environment.[8]

Table 2. Global Competitiveness Index, 2004
(Rankings among 104 Countries)

Elements of Competitiveness	*Bolivia*	*Argentina*	*Brazil*	*Chile*	*Colombia*	*Mexico*	*Peru*	*Botswana*
General Index	95	75	49	29	69	60	76	58
Institutions	101	83	55	29	67	69	81	38
Physical Infrastructure	100	59	58	34	73	62	81	51
Macroeconomic Stability	93	39	96	15	67	36	55	13
Security	72	79	75	39	103	83	84	40
Basic Human Capital	76	38	61	28	52	45	69	90
Advanced Human Capital	85	49	48	41	70	66	72	71
Efficiency of the Market for Goods	99	88	48	29	73	76	85	47
Efficiency of the Labor Market	103	97	52	26	73	69	79	22
Efficiency of the Financial Market	95	89	33	19	55	65	48	46
Availability of Technology	97	59	42	32	71	52	75	65
Openness and Size of the Market	97	80	28	59	55	27	77	71
Business Sophistication	98	65	27	32	53	51	73	80
Innovation	101	85	32	49	62	59	94	57

Source: WEF, *Global Competitiveness Index 2004.*

II. Issues of Competitiveness and the Investment Environment

Property Rights, Institutions, and the Rule of Law

Property rights, the rule of law, and the institutions that ensure their application are the foundations for a market economy. Potential investors assess how well property rights are defined by law, how protected they are by the judicial system, and whether the judicial system is immune to pressure from the government, citizens, and companies.

The World Bank's *Country Economic Memorandum* (2005) for Bolivia argues that growth is limited by uncertainty regarding property rights, contractual performance, and application of the rule of law. Most international surveys on these issues give Bolivia a poor rating. In a subjective survey focused only on property rights, the WEF ranked Bolivia 103 out of 104 countries.[9]

In general terms, Bolivia performs poorly when compared with other Latin America countries or the world in terms of independence of the judiciary, efficiency of the legal framework, and protection of intellectual property (Annex Figure A1). Table 3 examines three indicators for a sample of countries from Latin America and elsewhere:

(a) the WEF Contracts and Law Index (which reflects judicial independence, protection of property rights, neutrality of the government in the award of contracts and prevalence of organized crime); (b) the WEF Corruption Index focuses on the prevalence of extortion by government officials in trade transactions, public services, and the tax administration; and (c) Transparency International's Corruption Perceptions Index.

Bolivia also rates poorly in the corruption index, although businesspeople have reported recent improvements, particularly in customs service and tax administration. The country also rates poorly in terms of the time and number of procedures needed to enforce a contract (Annex, Table A2).

The Regulatory Environment for Trade

Bolivia has few price controls and the trade regime is relatively open, but the regulatory environment continues to be burdensome. Despite some recent improvements, there is still room for progress. In a country that needs new investment in the formal sector, starting and registering a company is very expensive and time consuming. Though procedures have been simplified on several fronts, they are still costly. Registering a business takes 15 steps, including the preparation of a notarized,

Table 3. Ranking in the Public Institutions Index, Selected Countries, 2004

Country	*WEF Contracts and Law Index*[a]	*WEF Corruption Index*[b]	*Transparency International's Corruption Perceptions Index*[c]
Norway	3	12	8
Singapore	10	7	5
Hong Kong (China)	13	4	16
Chile	27	15	20
Taiwan (China)	31	24	35
Malaysia	33	44	39
Botswana	35	47	31
South Korea	43	50	47
Slovenia	47	23	31
Mauritius	50	82	54
Brazil	53	45	59
Peru	86	39	67
Bolivia	**94**	**74**	**122**
Argentina	100	55	108
Paraguay	101	90	140
Venezuela	104	69	114

Sources: WEF, *Global Competitiveness Report, 2004–2005*; Transparency International, Corruption Perceptions Index, 2004.

Note: a. and b. Components of the WEF Competitiveness Growth Index of 104 countries.

c. Transparency International's Corruption Perceptions Index, which rates 145 countries.

publicly recorded document and its application, publication of that document, the submission of an affidavit of opening of accounts, tax registration, municipal approval, and registration with public or semi-public institutions (including FUNDEMPRESA, the Chamber of Commerce, the national health system, the pension system, and the Ministry of Labor).

The average time to open a business in 2005 (50 days) is better than in 2000, when it involved 18 entities (each of which had several procedures) and an average of 66 days.[10] Bolivia is not among the worst countries in Latin America, but is quite far from the best (Chile), and is behind with respect to other, more developed countries (Table 4 presents comparable country information for 2004). [11] There are no *a priori* reasons why Bolivia cannot emulate leaders such as Australia, Hong Kong, and Singapore. Table 4 illustrates that many countries find minimum capital requirements unnecessary for establishing new companies.

The main problem for informal companies is not that of opening and registering a company, but of making it work. In addition to a loss of competitive advantages, since formal companies must pay taxes and comply with the Labor Act, the country requires licenses and permits. Complying with government procedures consumes time and is costly, as the formal companies frequently complain. The burdensome

Table 4. Starting a Company, Selected Countries, 2005

Country/Region	*Number of Procedures*	*Time (days)*	*Cost (% of per capita GNI)*	*Minimum (% of per capita GNI)*
Argentina	15	32	13.4	6.6
Australia	2	2	1.9	—
Bolivia	**15**	**50**	**154.8**	**4.1**
Botswana	11	108	10.9	—
Brazil	17	152	10.1	—
Chile	9	27	10.3	—
Colombia	12	43	25.3	—
Ecuador	14	69	38.1	9.2
Hong Kong (China)	5	11	3.4	—
South Korea	12	22	15.2	308.8
Malaysia	9	30	20.9	—
Mexico	9	58	15.6	13.9
Nicaragua	8	42	139.1	—
Paraguay	17	74	147.8	—
Peru	10	102	38	—
Singapore	6	6	1.1	—
Taiwan (China)	8	48	6	216.3
Venezuela	13	116	15.7	—
LAC Countries	11.4	63	56.2	24.1
OECD Countries	6.5	19.5	6.8	41

Source: Doing Business in 2005 (World Bank and IFC, 2005).

requirements of the tax administration also reflect this situation. In terms of the overall regulatory burden, Bolivia rates poorly (Annex Figure A2).

In addition to regulatory problems, more difficulties are faced when a company becomes involved in international trade. Despite the trade liberalization policy introduced in the mid 1980s and the recent customs reforms, cross-border trade in Bolivia is among the most complicated in the world. Bolivia ranks 116 among 155 countries for this indicator (Annex, Table A3). Among Latin American countries, only Haiti and Honduras rank lower. For exports, nine different documents and 15 different signatures are needed, and executing it all requires an average of 43 days. Imports demand even more authorizations and time. It comes as no surprise that contraband is a problem in the country.

It is also difficult to close a company. Closing a company was not legally possibly until a few years ago, and is still difficult and costly. There is no effective bankruptcy law, which complicates the credit extension by the financial system, since it is difficult for a lender to liquidate the assets of a failed company.

Labor Market Regulations

Regulations for the labor market in Bolivia appear to hinder competitiveness and discourage investment. Costs other than wages for employees covered by the Labor Code (a minority of workers in the country) are 54 percent of the amount of wages paid.[12] The biggest distortion in the labor market comes from the Labor Act. Enacted in 1939, it is similar to the Labor Act of other Latin American countries, all of which were modeled after the Italian labor laws of the era. This law establishes inflexible rules, prohibits part time or temporary employment, mandates special benefits, and restricts the free choice of employers and employees. Ironically, the people who ought to benefit from labor laws often find themselves at a disadvantage. In general, this law tends to excessively increase labor costs for formal employers and reduces the flexibility of the labor market.

Termination costs, in terms of weeks of wages, are modest in comparison with some countries, such as Brazil or Colombia, but larger than average for Latin America.[13] The 2004 WEF survey reports that Bolivia enjoys relative flexibility in determining wages (27 out of 104 countries) and in the ease of hiring foreign workers (32 out of 104). These relatively high ratings suggest that the Labor Act is being effectively eluded by local companies. Labor relations at companies are generally reported to be good.

III. Policy Options and Choices

The World Bank *Country Economic Memorandum* (2005) recommends that the government's policy ensure the application of clear, stable, appropriate rules for the private sector. This is indispensable to attract the investment needed (18-22 percent of

GDP) in order to improve productivity (an annual increase in total productivity of 1.5 percent to 2.0 percent) and generate enough growth and jobs, with the ultimate objective of reducing poverty. For that, it is recommended that the government's economic team lead a program to improve the regulatory environment. Table 5, at the end of the chapter, summarizes the suggested measures, which are briefly described in the following paragraphs, together with a corresponding provisional scheduling.

General Policy Environment

The principal areas that significantly impede competitiveness and the investment environment include macroeconomic policies, trade policies, and policies on the financial market, credit, infrastructure, and human capital. Deepening trade liberalization is important to improve the overall investment environment and increase competitiveness and growth. The promotion of exports, among other things, would include measures to: (i) advance on the Free Trade Agreement with the United States; (ii) simplify the tax administration for exports, for example, by improving the efficiency of the Temporary Importation Regime for Exports Development (RITEX); (iii) make the use of free trade zones effective (as analyzed below); (iv) improve quality controls by reactivating the National Quality Control Council (CONOCAL) and supporting the National Standards, Measurements, Accreditation, and Certification System (SNMAC); and (v) improve export promotion and marketing by strengthening the SNMAC and the Bolivian Promotion Center (CEPROBOL). In addition, contraband should be fought more effectively through increased customs and police control.

Strengthen Property Rights, Institutions, and the Rule of Law

The new government is facing major decisions on preexisting contracts with the private sector related to investments in hydrocarbons and water concessions. The reaction of the national and international business community will depend upon how the government responds in this process. Other steps that could be taken immediately as part of a long-term strategy to strengthen property rights include:

- *Adopt a bankruptcy act.* Having a modern bankruptcy act would help overcome several problems. A multi-ministerial commission, comprised by the Central Bank and the Sector Regulation System (*Sistema de Regulación Sectoral*—SIRESE), could be a first step in that direction.
- *Modernize property registration.* Using computer technology, the current number of steps (seven), time, and cost required to register property could be reduced. It would be advisable for the government to evaluate how to better use electronic procedures and a "single window," that is, a central location for managing the procedures and authorizations of the various public entities.

Simplify and Improve the Regulatory Environment

There is an urgent need to simplify and improve the business environment in order to encourage investment in production. In this regard, the following measures could be considered:

- *Simplify the steps required to register and start up a company.* Extend the simplified procedures approved by the municipality of La Paz to other regions; make greater use of "one-stop establishments" for the registration of companies; and eliminate the minimum capital requirement for starting up a business.
- *Optimize and simplify licenses and authorizations for companies.* First, decide whether the authorization in question is essential or not. In many cases, the need is questionable, and the requirement serves only to open the way for government officials to exert their power and obtain informal payments.
- *Reform the procedures for export and import transactions.* The current procedures are excessive. Simplifying regulations that affect international trade transactions would reduce business costs, encouraging formality and reducing contraband.
- *Make better use of e-government.* E-government methods can increase the government's efficiency, reduce the cost of compliance for companies, increase transparency, and remove opportunities for corruption.
- *Improve tax administration.* There are problems in the way the tax system is administered, including difficulties in paying taxes[14] and the abuse of the system by tax administrators and inspectors for bribery. At the same time, Bolivia rates poorly on the international scale in terms of irregular tax payments.[15] The tax administration's requirements particularly penalize small companies. A simplified system could be designed and implemented for small businesses, following international examples. Such a system could include simplified registration requirements, e-government techniques, and estimated tax payments based on sales.
- *Track business indicators and make that information available.* A list of indicators, alongside comparisons with other countries, should be reviewed once every six months, with clear responsibilities and specific goals to ensure improvements are made. Indicators could include some of the 24 that the World Bank supervises around the world in relation to ten issues: (i) creating a company; (ii) handling licenses; (iii) hiring and terminating workers; (iv) registering property; (v) obtaining credit; (vi) protecting investors; (vii) paying taxes; (viii) promoting cross-border trade; (ix) contractual performance; and (x) closing a business.
- *Reduce informality.* Reducing informality requires lowering disincentives to formality, including the cost of preparing business taxes resulting from a burdensome regulatory and tax administration environment. The government could consider allowing businesses to register or operate even if they do not meet all the requirements.

- *Consolidate improvements in the regulatory agencies.* Prior administrations succeeded in establishing regulatory agencies under the SIRESE system. Assurance of the SIRESE system's independence, operating efficiency, and overall effectiveness should continue to be an important objective for the government.

Simplify Labor Regulations

It would be useful to enact a more modern labor code. However, this is a very sensitive matter, and there is no consensus to change the existing legislation. Interim steps to promote the reform could include the following measures:

- *Establish a commission* to study the impact of the current labor laws, examine alternatives, and prepare legislative reform proposals.
- *Disseminate more information.* To support potential legislative changes, greater public awareness and understanding is important. Accordingly, information needs to be provided to the communications media, trade unions, schools, and community groups.
- *Liberalize the application of labor regulations in the modernized free-trade zones.* One way to evaluate the impact of labor regulations reform would be to use the free-trade zones. The free-trade zone of El Alto has been such a "laboratory"—and a very important one—to introduce changes. If, as expected, a series of more liberal labor regulations is seen to be more conducive to encouraging investment and creating jobs, its demonstrative effect could help generate a consensus to reform existing labor law.

Production Chains and Clusters

In recent years the government has taken important steps to promote production clusters or chains. This approach seeks to collectively identify restrictions on the growth of a given sector. With more efficient markets, clusters could develop naturally, but the government has to provide additional support in order to improve the efficiency of the market. Encouraged by the experiences of other countries, the government has developed plans to support production chains. Through the Bolivian Productivity and Competitiveness System (*Sistema Boliviano de Productividad y Competitividad*—SBPC), the government has sought to promote strategic alliances of the public and private sectors, together with the academic community, that would formulate and implement policies aimed at increasing productivity and competitiveness. Close to 20 production chains have been selected. This initiative has great potential to attract new investments and can be strengthened in several ways:

- *Simplify procedures.* Although the program for developing clusters has gotten off to a good start, the elaborate, burdensome package of government requirements could be simplified.

- *Place emphasis on private sector participation and media communications.* The program has the potential to develop public/private sector partnerships that could propose broad-based changes to the sector in question to increase production, investment, productivity, and competitiveness. An open dialogue is essential to identify and resolve government-imposed restrictions and problems noted by the productive sector.
- *Place greater emphasis on resolving problems in the sector.* The *Bolivian Competitiveness Agreements* have identified common problems such as judicial insecurity, transportation problems, and contraband; but little progress has been made at the sectoral level to respond to these specific problems. By placing more emphasis on these areas, the government will position itself to achieve measurable results that increase the competitiveness of private investment.

Free-Trade Zones

Over the past 30 years, many governments around the world have promoted free trade zones or export processing zones (EPZs) as a means to develop manufactured goods, jobs, investment, and, in some cases, promote regional development. Based on information from the International Labor Organization (ILO), there are approximately 1,200 EPZs in the world, and they employ more than 27 million workers.[16] Of the larger countries in the western hemisphere, only Bolivia and Brazil do not have EPZs. These zones are characterized by certain features, such as: (a) tax exemptions on imports; (b) exemption from indirect taxes on exports; (c) a simplification and reduction of domestic economic regulations and procedures applicable to the EPZs; (d) freedom to engage in capital and trade transactions with entities abroad; and (e) a promised stability in economic policy. Obviously, there can be major variations in these characteristics. In some countries, access to communications and other infrastructure services is a principal attraction.

In general, the experience with EPZs has varied. Some countries have been very successful with EPZs, increasing exports, creating jobs, attracting investment, and creating links to their economies as a whole. China, Costa Rica, Mexico, Senegal, Ireland, Taiwan, and the Republic of Korea have all had successful experiences. The lessons and difficulties are many, as noted in Box 1. One lesson in particular stands out: the establishment of an EPZ is no substitute for good economic policies.[17]

The Bolivian government has established seven special economic zones or free-trade zones. The majority were originally intended to be trade zones, and only two were designated as industrial zones. None of them is functioning at present.

Given that the free-trade zones are not operating as originally intended, some reconsideration of them would appear appropriate. Such reconsideration could include:

- *Reorganization of the Industrial Free-Trade Zone located in El Alto into a modern Export Processing Zone (EPZ).* To achieve this goal, it would be necessary to reexamine the current tax administration. In principle, the payment of all

Box 1. Lessons from International Experience with EPZs.

The varied experience with EPZs allows some lessons to be learnt, among them:

- *EPZs cannot replace an adequate policy and framework of incentives for exports.* Having an appropriate policy framework for increasing exports is indispensable for the satisfactory performance and growth of exports. Even in a distorted policy environment, however, EPZs can limit some of the adverse effects of such policies. Though clearly a second best option, EPZs can provide demonstrative effects and some results, until a policy environment free of distortions and imperfections can be introduced.
- *Public sector EPZs can be expensive.* Experience shows that EPZs administered by the private sector work better. When preference is given to private sector ownership and management of EPZs, utilities and other infrastructure should not be subsidized.
- *EPZs work best in countries where there is a reasonably solid industrial base.* In those countries, linkages have more of an effect.
- *The fiscal costs of EPZs should be carefully analyzed.* As a general principle, EPZs and the companies that operate in them should pay taxes. Any fiscal incentive other than on trade-related taxes should be brief in duration.
- *The clustering of economies attained through EPZs can be a major attraction for investment.* Companies located in EPZs—and actually in any other industrial park—often benefit from easy access to infrastructure services and fewer barriers for entry.

See Madani (1999), Braga (2001) and Tyler (2003).

indirect taxes should be suspended or, if their collection is unavoidable, there should be prompt reimbursement for the production and sale of exports. In general, the best international practices for management of EPZs should be followed and adapted to Bolivia's circumstances. As suggested above, labor regulations should be more flexible. In organizing EPZs, foreign direct investment should be sought, and measures should be taken to facilitate the registration of companies and their establishment within the EPZs.

- *Consider extending the El Alto EPZ to other free-trade zones.* Depending upon the success of the future El Alto EPZ, the government could try to extend the model. In any transformation, special attention will have to be paid to restricting contraband activities.

Table 5. Suggested Policy Measures, in Chronological Order

Policy Category	*Chronology* *First 100 days*	*First year (2006)*	*Five-Year Period*
A. General Policy Environment			
Macroeconomic policies	• Announce the continuation of the macroeconomic stability program, including the fiscal adjustment.	• Continue sustainable macro-economic policies with external and monetary fiscal stability.	• Continue sustainable macroeconomic policies consistent with fiscal, external and monetary stability.
Trade policies	• Announce an intention to continue seeking open trade policies, including the consolidation of a series of existing particularities.	• Actions could include: simplification of the RITEX regime; improvement of tax refund mechanisms; timely issuance of CEDEIM certificates; reactivation of CONOCAL; and institutional improvements for SNMAC and SEPROBOL.	• Continue improving institutions and the tax administration framework with respect to trade.
	• Define a national anti-contraband program.	• Implement the anti-contraband program.	• Implement the anti-contraband program.
B. Strengthen Property Rights and the Rule of Law			
	• Announce vigorous support for the principles of the rule of law, including the performance of contracts.	• Adherence of the government to law, protection of property rights, and enforcement of the law.	• Adherence of the government to law, protection of property rights, and enforcement of the law.
	• Draft a new bankruptcy act.	• Submit the bankruptcy act to the legislature.	• Implement the new bankruptcy act.
	• Develop a plan for more extensive judicial reform.	• Implement judicial reform.	• Implement judicial reform.
	• Announce a plan for modernizing property registration.	• Implement a program to modernize property registration, making use of e-government procedures.	

C. Simplify and Improve the Regulatory Environment			
	• Simplify the steps to register and start up a company, including simplification of procedures, use of "one-stop establishments," and elimination of the minimum capital requirement.	• Monitor the registration of companies, introducing the appropriate improvements.	• Monitor the registration of companies, introducing the appropriate improvements.
	• Develop a plan to rationalize and simplify licensing and authorizations for companies.	• Implement a plan to rationalize the licensing of companies.	• Monitor the progress of the company licensing program, making any corrections needed.
	• Develop a program to reform procedures for import and export transactions.	• Implement a program of procedural reform for exports and imports.	
	• Develop a plan to introduce e-government methods.	• Implement an e-government program.	• Continue to implement the e-government program.
	• Develop a program to reform the tax administration, including better tax enforcement, less corruption, and special provisions for small and medium enterprise.	• Implement the tax reform program.	• Continue implementing the reform program of the tax administration, with additional improvements.
	• Announce a program to track and publish information on business indicators.	• Implement a program on business indicators.	• Continue implementing the business indicators program.
	• Announce a program to reduce economic informality.	• Implement a program to reduce economic informality.	• Continue implementing the program to reduce economic informality.
	• Announce an intention to consolidate progress in the formation and operation of regulatory agencies under the SIRESE system.	• Schedule meetings aimed at ensuring the independence of the agencies and improve their operational efficiency.	• Continue strengthening the SIRESE system.

(*Table continues on the following page.*)

Table 5. Suggested Policy Measures, in Chronological Order *(continued)*

Policy Category	*Chronology* *First 100 days*	*First year (2006)*	*Five-Year Period*
D. Simplify Labor Regulations			
	• Establish a Presidential Commission for the Reform of the Labor Market.	• Prepare legislative proposals, and host a public debate on labor reform.	• Submit the bills on labor reform to the legislature.
	• Commence a public awareness and educational campaign on labor market issues.	• Conduct a public relations campaign on labor market issues.	
	• Liberalize the application of labor regulations in the modernized Free-Trade Zones.		
E. Develop Production Chains and Clusters			
	• Announce an intention to strengthen and continue the existing Production Chains program.	• Simplify program development procedures.	• Continue the implementation.
	• Emphasize participation and communication with the private sector.	• Continue the implementation.	
	• Emphasize the resolution of problems at the sector level, with emphasis on common problems (e.g., judicial security, property rights, transportation, contraband, etc.).	• Continue the implementation.	
F. Develop the Free-Trade Zones			
	• Announce an intention to modernize the program for developing Free-Trade Zones.	• Reorganization of the Industrial Free-Trade Zone in El Alto as a modern Export Processing Zone (EPZ); review the legislation, if necessary.	• Extend El Alto's EPZ model to other Free-Trade Zones.

Bibliography

Braga, Hélson. 2001. *"A Experiência Internacional com Zonas Francas: Um Novo Desafio para o Brasil."* Paper presented at a UERG seminar, October 23.

CONAPE. 2005. Interviews, La Paz, Bolivia.

Djankov, Simeon, and Caralee Mcliesh. 2003. *Doing Business in 2004: Understanding Regulation.* Washington, DC: Oxford University Press and World Bank.

Gomes, Victor, Samuel de Abreau Pessoa, and Fernando Veloso. 2003. "*Evolução de Produtividade Total dos Fatores na Economia Brasileira: Uma Análise Comparativa.*" Economics Working Papers (Ensaios Economicos da EPGE) 483, Graduate School of Economics, Getulio Vargas Foundation (Brazil). Brasila.

International Labor Organization (ILO). 2003. Database on Export Processing Zones. Geneva: ILO.

Kreidler Guillaux, Walter. 2005. "*Plan Bolivia Competitiva,*" Ministry of Economic Development, Working Paper, La Paz, Bolivia.

Loayza, Norman. 1996. "The Economics of the Informal Sector: A Simple Model and Some Empirical Evidence from Latin America." *Carnegie-Rochester Conference Series on Public Policy* 45: 1996, pp. 129–162.

Loza, Gabriel. 2004. "*Estrategia de Crecimiento y Empleo—Bolivia,*" UDPE/Ministry of Economic Development, Working Document DT 01/04.

Madani, Dorsati. 1999. "A Review of the Role and Impact of Export Processing Zones," World Bank, Policy Research Working Paper No. 2238, November.

Monterry Arce, Javier. 2004. "El Sector Informal Urbano en Bolivia." INE working paper.

Sala-i-Martin, Xavier and Elsa Artadi. 2004. "The Global Competitiveness Index," in World Economic Forum (2004).

Schneider, Friedrich. 2002. "Size and Measurement of the Informal Economy in 110 Countries around the World." Department of Economics, Johannes Kepler University, July 17.

Transparency International. 2004. "Corruption Perceptions Index," London, England.

Tyler, William. 2004. "Strengthening the Policy Environment for Export Growth in Brazil." Versão Preliminar (UERG, Outubri 2003), published as Part III of World Bank, *Brazil: Trade Policies to Improve Efficiency, Increase Growth and Reduce Poverty.* Report No. 24285-BR (Washington: World Bank, 2004).

World Bank. 2001. *Bolivia: Restricciones y oportunidades macroeconómicas para mayor crecimiento. Evaluación del clima de inversión.* Washington DC: World Bank.

———. 2004. *Bolivia: Challenges in the Corporate and Banking Sectors.* Report prepared in the Latin America and the Caribbean Region. January.

———. 2005. "Bolivia Country Economic Memorandum: Policies to Improve Growth and Employment," Report No. 32233-BO. Washington DC: World Bank.

World Bank and IFC. 2005. *Doing Business in 2005.* Washington, DC: World Bank.

———. 2006. *Doing Business in 2006.* Washington, DC: World Bank.

World Economic Forum. 2004. *The Global Competitveness Report, 2004–2005.* New York: Palgrave Macmillan.

———. 2005. *The Global Competitiveness Report 2005–2006.*, New York: Palgrave Macmillan, p. 566.

ANNEX

Annex Figure A1. Property Rights and Judicial Performance Indicators

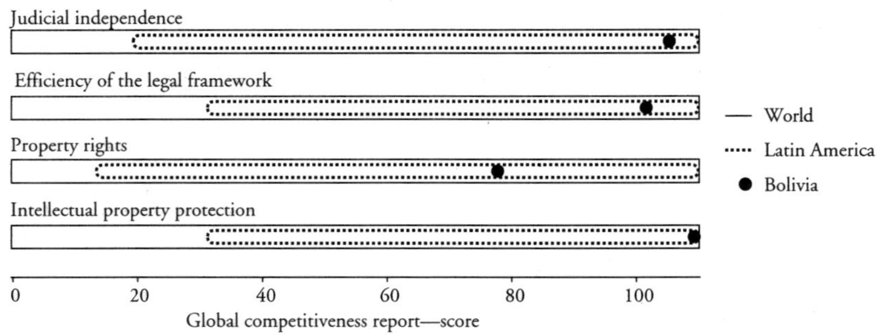

Source: WEF, *Global Competitiveness Report 2003–2004.*

Annex Figure A2. Public Regulation Indicators

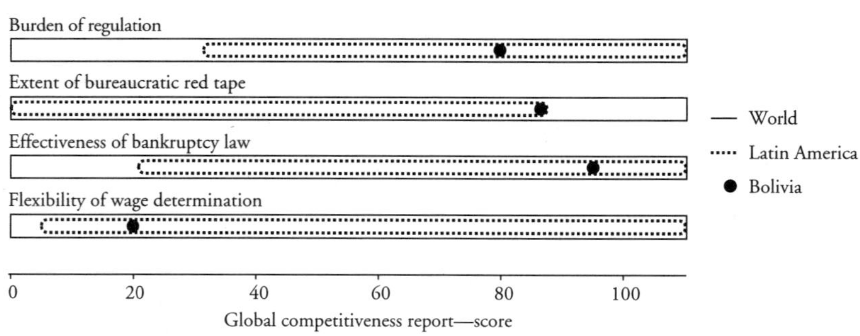

Source: WEF, *Global Competitiveness Report 2003–2004.*

Annex Table A1. Annual Growth of Per Capita GDP for Selected Countries, 1950–2000
(expressed as a %)

Developing Countries		*Industrialized Countries*	
Argentina	1.1	Australia	2.1
Bolivia	**–0.02**	Austria	3.5
Brazil	3.0	Belgium	2.8
Chile	2.2	Canada	2.2
Colombia	1.8	Denmark	2.3
Costa Rica	1.7	France	2.9
Ecuador	1.5	Ireland	3.7
Mexico	2.2	Italy	3.4
Paraguay	1.4	Japan	4.9
Peru	1.2	Portugal	4.0
Uruguay	1.2	Norway	2.9
Venezuela	0.2	Spain	3.8
Korea, Rep. of	5.4	Sweden	2.3
Taiwan	6.3	United Kingdom	2.2
Thailand	3.9	United States	2.3

Source: Calculated using data from the Penn World Tables, provided by Samuel Pessoa. (For a description of the panel of data, see Gomes, Pessoa, and Veloso, 2004).

Annex Table A2. Contractual Performance, Selected Countries, 2005

Country/ Region	*Number of Procedures*	*Time (Days)*	*Cost (% of debt)*
Argentina	33	520	15.0
Australia	11	157	14.4
Bolivia	**47**	**591**	**10.6**
Botswana	26	154	24.8
Brazil	24	546	15.5
Chile	28	305	10.4
Colombia	25	241	25.5
Ecuador	37	363	18.6
Hong Kong (China)	51	909	256.8
Korea, Rep. of	31	300	20.2
Malaysia	28	434	8.7
Mexico	28	340	34.6
Nicaragua	34	440	95.9
Paraguay	28	410	29.3
Peru	17	367	8.6
Singapore	37	421	20.0
Taiwan (China)	28	410	124.4
Venezuela	36	461	23.3
LAC Countries	39.5	432.1	17.7
OECD Countries	33	520	15.0

Source: World Bank and IFC, *Doing Business in 2005* (2005).

Annex Table A3. Trade Across International Borders, Selected Countries, 2005

	Exports			*Imports*			
Country/ Region	***No. of Forms***	***No. of Signatures***	***No. of Days***	***No. of Forms***	***No. of Signatures***	***No. of Days***	***Trade Rating***
Argentina	6	6	23	7	9	30	43
Bolivia	**9**	**15**	**43**	**6**	**16**	**49**	**116**
Brazil	7	8	39	14	16	43	107
Chile	6	7	23	8	8	24	42
Colombia	6	7	34	11	12	48	81
Costa Rica	7	8	36	13	8	42	88
Haiti	8	20	58	9	35	60	124
Honduras	7	17	34	15	21	46	119
Jamaica	5	7	20	8	7	26	37
Mexico	6	4	18	8	11	26	39
Nicaragua	6	4	38	7	5	38	50
Paraguay	9	7	34	13	11	31	97
Peru	8	10	24	13	13	31	93
Botswana	6	7	37	9	10	42	66
Korea, Rep. of	5	3	12	8	5	12	16
Mauritius	5	4	16	7	4	16	20
Malaysia	6	3	20	12	5	22	36
Singapore	5	2	6	2	8	8	6
LAC Countries	7	7	30	10	11	37	
African Countries	8	18	48	12	29	60	
Asian Countries	6	7	25	10	8	27	
OECD Countries	5	3	12	6	3	14	

Source: World Bank and IFC, *Doing Business in 2005* (2005).

Note: General rating on the ease of trade across borders of 155 countries rated. Number of days is the average.

Endnotes

1. See Annex Table A.1 for a comparison of growth in per capita income in selected countries during the period of 1950-2000.
2. WEF (2004, p. 540).
3. World Bank (2001, p. 125).
4. Loayza (1996), Schneider (2002).
5. Monterrey (2004).
6. Haiti was omitted from the 2004 survey.
7. This chapter is fundamentally based on two World Bank reports (2001 and 2005), especially the 2005 report.
8. Botswana, a country very rich in natural resources, provides useful data for Bolivia. In 2004, its per capita income was slightly higher than that of Uruguay or Brazil. Today, Botswana has improved its competitiveness in a number of important areas and has grown in large measure because of its institutional adaptability, a stable macroeconomic policy environment, and market efficiency. These factors have helped Botswana overcome disadvantages associated with unskilled human capital, the its small market size, and unsophisticated businesses.
9. WEF (2004, p. 524).
10. World Bank and IFC (2006), World Bank (2001, p. 12).
11. According to the World Bank survey entitled *Doing Business in 2006*, Bolivia ranked 134 out of 155 countries, one of the lowest positions in the world.
12. World Bank (2001).
13. World Bank (2005).
14. According to *Doing Business in 2006,* Bolivia ranked 146 among 155 countries in terms of facilitating the payment of taxes.
15. World Bank (2005, p. 33).
16. ILO (2003).
17. For example, see Madani (1999, p. 108).

8

Rural Development

David Tuchschneider
with the collaboration of Vivian Viaña

Summary

Fifty years after Agrarian Reform, approximately eight out of every ten rural inhabitants of Bolivia live below the poverty line. Poverty's persistence indicates that substantial change is needed in rural development policies. Experience on a global level over the last half century has confirmed that there are only three ways to reduce rural poverty: (i) creating jobs in rural areas through competitive insertion of rural producers (agricultural and non-agricultural) into dynamic markets; (ii) facilitating insertion into the labor market through migration; and (iii) improving the income of the poorest and most vulnerable groups through direct monetary transfers. In Bolivia, the repertoire of policies to meet these objectives requires a careful differentiation, based on the specific characteristics of the rural population, their material and agro-climatic conditions, their skills and assets, and their lifestyles, all of which, in turn, must be spatially differentiated over Bolivian territory. Trends in the composition of rural income already show the increasing role of non-agricultural activities and migration in lifestyle strategies. The most successful policies, therefore, will be the ones that reinforce these strategies and improve the capacities of migrants and the assets of producers. In addition to the agro-climatic limitations faced by most farmers in the highlands, the shortage of public goods and services in the rural areas continues to be the principal factor limiting improved income in the medium and long term, both within agriculture and elsewhere. Bolivia has taken major steps to reverse anti-rural bias in the allocation of government funds and the provision of public goods and services through the Popular Participation Act and other related reforms. Yet rural public investment is still inefficient due to the low synergy between sector-based and territorial-based policies. Results can be improved through a re-orientation of government spending coupled with institutional changes that influence the behavior of public and private stakeholders at the three levels of government. Even so, the greatest challenge for rural development is to improve opportunities outside the rural area through sustained, inclusive economic growth that creates urban and non-agricultural jobs and increases access to foreign markets.

I. Introduction

A quick look at poverty and development indicators for rural areas demonstrates the need for a major shift in the policies applied over the past 50 years. This document first provides a summary diagnostic of trends in the sector and discusses the principal challenges facing the country. It then proposes measures to improve the assets and opportunities of rural inhabitants. The changes proposed in this document are complemented by the notes on specific sectors included in this volume but emphasize policy differentiation based on peasant and indigenous lifestyle strategies, institutional contexts, available natural resources, and territory. Much of what is needed to achieve a good interfacing of sectors and players at different territorial levels is already present, but without sufficient effectiveness due to a lack of clarity in assigning responsibilities and a low correlation between the incentives and functions of the sub-national levels of government. There are also fiscal restrictions. Therefore, many of the proposed measures are for institutional adjustments and a re-prioritization of public expenditures rather than new programs.

Persistence of Rural Poverty[1]

More than half a century after one of the most far-reaching agrarian reforms in the history of Latin America, rural poverty in Bolivia still shows no signs of significantly decreasing. In the past decade, as part of a larger reform process, Bolivia has progressed in implementing a decentralization and participation model, which is fundamental for rural development and the fight against poverty and social exclusion. These changes have improved social indicators and local governability, but not income or consumption rates for the poor. Poverty, basic unsatisfied needs, inequality, and exclusion still characterize the situation of most Bolivians, particularly in rural areas.

According to data from early 2000, approximately eight out of every ten inhabitants in rural areas are poor and six out of every ten live in extreme poverty. Average income in the rural area is approximately US$18 per person per month,[2] that is, barely 30 percent of urban income.[3] Over the past 50 years, Bolivian society has urbanized, and the proportion of rural inhabitants has declined by almost 50 percent (Table 1). While the urban population increased in absolute terms by approximately 730 percent, the rural population has increased by only 56 percent.

While growth in the urban population was accompanied by a significant reduction in poverty, the same cannot be said for the countryside. Rural poverty is more than 30 percent higher than urban poverty.[4]

Table 1. National Population, by Geographic Area, Censuses of 1950, 1976, 1992, and 2001

Population	*1950*	*1976*	*1992*	*2001*
Bolivia	**2,704,165**	**4,613,486**	**6,420,792**	**8,274,325**
Urban Area	708,568	1,925,840	3,694,846	5,165,882
Rural Area	1,995,597	2,687,646	2,725,946	3,108,443
% Rural Area	74	58	43	38
% Urban Area	26	42	57	62

Source: INE.

Eliminating Anti-Rural Bias in Funding Allocations

With the enactment of the Popular Participation Act (*Ley de Participación Popular* - LPP), the Administrative Decentralization Act (*Ley de Descentralización Administrativa*—LDA), and the National Dialogue Act (*Ley del Diálogo Nacional*—LDN), which initiated the return of functions and funds to the municipalities and prefectures, Bolivia introduced the most extensive rural development reform since the Agrarian Reform of 1953. These laws made major changes to the spatial and social distribution of power and public funds. The enormous skew in public expenditures, which had favored the departments and cities of the "axis" (along the country's main road, specifically La Paz, Cochabamba, and Santa Cruz) was replaced by automatic transfers to municipalities and departmental governments based on population and poverty formulas, which notably improved the distribution and use of public funds.

These asymmetries started to be eliminated in 1994 with the LPP, under which shared revenue is distributed in accordance with the number of inhabitants, and the LDN, which since 2001 has distributed external debt relief funds, with an emphasis on the poorest areas (Table 2). Accordingly, in 1992, more than 96 percent of shared tax revenue reached only 45 percent of the population, concentrated in the nine departmental capitals and in El Alto, while the areas corresponding to the predominantly rural municipalities,[5] with a population weight of almost 47 percent, received only 1.7 percent of the shared revenue. The change was notable. In the period of 1994-2004 the nine capital cities and El Alto received 46 percent of the shared revenue, a percentage similar to what the predominantly rural municipalities obtained. The percentage of funds from the public debt relief plan for Highly Indebted Poor Countries (HIPC) received by Bolivia's principal cities between 2001 and 2004 was almost 24 percent, while the percentage received by predominantly rural municipalities was close to 68 percent. This means that the HIPC transfers prioritize the allocation of funds to the poorer municipalities—which are generally rural.

This represents an injection of approximately US$1 billion from the Treasury, an amount without precedent in the history of rural development.

The impact of these two laws goes beyond improvements in the distribution of tax revenue. Their emphasis on non-discretional funding allocations, using popula-

Table 2. Distribution of Shared Tax Revenue and HIPC II, by Geographic Area

	Shared Tax Revenue 1994–2004			*HIPC II Funds 2001–2004*		
Description	*Thousands of US$*	*%*	*per capita US$*	*Thousands of US$*	*%*	*per capita US$*
Capital Cities and El Alto	840,341	46	226.5	49,957	24	12.1
Predominantly Rural Municipalities	840,376	46	241.4	142,694	68	38.3
Predominantly Urban Municipalities	993,395	54	225.7	68,334	32	13.9
National Total	1,833,771	100	232.6	211,028	100	24.4

Source: Prepared by the author with information from the Ministry of Finance, INE, and UDAPE.

tion- and poverty-based formulas, ushers in an explicit equal opportunity policy, that is, an attempt to reduce inequities between rich and poor in access to public goods and services.[6]

Dynamics of the Agricultural Sector

Despite a relentless urbanization process, the agricultural sector's share in the GDP (including forestry, hunting, and fishing) has remained constant (15-16 percent) over the past 15 years. This behavior reflects not only the low growth rates of other sectors of the economy, but also the rise in commercial agriculture in the lowlands; in particular, the so-called edible oil industry. The share of industrial agricultural products (basically soybeans) in the composition of the agricultural GDP grew from 9 percent in 1989 to 20 percent in 2004. This growth partially offset losses due to the coca leaf eradication program (see Annex). The share of the rest of the sub-sectors, including traditional agricultural products, remained practically unchanged.

In short, we observe a dual tendency in agriculture. One sub-sector, devoted especially to the food production for the domestic market, is apparently stagnating. The other sub-sector, devoted to agricultural products for export, is highly dynamic and accounts for the bulk of growth in the sector. As seen in Figure 1, the only crop that has significantly increased its cultivated area is soybeans, which, as of the mid 1980s, became the base for a new agro-industrial sector.

The importance of commercial agriculture is reflected in its ties to other sectors of the economy. Trends in the manufacturing industry reflect that the only industrial sub-sector that has grown in Bolivia over the past 15 years is the foodstuff industry (Figure 2). Indeed, the expanded agricultural sector, including its links to

Figure 1. Trends in the Cultivated Surface Area of Major Crops (1985–2004)

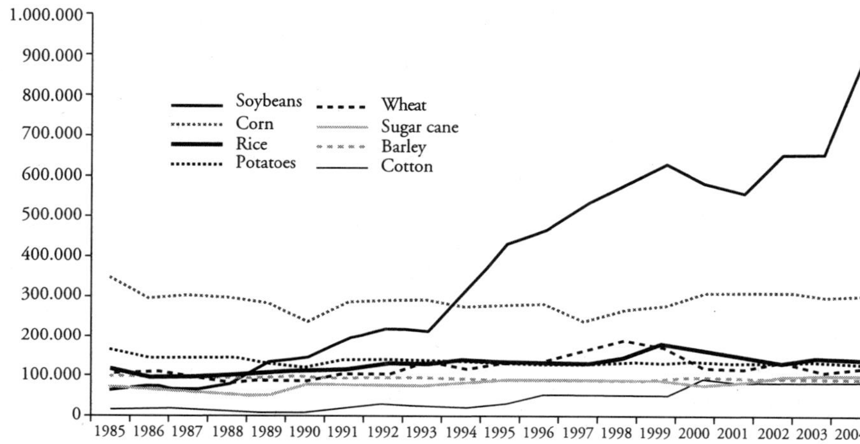

Source: INE.

Figure 2. Trends in GDP of the Manufacturing Sector, by Sub-sector (1989–2004)
(Millions of 1990 bolivianos)

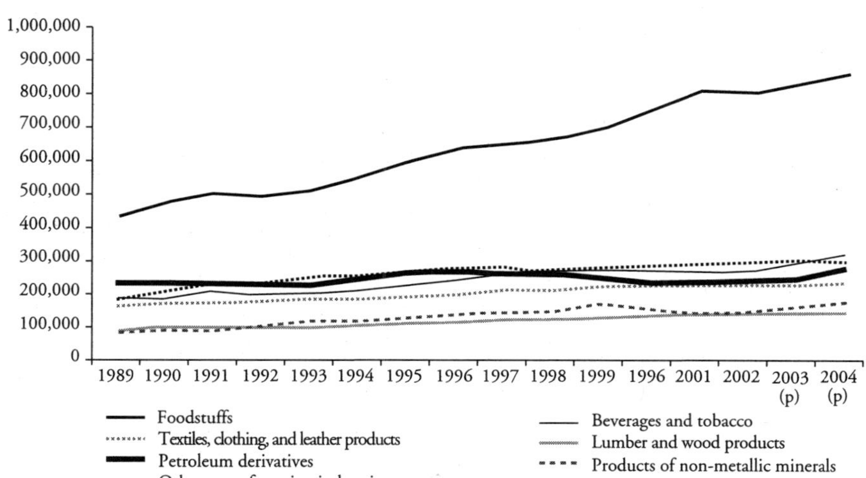

Source: INE.
(p) = projected.

agro-industry, contributes to 27 percent of GDP. This percentage would be even greater if transportation, trade, and other services directly related to agricultural and agro-industrial activities were included.

The agricultural sector plays an important role in non-traditional exports (and consequently in the generation of foreign currency reserves). In the 2000s, more than 70 percent of non-traditional exports were agricultural and forestry products. Almost 50 percent of those products, in turn, were soybeans and soybean products.[7] Moreover, growth of the edible oil industry underlies certain phenomena that are crucial for understanding current social and political dynamics, in particular, the concentration of land and a shift in the driving forces of the domestic economy to the lowlands. Though production of oil-producing crops is concentrated in mid- to large sized estates, a large number of peasant families in the lowland region, most of whom are Andean migrants and their descendents, have succeeded in joining dynamic markets. This translates into better income than the peasants had in their zones of origin. In contrast, in the highlands, only a minority of peasant families have increased their income through agricultural activities.

Policies for the Sector

In the past few decades, rural development policies in Bolivia have been fragmented, unstable, and marked by improvisation. Since 1990, a trend was reinforced of dividing the rural sector into two groups: peasants/indigenous peoples and businesspeople. Rural development policies regarding the first of these groups mainly, though not exclusively, targeted social aspects (although in practice their role was essentially political). Whereas agricultural development policies were established with businesspeople in mind, targeting production and marketing. In addition, three cross-cutting rural issues, namely land distribution, renewable natural resources, and indigenous affairs, gave rise to new agencies within the structure of the state. This irrational division and dispersion of functions held back the development and implementation of policies differentiated in accordance with the specific situations and potential of the different groups of rural producers in the highlands and lowlands.

Finally, the administrative decentralization process and popular participation reduced the jurisdiction of the central government, transferring power to the departments and municipalities, in a process still marked by overlapping responsibilities and lack of coordination among those involved. Through shifts in jurisdiction, transfers of funds, and recognition of the rights and obligations of civil society organizations, the LPP provides a basis for implementing inclusive rural development policies by linking sector-based policies to the territories' conditions and potential. For the past decade, rural development policies have focused above all on lending viability to the opportunities created by the LPA and the LDA. Given that most of the new municipalities are rural, the LPP gave an important impetus to rural development. The instruments chosen by the government to implement this reform, with strong support from the international cooperation community, were participatory planning, institutional strengthening of local governments and civil society organizations, and the provision of financial incentives for investments by the municipalities in productive infrastructure. From the start, there was concern over the sustainability of the rural municipalities, given their small tax base and almost total dependency on transfers from the central government. Therefore, the national government attempted to stimulate local growth through the provision of infrastructure and through improved access to services and assets for the rural poor.

It soon became clear that it was easier for the municipal governments to build schools, healthcare posts, and potable water systems than to provide productive infrastructure and production support services. Therefore, central government co-financing to the municipalities was attempted as a first step toward improving the supply of investments in production, by expanding the peasant development fund. This idea failed, however, due to problems of corruption. Organizations of peasant and indigenous producers soon started to express their dissatisfaction with the unkept promises of the LPP. They argued that by granting rights to Territorial Base Organizations (*Organizaciones Territoriales de Base*—OTB) over investments and public services, producers and their organizations were being marginalized from decision-making and funding offers. The second National Dialogue, which culminated with the enactment of the National Dialogue Act (2000), reflected these concerns. This law granted additional funds to the municipalities (transferring 70 percent of the funds from the second HIPC initiative), extended municipal jurisdiction to include the provision of production infrastructure and production support services to producers, and granted producer organizations the right to participate in local planning processes. In addition, it implemented the National Compensation Policy (*Política Nacional de Compensación*—PNC), which regulates the transfer of additional funds to local governments based on the same formula, through the new Production and Social Investment Fund (*Fondo de Inversión Productiva y Social*—FPS). The Second HIPC Initiative Funds and the FPS funds can both be invested in social or productive priorities, as determined by the participatory planning process.

Several governments have attempted to stimulate rural growth through Local Development Endeavors (*Esquemas de Desarrollo Local*—DEL) and a new emphasis on production chains. Recently, a Third National Dialogue was held; more than 60,000 persons participated in workshops and discussions covering all of the country's municipalities, followed by a similar process at the department level, and then a national assembly. Producer organizations dominated the discussions. Each municipality determined three priorities for production. Given the predominance of rural municipalities, most of the priorities involved agriculture and rural development. Producers sought greater support for production and basic transformation through financing for technical assistance, production infrastructure, and subsidized credit. At the municipal level, they demanded that a portion of the funds from the Second HIPC Initiative be earmarked exclusively for their needs.

Extensive poverty in rural areas demonstrates the failure of the rural development policies applied in Bolivia over the past 50 years. New policies are therefore needed that will allow rural inhabitants to overcome poverty in the coming decades. This policy shift should include the following lines of action: (i) a differentiation of policies in accordance with the lifestyle strategies of rural stakeholders, with particular emphasis on generating non-agricultural income (including migration); (ii) clarification and reinforcement of the role of the municipalities as coordinators in the provision of public goods and services for human and productive development; and (iii) the development of instruments that interface sector-based approaches with territorial approaches, focusing their interventions on the poorer and more vulnerable segments of the rural population.

II. The Principal Challenges

Ways to Overcome Poverty in the Highlands

Though rural poverty is still extremely high, there are regional variations. Significant differences in agro-ecological conditions, demographics, and social factors have a bearing on the lives of the population. Nonetheless, policies are not taking those differences into consideration. In the Andean zone (highlands and valleys), which is affected by agro-climatic limitations that increase with altitude, approximately 80 percent of the producers are caught in a vicious circle of owning ever-smaller parcels of land, the expansion of crops to zones more apt for animal husbandry, a decrease in animal fertilizer use, impoverishment of soils, and, consequently, declining yields.[8] These conditions have led to migration (temporary and permanent) to other countries, to the cities, or to other rural zones as a key family strategy. Access to land in settler-project zones in the Andean foothills and the eastern plains has provided a much-needed safety valve for Andean peasants, but these opportunities are drying up due to a shortage of land suitable for agriculture and unequal distribution of such lands. (For more information see the chapter on Land Policy).

The stagnation of the agricultural economy in the Andean region is reflected in the incomes of rural families.[9] Families derive barely more than half their income (52 percent) from agricultural activities, with subsistence agriculture still playing an important role in the highlands (28 percent) and in the valleys (19.5 percent). The relatively low monetary agricultural income is offset with the sale of one's labor, participation in other non-agricultural activities, remittances, and other income (public and private). In response to falling yields and productivity, Andean peasants find that their only way out is to diversify their income through non-agricultural activities, in the rural area or elsewhere. Nonetheless, there are major variations in total income—for example, the Gini index (which measures inequality) for the highlands (0.67) and the valleys (0.64) is significantly higher than for urban areas (0.54). In both the highlands and the valleys, the principal factor that explains the difference in income is non-agricultural activity and/or income. Briefly stated, family strategies to overcome poverty favor non-agricultural activities, but due to a lack of job opportunities outside the community, the benefits of this strategy are still limited to a relatively small portion of the population.

What role can agriculture play in the fight against poverty in the highlands? The principal goal should be focused on reducing the impact of catastrophic risks and helping peasant families break the vicious circle that leads to soil degradation and loss of productivity. In other words, the factors that create poverty need to be counteracted. This can be accomplished by promoting technologies to increase agricultural production and sound soil and water management, which would contribute to recovery of vegetation coverage and soil fertility and also increase income. Though more research is needed in this regard, many of these technologies already exist and have even been successfully applied in several highland communities.

Not all Andean peasants are caught in vicious circles of poverty. It is estimated that approximately 20 percent of them have increased their productivity and income through a better foothold in the foodstuffs markets. These markets provide most of the foodstuffs consumed in the cities, and many are linked to international markets, which demonstrates that Andean agro-ecological conditions do not place an absolute limit on competitiveness. Territorial competitiveness is concentrated in more or less well developed market niches. Of particular note are mountain-grown coffee, quinoa, and other high-Andean crops along with llama production. Therefore, support to high-Andean agriculture needs to focus on products that will help build specific territorial competitiveness based on the insertion of production into dynamic markets.

Agro-industry also plays an important role in the fight against poverty in the highlands. International experience demonstrates that chains forged through the transformation of agricultural products have a major impact on increasing income for the poorer strata, in particular, because they affect the demand for unskilled labor. The precariousness of agro-industry in the highlands comes, on the one hand, from insecurity in the supply of products, resulting from technological backwardness in agriculture (which effects quality, quantity, and the timeliness of deliveries). But it is also due to high costs, numerous bureaucratic obstacles, and legal and administrative penalties, which make the founding, growth, and formalization of companies quite difficult. Both in primary production and in transformation, limitations are also derived from shortages in other public goods and services, starting with the almost non-existent applied research, precarious markets for technical assistance and associated services, as well as the poor road infrastructure.

Though an emphasis on agriculture and the management of natural resources is fundamental, any strategy for the fight against poverty in the highlands must focus on increasing non-agricultural income. Non-agricultural income is divided into two principal areas of opportunity: rural non-agricultural activities and migration. As demonstrated by the priorities that the rural municipalities mutually formulated in the Productive Bolivia National Dialogue, many rural stakeholders have identified non-agricultural activities (among them tourism) as a central element in their strategies for creating wealth. On the other hand, migration is still frowned upon, despite being a historically central element in the strategy of the majority of Andean peasants. Large sums of public and non-governmental funds are earmarked for increasing income and restraining migration without taking into account that all productivity increases involve the freeing of labor. Rural migrants generally come from the most vulnerable municipalities. Levels of poverty and extreme poverty are lower for the migrant population than for non-migrants (Table 3). Likewise, migrants receive a higher income in their current places of residence (both in aggregate terms for the country as a whole, and in the urban and rural areas), than non-migrants. It is also worth noting that migrants increase not only their own incomes, but also those of their relatives in their places of origin through remittances.

To support migration, it is necessary to understand the labor markets that attract rural inhabitants and find ways to improve the insertion of migrants into those markets, either through improved skills or through a diversification of opportunities. Given that the urbanization of society is an irreversible long-term process, policies that improve accumulation of migrants' physical and human capital through education and a reduction in malnutrition, among other ways, take on enhanced importance. The accumulation of human capital has demonstrated major improvements over the past decades, but much is left to do. Beyond the fact that all inhabitants in rural areas need to improve their capital, a differentiated policy in the fight against poverty calls for reinforcement of successful strategies that the rural families themselves use, whether that strategy is migration or the diversification of production in agricultural and non-agricultural activities.

Decentralization: Opportunities and Limitations

The improvement of human capital is the most important factor for overcoming poverty in the medium and long term, and decentralization plays a major role in this

Table 3. Poverty Indicators for 2002, by Geographic Area and Recent Migration

Population	*Persons (%)*	*Household Per Capita Income (bolivianos)*	*Incidence of Poverty (%)*	*Incidence of Extreme Poverty (%)*
National Total	100	378	65	41
Non-migrant	92	385	64	41
Migrant	8	480	56	32
Urban Area	100	522	54	26
Non-migrant	91	535	52	24
Migrant	9	568	52	25
Rural Area	100	142	83	67
Non-migrant	94	140	84	68
Migrant	6	260	65	47

Source: UDAPE, with information from INE (Survey of Households Measuring Living Conditions, November 2002).

regard. As noted, the LLP and the National Dialogue Act have contributed to eliminating an anti-rural skew in public spending, creating a significant flow of funds to areas that had barely been serviced by the government in the past. One would expect the shift in responsibilities, coupled with an improved distribution of funds, to be reflected in the indicators most sensitive to public investment (for example, unsatisfied basic needs), in terms of both absolute improvements in each municipality or region and in a convergence among the indicators. The results show interesting improvements, but certain gaps continue to widen.

According to census data, between 1992 and 2001,[10] achievements were made in satisfying basic needs, expressed as a reduction of the population living in extreme poverty, and, in turn, an increase in the proportion of the non-poor population.

The change in the extreme poverty indicator for unsatisfied basic needs during 1992-2001 demonstrates significant progress, especially in the rural municipalities (Figure 3). Given that the rural municipalities started the period with dire indicators, it is not surprising that the improvements in unsatisfied basic needs are seen the most in the lowest strata for the indicator. Accordingly, extreme poverty in the rural areas declined by 2 percentage points every year between 1992 and 2001, a change that is considerably greater than the reduction in urban poverty (0.6 percentage points). This demonstrates that the LLP has improved the channeling of funds to the poorer population, which is reflected in a convergence between the urban and rural areas (Table 4).

Though poverty has declined, the reduction has not been sufficient to narrow the existing gap between the urban and rural areas. In fact, available data from the last three national censuses show that the increase in the population with satisfied basic needs is clustered, particularly in the urban areas of the country. Between 1976 and 2001, the percentage of the population with unsatisfied basic needs at the national level declined, on average, by approximately 27 percent. Nonetheless, while the improvement was 27 percent in the urban area, in the countryside it was only 7 percent (see Table 5). As a result, the urban/rural gap in unsatisfied basic needs grew from 32 percent in 1976 to 42 percent in 1992, and to 52 percent in 2001.

International experience shows that to improve the efficiency of public expenditures within a framework of decentralization, the responsibilities of the players must be delineated, and transfers must be linked to results and to local efforts.[11] Currently, fractured jurisdictions and transfers in block (revenue sharing and HIPC) or through projects (National Compensation Policy and others) create incentives for constructing public works, but not for the sustainable provision of services. For the municipalities, it is relatively simple to build schools, health care posts, roads, potable water systems, and other similar structures. More complicated is ensuring the quality of the services provided through these works. It is rare to find a municipality that, when making an investment, calculates the future fiscal impact resulting from the operation and maintenance costs of the works.

The shift in jurisdiction and the transfer of funds, coupled with certain sector-based reforms,[12] have had a major impact on the provision of public goods and services.

Figure 3. Basic Unsatisfied Needs: Population by Poverty Strata, 1992–2001
(as a percentage)

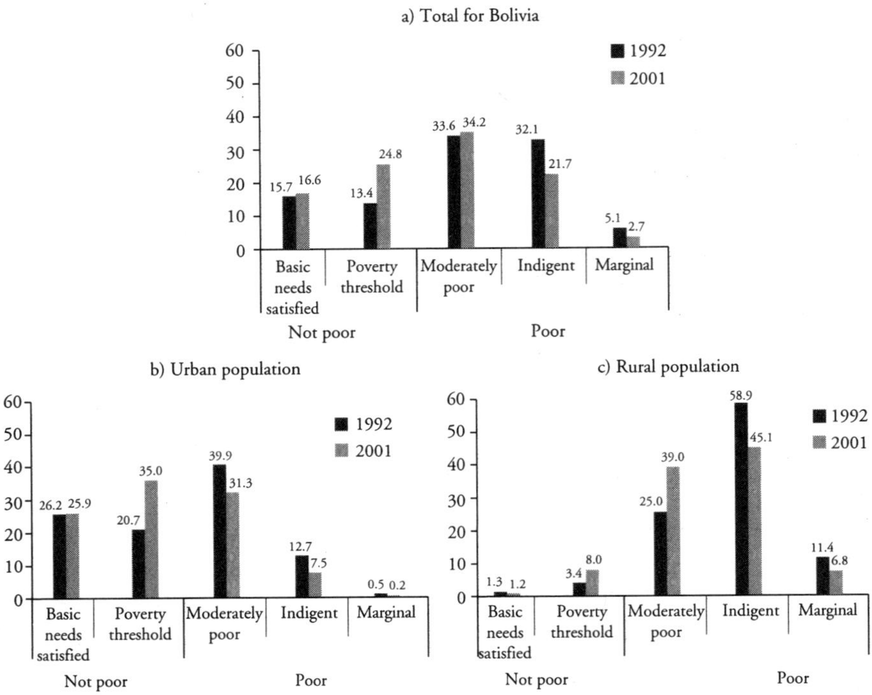

Source: INE.

Whether the population stays where it is or migrates, in the long run, their level of education and their health will play a determinant role in their chances of escaping poverty. Nonetheless, how can one explain that certain gaps continue to widen between the well-being of individuals residing in urban and rural zones, among municipalities and among regions, despite the fact that public spending is geographically better distributed

Table 4. Average Annual Variation in the Incidence of Poverty and Extreme Poverty, by Unsatisfied Basic Needs
(in percentage points)

Population	*Poverty* 1976–1992	*Poverty* 1992–2001	*Extreme Poverty* 1992–2001
National	−0.93	−1.33	−1.39
Urban	−0.84	−1.52	−0.59
Rural	−0.21	−0.48	−1.99

Source: Prepared by the author with information from INE.

Table 5. Incidence of Poverty, by Unsatisfied Basic Needs 1976, 1992, 2001
(as a percentage)

Population	*1976*	*1992*	*2001*
National	86	71	59
Urban	66	53	39
Rural	98	95	91
Urban/Rural Gap	32	42	52

Source: INE.

as a function of the size of the population and poverty? Rather, this points to inefficiencies in decentralized public spending. The differences would demonstrate that the decentralization policies have had unequal effects.

Expanded decentralization will be one of the core issues to be discussed in the coming years (starting with the Constitutional Reform Assembly). Bolivia will have an unsurpassed opportunity to adjust the relationship between funding and operations at the different levels of government. The critical objective is to align institutional incentives with the achievement of results, both in the social area and in production.

Decentralization and Production Development

There is a growing recognition that the current institutional and financing arrangements have not succeeded in promoting rural growth. In the first place, transfers to the municipalities (revenue sharing, HIPC II, FPS) are made with objectives of equity (and equalization formulas); that is, they are intended to offset horizontal differences and provide funds to equalize opportunities. However, they also include efficiency objectives (the direct promotion of economic activity). This mixture of objectives has confused the incentives for local authorities, who have to choose between allocating funds to public goods and services or the economic promotion of producers. It is not surprising that, in general, council members have preferred to allocate funds to social investment, public infrastructure and, occasionally, collective goods (for example, irrigation systems), which has left the producers devoid of support, despite the promises of the popular participation process.

In the second place, when investments do reach producers, they have generally financed their *needs* and not their *opportunities.*[13] That is, increased production or transformation has been promoted, taking into account only the potential to generate physical surpluses or products derived from them, not competitiveness in the market. In such a case, in the short term, investments often have a harmful effect on other private initiatives (including those of other peasant and indigenous producers), because private parties cannot compete with initiatives that enter the market with subsidized costs. In addition, subsidies to needs ("support to production") have a great potential to negatively affect not only fiscal balance, but even the producers who receive them, since the benefited producers cannot compete in the medium term on the market and end up devoting their energies to unsustainable endeavors. Subsidies to specific activities, in particular locations, tend to tie jobs to activities that show little promise. The rural areas are plagued with failed production projects: rusted processing plants, silos in ruins, and underutilized irrigation systems, because the "support to production" did not take into account that what makes a production initiative viable is market demand.

Finally, risks of waste increase when responsibility for granting private subsidies falls on the local public sector. Given their closeness to the producers and their organizations, municipal councils can be pressured to make investments of dubious use to the public, but that mainly benefit groups with a capacity to exert pressure or who function as clients (or patrons) of the political authority. Given the great variety of responsibilities of the council members and the still precarious institutionality of the rural councils, it is doubtful that they will have the capacities needed to manage lines of financing earmarked for market opportunities. Nonetheless, considering the positive impact on jobs and income offered by chains of primary activities with agroindustry, as well as potential agricultural and non-agricultural endeavors dispersed throughout rural areas, it would also be useful to implement a line of competitive financing that is focused on support to poor producers who can increase their income through their insertion into dynamic markets. The key here is the market test: the subsidy should be given to producers to support them in meeting the purchasers' contractual demands (quality, quantity, and delivery time). The operation of a mechanism of this type must contemplate a realm greater than the local one.

In the case of financing basic public goods and services to improve the competitiveness of rural producers, council members have two types of functions that could boost local economic dynamics: first, the building and maintenance of rural roads and potable water systems, and second, coordination of the provision of electricity, telephony, research, and technical assistance services. National and international experience demonstrates not only that such public goods and services are highly profitable, but also that they form the basis on which market opportunities are built. In all these areas there are experiences using innovative approaches to bring services to poor rural populations at low cost.[14] In the short time since their creation, the rural municipalities have demonstrated that with a small amount of funds, sufficient capacities can be assembled to handle a wide range of activities within a framework of confusing incentives and unclear responsibilities in certain sectors. Therefore, the role of local governments in coordinating strategies for local economic development will be fundamental in the future, but this role will also require the involvement of other players, at a larger scale, in a manner that complements local efforts.

National Agricultural Services

Research and agricultural extension services,[15] as well as plant and animal health services, are crucial to improve competitiveness, reduce vulnerability, protect the environment, ensure the quality of food, and decrease health risks for the citizenry. Considering the public well-being and the high performance these services offer a country, we recommend that their provision by the state be considered a priority.

As has been seen, the agricultural sector's contribution to GDP has hardly changed over the past 15 years. Despite that, there has been growth in edible oil-producing crops, based on soybeans and the agro-industrial activity associated with them. However, yields on soybeans and on the other 18 crops, which together represent 90 percent of the cultivated area in the country, have not grown significantly in this same period.[16] This stagnation in crop productivity is due, on the one hand, to environmental factors (loss of soil fertility, droughts, and floods) that also reflect weaknesses in research and extension services. In the highlands, low productivity and the vicious cycle of land use increase the poorest peasants' vulnerability to the climatic fluctuations that characterize the region. On the other hand, low productivity limits access to foreign markets (which are increasingly exposed to international competition) and access to domestic markets (which are increasingly exposed to imports of agricultural products from neighboring countries, whose yields are higher than those of Bolivia) (see Figure 4).

The need to strengthen key agricultural services (especially the development of agricultural technology, extension, and phytosanitary control) is widely recognized, and such efforts are taking place. The innovative methods introduced include active roles for producer organizations in health protection activities (for example, fighting livestock diseases) and competitive allocation of research funds through regional foundations. Nonetheless, progress in the implementation of these programs has been very slow. For example, in the case of the National Agricultural Health and Food Safety Service (*Servicio Nacional de Sanidad Agropecuaria e Inocuidad Alimentaria—*

Figure 4. Comparative Yields
(Metric Tons/Hectare)

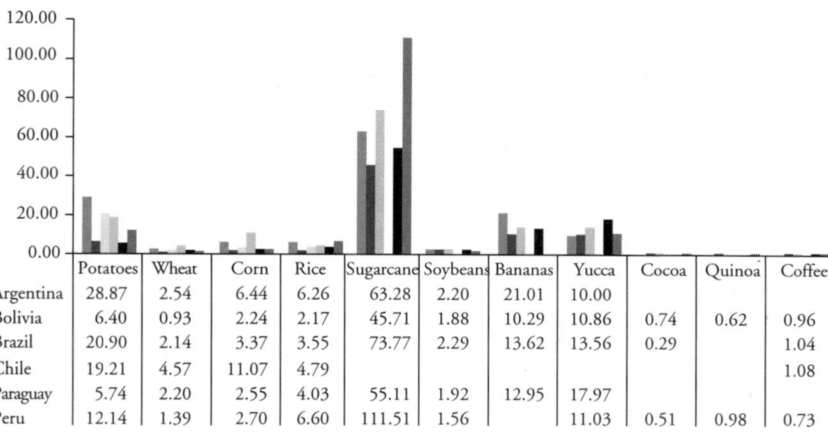

	Potatoes	Wheat	Corn	Rice	Sugarcane	Soybeans	Bananas	Yucca	Cocoa	Quinoa	Coffee
Argentina	28.87	2.54	6.44	6.26	63.28	2.20	21.01	10.00			
Bolivia	6.40	0.93	2.24	2.17	45.71	1.88	10.29	10.86	0.74	0.62	0.96
Brazil	20.90	2.14	3.37	3.55	73.77	2.29	13.62	13.56	0.29		1.04
Chile	19.21	4.57	11.07	4.79							1.08
Paraguay	5.74	2.20	2.55	4.03	55.11	1.92	12.95	17.97			
Peru	12.14	1.39	2.70	6.60	111.51	1.56		11.03	0.51	0.98	0.73

Source: INE and United Nations Food and Agriculture Organization.

SENASAG), the efforts are starting to bear fruit, but the institution still lacks the capacity, technology, and funds needed to ensure its continued success, especially considering the risk of transmitting diseases to the general population. In the case of the Bolivian Agricultural Technology System (*Sistema Boliviano de Tecnología Agropecuaria*—SIBTA), progress has been considerable, but it is necessary to expand the system's mandate to include environmental protection and adaptation, management of natural resources, and general research on basic food crops that provide the bulk of the agricultural income for peasants in the Andean region. Given the importance of ensuring the sustainability of these services in the long term, the government should design a mechanism to ensure funding, at least for basic operating expenses. The life cycle of the former Bolivian Agricultural Technology Institute (*Instituto Boliviano de Tecnología Agropecuaria*—IBTA) and the ups and downs of research demonstrate the importance of a reliable flow of funds to finance these essential services.

III. Policy Options

The following recommendations focus on overcoming the insufficient availability of public goods and services and production assets to benefit rural inhabitants. They also emphasize the need to differentiate policies in the fight against rural poverty as a function of territorial factors and the life strategies of the poor. Experience on a global level over the last half century has confirmed that there are only three ways to reduce rural poverty: (i) by creating jobs in rural areas through competitive insertion of rural producers (agricultural and non-agricultural) into dynamic markets; (ii) by facilitating insertion into the labor market through migration; and (iii) by improving the income of the poorest and most vulnerable groups through monetary transfers. In the medium and long term, only adequate growth rates in the national economy will make it possible to create enough jobs to absorb the rural (and urban) population. To accomplish that, priority must be placed on removing barriers for opening new companies and creating jobs. The recommendations are ordered by area of intervention and are accompanied by a suggested chronology. To the extent possible, given the context of budget restrictions, adjustments are suggested in the composition of the spending or in institutional arrangements. Recommendations on land policy are included in the chapter entitled Land Policy.

Financing of Rural Development

The most important step the government can take to support rural development is to rationalize and improve the efficiency of funding flows to the municipalities, communities, and producers. To accomplish that, two groups of measures are suggested: (a) clearly differentiate between the financing of public goods and services and the financing of subsidies; and (b) adjust co-financing mechanisms for municipal and community infrastructure.

Financing that Differentiates between Public Goods and Services and Subsidies to Producer Organizations

The best way to eliminate the confusion resulting from the mixed objectives of efficiency and equitability in municipal transfers is to clearly differentiate their sources and modes of financing. A sequence of measures that could be implemented for this purpose include: (i) agree with the various financiers on an explicit, transparent policy that defines eligibility criteria for potential beneficiaries, competitive rules for filtering access to funds, financing modes, and types of eligible initiatives; (ii) bring the various existing projects in line with this policy; and (iii) use municipal transfers solely for financing public infrastructure and the institutional strengthening of civil society organizations.

SUPPORT TO OPPORTUNITIES

The primary objective is to focus the financing on support for opportunities that allow producers to integrate themselves into dynamic markets. In other words, the financing should shift from support for production to support for competitiveness, from support to producer needs to support for their opportunities. Given the multidimensional character of the lifestyle strategies of rural inhabitants and the diversity of market opportunities, the financing should be open to both agricultural and nonagricultural activities. Only poor producers should be able to access this co-financing, and they should assume part of the costs of the projects to ensure a minimum profitability on their part. The financing should be limited over time and there should be restrictions on its use. To avoid distortions, support to producers should be strictly limited to meeting the technical specifications demanded by the market in terms of quality, quantity, and the timeliness of deliveries.

AGRICULTURAL SERVICES

The primary objective should be to consolidate the financing of the SENASAG and the SIBTA. Currently, both institutions depend almost exclusively on external financing. Thus, their institutional vulnerability is high. Horizons for maturity of the investments are long and the potential beneficiaries are disperse. By taking advantage of institutional progress, particularly of the SIBTA, funds could be reallocated to these basic services to support environmental management, reduction of vulnerability, peasant crops, and food surveillance. In exchange for the funds received from the Treasury, public universities can be involved in basic agricultural research, and departmental governments can be involved in financing adaptive research, extension, and plant and animal health programs.

Co-Financing of Municipal and Community Infrastructure

Mechanisms for co-financing infrastructure projects need to be reformulated. A sequence of proposals that could be implemented in a new financing policy include: (i) If the FPS continues, subcontract its operations to the private sector, reinforcing its supervision and control capacity; (ii) focus the co-financing on a limited number of priority sectors, making sure that the guidelines are implemented and that the institutions are strengthened to ensure their success; (iii) consider direct financing to the communities for community projects as a way to get around the bottleneck at the municipal level, reduce project costs, encourage creativity and accountability in the local community, and focus the impact on the poorer segments of the population; and (iv) in some sectors, design performance-based program transfers rather than financing individual investments.

PROVISION OF PUBLIC GOODS AND SERVICES

Responsibility for rural infrastructure is shared by municipalities, departments, and the national government, depending on the sector involved. Public financing of investments in and maintenance of rural roads, irrigation, and electrification is channeled principally through national government funds and projects for the departments or municipalities (sometimes to both), depending upon the sector. The effective use of these funds is crucial, but experiences to date have been extremely varied. Due to the distinct technical and institutional nature of each sector, an analysis of issues and recommendations for each of them is presented in separate chapters. Nonetheless, the primary conclusion is that a policy needs to be articulated that covers all the sectors with the objective of improving the development of rural infrastructure, through a clear link to the territorial level.

The following are basic principles to orient the definition of policies and modes of intervention in the rural infrastructure sectors: (i) an approach fundamentally based on the sustainable provision of services and not on new construction; (ii) financial policies that optimize the use of transfers, create incentives for the financial participation of users and the private sector, and consider the capacity and willingness to pay of the population to be attended; (iii) simplification and relaxation of rules and regulations for the sector and for design criteria, in order to optimize investment costs by using the lowest cost technologies; and (iv) clear rules for each level of government based on established roles and respect for the distribution of jurisdictions to the different levels of government, with criteria that increase transparency and efficiency (supported with technical assistance programs). This final aspect is particularly relevant in the case of departments, since it could lead to the effective articulation of national policies toward the municipal entities, and because these entities, in the future, could assume direct responsibility for providing services, when economies of scale and networked relationships so justify.

COMMUNITY PROJECTS

Directly financing certain projects in the communities would require a prioritization and selection of small projects by the communities themselves (note that the definition of communities is flexible and includes peasant associations and associations of small producers) in each municipality within the limits of a budget cap and in keeping with the framework of participatory municipal planning. Project funds would be administered by the communities, who would be in charge of preparing and implementing investments and would receive the corresponding technical assistance. This mechanism could be applied to projects for micro-irrigation, improvement of pathways (that is, pathways that feed into the rural roads exclusively for the benefit of communities or dispersed producers), foot bridges, and the management of natural resources.

The results of community administration include: (i) a reduction in project costs, because the communities directly supervise the use of funds; (ii) better quality implementation; and (iii) a better reflection of demand and a consequent increase in sustainability, because the prioritization involves funding allocations made by the communities themselves. Nonetheless, several points should be taken into consideration: (i) the communities must have access to the technical aid needed for projects of medium-to-high complexity; (ii) the community members must be properly informed of the rules of play, including transparent and participatory processes for the administration of funds; and (iii) projects with a wider geographic approach or a high complexity must be implemented at the municipal level.

RURAL ROADS

Out of the extensive system of 40,000 kilometers of rural roads,[17] only 12,000 are in usable condition year-round. The municipalities are responsible for the construction, restoration, and maintenance of the rural roads system, but the roads continue to be in poor condition due to inappropriate design criteria, lack of planning, investments that are frequently disperse and erratic, and lack of maintenance. The rural roads system takes up the majority of the municipalities' rural development investments. In budget terms, it requires more than half of the funds included in municipal plans and accounts for more than half of the proposals for FPS rural development financing. The rural roads strategy should be based on the principles of sustainability, participation, and integration of the roads system. A good basis for applying these principles are the roads-planning processes being promoted in more than 100 municipalities, which should come under a specific sector-based strategy that is as yet nonexistent. A rural roads strategy needs to focus on designing systems and procedures so that municipalities and communities can provide a sustainable transportation system to the rural communities of Bolivia. With these principles and objectives in mind, strategic actions that make it possible to establish the rules of play at the central level should take priority, as should incentives for the municipalities to strengthen their functions and responsibilities in managing the road networks over which they are in charge. This approach would require the establishment of a central technical unit to orient the actions of the municipalities. Such a technical unit would establish criteria for participatory roads planning, design intervention modes with an emphasis on points and spans, determine criteria for selecting priorities, and develop mechanisms for timely road maintenance. In the case of pathways, the communities themselves could become the implementation units for the interventions.[18]

MUNICIPAL STRENGTHENING

Rural municipalities need to consolidate the institutional progress of the past decade. Municipalities play a central role in the fight against rural poverty on account of both their coordinating role, which allows them to exploit the potential complementarities of public goods and services, and their jurisdiction over the provision of essential goods and services for human development and for fomenting production. Given its impact on municipal efficiency and transparency, a municipal strengthening policy must focus on improving and extending: (i) processes to involve the participation of communities and beneficiaries and to define prioritization criteria in the annual municipal program; (ii) a results-oriented citizen oversight; and (iii) quality in the provision of services, including the proper maintenance and operation of the existing infrastructure. Experiences with co-financing training and technical assistance at the municipal level have generally been successful when municipalities define and manage the lines of support, contracting them in the market. This, in turn, has developed a good supply of private services (individuals, firms, and non-governmental organizations). Considering that the majority of municipalities have sufficient funds to take charge of their own strengthening, a uniform policy should be adopted for the co-financing of services. This co-financing should incorporate differentiated rates based on the availability of funds, and incentives based on explicit, transparent requirements regarding levels of capacity for the co-financing of investments.

FOCUS ACTIONS ON THE COUNTRY'S POOR AREAS AND POOR INHABITANTS

The degree of focus on poorer inhabitants and areas in government programs and projects for the rural sector require corrections in the short term. What is needed is not so much to increase the quantity of funds to the most poor, but to improve interventions to strengthen their lives or eliminate barriers that restrict their opportunities and capacities.

As noted, in the Andean highlands and valleys, many peasant families are trapped in vicious cycles of environmental degradation, loss of soil fertility, declining yields, and, consequently, declining income from sales or subsistence agriculture. These same conditions also increase vulnerability to the climatic phenomena found at these latitudes and altitudes. To respond to this, three priorities are suggested.

First, develop and implement a natural resources management program that works to increase income in the Bolivian highlands. This program would endeavor to break the vicious cycles that create poverty in the highlands and valleys. Though these phenomena are widespread in the highlands, the program should focus on municipalities with high vulnerability to food shortages.[19] The most successful and efficient mode of intervention appears to be community and family competitions for the management of natural resources and production technologies. This intervention should be complemented by new research on Andean crops and environmental risks that could be implemented by SIBTA.

Second, develop and implement a program to help migrants find jobs. This program would reduce the costs of entry into the migrants' places of destination by providing information on accommodations and job references. Another important effort would be training to increase labor skills and facilitate access to a greater diversity of job opportunities.

Third, develop and implement a program of conditioned transfers that focuses on the poorest inhabitants and seeks to reduce the incidence of malnutrition among children under the age of two. Early detection and treatment of malnutrition in children is essential for avoiding the varying degrees of retarded physical and mental development (such damage is irreversible after the age of two, long before the children are eligible for school breakfasts). In 2000, more than 26 percent of children were suffering from chronic malnutrition and 12 out of every 100 children under the age of two were at nutritional risk;[20] in the case of the rural population, this figure increased alarmingly to 26 out of every 100 children between 1999 and 2002. The program could be implemented by redirecting existing funds and using established capacities.

Bibliography

Central Intelligence Agency of the United States. 2006. *Cultivation of Coca in Bolivia 2005*. CIA: Washington, DC.

Instituto Nacional de Estadística (INE). 2002. *Encuesta de Hogares, Medición de Condiciones de Vida*. INE: La Paz, November.

———. 2004. *Cuentas Nacionales*. INE. La Paz

International Crisis Group. March 3, 2005. *Drugs and Social Protest in Bolivia and Peru*. ICG: Washington, D.C.

Jiménez Pozo, Wilson and Susana Lizárraga. 2004. "Ingresos y desigualdad en el área rural de Bolivia." *Revista de Análisis Económico* Vol. 19: Agosto. UDAPE: La Paz.

Ministerio de Participación Popular (MPP). 2003. *Más allá de las cifras: La visión campesina de los cambios estructurales en la productividad rural y los recursos naturales*. La Paz.

Thoumi, Francisco E. 2003. *Illegal Drugs, Economy and Society in the Andes*. Woodrow Wilson Center Press: Baltimore.

UNICEF, UDAPE. 2005. *Bolivia: Equidad y derechos de la niñez, Índice Municipal de Desarrollo de la Infancia, Niñez and Adolescencia*. UNICEF: New York.

United Nations, FAO, PMA, SINSAAT, and MDSP. 2002. *Food Vulnerability Map*. UN: New York.

United Nations Office on Drugs and Crime (UNODC). 2005. *Survey on the Coca Leaf Crop, Bolivia 2005*. UN: New York.

Annex: Some Characteristics of the Coca Leaf Sector

Introduction

Coca leaves are an important agricultural product for Bolivia. In 2004, the total estimated value of coca leaf production, at market prices, was approximately US$240 million. This volume represents 2.8 percent of the total GDP (US$8.7 billion in 2004) and 20 percent of the agricultural GDP (US$1.17 billion in 2004). Approximately 20-25 percent of this amount is estimated to have been produced legally, with authorization from the government. Although the estimated income resulting from the harvest of coca leaves without governmental authorization is significant, a reduction in this production would not create an economic crisis on a national level, but it could have a major impact in the regions where coca leaves are produced. The strategy announced by President Morales to combat illegal cocaine trafficking and, simultaneously, support the legal production of coca leaves, would require a completion of the study currently underway regarding legal demand for coca leaves, and the formulation of strong alternative development programs in the producer regions.

Background

The coca plant (*erythroxylum coca*), which originated in the Andean region, has been cultivated in Bolivia for centuries. When chewed, the leaf of this plant acts as a mild stimulant, particularly useful for persons working at high altitudes. It is also rich in vitamins and minerals. These characteristics made this plant a key part of the Andean economy, in the time of the Inca empire and of pre-Inca civilizations, during Spanish colonial times, and following independence. The first sources that mention the existence of coca leaf plantations in Bolivia date back to the seventeenth century.[21] Coca leaves are still frequently used today in Bolivia as a mild stimulant and appetite suppressant, as well as in medicine and religious rituals.

In the nineteenth century, western chemists started producing cocaine—a stimulant much more powerful than the chewed leaf—using coca leaves as one of the raw materials. In the 1970s, cocaine started to be used increasingly for recreational purposes in several developed countries, which led to a spectacular increase in demand for the product and, as a consequence, increased demand for cocaine inputs, including coca leaves cultivated in the Andes, particularly in Bolivia and Peru. Prior to this increase in demand, almost all coca leaves in Bolivia were grown in the Yungas region north of La Paz, but during the 1980s their production started to expand to Chapare in northeastern Cochabamba. Chapare production grew even higher after the highland tin mining industry went into decline in the mid-1980s, with many laid-off workers moving their families to the Chapare. During the 1980s and the early 1990s, most coca leaves produced in Bolivia were converted into base paste and then sent to Colombia, where the paste was processed into cocaine and shipped to the United States or Europe. The flow of income from this trade was very important for the Bolivian economy and, according to some estimates, amounted to somewhere between 10 and 15 percent of the GDP.[22]

In the late 1990s, the government launched a campaign (the Dignity Plan) to reduce the production of coca leaves in Chapare and cut the traffic between Bolivia and Colombia. Estimates indicate that production dropped from approximately 48,000 hectares in 1996 to approximately 14,500 in 2000. The crop was controlled in Chapare, but in Yungas its eradication was not attempted. Implementation of the Plan was accompanied by conflicts between producers and the security forces. In recent years, the cultivation of coca leaves has expanded, but it still represents only about half of what was produced in the early 1990s.

Law 1008 (enacted in 1988), authorizes the cultivation of 12,000 hectares of coca leaves, which are then sold in markets authorized by the government. The crop is legal in the Yungas region, though the government has never precisely delineated the allowed zone, which makes it difficult to distinguish the illegal crop from the legal one. In 2004, the government allowed coca leaf cultivation, on an interim basis, on 3,200 new hectares of Chapare, whose limits were precisely delineated. To clearly establish the number of hectares needed for traditional consumption, the government, through the INE, plans to conduct a study to determine legal demand. This study, supported with financing from the European Union, will consist of a household survey on the use of coca leaves in Bolivia. This will be accompanied by research that is narrower in scope regarding industries that legally use coca leaves (for example, producers of *mate de coca* tea). The study is expected to be completed in the fall of 2006.[23]

Cultivation

Recent estimates by the United Nations[24] and the United States government[25] indicate that there are currently between 26,000 and 28,000 hectares of coca plants in Bolivia. This area represents less than half of the area cultivated ten years ago. At present, Bolivia only has 17 percent of the territory worldwide devoted to the coca leaf crop, following Colombia (50 percent) and Peru (33 percent).

Coca leaves are cultivated in two principal regions in Bolivia: Yungas and Chapare. In the Yungas region, coca leaves are grown in ten municipalities with a total population of 160,000 persons. This region accounts for 60 percent of the coca leaves produced in the country, which represents a highly significant change with respect to the 1980s and 1990s, when the region of Chapare was the area with the largest production. Nonetheless, the eradication campaigns of the late 1990s and the start of the decade of 2000 have made an impact. Since then, production in Yungas has experienced a slow but sustained growth—in 2004, it is estimated that there were approximately 17,000 hectares producing coca leaves in Yungas. Most coca leaves from Yungas are traded in the Villa Fátima market of La Paz, controlled by the General Directorate for the Control and Marketing of Coca Leaves (*Dirección*

Table A.1. Coca Leaf Production in the Andes, Hectares, 1994–2004

	1994	*1995*	*1996*	*1997*	*1998*	*1999*	*2000*	*2001*	*2002*	*2003*	*2004*
Bolivia	48,100	48,600	48,100	45,800	38,000	21,800	14,600	19,900	24,400	23,600	27,700
Peru	108,600	115,300	94,400	68,800	51,000	38,700	43,400	46,200	46,700	44,200	50,300
Colombia	45,000	51,000	67,000	79,000	102,000	160,000	163,000	145,000	102,000	86,000	80,000
Total	201,700	214,900	209,500	193,600	191,000	220,500	221,000	211,000	173,100	153,800	158,000

Source: Estimates of the crop for 2002 and before (Bolivia); 1999 and before (Peru); and 1998 and before (Colombia) are from the U.S. State Department. Data for subsequent years are from the UNODC, *Survey on the Coca Leaf Crop in Bolivia* (2005). Accordingly, the figures for Bolivia before and after 2002 are not directly comparable.

Note: According to preliminary data from the CIA, Bolivian coca production declined slightly to 26,500 hectares in 2005.

General de Control y Comercialización de Coca—DIGECO), the public entity that supervises their cultivation and sale. Strong resistance from the coca producers, extreme terrain, and the difficulty in distinguishing between legal and illegal coca leaves have made eradication efforts in Yungas difficult. The international cooperation community, in particular the United States Agency for International Development (USAID) and the European Union, continue to finance alternative development projects in Yungas in an effort to promote other sources of income.

The second largest coca leaf producing region is Chapare, where the Andes give way to the tropical savannah that leads to the Amazon basin. Coca leaves were almost unknown there until the early 1980s, when a rise in demand coupled with economic difficulties in the country induced the poorest people to cultivate coca leaves. Following an explosive growth during the 1980s and 1990s, coca leaves were almost entirely eradicated from Chapare during the intense and frequently violent campaigns of the late 1990s and the start of the decade of 2000. Although the cultivation of coca leaves is increasing in Chapare, production is still much lower than levels in the 1990s—it is estimated that, in 2004, approximately 10,000 hectares of coca leaves were cultivated. Most of the production is concentrated in the municipalities of Villa Tunari, Entre Ríos (formerly Pojo), and Porto Villarroel. The total population of this zone is 190,000 inhabitants. Both in Yungas and Chapare, the USAID and the European Union have intervened in a number of alternative development projects. A notable difference between the two efforts is that participation in the USAID programs is linked to eradication, which is not the case with the European Union.

A much lesser quantity is cultivated in Apolo (with a population of 13,831 persons) close to the Peruvian border, in the department of La Paz. The 300 estimated hectares of coca leaves cultivated there are generally grown on small farms and are used for traditional consumption.

No systematic study has been made of the social characteristics associated with the production of coca leaves (what kind of people are growing the crop, their background, how much they earn from this activity, etc.) in Bolivia. The most recent study of this type dates back 20 years; the USAID is now working on such a study, which it hopes to finish within one year.

Production, Prices, and Marketing

According to studies made by the Bolivian government and the United States Drug Enforcement Agency (DEA), yields of the different producer regions in Bolivia vary considerably, based on the production techniques used. The least profitable farms are those that use traditional techniques, in particular, the authorized regions of Yungas and Apolo. These farms produce an average of 936 kilos of leaves per hectare per year. The unauthorized farms of Yungas produce an average of 1,798 kilos per hectare per year, while in Chapare the harvest is 2,764 kilos per year per hectare. As one can see, the unauthorized farms are clearly more profitable. This is due in part to the fact that in the legally authorized areas, coca leaves are grown using traditional procedures that date back several centuries. In contrast, the new regions have more funds for fertilizers, pesticides, and ever more sophisticated irrigation techniques, and grow several varieties of the crop. The rate of conversion of coca leaves into cocaine also varies from one region to another: in Chapare, 370 kilos of leaves are needed to obtain one kilo of cocaine, while in Yungas only 315 kilos are needed.

Coca leaves produced with authorization from the DIGECO are sold in the markets of Villa Fátima (La Paz) or, on a lesser scale, in Sacaba (Cochabamba). One kilo of leaves, on average, costs 31 bolivianos (US$4.40) in Villa Fátima and 27 bolivianos (US$3.90) in Sacaba (data from 2004). The total value of authorized coca leaves was almost US$55 million in 2004.[26] The principal market for this product is workers from the agro-industrial sector in and around Santa Cruz or the mining regions of La Paz, Potosí, and Oruro. Coca leaves sold other than at the two official markets generally go for a slightly higher price: approximately US$5 per kilo. Prices are somewhat higher in Chapare (US$5.20 per kilo) than in Yungas (US$4.70 per kilo). In Apolo, the price is nearly half, probably due to Apolo's remote location and transportation difficulties. Considering estimates of the quantity of leaves produced (49,000 metric tons),[27] and the prices cited above, the coca leaf harvest of 2004 was worth approximately US$240 million. This figure represents almost 3 percent of the national GDP (US$8.7 billion in 2004[28]), and 20 percent of the agricultural GDP (US$1.18 billion in 2004[29]).

During the past decade, there has been a clear relationship between the supply of coca leaves and their price. Prior to 1998, prices held steady at US$1 or US$2 per kilo, with a certain variation depending on the season. Nonetheless, in 1998, passage of the Dignity Plan and the resulting eradication efforts in Chapare caused a drop in production, which raised prices to US$5 per kilo. This price increase has, naturally, translated into an incentive for coca leaf cultivation, and the evidence suggests that coca farming is growing. Since it takes several years for the plants to produce leaves, this new production might not be reflected in the figures for some time.

Some Conclusions

The cultivation of coca leaves is no longer the economic powerhouse it was in the 1980s or the early 1990s. The strategy announced by President Morales to fiercely combat the illegal cultivation of coca leaves and promote its legal cultivation and sale could benefit Bolivia. The fight against the illegal coca leaf crop requires intensive alternative development programs, beyond what currently exists. Although the industry is relatively small for the national economy, it is important for the 350,000 persons who live in the producer regions. In order to promote the legal cultivation of coca leaves, it is essential to conduct a study of demand. Otherwise, the government will have no way to ascertain what amounts should be allowed, and could open the door to more illegal production. Such a study should be conducted periodically, thereby making it possible to change authorized quantities as the legal demand for coca leaves varies.

Endnotes

1. For more information, see the chapter on the Dynamics of Poverty and Inequality.

2. If subsistence production is included, the average income increases to approximately US$25 (Jiménez and Lizárraga, 2003).

3. Economic Policy Analysis Unit (*Unidad de Análisis de Política Económica*—UDAPE), with information from the National Statistics Institute (INE, 2002). (*Instituto Nacional de Estadística*—INE) (Survey of Households, Measurements of Living

4. A similar phenomenon is seen in the incidence of extreme poverty and the poverty gap—a differential of approximately 42 and 31 percentage points between urban and rural areas, respectively.

5. To facilitate the analysis on predominantly rural municipalities, all municipalities with populations less than 50,000 inhabitants are included.

6. It has been impossible, for purposes of this note, to determine the urban/rural distribution of total public spending, including investments in prefectures and sectors, as well as wages for education, health, etc., in order to determine the absolute effects of public spending allocations on inequalities of access.

7. Non-traditional products amounted to 43 percent of exports in 2003, reflecting notable growth since 1980, when they accounted for approximately 14 percent of total exports. Also important to note is the dynamic, though lesser, growth in exports of other agricultural products such as chestnuts, cocoa, and sugar.

8. Ministerío de Participatión Popular, 2001.

9. See Jiménez and Lizárraga (2004).

10. The period between the two censuses reflects the first decade of the LLP, although the seven actual years of its application (measured here) are not sufficient to fully assess such a major reform. In this section, the terms "poverty" and "extreme poverty" are measured by unsatisfied basic needs, rather than income or consumption.

11. These issues are discussed in greater depth in the chapter on Decentralization.

12. Fundamentally Educational Reform, Health Reform, and, to a lesser extent, measures in Basic Sanitation and Electrification.

13. This bias comes from the traditional offer of "support to production" and is reinforced by the limitations of participatory planning in the proper identification of competitive factors.

14. See, for example, the rural roads program or investments in electrification and rural telephony.

15. "Extension" is understood to mean the range of technical assistance services to producers. These services can be provided under a variety of modes, from demonstrative farms to technical assistance contracts managed by the producers and co-financed by the government.

16. With the notable exception of potatoes, due to technological improvements introduced in the highlands and valleys and to an increase in their cultivation on the plains.

17. This estimate does not include community roads or pathways.

18. Many of the technical guidelines (points and spans) for planning and maintenance have already been formulated by the Ministry of Popular Participation.

19. See United Nations, FAO, PMA, SINSAAT and MDSP (2002) Análisis y cartografía de la Vulnerabilidad a la Inseguridad Alimentaria.
20. Nutritional risk includes the combination of educational and physical capital in the family as factors that are determinant for children's health. This makes it possible to measure a household's capacity to transform their assets into appropriate food and medical care. (UNICEF, UDAPE 2005, IDINA [Children's Equity and Rights the Municipal Index of Infant, Child and Adolescent Development]).
21. Thoumi, Francisco (2002), cited in "Drugs and Social Protest in Bolivia and Peru," International Crisis Group, March 3, 2005.
22. Ibid.
23. European Commission, office in La Paz.
24. UNODC (2005).
25. Central Intelligence Agency (2005).
26. INE, national accounts.
27. UNODC (2005, p. 43).
28. INE, national accounts.
29. INE, national accounts.

9

Trade and Integration Policies

Bruno Giussani
Marcelo Olarreaga

Summary

The export sector has not been a driving force for growth in the Bolivia due to four principal factors. First, there is a serious lack of diversification of products and markets for Bolivian exports. Traditional exports (hydrocarbons and minerals) and soybeans represent more than 75 percent of exports, while primary products represent more than 90 percent of exports. With respect to markets, Mercosur and the Andean countries account for more than 60 percent of exports. Second, there is little integration between the export sector and the rest of the economy. There are a small number of exporting companies that are highly volatile and export very low amounts. Third, contraband and tax evasion are a major source of unfair competition for the formal sector (including exporters). Contraband in 2003 was estimated at US$700 million, almost 50 percent of the official value of exports. This implies a revenue loss of US$100 to US$150 million for the government. Fourth (which contributes to the first three factors), given the country's extreme institutional and legal volatility, there is an absence of laws needed to regulate trade and existing laws are not applied. Laws or institutions undergo frequent changes due to a lack of long-term vision for the sector. This chapter illustrates the importance of these four factors and proposes possible alternative solutions.

I. Background—Characteristics of the External Sector

In economies with small internal markets, exports tend to be the principal driving force of economic growth. This has not been the case in Bolivia, where rapid growth of exports has not always translated into strong growth of GDP. When GDP was growing rapidly, exports were growing slowly, and vice versa. This is due to the high concentration of Bolivia's exports, as well as a lack of integration of the export sector into the rest of the economy.

The historic growth of Bolivian exports has been less than that of other countries in the region. Furthermore, rapid recent growth is due to external factors as opposed to structural factors within the economy. In 2004, more than 75 percent of exports were traditional products or soybeans and soybean products, and almost 90 percent of exports were primary products (including chestnuts, coffee, sugar, fruit, and cotton). Geographic concentration is also high, with 60 percent of exports channeled to the Common Market of the Southern Cone (Mercosur) and the Andean Community (CAN). Bolivian exports to markets such as the United States are more diversified and have a higher labor content (three times more than exports to Mercosur) but represent only 10 percent of total exports. Even more problematic is the fact that there are very few exporting companies, while those that do exist export very small amounts and are characterized by high volatility over time. These are symptoms of the weak integration of the export sector into the rest of the economy. On the other hand, the demand for Bolivian export products is great, and there is a high potential for Bolivia to increase its market share with its trading partners.

The trade liberalization embarked upon in the mid 1980s made a modest contribution to the diversification and growth of exports. Over the past 20 years, exports per capita in Peru, Colombia, Brazil, and Ecuador grew at least twice as quickly than those of Bolivia; in Argentina this figure was 4.5 times greater, and Venezuela and Chile it was seven times greater.

The rapid recent growth of exports (34 percent in 2004 and 25 percent in 2005) is more the result of exogenous factors than internal reforms or government policies. High prices and strong demand for products such as soybeans, natural gas, and other mineral products are behind the 67 percent increase in exports over the past two years. Prices of raw materials are volatile. In order to achieve lasting, sustainable growth that contributes to alleviating poverty, it will be necessary to broaden the export base to products better linked to the rest of the economy.

The trade reforms that commenced in 1985 helped to diversify exports, albeit modestly. Non-traditional exports rose from less than 10 percent of total exports in 1985 to 50 percent in the first part of the decade of 2000. However, the reason behind that was mostly a drop in traditional exports (minerals), rather than a significant increase in non-traditional exports. Non-traditional exports are also highly concentrated in a small number of products (Figure 1).

The Herfindhal index of product and market concentration[1] shows an increase in concentration in Bolivia around 1985, with a movement toward diversification following the trade reforms commenced in 1985 (Figure 2). Nonetheless, in 2003, the only concentration index that surpassed that of Bolivia was that of Peru. The Herfindhal index for Chile, Colombia, and Ecuador is one-third to one-half percent that of Bolivia. Bolivia's higher indices are essentially due to high product concentration, though a higher concentration of markets is also a contributing factor.

Figure 1. Composition of Non-Traditional Exports, 2004

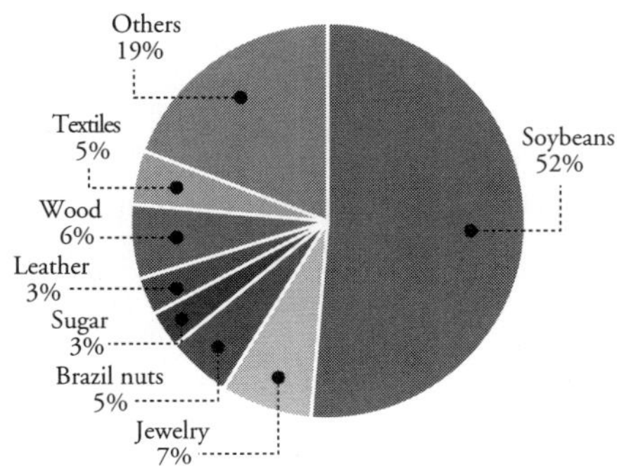

Source: National Statistics Institute (*Instituto Nacional de Estadística*—INE), La Paz.

The principal export markets are Mercosur and the CAN; together they comprised 60 percent of Bolivia's exports in 2004. Exports to Mercosur are principally traditional exports: natural gas to Brazil and Argentina, and crude oil to Argentina. The predominant exports to the CAN are soybeans and soybean products such as soybean oil and "*torta de aceite*" (oil-cake).

The United States, a relatively small market for Bolivia, represents about 15 percent of exports. The International Trade Center (ITC) of Geneva has stated that the U.S. market's potential is being underexploited by Bolivia. According to the *Tradesim* model developed at the ITC, Bolivian exports to the United States are 44 percent below their potential.[2] However, exports to the United States represent a significant portion of non-traditional exports (approximately 75 percent of Bolivian exports of clothing, jewelry, and wood products).

Figure 2. Concentration of Exports, 1962–2003

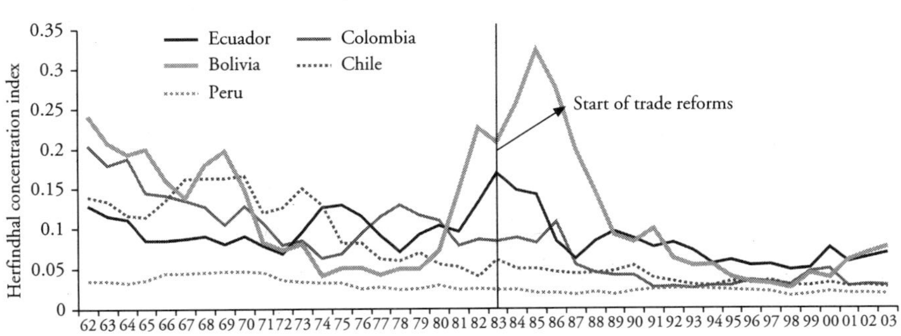

Source: United Nations Comtrade.

The labor content of manufacturing exports to the United States is higher than the labor content of manufacturing exports to other regions. This is significant, since manufacturing exports are associated with more than 40 percent of jobs in the Bolivian manufacturing sector. Manufacturing exports to the United States represent 16 percent of all manufacturing jobs, followed by exports to the Andean countries that create 11 percent of jobs in the sector (Figure 3).

The share of non-traditional exports in the markets of most of Bolivia's trading partners is very small. This indicates that the need to increase non-traditional exports is a problem not of demand, but rather of supply. Figure 4 illustrates market shares by place of destination and the principal competitors in each of the major markets for certain non-traditional export products. Bolivia has an insignificant share of the market with its principal trading partners to which it exports clothing, sawn wood, leather (except in Peru and Chile), and sugar (except in Colombia and Peru). Its principal competitors tend to be the other Andean countries, the Mercosur countries, the United States or the European Union, and, in the case of textiles, China, India, and Pakistan.

Bolivian exports are limited by the small number of companies capable of servicing major demand. In 2003 there were approximately 700 exporting companies,[3] only a few of which were capable of exporting significant amounts.[4] Using data provided by the National Customs Service, the average value of exports fell from an average of US$29,000 in 2001 to US$20,000 in 2004. These are very small amounts, reflecting the limited productive capacity of Bolivian companies, which limits the potential for exporting to large foreign markets.

Figure 3. Labor Content of Manufacturing Exports by Region, 2003
(Percentage of Total Employment in Manufacturing)

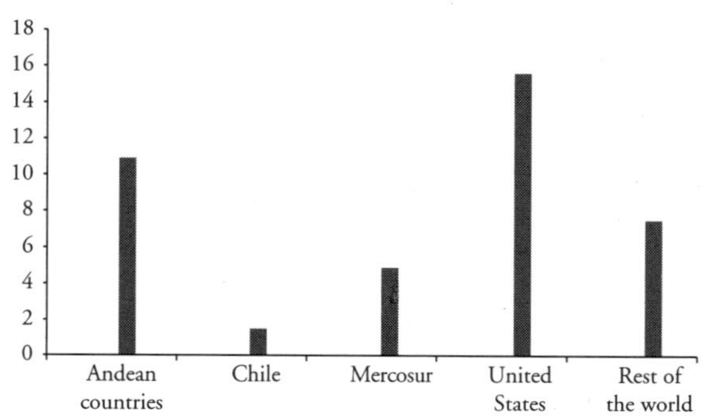

Source: INE.
Note: The content is calculated using the ratio between jobs and production for each manufacturing industry based on the three-digit International Standard Industrial Classification system (ISIC) (compiled by the INE for the year 2000), and then applying that ratio to exports for 2003.

Figure 4. Non-Traditional Exports by Principal Market and Competitors, 2003

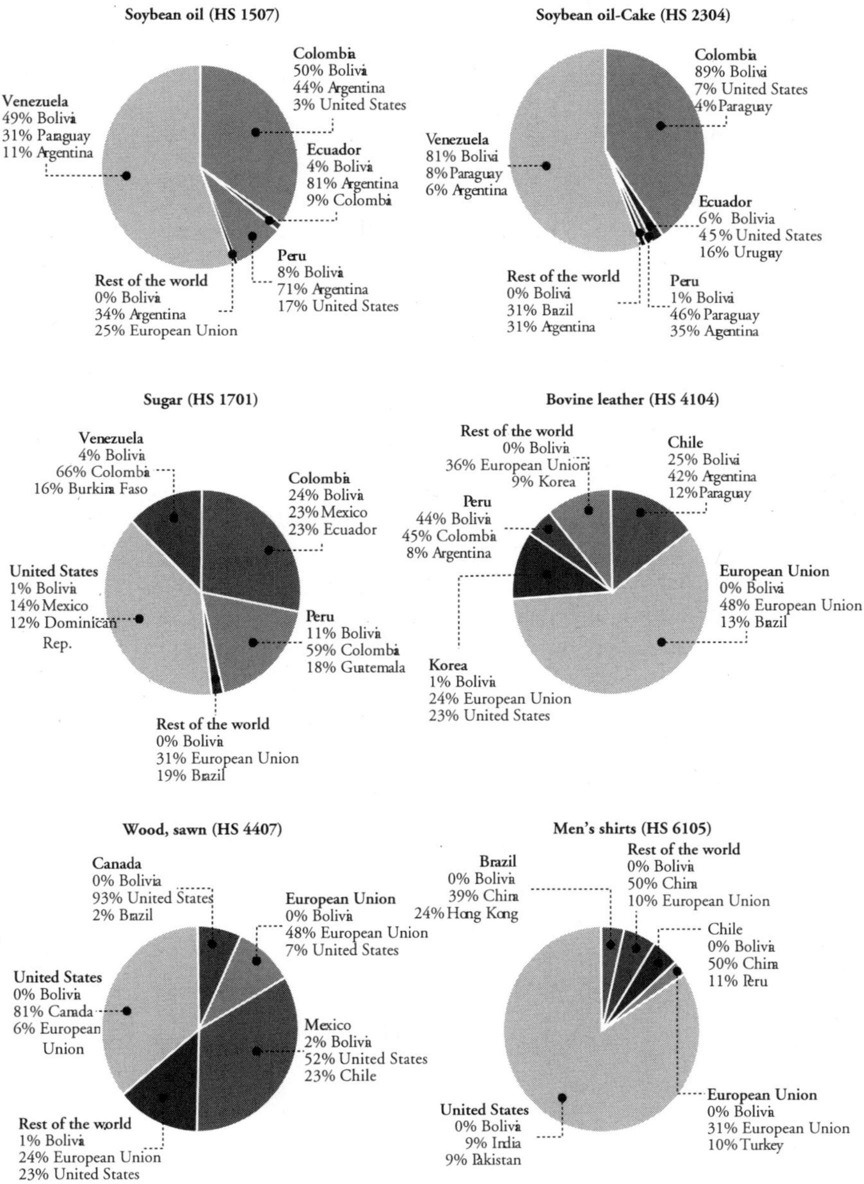

Source: United Nations Comtrade.

These restrictions translate into high export volatility. On average, Bolivian export products last a lower number of continuous years on a given market than the products of neighboring countries: 2.5 years for Bolivia in the period of 2000-2004, as compared with more than three years for the neighboring countries. Nonetheless, regional differences appear to be diminishing. During 1980-2004, exports from Chile, Colombia, and Peru lasted 50 percent longer than Bolivian exports, while products exported to a market during that 25-year period were present for an average of four continuous years (Figure 5).

The lack of productive capacity to compete on international markets can be overcome only by increasing private investment. Other chapters describe the problems faced by companies in unfavorable investment climates. Unless there is an overall change in the investment climate and there are institutions in support of export modernization, exporters will continue to be too small to increase Bolivia's market share on world markets. The National Exports Strategy 2005-2015 identifies these problems as a priority[5] and Supreme Decree 28124 of April 2005 proposes ways for solving these shortcomings.

Bolivia's tariff system has one of the simplest structures in the hemisphere, with the exception of Chile.[6] Most of the tariff lines are 10 percent. About 20 percent of the lines (principally capital goods) have a 5 percent tariff, while 5 percent of the lines have a zero tariff (books, magazines, scientific materials). Median tariff rates are 9 to 10 percent. Yet duties represent 4 percent of the price of imports, because capital goods account for a high percentage of total imports. This is also partially due to tariff preferences under regional agreements.

Bolivia does not use quotas and seldom applies anti-dumping measures. Import licenses are used only for health, environmental, or sanitary reasons and are regulated by Supreme Decree 24440. About 20 percent of tariff lines are affected by this

Figure 5. Percentage of Average Exported Years of a Product, 1980–2000

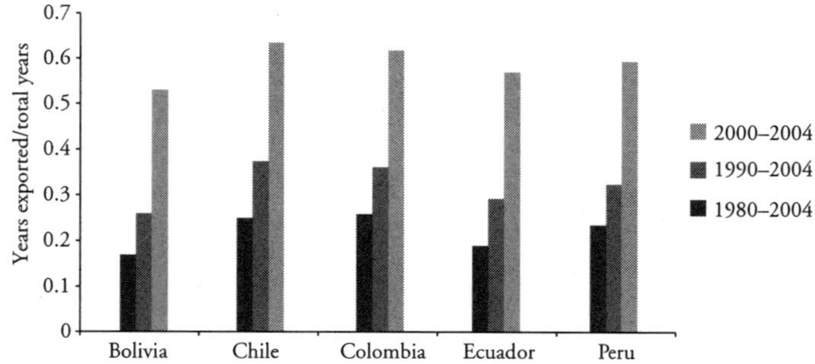

Source: United Nations Comtrade.
Note: The consecutive years of exportation (as a percentage) are measured as the ratio between the number of years during which a product is exported and the total number of years in the period.

type of barrier; these account for 30 percent of imports. The legal framework of sanitary measures, inspection, and certification is set forth in Supreme Decree 24498, and the Standards, Measurements, Accreditation, and Certification System (*Sistema de Normalización, Metrología, Acreditación y Certificación*—SNMAC) is in charge of its implementation. This translates into a relatively open system of non-tariff barriers. Bolivia's *ad valorem* equivalent of non-tariff barriers is 6 percent, the lowest in the hemisphere: Chile has an *ad valorem* equivalent of 7 percent, while Brazil's is 16 percent.[7]

Custom revenue is a major source of fiscal income in Bolivia. In 2004 duty revenue was US$83 million (US$98 million in 2005), but if one includes Value Added Tax (VAT), Specific Consumption Tax (*Impuesto a los Consumos Específicos*—ICE), and the Specific Tax on Hydrocarbons and their Derivatives (*Impuesto Específico a los Hidrocarburos y Derivados*—IEHD) collected at customs, then customs revenue was nearly US$370 million, or 16 percent of government revenue, equal to 4 percent of GDP. VAT represents more than 70 percent of customs revenue, and in 2004, 50 percent of VAT was collected at customs. Given that imports represent only 23 percent of the formal economy,[8] the rate of collections at customs is two to three times higher than the rate for the rest of the economy.

Contraband is estimated at almost US$700 million in 2003.[9] This implies a loss of customs revenue of approximately US$100 to US$150 million.

II. Diagnosis— Principal Restrictions in the Foreign Trade Sector

The two principal problems of Bolivia's foreign trade sector are (i) a lack of diversification of exports and (ii) a lack of integration of the export sector with the rest of the economy. In addition, contraband, tax evasion, and unfair competition against producers in Bolivia's formal sector limit its development. These problems reflect a general situation of weak institutions and extremely volatile institutional strategies that hinder long-term, reliable implementation of reforms.

Bolivia lacks comprehensive development planning. Most exporters agree that the various governmental administrations have placed most of the burden of the country's development on the production and export of extractive raw materials, particularly minerals and hydrocarbons. The enormous quantity of time and resources that the executive and legislative branches devote to promoting these two sectors is a clear sign of the importance and priority placed on them. In contrast, little attention is paid to other potential areas of the economy, such as forestry, agrobusiness, tourism, and manufacturing.

The growth and diversification strategy for non-traditional exports has been inconsistent and inefficiently implemented. Despite the creation of a few trade-promotion mechanisms in the 1990s and countless efforts to develop a long-term strategy for promoting non-traditional exports, Bolivia has yet to implement even one of them in a consistent and effective manner. Most of the strategies are collecting dust on the shelf or are implemented only during their authors' ministerial term of office.

Legislation on foreign trade is lacking; and when it does exist, it is ineffective. Most notably, the country has no foreign trade act or legislation regulating the country's position on issues such as technical barriers to trade, dumping, e-trading, trade in services, certification, and trade negotiations. The authorities also fail to comply with existing legislation for the promotion of exports or the control of imports. An example is the situation faced by exporters regarding fiscal neutrality and refunds (Law 1480 of April 1993). The refund in question is regulated by Supreme Decree 25465 of August 1999. That Decree states that the limit for issuing a refund or a Tax Refund Certificate (*Certificado de Devolución Impositivo*—CEDEIM)[10] must not exceed 35 days (20 working days for issuance of the certificate and 15 days for acceptance of the refund).[11] In practice this process can take up to six months. Such a delay can be prohibitive for a small or medium enterprise with little and/or costly access to the capital market.

A second problem with the tax refund system for exporters is a differentiation in the refund rate between small and large exporters. The automatic mechanism,[12] which applies to companies with exports of less than US$3 million during the prior year in accordance with the Harmonized System 10-digit codes (close to 97 percent of exports in 2004), distinguishes between companies that exported more than US$100,000 and those that exported less than US$100,000. For companies with export amounts in excess of US$100,000, the refund rate is 2 percent; for companies that exported lesser amounts, the rate is 4 percent. This creates incentives to divide large shipments into several parts under the names of several companies, which causes costly and unnecessary distortions to the economy (Figure 6).

The second pillar of the tax neutrality policies for Bolivian exporters is the temporary importation regime for the development of exports (*Régimen de Internación*

Figure 6. Impact of Article 6 of Supreme Decree 24565

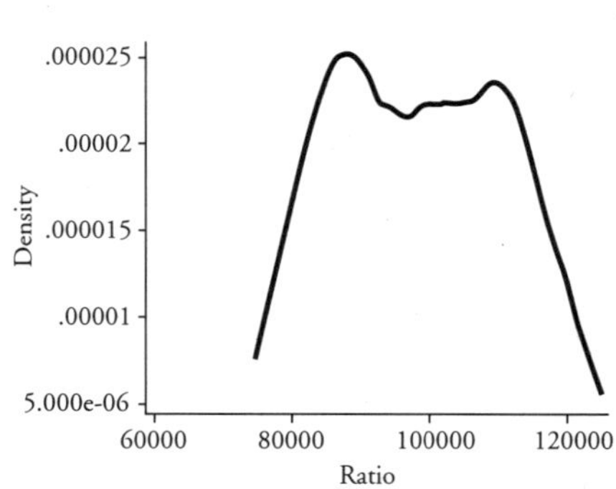

Source: Export data from 2004, Customs Service, La Paz.
Note: The figure demonstrates the Kernel density of the average export transaction by tariff line (approximately US$100,000).

Temporal para Exportación—RITEX), which is regulated by Supreme Decree No. 25706 of March 2000. The imported inputs (raw materials and intermediate merchandise) must be incorporated into a production and re-exportation process within 180 days, extendable for another 180 days. Use of the RITEX regime has been quite rare, but it does offer advantages over the tax refund system (there is no need to wait for the refund or issuance of the CEDEIM certificate). Less than 10 percent of Bolivian exports are estimated to benefit from the RITEX regime. In 2003, only US$82 million in imports entered under the RITEX regime; this represented some US$25 million in tax exemptions. This amount may seem low, but when compared with the alternative of a tax refund with a CEDEIM certificate one year later (considering an interest rate of 10 percent), exporters using the RITEX regime instead of the refund system gained US$2.5 million.

Part of the reason why use of the RITEX regime has been limited is the instability of long-term policies in this area.[13] The first tax incentives were introduced in 1977 to promote export diversification. Up until 1993 the coverage (traditional or non-traditional exports), the type of tax covered by the refund, or the refund system changed every two years. Since 1993 the system has been stabilized and the limited use of the RITEX regime is perhaps primarily due to administrative and processing costs, which are relatively high for the user, especially for small and medium enterprises. The most recent reform of the RITEX regime introduced the possibility that associations of businesspeople or farmers could apply for the RITEX exemption, thus facilitating access for small and medium enterprises.

In general, the infrastructure for promoting exports is weak. The Bolivian Promotion Center (*Centro de Promoción Boliviano*—CEPROBOL) is poorly financed. CEPROBOL's budget is US$300,000; three-fourths of this covers salaries, which leaves little margin for technical assistance programs targeting exporting companies. This represents 0.02 percent of the value of Bolivia's exports. Successful export promotion agencies in the region have budgets in the neighborhood of 0.10 to 0.15 percent of exports (Chile, Colombia, Costa Rica, Mexico). Proexport in Chile started with a budget of US$2 million in 1974 and currently has a budget of US$29 million. In addition, changes in the institutional structure of CEPROBOL are too numerous to describe here (as one example, since 1985, CEPROBOL or its predecessors changed the ministry to which they reported five times).

Trade agreements are multiplying but lack trade vision. Producers and exporters find that the country is continually signing agreements without the needed connection to economic reality or trade interests. Many non-tariff barriers imposed upon Bolivia by its trading partners in Mercosur or the Andean nations are not negotiated, which means that the opportunity is lost for many tariff preferences that could benefit Bolivian exporters. The private sector is asking to be consulted more during trade agreement negotiations and requesting that the agreements be based on trade needs rather than politics.

In terms of recent agreements or those pending negotiation, analysis using trade models in partial equilibrium[14] suggests that the CAN-Mercosur Agreement would reduce Bolivian exports by 1 percent. This is because Bolivia already receives preferential treatment from Mercosur under a bilateral agreement, which would be partially eroded by its extension to other Andean countries. Moreover, Bolivia's preferential treatment in the Andean market would be eroded due to increased competition with Mercosur exports to the other CAN countries. The greatest losses for Bolivia would be in its exports of soybeans and soybean products to Colombia and Venezuela. These losses could be offset if a better regulation of non-tariff barriers were negotiated within these agreements, which would prevent an arbitrary protection of certain Bolivian products exported to Mercosur and the CAN.

Even if ambitious agreements are reached for opening markets, the Doha round would have very modest effects on the Bolivian economy for three reasons: (i) the majority of its trade is preferential; (ii) the economy is already relatively open and has low protection levels; and (iii) the majority of its exports (traditional) face few barriers in the rest of the world.

The Andean-United States agreement has attracted notable attention, though Bolivia's participation has been as an observer. The effects on the country's welfare are modest in either case, but Bolivia would be better off participating in the agreement. If Bolivia participates, the model developed by Francois and Hall (2003) suggests that its exports to the United States would increase by 30 percent, or some US$51 million. If Bolivia does not sign the agreement, its exports would drop by 10 percent. If Bolivia participates in a bilateral agreement, the products whose export to the United States would increase by at least 10 percent would be jewelry, carpentry for construction, wood, tin, men's shirts, sweaters, and T-shirts. It is important to note that Bolivia does not import agricultural products, which are exported massively to the United States. The increase in agricultural imports by Bolivia would be insignificant. As for agricultural exports, soybeans and soybean products would have to compete with exports from the United States in Colombia, Peru, and Ecuador at the same time that competition would be increasing from the members of the Mercosur in the CAN. But this increase of exports from the United States to the Andean markets would occur whether or not there were a trade agreement between Bolivia and the United States.

Even more important is that the agreement with the United States would go beyond traditional market-access negotiations. The agreement would comprehensively regulate trade and the investment relationship between the Andean countries and the United States, with the objective of increasing investment and the economic and social development of the signing countries. Full implementation of a free trade agreement with the United States would lead to modernization of Bolivia's legislation, regulations, and institutions. Bolivia could also benefit from technical assistance that the United States might provide within the framework of an agreement, as it did in the case of the Central American Free Trade Agreement (CAFTA) with the creation of the Institute for Trade Capacity Building in New Orleans, which was devoted to developing capacities to strengthen programs for small and medium enterprises. A complete analysis of the implications of these texts goes beyond the scope of this note, but it is necessary to study them in detail.

Despite significant progress in developing national quality control standards and improving requirements in Bolivia for calibration services, along with a major increase in the number of companies that must demonstrate compliance with pre-established quality standards, the SNMAC has not yet received the attention it deserves from the government. The SNMAC should be regulated by Law and not by a simple Supreme Decree. The need for a law is evident given the proliferation of institutions in this area. The relationship between the SNMAC and these institutions must be clarified. It is also necessary to reactivate the National Quality Control Council (*Consejo Nacional para el Control de Calidad*—CONACAL), which has not met since 2001. This was also identified as a priority in the recent National Exports Strategy 2005-2015.

With respect to customs, the reforms over recent years were highly successful, but there is still room to improve certain technical aspects, such as physical inspections.[15] The law requires inspection of 20 percent of the merchandise. But on average these inspections discover only 1 percent of the fraud. Improving the risk system would subtly pressure importers. Administrative processing could also be simplified.

The relative success of the reform project at the institutional level has been undermined by a lack of capacity to counteract smuggling. From the very start, the customs reform process was associated, in the opinion of the general public, with the fight against contraband. The General Customs Act (*Ley General de Aduanas*—LGA) entrusts this task to the Bolivian Customs Service, but in order to be able to handle this problem, the Customs Service would need other national institutions to be involved as active participants. The creation of the Customs Operating Control police unit against contraband (*Control Operativo Aduanero*—COA) has been an important first step, but COA has neither the personnel nor the funds needed to fulfill its mission. Even so, the solution does not consist of merely increasing COA's staff or providing the unit with more sophisticated equipment for the fight against contraband. An effective policy of fighting against contraband requires the elimination of incentives to smuggle. Implementation of a consistent policy of fighting contraband must begin by eliminating Article Four of the LGA and other related legislation, which prohibits the COA and the Customs Service from conducting control operations on retailers of contraband merchandise. Taxes on imports, particularly the VAT, should also be reviewed, since the tax burden could be excessive (40 percent for whisky, 90 percent for cigarettes, and 50 percent for automobiles). It is also necessary to define and improve the requirements for sanitary and phytosanitary certificates, and for other import licenses, in order to prevent major costs and at times arbitrary decisions by the institutions involved. All import trade operations must be governed under a unified Tax Identification Number (*Número de Identificación Tributaria*—NIT). It is therefore necessary to improve coordination with the National Tax System (*Sistema de Impuestos Nacionales*—SIN) and to engage in combined operations.

III. Policy Recommendations

The trade reforms that Bolivia commenced in the mid 1980s focused on what was easiest. They reformed policies, but not institutions, with the exception of a customs reform in recent years. Duties were lowered, dispersion in the customs structure was reduced, and non-tariff barriers were eliminated. Tax neutrality for exporters was legislated, taxes on exports were eliminated, a quality control system was introduced, and several bilateral and regional preferential trade agreements were signed. But the institutional reforms did not have continuity or were less successful. Support for exports through microeconomic policies is almost nonexistent, and the capacity of customs to fight against contraband is meager, which leaves Bolivian producers in a very weak position to compete in both international and local markets. The most difficult part of the reforms still lies ahead: to fully integrate the export sector into the rest of the Bolivian economy.

Recommendations are divided into those that require immediate action and those that require action in the medium term.

Immediate Action

- Promote the use of the RITEX regime among exporters to streamline procedures and reduce unnecessarily burdensome costs, above all for small and medium enterprises (SMEs). The recent reform that allows associations of farmers or businesspeople to use RITEX is welcome, and its implementation will be key. Explore the possibility of introducing a system of customs duties exemptions for indirect exporters.
- Simplify the automatic refund system on duties and internal taxes (VAT and ICE) for exporters. Introduce a single tax refund rate at 3 percent for all exporters without distinguishing between established or new exporters.
- Abide by the law with respect to the time for issuing the CEDEIM certificates.
- Explore the possibility of eliminating the traditional sector from the refund system, in order to restore this system's original purpose. This would allow for more financing of the system, and would reduce the average tax rate as exemptions are phased out.
- Support and correctly fund the CEPROBOL and other export promotion infrastructure. Under current conditions, CEPROBOL cannot be effective. A study should be made to explore financing sources for CEPROBOL. Alternatives include: (i) a tax on exports of 0.1 percent; (ii) financing from a bilateral aid agency, since an important part of the benefits associated with the promotion of exports are reaped by the rest of the world (by reducing asymmetric information); and (iii) greater private sector participation.
- Study the possibility of joint activities for promoting exports among the members of Mercosur, since the members have a common mechanism for this purpose.

- Consolidate and expand export markets in the CAN, Mercosur, the United States, and Europe. Scarce negotiating capacity should focus on eliminating non-tariff barriers from existing agreements in the region.[16]
- Make a detailed study of the effect on law and regulations of an Andean-United States agreement that would include Bolivia, while also studying the possibility of creating something similar to CAFTA's Institute for Trade Capacity Building, devoted to developing the export capacity of SMEs.
- Define a clear national policy that would fight against contraband and involve all relevant institutions of the public and private sectors.
- Reduce the tax burden on Bolivian importers and companies to lessen incentives for contraband and informality. Suggestions include:
  - Eliminate the Specific Consumption Tax (*Impuesto a los Consumos Específicos*—ICE) on imports. This tax should be charged in the internal market or be eliminated.
  - Charge VAT on C.I.F. (Cost, Insurance, Freight) prices, but not on duties.
  - Facilitate access to the VAT exemption mechanism for small and medium enterprises.
  - Eliminate the simplified system for importers. Importers should enroll in the general system and have an enrollment number (NIT).
- Eliminate the legal restriction against allowing the Customs Service to take action against retailers of contraband merchandise.
- Consolidate COA in the fight against contraband and provide it with more personnel, appropriate training, and state-of-the-art communications technology. This could be financed in part by auctioning seized merchandise.
- Promote cooperation with customs administrations of neighboring countries in order to exchange information on exports and imports; and also, in the medium term, establish a shared border infrastructure.
- Create mechanisms for greater cooperation between the Customs Service and the SIN to fight contraband and tax evasion.
- Prepare legislation regarding imported used items and imported items that are dangerous for consumption, with a particular focus on evaluating the customs value of used items.

Actions for the Medium Term

- Define a clear, consistent strategy to promote exports and growth to reduce poverty. This would include a foreign trade act.
- Improve the stability and continuity of commercial laws and regulations, as well as the overall institutional climate.
- Negotiate more reliable rules on non-tariff barriers with certain preferred trading partners in Latin America (eliminate reference prices and non-automatic licenses in Mercosur and the CAN).

- Enact a law that regulates quality issues for exporting companies and disseminate information on technical barriers to trade in export markets.
- Define support and financing mechanisms for non-traditional exports of small and medium enterprises.
- Explore the possibility of combining the Customs Service and the SIN into a single institution.

Bibliography

ALADI/LAIA. 2004. "*Informe sobre el comportamiento registrado en las condiciones de acceso de los productos de Bolivia al mercado interregional.*" LAIA Secretariat, Montevideo.

Bolaky, B. and Caroline Freund. 2004. "Trade, Regulations and Growth." Policy Research Working Paper No. 3255, Washington DC: World Bank.

Castillo Garay, Antonio. 2002. "*Infraestructura institucional – Apoyo a CEPROBOL.*" Report No. 2, pp. 2-3, Project BOL/61/80, Multifunctional Technical Cooperation for Promotion and Expansion of Exports, ITC (UNCTAD-WTO).

Fanta, Enrique. 2005. "*Evaluación de la Aduana Nacional de Bolivia, su proceso de modernización y reforma institucional 1999-2005 y recomendaciones para su fortalecimiento,*" mimeo, Institutional Reform Program, Ministry of the Treasury, Bolivia.

Francois, Joseph and H. Keith Hall. 2003. "Global Simulation Analysis of Industry-Level Trade Policy," Version 1.5: March, mimeo. World Bank.

Hoekman, Bernard, Alessandro Nicita, and Marcelo Olarreaga. Forthcoming. "Can Doha Deliver a Development Round?" In Bernard Hoekman and Marcelo Olarreaga. eds., 2007. *Global Trade Liberalization and Poor Countries: Poverty Impacts and Policy Implications.* Brookings Institution and Institut d'Etudes Politiques, Paris.

INE (National Statistics Institute). 2005. "Comercio exterior de Bolivia, 1981-2003," available at www.ine.gov.bo.

Kee, Hiau Looi, Alessandro Nicita, and Marcelo Olarreaga. 2005. "Estimating Trade Restrictiveness Indices," mimeo. World Bank.

Kreidler Guillaux, Alfonso and Antonio Rocha Gallardo. 2004. *El contrabando en Bolivia: una visión heterodoxa.* Bolivian Foreign Trade Institute, La Paz.

Ministry of Economic Development. 2005. "Estrategia Nacional de Exportaciones."

Rodríguez Álvarez, Gary Antonio. 2004. *Apertura económica y exportaciones en Bolivia: el papel del Estado (1980-2003).* Bolivian Foreign Trade Institute, La Paz.

Rose, Andrew. 2005. "The Foreign Service and Foreign Trade: Embassies as Export Promotion." NBER Working Paper 11111, Cambridge.

Silva, Claudia. 2004. "Programa de reforma y modernización de la Administración aduanera: evaluación intermedia." Inter-American Development Bank.

World Trade Organization. 1999. *Trade Policy Review: Bolivia.* Geneva.

Endnotes

1. The Herfindhal concentration index is computed as $H = \sum_i s_i^2$, where s_i is the portion of product i in Bolivia's total exports (that is, $\sum_i s_i = 1$). H increases with the concentration of exports. The Herfindhal index is calculated using each product in each market as a unit of observation. It therefore reflects concentration by product and by market.

2. *Tradesim* is an econometric weighting model in which exports are explained by economic and geographic variables (See www.intracen.org).

3. Compared with 6,500 in Chile and 1,650 in Costa Rica (Rodríguez Álvarez, 2004).

4. According to the Exporters' Association, 50 percent of exporting companies closed in 2005. These were small companies (especially in the non-traditional sector) whose sales volumes had little impact on total export amounts, but this did have an effect on the potential for diversifying production.

5. Ministry of Economic Development, 2005.

6. Prior to the reforms that began in 1985, Bolivia's trade policy was very restrictive. Tariffs were more than 70 percent on cigarettes and textiles, 60 percent on automobiles, and 50 percent on liquors and furniture. Import licenses were also frequent. The tariff system of the mid 1990s was similar to today's, and import licenses were eliminated except for health or sanitation purposes.

7. Kee et al., 2005.

8. The informal economy is estimated at 67 percent of GDP, which means that if those activities were incorporated into the formal economy, the locally collected VAT could be almost double, or the VAT rate could nearly be cut in half without affecting total VAT revenue.

9. Kreidler and Rocha, 2004.

10. The CEDEIM is a transferable security, negotiable on the Bolivian stock exchange, that can be used to pay any tax owed to customs or other tax authorities.

11. Unless there is no bank guarantee for the sums associated with the tax refund, in which case it should take between three and four months.

12. The non-automatic mechanism applies to products for which exports exceeded US$3 million. The refund rate is calculated each year based on industry-wide cost information. There is also a system under which companies can challenge the rates decided upon by the government.

13. Rodríguez Álvarez, 2004.

14. For more details on these models, see Francois and May, 2003, and Hoekman, Nicita and Olarreaga, forthcoming.

15. Fanta, 2005.

16. Latin American Integration Association—ALADI/LAIA, 2004.

Part II

With Benefits for All

10

The Dynamics of Poverty and Inequality

Omar Arias

Summary

The majority of Bolivia's population subsists in the face of shortages and inequality. According to data from the first part of this decade, approximately 65 percent of Bolivians are poor and almost 40 percent live in extreme poverty. In addition, income distribution in the country is one of the most unequal in Latin America. This chapter explains some of the reasons for this persistent stagnation and proposes certain policy options designed to address these problems.[1] *In synthesis, the three principal reasons for the high levels of poverty and inequality are:*

First: *Growth during the 1990s focused on exports of natural resources, which generally create few jobs. The labor-intensive sectors and the poorer regions grew little. More important, starting in 1999, negative factors such as loss of investor confidence, deterioration of the terms of exchange, reduced exports, and the coca leaf eradication program slowed growth, which reversed the progress achieved in poverty reduction. In addition, high returns on capital compared with low returns on labor (especially unskilled labor) exacerbated the already deep-rooted inequality in income.*

Second: *Low productivity, especially in the labor-intensive informal sector, has impeded job creation and wage growth. This, in good part, is due to a legal and institutional framework that limits entrepreneurial initiatives, as well as a lack of effective policies to encourage access to the formal economy by smaller firms.*

Third: *Despite expanded access to basic education, the poor, and in particular indigenous groups, have few opportunities to improve their human capital. The result is low labor productivity and restricted access to better paying jobs. Moreover, due to high opportunity costs and an inadequate social welfare system, many drop out of school and end up in low paying jobs.*

Strong, broad-based sustainable economic growth is fundamental for reducing poverty and inequality, but policies for improving labor productivity and job creation are also required. Public policies that would help the government to accomplish this include: (i) remove obstacles to modernization and growth of firms, promoting their integration into the global economy; (ii) modernize labor and business regulations, and provide a framework of incentives so that firms, especially small and medium sized firms, will participate and remain in the formal sector; and (iii) strengthen human capital and social welfare so that the poor can increase their productivity and their ability to access better paying jobs.

I. Poverty and Inequality: Growth and Trends

During the 1990s, poverty and inequality declined; but since 1999, this trend has reversed. During the period of growth, 1993-1999, poverty declined from 52 to 46 percent in the principal urban centers, although urban income inequality remained unchanged. While country-wide data is not available, there is evidence that both national and rural poverty may have also declined in the 1990s (Table 1).

The economic deceleration of the late 1990s reduced growth and reversed progress on the poverty front. Between 1999 and 2002, the population living in poverty increased from 62 to 65 percent, while extreme poverty grew from 36 to 37 percent. The urban poor households were the most affected. Urban unemployment increased from 6 to 9 percent, and urban poverty reverted to the levels of the early 1990s.

Income inequality increased significantly between 1997 and 2002. Bolivia currently has a Gini coefficient greater than 0.55, making it is one of the most inequitable country in the region, together with Brazil and Chile, which both have much lower poverty rates (Figure 1). This inequality reflects significant disparities in assets (such as education and land), household size, and earning gaps based on gender, ethnicity, location, and type of employment. Nine out of every ten Bolivians (both poor and non poor) consider the income distribution "unfair" or "very unfair."

Growth in the 1990s reduced poverty and improved social indicators. Between 1993 and 1998, growth was 4.7 percent per year (2.2 percent per capita), a rate that surpassed other Andean countries for the first time in 40 years. Exports diversified beyond minerals and hydrocarbons, to soybeans, coffee, sugar, and lumber. Investment surpassed 16 percent of GDP, more than two percentage points above the average of the 1980s. Macroeconomic stabilization and structural policies explain most of the growth of the 1990s, which was accompanied by increased labor participation (especially of women) and an improvement in productivity (1.2–1.7 percent per year).

This growth raised income (per capita income grew 13 percent altogether between 1993 and 1997) and reduced poverty. Specifically, the income of the poor in the capital cities grew at the same rate as average income, and poverty diminished from 52 percent in 1993 to 46 percent in 1999 (Figure 2). At the same time, better living and

Table 1. Measures of Poverty, 1993–2002

		Income-Based Estimates			
		Poverty		*Extreme Poverty*	
		Rate	*Gap*	*Rate*	*Gap*
National	1997	63.6	33.7	36.5	18.9
	1999	63.5	36.0	40.7	22.2
	2002	65.2	36.7	41.3	22.3
Capital Cities*	1993	52.0	22.2	23.7	8.4
	1997	50.7	21.0	21.3	7.5
	1999	46.4	18.8	20.7	7.02
	2002	51.0	22.1	23.5	8.8
Urban	1997	54.5	23.8	23.8	9.1
	1999	51.4	22.4	23.5	8.9
	2002	53.9	23.8	25.7	9.4
Rural	1997	78.0	49.4	59.0	34.4
	1999	84.0	59.4	69.9	45.1
	2002	83.5	57.6	67.0	43.3
		Official Estimates			
		Poverty		*Extreme Poverty*	
		Rate	*Gap*	*Rate*	*Gap*
National	1999	62.6	31.3	36.8	15.0
	2000	66.0	34.1	39.8	17.2
	2001	64.0	31.6	37.0	19.6
	2002	64.3	31.0	36.6	14.4
Urban	1999	51.5	22.5	23.6	8.9
	2000	54.8	25.7	28.4	11.0
	2001	54.9	24.4	25.9	14.7
	2002	53.5	23.6	25.5	9.4
Rural	1999	81.6	45.8	59.1	25.4
	2000	85.6	48.7	59.9	28.0
	2001	80.9	43.5	55.5	27.8
	2002	82.1	43.3	54.9	22.6

Source: Economic Policy Analysis Unit (*Unidad de Análisis de Política Económica*—UDAPE), based on the Integrated Household Survey (*Encuesta Integrada de Hogares*—EIH) (1993); National Employment Survey (*Encuesta Nacional de Empleo*—ENE) (1997); and Survey on Improvement in Living Conditions (*Encuesta de Mejoramiento de Condiciones de Vida*—MECOVI) (1999–2002).
Note: Based on per capita household expenses in rural zones and per capita household income in urban zones I: Rate = % of the population. Gap = Poverty Gap (% of difference between the average income of a poor person and the poverty line).
*Capital cities include: Sucre, La Paz, Cobija, Cochabamba, Oruro, Potosí, Tarija, Santa Cruz, Trinidad, and El Alto.

educational conditions in the rural areas suggests that rural poverty might also have diminished.

Despite these achievements, growth was insufficient to pull many Bolivians out of such severe poverty. In 1997, 37 percent of Bolivians were still far from attaining

Figure 1. Gini Coefficients in Latin America Distribution of Equivalent Household Income, Approximately 2000

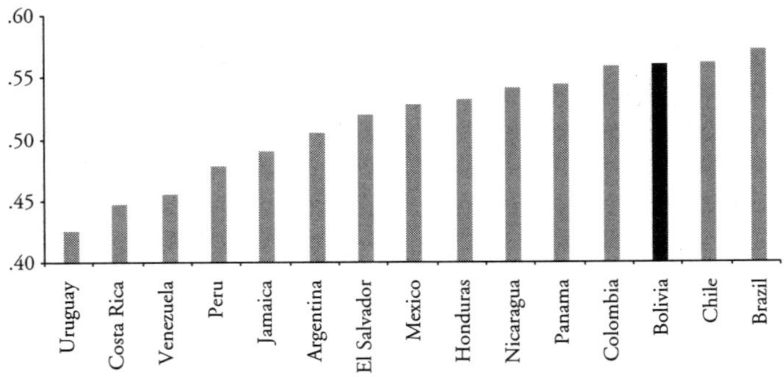

Source: Gasparini et al. (2004).

Figure 2. Growth Rate Curves, 1993–2002
(% of change in household per capita income, by percentile)

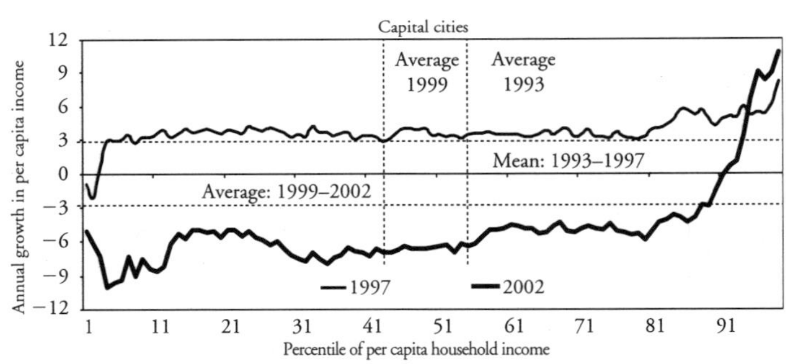

Source: Estimates based on household survey information.
Note: Based on per capita household spending in rural zones and per capita income from the principal occupation of the household in urban areas to improve the comparison among surveys of 1990–2000.

sufficient income to escape poverty. Bolivia has a poverty/growth elasticity of 0.3 to 0.5, while the average elasticity for the region is 1.0. This means that a one percent increase in per capita income contributes to moving less than one-half of a percent of Bolivians out of poverty.

Poverty reduction would have been greater if growth had been sustained, more broad-based, and more labor-intensive. Capital- and skilled-labor intensive sectors such as hydrocarbons, telecommunications, and financial services grew more rapidly, with limited spillovers to agriculture and manufacturing, which employ more than 50 percent of the employed population. Exports diversified, but that did not stimulate the labor-intensive sectors producing for export. The share of exports in the GDP remained unchanged. Growth in these modern resource sectors—in the lowlands around Santa Cruz—did not spread as vigorously to subsistence agriculture and low-productivity artisans, particularly in the highlands.

Bolivia's high poverty and inequality transcend rural-urban and regional boundaries. In addition to the overwhelming portion of the rural population that lives in poverty, there are also large pockets of urban poverty (Figure 3). Urban poverty is concentrated in the valleys and in the central highlands, especially Potosí and Chuquisaca, followed by Beni, La Paz, and Oruro. Santa Cruz and Cochabamba have lower poverty rates, but due to their large populations, they have many poor citizens. Nearly 40 percent of the inhabitants of the department of Santa Cruz are poor, but the city's poverty rate is only 20 percent. Many intermediate cities and small municipalities also have low poverty rates.

Indicators of non-income poverty show more improvement than poverty measured by income, but great challenges remain. Social indicators measuring Unsatisfied Basic Needs (UBNs) and progress toward the Millennium Development Goals (MDGs) improved significantly during 1992-2001. For example, child and infant mortality declined by 30 percent, net enrollment in primary education is approaching 100 percent, and the number of households without potable water and adequate sanitation fell from 50 to 30 percent. Nonetheless, Bolivia is still among the countries with the worst malnutrition and maternal and infant mortality rates in the region, and is off track for meeting the MDG of having all boys and girls complete their primary education.

People's self-perception of their well-being is generally aligned with income poverty. Peoples' self-perceptions of their poverty and measures of income poverty are both largely determined by employment, education, access to assets and basic

Figure 3. Distribution of Per Capita Income by Household, 2002, Urban and Rural

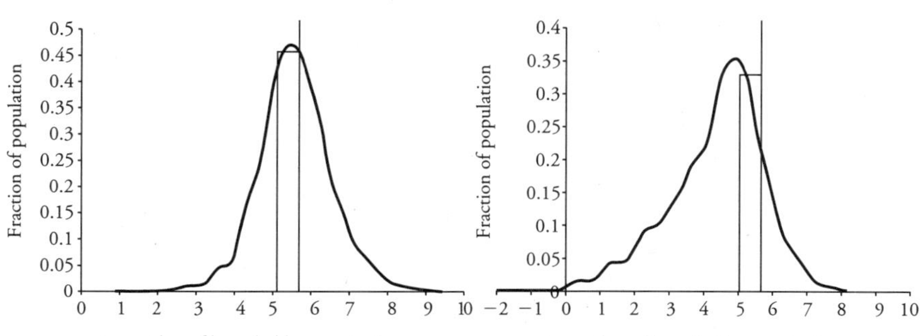

Source: Estimations of the author based on household survey information.

Note: The vertical lines in each figure represent the line of poverty in each area. The figures show the fraction of people in each income level; the area under the curve to the left of the line of poverty is the fraction of poor. The vertical bar gives an idea of the fraction of people with incomes barely under the line of poverty.

services, ethnicity and location. Bolivians tend to fall into income poverty—and also consider themselves poor—when they are young, uneducated, unemployed or underemployed, indigenous, rural dwellers, and lacking basic services.

There are, however, some differences in income and self poverty perception surrounding ethnicity and location. Bolivian Quechuas tend to self-rate poorer than is suggested by income poverty profiles, while the converse is true for Aymaras. With equal access to basic services, rural residents perceive themselves as less poor than urban inhabitants, although they are more likely to be income poor. Thus, exclusion and/or cultural factors (such as sense of empowerment or identity) as well as location-specific characteristics (such as inequality, social capital, or crime) may have meaningful effects on Bolivians' self-perceptions.

One of the main factors that explains the persistence of poverty and inequality is low productivity, particularly of labor, which limits the development of economic activities that are more labor intensive. Factors holding back productivity include: (i) labor demand—the ability of firms and producers to adopt new technologies and production processes, train workers, and actively develop new products and markets; and (ii) labor supply—the ability of the poor to accumulate human capital and effectively utilize it in labor markets.

II. Constraints to Employment Creation—the Demand for Labor

Bolivia's weak business climate hinders investment, productivity, and the creation of jobs. Progress in total productivity in the 1990s did not represent technological improvements or innovations as much as a better allocation of funds following the economic reforms. Physical accumulation of capital (linked to the adoption of new technologies) contributed little to growth, and general labor productivity (GDP per worker) increased by only 0.5 percent per year during the economic upswing. That was reflected in limited improvements to labor productivity in the most productive sectors, such as oil and gas, foodstuffs, and textiles.

Few small and medium enterprises (SMEs) are successfully expanding. Small firms, with 10 employees or less, represent 83 percent of jobs (mostly unskilled jobs) and 25 percent of output; while a few large firms, which employ 50 or more workers, generate two-thirds of output and only 9 percent of jobs (mostly skilled jobs). In addition, labor demand in manufacturing firms takes over a year to adjust to changes in economic conditions. Such a time frame is in the high range for the Latin American countries and is 2.5 times the OECD average. Moreover, there is a high wage-employment trade-off. For each 10 percent increase in real wages, demand for unskilled labor in manufacturing goes down by 6.4 percent (twice the international average and in the high range of the Latin American countries).

A small output market, burdensome regulations, limited and costly credit, and deficient transportation infrastructure limit capacity utilization rates, prospects for

Table 2. Comparison of Investment Climate Indicators in Bolivia and Other Selected Countries of Latin America, 2004

		Country						
		Bolivia	*Chile*	*Colombia*	*Ecuador*	*Honduras*	*Nicaragua*	*Peru*
Starting a Business	Number of Procedures	15	9	10	12	14	13	8
	Time (days)	50	27	102	43	69	62	42
	Cost (% of per capita income)	154.8	10.3	38.0	25.3	38.1	64.1	139.1
Hiring and Firing Workers	Hiring Difficulty Index	61	33	44	72	44	22	11
	Termination Difficulty Index	0	20	40	40	30	40	50
	Employment Rigidity Index	40	24	48	57	44	34	47
	Termination Costs (weeks)	98	51	56	44	77	46	24
Registering Property	Number of Procedures	7	6	5	7	10	7	7
	Time (days)	92	31	33	23	21	36	65
	Cost (% property value)	5.0	1.3	3.2	3.5	6.7	5.8	6.5
Getting Credit	Cost of creating collateral (% of per capita income)	51	5.3	16.0	38.9	10.8	36.6	2.0
	Legal Rights Index	3	4	2	4	3	5	4
	Credit Information Index	4	6	6	4	4	4	4
Protecting Investors	Disclosure Index	1	8	7	7	1	1	4
Enforcing Contracts	Number of Procedures	47	28	35	37	41	36	20
	Time (days)	591	305	381	363	388	545	155
	Cost (% of debt)	10.6	10.4	34.7	18.6	15.3	33.1	16.3
Closing a Business	Time (years)	1.8	5.6	3.1	3.0	8.0	3.8	2.2
	Cost (% assets)	14.5	14.5	7.0	1.0	63	8.0	14.5
	Recovery Rate (cents per dollar)	36.9	23.1	31.3	55.1	20.7	21.9	33.8

Source: Djankov and Mcliesh (2003).

expansion, and therefore, the employment creation in manufacturing (see Table 2). For smaller firms, regulatory restrictions (for example, registration and operating licenses), high collateral requirements to obtain credit and skilled labor shortages are the most restrictive factors. For larger firms, input costs, including credit and access to technology, along with market size, are the most binding constraints.

More specifically:

- *A thin, localized market.* Domestic trade is highly concentrated and there are few exporting firms (for example, while almost 50 percent of the large firms export their products, only 20 percent of small-medium firms export).
- *Burdensome business regulation and weak institutions.*
  - Registering a business is a very slow and expensive process, despite recent improvements.
  - Property is difficult to register and enforcement of contracts and property rights is uncertain.
  - Transaction and information costs are high, particularly those related to credit, technology, and information on domestic and foreign markets, accreditation, and contractual conflicts.
- *Limited access to credit.* The costly collateral required to obtain a loan, especially for smaller firms (over twice the loan amount owed, and above all the required property collateral), reflects thin credit markets, ineffective assets registries, and insecure and costly debt recovery.
- *High logistics costs and risky market conditions.* Supply chains are weak due to slow and costly transportation (on a unit basis, transport in Bolivia is 20 times costlier than in Brazil). Custom clearance remains cumbersome and costly despite some recent improvements, and the quality of domestic services and inputs is poor (for example, unreliable supply of power). As a result, inventories/stock on material are high (36 to 50 days).
- *Restrictive labor regulations.* Labor legislation dating from 1939 mandates conditions for workers that are favorable compared with those of other countries in the region and elsewhere (Figure 4). This legislation—intending to protect workers—ends up increasing the total labor cost, makes firms less competitive, and discourages equitable hiring in the formal market. As a result, it encourages informality and hinders productivity and employment creation. More specifically:
  - Severance pay results in termination costs two to three times higher than in most Andean countries.
  - Benefits (such as retirement or healthcare) represent close to 50 percent of labor costs.
  - Regulations restrict layoffs (including those resulting from economic shocks), seasonal work, overtime, the duration of the work week for women, and work at night.

Faced with few incentives to comply with the rules and regulations, many firms, particularly micro and small enterprises, remain outside the formal sector and lack access to formal institutions (for example, credit and export markets). This situation restricts their potential for expansion, since they cannot capitalize on productivity gains from innovation and economies of scale. More specifically,

- *Smaller firms face low benefits and tax disincentives to become and remain formal because:*
  - Regulatory costs for incorporation of partnership are high.
  - Businesses cannot deduct Value Added Tax when they make purchases from firms registered under the simplified tax regimen (*Servicio de Impuestos Internos*—SII), which covers the majority of small firms.
- *One-size-fits-all labor regulations are not conducive to improving productivity for smaller businesses because:*
  - Benefits mandated by law (principally for social security health services) are expensive for small businesses and can amount to as much as 8 percent of sales. This encourages firms to remain in the informal sector, by which they forgo access to formal credit institutions, training, and exports. Even small firms registered to operate and report taxes often violate the labor laws.

Figure 4. Index of *De Jure* Employment Conditions in Bolivia and around the World, (0–1)

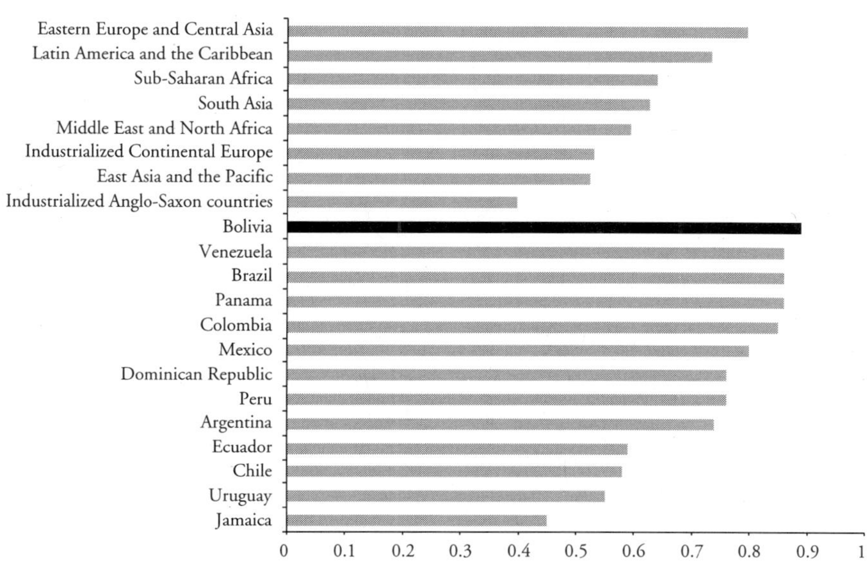

Source: Based on Djankov et al. (2003), taken from the IDB (2004). 1= most protection for workers, 0 = least protection.

III. Constraints to Human Capital Accumulation—The Supply of Labor

Getting a high quality education is harder for the poor, and labor market returns to education are not equal. The combination of high opportunity costs and low returns on education discourage children from poor families from staying in school. The public education system, especially at the secondary level and in rural areas, offers low quality education, which limits the capacity of the poor to accumulate human capital and improve their earning opportunities. Further, poor families face high opportunity costs and are often unable to afford to keep their children in school because they need them to help the family, either through income-generating activities or domestic and agricultural chores. As a result, the distribution of education in Bolivia is unequal and has a very narrow base at the secondary level.

Returns on education are low—six out of ten high school graduates are at risk of poverty because of these low returns. In rural areas, only a post-secondary education offers a significant boost to earnings. Furthermore, education does not carry equal returns for all workers. Education returns range from 0 to 60 percent for the least to best paid workers with primary education, 20 to 30 percent for those with a secondary education, and from 50 to 150 percent for the college-educated. Workers from poor families tend to receive lower returns on education due to limited learning outcomes by the poor (because of low quality schooling in poor areas, as well as health and nutrition deficiencies that impede early-childhood development) and limited access to the better paying jobs for their skills. The employment gaps faced by women, youths, and low educated workers and the earnings disparities solely related to gender, ethnicity, location, and employment sector are above regional averages. Although the income of indigenous workers averages approximately half that of non-indigenous workers, most of these differences are explained by low levels of human capital (quantity and quality of education) for indigenous workers.

The country's demographic trends provide a unique opportunity to improve labor productivity and reduce poverty. Together with Haiti, Bolivia is the only country in Latin America and the Caribbean that is entering the stage of demographic transition where the rate of dependency (the fraction of the population that is too young or too old to work) will be decreasing over the next two decades (Figure 5). As Bolivia enters this stage, an increase is expected in labor force participation. This provides a unique opportunity for educational investments to immediately translate into a more productive labor force and into greater potential to reduce poverty, based on better quality work in the medium term.

Low opportunity costs for self-employment and non-wage benefits encourage large employment in the informal sector. Bolivia's urban informal sector is large and heterogeneous. In 2002, more than 55 percent of the labor force was in the informal sector, either as self-employed (40 percent) or salaried workers (15 percent). An additional 10 percent of workers were unpaid, principally working in family businesses

Figure 5. Demographic Transition and Accumulation of Capital in Bolivia and Latin America

Window of Opportunity (Rate of Dependency)

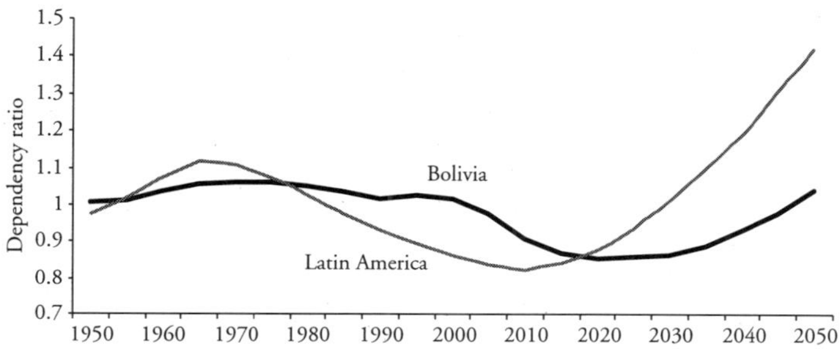

Percentage of the Labor Force by Educational Level

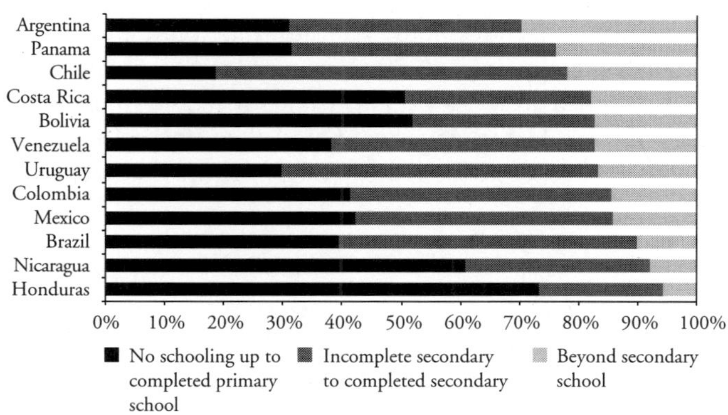

Source: IDB (2004).

or as apprentices. Informal employment largely reflects the low opportunity costs and non-income benefits of informality. For many Bolivians it offers a competitive alternative to low-productivity formal sector jobs or no work at all. Moreover, self-employment may be more attractive to certain sectors of the population, such as women seeking flexible work hours to balance their work and family obligations, or the indigenous who may face less discrimination as independent workers than they might as employees in a company. In fact, the self-employed perceive themselves as less poor than salaried workers with similar characteristics, an indication of the importance of non-monetary benefits of self-employment.

Due to low labor productivity of workers in the informal sector, those who work for wages in the informal sector appear to be at a great disadvantage compared to those working for wages in the formal sector with the same capabilities and job characteristics, particularly for those at the bottom of the salary scale. In part, this is due to lower access of informal firms to programs for labor training, technological adaptation, and other interventions that can improve productivity.

Migration has increased income opportunities but has had limited impact in reducing poverty. Although a certain amount of migration has been present from the less developed regions to the more developed ones, it has remained small among the rural poor. There is also significant migration toward the rural areas, which are experiencing an economic boom, especially in the region around Santa Cruz.

Those who emigrated to urban areas improved their income upon moving (this was particularly true for those on the lower end of the earnings scale). Despite migrants lacking contacts and urban experience, they were able to obtain competitive urban jobs. Therefore, it is probable that rural to urban migration directly helped to reduce poverty, and might also have helped indirectly through remittances.

However, the small flows of migration are not providing a safety valve for the poor in rural areas. Nearly 350,000 persons migrated during the 1993-1997 boom, of which only 69,000 were rural-to-urban migrants. Individuals from the poorest locations and indigenous household heads are more prone to rural-to-rural migration. The young, more educated, women, and small families are more likely to migrate to urban areas. As a result, while urban and rural labor markets seem interlinked, the absolute magnitudes of cross flow remain small. This partly reflects the high costs and possibly non-pecuniary factors that affect settlement decisions.

IV. Selected Policy Recommendations to Reduce Poverty and Inequality

Restoring sustainable economic growth and facilitating development of labor-intensive sectors are essential to reducing poverty and inequality in Bolivia. The country could have higher growth in the medium and long term if it works on developing the gas industry. Nonetheless, in order to have a significant impact on poverty reduction, such efforts must be accompanied by a series of policies that, among other things, promote broader investment, increase productivity, and create jobs.

Policy reforms would be well positioned to accomplish this by focusing on: (i) removing obstacles to firm modernization and growth while promoting integration into the global economy; (ii) modernizing business and labor regulations and providing a proper framework and incentives for firms, especially small and medium enterprises, to participate and remain in the formal sector, and thereby increase their productivity; and (iii) strengthening human capital and social protection for the poor to enhance their productivity and ability to obtain better paying jobs. Specific policy recommendations are elaborated below.[2]

Measures to remove obstacles to firm modernization and growth while promoting increased productivity and integration into the global economy include:

- Simplify procedures and reduce the cost of business registration, especially in large municipalities, emulating the efforts of the municipality of La Paz and other local governments.
- Implement incentives (for example, partial tax credits) for the acquisition of new technologies (including in the manufacturing sector). This should include not only computer hardware and information technologies, but also management techniques and labor training, and, in the case of agriculture, incentives for the acquisition of small-scale rural technology and new crop varieties.
- Promote broader access to prudent financing for SMEs, among other methods, through an overhaul of laws on collateral.
- Increase participation in global markets, in particular through the adoption of free-trade agreements that will deepen exports and promote investment and technology transfers.
- Encourage the creation of producer and exporter associations to reduce information costs and take advantage of the benefits of trade and other market opportunities.

Modernize labor and business regulations to facilitate formal sector participation by implementing measures to:

- Reduce the cost of registering and expanding businesses for microenterprises and SMEs, particularly the cost of incorporating partners, General Tax Regimen registration, and obtaining export licenses. This could be accomplished by rationalizing documentation requirements (for example, notary registration) and licensing processes, and by optimizing on-line business portals for registrations and licenses at municipal government offices.
- Establish pilot initiatives to promote the formalization of small firms, including initiatives to: encourage small businesses and producers to participate in public tender processes,[3] grant partial credits on added value taxes for eligible firms, and offer business development services (access to private credit, court services, administrative and accounting practices). Priority should be given to supporting initiatives for innovation and export-oriented production. Bolivia could benefit from the successful experience of small business development bureaus, such as in Chile, Italy, and the United States.
- Streamline labor regulations, which currently limit the ability of firms to expand and contract along with economic cycles. Align regulations with international practices and reduce the cost of mandated labor benefits, which are currently about 50 percent of labor costs and only benefit a minuscule proportion of Bolivian workers.

- Simplify, reduce the cost of, and increase the transparency of government bureaucratic procedures required to access technology, quantify certification of quality, accreditation, and dispute resolution.
- Strengthen institutions and coordinate public offices to reduce duplication and transaction costs, particularly at the Superintendency of Enterprises and the Labor Ministry.

Strengthen human capital and social protection for the poor to enhance their productivity and ability to get better jobs with the following measures:

- *Raise the quality of the education system, particularly for the poor.* An educational strategy needs to be implemented that targets developing basic cognitive capacities and improving the labor force's productivity. The key elements of this strategy, discussed in detail in the chapter on the education, should include measures to:
  - Reduce the coverage gap in universal basic education, improve transitions to secondary education and access to private higher education for poor students, and address the problem of low quality and inequalities in educational performance at all levels. This can be achieved through results-based management, especially in municipalities with the poorest educational results.
  - Implement a conditional cash transfer program that provides sufficient incentive to very poor families with children at risk, in order to promote preventive health and nutrition and to keep children in school. To accomplish this, recent national experience in El Alto and international experiences, especially in Brazil (*Bolsa Escola*) and Mexico (*Oportunidades*) can be drawn upon, bearing medium-term fiscal restrictions in mind to ensure sustainability. The cost of similar programs in the region ranges from 0.5 to 1 percent of GDP.
- *Improve labor market equity and job opportunities.* This could be achieved by implementing measures to:
  - Reduce employment obstacles by expanding pre-school installations and child care centers in order to facilitate the participation of women and migrants in the labor force. Community-led crime prevention efforts should also be promoted, particularly in marginal urban neighborhoods, to allow workers, especially women, to take advantage of available job opportunities.
  - Provide training at secondary schools and colleges in relevant skills demanded by the labor market, and encourage the private provision of job placement services.
  - Use the recently developed consumption-based poverty map to target interventions aimed at income generation for the poor. These actions could include investments to stimulate growth; programs to develop human cap-

ital, community assets, and income generation; and investments that promote a gradual integration of migrants.

- Strengthen investments in basic utilities and transportation infrastructure in poor communities, in coordination with temporary job creation initiatives.

V. Synergies in Policies for Growth and for the Reduction of Poverty and Inequality

The outlook for growth depends more on internal stability than on favorable external circumstances. The country has an opportunity to promote more inclusive economic growth that creates a "virtuous circle" of economic growth and poverty reduction. International experience shows that Bolivia's growth potential can improve if major reforms are adopted and the needs of the poor and marginalized sectors are addressed.[4]

Impact simulations of some of the above-cited policy options suggest that if growth indicators were to improve significantly, per capita GDP growth could be sustained at, or even surpass, 4 to 5 percent per year. Given how deep and extensive poverty is in Bolivia, and the skewed income distribution, these growth rates are needed in the medium and long term to reduce poverty in the country. Indeed, the MDG of halving the incidence of extreme poverty by 2015 could be attained with such growth rates, especially in conjunction with other pro-poor policy interventions. Economic simulations indicate that individual policy reforms will have a relatively small impact on growth and poverty by themselves but will have a much larger impact if the reforms are implemented as part of a comprehensive strategy of mutually reinforcing reforms that includes macroeconomic stability.

Bibliography

Andersen, L., A. Brooks and A. Mercado. 2004. "Macroeconomic Policies to Increase Social Mobility and Growth in Bolivia." Institute for Socio-Economic Research, Catholic University of Bolivia, La Paz, Bolivia.

Andersen, L. and R. Faris. 2002a. "Natural Gas and Income Distribution in Bolivia." Institute for Socio-Economic Research, Working Paper n. 1/2001, Catholic University of Bolivia, La Paz, Bolivia.

———. 2002b. "Reducing Volatility Due to Natural Gas Exports: Is the Answer a Stabilization Fund?" Institute for Socio-Economic Research, Working Paper n. 11/2001, Catholic University of Bolivia, La Paz, Bolivia.

Arias, O. and W. Sosa. 2004. "Subjective and Objective Poverty in Bolivia." Background paper for the 2005 World Bank Bolivia Poverty Assessment.

Bossert, T. 2000. "Decentralization of Health Systems in Latin America: A Comparative Study of Chile, Colombia, and Bolivia." Harvard School of Public Health. Boston, Massachusetts.

De Ferranti, D., G. Perry, F. Ferreira and M. Walton. 2003. *Inequality in Latin America & the Caribbean: Breaking with History?* Washington D.C.: The World Bank.

Djankov, Simeon, and Caralee Mcliesh. 2003. *Doing Business in 2004: Understanding Regulation.* Washington, DC: Oxford University Press and World Bank.

Doria Medina, S. 1990. "Características y perspectivas de la industria boliviana." *La industria: problemas y perspectivas.* La Paz, Bolivia: ILDIS.

Faguet, J. 2004. "Does Decentralization Increase Government Responsiveness to Local Needs? Evidence from Bolivia." *Journal of Public Economics* 88: 867–893.

Gasparini, L., M. Cicowiez, F. Gutiérrez and M. Marchionni. 2004. "Simulating Income Distribution Changes in Bolivia: A Microeconometric Approach." Background paper for the 2005 World Bank Bolivia Poverty Assessment.

Inter-American Development Bank (IDB). 2003. *Good Jobs Wanted: Labor Markets in Latin America. 2004 Economic and Social Progress Report.* Baltimore: The Johns Hopkins University Press.

International Monetary Fund. 2004. "Bolivia: Second Review under the Stand-By Arrangement and Request for Waiver of Applicability and Modification of Performance Criteria. IMF Country Report 04/5. International Monetary Fund, Washington, D.C.

Jiménez, W. and F. Landa. 2004a. "Poverty and Indigenous Peoples in Bolivia, 1989-2002." Background paper for report: Indigenous People, Poverty and Human Development 1994-2004. World Bank, Washington, D.C.

———. 2004b. "*¿Bolivia Tuvo Crecimiento 'Pro-Pobre' entre los años 1993 y 2002?*" UDAPE Working Paper for the World Bank Bolivia Poverty Assessment.

———. 2004c. "*Empleo y Productividad de la Pequeña y Mediana Empresa de la Manufactura en Bolivia 1995-1999.*" UDAPE background paper for the World Bank Bolivia Poverty Assessment.

Kaufmann, D., M. Mastruzzi and D. Zavaleta. 2002. "Sustained Macroeconomic Reforms, Tepid Growth: A Governance Puzzle in Bolivia?" Processed. The World Bank, Washington, D.C.

Klasen, S, M. Grosse, R. Thiele, J. Lay, J. Spatz and M. Wiebelt. 2004. "Operationalizing Pro-Poor Growth Country Case Study: Bolivia." University of Göttingen and Kiel Institute for World Economics.

Landa, F. 2003. "*Las Dotaciones de la Población Ocupada ¿Son la Única Fuente que Explica la Desigualdad de Ingresos en Bolivia?: Una Aplicación de las Microsimulaciones.*" Draft, UDAPE.

Lay, J. 2001. "Segmentation and Informality in Urban Labor Markets: Evidence from Bolivia and Implications for Poverty Reduction." Kiel Institute for World Economics.

Loayza, N., P. Fajnzylber and C. Calderón. 2002. "Economic Growth in Latin America and the Caribbean: Stylized Facts, Explanations, and Forecasts." World Bank, Regional Study LAC.

Maloney, W., "Informality Revisited." *World Development* 32, No. 7:1159-1178.

Muñoz, R. and A. Palma. 2003. "Determinants of Firm Size and Capacity Utilization in Bolivian Manufacturing Sector." Background paper for the World Bank Bolivia Poverty Assessment. Mimeographed. The World Bank, Washington, D.C.

Muñoz, R., A. Palma and O. Arias. 2004. "Determinants of Firm Size and Capacity Utilization in Bolivian Manufacturing Sector." Background paper for 2005 World Bank Bolivia Poverty Assessment.

Nina, O. and A. Brooks de Alborta. 2001. "Vulnerabilidad macroeconómica ante shocks externos: el caso boliviano." Institute for Socio-Economic Research Working Paper n. 10/2001, Catholic University of Bolivia, La Paz, Bolivia.

Ravallion, M. and M. Lokshin. 2002. "Self-Rated Economic Welfare in Russia," *European Economic Review*. Processed.

———. 2001. "Identifying Welfare Effects Using Subjective Questions," *Economica*, 68: 335-357.

Rodrick, D. and R. Hausman. 2003. "Economic Development as Self-Discovery," *Journal of Development Economics* (Netherlands) 72, No. 2:603-33, December.

Saavedra, J. and M. Torero. 2000. "Labor Market Reforms and their Impact over Formal Labor Demand and Job Market Turnover: The Case of Peru." Research Network Working Paper R-394. Inter-American Development Bank, Washington, D.C.

Tannuri-Pianto, M., D. Pianto and O. Arias. 2004a. "Informal Employment in Bolivia: A Lost Proposition?" Background Paper for the 2005 World Bank Bolivia Poverty Assessment.

———. 2004b. "Rural-Urban Migration in Bolivia: An Escape Boat?" Background paper for the 2005 World Bank Bolivia Poverty Assessment.

Unidad de Análisis de Políticas Sociales y Económicas (Economic and Social Policies Analysis Unit - UDAPE). 2003a. "Estrategia Boliviana de Reducción de la Pobreza: Informe de Avance y Perspectivas." La Paz, Bolivia

———. 2003b. *"Pobreza y Desigualdad en Municipios de Bolivia: Estimación del Gasto de Consumo Combinando el Censo 2001 y las Encuestas de Hogares."* La Paz, Bolivia.

United Nations Development Programme, (UNDP). 2000. *Human Development Report 2000: Human Rights and Human Development.* New York: Oxford University Press.

———. 1999. *Human Development Report 1999: Globalization with a Human Face.* New York: Oxford University Press.

World Bank. 2006. *Growth and Poverty Reduction: Vicious and Virtuous Circles.* Latin America and Caribbean Region, World Bank, Washington D.C.

———. 2005. "Bolivia—Poverty Assessment: Establishing the Basis for More Pro-Poor Growth." Report No. 28068, Washington, D.C.

———. 2004a. "Public Expenditure Report." Washington, D.C.

———. 2004b. "Social Sector Programmatic Credit Document." Washington, D.C.

———. 2001. "Bolivia Microeconomic Constraints and Opportunities for Higher

Growth." Climate Investment Assessment, Report No. 24746-BO, Washington, D.C.

———. 2000. "Bolivia: Poverty Diagnostic." Washington, D.C.

———. 1999. *"Consultando con los Pobres: Reporte de Síntesis Nacional."* Washington, D.C.

———. 1996. "Bolivia; Poverty, Equity, and Income: Selected Policies for Expanding Earning Opportunities for the Poor." Report No. 15272-BO. Vol. II: Background papers. Washington, D.C.

Endnotes

1. World Bank, 2005.
2. These options complement others contained in other chapters of this volume and recent World Bank reports for Bolivia.
3. Presidential Decree 27328 "*Compro Boliviano*" ("I Buy Bolivian") establishes the legal basis for this.
4. World Bank, 2006.

11

Social Inclusion of Indigenous Peoples

David Tuchschneider
with the collaboration of Gillette Hall, Ruth Plains, McDonald Benjamin, and Vivian Viaña.

Summary

This chapter examines the social exclusion faced by indigenous peoples in Bolivia.[1] *The starting point of the discussion is the income gap between indigenous and non-indigenous peoples. This gap is a legacy of centuries of exclusion and discrimination, imposed through inequitable institutions that favored privileged groups of society, that keeps funds from being allocated to the most socially successful uses. This chapter is divided into three sections. The first section presents a summary diagnosis of the situation of indigenous peoples. This section points out that most of the current income differential is explained by intergenerational inequality traps—the negative accumulation of historic exclusion and discrimination. The second section addresses two challenges: to correct imbalance in personal development (equality of means) and to overcome discrimination (partiality in processes). The third section focuses on concrete policies to complement recommendations for the fight against poverty formulated in other chapters of this volume.*[2]

I. Diagnosis

What proportion of the Bolivian population is indigenous?

The history of Bolivia is marked by major economic and social inequalities. For example, according to figures from the National Household Survey of 1999, the richest decile of the population absorbs almost 43 percent of the nation's income, that is, 140 times more than the poorest decile, which receives only 0.3 percent. These figures rank Bolivia among the most unequal countries in the Latin America and Caribbean region. Such enormous differences can be explained, in part, by social exclusion. Income differences, access to public goods and services, and political power all appear to be associated with ethnic, racial, regional, and gender differences, that is, with factors beyond the control of the individual.

Social exclusion tends to be determined by the historic construction of "inequality traps"[3] and is manifested through the stratification of society into groups that have unequal access to opportunities, institutions, and political power. Economic, social and political inequalities restrict social mobility and form an obstacle for development and the fight against poverty.

According to data from the National Population and Housing Census of 2001, more than half the population of Bolivia is indigenous. Depending upon the identification criteria used, the percentage varies from 53 percent (by language spoken) to 62 percent (by self-identification). Not unlike the rest of the Bolivian population, indigenous peoples have been urbanized; today approximately half of the indigenous population lives in urban centers,[4] though the rural area continues to be predominantly indigenous (Table 1). The indigenous population is not homogeneous—there are 36 recognized ethnic groups,[5] although the Quechuas and Aymaras form the majority of the population (Table 2).

Although the indigenous population has grown in absolute terms over the past 50 years (from 1.7 million in 1950), their percentage of the total population has diminished over that same period. Based on language spoken, between 1976 and 2001, the annual rate of growth of the non-indigenous population was 4.2 percent, compared

Table 1. Percentage of Indigenous Population, Using Different Indicators

Identification Criterion	*Total*	*Urban*	*Rural*
Self-identification[a]	62.0	53.4	77.7
Language spoken[b]	53.2	39.3	77.1
Language in which the person learned to speak[c]	35.5	19.2	63.3

Source: National Statistics Institute (*Instituto Nacional de Estadística*—INE): National Population and Housing Census 2001.
Note: a. Population age 15 or older; b. Population age 6 or older; c. Population age 4 or older.

Table 2. Self-Identification as Indigenous Peoples for the Population Age 15 or Older
(as a percentage of the indigenous population)

Area	*Quechua*	*Aymara*	*Guaraní*	*Chiquitano*	*Mojeño*	*Other Native*	*Total Indigenous*
National	49.5	40.7	2.5	3.6	1.4	2.4	100.0
Urban	45.3	43.6	2.5	4.4	1.9	2.4	100.0
Rural	54.8	37.0	2.5	2.5	0.8	2.4	100.0

Source: Prepared by the author based on information from the INE.

with 1.4 percent for the indigenous population. Due to this difference, during this period the percentage of the population that was indigenous declined by almost 17 percent (Table 3).

This trend is one of the least studied phenomena of Bolivia's demography. There are three factors that can explain this relative decrease: differences in fertility and mortality rates, migration out of the country, and cultural assimilation processes (*mestizaje*).[6] It is not possible to reach a definitive conclusion without more detailed research, but there are indications that changes in identity and the abandonment of one's native language, possibly correlated with social mobility, transform a large proportion of the indigenous population.[7]

The data demonstrate that, regardless of the indicator used, the proportion of the population identified as indigenous decreases with each new generation (Table 4). This is not surprising considering that cultural change is promoted in numerous social and governmental realms and is reinforced through discrimination.[8] Identity is generated or changes as a function of the interaction of internal and external processes experienced by persons and groups. Individuals can reject their cultural legacy and adopt lifestyles different from those of their parents. Sometimes, these

Table 3. Percentage of the Population Age 6 or Older who Speak a Native Language

Year	*National*	*Urban*	*Rural*
Census 1976	69.9	53.3	82.1
Census 1992	60.0	45.8	80.1
Census 2001	53.2	39.3	77.1

Source: Prepared by the author based on information from INE.

Table 4. Percentage of the Indigenous Population by Different Indicators and Age Groups

Population by Age Group	*Learned to Speak in a Native Language*	*Speaks a Native Language*[a]	*Indigenous Self-Identification*[b]
Age Group			
Children (4–12)	25	37	No data available
Adolescents (13–18)	28	40	55
Youth (19–25)	30	48	58
Adults (26–44)	40	61	63
Adults (45–64)	52	76	66
Elderly Adults (65 or more)	63	85	70

Source: INE, National Population and Housing Census 2001.
Note: a. The first age group includes children ages 6 to 12; b. The second age group includes adolescents ages 15 to 18.

changes take place through imitating society's cultural models. Other times, they take place as the result of explicit policies aimed at generating national identities, such as the policies that characterized the 1952 revolution. Finally, they sometimes take place in an attempt to escape discrimination by integrating into a more homogeneous group. Nonetheless, discrimination can have several different effects on identity, as a function of individual and group processes in which people are living. In response to these processes, sometimes identities are reaffirmed or are abandoned, although never unidirectionally. If the existence of a direct relationship were shown, however, between social mobility and changes in identity, this would affect the relationship measured between poverty and membership in an ethnic group. Social mobility has experienced a gradual increase since colonial times, but it has accelerated considerably since the early 1950s.

II. Incidence of Poverty in the Indigenous and Non-Indigenous Population[9]

The percentage of indigenous persons whose income is below the poverty line is notably greater than that of non-indigenous persons. On a national level, seven out of every 10 indigenous people are poor, as compared with five out of every 10 non-indigenous people. Both the incidence of poverty and the difference between the two groups is less in urban areas. Likewise, extreme poverty affects a greater percentage of indigenous people. This is even more notable in the rural areas, where the gap between the indigenous and non-indigenous population living in extreme poverty is almost 20 percentage points (Table 5). The incidence of poverty is even greater among monolingual indigenous people, 84 percent of whom are living in poverty.

An important statistic is that the probability of being poor on account of being indigenous in Bolivia has declined from 16 percent in the mid 1990s to 13 percent

Table 5. Incidence of Poverty and Extreme Poverty by Income Method
(as a percentage)

	Incidence of Poverty (%)			*Incidence of Extreme Poverty (%)*		
Population	*Total*	*Indigenous*	*Non-Indigenous*	*Total*	*Indigenous*	*Non-Indigenous*
National	63.1	73.9	52.5	39.5	52.5	26.9
Urban	51.5	59.1	47.3	23.9	29.9	20.6
Rural	82.8	86.3	73.6	66.2	71.6	52.1
Capital Cities	48.6	56.8	44.0	22.2	28.6	18.7

Source: Jiménez, Landa and Yáñez, based on the Integrated Household Survey (*Encuesta Integrada de Hogares*—EIH, National Employment Survey (*Encuesta Nacional de Empleo*—ENE), and the Survey on Improvement in Living Conditions (*Encuesta de Mejoramiento de Condiciones de Vida*—MECOVI), in Hall and Patrinos (2006).

in 2002.[10] Nonetheless, the degree of disparity for indigenous poverty (which measures the depth of poverty) is approximately twice as large as for non-indigenous people, which suggests the magnitude of the effort needed to correct this situation.[11] These levels of poverty and their probabilities are directly related to the income gap among the various population groups. According to data from the MECOVI Survey 2002,[12] the monthly average income of non-indigenous men (US$189) is practically double that of indigenous men (US$92). In the case of women, the income of non-indigenous women (US$112) is almost two and a half times higher than that of indigenous women (US$46).

How can the income gap between indigenous and non-indigenous peoples be explained?

According to a study by Hall and Patrinos (2006), 73 percent of the gap is due to "observable" factors, such as years of schooling, experience, hours worked, health, marital status, and job situation; but 27 percent of the gap between the average income of indigenous and non-indigenous peoples is due to "non-observable" factors, such as discrimination.[13] A first conclusion in this regard is that almost three quarters of the income gap among the population is explained not by problems of actual discrimination in the labor market, but by educational differences (and hence, differences in qualifications) of workers. Therefore, efforts to equalize income should principally focus on access to education, among other observable factors. At the same time, "non-observable" factors, such as discrimination, also merit a more detailed analysis, with the aim of developing policies to meet these challenges (see the following two sections).

It should be underscored that the "observable" factors themselves have their origin in a long history of social exclusion; that is, policies and institutions that have maintained and reproduced inequality of opportunity over time, resulting in limited access for the indigenous population to services as basic and important for their personal development as education and health.[14] The fact that income and capacities are related to circumstances of birth, such as membership in an ethnic group, gender, or place of birth (predetermined factors), clearly demonstrates the existence of inequality traps.[15] Such traps tend to be the fruit of complex relationships among several factors, including an unequal distribution of access to services and markets through which to develop human capacity, a lack of infrastructure services, partiality of the justice system, and concentration of political power. Based on these factors, certain power groups can attempt to appropriate state funds and institutions for themselves, with the aim of guaranteeing that public spending will be allocated in a manner that favors their interests, thereby resulting in inequality of opportunity.

One of the consequences of the institutionalization of inequality is that the unequal formation of human capital is transmitted from generation to generation, thereby perpetuating the obstacles and limitations that individuals face upon being unable to transform their human capital into social achievements. In this way, inequality becomes consolidated over time. These trends provoke not only injustices, but also persistent inefficiencies, since they keep the country's scarce funds, whether allocated by governments or markets, from being put to best use (for example, when the educational system favors youth with higher income rather than those with greater talent and potential). Finally, a very unequal environment diminishes the impact of economic growth in poverty reduction, since the poor population does not easily benefit from growth.[16]

As discussed in the following two sections, this distinction between observable factors that result from historic social exclusion (an accumulation of the effects of inequality of opportunity and of historic discrimination) and "non-observable" factors, such as current discrimination, lead to different policy recommendations.

What factors influence social exclusion and poverty?

When certain indicators of results (for example, income level and education) are correlated with ethnic origin (or other predetermined factors), we can conclude that the differences are caused by inequality of opportunity.[17] Other chapters in this book go into greater detail on the statistical results of inequality of opportunity. Accordingly, at this point, we will highlight only certain key factors.[18]

Human Capacity

The first opportunity that must be considered is the opportunity to live. The great accomplishment of reducing national infant and child mortality rates (by almost 40 percent between 1989 and 2003) is overshadowed by the persistence of high rates in the rural areas of the highlands and valleys, which have mainly indigenous inhabitants. In the most extreme case, for example, the infant mortality rate in the Andean rural area is practically double that of the eastern urban area.[19]

A second opportunity refers to infant development. The development of capacities is highly related to infant nutrition. The 24 months following birth are a key period to prevent or correct the effects of malnutrition.[20] Early detection and treatment of infant malnutrition makes it possible to avoid the damage that takes the form of varying degrees of physical and mental retardation. This damage is irreversible after age two, long before children are eligible for school breakfasts. According to 2002 data, 12 out of every 100 children under the age of two are at nutritional risk. This figure, in the case of the rural population, which is majority indigenous, rises to the alarming rate of 26 out of every 100 children.[21]

The third realm of opportunity is education. Its importance is vital, as is demonstrated by the fact that the income gap responds above all to differences in access to education. The gap in school attendance between indigenous and non-indigenous peoples has been closing in recent years with greater coverage of the educational system, but it continues to be startling. On the other hand, the data demonstrate that the performance of indigenous students is lower than that of non-indigenous students, but no studies make it possible to confirm to what degree this result is related to differences in the quality of schools (especially in the rural areas), discriminatory bias in the classroom, or family dynamics (which, in turn, can result from the discrimination previously endured by the parents).[22] In all events, it is necessary to improve the quality of education. For purposes of this work, bilingual, intercultural education appears to be a very important option, in light of international studies that suggest students who study in their native language during the first years of their basic education perform better.

Economic Opportunities

International evidence demonstrates that to escape poverty, in addition to improving human capacities, people need access to several public goods and services.[23] A first fundamental need is the provision of infrastructure services. Despite the investments made in the past two decades in the construction of roads, electricity services, potable water, and telecommunications, there are still enormous gaps, particularly in the countryside.[24] It is important to close these gaps with more basic infrastructure in rural population centers, given the impact of such infrastructure on the quality of life and rural productivity. Indeed, such services provide access to potable water, rural electrification, and better access to markets through a more extensive rural roads network.

A fundamental requirement for indigenous communities is access to land, given the importance of land both in production and in community, culture, and life. The chapter on land contained in this volume makes a more thorough examination of unequal land distribution and important market failings that reduce access to this resource.[25] In this research on social inclusion, of note is the major advance represented by the Law on the National Agrarian Reform Institute (*Instituto Nacional de Reforma Agraria*—INRA), with the recognition of Original Community Lands (*Tierras Comunitarias de Origen*—TCO). As of the enactment of this law, 49 TCO claims have been filed in lowlands (including eight indigenous territories created by supreme decree), for a total of more than 14 million hectares, that is, more than 10 percent of the total area of the country. With the encroachment of the agricultural border into ancestral lands, legal/agricultural dynamics in the lowlands jeopardize the social and economic reproduction of the indigenous peoples, who depend on multiple forms of land use. In the highlands, this issue is slightly more complex, since the principal problems are not related to legal insecurity over land ownership.[26] In the highlands and valleys, the central problem is related to a vicious circle of agricultural intensification, loss of soil fertility, and falling yields, which directly affect income (from sales and subsistence agriculture).[27] In addition, there is a high potential for jurisdictional conflicts over land in these areas, given the superposition of TCOs, indigenous municipal districts (*Distritos Municipales Indígenas*—DMI), and municipalities.[28]

Given the importance of employment as a source of income in poor families (since they do not derive a significant proportion of their income from dividends, rents, or interest), it is essential to stimulate job creation through an attractive investment climate, a legal framework that favors the creation and financing of businesses, and policies that promote labor training and access to technology.[29] To ensure the faithful performance of contracts and encourage production and trade, an effective legal system is essential. The cost of access to justice can be high, therefore it is advisable to promote greater efficiency in the system through alternatives that are accessible to the population.

Finally, it should be noted that social prestige and indigenous culture provide important comparative advantages to indigenous organizations and communities through which they could improve their insertion into the market. A promising policy line is support for culture-based production initiatives. These initiatives consist of a wide range of potential endeavors, including crafts, ethno-ecotourism, traditional medicine, and cosmetology. Given their unique characteristics, it would be difficult for such endeavors to attain a very large scale, but they could contribute to strengthening the characteristic culture of the communities and grant indigenous culture a more prominent place in national society, where it has often been argued that development requires an abandonment of identity.

III. The Challenge of Discrimination

Innumerable personal testimonies of Bolivian indigenous people, anthropological studies, and participatory observation provide evidence of the presence of stereotypes and hierarchical assumptions based on ethnicity in the daily practice and discourse that characterize social relationships. This section highlights the possibility of discrimination, that is, of negative treatment that individuals can receive when characteristics are ascribed to them that have nothing to do with their personal development (for example, their level of education), but rather with their alleged group condition (for example, ethnicity, religion, and gender). This type of discrimination can considerably affect the development of indigenous persons and limit their job opportunities and wages, despite progress achieved in their qualifications and education (which reduces the benefits of education for indigenous peoples, as compared with non-indigenous peoples).

The average income of indigenous peoples is less than that of non-indigenous peoples with the same level of education (Table 6). The gap is explained by several non-observable factors, of which discrimination is only one. Discrimination, on an average, explains up to a maximum of 27 percent of the income gap.[30] Due to their possible importance, it is worthwhile to understand the extent and nature of discriminatory practices in Bolivia, and the experiences of other countries that have confronted this problem, with the aim of defining possible solutions. For example, there might be a difference in access to basic services between indigenous and non-indigenous peoples, due not so much to discrimination but rather to the greater incidence of public investment in urban areas, where the indigenous peoples have less of a presence.

Given that the studies in Bolivia demonstrate discrimination in the labor market only indirectly, without definitively determining its existence, nature, or scope,

Table 6. Incidence of Poverty by Educational Level (2002)

	Indigenous		*Non-indigenous*	
Educational Level	*Poverty*	*Extreme poverty*	*Poverty*	*Extreme poverty*
No Education	84.9	65.4	69.5	41.9
Incomplete Elementary School	79.2	58.8	64.8	36.3
Completed Elementary School	70.6	50.6	53.6	24.6
Incomplete Secondary School	67.5	40.3	48.9	21.6
Completed Secondary School	55.6	29.2	37.6	13.3
At Least Some University	29.0	7.9	18.6	5.4

Source: Hall and Patrinos (2006) from INE (2002b).

it is advisable to conduct a more in-depth analysis by applying the techniques used in other countries to obtain more precise and useful data on discrimination. For example, a study in the United States[31] detected notable discrimination between whites and Afro-Americans. The authors answered announcements for personal interviews published in newspapers by sending fictitious résumés with certain names common to whites and others more common among Afro-Americans, but always with identical qualifications in terms of education and experience. The study concluded that the 'whites' received 50 percent more calls for interviews than the Afro-Americans. Similar studies conducted in the United States and Europe regarding financial markets (access to mortgages), housing markets, and car sales have suggested the presence of significant racial discrimination that is not observable without the studies. These studies use techniques that are easily applicable to Bolivia to prove where and how discrimination is practiced. Application of such techniques would make information available for potential anti-discrimination programs or legislation.

Finally, once discrimination has been directly corroborated, alternative policies can be considered to meet this challenge. Such policies could take the form of: (i) "color-blind" laws, that is, the application of penalties for discriminatory behavior (whether in favor of or against an individual based on his or her membership in a given group); (ii) "positive policies," such as informational announcements or campaigns that encourage candidates from ethnic minorities to compete for jobs or aspire to positions of employment from which they have been marginalized, but without offering them any particular advantage in the selection process; or (iii) affirmative policies, through more aggressive programs, such as quotas, funds, or preferential scholarships. When working to offset past discrimination and offer assistance with great speed and diversity, the more aggressive the approach, the greater the risk of promoting reverse discrimination and creating incentives contrary to performance, since the point could be reached of granting aid to the selected groups without respecting merit and, at the same time, by law, excluding members of groups not selected who exhibit better performance.[32] Anti-discriminatory policies vary in the

Table 7. Global Approaches to Affirmative Policies or Positive Policies

Bolivia, Ecuador, Greece: Quotas for female participants on the electoral slates of political parties.

China: Quotas for minority representatives in the National Assembly.

Germany: The Constitution provides for equality of rights for all citizens, regardless of race or sex. The new anti-discrimination law aspires to provide greater protection to minorities.

India: Certain university and government positions are reserved for castes that were formerly oppressed.

Malaysia: The Bumiputra Act is an affirmative policy that aspires to grant more opportunities to majority ethnic groups, given historical and financial domination in Malaysia by the minority populations of Chinese or Hindu descent.

New Zealand: Maoris and persons of Polynesian descent are granted preferred access to university courses and scholarships.

Slovakia: Affirmative policies are considered to be reverse discrimination, and are therefore unconstitutional.

South Africa: The Employment Equity Act aims to achieve equality at the work place; it includes efforts to identify the causes of inequality in access to jobs and to increase the hiring rate for previously under-represented groups in order to achieve greater equality on the labor market.

United States: Laws promote "color-blind" (and gender-blind) equality of opportunity in access to education, employment, housing, and credit. Affirmative policies exist that offer preferred treatment to students from minority groups; on the other hand, quotas are illegal except in proven cases of extreme discrimination.

world due to the advantages and disadvantages mentioned above (Table 7), and, of course, because they are decided upon independently by each nation. An assessment of international experience regarding anti-discriminatory policies could allow the authorities to identify the best way to meet this challenge in Bolivia.

IV. Conclusions and Options for the Future

Given that they have been excluded for centuries, the country's indigenous population would be the principal beneficiary of an explicit equal opportunity policy aimed at reducing poverty and promoting social inclusion. Nonetheless, it should be emphasized that not all indigenous people are below the poverty line and not all non-indigenous people are above it. In addition, there are other groups that, on account of their gender, age, or geographic location, have suffered from social exclusion.[33]

This suggests that an equal opportunity policy should be based, in the first place, on poverty, regardless of ethnic origin. In the context of a decentralized administration, such a policy could be based on setting clear goals, expressed through sector-based indicators that the level of government entrusted with such goals would define.

Transfers from the central level to sub-national levels in this context could represent an incentive for accomplishing such local goals.[34]

None of this means that indigenous policies should be abandoned. On the contrary, they should play a role within the framework of sector-based goals, because quality and effectiveness in the provision of public goods and services is intimately linked to the linguistic and cultural characteristics of the individuals, communities, and peoples who benefit from them. Accordingly, two types of social inclusion policies can be distinguished: those that place their emphasis on *equality*, such as the ones described above, and those that emphasize *difference*. The distinction between the two types of policies is not always clear, but difference-based policies generally tend to focus on the social, cultural, economic, and/or political particularities of social groups such as indigenous peoples. Differenced-based policies include indigenous development, ethno-development, and identity-based development in their various modes. Highlighting specific cultural characteristics (reciprocity, the earth as a living being, etc.), many of these approaches emphasize the importance of quality of life more than the monetary income of indigenous communities and peoples.[35] Other such approaches emphasize differences as a means of recovering or preserving a way of life or a set of traditions to achieve a better insertion in a world that is ever more globalized and competitive.[36] It is important to bear these options in mind in order to select sound social inclusion policies for indigenous peoples.

This chapter is intended to serve as a complement to other chapters in this volume regarding specific sectors in the fight against poverty. Social exclusion is not synonymous with poverty; it is a more complex phenomenon that includes all dimensions of life. Social exclusion of indigenous peoples in Bolivia has particular characteristics that condition applicable policies. To start, indigenous peoples comprise the majority of the population. Barriers between indigenous and non-indigenous peoples have been eased. International experience suggests that equality in the balance of power and political influence constitutes the institutional basis for prosperity.[37] Upon electing its first indigenous president in history, Bolivia has a new chance to reduce social exclusion in the country and progress along the road of equal opportunity and impartial processes.

Equal Opportunity Options

The basic recommendation regarding equal opportunity is equity in access to public goods and services. Both the Popular Participation Act and the National Dialogue Act introduced equality promotion policies in the country through funding transfers, determined by population and poverty formulas. These two laws transfer jurisdiction but do not specify the results to be achieved. Accordingly, they provide an as yet incomplete basis for equitable, effective action. These newly introduced changes have confused the institutional players and have displayed a bias toward investment per se as opposed to results. Not only are incentives unclear under these new laws, but jurisdictions are fragmented, responsibilities overlap, and block transfers are unconditional. An effective equality policy would require: (i) the establishment of clear, measurable sector-based goals; (ii) specification of the entity directly in charge of fulfilling those goals; (iii) allocation of sufficient funds and adequate incentives to achieve those goals; and (iv) supervision of progress and results.

In relation to the large number of children at nutritional risk, the government could obtain rapid, effective results by implementing a conditional monetary transfer program. The information needed to apply such a program already exists, and Bolivia could take advantage of lessons learned in several countries (among them Brazil and Mexico) that have implemented similar programs to address access and participation issues in education and health. To improve social inclusion, a complementary program for improving the quality and coverage of education is essential.

With respect to opportunities, several areas have been mentioned where social inclusion programs could be applied (such as access to financial services, training and technology, an investment climate favorable to job creation, etc.). Here, rural development is of special importance in the fight against social exclusion. In addition to the policies proposed in the *Rural Development* chapter, the government could consider a program of support to production initiatives based on indigenous cultural knowledge. Part of the funds from the Direct Tax on Hydrocarbons (*Impuesto Directo sobre los Hidrocarburos*—IDH) earmarked for the "indigenous fund" (which has not yet been created) could be allocated to such a program, with the advantage that prior experience in the country through the LIL/Indígena Project has amassed important lessons that would help ensure successful implementation.

Beyond improving the provision of services, the institutional realm must also improve social oversight and accountability. Bolivia has progressed considerably in social oversight through recognition of the legal status of entities, participatory municipal planning, and the formation of oversight committees; but accountability on the part of local governments continues to be insufficient and lacking in transparency. By defining sector-based goals, applicable in the various geographic areas, social control would be improved, because it would be more closely tied to the expected results of governmental actions.

Options to Address Discrimination

Although the most effective measures to equalize income are sector-based policies that contribute to the formation of human capital, a good part of the income gap probably has its origin in discriminatory practices. Accordingly, the principal recommendation to address discrimination would first be to study discrimination using techniques capable of bringing its presence to light in the various realms. Based on this, concrete affirmative action or anti-discriminatory policies could be adopted, appropriate to their respective realm of application (for example, access to services or opportunities). One measure that could be contemplated in the short term, given the need to develop indigenous technical personnel and the importance of strengthening role models for society, is a competitive program of university scholarships that seeks out the best indigenous students graduating from the schools of poor municipalities in the rural areas.

Over the past decade, Bolivia has had little success with its office on indigenous affairs. In fact, generally speaking, the counterpart agencies of other Latin American countries have also failed to demonstrate their effectiveness. They usually have little influence on government institutions that provide the main goods and services needed by indigenous communities and peoples, and they end up playing a political or symbolic role rather than providing an effective service for their intended beneficiaries.[38] The relevance of an agency of this type in Bolivia, where the majority of the population is indigenous, is even more debatable. In addition, it must be ensured that the ministries for each sector incorporate the indigenous dimension as an element of their work. This is because consideration of linguistic and cultural factors is important to ensure quality services. Furthermore, it is necessary to closely monitor the definition of goals to ensure that they incorporate an indigenous world view and that sufficient funds are allocated to reverse the accumulated effects of social exclusion.

Bibliography

Bertrand, Marianne and Sendhil Mullainathan. 2004. "Are Emily and Greg More Employable than Lakisha and Jamal? A Field Experiment on Labor Market Discrimination." *American Economic Review*, vol. 94, no. 4, pp. 991-1013.

De Ferranti, D., G. Perry, F. Ferreira, and M. Walton. 2003. *Inequality in Latin America and the Caribbean: Breaking with History?*, World Bank, Washington, DC.

De Ferranti, D., G. Perry, W. Foster, D. Lederman and A. Valdés. 2005. *Beyond the City: The Rural Contribution to Development.* World Bank, Washington, D.C.

Economic Policy Analysis Unit (*Unidad de Análisis de Política Económica*—UDAPE), (Pan American Health Organization—PAHO), World Health Organization (WHO). 2004. *Caracterización de la exclusión en salud en Bolivia.* La Paz.

Gurin, Patricia. 1999. "The Compelling Need for Diversity in Higher Education: Expert Testimony." *Michigan Journal of Race and Law*, 5, pp. 363-425.

Hall, Gillette and Harry Patrinos (*eds*). 2006. *Indigenous Peoples, Poverty and Human Development in Latin America.* Palgrave Macmillan. UK.

Instituto Nacional de Estadística (National Statistics Institute—INE). 2002a. *Censo nacional de población y vivienda 2001 Bolivia: Distribución de la población.* La Paz.

———. 2002b. *Encuesta continua de hogares* (2002). (Survey on Improvement in Living Conditions (*Encuesta de Mejoramiento de Condiciones de Vida*—MECOVI)). Available at www.ine.gov.bo/mecovi/index.htm.

Sowell, Thomas. 2004. *Affirmative Action Around the World.* Yale University Press. New Haven.

Strobele-Gregor, Juliana. 1986. *Indios de piel blanca: Evangelistas en chuquiyawu.* HISBOL, La Paz.

UNICEF, UDAPE. 2005. *Bolivia, equidad y derechos de la niñez, Índice municipal de desarrollo de la infancia, niñez y adolescencia (IDINA)*. La Paz.

Uquillas, Jorge E. and Melanie A. Eltz. 2004. "The Quest and Practice of Indigenous Development," in *Lessons of Indigenous Development: the Proceedings of a World Bank Workshop on Indigenous Peoples Development*. World Bank, Latin America, and Caribbean Region, Sustainable Development Working Paper No. 20.

World Bank. 2001. "Indigenous Peoples Development Project," Report No. 21345-BO. World Bank, Washington, D.C.

———. 2002. "Poverty and Nutrition in Bolivia," Report No. 24691-BO. World Bank, Washington, D.C.

———. 2005. "Bolivia Poverty Assessment: Establishing the Basis for Pro-Poor Growth." Report No. 28068-BO. World Bank, Washington, D.C.

———. 2006. *Equitability and Development. World Development Report*, World Bank, Washington, D.C.

Endnotes

1. To simplify the terminology, the word "indigenous" is used indistinctly to refer to persons in Bolivia who identify themselves as "indigenous," "original peoples," and/or "peasants," depending upon the region or even the particular situation of that person.

2. The concept of poverty used in this chapter is measured only in relation to the threshold of monetary income or access to basic goods. There are other important dimensions of wealth, such as cultural or social wealth; and it is possible to have a low income but be rich in those other dimensions.

3. The relationship between equity and prosperity is examined in detail in the World Bank Development Report for 2006, which addresses the relationship between equity and development (World Bank, 2006).

4. The urban percentage is 56 using the criterion of self-identification, and 47 when calculated based on language spoken (author's calculation based on the 2001 Census).

5. Including Afro-Bolivians, who were not identified in the Census, but whose population is estimated at approximately 31,000 inhabitants.

6. There is no reliable information, much less desegregated by ethnic group, on migration out of the country. According to the 2001 Census, fertility and infant mortality rates for the indigenous population are 5.0 children per woman and 75 per thousand live births, while for the non-indigenous population these rates are 3.6 and 52, respectively (INE, 2002a).

7. This phenomenon appears to particularly characterize the urban indigenous population as of the second generation.

8. With very few exceptions, most of the policies and projects implemented in Bolivia have paid little attention to the multi-ethnic composition of society. Discrimination and stereotypes are common in discourse and everyday practice.

9. The data on poverty and income in this section are taken from Hall and Patrinos (2006), unless indicated to the contrary. See also World Bank (2005).

10. In Ecuador, Guatemala and Mexico, being indigenous increases the probability of being poor by 16 percent, 14 percent, and 30 percent respectively. In Guatemala and Mexico, this probability has increased over the past decade (Hall and Patrinos, 2006).
11. For a more detailed analysis, see the chapter on the Dynamics of Poverty and Inequality in this volume.
12. INE (2002b).
13. These studies use the "Oaxaca-Blinder" technique to obtain a breakdown of factors that determine labor income, using samples of wage data and individual characteristics such as age and educational level to estimate up to what point the income gap between indigenous and non-indigenous workers is explained by observable factors, such as educational level. The remaining income gap (the part that cannot be explained by these factors) is attributed to less observable factors, such as discrimination. On the other hand, the magnitude of this remaining gap is considered to be the 'upper limit' or estimated maximum of the impact of discrimination, because there are also other non-observable factors, such as quality of education, individual ability, etc., which might play a role in the unexplained portion of the income gap.
14. For more information, see the chapters on Dynamics of Poverty and Inequality, Primary and Secondary Education, and the Health Sector in this volume.
15. See World Bank (2006).
16. De Ferranti et al. (2003) indicate that the reduction of poverty in a country with a Gini index of 0.3 (such as that of several European countries) can be as much as four times higher than in another country with an identical economic growth rate, but a Gini index closer to 0.6 (such as that of Bolivia).
17. Opportunities themselves are difficult to measure, since, by definition, they are potential.
18. See, in particular, the chapters on Primary and Secondary Education, the Health Sector, Transportation Systems, and Rural Development, which address differences in opportunity by ethnic group and gender.
19. Economic Policy Analysis Unit (*Unidad de Análisis de Política Económica*—UDAPE), Pan American Health Organization (PAHO), World Health Organization (WHO) (2004).
20. World Bank (2002).
21. Nutritional risk includes the combination of educational and physical capital in the family as factors that are determinant for children's health. This makes it possible to measure a household's capacity to transform its assets into appropriate food and medical care. (UNICEF, UDAPE, 2005).
22. Especially in the rural areas, families continue to place priority on the education of boys.
23. De Ferranti et al. (2003) and De Ferranti et al. (2005).
24. See the chapters on Water and Sanitation, Transportation Systems, and Rural Development.
25. The chapter on Land Policy goes into more detail on title clearance and land distribution.
26. With the exception of boundary conflicts among *ayllus* or among communities, often dating back "to time immemorial," which could be handled in a simpler fashion.
27. See the chapter on Rural Development in this volume.
28. The problem is even more complex in protected areas, since they come under national jurisdiction.

29. See the chapters on the Dynamics of Poverty and Inequality, Challenges and Opportunities for the Financial System, and Justice and Public Security, among others.
30. Comparatively, the percentage that represents the maximum for potentially discriminatory effects is higher in Ecuador (45 percent), Guatemala (42 percent), Mexico (42 percent) and Peru (58 percent) than in Bolivia (27 percent). Furthermore, in Peru and Ecuador, unlike the other countries mentioned, this percentage has grown over the past decade.
31. Bertrand and Mullaithanan (2004).
32. Sowell (2004).
33. Data from the 2002 MECOVI indicate that one out of every four indigenous persons in the country is above the poverty line, while five out of every ten non-indigenous persons are below the poverty line.
34. See the chapter on Decentralization in this volume.
35. Uquillas and Eltz (2004). In general, attempts to implement these types of policies have been limited to areas where indigenous groups form territorially distinguishable minorities with varying degrees of political autonomy, or to projects financed by the international cooperation community.
36. Such are the cases of Quebec, in Canada, or of Belgium, where the linguistic/cultural communities, within a framework of federalism, pursue ever increasing degrees of territorial and political autonomy.
37. World Bank (2006).
38. A highly successful recent experience was that of the Indigenous Development Commission of Mexico, which has received a large budget (approximately US$250 million per year) to leverage state and municipal investments in basic infrastructure, concentrating on areas with high poverty rates and an indigenous presence.

12

Gender Issues

Ruth Llanos

Summary

This chapter presents the progress achieved over the past decade on gender issues in Bolivia, describes changes in public policy, and correlates them with women's conditions and quality of life. Although there have been achievements and progress in the implementation of corrective measures with a gender approach, they have been insufficient to meet the demands built up over recent years. This chapter first provides an overview of the profile of the population. It describes the current situation, progress, and limitations on the citizenry in social, economic, and political terms and then assesses the situation from a gender perspective on education, health, housing, and basic services as well as in terms of poverty and a lack of equal job opportunities. The diagnosis emphasizes the violence that affects seven out of every ten Bolivian women and analyzes its costs. With respect to political participation, the chapter evaluates the potential and shortcomings of affirmative action policies, such as the law on quotas, and summarizes the progress and agendas of women's movements and organizations in different arenas of parliamentary and local representation. It also examines institutionality in public administration and outlines progress in laws and in national and international standards, along with obstacles to their implementation. The final part of the chapter analyzes the reasons for the poor performance of myriad laws and policies as well as the inefficiency and weakness of various specialized agencies. In addition, a summary is given of the debate on institutional alternatives that could serve to fight against discrimination, inequality, and gender violence: a strong government body, with funds, a hierarchy, and the capacity to institutionalize a gender approach in the public management process for the different sectors and levels of the state; or a single agency that combines and integrates the demands and rights of other excluded groups.

I. A Gender Diagnostic

Profile of the Population

During 1976-2001, the Bolivian population grew from 4.6 million to 8.3 million inhabitants. In this same period, the population's gender composition remained almost unchanged and balanced at about 50 percent.[1] Between the 1992 census and the 2001 census, the annual rate of growth for women was 2.6 percent, slightly less than the rate for men (2.8 percent), which reduced the slight gap between the number of men and the number of women.

According to the 2001 census, in rural zones 48 percent of the population is female, while in urban zones this percentage is 51 percent. Geographic differences are observed not only in the composition of the population, but also in its distribution. Rural zones account for only 38 percent of the population in Bolivia; the remaining 62 percent inhabits urban zones. The magnitude of country-to-city migration in Bolivia is evident: in 1950, 74 percent of the population inhabited rural zones, in 1976, this figure was 58 percent, and in 1992, 42 percent. This phenomenon has a significant effect on the form and composition of households, the demand for public services, economic conditions, and participatory processes.

Primary Socialization: Households and Families[2]

The behavior of the economy is one of the variables that most influence the composition and typology of Bolivian households. In 2001, 32 percent of total households in Bolivia were nuclear two-parent families with children (a mother, father and children), 16 percent were single-parent nuclear families (a mother or father and children), 15 percent were one-person households, and 10 percent were extended two-parent families (a mother, father, children, and other relatives), among the most representative types.

In 31 percent of total households, the head of the family was a woman, while only 16 percent of households had unmarried heads of households. Seventy-eight percent of single-parent households are led by women and only 22 percent by men. In urban zones, the percentage of single-parent households headed by women is 81 percent, and in rural zones it is 71 percent. This persistent presence of female heads of households is a variable that needs to be taken into account in the design and content of public policies on gender equality.

II. The Gender Outlook[3]

Illiteracy, Average Years of Study, and Levels of Schooling

At a national level, the illiteracy rate among the population age 15 or older dropped from 37 percent in 1976 to 20 percent in 1992 and to 13 percent in 2001. Nonetheless, there are significant gender gaps. In 1976, illiteracy was 49 percent among women and 24 percent among men; in 1992, it was 28 percent among women and 12 percent among men; finally, in 2001, it was 19 percent among women and 7 percent among men.

These differences are even greater if broken down by geographic zones. According to the 2001 Census, 10 percent of women in the urban zones are illiterate, as compared to 2.4 percent of men. In the rural zones, the situation is particularly dramatic, since 38 percent of women are illiterate, and the gap as compared to illiteracy among men (23 percentage points) is very high. These data are indicative of the serious limitations in access to goods and services for illiterate women, a situation aggravated by the large percentage of illiterate women who speak only a native language.

There are also important differences between men and women in terms of the average number of years of education. According to the 2001 Census, women study an average of 6.6 years, while men study an average of 8.2 years. In rural zones, women study only 3.1 years and men 5.2 years. On a national level, the data shows that, generally, the total population finishes primary school, while in rural zones women reach only the third grade. Among the adverse factors that affect the enrollment of girls in school are cultural relegation, which undervalues their education, as well as their early incorporation into domestic work and their families' fears of the difficulties they will face if they go to study at academic centers far from home. These situations negatively affect future job opportunities and earnings potential.

At the level of higher education, gender differences are not as marked, though there are large differences based on geographic factors. Of the 15 percent of the total population that enrolls in universities, 45 percent are women and 55 percent are men. Nonetheless, 21 percent of the urban population enrolls in a university, as compared with 3 percent of the rural population. There are marked differences, however, in the selection of college majors, unquestionably motivated by the maintenance of structures that are still conservative and sexist in academic circles and in the job market. Women in higher education tend to major in nursing, biochemistry/pharmacy, and social work; other lesser preferences are financial auditing, tourism, linguistics, psychology, communications, and education sciences.

Gender Considerations in Health

Implementation of Universal Mother/Child Insurance (*Seguro Universal Materno-Infantil*—SUMI) has contributed to great progress in the health of both women and children. The maternal mortality rate on a national level was reduced from 390 deaths per hundred thousand live births in 1994 to 229 in 2003.[4] Although this reduction represents an advance, the rate observed continues to be high: in Potosí, one of the departments with the largest indigenous population, this figure is 496 deaths. It is high compared with other Latin American countries such as Uruguay, where the rate is 11.1 deaths. Another significant result of the Bolivian government's health policy is a reduction in the overall fertility rate for the population: from 6.5

children per woman in 1976 to 3.8 in 2003. However, geographic differences are also substantial, in 2003, the fertility rate was 3.1 children per woman in urban zones compared with 5.5 in rural zones.

Housing, Female Heads of Households, and Basic Services

According to INE data,[5] 31 percent of households were living in overcrowded conditions, that is, they did not meet the standard of 2.5 persons per room. This is a high figure considering that overcrowding has an adverse effect on socialization processes in the family; it also increases domestic violence. The majority of sexual crimes are committed by persons close to the victim, in their own homes.

The data demonstrate significant advantages in favor of women regarding basic services. Nonetheless, the historic data show that these advantages are, to some extent, losing ground. According to INE data, the greatest unmet need is a lack of sewage services. Segregating on the basis of head-of-household status, it can be seen that, in 2001, 49 percent of households headed by men had no sewage services, as opposed to 21 percent of households headed by women. Nonetheless, compared to 1992, the percentage of households headed by women that lacked sewage services (19 percent) increased by 2 percentage points, while for households headed by men (61 percent) the rate decreased by 11 percent.[6]

The relationship between female head-of-household status and access to basic services should be carefully studied. It is important to determine what factors—cultural, social, etc.—influence this phenomenon. It also must be noted that having better services than households headed by men does not mean the services are good, since the percentage of households lacking these services is still high for both men and women. Overcrowded housing conditions and limitations in the consumption of basic services influence the quality of life of women, who, in addition to their role in production, must carry out additional daily tasks, such as the search for water, firewood, and other energy-producing materials.

III. Economic Characteristics of the Citizenry

Gender, Ethnicity, and Poverty

In the most recent census (2001), 62 percent of the population age 15 or older (that is, close to 3.1 million Bolivians) self-identified as indigenous.[7] Forty-four percent of this population lives in rural zones. According to data from 2002, the incidence of national poverty was much higher among the indigenous population than among the non-indigenous population (74 versus 52 percent on a national level). On the other hand, the incidence of poverty is higher among the indigenous population in rural areas (86 percent) and lower among the non-indigenous population in capital cities (44 percent).[8]

Gaps in poverty and income for indigenous populations are detailed in the Hall and Patrinos study (2005).[9] The authors maintain that the poverty gap in Bolivia in 2002 was approximately 0.40. For indigenous populations, the poverty gap is double that of the non-indigenous population. In other words, the indigenous population would need twice the income of the non-indigenous population to escape poverty. The gap in the poverty rate for the monolingual indigenous population of Bolivia is also substantially greater than the gap for the bilingual indigenous population.

The case of indigenous women is very particular, since they are the most vulnerable. According to Hall and Patrinos, they are most likely to work in the informal sector, a sector highly correlated to extreme poverty. In addition, 45 percent of indigenous women who work do not receive any remuneration whatsoever.

The feminization of poverty confirms that women lack access to material resources on an equal footing with men; they also lack participation in the principal decision-making venues. This places the indigenous population and persons of African descent at a greater disadvantage. The lack of visibility of this latter group is even greater. The most recent census (2001) acknowledged the existence of only two Afro-Bolivians, a failure to recognize approximately 31,000 persons.

Lack of Equal Job Opportunities

In the job market, the composition of employment shows that women represent 41 percent of the employed population, as compared with 59 percent for men.[10] However, the contribution of women is often "invisible," since no value is placed on work in the home and on agricultural tasks, which are incorporated into the roles assigned to women.

One of the most significant variables with negative impact on women is their low level of education, especially when compared with men. This affects access to quality jobs that offer stability, a salary sufficient to meet the family's basic consumer needs, and access to the public social security system in the short and long term. According to Hall and Patrinos, 70 percent of women are self-employed; they work principally in agriculture, trade, and informal services.

Another important factor is the "double shift" generally performed by female workers, meaning the need to work and also attend to household chores. In the urban zones, above all, this makes it hard or impossible for women to participate in extra training activities that could translate into better job and income opportunities.

Access to jobs and remunerations on the job market are also discriminatory. For example, women in the manufacturing industry in rural zones receive 25 percent of what a man earns for the same work;[11] in the urban zones, they receive 56 percent. Similarly, a female rural worker receives 36 percent of what a man receives for his work; and a female urban worker receives 61 percent of a man's wages.

The preceding data show that several interrelated factors cause women's poverty: low levels of education deny equal job opportunities, lead to differences in economic participation, and result in gender gaps in the distribution and redistribution of income.

Gender Equity and Access to Land

The implementation of the first Agrarian Reform Act in Bolivia (1953) excluded women. Of the total deeds granted while this act was in force, only 1.2 percent were granted to women. The Law on the National Agrarian Reform Institute (*Instituto Nacional de Reforma Agraria*—INRA, 1996) explicitly set forth a woman's right to property ownership, regardless of her marital status. Nonetheless, in the first years of its application, its implementation and supervision procedures were not specified.

Afterward, the INRA developed internal rules for granting joint deeds, regardless of the legal situation of the couple; joint deeds would include both names, recording the woman's name first. Efforts were also made to provide information to women through which they could gain increased access to clean water and better sanitation. The inclusion of female technicians who spoke an indigenous language facilitated the process in some regions.

The number of female deed holders has progressively increased, although the parcels in question are small. Men have maintained access to and control over the larger properties. In addition, inheritance continues to be the principal access mechanism, which is a limited right for women in certain indigenous communities that favor men under the traditional system. Furthermore, a lack of personal documentation limits the possibility for women to claim their rights.[12]

IV. Violence against Women

Domestic violence is one of the most serious problems affecting Bolivian women, despite the enactment and subsequent application of Law 1674 against Family and Domestic Violence (1998), which revealed a commonplace practice and facilitated the implementation of several government measures to prevent, respond to, and punish such violence.

Seven out of every ten women suffer from some type of violence in their homes. Such violence "in 75 percent of cases, tends to be repetitive and to go unreported by the victims. Accordingly, out of all women who stated that they had suffered violence in their homes, 53 percent did not take any action and only slightly more than 17 percent filed reports. The remaining 30 percent opted to find solutions within the framework of their own nuclear families." [13]

According to comparative data on cases of domestic violence (sexual, psychological, and physical) in the cities of La Paz, Cochabamba, Oruro, El Alto, and Potosí, in the second half of 2003, 4,585 cases were handled. This figure increased to 8,510 in the first half of 2004, an increase of 86 percent.[14] These data might reflect a greater trend to file reports, but they also indicate the persistence of violence against women and girls.

The 2003 National Demography and Health Survey (*Encuesta Nacional de Demografía y Salud*—ENDSA)[15] confirms the above-cited data. This survey shows that more than half of married women and women living in common-law relationships reported that they had been victims of some type of psychological violence (52 percent) or physical violence (52 percent) from their spouse or partner, either frequently or sporadically. The percentages of men who reported having been victims of some type of psychological or physical violence are 37 percent and 27 percent, respectively. The percentages are higher in urban areas than in rural areas, but this could be explained by failure to file reports in the rural zones.

The 2003 ENDSA survey establishes the types of violence, its characteristics, and the different situations of violence that victims suffer in the various regions of the country. It can be inferred from the results that psychological violence against women is greater the lower their socioeconomic status. On the other hand, violence is greater against men when their socioeconomic conditions are better. Such a situation could be explained by women in higher positions defending themselves. One frequent form of violence is verbal abuse against women, which increases with the age of the victim. The percentage of cases for the various types of physical and sexual violence increases with the age of the interviewee and decreases in proportion to her level of education.

Coordinated action by women's movement organizations and the state led to the passage of important laws and regulations. Despite several changes in the government, a number of mechanisms were institutionalized to respond to and prevent family violence, such as Integral Legal Services (*Servicios Legales Integrales*—SLIM), administered by the municipal governments, and the Family Protection Brigades under the National Police.[16] In addition, the Violence Response and Prevention Networks coordinate community entities.[17] Despite that, impunity persists and crimes against women go unpunished. "Conciliation" mechanisms and "settlements between parties" are misused or abused. Cultural practices of discrimination and stigmatization persist, and the exercise of individual liberties (dress, speech, going out, etc.) is curtailed and restricted. Institutional services lack specialized human resources, the scope of the services is limited by budget problems, consciousness-raising work for government officials is not done, and dependency on the international cooperation community persists for the implementation of programs and projects.

V. Civic Involvement

Women: Participation and Political Power on the Local and National Level

The women's movement mobilized to achieve equality in participation and representation. These demands for participation led to the development and enactment of laws such as the Law on Political Parties (whose Article 19 guarantees a 30 percent quota of women on party slates), the Electoral Code (whose Article 112 incorporates the granting of precedence to women on party slates and an every-other-candidate listing on the slates for municipal elections), as well as the most recent Law on Civic Groups and Indigenous Peoples of 2004 (whose Article 8 establishes a quota of not less than 50 percent for women in all campaigns for elected office).

Therefore, the search for equality through affirmative measures in Bolivia takes the form of two types of quotas that obligate political parties and civic groups to incorporate women at a rate of 30 percent and 50 percent, respectively, with the National Electoral Court being responsible for controlling and enforcing this rule. Since 1992, there has been a certain increase in representation by women, but in reality, the minimum quotas established have not been achieved. Parties have used the weak argument that it is difficult to "find capable women candidates."

Thus, even though women actively participated in restoring democracy in the 1980s and in building a democratic culture, the application of quotas has come up against myriad difficulties, such as an absence of instruments, "faults in the terms of the legal provisions themselves, deficiencies in the political system that prevent effective enforcement of the laws, and self-exclusion by women themselves."[18]

The composition of registered voters has improved. The percentage of women registered to vote in the national elections of 1997 was 46 percent, as compared to 54 percent for men.[19] In the most recent elections for national and prefect offices of December 2005, the percentages came even closer: 49.6 percent of women and 50.4 percent of men were registered to vote. [20, 21]

In the Senate, neither the 30 percent quota nor parity of representation has been achieved. In the 1993-1997 term, out of 27 senators, only one was a woman; for the unconcluded term of 2002-2007, four senators were elected; and in the incoming term for 2005-2010, there will be only one female senator.

It is in the multi- and single-candidate slates for the House of Representatives where the differences introduced by the parties in the application of quotas are most clearly seen. Due to the mode of personalized single-candidate elections for the various jurisdictions, the parties and associations do not meet the percentages and do not risk running women candidates. In the most recent elections, the eight participating entities ran only 221 female candidates, as opposed to 745 men. Sixty-three seats were won for men, but only five women were elected as representatives on single-candidate slates.

The number of representatives who won on multi-candidate slates is greater, because the parties rely on the presidential candidate's victory to sweep the other candidates in, depending upon their location on the slate. In the last elections, civic groups and parties ran 362 women candidates and 434 men. Of them, 17 women were elected as representatives, compared with 43 men.

The composition and participation of women has increased slightly over the various legislative periods. In the June 2002 elections, for the first time in the history of the Republic, indigenous men and women, representing new political movements, were elected to parliament.

The use of quotas has not brought about substantial changes or resolved the problem of under-representation of women in parliament. Several factors explain this lack of progress: failure to abide by the quotas, the distribution and location of candidates on the slates, the type of election, the electoral districts' characteristics, women's lack of documentation, and the commonplace exercise of discrimination.

The key posts and positions of the Executive and Judicial branch continue to be filled by men, although some changes have been seen. In the unconcluded term of 2002–2007, there were three women ministers. The first cabinet of recently elected President Evo Morales includes four women ministers out of 16 cabinet members. One of them, for the first time, will be the Minister of the Interior with authority over the National Police.

Despite the fact that only 20 percent of city council members worldwide are women, the participation of women in local politics continues to grow.[22] In Latin America, Bolivia ranks second in the percentage of women mayors (11 percent) and third, after Argentina and Chile, in the percentage of women council members (34 percent).

The ascending curve of the past five years in increased female local representation is explained by the gradual application of the principles of equity and equal opportunity included in several laws and regulations (such as the Popular Participation Act and the Municipalities Act), reinforced by several actions taken by social organizations and female council members. These policies facilitated the election of 21 female mayors out of a total of 314 in 2000. The presence of female council members has also increased, particularly in the municipalities of La Paz, Santa Cruz, and Cochabamba, in addition to Beni and Pando. The number of female mayors elected by their councils increased by one hundred percent in the last municipal elections (2004).

The local arena provides important opportunities for the participation and empowerment of women. Nonetheless, harassment and political violence impede and restrict women in the exercise of their positions, and women are forced out of office using various means (such as obligating some women council members to sign their resignations, "with a knife to their throats, after having their homes burned down, or after their relatives have been taken hostage."[23]) On account of the persistence of these patriarchal, authoritarian practices, a collective comprised of several government and civil society entities has introduced a Bill Against Gender-Based Harassment and Political Violence.

Finally, the upcoming Constitutional Reform Assembly is the avenue through which women will call for proposals geared toward a new design for the country, in which its diverse ethnic, economic, and cultural composition finds common avenues for representation, dialogue, and policy development. Such measures seek reforms on issues including political reform, ownership of natural resources, and land/territory, among others. There are a series of initiatives to discuss the proper content and scope of these issues. In addition, women's organizations, together with the Vice Ministry on Women, have made a proposal to the Special Commission for Convening the Constitutional Reform Assembly (*Comisión Especial de Constitución de la Asamblea Constituyente*—CECAC) of the Senate, regarding the issue of parity in the election of assembly members by electoral district. Nonetheless, this demand, as well as other women's proposals, will continue to face a policy of discrimination, the marginalizing nature of the political system, and the non-existence and/or weakness of the network of alliances in the women's movement.

VI. Legal Framework, Gender-Related Policies, and Public Institutions

Gaps between International Instruments and Enforcement of Women's Rights

In the twentieth century, in the framework of systems going beyond the national level, such as the United Nations and the Organization of American States, Bolivia ratified approximately 90 international instruments (conventions, protocols, and pacts). Many of them favor the exercise of women's individual and collective rights. Bolivia has also ratified the majority of binding and non-binding conventions related to gender and the rights of women; thus it has committed to complying with instruments such as the Convention on the Elimination of All Forms of Discrimination against Women (1989); the Optional Protocol to the Convention on the Elimination of All Forms of Discrimination against Women (2000); the Convention on the Political Rights of Women (1979); the Convention on the Nationality of Married Women (1970); the Inter-American Convention on the Granting of Civil Rights to Women; and the Inter-American Convention on the Prevention, Punishment, and Eradication of Violence Against Women ("Convention of Belem do Pará," 1984). In addition, other pacts and conventions, such as ILO Convention 169 of the International Labor Organization, also protect the specific rights of indigenous women.

Nonetheless, delay tactics persist, and long periods go by between adhesion to and ratification of these international instruments. In addition, incorporation into national legislation comes up against a vacuum, since the Constitution of Bolivia does not contain express provisions that define the hierarchy of these conventions.[24] Harmonization and the adaptation of these international standards to Bolivian law, as well as the real application of these commitments, are additional pending issues.

Progress and Setbacks in Institutionality and Public Policy

Incorporation of gender into Bolivia's public policies started with the signing of the Convention on the Elimination of All Forms of Discrimination against Women (CEDAW) and the Global Platform for Action of the Fourth World Conference on Women held in Beijing in 1995. Bolivia, as a signatory, chose seven fields of work through which to improve the living conditions of women.

Institutionalization began with the creation of the Vice Secretariat on Gender Affairs (*Subsecretaría de Asuntos de Género*—SAG) in 1993. In the first administrative term (1993-1997) its location and jurisdiction were designated. The policies it addressed focused on issues such as violence, political participation, the right to property, and land use. The rights of boys, girls, and adolescents were also recognized. With support from the international cooperation community, a technical team was formed, and several media resources were used to reinforce public opinion on the gender issue. Mainstream gender equality also was sought through certain laws, such as Educational Reform, Health Reform, the Popular Participation Act, and the Law on the National Agrarian Reform Institute. In addition, equal opportunity plans were designed and, in the framework of decentralization, gender and women's units and offices were created in departmental governments and in some municipalities.

In a second administrative term (1997-2002), the SAG disappeared and the General Directorate on Gender Affairs (*Dirección General de Asuntos de Género*—DGAG) was created, with a lower hierarchy. Through that new structure, progress was made on incorporating the principle of alternation (every-other-candidate slate listings) in the municipal elections. In addition, national plans were formulated to achieve gender equality, prevent and eradicate violence, and reduce women's poverty. Some of these plans and policies present conceptual and methodological deficiencies and, on the operating level, their integration with the rest of the policies for the different sectors is not addressed.

As of 2000, political and social instability affected continuity. Despite that, the Vice Ministry on Women developed a National Public Policy Plan for the Full Exercise of Women's Rights 2004-2007. Financed through a common fund of several agencies, the plan seeks to reduce inequality and incorporate a gender approach into the public management model.

In sum, significant progress has been made by women in the form of several laws, but with a precarious correlation in terms of budgets and implementation. With respect to the various institutional mechanisms created with different names by the various administrations, their weaknesses involve the existence of several hierarchical levels, a lack of autonomy and authority, shortages of funds and technical resources, a constant turnover in their human resources, and very little capacity to influence the remaining sectors of the government.

It is difficult to quantify funds provided by the international cooperation community for gender issues in Bolivia. The task becomes even more complicated if one tries to systematize the funds provided by non-governmental organizations and international foundations. Nonetheless, funds from abroad were clearly a fundamental factor for progress on the governmental level and among the organizations of civil society, above all in the 1990s.[25] Finally, a significant proportion of agencies consider the mainstreaming of a gender outlook to be an important condition for reducing poverty.

VII. Conclusions and Policy Options

The diagnostic data show that important progress has been made on gender equality in some sectors but that the progress has been unequal and dispersed. Although the number of women who enter universities has increased, there is a high percentage of illiteracy among women. This situation is aggravated by the retrogressive effects of gender- and ethnic-based discrimination, which adds to disadvantages and inequities in income levels and in access to productive resources such as land, loans, and capital.

At the same time, several data demonstrate that violence is one of the most serious problems affecting Bolivian women: seven out of every ten women suffer from some type of violence in their homes. Violence is not only a social problem, given its psychological effects, but also an economic problem, given the days lost from work on account of physical injuries. The increase in murders of women and impunity for these crimes is also cause for concern. Given the severity of this situation, a wide range of public and private alliances needs to be formed to improve prevention mechanisms, as well as the quality of the services and operators.

As in other Latin American countries, Bolivia has ratified the majority of binding conventions related to gender and women's rights. In addition, the past decade has been characterized by the enactment of an increasing number of laws promoting greater equity, though some discriminatory laws remain in effect. This extensive legal framework is not applied, either because it is unknown, or due to lack of access to services, or because the instruments lack a corollary in Bolivian law, since they are not granted an express hierarchy by the Constitution. Therefore, it is necessary to implement harmonization, reformulation, training, and dissemination policies.

For more than a decade, the design and execution of gender-based public policies have inevitably had to struggle through a governmental labyrinth of mechanisms and agencies created with various hierarchies by the different administrations in office. There has been a huge turnover of human resources in these agencies, both among the more skilled personnel or experts and among the unskilled, who get their jobs on the basis of political connections rather than their capacities and/or skills. This situation has affected efficiencies and results, although no systematic evaluations have been made of this "national machinery" to measure its effectiveness and impact. [26]

To progress in social inclusion, Bolivia has constructed a labyrinth of laws and policies that are not applied or enforced. The functionality and results of the specialized agencies have failed to meet expectations, and, finally, affirmative measures (such as quotas of participation) have not achieved significant changes. What, then, are the best options to overcome discrimination, inequality, and the gender violence that affects more than 50 percent of the population? At present, two options are being discussed. The first considers that the country has binding commitments through several international instruments and that, therefore, the quality and governmental management capabilities of the current government agency, the Vice Ministry on Women, should be reinforced, providing it with human resources and funds and improving its hierarchy, so that it can intervene in the public system as a decisive player. The Vice Ministry should have the capacity to institutionalize a gender approach for public management processes in the other sectors and levels of the state.

The second alternative proposes that no specialized agencies are needed on indigenous or gender issues. With respect to indigenous issues, it indicates that, since the country is indigenous in its majority, no discriminatory mechanism is needed to address indigenous affairs. In relation to gender issues, it proposes to do away with the Vice Ministry on Women and develop another body, with different spheres of actions and jurisdiction, to formulate and implement policies, not only for women but also for other groups (such as children, adolescents, and the elderly). This option is criticized by some organizations, which consider it more of a setback than an advance.

Given these opposing approaches, it would be necessary to analyze experiences and lessons learned in other countries that have established an umbrella organization to take charge of policy development and promote the rights of several marginalized groups (for example, Mexico).[27] Also notable is the emergence of other international institutional trends in the fight against social exclusion, such as Norway's Gender Equality Act and its Anti-Discrimination Act. The experience of Argentina is also highly significant. Accordingly, before creating a new government body, a participatory process could be commenced by organizing a National Equality and Non-Discrimination Commission, whose hierarchy would surpass that of the Ministries, at the highest level. Within a set term, that commission would issue a status report on discriminatory and marginalizing practices across the board, propose multi-dimensional social inclusion policies, develop plans, and propose a series of concrete measures to fight against discrimination and turn equal opportunity into a reality.

Bibliography

Auza, V., P. Estenssoro, and V. Diaz Romero. 2003. "Alteridades de la feminidad: Un Análisis en las Discursividades de Mujeres Recoveras, Artistas y Locas". Cuadernos de Resumen, Actores e Identidades Culturales. Programa de Investigación Estratégica en Bolivia (PIEB). La Paz.

Bouta, T., Freks, G., and I. Bannon. 2005. "Gender, Conflict and Development." The International Bank for Reconstruction and Development/The World Bank. Washington, DC.

Buvinic, Mayra, and Jacqueline Mazza. 2005. "Gender and Social Inclusion: Social Policy Perspectives from Latin America and the Caribbean." Draft working paper for The World Bank Conference, New Frontiers of Social Policy: Development in a Globalizing World.

Centro de Información y de Desarrollo de la Mujer (CIDEM). 2005. "Sistema de Información para la Vigilancia Ciudadana Desde una Perspectiva de Género." CIDEM. La Paz.

Comité Impulsor de los Derechos Políticos de las Mujeres. 2005. "Anteproyecto de ley contra el acoso y la violencia política en razón de género."

Consejo Interinstitucional de Derechos Humanos. 2005. "Plan de Acción de Derechos Humanos 2006-2010." Consejo Interinstitucional de Derechos Humanos. Bolivia

Corte Nacional Electoral. Estadísticas del Padrón Electoral. CNE.

Coordinadora de la Mujer. 1998. Convención Sobre la Eliminación de Todas las Formas de Discriminación Contra la Mujer. Plataforma de Acción Mundial – IV Conferencia Mundial sobre la Mujer Bejing, 1995. Coordinadora de la Mujer. La Paz.

Farah, I. 2000. "Género y Pobreza: Una Relación Difícil. La Pobreza en Bolivia: Dimensión, Políticas y Resultados (1985 – 1999)" – Documentos de Trabajo. Instituto Prisma. La Paz.

———. 2002. *Familias Bolivianas y Trabajo de Hombres y Mujeres.* CIDES/UMSA. Publicidad e Impresión Génesis. La Paz.

Fríes, L., C. Portaluppi, and Lola Valladares-Tayupanta. 2005. "Análisis y contribución feminista a los derechos económicos, sociales y culturales". Corporación Promoción de la Mujer / Taller Comunicación Mujer, Quito, Ecuador; Coordinadora de la Mujer, La Paz, Bolivia. Plural Editores. La Paz.

Gutiérrez de Toranzo, Martha. 2004. *Presupuesto Público con Enfoque de Género.* Ediciones Excelsior. La Paz.

Hall, Gillette, and Harry Patrinos, eds. 2005. "Bolivia" in *Indigenous Peoples, Poverty and Human Development in Latina America 1994-2004.* The World Bank. Washington, DC.

Instituto Nacional de Estadísticas. Website: http://www.ine.gov.bo.

———. 1976, 1992, 2001. *Censo Nacional de Población y Vivienda.* Instituto Nacional de Estadísticas.

———. 2002. Proyecto Construcción del Sistema de Información de Igualdad de Género: Enfoque de Género en la Producción Estadística. INE. La Paz.

———. 2003. "Características de la Población con Enfoque de Género". Serie IV: Estudios Temáticos. Instituto Nacional de Estadísticas. La Paz.

———. 2004a. "Bolivia: Carencias, Déficit Habitacional y Acceso a Servicios Básicos". Serie IV: Estudios Temáticos. Instituto Nacional de Estadísticas. La Paz.

———. 2004b. "Encuesta Nacional de Demografía y Salud 2003" Instituto Nacional de Estadísticas. La Paz.

Katz, E., and M. Correia, eds. 2001. "The Economics of Gender in Mexico: Work, Family, State, and Market." The International Bank for Reconstruction and Development/The World Bank. Washington, DC.

Lanza, M. 2003. "Reconstruyendo Saberes: El Enfoque de Género en el Proyecto de Bi—alfabetización en Salud Reproductiva." Viceministerio de la Mujer; Fondo de Población de la Naciones Unidas. Talleres Gráficos Gaviota del Sur S.R.L. La Paz.

Lanza, M., and M. Herrera. 1997. "La Situación de la Mujer en el Área Educativa: Avances y Perspectivas." Subsecretaría de Asuntos de Género; UNICEF. Grupo Design. La Paz

Ministerio de Desarrollo Sostenible y Planificación, Viceministerio de Asuntos de Género, Generacionales y Familia. 2000. "Bolivia 5 años después de Beijing: Poder, Oportunidades y Autodeterminación para las Mujeres en el Nuevo Siglo." VAGGF. La Paz.

Ministerio de Desarrollo Sostenible y Viceministerio de la Mujer, 2005. "Encuentros Departamentales con Mujeres Indígenas Originarias y Afrodescendientes sobre la Asamblea Consituyente." MDS

Ministerio de Desarrollo Sostenible, Viceministerio de la Mujer e Instituto de la Judicatura Sucre. 2005. "Módulo Instruccional de Género." Viceministerio de la Mujer e Instituto de la Judicatura. La Paz.

Ministerio de Desarrollo Sostenible, Viceministerio de la Mujer y Red de Atención y Prevención de la Violencia Intrafamiliar El Alto, 2005. "Encuentros Departamentales con Mujeres Indígenas Originarias y Afrodescendientes sobre la Asamblea Constituyente." Ministerio de Desarrollo Sostenible. Imprenta Santana. La Paz.

Moser, C. 2001. "Fortalecimiento de la Capacidad de DFID para Promover la Igualdad de Género y el Empoderamiento de las Mujeres en Bolivia." Informe para DFID en Bolivia. Overseas Development Institute. London.

Noya, M., J. Monterrey, and F. Vilaseca. 2005. "Informe CEDAW." Coordinadora de la Mujer. Artes Gráficas Sagitario. La Paz.

Red de Educación Popular entre Mujeres de América Latina y el Caribe (REPEM). 2005. "Memoria: Foro Internacional por los Caminos del Empoderamiento de las Mujeres." REPEM. Uruguay.

Romero, R., and B. Soruco. 1997. "Guía de capacitación: Género y Participación Popular. Serie Mujer y Participación." Subsecretaría de Asuntos de Género. Ediciones Gráficas E.G. La Paz.

United Cities and Local Governments. Website www.cities-localgovernments.org.

Velásquez Clavijo, G., C. Luna, and G. Velásquez. 2002. "Mujeres Concejalas: Empoderamiento, Desempeño y Liderazgo." Cuadernos de Resumen, Municipio y Participación La Paz: Programa de Investigación Estratégica en Bolivia (PIEB).

Viceministerio de la Mujer. 2004. "Las Mujeres Tenemos Derecho a Ser Propietarias de la Tierra y a la Distribución de las Tierras Fiscales." Viceministerio de la Mujer. La Paz

———. 2005a. Por el Ejercicio Pleno de los Derechos de las Mujeres: Beijing + 10, Informe Bolivia. Viceministerio de la Mujer. EDOBOL. La Paz

———. 2005b. "Mujeres y Hombres en Cifras: Brechas de Género." Viceministerio de la Mujer. La Paz.

———. 2005c. "Informe país Bolivia: Convención sobre la Eliminación de todas las Formas de Discriminación Contra la Mujer." CEDAW 2005. Viceministerio de la Mujer.

———. 2005d. "Plan Nacional de Políticas Públicas para el Ejercicio Pleno de los Derechos de las Mujeres, 2004-2007" Viceministerio de la Mujer. La Paz.

———. 2005e. "Plan Nacional de Políticas Públicas para el Ejercicio Pleno de los Derechos de las Mujeres 2004-2007." Viceministerio de la Mujer. Grupo Design. La Paz.

Viceministerio de la Mujer y Secretaría Técnica del Diálogo Nacional. 2004. "Informe Memoria Encuentros Departamentales de Mujeres Productoras Rurales de Bolivia." Viceministerio de la Mujer. La Paz

Wanderley, F. 1995. "Discriminación ocupacional y de ingresos por género." Ministerio de Desarrollo Humano, Secretaria Nacional de Asuntos Étnicos, de Género y Generacionales, Subsecretaría de Asuntos de Género. La Paz.

Winkler, D., and S. Cueto, eds. 2004. "Etnicidad, Raza, Género y Educación en América Latina." PREAL (Programa de Promoción de la Reforma Educativa en América Latina y el Caribe). Washington, DC

World Bank. 2005 "Gender Issues and Best Practices in Land Administration Projects: A Synthesis Report." Preparado para (PREM/ARD) del Banco Mundial. The World Bank. Washington, DC.

Endnotes

1. 1976 National Population and Housing Census (*Censo Nacional de Población y Vivienda*—CNPV): men 2,276,029 (49.8 percent) and women 2,337,457 (50.2 percent); 1992 CNPV: men 3,171,265 (49.3 percent) and women 3,249,527 (50.7 percent); and 2001 CNPV: men 4,123,850 (49.4 percent) and women 4,150,475 (50.6 percent).

2. Based on the National Statistics Institute (*Instituto Nacional de Estadística*—INE), *Características de la población con enfoque de género*.

3. Ibid.

4. Information from the web page of the INE.

5. INE (2003, p. 107).

6. This pattern is repeated in households without running water. The percentage for households headed by women is 14 percentage points less than for households headed by men. However, for female heads of households, this percentage increased from 10 percent in 1992 to 11 percent in 2001, while for male heads of households it decreased over the same period from 36 percent to 27 percent. INE (2003, p. 201).

7. Other official sources estimate the indigenous population at approximately 50 percent.

8. Integrated Household Survey (*Encuesta Integrada de Hogares*—EIH), National Employment Survey (*Encuesta Nacional de Empleo*—ENE), Survey on Improvement in Living Conditions (*Encuesta de Mejoramiento de Condiciones de Vida*—MECOVI). Cited in Hall and Patrinos, eds. (2005, p. 52).

9. Ibid.

10. Vice Ministry on Women (2005b, p. 26).

11. Ibid, p. 30.

12. Some results and lessons learned from the National Land Management Project (*Proyecto Nacional de Administración de Tierras*) (1995-2005) are described in the report entitled *Gender Issues and Best Practices in Land Administration Projects* (World Bank, 2005), which studies the case of Bolivia together with programs in Azerbaijan, Ghana, and the Lao People's Democratic Republic.

13. Vice Ministry on Women (2005e, p. 27).

14. CIDEM) (2005), based on data provided by Comprehensive Municipal Legal Services (*Servicios Legales Integrales Municipales*).

15. National Demography and Health Survey, conducted periodically by the INE (2004b and other years).
16. See "Convention on the Elimination of All Forms of Discrimination against Women," Vice Ministry on Women (2005c).
17. These services have gradually been extended. In 2005 128 SLIMS were in operation, along with 24 Family Protection Brigades and 53 Protection and Prevention Networks throughout the country.
18. Vice Ministry on Women (2005c, p. 36).
19. Out of a total of 3,168,989 registered voters.
20. National Electoral Court, total registered voters as of October 2005: 3,679,886. Men: 1,855,090. Women: 1,824,796.
21. A significant statistic is the percentage of registered men to registered women in relation to the country's regional differences. Women in the highlands (La Paz, Cochabamba, Oruro) are registered in greater numbers than men. On the other hand, in the lowlands (Santa Cruz, Beni, and Pando), more men than women are registered.
22. United Cities and Local Governments, www.cities-localgovernments.org.
23. Committee to Promote the Political Rights of Women (*Comité Impulsor de los Derechos Políticos de las Mujeres* (2005). "Bill against Gender-Based Harassment and Political Violence."
24. Inter-Institutional Human Rights Council (2005). *Estrategia nacional de derechos humanos*, December.
25. Unfortunately, updated information is not available in this regard.
26. Buvinic and Mazza (2005).
27. Ibid, pp. 13 and 14.

13

Primary and Secondary Education

Raja Bentaouet Kattan

Summary

In the past decade, Bolivia has taken great steps forward in expanding its educational system, which has been reflected in the educational achievements of its population. Though educational coverage has increased, universal coverage continues to be a pending goal, especially for the most vulnerable groups. Bolivia is facing serious challenges: access to the final years of elementary school and secondary school is limited and unequal, academic performance is still deficient, and the system is inefficient. Low enrollment levels at the secondary level translate into major gaps in capabiliities within the Bolivian labor force and an insufficient number of highly trained individuals. In the end, these barriers create obstacles tor achieving sustained growth in the near future. It will be important for the government to improve quality and coverage and to increase the efficient, equitable use of funds in primary and secondary education. Moreover, measures need to be taken to ensure that students will be able to complete secondary school. The success of measures aimed at strengthening the supply of education will depend on their being accompanied by financial interventions on the demand side that can address poverty in the short term and guarantee that children enroll in and complete their education through the end of secondary school. In addition, commitments could be obtained from the small but important private educational sector to guarantee access to schooling for the more disadvantaged. It might also be useful to promote greater decentralization in order to increase the efficiency and effectiveness of the educational system.

I. Background

During the past decade, Bolivia has significantly extended the scope of its educational system; this is reflected in the educational achievements of its population. Average years of schooling have increased from 6.1 in 1992 to 7.4 in 2001. This increase in educational coverage can be attributed to major public policy initiatives. The Education Reform Program of the 1990s contributed to increasing rates of enrollment and completion in primary education. In Bolivia, 95 percent of children between 7 and 14 years of age are currently in school, a figure that places the country in the same range as some of its richer neighbors, such as Brazil or Peru. In other countries with similar per capita incomes, such as Guatemala and Honduras, the school attendance rate is considerably lower, in the range of 85 percent or less. In addition, between 1997 and 2002, the dropout rates at the primary level have fallen from 10.5 to 7.3 percent in the rural areas and from 9.9 to 5.9 percent in urban areas during the past six years. Similarly, the number of children who have had to repeat a grade has been cut in half. Completion rates have increased from 56 percent in 1996 to 71 percent in 2001 and are projected to reach 85 percent in 2010, which would place Bolivia very close to the Millennium Development Goal of universal primary education.

Despite these achievements, universal coverage continues to be a pending goal, especially for the less privileged groups, who still have high dropout and repetition rates. Access to secondary education is also markedly reduced for this group. In contrast to the high enrollment rates for primary education, in 2001, secondary school enrollment rates were only 51 percent.

Another important factor is that the quality of education has not improved at the same pace as the expansion of coverage, as is seen in Bolivia's results in national tests of the Educational Quality Measurement System (*Sistema de Medición de la Calidad Educativa*–SIMECAL) and international testing through the Latin American Laboratory for Assessment of Quality in Education (*Laboratorio Latinoamericano de Evaluación de la Calidad de la Educación*—LLECE). Spending in education has grown steadily since 1995, from 5.3 percent to the current 7.0 percent of the GDP, but this does not mean that funds have been allocated efficiently to improve academic performance. The relative success of the small private sector shows that there is no internal reason keeping Bolivia from developing a successful educational system.

This chapter describes the current situation of education in Bolivia. It is based on analyses and recommendations found in previous reports, especially the draft of the World Bank's 2006 study on the education sector (*La educación básica en Bolivia. Desafíos: 2006-2010).*

Recent Policy Initiatives

The challenges described above have led recent administrations to focus on improving the performance of the education sector, especially at the secondary level, which was given little priority during the former reform process. The recent National Education Strategy[1] pursues three main objectives: (i) improve access and keep children in school during their final years of primary and secondary education, (ii) improve the quality of teaching and learning, and (iii) strengthen decentralized educational administration.

The precedent for these proposals was the primary education reform of the second half of the 1990s. The Educational Reform Act of 1994 was an ambitious plan and has been implemented by four consecutive administrations. The comprehensive reform package considered the expansion and improvement of primary education to be essential for the development of human capital; it covered the following areas.

a) Modification of the grade structure and an increase in the number of mandatory years of basic education. Prior to 1994, there had been three levels: 1-5 (basic education), 6-8 (middle school education), and 9-12 (secondary education). Only the five years of basic education were mandatory. The reform provided for eight years of mandatory primary school and four years of secondary education.
b) New institutional development through optimization and professionalization of the Ministry of Education (*Ministerio de Educación*—MINEDU) and the creation of: (i) the SIMECAL; (ii) an administrative system for education; and (iii) a new system for payroll and other administrative functions, known as the Administrative Teaching Staff Registry (*Registro Docente Administrativo*—RDA).
c) Curriculum changes, with a total overhaul of curricula and new teacher guides, text books, and updated teaching materials.
d) The official recognition and gradual implementation of Intercultural Bilingual Education (*Educación Intercultural Bilingüe*—EIB) in Bolivian schools with a large presence of Quechua, Aymara, and/or Guaraní students.
e) The creation of popular participation councils at several educational administration levels to support decentralization. Similarly, parents' councils at the school level were strengthened to promote parental commitments and contributions to education. Particular importance was placed on the Educational Councils of Original Peoples (CEPO). As part of a pyramid system of school boards, four cross-geographic CEPOs were created in 1998, one each for the Aymara, Quechua, and Guaraní, and one for the other 30 Amazon peoples (at present, this fourth CEPO is being subdivided). The councils' representatives were elected by their respective peoples. Currently, the CEPOs play a fundamental role in civil society, in the initial formation of teachers through the reform of the former normal schools, and within the MINEDU to support and disseminate bilingual education.
f) Transformation of the current 18 Teacher Training Institutes (*Institutos Normales Superiores*), half of which are using a bilingual, intercultural approach, as well as the establishment of a system of pedagogic advisors to introduce reforms and train in-service teachers.

An evaluation of the reform shows major improvements, above all in primary education, with more extensive, equitable, and efficient education. The same can be said for Intercultural Bilingual Education. However, there is no evidence that the reform has improved academic performance. One criticism of the educational reform of the 1990s is that it was instituted from the top down, that is, with relatively few contributions from the principal stakeholders, such as teachers and their trade unions, school administrators, teacher training institutes, and other key persons.[2]

The Current State of Educational Coverage

At present, formal education, which starts at age five, is far from achieving universal access and coverage. Initial education in Bolivia is underfinanced and inaccessible for most children. Enrollment of children between the ages of five and six is approximately 30 percent; only 10 percent of children between the age of three and four are enrolled. Unfortunately, those most in need of pre-school education are those who have the least access to it. While 32 percent of children in the urban zones between the ages of five and six attend the initial level of school, only 24 percent of children in the rural zones do. While 34 percent of boys and girls between the ages of five and six from non-poor households have access to that level of education, only 27 percent of the poor benefit from early childhood education.[3]

In 1994, primary education was extended from a mandatory five-year cycle to a mandatory eight-year cycle for children between the ages of six and 13. With that, 97 percent enrollment was achieved, which ranks Bolivia higher than richer neighbors such as Venezuela or the Dominican Republic, and very close to Brazil (Figure 1). At the same time, primary school completion rates increased from 56 percent in 1996 to 71 percent in 2001. They are projected to reach 85 percent in 2010, which will bring Bolivia close to the Millennium Development Goal of universal primary education.

Secondary education lasts four years and serves students between 14 and 18 years of age who have completed primary school. At present, secondary school is characterized by limited overall access (only 51 percent in 2001), unequal access for male and female students, and poor quality.

Figure 1. Enrollment Rates and per capita GNP

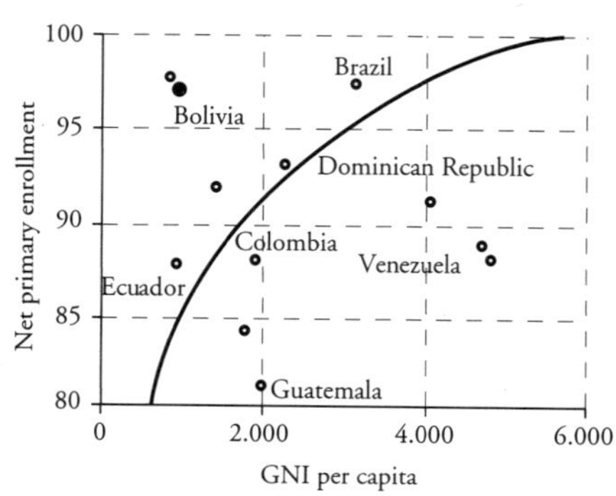

Source: EDSTATS, UNICEF, LLECE/OREALC.

The great majority of students are at the primary level, especially in the first three grades (Figure 2). In contrast to 300,000 students registered in the first year of primary school, there are fewer than 90,000 in the final year of secondary education. The broken lines show the size of the groups corresponding to 1994, 1987, and 1983 that should have, respectively, been in first grade, completed primary school, and completed secondary school. These figures show an excess of 63,000 (22 percent) children in first grade and a loss of 18,000 and 72,000 children (11 percent and 81 percent) at the end of primary and secondary school, respectively.

During the past ten years, the greatest increase in enrollment in secondary schools was concentrated in urban schools, which are characterized as having overcrowded classrooms, outdated curricula, and poorly trained teachers. While the Education Reform Program prioritized the primary level, the secondary level was overlooked. Secondary schools continue to work with outdated curricula and teaching materials. Their infrastructure is inappropriate; their teaching methods are conventional; funds for instructional purposes are very limited; and classroom size is inefficient (some schools have overcrowded classrooms, while others—especially in the rural areas—have a very low student/teacher ratio). In addition, an estimated 45 percent of secondary school teachers are not trained to teach at that level; in rural areas, that figure runs as high as 70 percent.

University enrollment in Bolivia is a relatively high 33 percent. This rate is higher than that of Brazil or Jamaica, whose rate is only 14 percent, and is similar to the rates for Argentina (36 percent) and Chile (37 percent). Nonetheless, though access to higher education is relatively equitable, the quality and internal efficiency of the system are very low.

Figure 2. Enrollment by Levels

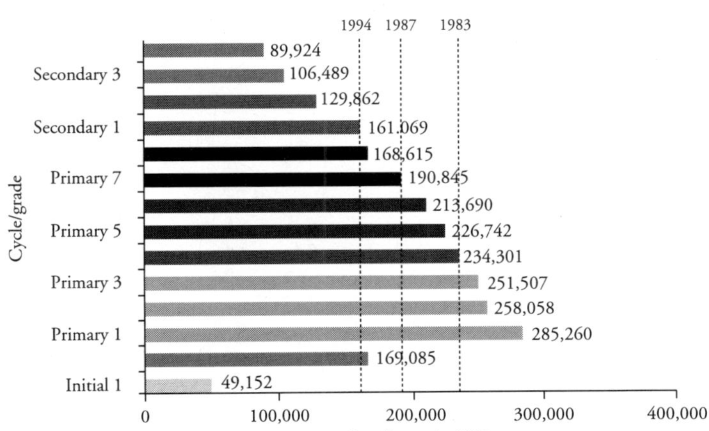

Source: MINEDU.

With the exception of higher education, the highest expenditures per student are for primary school (774 bolivianos), which represents close to 70 percent of the total spending of the MINEDU on education other than for college credit courses (Table 1).

Despite growing evidence on the long-term benefits of early childhood education, particularly for the poor, the table shows that this is not a priority for the Ministry of Education's budget, since expenditures per student at that level are very low (446 bolivianos). On the other hand, with 27 percent of all educational spending, the financing of higher education is quite elevated when compared with that of other Latin American countries.[4] It is alarming that secondary education receives less funding per student (669 bolivianos) than does primary education. Secondary schooling requires specialized teachers and more expensive installations, which should result in a higher cost per student, as occurs in most countries. This evidence, together with a broad consensus of public opinion on the issue, suggests that this level of education is in urgent need of attention.

II. Principal Issues to be Addressed

Although educational coverage has increased, Bolivia still faces a series of major challenges. These include: limited, unequal access to the final years of primary education as well as secondary education, low levels of academic performance, and inefficiency of the educational system.

Table 1. Educational Spending as a Percentage of the GDP in 2002

Level or Item	*Percentage of spending by the Ministry on education other than for college credit courses*	*Percentage of the central government's recurring expenditures in education*	*Expenditures per student (recurring), in bolivianos*
Administration (central or departmental)	4.0	2.9	
Initial	4.7	3.4	446
Primary	69.4	50.6	774
Secondary	15.5	11.3	669
Other*	6.4	4.7	
Total other than for college credit courses	100.0	73.0	
Public University System		27.0	3,342
Total for the Ministry		100.0	1,019

Source: MINEDU/UDI.

Note: * "Other" includes alternative education, special education, technical education, and non-credit courses at universities.

Limited, Unequal Access to the Final Years of Primary School (Seventh and Eighth Grades) and to Secondary School.

Although access to school, measured through enrollment rates, indicates that schooling is universal for male and female students up to 11 and 12 years of age, there are significant gaps after that age for indigenous and non-indigenous students, rural and urban students, and rich and poor students. Between seven and 11 years of age almost all boys and girls are in school (Figure 3). Even in the rural areas, in the lowest quintiles, and among the Quechua speaking population, attendance rates are above 90 percent. However, starting at 12 years of age, enrollment falls significantly and the gap grows. At that age, students in the urban areas, Spanish speakers, and families from higher income brackets have more possibilities to enroll in school. The enrollment rate for students 14 years of age from the highest income quintile is 14

Figure 3. School Attendance by Ethnic Group, Income Quintile, Gender, and Urban or Rural Residence

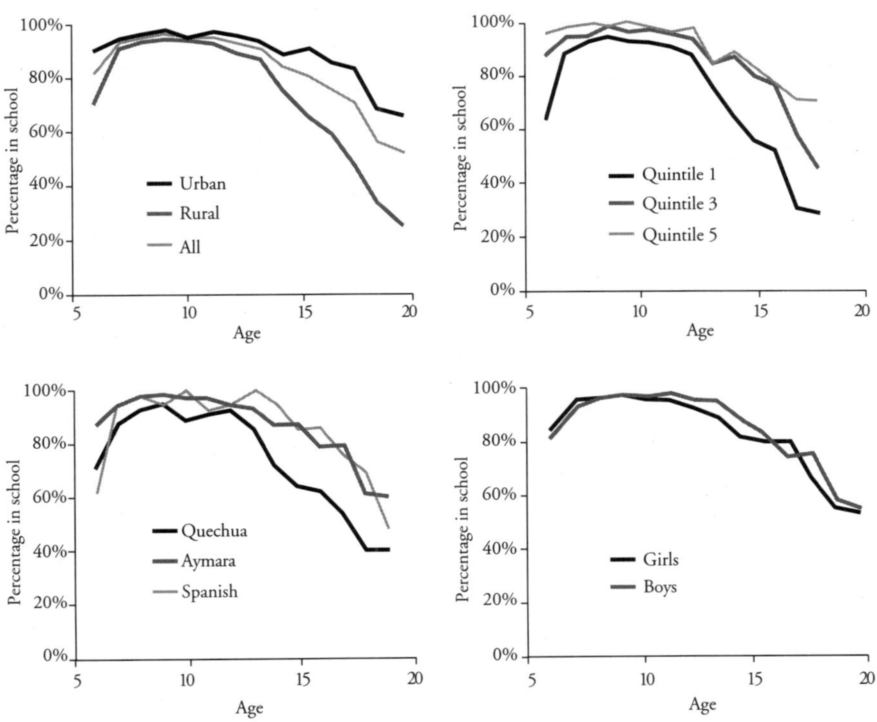

Source: Survey on Improvement in Living Conditions (*Encuesta de Mejoramiento de Condiciones de Vida*—MECOVI) 2002.

percentage points higher than that of their counterparts from the lowest income quintile. Quechua speaking boys and girls 14 years of age are 16 percentage points below their Spanish speaking counterparts, and the difference between urban and rural areas is 14 percentage points. At age 15, when teenage boys and girls should be entering secondary school, the differences grow and enrollment diminishes drastically. At age 16, the differential in attendance rates is 27 percentage points between urban and rural areas, 26 percentage points between students of the poorest and richest quintiles, and 17 percentage points between Quechua and Spanish speakers. This suggests that access to the final cycle of primary school and especially to secondary school is particularly low among vulnerable or disadvantaged groups.

The significant drop in enrollment after age 12 is attributed to various factors. The first and most obvious is the lack of available schools. While there are approximately 13,000 schools that serve children from first to third grade, only 8,000 serve fourth and fifth grade, fewer than 5,000 offer the final grades in primary school, and fewer than 2,500 schools offer the secondary level. This demonstrates that schools offering the highest grades are the scarcest and that distances between schools become greater as the students move up to the higher grades.

Data from the Geographic Information System (SIG) show that children who do not attend school live an average of twice as far from the closest school than those who do attend. Although this is due in part to other factors related to distance, an econometric analysis shows that distance is a decisive factor and that each kilometer of distance from the closest school reduces the probability of school attendance by 1.3 percentage points. It is not surprising to find that, if all other factors remain constant, children who have to walk great distances have a significantly higher probability of dropping out of school.

Participation in the labor market is another factor that takes children out of school, especially in the poorer rural zones. Twenty percent of children between the ages of ten and 14 work, which coincides with the age when they start to abandon the classroom. The diagnosis shows that a 1.0 percentage point increase in the probability of working reduces the probability of going to school by 0.75 percentage points. Of course, other factors not reflected in the household surveys influence the decision to drop out of school; these need to be covered by future research. Programs to prevent school desertion in other countries are taking such factors into account (Box 1).

Limited, Unequal Quality of Education

Bolivia has participated in only one international assessment of academic performance, by the LLECE,[5] in which Bolivia ranked close to average in academic performance (Table 2). Given its per capita income, it does somewhat better than expected. However, a detailed analysis shows that such an interpretation is limited.

The results of the LLECE in mathematics are especially good for the country, since Bolivia ranked even with Colombia in fifth place among the 11 participating countries. Bolivia not only obtained better results than Honduras (the only country

Box 1. Chile's "Secondary Education for All" Program

Chile's "Secondary Education for All" program (*Educación Secundaria para Todos*), which began in 2000, is designed to resolve the problem of school desertion by students at the secondary level. Schools are selected using a vulnerability risk index to estimate the probability at each school that students will drop out, based on the mother's years of schooling and the students' rate of repetition of grades. That same index serves to define the number of scholarships for each school. This is complemented with a student report card that allows the beneficiaries to be selected based on their class attendance, their average grades, and their situation in terms of excess of age (being behind in school or age to grade/course ratio).

The program is based on an intervention strategy that combines two dimensions: quality of life and quality of education. The first includes access to social services (especially scholarships for the most vulnerable students), improvement in the conditions of schools, and implementation of a school health program designed to keep young persons in school. As for the quality of education component, each center must formulate and implement a plan of action to prevent school desertion, based on a process of analysis and reflection. The center then receives: (i) scholarships in the amount of 148,000 Chilean pesos per year (equivalent to some US$200 per beneficiary); (ii) a teacher training plan; (iii) a psycho-social development plan; and (iv) improved mentoring.

The program has not yet been evaluated and its coverage is still relatively limited. In 2001 the program granted approximately 6,000 scholarships. Nonetheless, similar programs (including those in the United States) have been highly cost effective.

Sources: Economic Commission for Latin America and the Caribbean (ECLAC), 2002; Greenwood et al., 1998.

with comparable per capita income in the sample) but also better than other, much richer countries, such as Venezuela and the Dominican Republic. In language, however, Bolivia's score was lower than six of the 11 countries.

These results could lead to erroneous conclusions if the only thing considered is the average. An in-depth analysis of the international LLECE assessment and of the SIMEÇAL reveals major differences in academic performance between children at the highest and lowest percentages. The LLECE results for students in the 90th performance percentile in Bolivia are less than half the results for students in the 10th performance percentile. The results of the national assessment tests in Bolivia are

Table 2. Average Ratings in Mathematics and Language on the LLECE for the Third Grade
(Ranking in parentheses)

Country	*Language*	*Mathematics*
Argentina	263 (2)	251 (2)
Bolivia	**232 (7)**	**240 (6)**
Brazil	256 (4)	247 (3)
Chile	259 (3)	242 (4)
Colombia	238 (6)	240 (5)
Cuba	343 (1)	351 (1)
Dominican Republic	220 (10)	225 (9)
Honduras	216 (11)	218 (11)
Mexico	224 (9)	236 (7)
Paraguay	229 (8)	232 (8)
Venezuela	242 (5)	220 (10)

Source: LLECE.

even more compelling with respect to the low quality of education. The results of the SIMECAL tests conducted in 1998 on students from the eighth grade revealed that only half the students attain satisfactory results (pass) in reading and less than one third pass in mathematics.

A regression analysis shows that a good part of this difference either is not explained or is related to variables of the home, such as the educational level of the parents. However, the analysis also suggests that better accountability and school administration can lead to improved results. An educational production function[6] suggests that test results improve when the teacher has graduated from a teacher training institute. For public schools, this result is weak and has little significance; moreover, a reverse causality could be taking place, since the teacher training institute graduates may be choosing the best schools in which to teach. The evidence is strong and significant with respect to private schools. The fact that private schools are obtaining better results (even when controlling the characteristics for students observed), suggests that some of the characteristics of private schools in Bolivia may be significant determinants of academic performance. Selection processes, grouping by levels, and non-observable characteristics of the students probably play an important role in the success of private schools that charge tuition and serve the richer population. In institutions such as "*Fe y Alegría,*" both selection and non-observed characteristics play a limited role. This suggests that administrative factors, for example better pedagogic support to teachers, more supervision of teachers, and, in general, a higher degree of accountability, can have an influence.

In addition to the lack of preparation of teachers and less effective school administration, the poor results can be explained by absenteeism, both of students and of teachers. While 95 percent of school-age students are enrolled in primary school, information from the household survey shows that on any given day, close to 40 percent of those boys and girls are not in school. Although this phenomenon has not been sufficiently addressed to date, institutional variables may be at play. School principals reported that institutional reasons are behind a good part of teacher absenteeism, such as training and planning time, as well as other non-instructional activities that could be scheduled for any given time.[7] The six panels of Figure 4 show enrollment (darker line) and class attendance (lighter line), by age, for all Bolivian students, for women, for Quechua and Aymara speakers, and for urban and rural areas. These panels were developed by including questions regarding attendance in the MECOVI surveys.[8] Figure 4 shows a large gap between enrollment and attendance, especially for students in rural areas. The difference between enrollment and attendance in the panel for all students is 40 percentage points for children between the ages of eight and ten. In the case of the rural population, that differential increases to 50 percentage points for children between ages nine and ten. Quechua students show especially low results, while the Aymara students do a little better in terms of attendance. The attendance/enrollment gap is lower in the urban areas than in the rural ones and does not appear to be related to gender differences.

Inefficient Educational System

Even though a good part of GDP is invested in education, Bolivia is not succeeding in producing the citizens or production workers it needs to compete in the global economy. In 2004, educational spending represented 7.0 percent of GDP (the highest level in the past ten years). This is much higher than the 1995 level of 5.3 percent, and far higher than investments made by neighboring countries such as Ecuador (2.9 percent), Peru (3.3), or Brazil (5.6). Nonetheless, these funds are not used efficiently. Spending on instructional materials is low, while the part allocated to administrative expenditures is excessively high. The assignment of teachers to the various schools is also alarmingly inefficient.

Decentralization

The central government has recognized that the national educational system is too large to be managed from a single administrative center. Given that the government has too many tasks to perform and is too centralized, it cannot perform all its functions in an efficient and effective manner. As a result, many local matters are neglected or overlooked, because they have to be decided upon by the upper echelons of the Ministries. In such a context, the communities do not have access to decision making (because the decisions are made too far away) and, therefore, many problems that could be resolved at a departmental or municipal level (if that were possible), remain unresolved.

In the 1990s, the Educational Reform Act and the Popular Participation Act reallocated education resources and reassigned jurisdictions to the departments and,

Figure 4. Enrollment (darker line) and Attendance (lighter line) by Age and Demographic Group

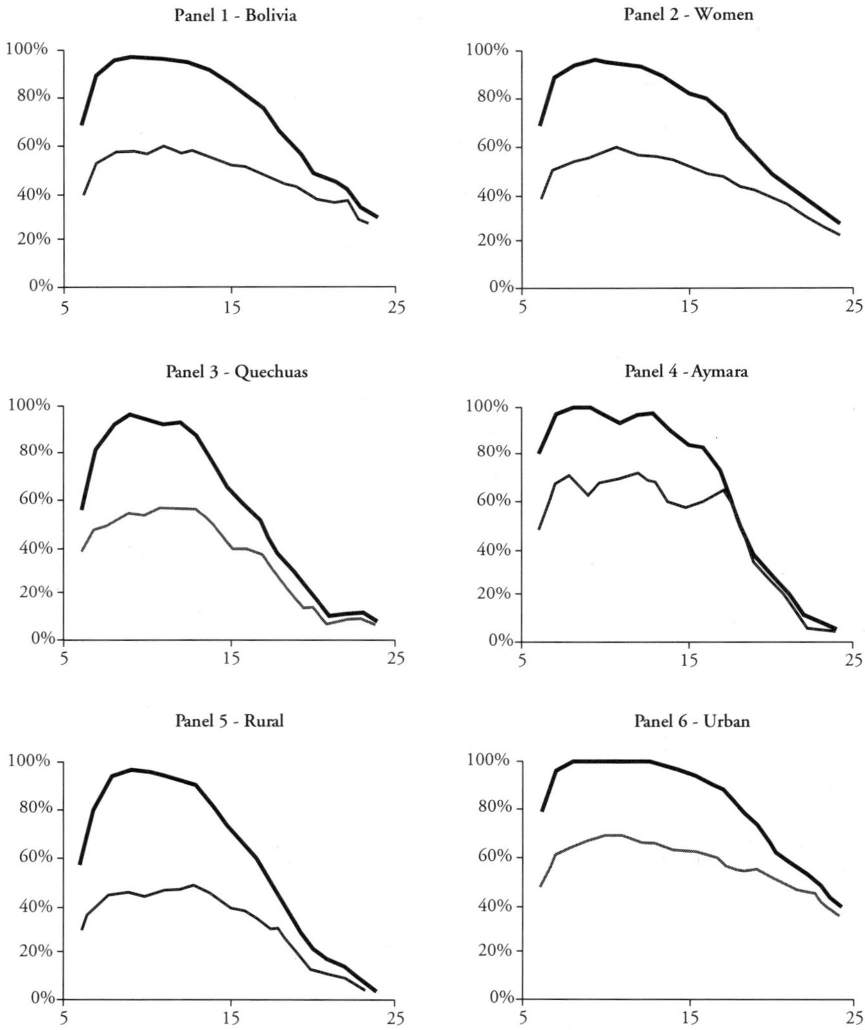

Source: MECOVI, 2002.

above all, to the municipalities. Although decentralization has positive results in many respects, it has also provoked a dispersion of jurisdictions and budgets. Despite many institutional deficiencies, it would appear that the educational inequalities from one department to another do not constitute a significant problem. Although expenditures per student are reasonably similar among departments, they are much less equitable within the departments and among districts, which leads one to think that the future autonomous departmental governments will need to take measures to better redistribute their money within the departments.

The municipal governments have transitioned from playing almost no role whatsoever in financing education to being responsible for 7 percent of ordinary current expenditures in education and 1 percent of total non-financial public sector expenditures. Revenue sharing takes up 20 percent of the central government's tax revenue earmarked for the municipalities plus 5 percent earmarked for public universities. Total revenue sharing is relatively large and represents close to 17 percent of GDP[9] (approximately 9 billion bolivianos, or approximately US$1.1 billion), which means that these transfers alone represent close to 3.4 percent of GDP for municipalities and 0.85 percent of GDP for universities.

HIPC resources are smaller; they amount to approximately 1 percent of GDP (582 million bolivianos, or nearly US$7.2 million). HIPC funds go directly to the municipal councils and are divided as follows: 20 percent for education, 10 percent for health, and 70 percent for productive investments. Within these areas, municipalities can invest the funds as they see fit. Nonetheless, this money is not always spent when transferred to the municipalities and, in many cases, is accumulating in bank accounts.

With these revenue sources, municipalities also have an obligation to provide infrastructure for health and education, as well as inputs and certain recurrently used materials for both sectors. There is little coordination between the municipalities and the MINEDU regarding the use of funds in education. This situation needs to be addressed through better communication.

The internal organization of the education sector is similar to that of the Bolivian State. In addition to the Ministry of Education, there are nine decentralized units, named SEDUCAs (Departmental Education Service—*Servicio Departamental de Educación*). The SEDUCAs take charge of managing the teaching personnel. Most of the everyday administrative efforts are carried out in the district by the District Director. Each Educational District contains educational clusters, which are sets of six to nine schools that share their funding. Each cluster, in turn, has a central school where the teaching materials are concentrated for support to the rest of the schools.

The principal challenge in the sector is to restore the disjointed, fragmented decision making process. As in other countries, certain of the system's functions were decentralized, but the central level continued to have responsibility for and jurisdiction over the most important issues.

As indicated above, most of the everyday administrative tasks are handled at the district level. Educational districts tend to coincide with the municipalities, but not always. There are 327 municipalities and only 275 districts, since smaller municipalities are grouped into a larger educational district. The district director handles basic functions such as the distribution of textbooks and teaching materials (provided by the central level) and the selection and assignment of school principals and teachers. On the other hand, the councils are responsible for physical elements such as school maintenance and the provision of electricity, water, and teaching materials. However, there is a fuzzy area where the tasks of the district directors and the council members are not clear. For example, many schools are in need of basic supplies such as paper, pencils, or chalk, because neither the directors nor the councils assume responsibility for providing them; frequently they do not have a sufficient budget for these types of expenditures.

Municipalities receive significant resources for educational infrastructure (close to 0.4 percent of GDP). MINEDU creates educational projects and encourages council members to plan the use of those funds in the framework of such projects with the participation of local stakeholders. Since 2000, educational projects have been developed to support decentralized management at the local level and to better coordinate with other levels. The projects start with the plans of each school, known as Instructional Unit Educational Projects (*Proyectos Educativos de Unidad Educativa*—PEU), which are then grouped under Cluster Educational Projects (*Proyectos Educativos de Núcleo*—PEN, in the rural areas), School System Educational Projects (*Proyectos Educativos de Red*—PER, in urban areas) or Indigenous Educational Projects (*Proyectos Educativos Indígenas*—PEI, in indigenous districts), as applicable. These projects are integrated into the Municipal Educational Projects (*Proyectos Educativos Municipales*—PROME) and then go on to form a part of the annual operating budgets of the municipalities. These projects allow for greater community participation in educational decision making as well as coordination of various stakeholders in education. At the same time, they leverage funds, which makes it possible to combine both centralized and decentralized municipal funds. Despite this, the educational projects have not been as useful as anticipated due to a lack of communication between the municipalities and MINEDU. Municipalities spend 81 percent of their money on physical infrastructure and only 19 percent on teaching materials or training materials, even though experience suggests that better quality requires more investments in the latter. Even more worrisome is that infrastructure policy is out of line not only with investments in pedagogical needs, but also with personnel policy.

The administration of teacher designation is ineffective. The task of hiring and firing teachers, as well as their assignment to the educational districts, was delegated to the SEDUCAs that, as noted above, report simultaneously to the department government and to the MINEDU. The SEDUCAs have become politicized and have little jurisdiction over administrative and technical matters. This problem is seen more clearly when one examines the poor distribution of teachers in the districts. Teachers are paid by the central administration, but their location assignment is decided at the departmental level. A detailed analysis of how they are assigned shows that the distribution of teachers is extremely inefficient. One statistic suffices to illustrate this: more than 9,000 teachers are not truly needed by the schools in which they work, as is seen by the low teacher/student ratio. It is essential to improve the efficiency of the system through a greater assumption of responsibilities and to perfect accountability at the departmental and municipal levels. Substantial gains could be obtained through better teacher assignment policies.

III. Policy Recommendations

Some policy alternatives are presented below to respond to the issues discussed.

Improve Access and Staying in School for the Final Years of the Primary Level and at the Secondary Level

In order to consolidate progress at the primary level, expand achievements to the final years of primary school and secondary school education. Greater access to the classroom, an increase in the completion rate at the primary level, and natural pressure from the growing population will inevitably lead to a growth in the demand for schooling, especially in rural zones. The demand for enrollment in secondary school will likely double by the year 2010. To succeed in having more youth attend secondary school, sufficient supply is needed. Schools need to be located close to most population centers, and they must have teachers and books.

Improving access involves investing more in the existing conventional systems, in addition to exploring alternative methods for providing services to satisfy the specific needs of rural students. For children who live far from school, and who drop out or fail to attend school due to long distances, methods such as education by radio and/or home/school tutorial combinations are especially promising. Both options, which have gained much recognition in Ecuador, can be effective and efficient in terms of their educational impact. Under tutorial programs, once or twice a week a teacher visits an isolated community or the children travel to a distant school. The rest of the days, the students follow a work program supervised by an adult of their community. If this is complemented with education by radio, provided that there are batteries available if there is no electricity, the model can work even better.

Given the complicated fiscal situation, the use of school infrastructure and existing personnel at the primary level to implement alternatives such as tele-secondary education in areas with access to electricity is a promising possibility to bring secondary education to the rural areas at a low cost. This uses existing infrastructure and teachers to extend secondary education. A generalist teacher, with training in secondary education, acts as the facilitator for the process, while teachers specialized in the content take charge of the instructional processes using videos or television channels. In Mexico, where this model has already been evaluated, tele-secondary students achieve levels of performance similar to those achieved using other models.[10]

Given the economic slowdown and growing poverty, especially in the countryside, interventions are also needed on the demand side to attract and keep children in school. Such measures include conditional cash transfers to families in exchange for enrolling their children in school and maintaining high attendance rates. These programs have proven to be highly successful in other countries of Latin America (see Box 2).

Mexico has had great success in enrolling students and keeping them in primary school through a conditional monetary transfer program called *Oportunidades*. Rig-

Box 2. Increased School Attendance through Monetary Transfers in Brazil: the *Bolsa Escola* Program

In 1995, the municipality of the Federal District of Brasilia launched an innovative program named *Bolsa Escola* with the aim of improving education and reducing the impact of child labor. The relevance of this program for lifelong learning is based on the use of coupon-type instruments, including scholarships to offset the cost of attending school.

This initiative also includes a savings program that creates an incentive to stay in school. If a child whose family benefits from the scholarship program is promoted to the next grade, the school savings program deposits money into that student's account. Half of the deposit can be withdrawn when the child reaches fifth grade. Other withdrawals can be made once the student completes primary school and then secondary school.

orous evaluations of the program's impact indicate that enrollment has grown significantly, particularly among females, and above all in secondary school. The results indicate that children will have an average of 0.7 extra years of schooling thanks to *Oportunidades*. This effect could increase if, motivated by the initial incentive, children also attended high school. The data on Mexico for 1997 to 1999[11] show that *Oportunidades* resulted in superior academic performance among indigenous students and a significant reduction in the gap between indigenous and non-indigenous children[12]. The results also show that indigenous children are less likely to work and abandon their studies after having participated in the program. However, indigenous children also displayed lower academic performance than did children who spoke only Spanish or who were bilingual. For that reason, it is important that these actions carefully target the poorest children and the most vulnerable indigenous populations. Household surveys can be useful to obtain information about the most disadvantaged groups.

Together with the demand-side financing approaches described above, Chile's "Secondary School for All" (*Escuela Secundaria para Todos*) program (Box 1), designed to stop secondary school students from dropping out of school, could be considered for Bolivia. Similar programs in the United States have been proven highly effective.[13]

In addition to the subsidies program indicated above, the MINEDU could contract the private sector, which tends to be more efficient in the provision of quality education among those most disadvantaged. Alternative schooling models such as *Fe y Alegría* (Box 3), which is being implemented in 14 Latin America countries, including Bolivia, show tangible results. An evaluation of the program in nine countries

Box 3. ***Fe y Alegría***

Fe y Alegría is a non-governmental organization associated with the Catholic Church. Based on an agreement with the government, teachers' wages are paid by the state, while other costs are covered by the communities and the private sector. In 2001, more than 1 million students throughout Latin America attended 2,188 learning centers through this program, including 922 schools. The national office of *Fe y Alegría* in each country supervises the quality of the education imparted, trains its own teachers and principals, manages the educational centers, and coordinates activities to turn the program into a development strategy for the local area. *Fe y Alegría* has developed strategies to reduce the repetition of grades and school desertion during the first years of schooling for children from the most disadvantaged areas. The strategies include: preventive programs designed to improve and change the health and nutrition situation, therapeutic programs for children with learning disabilities, flexible or multiple promotion programs, plans for reinforcing demand, active community participation, and technical secondary education programs. In these programs, the most effective strategies are those that focus on the parents, based on an open academic environment that promotes the effective participation of parents in the learning process, community participation in the administration of schools, and strategies around the students based on an interactive teaching method and recognition of various modes of learning. In addition, the general organizational strategy of providing a broad education includes pre-school, primary, and secondary education. Such a strategy provides a major incentive for parents to keep their children in school.

Source: Swope and Latorre 1998a, 1998b, 1998c.

indicates that these schools stand out over traditional public schools, with fewer repeated grades, a lower dropout rate, more academic progress, and greater average overall rates of keeping children in school.[14] This strategy saves money for the government while improving the rates of keeping disadvantaged children in school.[15]

Other Latin American countries' successful school system programs should be taken into consideration. For example, Santiago's Matte Schools of the Primary Instruction Society (*Sociedad de Instrucción Primaria*—SIP) are an example of a successful system of private subsidized schools. The entities affiliated with the SIP are located in poor neighborhoods, have complete autonomy, and were initially supported by private contributions. They were among the first to take advantage of the opportunity to become private when Chile's national coupon system was established in 1980. In national evaluations, the SIP schools obtain better results than public (municipal) schools and the private subsidized schools and do almost as well as the most selective and costly centers. This is an important finding considering that SIP schools serve children of poor families.[16]

Improve Educational Results

Increase the provision of quality teaching materials, especially in low-income areas, in order to improve student learning. Low educational quality can be due to family environments, but also to factors related to schools. Among them, the quality of teaching materials, together with a positive academic climate, are the factors that most influence performance.[17] The lessons learned in educational experience worldwide reveal that results can be substantially improved through well-focused interventions, provided that they are properly implemented. If they are adapted to the needs of the most disadvantaged children, these actions can reduce the gap between these children and their counterparts. Therefore, a substantial improvement in learning can be attained in rural schools and among indigenous populations if the use of better quality supplies is well distributed. Despite the improvements gained through institutionalization of Intercultural Bilingual Education (EIB) as part of the Educational Reform, its implementation is far from perfect. Many tasks are still pending, including the development of adequate teaching materials. Thus, many children have not received the instructional materials required. Perhaps the greatest failure of EIB was its application against the will of families and students, which led to an unnecessary resistance among those who wanted their children to learn Spanish as soon as possible. This ended up isolating the advocates of bilingual education. One important recommendation is to make bilingual education optional, and not have the government impose it.[18]

National evaluations (such as SIMECAL) need to be used to establish standards for future follow-up on trends in achievement, and the results need to be linked to teacher training and the curriculum. Bolivia has established a comprehensive evaluation system initially intended to make systematic use of available information. Nonetheless, the SIMECAL's results have not been used to provide feedback to educational planners. Initially the results of the SIMECAL were supposed to be used to improve curriculum reform and teacher training, which would be conducted in parallel, thereby leading to changes in the classroom. This has not occurred. Due to budget limitations, SIMECAL tests in the primary grades are taken only sporadically (1997, 1999, and 2000); each time in a different grade, using samples that are representative, but nonetheless very small. These characteristics limit the value of its conclusions and impede rigorous comparisons. The recent suspension of the SIMECAL evaluations is cause for concern. Although the SIMECAL has not been eliminated, its staff has been cut and no new evaluation has been made at the primary level since 2000. Despite those obstacles, this consultation system provides Bolivia with an excellent opportunity to establish national standards regarding what the students should be learning each year, teacher qualifications, curriculum evaluation and development, and incentives for improving education in general. The transformation of an evaluation system on student performance from a political tool to a tool for pedagogic support is a first step toward establishing mechanisms to ensure greater responsibility and accountability in the educational framework and to improve the quality of education.

Moreover, it is important for Bolivia to participate in international evaluations such as TIMSS and PISA. The results should be used to compare Bolivia's performance with that of other countries and evaluate its education system. This has been done by Singapore and Jordan, where the data is used for curriculum reform, teacher training, and research on the elements that impact learning. In both cases, but especially for Singapore, this approach has led to important benefits.

Promote Decentralization to Improve Efficiency and Effectiveness

To improve quality, continue its efforts to move the decision making process to the local level (that is, to the schools) while increasing and strengthening their autonomy. In most countries that have good results in international evaluations, local and school authorities have a very high degree of responsibility for the content of the instruction and/or the use of funds, and much content is developed specifically to work with heterogeneous groups of students. To improve the academic results, the empowerment of schools must be accompanied by a clear framework of jurisdiction and accountability that leads to the participation of society and parents in schools. Finally, accountability for educational actions can improve the quality of education, by increasing the involvement of the family and community, and by establishing goals for the educational system.

The government can increase the efficiency and effectiveness of the education system by decentralizing the system to promote greater parent and community involvement. Educational decentralization, as applied in New Zealand, Victoria (Australia), Brazil, Colombia, and Chile, will probably improve the performance of the education system. On the other hand, a decentralized financing system, without an effective offsetting mechanism, could be detrimental to children from economically disadvantaged sectors. With sound policies, the benefits of decentralization can be enjoyed without losing equity. One of the policies needed would be a guarantee by the federal government that the most vulnerable departments or states will receive more funds than others. Decentralization makes it possible to review the distribution of federal money and make it more simple and transparent. Especially interesting are budget distribution processes based on standard formulas—with the corresponding framework for defining responsibilities and the levels and instances where such responsibilities are discharged—as a step toward opening the way for more effective alternatives to address issues of equity and efficiency. Many of the major achievements leading to improved academic results in Chile were attained only once the decentralization policy was accompanied by the implementation of programs to improve public schools. These measures increased support in the form of materials intended for poorer schools and strengthened the professional development of teachers. The best administrative and budget reforms in the world have been those that assure schools and teachers that they will obtain the professional competency, authority, funds, and incentives required to design and carry out their own academic and teaching activities in keeping with the needs of their students. There are certain activities—such as supervision and coordination to ensure equity among different locations within a state—that the government cannot handle efficiently, because it is too far from the specific problem.

Given the current management system, the best solution might be a change in the financing rules. Funds could be linked to students or be assigned according to each student ("funds follow students"). If the MINEDU finances the departments or the municipalities (or both) in accordance with a formula based on the place where the students are (adjusted to special conditions such as when a rural area is very remote or if there are transportation difficulties), it could then assume the tasks of setting performance standards, conducting performance evaluations, and providing technical assistance to the departments and municipalities that administer the schools. In that way, the MINEDU would be able to create the incentives to have the largest possible percent of students in school.

Bibliography

Banco Central de Bolivia. 2002. *Boletín Estadístico* No. 316. December. La Paz.

Bando, R., L. F. Lopez-Calva, and H. A. Patrinos. 2005. "Child Labor, School Attendance, and Indigenous Households: Evidence from Mexico." World Bank Policy Research Working Paper No. 3487, Washington, DC.

Behrman, J., P. Sengupta and S. Parker. 2005. "*Progresando a través de PROGRESA: Una Evaluación del Impacto de un Subsidio Escolar Experimental en México.*" *Desarrollo Económico y Cambio Cultural* (publication pending).

Bolivian Ministry of Education. 2004. *La Educación en Bolivia: indicadores, cifras y resultados.*

Contreras, Manuel and Maria Luisa Talavera. 2004. *Examen parcial: la reforma educativa boliviana, 1992-2002.* La Paz: Fundación PIEB.

Fiske, E.B. 1996. *Decentralization of Education: Politics and Consensus.* Washington DC: World Bank.

Greenwood, P.W., K.E. Model, C.P. Rydell and J.R. Chiesa. 1998. *Diverting Children from a Life of Crime: Measuring Costs and Benefits.* Santa Monica: RAND.

Kremer, Michael, Karthik Muralidharan, Nazmul Chaudhury, Jeffrey S. Hammer and F. Halsey Rogers. 2004. "Teacher Absence in India: A Snapshot" en *Journal of the European Economic Association* 3:2-3.

McMeekin, R. 2003. *Red Escolar. Documentos de Análisis de Política Educativa.* 11(16).

National Statistics Institute (*Instituto Nacional de Estadística*—INE). 2003 *Bolivia: características educativas y cambios entre 1992 y 2001.* La Paz: INE, October.

Patrinos, H.A. 2002. *Subcontratando en Educación.* Washington DC: World Bank.

Schultz, T.P. 2004. "School Subsidies for the Poor: Evaluating the Mexican PROGRESA Poverty Program." *Journal of Development Economics* 74(1): 199-250.

Skoufias, E. and S. Parker. 2001. "Conditional Cash Transfers and Their Impact on Child Work and Schooling: Evidence from the PROGRESA Program in Mexico." *Economía* 2(1): 45-96.

Swope, J.Y and M. Latorre. 1998a. *Estudio de eficiencia interna de las escuelas formales de Fe y Alegría.* CIDE Santiago, Chile.

———. 1998b. *Comunidades educativas, Donde Termina al Asfalto; Escuelas Fe y Alegría en América Latina.* CIDE-PREAL-USAID-IABD, Santiago.

———. 1998c. *Fe y Alegría: una propuesta alternativa de educación primaria en América Latina.*

UNESCO (2000). *Latin American Laboratory for Assessment of Quality in Education: First International Comparative Study of Language, Mathematics, and Associated Factors for Students in the Third and Fourth Years of Primary School. Second Report.* Santiago: UNESCO.

Urquiola, M., W. Jiménez, M. L. Talavera, and W. Hernany. 2000. *Los maestros en Bolivia: impacto, incentivos y desempeño.*

World Bank. 1996. "*Colombia. Reformando la Ley de Descentralización: incentivos para una efectiva provisión de servicios.*" Mimeo.

———. 2003. "*Bolivia. Revisión del gasto público.*" Mimeo.

———. Bolivia Country Office. 2003. *Bolivia. Resumen del Sector Educación.* Mimeo

———. 2004. "*Evaluación del impacto de la educación intercultural bilingüe.*" Mimeo.

———. 2005. "Mexico. Determinants of Learning. Policy Note." Report No. 31842-MX. World Bank, Washington, DC.

———. 2006. *La educación básica en Bolivia. Desafíos: 2006-2010.* Draft.

Endnotes

1. MINEDU, 2004.

2. More information about the evaluation of the reform can be found in Contreras and Talavera (2004).

3. Although a detailed analysis of the challenge to expand initial education exceeds the scope of this chapter, international experience has shown that access to early childhood education and improved academic performance provide significant benefits.

4. Bolivia's university system has a graduation rate of only 40 percent and consumes 27 percent of total spending on education. Although a rigorous analysis of the challenges in higher education are beyond the scope of this chapter, it is important to note that an improvement in the internal efficiency of the Bolivian university system could lower costs without reducing the number of university graduates.

5. The LLECE testing was conducted between June and November 1997 in Argentina, Bolivia, Brazil, Chile, Colombia, Cuba, the Dominican Republic, Honduras, Mexico,

Paraguay, and Venezuela. Students from the third and fourth grade were tested in mathematics and writing. Bolivia has not participated in more modern tests such as PISA (Programme for International Student Achievement), TIMSS (Trends in International Mathematics and Science Study) or IALS (International Adult Literacy Survey). The LLECE is based on classic test theory and not Item Response Theory; it uses identical questions to compare various countries or groups. The number of items is relatively low and the test does not use the problem-solving approach employed by the PISA and other modern testing programs.

6. Estimated by Urquiola et al., 2000. The complete specification also included controls on an individual basis, on a household basis, and other socio-economic factors.

7. According to Kremer et al., 2004.

8. This question is quite new for the household surveys. Accordingly, it is as yet unknown how the interviewees are interpreting the question, but the results are worrisome.

9. All the figures for the financing of education refer to 2002.

10. See World Bank, 2005.

11. Behrman and other, 2005; Skoufias and Parker, 2001; Schultz, 2004.

12. Bando et al., 2005.

13. Greenwood et al., 1998.

14. Patrinos, 2002.

15. McMeekin, 2003.

16. Ibid.

17. UNESCO, 2000.

18. Obviously, the selection of the bilingual option would call for planning on the part of the MINEDU. For example, the materials and trained teachers cannot be provided overnight.

14

The Health Sector

José Pablo Gómez

Summary

The health situation in Bolivia is one of the most unfavorable in Latin America. Improvements during the 1990s were moving the country toward attaining the Millennium Development Goals for the sector, but essential measures have failed to move forward or have taken a downward turn, thereby jeopardizing that objective. The sector's lack of progress has three causes: First, the country's institutional crisis has prevented implementation of stable policies, adequate coordination, and monitoring. Second, the sector has been decentralized, which has not always been beneficial and has resulted in high transaction costs. Third, inappropriate allocation of funds resulting from decentralization keeps equity gaps from being closed. In order to overcome these problems, several measures should be considered. One is to support the Ministry of Health in its role as the administrative entity with the final responsibility for what happens in the sector. Next, with respect to decentralization, the new departmental governments need to play a specific role in the provision of healthcare services in a manner that complements the national and municipal levels. Finally, resources need to be more closely conditioned upon performance in healthcare within the departments and service networks through effective incentives and better accountability.

I. Background

The Health Status and the Millennium Goals

The health status of the Bolivian population is among the most complex in Latin America. Indicators such as infant mortality and maternal mortality rates rank

Bolivia as the worst country, after Haiti. On the Human Development Index (HDI), Bolivia is among the mid-income countries with the lowest levels of development—in 2005, it ranked 113 on the HDI list, close to Honduras (116) and Guatemala (117). Nonetheless, both Honduras and Guatemala have better health indicators than Bolivia (Table 1).

In the health sector, during the 1990s and the start of the current decade, Bolivia engaged in notable efforts and made progress, as is seen in the aggregated data presented in the following table. Of particular note was the progress made in the late 1990s, observed in a study on the reform of the health sector.[1]

Bolivia could meet its Millennium Development Goals for the health sector if it keeps up its current pace of progress and also takes actions to improve data collection, follow-up, and supervision (Table 2).[2] Unfortunately, the indicators for these activities over recent years reveal stagnation and even regression or excessively slow progress (Table 3).

The communicable diseases situation in the country has not improved. Chagas is endemic, and malaria continues to be present, even though the malaria rate has diminished thanks to anti-malaria programs. The incidence of yellow fever has diminished, but this disease continues to affect the departments of Santa Cruz and Pando. Among emerging and reemerging diseases, most notable is the reappearance of dengue fever (serotypes I and II)[3], especially in the departments of Beni and Pando.[4]

Table 1. Indicators in Latin America

Selected Countries	*Per Capita GDP (Purchasing Power Parity) 2003*	*Human Development Index Ranking 2005*	*Maternal Mortality Rate**	*Infant Mortality Rate 2003*	*Life Expectancy*	*Urban Population 2005 (%)*
Central America						
Guatemala	4,090	117	153	30.8	71.6	47
Honduras	2,590	116	108	34.0	70.7	46
Nicaragua	3,180	112	82.8	35	72.9	58
Panama	6,420	56	68	15.2	77.9	58
Andean Zone						
Colombia	6,410	69	84.8	18	75.9	77
Ecuador	3,440	82	77.8	22.3	77.7	63
Peru	5,080	79	185	33.4	73.3	75
Venezuela	4,750	75	57.8	18.5	76.4	88
Southern Cone						
Paraguay	4,690	88	174.1	19.4	73.8	58
Uruguay	7,980	46	no data	15	79.5	93
Bolivia	**2,490**	**113**	**230**	**54.0**	**67.0**	**65**

Source: PAHO, 2005, *Basic Indicators;* and UNDP, *2005 Human Development Report.*
Note: * = most recent year for which data is available (Bolivia is for 2003).

Table 2: Progress towards the Millennium Development Goals

Objective	*Goal*	*Starting Point (1990)*	*Progress (most recent year)*	*Expected by 2015 (estimated)*
4. Reduce infant mortality (Goal for 2015 = reduce the 1990 mortality rate among children under age 5 by two-thirds)	Mortality rate for children under age 5	120	75 (2003)	40
	Infant mortality rate (for each 1,000 live births)	89 (1989)	54 (2003)	30
5. Improve maternal health (Goal for 2015 = reduce the 1990 maternal mortality rate by three-fourths)	Maternal mortality rate (for each 100,000 live births)	416 (1989)	235 (2003)	138

Source: UDAPE, 2005.

As for the coverage of the health system, 27 percent of the total population was affiliated with the social security health system in 2004. About 10 percent of the population has private health insurance to supplement coverage from the social security system or the Ministry of Health and Sports (*Ministerio de Salud y Deportes*—MSD).[5] Approximately 70 percent of Bolivians make use of the public health sector.

Table 3. Progress in Health Indicators

Indicator	*1999*	*2000*	*2001*	*2002*	*2003*	*2004*	*2005 (e)*
Coverage of hospital births (%)	48	54	51	58	59	60	62
Coverage of at least 4 prenatal checkups (%)	36	42	43	42	46	50	50
3rd dose of the pentavalent vaccine and DTP vaccine in children under 1 year of age (%)	85	91	92	88	81	85	84
Women using some family planning method (%)	48				58		
Percentage of children with chronic malnutrition (%)	27				27		

Source: Ministry of Health, World Bank (2004, 2005) and National Statistics Institute (*Instituto Nacional de Estadística*—INE).

Table 4. Trends in Health Expenses as a Percentage of GDP
Health Spending Indicators (% of GDP)

	1995	*1996*	*1997*	*1998*	*1999*	*2000*	*2001*	*2002*
Total National Spending	4.38	4.64	4.71	4.97	6.20	6.08	6.40	6.95
Public Spending	1.21	1.13	1.04	1.15	1.41	1.39	1.32	1.46
Social Security	1.64	2.01	1.97	2.11	2.36	2.42	2.63	2.86
Private Spending	1.52	1.50	1.70	1.71	2.42	2.27	2.46	2.64

Source: Cárdenas, 2004.

The rest use the social security health system, and some use private providers. Despite that, the public sector covers only 25 to 28 percent of expenditures. Between 37 and 40 percent of expenditures is covered by social security funding, 5 to 10 percent by the private insurance sector, and the rest directly by families. At the aggregate level, this is not much different from what is observed in the other Andean countries.

Health expenses in Bolivia amount to around 7 percent of GDP (approximately US$550 million) and have been growing due to expenses on medications (based on spending groups), in the social security system and the private sector (which includes family expenses). Public spending on health is estimated to represent approximately 1.4 percent of GDP, part of which is covered by funds received through the Highly Indebted Poor Countries Initiative (HIPC) (Table 4).

II. Organization of the Sector

The MSD is the highest authority in the health sector. It is responsible for the general supervision of the public and private healthcare system and for implementing public health actions on a national level. It is exclusively financed by the fiscal budget, which includes grants and projects that receive multilateral financing. The MSD controls close to 25 percent of the public budget for health. The majority of these funds are earmarked for public health actions and for financing staff at the central level (Table 5).

In recent years, the MSD has received support from several international initiatives and multilateral entities. Accordingly, in connection with the debt relief initiative under the HIPC program, new indicators and goals have been set for the country. In the health sector, the National Health Information System has been strengthened to monitor progress on these indicators. As a follow-up method, management commitments are being used, each signed with Departmental Health Service (*Servicio Departamental de Salud*—SEDES). These entities are also supervised by the Comptroller General of the Republic. In addition, the use of basic follow-up indicators has been promoted in the different health sector support projects (for example, indicators of coverage for institutionalized childbirth, vaccinations, prenatal care, etc.).

Table 5. Health Budget as Executed, by Elements (2003)
(in millions of bolivianos)

	Operating Costs				*Capital Expenditures*		
	Consumption Expenditures		*Others*				
	Wages	*Services Other than Personnel*	*Transfers and Misc.*	*Total*	*Investments*	*Total*	*Total*
MSD	44.2	204.2	2.1	250.6	16.2	16.2	266.8
Departments	460.6	22.8	0.0	483.4	8.4	8.4	491.8
Municipalities	11.9	90.3	35.7	138.2	169.0	169.5	307.7
Total	516.7	317.3	37.8	872.2	193.5	194.1	1,066.3

Source: Public Accounting, Ministry of Finance.

The MSD has partial control over the public system funds earmarked for the provision of services. In practice, jurisdiction over the provision of services is not clearly defined. A significant part of the operating budget for financing the human resources payroll has been transferred to the departmental governments.

The Role of the Departments

Based on this budget, the departments are responsible for paying personnel. In addition, based on a mutual agreement with the municipalities, they evaluate the performance and location of health services.[6] In practice, the departments' activities are limited to the payment, since so far they cannot hire or fire personnel or reallocate funds received from the MSD. The departments collaborate with the SEDES and regional offices of the MSD on public health campaigns and epidemiological control, facilitate certain logistical resources, and cooperate on the maintenance of certain establishments such as the national institutes. The departments also have another significant role of co-financing investments on approved projects or loans for the municipalities.

The Role of the Municipalities

The municipalities are the owners and managers of the service establishments. They are in charge of investment, maintenance, and administration. However, since they lack the personnel and funds for these tasks, they have to come to an agreement with the departments on the assignment of human resources. This is accomplished through an institutional agreement for what are known as Local Health Boards (*Directorios Locales de Salud*—DILOS). The municipalities are represented on and preside over the DILOS. Also represented on the DILOS are the SEDES and the community. This mechanism plans healthcare services and evaluates their delivery.

To make investments, the municipalities must use their own funds or request funds from the central level, which requires support from the departments. This

Box 1. The Experience of *Extensa*

The MSD's *Extensa* program targets providing direct basic services to populations in difficult to access areas in the country. The program deploys multidisciplinary health teams (a doctor, nurse, dentist, and assistant) for preventive care actions and health control, especially in the area of infant and maternal health. Each "brigade" performs its task in a series of 40 to 50 locations, which they cover every two months in rounds of 20 to 25 days. As of June 2005, the 59 existing brigades were serving a population of nearly 300,000 people, most of whom were indigenous, in close to 300 locations in the nine departments.

At first, all of *Extensa's* financing came from the Reform Project, but gradually, this financing was complemented with human resources and inputs from existing healthcare systems in the municipalities and departments serviced. At the same time, the modus operandi of the brigades has been changing. Originally, they were organized at the central level. Now, 40 new brigades have been created exclusively with personnel from existing healthcare systems. The initiative's sustainability will depend on authorization from the departments and municipalities to finance these brigades with funds from the hydrocarbons tax. The supervision and control of all the brigades is being conducted at the central level.

makes the departments de facto guarantors of credit for investment, whether through the Production and Social Fund (*Fondo Productivo y Social*—FPS) or any other fund. The municipalities can also use funds from revenue sharing for health, allocated to the Universal Mother/Child Insurance (*Seguro Universal Materno-Infantil*—SUMI).

Universal Mother/Child Insurance (Seguro Universal Materno-Infantil—SUMI)

SUMI is one of the innovations of the healthcare system. SUMI provides financial protection around a package of services to mothers and infants. The services, which are available for the entire potential beneficiary population, are provided through public and private systems. They are financed through the following mechanism: the municipalities receive revenue sharing funds "earmarked" for the SUMI. The percentage of funds from this source has been 10 percent since 2005. However, in order to obtain these funds, the recipient establishment must provide an accounting of the services provided. Furthermore, the establishment's prices must be as defined by a central unit of the SUMI, which is an agency of the MSD. As such, the SUMI makes it possible to define priorities for the services offered to the beneficiaries.

Use of SUMI funds by the municipalities is unequal and incomplete. The SUMI is intended to finance operating costs other than staff payroll (medications, inputs), although certain expenses for investments and administrative support are allowed. Nonetheless, the average use of the SUMI in 2004 was 75 percent.

SUMI financing is complemented by the National Solidarity Fund (*Fondo de Solidaridad Nacional*—FSN), whose purpose is to supplement financing for municipalities when the services the municipalities provide, as confirmed by the SUMI, exceed what is financed through the allocation of revenue sharing funds. Not surprisingly, the municipalities that apply for this funding either have the most complex healthcare systems or are poles of incoming migration not reflected in the censuses. In 2004, 47 of the 327 municipalities applied for these funds.

III. Principal Problems in the Sector

Among the health sector's principal problems are its low performance (as compared with the rest of the countries in the region) and the slow rate of improvement. Efforts to improve the health of Bolivian citizens have been losing ground despite an increase in funds. An example of this is seen regarding childbirths at a healthcare establishment (Figure 1).

The problem is even more severe if analyzed from the point of view of equity. There are major differences in healthcare among regions (highlands, valleys, and plains) (Table 6). There are also differences between healthcare for the indigenous vs. the non-indigenous populations. For example, in terms of childbirths at a healthcare establishment, the gap is 20 percentage points to the detriment of the indigenous population. Healthcare for pregnant mothers also varies notably by income groups: while 23 percent of deliveries in the poorest quintile were receiving government-provided healthcare at the start of the millennium, 53, 71, and 67 percent of the upper quintiles (quintiles 2, 3 and 4), and 89 percent of the richest quintile received such care.

Figure 1. Coverage of Childbirths at a Healthcare Establishment (1995–2005)

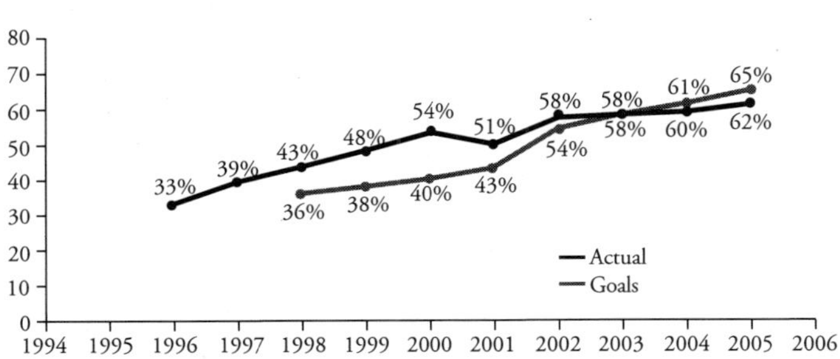

Source: MSD.

Table 6. Differences in Healthcare by Region

Geological Region *Departments*	*Highlands* *La Paz, Potosí, Oruro*	*Valleys* *Cochabamba, Chuquisaca, Tarija*	*Plains* *Santa Cruz, Beni, Pando*	*All Bolivia*
Chronic malnutrition (size/age) for children under the age of 5 (%)	32	29	16	27
Infant mortality (per 1,000 live births)	61	58	38	54
Childbirth at a healthcare establishment (last 5 years) (%)	41	59	78	57
Maternal mortality (per 100,000 live births)	320	147	206	234

Source: INE, 2003 and 2004.

Inequality affects not only access, but also health insurance protection. To analyze the percentage of affiliates of the social security healthcare system by income strata, the population is divided into quintiles, where Q1 corresponds to the poorest quintile. Only 3 percent of those receiving social security healthcare belong to Q1, while 15 percent belong to Q2, 10 to Q3, 29 percent to Q4, and 43 percent to Q5 (the richest quintile) (Table 7).

Bolivia's performance in health, and, in particular, its slowness in implementing actions has been affected by (i) administrative difficulties owing to the country's institutional crisis, which has created obstacles for stable policies and a proper coordination and supervision of actions on the departmental level; (ii) decentralization, which has resulted in high transaction costs and a loss of control over essential activities; and (iii) poor allocation of funds resulting from (i) and (ii), which has weakened priorities and accountability.

Administration of the Sector

Bolivia's economic and political instability has affected the health sector since the late 1990s.[7] Protests have hindered the implementation of measures that require logisti-

Table 7. Expenditures in Health by Quintile, 1999
(in bolivianos per capita)

Quintile Sector	*Q1*	*Q2*	*Q3*	*Q4*	*Q5*
Public	80.3	84.4	81.9	73.1	65.4
Social Security	30.5	45.5	136.9	241.1	242.8
Private	30.9	66.5	127.3	186.5	366.6

Source: World Bank, 2004.

cal preparation at the central level, such as vaccines and epidemiological monitoring. The crisis has created instability in the sector's administration, because there has been an increased turnaround of personnel among the national and even local authorities, due to repeated resignations and reorganization. Finally, general supervision of performance and coordination with the subnational and local governments has been highly restricted.

This crisis intensified during the second half of 2005, when, on account of administrative changes and financing problems, the MSD confirmed not only that management commitments in effect with the Departmental Health Services (*Servicio Departamental de Salud*—SEDES) were keeping them from fulfilling the goals agreed upon with international entities, but that they had not even perceived such a failing.

The new health authority then proposed an Immediate Action Plan (*Plan de Acciones Inmediatas*—PAI),[8] followed by an emergency decree designed to overcome the low immunization coverage. Figure 2 illustrates the supervision of childbirths at a healthcare establishment. The departments' performance was lower than what was agreed to in the management commitments. On the other hand, if not for the PAI, these commitments would not have fulfilled the goal of 65 percent coverage established for 2005.

Lack of timely information continues to be a major problem. The National Health Information System (*Sistema Nacional de Información en Salud*—SNIS) is the only entity with reliable data on public establishments, but its reports and the updating of its inventories of infrastructure and human resources have been interrupted by social problems. Population data by municipality, which is needed to obtain coverage and mortality indicators, are just now available for the second half of 2005. The

Figure 2. Difference in Healthcare Performance with and without Supervision

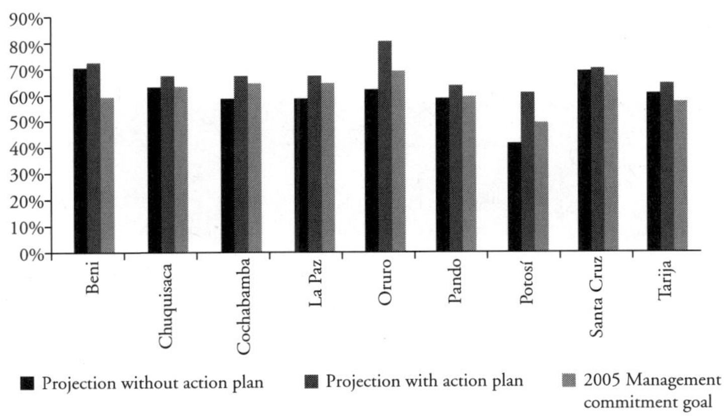

Source: MSD, 2005.

under-registration of deaths is approximately 75 percent at the national level, according to the United Nations Development Programme (UNDP). As a consequence, relevant data subsequent to 2000 come from specific surveys or estimates.

Decentralization

Decentralization of the sector has, in many ways, caused a regression since the system became very fragmented and lacks a clear delineation of jurisdictions. In territorial terms, there are four levels of management: national, departmental, municipal, and local. Jurisdiction over administration, financing, and, above all, the provision of services, is dispersed among the various strata of government.

The effect of this institutional structure is a dispersion of functions. It is not clear who is in charge of financing and who is in charge of providing health services. Under such circumstances, it is difficult to make better use of health sector funds; this difficulty hinders the population's ability to demand the right to access to, for example, SUMI.

The financial situation is similarly confused (Figure 3). The person in charge of the assistance system or of the establishments receives resources from several sources. Though that person does render financial accounts, nothing guarantees that access to services will increase in accordance with what is defined or expected.

The current system does not contribute to the effectiveness of the sector or to accountability. Administrative functions need to be strengthened, and serious organizational and financial problems persist in the provision of healthcare services; these may intensify as decentralization advances.

Figure 3. Basic Financing Elements for the Health Sector

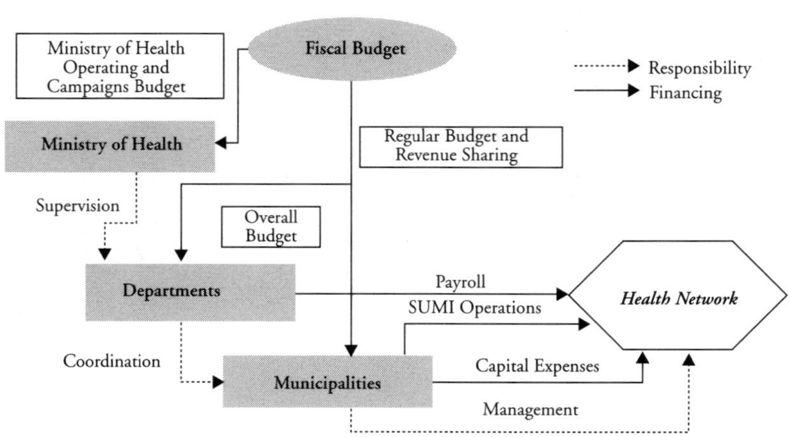

Source: Prepared by the author based on World Bank, 2004, 2005.

Financing and Inequality in the Public Sector

The SUMI has been a financial support tool for the municipalities in the provision of healthcare services. Since it is a universal insurance, it has increased equity in the system, because its distribution is based on the quantity of persons in each municipality. The SUMI has made it possible to focus actions and resources on the country's priorities, given that the package of services targets children under the age of five and their mothers.

Despite that, the effectiveness of the SUMI is questionable. The portion that it subsidizes, for example, finances only first- and second-level care in poor municipalities. Third-level care is financed only in wealthier, large municipalities. The high unit costs of hospital services explain why there is a tendency, in the large municipalities, to request extra funds from the FSN.

Figure 4 shows the results of the most recent municipal evaluation of the SUMI. The poor municipalities (P) do not finance third level care, unlike the non-poor municipalities (NP). The same occurs with municipalities with a majority indigenous population (I) as compared with other municipalities (O). Municipalities with fewer than 10,000 inhabitants (A) receive only primary care, while those with more than 30,000 (C) receive third-level care. If equity is based on references for which reliable information is not available, the SUMI would be badly concentrated and would not contribute to reducing inequality. The non-poor population in Bolivia is insured in a higher proportion than the poor population. Nonetheless, almost 45 percent of the care provided by SUMI is concentrated among the non-poor. Moreover, the indigenous population is located in municipalities that do not offer equal access to all their inhabitants, especially with respect to the third-level healthcare.

Given the inequality and inefficiency detected, the SUMI should be strengthened. The purpose of its creation, which was to support mothers and children, could be achieved if vulnerable groups are identified and well-focused policies are implemented.

Figure 4. SUMI Healthcare by Level and Type of Municipality

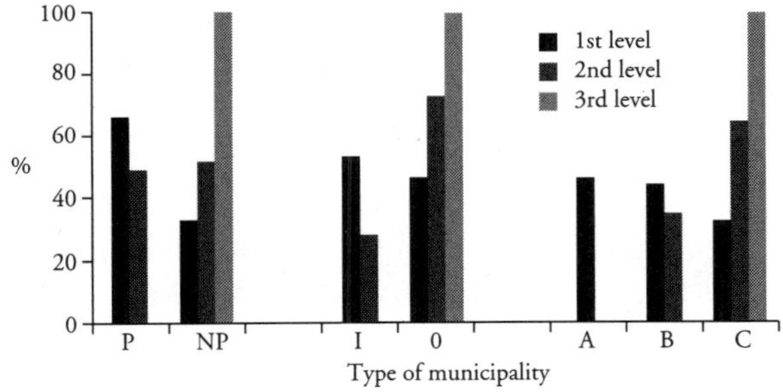

IV. Policy Options

Performance Based Administration

The MSD needs to be strengthened at the regulatory and technical levels. Recent experience, through which the sector advanced toward its goals under the active coordination of the MSD, demonstrates that the country can make rapid, effective progress. Political strengthening of the MSD means that its efforts must be backed by the Ministry of Finance and entities such as the Comptroller General, which supervises the fulfillment of management commitments.

The MSD should continue reinforcing its information technology and statistical systems, which are essential for better focusing its actions on the most vulnerable sectors. The MSD is upgrading the National Health Information System (SNIS) and is trying to make it compatible with other systems, such as that of the SUMI. However, the problem lies in attempting to improve everything gradually, when, in reality, most of the problems involve specific indicators, such as maternal mortality. That is why it is so important to prioritize tasks.

In addition, the MSD needs to set access and care standards, especially for the poorer population. The SUMI's experience could make a major contribution in this regard. Data from the SUMI (although secondary and imperfect) can be used to discover and prioritize the locations where there are coverage gaps in the package of services for that insurance. If enrollment data is cross-referenced with census information, it's possible to obtainan estimate, by department and by certain zones, of the number of potential beneficiaries. This information should be used to set specific indicators and goals, by department, that demarcate the government's priorities in what health problems need to be resolved, where those problems are found, and for whom they must first be resolved.

Organized Decentralization and Accountability

Given the political and administrative decentralization currently under discussion, it is necessary to clarify the organizational model for healthcare services. The first priority should be to clearly define the jurisdiction of each entity in terms of its responsibilities, financing, and above all, the services it will provide. In the medium term, a decision needs to be made as to whether departments or municipalities assume jurisdiction over the provision of services. The lack of management capacity that characterizes most of the municipal councils and the high costs of supervising and monitoring the provision of healthcare services lead to the conclusion that the departments should have a more decisive role. In addition, it is evident that: (i) it is more efficient to strengthen and supervise these nine units than the 327 municipalities, and (ii) future administrative policy steps contemplate a strengthening of the departmental level of government.

Thus, in order to create efficient assistance systems, it would be very useful to transfer full jurisdiction of the management of human resources in healthcare to the departments.[9] The second implication is that the departments, rather than the MSD, are better qualified to organize the healthcare systems. Finally, whether or not the DILOS are maintained, the departments must increase accountability for the operations of the healthcare systems.

All this implies a need to strengthen the institutional capacity of the departments. Particularly, to prepare and train departmental personnel regarding the organization of healthcare systems, program follow-up, and management of accreditation standards for healthcare centers.

A precise determination of jurisdiction for the sector would make it possible to avoid duplication of functions and excess bureaucracy. By knowing precisely who is in charge of financing healthcare services, and who is in charge of supervision and accountability, funds and jurisdiction could be better assigned.

Given existing regulatory restrictions and the need for institutional capacity, it is advisable that decentralization of functions be implemented gradually. One possible model is the following:

a. In a first stage, the departments would be trained in human resource administration, starting with hiring based on background selection, and continuing with the application of performance supervision standards. At the same time, functions related to human resources management would be transferred to the departmental level. This would include the hiring of new personnel, which would be financed through the regional budget.
b. During this stage, the MSD and the departments would develop indicators to supervise performance and goals for each department. At the same time, they would define accountability mechanisms.
c. In a second stage the remaining essential functions for the administration of human resources would be transferred to the departments, but with respect to staff already hired by the MSD.
d. Finally, powers would be transferred regarding the organization of healthcare systems. In addition, the organization of the DILOS would be made more flexible, in order to take better advantage of existing healthcare systems. This is important so that healthcare can be organized around population demand.

This redistribution of functions should entail only the financial costs of training and supervision, since spending on human resources would be decentralized. In fact, improved management might even result in savings or a better allocation of funds. In this way, decentralization could help improve fiscal expenditures, which means that the available funds would have a greater impact. At present, the sector pays wages, makes investments, and defrays the cost of inputs through its operating budget and through allocations such as the SUMI. A transfer of service provision functions to the departments would allow the MSD to improve its general control and would also bring financing more in line with the demand for healthcare services.

In support of this process, in addition to the regulatory functions, the MSD would have to strengthen management commitments. Furthermore, the delivery of funds from the central level to the departments would have to be established in accordance with the demands of equity by providing offsets to the regions based on their relative healthcare challenges or healthcare results. In this regard, it would be useful if the Ministry of Finance were to announce the availability of funds for each of the regions, to ensure full confidence that the new funds allocated to the health sector will be spent in accordance with priorities.

Giving more control to the departments would have the further advantage of allowing the population to have a greater influence monitoring the performance of the health sector.

Condition Financing to Healthcare Performance

In addition to the necessary administrative functions for setting standards, goals, and supervision, there must be proper incentives. In the Bolivian healthcare system, the SUMI has the best set of incentives and an ideal accountability mechanism for supervising the efficiency of healthcare providers. However, the SUMI must be strengthened so that the entire population in need will enjoy the same package of services. Along these lines, progress needs to be made on a system for identifying users, which will make it possible to follow up on the number and type of services received by each user. This is the only way to control what type of services are received and with what frequency and quality.

One important incentive mechanism is to correlate healthcare spending with the specific results obtained, whether by improving social indicators (such as maternal or infant mortality), a more extensive provision of healthcare services (for example, coverage of immunizations or childbirths at a healthcare establishment), or better access to healthcare services (better equity), such as access for indigenous peoples to the services of the SUMI.

To accomplish that, with a view toward strengthening the SUMI, it would be advisable to consider an institutional system in which the current revenue sharing transfers are combined with other sources (remunerations or old-age insurance, for example). There are alternatives, even without changing revenue sharing allocations to municipalities. For example: (i) municipalities could delegate the decision about what to pay and to whom to a departmental unit of the SUMI, which would reallocate funds that are currently earmarked for the payment of remunerations to providers; or (ii) the payment system could be divided so that primary care would be financed by the municipal councils as part of the DILOS, while second- and third-level care would be financed by a departmental SUMI, as occurs in Chile.

Finally, the MSD must be guaranteed an ongoing fiscal budget to enable it to carry out national programs such as the Immediate Action Plan (*Plan de Acciones Inmediatas*—PAI) and to control and monitor vector-transmitted diseases. These actions are essential, and there is no evidence that decentralization would lead to improvements in their management, because they involve the general welfare of the public. In other words, these are actions whose benefits are enjoyed by the population at large, which is why they are not suitable for appropriation at the regional level. Therefore, the departments would not have sufficient motivation to carry out these actions on their own.

Bibliography

Calvo, Luis. 2004. *Resumen del Análisis de Situación y tendencias de salud - Bolivia 2004*. In www.ops.org.bo/ais. La Paz, Bolivia: PAHO.

Cárdenas, Marina. 2004. *Estudio de cuentas nacionales de financiamiento y gasto en salud*, La Paz, Bolivia:MSD.

Gray Molina, George. 2004. *Desigualdad en Bolivia*, Presentation for UDAPE, February 2004.

INE. 2003. *Encuesta Postcensal de Mortalidad Materna* [Post-Census Maternal Mortality Survey] 2000. La Paz: INE.

———. 2004. National Demography and Health Survey (*Encuesta Nacional de Demografía y Salud*—ENDES) 2003. Bolivia.

———. 2005. *Información estadística de pobreza* at www.ine.gob.bo.

Ministerio de Salud y Deportes. 2005. *Boletín Semanal de Vigilancia*, No. 1, 36 and 40. La Paz, at www.sns.gov.bo.

PAHO. 2005. *Health Situation in the Americas. Basic Indicators.* Washington, DC: PAHO.

The Reform Project, Bolivia. 2005. "*Evaluación Externa del SUMI.*" Surveys and studies, October 2005.

UNDP. 2003. Second MDG Progress Report. La Paz, Bolivia: UNDP.

———. 2005. *International Cooperation at a Crossroads: Aid, Trade and Security in an Unequal World.* Human Development Report 2005.

World Bank. 2004. Health Sector Reform in Bolivia. A Decentralization Case Study (ESW). Washington, DC.

———. 2005. "Program Document for a Social Sector Programmatic Credit II Bolivia." Report 32066-BO. Washington, DC.

———. 2006. "Institutionality and Governance Review" (in preparation).

World Bank and Inter-American Development Bank. 2004. Bolivia Public Expenditure Management for Fiscal Sustainability and Equitable and Efficient Public Services. Washington, DC.

Endnotes

1. World Bank, 2004.
2. See Annex II, UNDP, 2003.

3. Calvo, 2004.

4. Ministry of Health and Sports, 2005.

5. Private insurance includes General Insurance (*Seguros Generales*) (58 percent), Mandatory Personal Accident Insurance (*Seguro Obligatorio de Accidentes Personales*—SOAT) (26 percent), and Personal Accident Insurance (*Seguros de Accidentes Personales*) (16 percent). Cárdenas, 2004.

6. This is accomplished through Local Health Boards (*Directorios Locales de Salud*—DILOS), described below.

7. The health sector's problems coincide with a fall in GDP growth. Though GDP has recovered, this has not benefited the informal and rural sectors, whose income continues to be depressed.

8. Decree of the Ministry of Health, September 9, 2005.

9. See the Institutionality and Governance Review, in preparation, World Bank, 2006.

15

Social Protection

Ian Walker

Summary

Bolivia's national social protection system is designed to respond to the needs of children and the elderly, as well as those who are of working age but cannot find a job and lack social security. In the past year, the country has been losing ground with respect to the progress achieved. This chapter makes an assessment of what has occurred in the sector, analyzes spending in each area, recommends ending the National Employment Plan (Plan Nacional de Empleo—PLANE), and sets forth a strategy for recovering lost ground.

I. Introduction

This chapter reviews recent trends in social protection programs and policies and analyzes the principal political questions that need to be faced in the immediate future. The core message is that over the past year, there has been a worrisome loss of dynamism in the implementation of institutional and programmatic reforms to improve the effectiveness of the social protection framework. This document suggests options to recover lost ground and emphasizes the importance of placing a priority on attending to the needs of Bolivia's most vulnerable citizens.

Social protection programs aim to reduce social exclusion for low-income families through:

- *A reduction of their exposure to shocks and risks,* through investments in human capital (education, health, and nutrition); greater access to housing and basic utilities, such as water, sanitation, electricity, and telecommunications; and an

improvement in their opportunities to participate in sustainable economic activities;
- *Aid, where possible, to insure them against the risks they face,* by promoting the expansion and sustainability of social security systems that provide coverage[1] for pensions, unemployment, disability, and health; and
- *Compensation for the cost of uninsured shocks and risks,* such as chronic diseases and disabilities, advanced age, natural disasters, and economic crisis (reflected in unemployment and reduced family income).[2]

Following this conceptual framework, social protection programs in Bolivia can be divided as follows: (i) those that propose to reduce vulnerability *ex ante,* by extending the coverage and quality of basic services and increasing economic opportunities for the poor; these programs work with agencies in the sector such as the Ministries of Health and Education, agencies responsible for water and sanitation, and the authorities that regulate labor, land, financial markets, and markets for goods, in order to increase opportunities for productive, sustainable jobs; (ii) the social security system; and (iii) social welfare programs to provide *ex post* mitigation of uninsured risks that affect vulnerable groups, including welfare labor programs for the unemployed, programs to ensure a minimum guaranteed income for the elderly, support programs for the chronically ill and disabled, and disaster relief programs.

This chapter examines programs and policies aimed at reducing vulnerability and compensating uninsured risks, except for the solidarity bonus program (Bonosol), which is analyzed in the chapter on the Pension System. The chapter is organized into four sections, following this introduction. Section II provides the relevant background and highlights recent developments in the government's social protection strategy, designation of institutional responsibilities for the strategy, and selection of target populations. Section III analyzes the main social protection programs and trends in expenditures. Section IV addresses some of the principal problems and issues facing the sector, while Section V summarizes policy recommendations that could be useful to the government.

II. Background: Social Protection in Bolivia

The economic crisis that started in 1999 resulted in a significant downturn in economic growth and an upswing in poverty.[3] Average real GDP growth was 4.7 percent per year during 1993-1998 (2.2 percent per capita) but fell to 2.6 percent during 2000-2004 (zero growth in per capita terms). Reflecting the trend in GDP, the poverty rate in the department capitals declined from 52 percent in 1993 to 46 percent in 1999 but then increased to 51 percent in 2002. Likewise, extreme poverty rates fell from 24 percent to 21 percent between 1993 and 1999 but then increased to 23 percent in 2002. In Bolivia as a whole, the poverty rate grew from 64 percent in 1997 to 65 percent in 2002; the extreme poverty rate increased from 36 percent to 41 percent over the same interval. The crisis also significantly increased urban unemployment, from 6 percent to 9 percent between 1999 and 2002.

In response to these trends, the government committed a growing amount of tax revenue to social protection programs. Total spending on social protection increased from US$77.8 million in 1999 to US$224.5 million in 2003, but then fell to US$191.8 million in 2004. Spending on social protection programs increased from 0.9 percent of GDP in 1999 to 2.2 percent in 2004. That year it amounted to approximately US$21.30 per year per capita, or 6.6 percent of total public expenditures and 13 percent of basic social expenditures[4] (Table 1).

Social Protection Strategy

While increasing expenditures on social protection programs, the government also worked to establish a coherent general framework for its social protection strategy. The goal is to establish a national social protection strategy that: (i) specifies the population groups, risks, and priorities that should be serviced; (ii) estimates the corresponding budget conditions; and (iii) provides an effective supervision and evaluation system. A preliminary version of the social protection strategy was prepared in 2005 by the Unified Funding Board (*Directorio Único de Fondos*—DUF) and the Economic Policy Analysis Unit (*Unidad de Análisis de Política Económica*—UDAPE), but it has not yet been implemented.[5]

The DUF oversees the principal components of the social protection system (Figure 1). These include the Production and Social Fund (*Fondo Productivo y Social*—FPS), which builds infrastructure in the health and education sectors in coordination with the Ministries of Health and Education; the National Compensation Fund (*Fondo de Compensación Nacional*—FCN), which transfers loans to the municipalities; and the Integrated Social Protection Network (*Red de Protección Social*—RPS).

Table 1. Indicators of Social Protection Expenditures in Bolivia, 1999–2004

	1999	*2000*	*2001*	*2002*	*2003*	*2004*
Total Social Protection Expenditures (US$ million)	77.8	90.2	139.6	156.3	224.5	191.8
Per Capita Social Protection Expenditures, US$/year	9.6	10.8	16.5	18.1	25.5	21.3
Social protection expenditures as a % of GDP	0.9	1.1	1.7	2.0	2.8	2.2
Social protection expenditures as a % of public expenditures	2.6	2.9	4.6	5.4	7.5	6.6
Social protection expenditures as a % of basic social expenditures	5.6	6.2	9.1	9.3	15.0	13.0

Source: World Bank Bolivia, 2004b and Economic Policy Analysis Unit (*Unidad de Análisis de Política Económica*—UDAPE).

Figure 1. Organization of Bolivia's Social Protection System

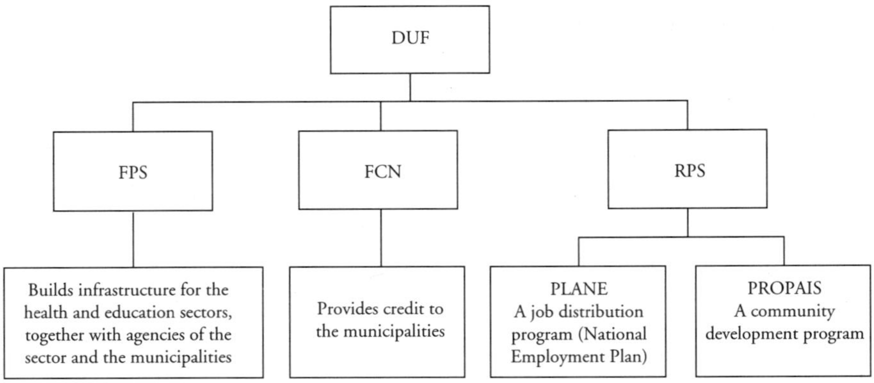

In turn, the Social Protection Network includes two subprograms: PROPAIS, established in 2005, which offers financing to small community projects; and the National Employment Plan *(Plan Nacional de Empleo*—PLANE), which dates to 2002 and finances temporary jobs to alleviate the effects of unemployment.

Institutional responsibility. The preliminary social protection strategy proposes a structure supervised by the National Economic and Social Policy Council (*Consejo Nacional de Política Económica y Social*—CONAPES), composed of the Ministries of the Presidency, Education, Health, Labor, Decentralization, and Popular Participation, among others. The DUF has been given the role of the system's supervisor and controller. An Executive Board will be responsible for technical and administrative implementation of the system, in coordination with the service providers, which include public national decentralized entities, prefectures, municipalities, and private companies. However, confusion arose over the roles of the different players in the second half of 2005, when the Ministry of Popular Participation, which supervises the DUF, assumed direct responsibility for the future development of the social protection strategy.

Target Populations and Risks

The social protection strategy identifies principal target populations as children under the age of 18; adults over the age of 65; and persons of working age (18 to 64) who are unemployed or do not have health insurance. The principal risks are as follows.[6]

- For *children up to five years*: malnutrition (which affects 24.2 percent of children under the age of three),[7] and infant mortality (with a rate of 54 deaths of children under the age of five for each thousand live births).

- For *children between six and 18*: premature desertion of school (which affects 14 percent of children between the ages of six and 14) and child labor (10 percent). The desertion rate in primary education is 7.3 percent and the net matriculation rate in secondary is barely 51 percent.
- For the *adult population between 25 and 64*: unemployment and health coverage. Nine percent of the economically active population is unemployed. For those between the ages of 15 and 24 who have entered the labor market, open unemployment is 15 percent. In addition, 83 percent of the adult population has no health insurance.
- Among the *group over 65*: the poverty rate is 62 percent (77 percent in rural areas); 81 percent have no retirement pension, and 73 percent have no health insurance.

Vulnerability tends to be greatest among the poor. For example, among families of the poorest quintile, the malnutrition rate for children under the age of five is 39 percent, compared with 6 percent in the highest quintile. Access to childbirth in hospitals or maternity centers is 23 percent for the poorest quintile, as compared with 89 percent for the highest quintile. Similarly, access to healthcare services for patients with acute respiratory infections in the highest quintile is more than double that of the lowest quintile (Table 2). Health insurance coverage is very low throughout the country (below 20 percent), but for poor and indigenous families it is half that (see Figure 2a).

Likewise, academic performance closely correlates to family income: members of families from the lowest quintile receive less than four years of schooling on average, as compared with nearly 10 years in the highest quintile (see Figure 2b).

Available evidence suggests that demand factors, such as lack of money or a need to work, are often behind school desertion, especially among children over the age of 11 (Figure 2c). This helps explain why the recent crisis resulted in a significant reduc-

Table 2. Bolivia: Vulnerability Indicators by Income Quintile

Percentages of the relevant population	*Income Quintile (1= poorest)* 1	2	3	4	5	*Ethnic Group* Non-indigenous	Indigenous
Chronic malnutrition (24 to 59 months)[a]	39	29	22	11	6	no data	no data
Institutionalized births[b]	23	53	71	67	89	72	54
Use of healthcare services for respiratory infections[b]	32	46	56	60	70	60	50
Rate of DPT immunization (% for ages 12-24 months)[b]	55	57	66	59	65	64	59

Source: a. Data from National Demography and Health Survey (*Encuesta Nacional de Demografía y Salud*—ENDSA) 1998, cited in World Bank, 2004a, Table B1.
b. MECOVI 2001, cited in World Bank 2004a, Table C2.

Figure 2a. Population with Health Insurance Coverage, 2002

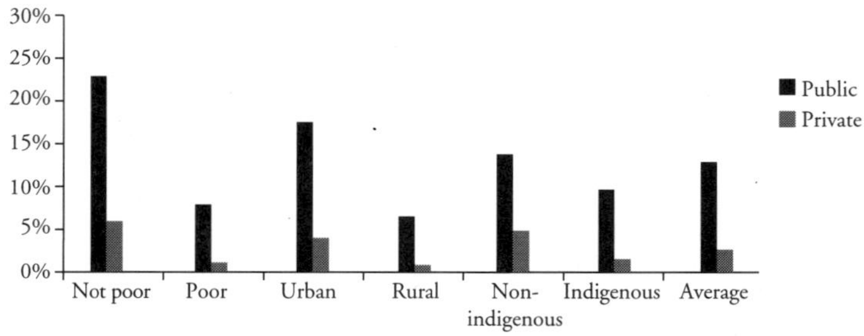

Source: MECOVI 2002.

Figure 2b. Years of Schooling, 2002

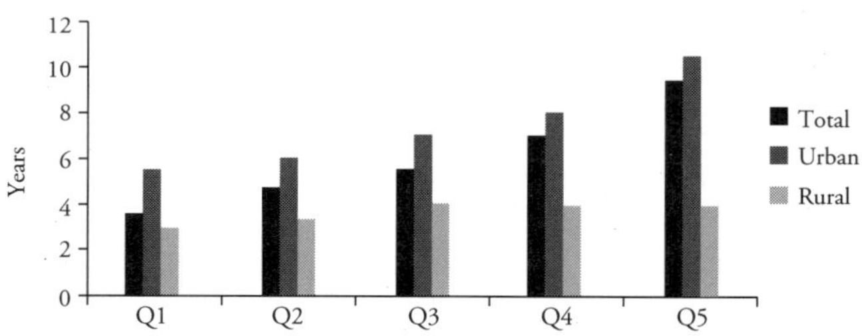

Source: MECOVI 2002.

Figure 2c. Main Reasons for Not Attending School

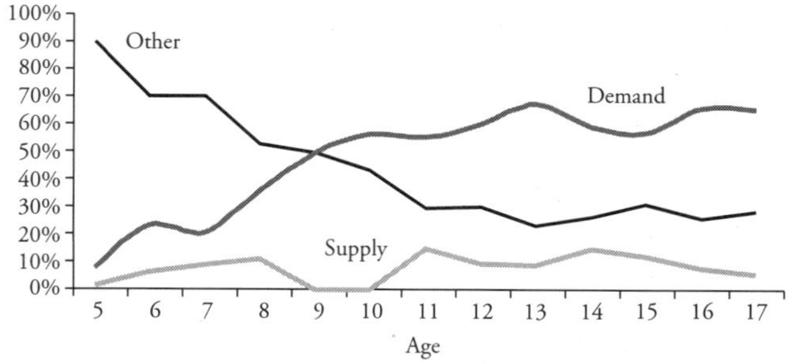

Source: MECOVI 2002.

Note: Demand related: lack of money, need to work, need to look after brothers and sisters; supply related: distance from school; others: illness, finished studies, pregnancy, not interested, or too old (excludes children who were on holiday from school).

tion in school enrollment and attendance rates between 2000 and 2002 (from 84 percent to 80 percent; and from 84 percent to 79 percent, respectively).

The indigenous population of Bolivia is more vulnerable than the rest of the population.[8] The poverty rate among indigenous peoples is 74 percent, as compared with 52 percent for non-indigenous peoples. Similarly, education indicators are worse for indigenous than non-indigenous Bolivians. The average income of an indigenous Bolivian is US$65 per month, as compared with US$142 for the average non-indigenous person. The incidence of child labor (for ages 9 to 11) is 31 percent for indigenous children and 8 percent for non-indigenous children. The average number of years of schooling for indigenous is 5.9 compared with 9.6 for non-indigenous.[9]

III. Principal Social Protection Programs and Projects

The most significant social protection programs are: Universal Mother/Child Insurance (*Seguro Universal Materno-Infantil*—SUMI); the Integral Health Program (*Programa Integral de Salud*—PROSIN); the Immediate Action Plan (*Plan de Acciones Inmediatas*—PAI); the PLANE; the BONOSOL (cash transfers to adults over the age of 65); housing improvement programs; social funds, principally for educational infrastructure and rural development; the plan for education of children below the age of six (*Programa Nacional de Atención al Niño y a la Niña*—PAN); and land tenancy programs to improve rural economic competitiveness. Table 3 illustrates the expenditures of the principal social protection programs.

Recent growth in social protection spending resulted, above all, from an expansion in economic programs (particularly PLANE and the BONOSOL), which rose from US$27.1 million (35 percent of the total) in 1999 to US$123.7 million (65 percent of the total) in 2004. Social protection spending on healthcare also rose considerably (from US$3.9 million in 1999 to US$18.7 million in 2004). On the other hand, spending in education declined sharply after 1999, although it recovered to US$12.7 million in 2004. There were also spending cutbacks within the relatively small disaster management programs. Also notable is the portion of social protection expenditures channeled through social funds, which dropped from 39 to 24 percent of the total during the period under review (Table 4).

Economic development programs. To promote more job opportunities, especially for the poor rural zones of Bolivia, the government is granting land titles (which make families take more of an interest in investing there and provide collateral for loans). For that purpose, the government is building productive infrastructure, such as roads, and is promoting rural production companies with support from the social funds.

Social protection programs in health.[10] Lack of access to health services is being addressed by the SUMI, a program launched in 2003 to replace the former Basic Health Insurance (*Seguro Básico de Salud*—SBS). SUMI aims to stimulate demand by providing free health services. At the same time, it channels part of the funds

Table 3. Social Protection Programs in Bolivia, 1999–2005
(In millions of current US$)

Program	*Sector*	*1999*	*2000*	*2001*	*2002*	*2003*	*2004*
Literacy Programs	Education	3.2	2.5	2.5	1.9	0.2	0.0
PAN (Program for children under age 6)	Education	11.7	12.9	10.6	6.7	1.9	4.8
PROSIN (Integrated Health Program)	Health	0.0	5.5	4.5	5.4	2.4	6.2
"Epidemiological Shield"	Health	1.1	3.0	6.6	6.6	5.5	2.7
SBS / SUMI (Health insurance)	Health	0.0	7.0	7.7	8.4	16.5	16.9
PAI (Vaccination Program)	Health	0.6	4.2	2.3	2.9	5.0	4.2
Gender projects	Governance	1.0	0.4	0.8	1.0	0.2	0.0
Indigenous projects	Governance	2.7	1.9	1.5	1.1	0.6	0.6
FDC (Infrastructure- production roads)	Economic	18.9	16.8	4.8	0.0	0.0	0.0
PLANE (Labor Assistance)	Economic	0.0	0.0	0.0	26.0	23.5	7.3
BONOSOL (Monetary transfers for the elderly)	Economic	0.0	0.0	41.7	21.0	103.5	93.7
Land tenancy projects	Economic	8.1	5.1	6.5	6.5	4.6	4.1
Housing improvement	Economic	0.1	2.9	6.5	13.3	18.8	5.2
Disaster Prevention and Response	Disaster Management	0.4	0.0	0.2	0.0	0.3	0.0
PROAGUAS (access to water)	Water & Sanitation	0.0	0.0	0.1	0.4	0.4	0.6
Social Funds		30.0	28.0	43.3	55.1	41.1	45.5
Educational Infrastructure	*Education*	*17.7*	*13.7*	*29.3*	*37.0*	*20.3*	*14.0*
Health Infrastructure	*Health*	*1.3*	*3.5*	*6.1*	*8.1*	*3.9*	*5.9*
Water Infrastructure	*Water & Sanitation*	*8.1*	*7.3*	*2.4*	*0.1*	*0.0*	*0.0*
Sewage Infrastructure	*Water & Sanitation*	*1.4*	*0.4*	*1.2*	*1.0*	*4.8*	*12.1*
Disasters	*Disaster Management*	*1.5*	*3.1*	*2.6*	*1.3*	*1.2*	*0.1*
Rural Development	*Economic*	*0.0*	*0.0*	*1.7*	*7.6*	*10.9*	*13.4*
Total		**77.8**	**90.2**	**139.6**	**156.3**	**224.5**	**191.8**

Source: Ministry of Finance.

Table 4. Principal Social Protection Programs in Bolivia, by Sector, 1999–2004

Sector[a]	*1999*	*2000*	*2001*	*2002*	*2003*	*2004*
	In millions of updated US$					
Economic	27.1	24.8	61.2	74.4	161.3	123.7
Education	32.6	29.1	42.4	45.6	22.4	18.8
Health	3	23.2	27.2	31.4	33.3	35.9
Water and Sanitation	9.5	7.7	3.7	1.5	5.2	12.7
Governance	3.7	2.3	2.3	2.1	0.8	0.6
Disaster Prevention and Response	1.9	3.1	2.8	1.3	1.5	0.1
Total[b]	**77.9**	**90.1**	**139.8**	**158.6**	**216.8**	**191.8**
	% of the total					
Economic programs	34.8	27.5	43.8	46.9	74.4	64.5
Education	41.8	32.3	30.3	28.8	10.3	9.8
Health	3.9	25.7	19.5	19.8	15.4	18.7
Water & Sanitation	12.2	8.5	2.6	0.9	2.4	6.6
Governance	4.7	2.6	1.6	1.3	0.4	0.3
Disaster Prevention and Response	2.4	3.4	2.0	0.8	0.7	0.1
Total	**100.0**	**100.0**	**100.0**	**100.0**	**100.0**	**100.0**
Covered by:						
Social Funds	38.5	31.1	31.0	34.7	19.0	23.7
BONOSOL	0.0	0.0	29.8	13.2	47.7	48.9

Source: Ministry of Finance.

a. Classifications by sector, see Table 3.

b. There are slight differences between the components and the totals, due to rounding off.

received by the municipalities under the Decentralization Act of 1994.[11] These funds are used as an insurance premium, payable by the municipality to health institutions under their jurisdiction.

Prior to the establishment of the SUMI, many municipal councils were not allocating the necessary funds for their health insurance. Later, the universe of treatments covered by that insurance was expanded to include third-level interventions. In addition, transfers to the municipalities earmarked for this health insurance have increased to 7 percent and, in the medium term, are scheduled to go up to 10 percent. At the same time, the new National Solidarity Fund (FSN) was created with money from the debt reduction program for Highly Indebted Poor Countries (HIPC). This fund provides additional revenue as an offset to municipalities that have spent all their funds earmarked for health under the legally mandated transfers. This is an incentive to allocate more funds to healthcare. Finally, the EXTENSA program was established to improve coverage in remote regions by organizing mobile brigades.

"Epidemiological Shield." Communicable diseases, such as malaria, tuberculosis, and Chagas disease, account for 40 percent of all diseases contracted by Bolivians and cost the country an estimated 7 percent of GDP. These diseases are being addressed through "vertical" programs of the Ministry of Health throughout the

country, clustered in the most vulnerable municipalities. This includes the Immediate Action Plan (*Plan de Acciones Inmediatas*—PAI) and the "Epidemiological Shield" program launched in 1999. These programs have significantly improved their coverage and quality over the past four years.

Malnutrition and anemia in children under the age of three and in pregnant women is a priority issue for the social protection strategy. These persons are serviced through the National Nutrition Program (*Programa Nacional de Nutrición*—PNN), which includes: a micro-nutrition program; a program to monitor nutritional and epidemiological conditions; and a food security program. A pilot plan has been established, implemented by the Ministry of Health, to intensify activities for treating malnutrition. This program will be implemented in 25 of the poorest municipalities, prior to establishing a larger scale program.

Education. The net coverage of primary education has increased considerably over the past 15 years and is currently 97 percent. However, the rate of completion for the 8th grade is still only 75 percent. The Millennium Development Goals propose that net coverage and completion rates for primary school reach 100 percent by 2015. Coverage in secondary education is low; the net matriculation rate is barely 51 percent. This threatens to undermine Bolivia's economic competitiveness and reduce job opportunities. The social funds are in charge of building infrastructure for education. The social protection system also covers literacy programs for adults, while the PAN includes a significant preschool education component. The PAN was created in 1997 for children up to six years of age. It covers attention to nutrition, health, and protection. PAN works through Centers for Families and Children (*Centros Infantiles Familiares*), where 15 children are brought together at the house of a volunteer. The children are educated by community volunteers trained by the program. Currently, the PAN is reaching the end of its financing and has no funds to continue.

Programs for indigenous groups. Even though few social protection programs are designated exclusively for the indigenous population, indigenous peoples benefit from interventions aimed at combating poverty in general. The SUMI and EXTENSA are intended to improve access and quality of healthcare service in the indigenous areas of Bolivia. The law on the SUMI specifically recognizes the intercultural dimension of healthcare. EXTENSA works with community agents (named "ASISTES"), and conventions have been signed with the principal indigenous organizations for the accreditation of traditional physicians. There are also specific programs on bilingual education that target the indigenous population.

Labor assistance. In response to the rapid increase in open unemployment (from 6 to 9 percent of the economically active population in urban areas during 1999-2002) and in underemployment (from 16 percent to 21 percent during the same period), the PLANE was established in 2002. This was intended as an anti-cyclical labor assistance program, to replace the Peasant Development Fund (*Fondo de Desarrollo Campesino*—FDC), which previously financed economic infrastructure works. PLANE has gone through three phases. The first was financed with US$25 million and was geared toward creating 380,000 jobs a month. Phase II received US$20 million to generate 390,000 jobs a month, and Phase III was initially financed with US$12 million dollars to create 200,000 jobs a month. Eighty percent of PLANE's financing comes from bilateral donors.

In 2005, the budget for Phase III of PLANE increased by US$7 million, making use of funds from the national government. At that time, the government proposed to create at least 200,000 jobs a month in the first half of 2005. Workers are employed for an average of two months and are paid less than minimum wage. Accordingly, participation results from a self-selection process among those who have been unable to find a job in the formal sector. PLANE has had certain positive effects. The income, for example, is significant, especially for women, and the majority of the workers employed in the program have increased their spending on food while also acquiring a new skill. It is estimated that 20 percent of the participants in the PLANE program later acquired a permanent job.[12]

BONOSOL. The principal social protection program to address the needs of adults over the age of 65 is the BONOSOL. This plan is analyzed in the chapter on the Pension System.

IV. Principal Issues for the Sector

This section discusses the principal policy questions that need to be addressed in the social protection sector. It first examines issues in the sector closely related to strengthening strategies. It then reviews the strategies for health, nutrition, and education, and finally analyzes regulations and issues involving the labor market with respect to creating jobs and sustainable income.

Strategy for the sector. Despite the significant progress achieved in defining a new social protection strategy for Bolivia, that strategy has not yet been officially implemented. The social protection budget is not yet allocated in accordance with priorities for the sector. A short while ago, confusion emerged on the roles of the various agencies in providing leadership for the system (specifically in relation to the respective roles of the Ministry of Popular Participation and the DUF). The social fund system works in coordination with the ministries to schedule infrastructure works. Nonetheless, there is room to improve the targeting mechanism for funds channeled through the FCN to the municipalities. Greater consistency is also needed between municipal and national priorities. In addition, while the economy is starting to recover and unemployment is diminishing, a discussion is underway on the future role of emergency employment and a possible role for monetary transfer programs that link income subsidies to basic social programs in education and health. These issues are analyzed in the following paragraphs.

Effective Targeting. Within the framework of the National Compensation Policy, the central government transfers funds to the municipalities through an FPS that coordinates with the ministries to allocate funds as a function of the unmet basic needs of the municipalities' inhabitants. Nonetheless, a recent evaluation concluded that a significant proportion of funds is still being earmarked to communities that are not poor. This suggests that improvements are needed in the targeting mechanism.[13] The current system takes criteria such as poverty (unmet basic needs) into account, as well as implementation capacity. Unfortunately, the scarce implementation capacity of the poorer municipalities tends to offset their higher level of unmet basic needs. Not long ago, the SUMI conducted an impact assessment to verify that the program is reaching the poorest households. This assessment will also serve as a guide for the program's future development.

The challenge of decentralization. A key challenge for Bolivia's social protection policy is that the decentralized administrations do not necessarily have to subscribe to national priorities in the allocation of local funds. Likewise, if the allocation rules do not adequately consider the relative poverty of the various regions, fiscal decentralization could reduce the impact of the redistributive measures. This concern will be even more significant if it intensifies in the course of the decentralization process. In 2005, the National Compensation Policy began a pilot exercise using counterpart grants (*Política de Transferencia Condicionales*—PTC) in order to encourage the municipalities to channel their funds toward accomplishing the Millennium Development Goals. During its first phase, the focus will be on infant and maternal mortality. The results of this pilot need to be carefully supervised and, if appropriate, scaled up. At the same time, Bolivia has not yet transferred certain major functions to local control that would probably improve the performance of basic services, such as the power to supervise personnel in the health sector.

SUMI. Several problems are undermining the effective and equitable operation of the SUMI, including the following.

(i) No detailed cost study is available, hence it is not known whether payments from the SUMI are covering the actual costs of the protocols required.

(ii) There is no information available on the distribution of the SUMI funds within the Ministry of Health, but it appears likely that a more than optimal portion is being consumed by third-level interventions.

(iii) Poorer municipalities find it difficult to spend their quota of health funds and therefore will run into obstacles for applying to the FSN, which could lead to a regressive distribution.

(iv) The SUMI originally focused on health insurance for mothers and children, which excluded other previously covered services, such as sexual and reproductive health and the identification and treatment of tuberculosis and malaria, all of which could be negatively affected.

(v) Due to the geographic segmentation between the hospitals of the Ministry of Health and those of the Social Security system, the law for the SUMI establishes that the Social Security hospitals must provide the SUMI insurance package to persons who live in their coverage area. Nonetheless, no incentive is granted to the Social Security system to do so.

Empowerment of indigenous users and the cultural relevance of the services. As follows from the data on health and access to services, the high level of exclusion of indigenous groups is a key issue for social protection intervention. Despite the progress described above, there are many gaps between declared intentions and the effective application of policies. In addition, there is still much work to be done with respect to cultural sensitivity in healthcare services. Progress is also sorely needed in promoting demand for the services among indigenous women under the Accord on the Rights of Pregnant Women (which includes the right to deliver a baby in the location of one's choice and to keep the baby's placenta).

Emergency employment. A satisfactory emergency employment program must always be temporary and anti-cyclical. It must also be self-focused and avoid distorting the labor market, which could occur if it were to "substitute" demand for other types of employment. PLANE seeks to be self-selective by establishing a wage below the legal minimum. But there is a risk that it could still be "substituting" for work in the informal sector, where the minimum wage is not enforced. During 1999-2002, the informal sector grew in importance due to the economic crisis, as is demonstrated by the increase in underemployment from 16 to 21 percent.[14] It could also be expected that PLANE would introduce certain people into the economically active population, for example, women who were not previously looking for a job because they had few hopes of finding one. This would offset its impact on the unemployment rate. Finally, an issue exists regarding the double advantage that the beneficiaries of other programs would have, such as those involved in grants to start up small businesses, who could also work through PLANE. In all events, as an anti-cyclical program, PLANE should be limited once the economy improves and unemployment diminishes. The intention to conclude the program was announced in late 2005.

Reform of the labor market. At present, labor regulations discourage jobs in the formal sector, given the high costs of termination. They also make it difficult to provide employees with productivity-based incentives. This results in a bias toward the selection of products and technologies that are capital-intensive, which helps perpetuate unemployment. This also pushes economic activity into the informal sector, where labor regulations are not effective. Given that employees in the informal sector do not have access to social security, such a phenomenon has a double negative effect on social protection. In fact, it produces jobs that are less secure and that generate increased vulnerability.

V. Policy Recommendations

Principal Program Areas for Social Protection in Bolivia

The social protection strategy in Bolivia should continue to focus on: (i) strengthening children's human development and improving poor families' access to education and good quality primary healthcare; (ii) supporting low income households that are exposed to economic instability; and (iii) establishing a sustainable, equitable system of support to old age. At the same time, indigenous populations should be empowered to participate in formulating social protection policies in general.

Human Development of Children

Strengthen the provision of primary healthcare. It is essential to strengthen the provision of primary healthcare within the framework of the SUMI. An option here is to establish a guardian system and mandate that access to SUMI services be obtained through primary level clinics. It is important to institutionalize the links between the EXTENSA brigades and the healthcare posts. One option the SUMI could consider is refunding transportation costs to healthcare posts for those who live in remote places. It would also be worthwhile to evaluate the possibility of expanding the package of SUMI benefits and consider whether all the services included are truly priorities given the restrictions on the available budget. By making payments to the Social Security system, the SUMI could help to offset the cost of its legally mandated services and provide the Social Security system with an incentive to provide those services. If the SUMI remains outside the health insurance system, it is important to guarantee a central financing budget adequate for such "vertical" programs as tuberculosis, Chagas, and malaria, as well as immunizations under the Immediate Action Plan (PAI), with the aim of improving the epidemiological shield. It is also essential to improve coordination between the epidemiological shield and the PAI programs and better define the responsibilities of other players in the system (especially SUMI and EXTENSA) in the implementation of vertical programs, in order to avoid a duplication of efforts.

Focus social protection actions in health on the first years of life. The most significant results in children's health are determined by the first 24 months of life. Thus, it is advisable that Bolivia place greater emphasis on monitoring pregnancy and on providing integrated support to primary healthcare and nutrition during the first 24 months of life. The lessons of successful programs from other countries, such as the Integral Attention to Community Childhood (*Atención Integral a la Niñez Comunitario*—AIN–C) program in Honduras and *Creciendo Bien* (Growing Well) in Guatemala, provide potential roadmaps. Lessons can also be taken from early stimulation programs that seek to offset deficiencies in the learning environment of poorer households, such as Colombia's *Hogares Comunitarios* (Community Households) program for children between the ages of two and four.

Improve the indigenous population's access to healthcare services. The measures recommended include: (i) implement an outreach strategy to promote the use of rights set by the Accord on the Rights of Pregnant Women; (ii) pay incentives for referring patients to the installations of the Ministry of Health in order to increase the use of institutionalized childbirth among indigenous women; and (iii) involve indigenous organizations in health planning, including at the local level.

Support for Adults Exposed to Economic Instability

Emergency employment. The anti-cyclical emergency.employment program (PLANE) has had positive effects but is best not viewed as a permanent solution. In fact, to the extent that the economy continues recovering, it is recommended that the government end PLANE and, in the future, develop strategies to respond to structural unemployment that consist of training programs to help the unemployed—and especially young people entering the labor market for the first time—find purposeful work in the recovering labor market.

Reforms to the labor market. Bolivia could find it productive to propose certain reforms in the labor market in order to maximize the impact of the economic recovery and encourage investment in labor-intensive products and technologies. For maximum impact, such reforms would include a reduction in the burden of social expenditures on the private sector, which discourages companies from entering the formal sector.

Conditional monetary transfers and registration of beneficiaries. Bolivia could also find it beneficial to make monetary transfers to the poorest households, provided that such households take advantage of basic health and education services, through conditional monetary transfer programs (see Box 1). Components of this strategy would be for the coverage of the national population registration to be improved and for identity cards to be issued to guarantee that the poorest households are not excluded from access to targeted services simply because they are not officially registered.

Crosscutting Issues

Institutional framework for the social protection strategy. It is necessary to go beyond the theoretical definition of social protection strategy and move on to implementation. The National Economic and Social Policy Council (CONAPES) is best equipped to assume the leadership in this process. The budget of the principal social protection programs should be debated considering the costs of the various results pursued. Stronger supervision and evaluation is a necessary condition.

Decentralization. Much remains to be done to improve the consistency between municipal and national priorities within the framework of Bolivia's decentralized governance model. This issue will grow in importance as decentralization intensifies. It is advisable that recent initiatives to use counterpart grants related to the Millennium Development Goals be considered as soon as possible. At the same time, we recommend that Bolivia transfer the supervision and control of its basic services personnel to local governments, which have a better capacity to supervise their performance and are less exposed to being manipulated by the trade unions.

Improve effective targeting. A review of the targeting rules of the National Compensation Policy could serve the aim of increasing the proportion of funds earmarked to poor communities. In health, there are indications that the SUMI is not yet sufficiently concentrating resources in the poorest municipalities or in the most important primary interventions. Similarly, careful monitoring of the SUMI's financial flows to see how the funds are being used could help determine how best to reallocate them to priority areas and interventions. Adding flexibility to the prioritization rules for healthcare financing from the FSN would help to ensure that the poorer municipalities can use those funds. Finally, EXTENSA requires better targeting in areas where there is a shortage of doctors.

Box 1. Conditional Monetary Transfers: Lessons from International Experience

There is growing international evidence regarding the effectiveness of conditional cash transfer programs, such as *Oportunidades* in Mexico, *Bolsa Familia* in Brazil, *Familias en Acción* in Colombia, and *Red Solidaria* in El Salvador. These programs provide cash subsidies to the poorest households while encouraging the use of health and basic education programs for the household's children. This offers the next generation an opportunity to break with the cycle of poverty. These programs work particularly well in situations where the supply of basic services is adequate, but where certain households cannot use them or are not sufficiently motivated to do so.

In addition to providing incentives to poor families to invest in the development of their children, conditional cash transfer programs also respond to the social and political demand for a public initiative to support the income of the poorest families. But this must be done without causing distortions in the labor market and without creating implicit interest groups that end up becoming a permanent drain on fiscal revenue.

Some of the principles for an effective conditional cash transfers program are:

- The terms and the amount of the monetary transfers are sized in such a way that they do not interfere with decisions in the labor supply, but are sufficient to influence the decision to utilize the basic services;
- The rules of identification by geographic area and/or characteristics of the household are clearly defined and strictly enforced;
- Participation in the program is temporary, depending upon the poverty situation of the household;
- The program is adequately coordinated with the agencies that provide basic services;
- The institutional structure must be sound, with first-hand information, and evaluation and supervision systems.

Bibliography

Aguilar Perales, Javier and F. Ruiz Mier. 2004. *Lineamientos de la política de transferencias condicionadas (PTC) a gobiernos municipales*. Unified Funding Board (*Directorio Único de Fondos*—DUF), November.

Economic Policy Analysis Unit (*Unidad de Análisis de Política Económica*—UDAPE). 2005. *Tercer Informe del Progreso de los Objetivos de Desarrollo del Milenio Asociados al Desarrollo Humano*.

Hall, Gillette and H. A. Patrinos (editors). 2005. *Indigenous Peoples, Poverty and Human Development in Latin America.* Palgrave Macmillan: United Kingdom.

Jiménez, Wilson and S. Lizárraga. (2003). "*Ingresos y desigualdad en el área rural de Bolivia.*" Economic Policy Analysis Unit (*Unidad de Análisis de Política Económica*—UDAPE). July.

Landa, Fernando and Wilson Jiménez. 2004. *Pobreza y pueblos indígenas en Bolivia, 1989-2002*, UDAPE.

Lya, Fernyo. 2003. *Transferencia de recursos hacia los más pobres. Un análisis de PLANE I con escenarios contrafactuales.* UDAPE, May.

National Statistics Institute (*Instituto Nacional de Estadística*—INE. (2003). *Bolivia: Características sociodemográficas de la población*, November.

Víquez, Roxana M. and Raúl Lima. 2005. *Una nueva red integral de protección social para Bolivia*, UNDP, March.

World Bank. 2002. "Poverty and Nutrition in Bolivia." Washington DC: World Bank.

World Bank. 2003. "Program Document for a Proposed Credit to the Republic of Bolivia for a Social Safety Net Structural Adjustment Credit." Report 25927-BO, May. Washington DC: World Bank.

———. 2004a. "Bolivia Health Sector Reforms in the Context of Decentralization." Washington DC: World Bank.

———. 2004b. "Public Expenditure Management for Fiscal Sustainability and Equitable and Efficient Public Services." Report 28519-BO, November. Washington DC: World Bank.

———. 2005a. "Bolivia Poverty Assessment 2005." Report 28068-BO, February. Washington DC: World Bank.

———. 2005b. "Program Document for a Second Social Sector Programmatic Development Policy Credit Project," Report 32066-BO, April. Washington DC: World Bank.

Endnotes

1. Many risks can be offset by expanding insurance coverage and sustainability in order to share risks across the insured population, an initiative that would be financed through premiums. Most countries have mandatory social insurance systems for the formal sector or labor market. These encompass health, disability, and retirement insurance but tend to cover only a small percentage of the population and demand high levels of fiscal subsidies due to a lack of equilibrium between benefits and contributions.

2. Risks of all types can no longer be insured once they have materialized. People who are already chronically ill or disabled, or who are too old to work, and who did not insure themselves against such a possibility before it occurred, cannot buy insurance, since the probability of the event is now equal to 1, so no insurance fund would cover it. But governments can decide to compensate their citizens for such costs when it is in the public interest to do so: for example, for reasons of equity (related to poverty and to excluding the affected groups

from vulnerability) or due to potential economic, social, or political consequences for the system if the affected groups were not assisted.

3. For more information see World Bank, 2005a.

4. In addition to the increased social protection expenditures noted here, the government also increased spending on the social security system. A 1995 reform introduced an individual capitalization system. The resulting fiscal transition costs far exceeded what was expected, due to the changes introduced into the reform model (see the chapter on the Pension System in this volume).

5. See Víquez and Lima, 2005.

6. The data cited in these paragraphs are from the World Bank, 2005b, p. 30, Table 6.

7. Economic Policy Analysis Unit (UDAPE), 2005, p.12.

8. The data for this paragraph come from Landa and Jiménez, 2004, who use data from the MECOVI conducted between 1999 and 2002. The study uses a definition based on the ability to speak an indigenous language.

9. For more information on indigenous issues in Bolivia in particular, and in Latin America in general, see Hall and Patrinos, 2005.

10. See World Bank, 2004. The health programs analyzed here are complemented by the reform efforts of the Ministry of Health and Sports.

11. The legislation enacted in 1994 required that the central government transfer 20 percent of its revenue to Bolivia's 314 municipalities. This included funds previously allocated to health services. It was stipulated that the municipalities would earmark at least 5 percent of the transfers received from the central government to pay for insurance from the health system in order to provide coverage for their populations. The municipalities became the owners of the health installations they administered and acquired jurisdiction to finance their equipment and supplies—but not human resources, which continue to be under the control of the regional offices of the Ministry of Health, Departmental Health Services (*Servicio Departamental de Salud*—SEDES). To improve the performance of the services provided by the nine SEDES, performance agreements (quasi-contracts) have been signed, supervised by the Local Healthcare Boards (*Directorios Locales de Salud*—DILOS). The budget for each hospital and health post is based on the cost of the scheduled services, which are linked to the Millennium Development Goals on health: for example, institutionalized childbirth and vaccination coverage. The Ministry has implemented a human resource policy to promote staff reassignments to areas in greatest need. These initiatives are described in greater detail in the chapter on Health.

12. Landa, 2003.

13. Aguilar Paredes and Ruiz Mier, 2004.

14. Underemployment is seen principally among workers in the informal sector, who earn less than the minimum wage.

16

The Pension System—Reforms of the Reform

Rafael Rofman

Summary

*Bolivia's pension system is facing serious problems related to its institutional framework, fiscal impact, coverage (including the "*BONOSOL*"), and management costs. Such deficiencies demand both immediate and medium-term actions. Fiscal problems will be overcome only through institutional improvements that define clear rules and protect the system from political and social pressure. The* BONOSOL *program can continue to be a creative response to the extremely low coverage of the contributive system, but only if its access and financing problems are corrected and its sustainability is ensured, regardless of what happens in the debate over the hydrocarbons policy. Finally, the private system has serious deficiencies in terms of jurisdiction and costs; these must be reviewed.*

I. Background

In 1996, Bolivia instituted a structural reform of its pension system. New legislation created a single pillar of capitalization, accompanied by an innovative universal benefit approach, under which a fixed amount was directly transferred to all Bolivians once they reached age 65. Prior to that time, the pension system had been an apportionment system with a defined benefit. Planned on a central level, it was managed by the national government and used several supplementary funds. The system was plagued by assets and liquidity problems and had little or no supervision.

The 1996 reform introduced three principal changes. First, it did away with the former system for the economically active population. Workers who had already retired or had met the conditions to receive that benefit retained their rights under the former legislation, but anyone who retired after the reform would have to do so under the new system. The second change was the creation of a capitalization system with mandatory participation of employees of any economic branch or sector, including government employees and the military, all of whose contributions were placed in privately-administered individual accounts. At the same time, the Solidarity Bond (BONOSOL) was created; this new program consisted of an annual, basic amount of money distributed to anyone over the age of 65. The BONOSOL is a non-contributive system but is completely pre-financed. [1]

In analyzing the impact of the reform and the new system's performance, five aspects can be considered. First, the system's institutional framework has played a detrimental role. In addition to its weakness, it has undergone constant changes and faced numerous problems. A second aspect is the burden placed by the pension system on government finances ever since the reform went into effect. The third aspect is the coverage of the pension system. Bolivia still has the highest percentage of uncovered persons and is characterized by the most extreme inequality in the region. Fourth, the creation, implementation, and impact of the BONOSOL are worth particular attention, as a creative example of how social programs can be applied. Finally, the situation of the private management pension system should be evaluated, in relation to its managers' performance and the financial management of the funds accrued. These five aspects will be analyzed in detail below; the subsequent section discusses the main challenges and offers policy recommendations.

Institutional Structure

The institutional structure has undergone several changes since the implementation of the new system in 1996. After several adjustments, policy design was entrusted to the Vice Ministry on Pensions and Financial Services of the Ministry of Finance (see Figure 1). The entire system was placed under its direction, including its apportionment components (old system), capitalization (new system), and distribution of the BONOSOL. The second institutional level was taken over by the Superintendency of Pensions, Securities and Insurance, an autonomous entity under the umbrella of the Ministry of Finance, whose function is to supervise the three components of the system through its Pension Divisions for apportionment system and BONOSOL and Pension Funds Administrators (*Administradoras de Fondos de Pensiones*—AFPs) for the new capitalization system.

On a third institutional level, the operating entities are divided according to the system's components. The National Apportionment System Service (*Servicio Nacional del Sistema de Reparto*—SENASIR) is in charge of managing the old system, including the payment of benefits to those who retired when it was in effect. SENASIR also verifies and pays compensation to those retiring under the new system who are entitled to compensation under the old one because they made their contributions prior to the reform. The SENASIR is an autonomous entity under the umbrella of the Ministry of Finance. The AFPs take charge of registering affiliations, administering the funds, and paying workers' benefits under the new system. In

Figure 1. Institutional Structure of the Pension System in Bolivia

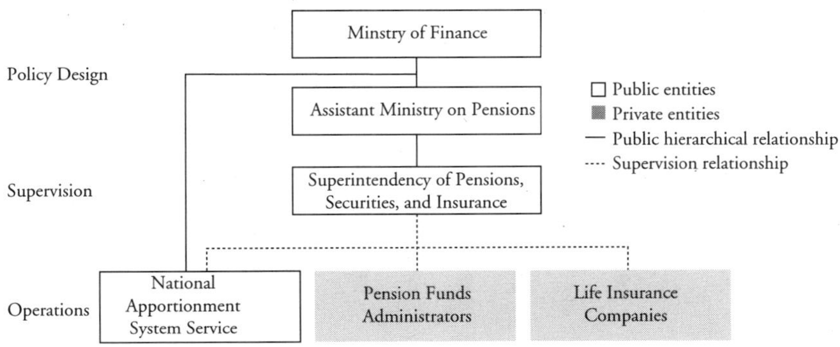

addition, they administer the Collective Capitalization Funds (*Fondos de Capitalización Colectivo*—FCC) and use those funds to pay the benefits of the BONOSOL. Finally, the life insurance companies administer death and disability insurance (with which those benefits are financed, in case active workers suffer such a loss) and annuities that the workers acquire under the capitalization system for collection of their benefits.

Public Expenditures on Pensions

At the time the reform was instituted, the annual expenditures of the public system amounted to approximately 2 percent of GDP, with a deficit of close to half a percentage point. This expense had started to accelerate in previous years and was cause for concern, since the government had predicted a sustained increase. When the reform was implemented, analysts and politicians expected that, with the elimination of the old system for active workers, expenditures would start to decline with the mortality of those who had already retired. Official projections indicated that, as an immediate consequence of the reform, the deficit would increase by up to 3 percent of GDP and then start to decline. By 2005, the deficit was expected to be approximately 1.5 percent of GDP.[2] According to these projections, by 2018 the deficit under the reformed system would be less than would have occurred without the reform, and by 2045, the total cost would be practically null.

Shortly thereafter, a permissive attitude in the process of phasing out the old system, coupled with the granting of major increases in benefits in response to political and social pressure, the accounting of special benefits for the Armed Forces, and compensations for public employees as part of pension expenditures, derailed the initial optimism. In fact, expenditures rose to more than 4.5 percent of GDP in 2004[3] and were predicted to be 5.1 percent of GDP by 2005, that is, more than triple the initial projections (Figure 2).[4]

Figure 2. Expenses in Pensions, as percent of GDP, 1997–2004

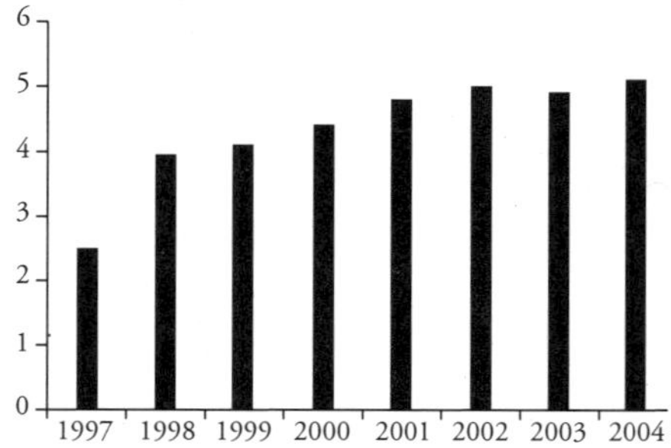

Source: Parra (2002) and Gamboa (2005).

One detailed analysis identified five causes for the great difference between the expenditures projected when the reform was implemented and what actually resulted.[5]

(i) **The number of pensioners**: according to initial estimates, the number of persons who had retired under the old system should have declined from 125,000 in 1996 to 107,000 in 2001. The reduction would have taken place at a rate of 3 percent per year. However, in 2001, the number of pensioners not only failed to diminish with respect to 1996, but had continued to increase; it reached 156,000, which means that initial projections were off by 46 percent. This difference was due to the ease with which workers close to retirement age could obtain recognition of their pension rights by falsifying identification documents (which made it possible to alter a person's age) and via continual extensions of the deadline within which to submit retirement applications under the old system.

(ii) **Amount of the benefits**: Following the approval of the new pension system, political and social pressures led to continual increases in the benefits. Two agreements, which took the names of the places where they were signed, "Caracollo" and "Patacamaya," provoked major increases in minimum pensions, which, by the end of 2002, were twice the minimum wage.

(iii) **Indexing benefits to the dollar**: As of 1997, the adjustment mechanism for pension amounts became indexed to changes in the United States dollar. Due to the constant loss of value of the bolivianos (which depreciated by 16 percent in real terms between 1997 and 2004), this decision resulted in a significant increase in average benefits.

(iv) **Decisions regarding the "sandwich generation**:" When the reform was approved, a hot debate ensued on the treatment to be given to those who had met the requirement of the number of years of contributions needed to retire

(12 years under the old system), but did not have the minimum age. Several measures taken after the new system went into effect relaxed the conditions for this group's access to the former system's benefits, thus increasing the sector's expenditures.

(v) Accounting criteria for expenditures: Under the reform, Armed Forces personnel came under the national system but retained the right to receive a benefit equal to 100 percent of their final salary. For that reason, an additional subsidy mechanism was designed that, in accounting terms, is considered part of pension expenditures. In the same way, when the workers' contribution rate changed, the government granted its employees a compensatory increase in wages. Known as the "wage merger contribution," this increase has been kept separate from the rest of personnel expenditures and, in various presentations, is considered part of pension expenditures.

The System's Coverage

Bolivia's pension system has one of the lowest levels of coverage in the region (Figure 3). Only 10 percent of the workforce in the country regularly contributes to pension funds, and even if one considers only those who receive wages and salaries, which is a relatively privileged group, the percentage that makes contributions does not surpass 30 percent. This low participation is reflected in the passive (benefit-receiving) stage: fewer than 15 of every 100 persons age 65 or older receive pension benefits.

Gender differences are significant. The coverage rate for males in the active (contributory) and passive (beneficiary) stages is 40 percent greater than among women. Similarly, most participants in the system reside in cities, since rural coverage is less than 3 percent among the economically active population and less than 5 percent among the elderly.

Figure 3. Coverage of the Pension System for the Economically Active Population and for Persons over the Age of 65, in 2002, Approximately

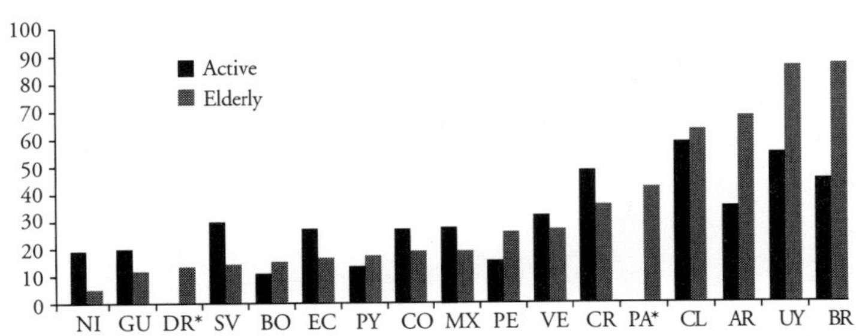

Source: Rofman and Lucchetti (2005).

* No data are available from the Dominican Republic or Panama regarding pension coverage among active workers.

The significance of inequity in access to the pension system can be clearly seen when considering the coverage of persons in the poorest quintile (which barely surpasses 0.5 percent) as compared with that of the richest quintile (36.5 percent). The gap between these two figures is defined as the "equity ratio," which demonstrates that the richest group has a rate of access to the system 63 times greater than that of the poorest one. In comparison, other countries in the region, such as Brazil, Ecuador, Chile, Uruguay, and Costa Rica, have much lower "equity ratios;" the coverage of the richest quintile differs from that of the poorest quintile by a factor of only ten Figure 4).

The Bolivian pension system is inequitable not only for those who participate in it, but also for the rest of society. In addition to the high cost of the old system in terms of its fiscal impact (which has been cause for concern), coverage is low and exclusive. This makes it an enormous subsidy that the entire society provides to a limited number of beneficiaries. The population favored by the system is less than 15 percent of all persons over the age of 65, equivalent to 0.6 percent of the total population. Nonetheless, this group absorbs close to 5 percentage points of GDP, with benefits that, on average, are almost four times the per capita GDP. These figures show that the system is very generous to those who participate in it,[6] and it also has an enormous regressive effect on income distribution.

The Role of the BONOSOL

Unlike other countries in the region and the world, the transfer of state-owned companies in Bolivia in the mid 1990s failed to completely privatize the companies. The new shareholders received only 50 percent of the shares, which were delivered at no charge to the private shareholders in exchange for a major investment commitment to capitalize the companies. At the same time, a lesser part of the capital stock (less than 3 percent, with only one exception) was turned over to the companies' workers, and the remainder was transferred "*to the citizens of Bolivia residing in the country who, as of December 31, 1995, had reached retirement age.*"[7] The capitalization

Figure 4. Participation of Active Workers in the Pension System by Income Quintile, and Equitability Ratio

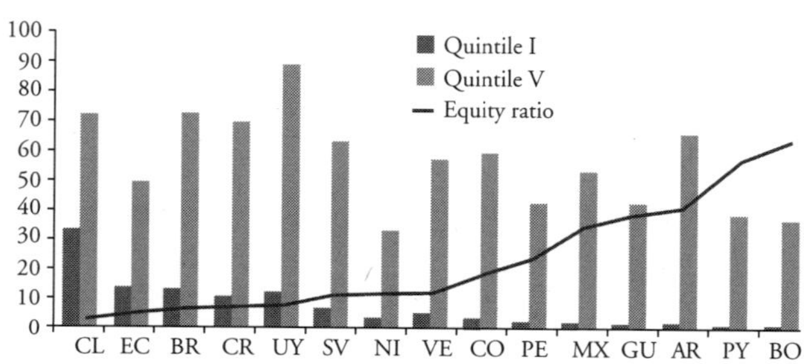

Source: Rofman and Lucchetti (2005).

and privatization process was applied to six companies in the hydrocarbons, telecommunications, electrical energy, air transportation, and railroads industries.

With the enactment of the new Pensions Act in 1996, the shares delivered to the citizens were deposited into FCCs and administered by the Pension Funds Administrators (*Administradoras de Fondos de Pensiones*—AFPs). Based on information on the amounts capitalized by the new private shareholders, it was estimated that the monetary value of all the shares was US$1.65 billion (22 percent of GDP). With these funds, the AFPs undertook a commitment to pay a BONOSOL of approximately US$250 per year to each Bolivian over the age of 65 (provided that they were born prior to 1974). The amount of the benefit is to be reviewed through an actuarial analysis every three years.

When payments of this benefit commenced, two problems arose. On the one hand, the personal identification documentation system in Bolivia has major failings. As a result, many potential beneficiaries did not have the necessary identification documents, while in other cases falsifications or fraud in the documents was suspected. At the same time, the AFPs had to pay close to US$100 million at a time when the FCC lacked liquidity. In addition, given the absence of markets and political restrictions, it did not appear viable to sell the shares of the capitalized companies. Therefore, the AFPs opted to increase the debt of the FCC. The amount of the debt was equal to half of the payments they had to make.

Given the serious liquidity problems, the AFPs suspended payments in early 1998, and the government replaced the BONOSOL program with another one called "Bolivida," which distributed the shares of the privatized companies among the population through individual accounts and reduced the amount of benefits to approximately 25 percent of their original value. The Bolivida benefits were paid between 1998 and 2001, but in late 2002 a new law was enacted that reinstituted the BONOSOL under its initial conditions. The new law also merged the assets of the FCC with the individual capitalization funds in order to increase the system's liquidity. This merger was never carried out in its entirety, although during 2003 transfers were made in an amount of approximately US$130 million, which significantly improved the liquidity of the FCC.

The government of President Mesa called a national referendum for July 18, 2004, that consulted with the citizenry regarding several aspects of the hydrocarbons policy. The third question on the plebiscite was: *"Do you agree with reestablishing Yacimientos Petrolíferos Fiscales Bolivianos, restoring government ownership to the shares of Bolivian men and women in the capitalized oil companies, so that the government can participate in the entire hydrocarbons chain of production?"* The question, whose language was quite similar to that of the law that created the BONOSOL, received a positive response from 67 percent of the eligible voters. Given the massive support for this measure, several sectors believed that the FCC assets would be transferred to the new YPFB. Although the government did not make such a transfer, the imminent possibility of doing so remains open, as was indicated by the new authorities elected in 2005. In this regard, Point 1.7 of the government program of the Movement to Socialism (*Movimiento al Socialismo*—MAS) calls for "*returning the shares of all the capitalized companies, so that the Bolivian State will have direct control over them. This entails a modification of the shareholding package of these companies. Furthermore, payment of the BONOSOL will be guaranteed with the yields of the FCC and with additional funds from the Treasury.*"

All Bolivians over the age of 65 are entitled to receive the BONOSOL. In accordance with estimates and demographic projections made by CELADE (*Centro Latinoamericano y Caribeño de Demografía*—2005), this group totaled approximately 300,000 persons in 1997 and increased to 390,000 in 2005. The number of beneficiaries of the program appears to have been somewhat greater than expected, since benefits were paid to 364,000 beneficiaries in 1997 and to 427,000 beneficiaries in 2004. No rigorous estimates have been made of the program's scope (that is, if it is reaching all its potential beneficiaries) or of the extent of fraud. Nonetheless, according to data from the 2002 Household Survey, 27.7 percent of those over the age of 65 reported that they were not receiving the money. These differences between the estimated population and the actual beneficiary population might indicate the existence of undue benefits.

Although the bonus is small, the program's effects on the population's conditions of life appear to be relevant. A study based on data from the period of 1999-2002 concluded that, especially in rural areas, households with at least one BONOSOL beneficiary significantly increase their consumption of food.[8] The cause of this impact appears to reside not so much in the purchase of more food by the beneficiaries, but in the possibility of acquiring the basic capital goods needed to increase their agricultural production, which previously were inaccessible due to liquidity restrictions and a lack of financing.

The New System

The capitalization introduced in 1996 is quite similar to what had been developing since 1981, inspired by the Chilean experience. Nonetheless, several differences should be mentioned. The new system requires the participation of employed workers, who must contribute 12.5 percent of their wages, with an additional two percentage points paid by the employers to finance worker's compensation insurance. The contributions are distributed in a pre-established manner. Ten percentage points are earmarked for pension funds, two percentage points are earmarked for financing death and disability insurance, and one half of a percentage point is earmarked for administrative costs. As in other countries of the region, workers accrue contributions and, when they reach retirement age (65 years), can convert the balance of their individual accounts into an annuity. The system does not provide for the payment of minimum pensions. Accordingly, there is no requirement regarding years of contributions to request a withdrawal. Despite this, the payment of "contribution compensation" was provided for workers who had made contributions into the system prior to the reform.

Rather than opening the market to the participation of any interested party (as occurred in Chile and in most countries in the region), or using a progressive system that guarantees a high degree of participation from a pension fund administered by a public entity (as occurred in Uruguay), the model elected by the Bolivian authorities took the form of a bidding competition. The market was divided into two identical parts, and workers were assigned to one of two AFPs. The selection of these administrators was made through a bidding competition, which created a duopoly whose members do not compete with one another. Though affiliation transfers from one administrator to another were authorized in 2002, this activity has been minimal, in part due to a lack of business ambition on the part of the AFPs. Between 2002 and 2004 there were slightly more than 11,000 transfers, which had almost no effect on the distribution of affiliates (the "net gain" by the favored AFP was approximately 200 affiliates over a three-year period). The number of total transfers is equivalent to an annual rate of approximately 0.4 transfers for each 100 members, far below the average for Latin American countries, which ranges from two to three transfers per year for each 100 affiliates.

The administrative fee charged by the Bolivian AFPs on the contributions (0.5 percent of wages) is the lowest in the region. However, the existence of other charges made directly on the funds, along with the relatively high cost of death and disability insurance, have generated controversy over the actual burden of the system, which, in reality, would be almost double the amount indicated[9]. Since there are no marketing or publicity expenses, Bolivian administrative companies obtain very positive results on their management. The return on equity, which measures a company's results as a percentage of its net equity, has been very high in Bolivia, both in absolute terms and as compared with other countries. Only Peru has surpassed Bolivian AFPs' return on equity since 2000.

The AFPs have a very conservative investment policy for the assets of the pension funds, due in part to legal requirements. At the same time, the fiscal problems of the old system have affected the new capitalization model, because the government obtains funds from the AFPs to meet the old system's financing needs. In March 2005, nearly 69 percent of the funds were invested in government securities. Furthermore, pursuant to a decree from the year 2000, the pension funds must annually acquire the equivalent of US$180 million in public debt. Given that collections in recent years have been approximately US$220 million per year, this rule means that the AFPs must invest at least 85 percent of their annual collections in public debt.

The investment portfolios of the pension funds have very little diversification. In addition to the 69 percent invested in public debt, 7 percent of their assets are invested in the shares and debt of *Petrolera Andina*, 5.7 percent in *Transredes S.A.*, and another 5.3 percent in shares of other companies privatized in 1996. In total, more than 85 percent of their assets are concentrated in public debt or securities issued by the capitalized companies. International diversification is also minimal, with only 1.4 percent of the funds invested in foreign assets.

The funds' earnings rate has been very stable since they started to run the system; it has averaged 8 percent per year, in dollars (Table 1). Given the composition of the

Table 1. Return on Equity for AFPs, by Country, 2000–2004

	2000	*2001*	*2002*	*2003*	*2004*	*Linear Average*
Peru	55.5	58.2	58.0	58.6	52.5	45.6
Bolivia	88.6	14.4	36.5	39.2	38.8	31.9
Chile	40.6	27.4	23.1	21.8	21.0	25.1
Mexico	21.6	30.5	32.9	30.7	25.2	22.6
Uruguay	1.3	30.8	92.0	31.9	39.0	17.4
El Salvador	4.9	17.9	24.7	27.8	30.8	8.7
Argentina	14.7	2.6	−18.6	−9.3	−10.0	1.5

Source: Statistical Bulletins of the International Organization of Pension Supervisors (IOPS).

investment portfolio, this rate is directly determined by the profitability of public securities, which, in turn, is set by the government. Therefore, it is difficult to establish a correlation between the funds' returns and trends in financial markets.

As occurs in other countries of the region, when considering new capitalization schemes, most analysts and politicians focus on trends in the pension funds and the performance of their administrators, the AFPs. However, life insurance companies play an essential role, since they cover the risks of death and disability, which can represent a high percentage of the benefits paid. They also absorb a good part of the system's costs. In Bolivia, two insurance companies cover all the activity related to the pension and welfare system. In 2004, the production of disability and survivor insurance was US$48 million, that is, almost 25 percent of the system's total revenue, while recorded losses were US$25 million. This notable difference reflects the immaturity of the system and, possibly, the existence of earnings for the insurance companies. Such earnings are not reflected on the balance sheets submitted to the Superintendency, however, because significant reserves are being set aside, which as of March 2005 amounted to more than US$260 million.

II. Challenges for the Sector

Fiscal Cost

The burdensome fiscal cost of Bolivia's pension system has been the focus of much debate, because the magnitude of the expense resulting from the reform jeopardizes the financial stability of the state as a whole. One of the principal objectives of the 1996 reform was to control and reduce that cost, but as noted above, that goal was not met.

The experience of Bolivia and of other countries in the region points toward the difficulty of reversing what has occurred since 1996. The adoption of measures to drastically reduce these expenses would come up against legal restrictions and, in many cases, violate vested rights. Such measures would also provoke social and political conflicts. The most feasible course of action appears to be to promote policies that keep such errors from recurring.

Using reasonable assumptions and modeling, projections can be made of trends in the system and the system's demand on fiscal revenue. During 2003 and 2004, two simulations were made of future expenditures, one for a study of the Inter-American Development Bank and another by a joint team of the World Bank and the government. These projections indicate that these expenditures should steadily decrease over the coming decades, thereby gradually reducing the pressure on fiscal revenue (Figure 5).

Although projections indicate that expenditures will tend to diminish over time, the system's principal fiscal risk continues to be its institutional fragility. For example, in 2004, two Supreme Decrees (27542 and 27543) were issued; they create three new benefits for those who applied for them under the former system but have not yet obtained a response. This additional expense, not included in the projection, was approximately US$5 million during the second half of 2004. Thus, its annualized value could represent 0.1 percent of GDP.

Successive administrations have granted benefits to groups and sectors in order to solve demands and conflicts, which means that the pension system has been used for years as a short-term social policy tool. Unless explicit agreements are reached on the limits of the system and the conditions for accessing it, the risk remains that this practice will continue in the coming years and will counteract the theoretical diminishing trend in expenditures.

In 2004, the government created a technical commission to analyze the cost of the apportionment system. That commission prepared a report and several action proposals that were adopted by the government through Decree 27991 of January 2005. Among the decree's principal measures are:

- Creation of an electronic data archive, with information on pensioners who are receiving payments or vesting rights, to which the Superintendency of

Figure 5. Projection of Fiscal Pension Expenditures, as a Percentage of GDP, 2005–2060

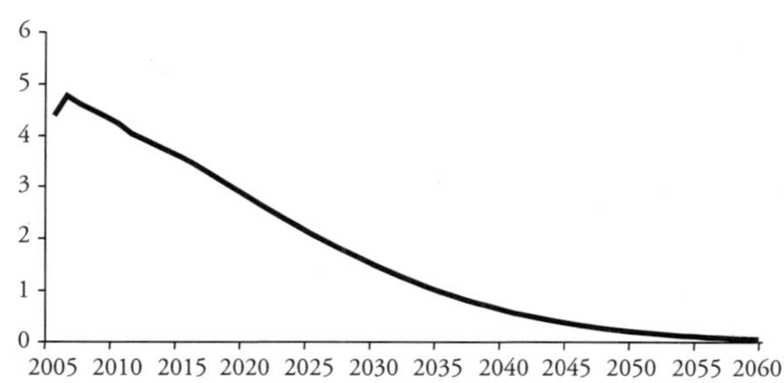

Source: Gamboa (2005).

Pensions, Securities and Insurance (*Superintendencia de Pensiones, Valores y Seguros*—SPVS), the Ministry of Finance, the Assistant Ministry of Pensions and SENASIR should have direct access.
- The review, by SENASIR, of pensioner records that display contradictions.
- Annual actuarial studies by the Ministry of Finance on the state of the pension system.
- The adoption by SENASIR of a system to incorporate all available information into the electronic data archive.
- Implementation of an emergency plan to service the insured, allowing interested parties to obtain information on the state of their processes with the SENASIR.
- The adoption of a plan to expedite the qualification process for pending annuity applications, in order to finalize the review of pending applications prior to December 31, 2005.
- A review by the SENASIR of qualifications for annuities and lump-sum payments that may have been granted irregularly.
- Evaluation of a proposal to create a fund with the property that originally belonged to the supplementary funds but was transferred to the state in order to finance the system's expenses.
- Preparation of an annual report on the liquidation of the former supplementary funds.

At the same time, the decree introduced several institutional reforms in the SENASIR that addressed the areas of debt collection, the fight against corruption and payment arrears, double benefits, and monitoring to ensure that the pensioners are still alive. However, one of the principal missions assigned to the commission—to search for alternative financing sources—was not carried out. Through a supreme decree, the government called upon the Vice Ministry of Pensions and Financial Services to search for alternatives to public indebtedness.

The measures set forth in the decree are aimed at improving the transparency and governability of the apportionment system, since these two areas had limited progress in the past. These measures appear to provide the conditions for better control of the system and reduced fraud and abuses. Though these measures are a step in the right direction, their effectiveness can be evaluated only in terms of the actual operation of the system over the coming years. As indicated above, the enormous cost of the current pension system is the result not of its planning or of the clarity of its standards and objectives, but of its nonperformance.

Access to and Sustainability of BONOSOL and its Connection to Hydrocarbons Policy

Since its creation, the BONOSOL has been the subject of debate, regulatory changes, and the concern of successive administrations. There has been much debate over the management quality of the FCC, adminstrative costs, access of the poorest and most vulnerable groups to its benefits, and the program's financial sustainability.

Pursuant to the Pensions Act of 1996, the AFPs are in charge of administering the FCCs, parallel to the pension funds. Nonetheless, while the individual capitalization funds receive a monthly flow of revenue to be invested, the opposite occurs with the FCCs. The AFPs received assets that they have to administer to generate earnings and liquidity with which to pay benefits, but they do not have a constant, regular inflow of revenue. From the start, the lack of liquidity was considered to be a problem for managing these funds. It was sometimes speculated that the dividends paid by the capitalized companies might be sufficient to finance the BONOSOL benefits. Yet those companies actually had relatively low profitability.[10] As a result, the funds transferred by the capitalized companies to the FCCs during those years averaged less than US$50 million per year, or approximately half the funds required.

The reason for the low profitability could be because the estimated value of the assets is incorrect (that is, the shares are overvalued); because the quality of management of the companies is less than expected; or because there are objective problems in running these companies that keeps them from achieving better results. In all events, the FCCs have a liquidity problem that can be solved only through the sale of part of their assets on the market. Nonetheless, such transactions have been very rare due to the political pressure that the administrators are under and due to the fact that there are no markets with sufficient liquidity to operate with large volumes of assets.

Although the AFPs have engaged in few financial management activities with respect to the FCCs, they have continued to collect fees for that service. The two administrative companies charged approximately US$2.2 million to manage the FCC portfolio in 2004.

Although the BONOSOL is a universal benefit for persons over the age of 65, there are signs that part of the population is not receiving that benefit. According to the 2002 Household Survey, 27.7 percent of the population over the age of 65 reported that they were not receiving this benefit.[11] At the same time, according to existing records, the number of solidarity bonds paid each year is higher than the official estimate of the population whose age qualifies them to receive this benefit. This indicates the existence of many errors or fraudulent collections that need to be reviewed.

The determination of the amount of the benefits has been discretional from the start, since actuarial studies were planned to be conducted at a later time. In 1996, it was decided that each BONOSOL benefit payment should be US$250, and this figure remained in effect until 2001. It was then determined that as of 2002, the Superintendency would conduct actuarial studies once every three years to correct that figure. When the BONOSOL was replaced by the Bolivida in 1998, the new legislation established that the benefit would be US$60. That law once again indicated that in "subsequent years" the corresponding actuarial corrections would be made. Finally, upon reinstating the BONOSOL in 2002, the law established a benefit of 1,800 bolivianos, which would be subject to a five-year review in 2008. As the result of this series of changes, there are no official studies that make it possible to evaluate the sustainability of the FCCs in the medium term, nor are there strategic proposals to guarantee that sustainability. The corrections have responded to political considerations, as opposed to technical reasons. Thus, it is unknown how many resources are needed to sustain the program in the coming decades, or whether the assets available at present will be sufficient to finance the payments.

Following the 2004 referendum and the proposals formulated during the 2005 presidential campaign, it is not clear whether the FCCs will continue controlling the shares of the capitalized companies or whether those shares will be transferred to the government. In such a case, the government must decide its policy for the BONOSOL, because if such a transfer is made, this benefit would lose its financing.

The AFPs' Market Conditions

In order to reduce superfluous expenditures in a relatively small market, the legislation on pensions enacted in 1996 introduced an innovative bidding competition system for distributing the pensions market between two administrators. Under this law, workers were distributed in identical proportions between the two AFPs. Transfers between administrators were not authorized until 2000, nor was the entry of new competitors into the market allowed until 2002. The fee the AFPs receive for administering the contributions is equivalent to 0.5 percent of taxable wages, but they also charge a portfolio administration fee (which is established by contract), another amount for the payment of retirements and, as of 2001, they receive a monetary transfer for the collection of premiums on disability and survivor insurance.

The most "visible" fees received by the AFPs (that is, the fees on contributions to the individual capitalization funds) represent less than 45 percent of their total revenue. Although these fees, as of 2002, are subject to change, no proposals have been made along such lines. Neither have new companies been incorporated into the market. As a result, there is practically no competition between the AFPs.

As indicated above, the investment portfolios were heavily concentrated in government debt and a few capitalized companies in the 1990s. This lack of diversification creates a dual risk for the contributors and society as a whole. On the one hand, the interests of the affiliates could be affected in the event of non-payment by the government, or if a forced renegotiation were to take place. At the same time, since there is such a large exposure to sovereign risk, and given that there are no explicit guaranteed earnings or minimum pension in the system, poor performance by the Individual Capitalized Accounts would open the possibility that those affiliated with the funds will demand a political solution. Thus, there might be an implicit guarantee operating whose scope cannot be evaluated, but that would be very costly for society as a whole.

A final problematic aspect of the new pension system is the disability and survivor insurance, including occupational hazards insurance (Figure 6). From the time

Figure 6. Structure of the Operating Revenue Received by the AFPs. Bolivia 2004

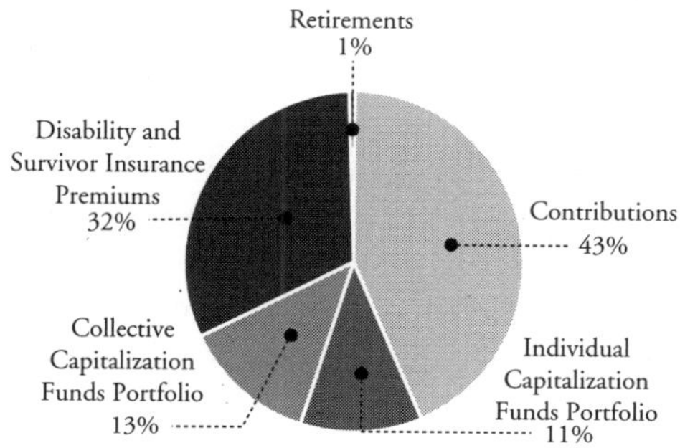

Source: SPVS.

the system began until late 2001, both AFPs were operating without insurance. In lieu of it, they held special reserve accounts with the same administrators where the contributions made by employees and employers to finance them were accruing. In late 2001 a bidding competition awarded the management of all the insurance to two companies: 75 percent of the market was granted to La Vitalicia Seguros and 25 percent to Seguros Provida. The system's affiliates were then distributed among these two insurance companies at random, and the AFPs proceeded to transfer the accrued reserves to them. Given differences in criteria over coverage of the affiliates, there has been very slow growth in the flow of beneficiaries, in particular due to disability losses. In late March 2005, only 1,200 persons received money on that account, while 3,250 affiliates died since the system started. The SPVS has worked to resolve this problem, because application of strict criteria designed to limit the population with a right to coverage would seriously obstruct access for many workers to the protection initially intended to serve them.

Policy Options

Bolivia's system for economic protection of the elderly is contradictory in its design and implementation. The traditional contributive pension system is costly and has very low coverage; the non-contributive universal protection system (BONOSOL) has limited access and sustainability; and the new capitalization system is facing problems in terms of its effectiveness and security.

Policy options in relation to these issues are discussed below; they highlight certain suggestions and evaluate their possible effect. As with any proposal, it is important to identify the restrictions that accompany their implementation, whether political, financial, or social.

Fiscal Cost

As described, the burdensome fiscal cost in Bolivia was due not to poor planning of the reform, but to poor implementation. Therefore, to ensure financial consolidation and long-term sustainability, it is crucial to develop a strategy that considers the issues of policy design and implementation.

Among the measures that merit adoption, a relatively simple one from a technical point of view, although possibly conflictive in political terms, would be to change the way in which pension expenditure statistics are presented in Bolivia. The "tradition" of including items such as guaranteed benefits to the retired staff of the Armed Forces, or the cost of compensation granted to government employees due to the 1996 changes in the contributions, have exaggerated the magnitude of the pension system's fiscal cost. The debate would be more transparent if these expenditures, as well as other minor ones, were correctly assigned to the budgets of the originating entities.

Certain measures were also defined in the January 2005 decree to control future expenditures. The government should ensure that these measures are implemented, and, where applicable, extended. A massive review of benefits granted since 1996 does not seem reasonable, due both to legal restrictions and the political and social conflicts that such an action would unleash. On the other hand, a systematic effort, based on analyzing available information and cross-referencing that data with other sources, could identify those individuals who may have received benefits in an irregular manner. Such an effort would make it possible to reduce the overall costs of the system and, at the same time, would send clear signals to society as a whole that the government takes this matter seriously.

Financial problems in the context of the current and short-term projected deficit can be addressed either as a specific, unique issue for the pension system (that is, through seeking a specific solution within the framework of the pension system) or as part of an overall strategy for government financing. In the first case, the strategy would focus on obtaining additional contributions from those who participate in the system, by creating a "solidarity contribution" for active workers. Here, a model similar to the Colombian one could be followed, by explicitly or implicitly reducing the benefits of retirees (in the latter case, through applying a contribution from retirees). The Peruvian example could also be followed for the government employee retirement system. If such an approach is integrated within a management strategy for the overall public sector deficit, including the expenditures generated by the pension system, it would be justifiable to search for low-cost financing sources, as is proposed in Decree 27991.

The BONOSOL

To reduce fraud and difficulties of access to BONOSOL, it is recommended that Bolivia conduct a specific survey to precisely assess the magnitude of these problems. Based on the results, the government could define a progressive strategy, correct the roster of beneficiaries by eliminating those individuals who have irregularly received the benefit and, at the same time, incorporating those who meet the requirements but have not been incorporated.

With respect to the system's financial management and sustainability, a first step, similar to the one mentioned in the preceding paragraph, is to conduct a rigorous review of the valuation criteria for the assets now registered in the FCCs. Strategies would then be proposed for the medium and long term to maximize the earnings of the FCCs while preserving high security. This should include a review of the government's business regulations and their application to ensure that the interests of the FCCs, and through them of all Bolivians, are being properly protected and represented. At the same time, conducting a demographic and actuarial analysis would serve to allow the government to project the flow of benefits payable in the coming years and decades and adjust the investment strategies and availability of liquid assets to that flow.

Although the BONOSOL was originally conceived as a mechanism to "return" ownership to Bolivians of part of the companies that were previously government-owned, the authorities could reconsider some aspects of the program and seek to make it more inclusive in terms of time (that is, by eliminating the requirement of being born prior to 1974), while also streamlining its distribution. Another possibility would be to integrate the BONOSOL into the contributive system by turning it into a minimum universal benefit that, as such, would not be paid to those who receive regular pensions. The financial viability of the first of these proposals could best be evaluated within the framework of an actuarial study, although with adequate profitability levels, the difference between the flow of payments over the next 45 years (the average life expectancy for the population born before 1974) and a perpetual flow is not very high. The second proposal, limiting the collection of the BONOSOL to those who do not receive another pension, would reduce the annual flow of payments by approximately 15 percent. Such a change would alleviate (though not solve) the BONOSOL's liquidity and sustainability problems.

The government's decisions regarding the ownership of the shares of the capitalized oil companies will be central in the debate on the BONOSOL and its future. If the FCC assets are transferred to the state, an alternative funding source will have to be defined, or else the program would have to be reformulated (by better targeting the benefits or reducing their amount) to keep the BONOSOL from definitively losing its financial backing.

The Capitalization System

Bolivia's individual capitalization system was designed as one with the lowest cost in the region, but the administration's payment of fees from the funds and disability and survivor insurance has generated higher than expected costs. The bidding competition mechanism for the system was effective in reducing excessive affiliate enrollment expenditures, but after five years of operations, the expected conversion to a competitive model has not taken place.

The problems of lack of competition are not exclusive to Bolivia. In fact, they have affected almost all the countries in the region. But the reduced size of the Bolivian market and the rules of play initially applied have created a system that is more closed than in the other countries, which benefits only the administrator companies.

The authorities in the sector now face a dilemma: whether to promote competition by, for example, facilitating affiliation transfers, as was successfully done in Peru in early 2005, or once again to make use of a bidding competition, renewing the process to incorporate new players. Affiliation transfers made as a block could also be promoted, through administered competition mechanisms, as has been recently proposed in Chile. Although given the reduced size of the Bolivian market and prior experience, the second option would appear to be more advisable, for its proper implementation, it would be necessary to revise the operating rules for the market and establish an announced mechanism for regular recurrence in the public bidding processes.

The problems in the field of insurance are relatively new, in part because insurance activities commenced only a few years ago. Nonetheless, it is urgent to resolve certain aspects related to workers' coverage, especially cases of occupational hazards, since the insurance companies have applied very restrictive criteria. In this case, it is advisable that the Superintendency take strong action in defining the objectives of the insurance and separating traditional business insurance from disability and survivor insurance, both on a conceptual and operational level.

Area	*Problem*	*Options (Recommendations in Bold)*	*Impact and Expected Difficulties*
Fiscal Cost	The cost of the pension system is high and has steadily grown	– **Formally review the criteria for determining pension costs to exclude items that are improper.**	Greater transparency and clarity in the debates.
		– **Apply the control and transparency measures included in Supreme Decree 27991.**	Progressive reduction of costs.
		– Consider the deficit as a problem of the pension system and seek internal solutions.	Savings would depend upon the measures taken, but it would be very difficult to obtain social and political support for measures with a significant impact.
		– **Consider the deficit as part of Bolivia's overall financing problems and seek funds from that perspective.**	This would not reduce costs, but would make it possible to discuss overall problems within a suitable framework.
BONOSOL	Possible problems of access and fraud	– **Conduct a specific survey to evaluate the program's coverage and the magnitude of irregularities in access. Implement a program to include the most vulnerable.**	Extension of the program to groups that are not currently receiving this benefit, coupled with major savings due to a reduction in fraud.
	Low earnings rate of the FCC and doubts as to sustainability	– **Review the valuation of assets and the performance of the capitalized companies, making sure that FCC interests are properly protected.**	Correcting the value of the assets will result in greater transparency, while a better defense of the interests of the FCC should result in higher dividends.
		– **Conduct actuarial and financial studies to adjust the parameters and plan long-term investment strategies.**	Adjustments to the values would make it possible to ensure BONOSOL's long-term sustainability
		– **Extend the benefit to the entire population, without age limits.**	This would improve political and social support for the program. It would reduce benefits, but not by a lot if profitability is reasonable.
	Duplication with pension benefits	– **Integrate the BONOSOL into the contributive system, turning it into a minimum universal pension.**	This would free funds (close to 15 percent), making it possible to improve benefits and/or sustainability.

(*Continues on the following page.*)

Area	*Problem*	*Options (Recommendations in Bold)*	*Impact and Expected Difficulties*
	Possible impact of a nationalization of hydrocarbons	– **Ensure the financial sustainability of the BONOSOL through the FCCs or through other funds, in case the shares in the possession of the FCCs are transferred to the State.**	Possible fiscal impact if general revenue funds are used to offset the cost of nationalization.
Capitalization System	Cost is growing and is greater than expected	– **Adoption of pro-active policies to encourage competition, by facilitating affiliation transfers and disseminating information on options.**	Possible impact if other aspects are corrected (such as "hidden" fees).
		– **Return to bidding competition mechanisms to reduce costs.**	More probability of success, but it would meet up with resistance from the industry.
	Disability and survivor insurance that is expensive and ineffective	– **Review of legislation, reducing fees when possible and making coverage criteria explicit.**	Possible reduction of costs, together with improvements in coverage.

Bibliography

CELADE (*Centro Latinoamericano y Caribeño de Demografía).* 2005. Santiago, Chile.

FIEL. 2005. *Comentarios críticos al trabajo del Banco Mundial, "Keeping the promise of old age income security in Latin America."* Mimeo. Buenos Aires.

Gamboa, Ramiro. 2005. *El costo fiscal del sistema de reparto:* Proyección 2004-2060. Economic Policy Analysis Unit (*Unidad de Análisis de Política Económica—*UDAPE), La Paz.

International Organization of Pension Supervisors (IOPS). Several years. Santiago, Chile.

Martínez, Sebastián. 2005. "Pensions, Poverty and Household Investments in Bolivia." Mimeo.

Parra, Juan Carlos. 2002. "Pension Reform in Bolivia: Five Years After." Mimeo.

Revilla, Ernesto. 2002. *El costo de la reforma de pensiones en Bolivia.* Inter-American Development Bank, Washington DC.

Rofman, S. Rafael. 2005. "Social Security Coverage in Latin America." Social Protection Discussion Papers No 0523. World Bank, Washington DC.

Rofman, S. Rafael, and Leonardo Lucchetti. Forthcoming. "Pension Systems in Latin America: Concepts and Measurement of Coverage." Social Protection Discussion Paper Series. The World Bank, Washington, DC.

Superintendency of Pensions, Securities and Insurance (*Superintendencia de Pensiones, Valores y Seguros* – SPVS). Several years. *Boletín Estadístico.* La Paz. Bolivia.

Von Gersdorff, Herman. 1997. "Pension Reform in Bolivia: Innovative Solutions to Common Problems." World Bank, Washington, DC.

World Bank. 2004. "Public Expenditure Review (PER)." World Bank, Washington, DC.

Endnotes

1. For a detailed description of the new system, see Von Gersdorff, 1997.
2. Gamboa, 2005.
3. SPVS, 2004.
4. Gamboa, 2005.
5. Revilla, 2002.
6. In Argentina, for example, the average benefit is approximately 75 percent of per capita GDP, and in Uruguay, 30 percent of per capita GDP.
7. Text of Article 6 of Law 1544, known as the "Capitalization Act," enacted on March 21, 1994.
8. Martínez, 2005.
9. FIEL, 2005.
10. The earnings obtained between 1997 and 2003 ranged between 2.5 and 4.2 percent of the amount of the capitalization.
11. Rofman, 2005.

17

Water and Sanitation—Serving People Better

Franz Drees-Gross, Franz Rojas Ortuste, and Alejandro Tapia

Summary

The basic sanitation sector in Bolivia is facing: (i) a crisis on which model to adopt for water utilities in the cities of La Paz and El Alto; and (ii) a series of structural challenges, such as low labor and operating efficiency, insufficient financing, regulatory deficiencies in the sector, and a lack of sustainability of services in rural areas. These two challenges need to be resolved in the short and medium term to ensure a sustainable increase in coverage and to improve service quality. The current situation demands an efficient, proven model that ensures supply continuity in a context of high population growth, such as La Paz and El Alto are experiencing. Operator efficiency must be maintained, while a substantial increase is needed in sewage service coverage in El Alto. At the same time, participatory channels must be opened for the municipalities and civil society. To accomplish that, it would be worthwhile to consider the possibility of a mixed public-private water and sanitation company that would be created through an increase in the capital of Aguas del Illimani earmarked for expansion works and with the participation of both municipalities. With respect to the general challenges in the sector, suggestions are to: (i) improve the quality of public financing for the water and sanitation sector; (ii) implement the financial policy for the sector and establish the Foundation in Support of Sustainability in Basic Sanitation; and (iii) strengthen and delineate the regulatory authority of the Superintendency of Basic Sanitation.

I. Introduction

The basic sanitation sector covers the services of potable water, sewage systems, solid waste management, and rainwater drainage. This study focuses on potable water and sanitation services,[1] given the importance these two services have taken on in Bolivia over recent years.

The reforms in the water and sanitation sector commenced in the mid 1990s with a redefinition of jurisdiction in the sector. The municipal governments were entrusted with ensuring the provision of water and sanitation services through the Potable Water and Sewage Systems Service Provider Entities (*Entidades Prestadoras de Servicios de Agua Potable y Alcantarillado Sanitario*—EPSAs). Through the Vice Ministry of Basic Services, the jurisdiction to formulate policies for the sector, approve standards, and develop plans and programs for provision of the service was transferred to the Ministry of Services and Public Works, while the Superintendency of Basic Sanitation (*Superintendencia de Saneamiento Básico*—SISAB) was placed in charge of matters regarding the regulation of the sector, among them the granting of concessions and licenses, registration for the provision of water and sanitation services,[2] follow-up on the obligations and rights of concessionaires, approval of the EPSAs' quality, expansion, and development targets, and protection of service users.

In the nine departments, Basic Services and Housing Units (*Unidades de Servicios Básicos y Vivienda*—UNASBVI) were created; these supervise the application of standards and policies in the sector. In the municipalities, Internal Technical Units of the Municipality (*Unidades Técnicas Internas del Municipio*—UTIM) take charge of the technical monitoring of water and sanitation projects. The development of these units has been uneven, depending upon the departmental or municipal support received.

In urban areas, the provision of potable water and sewage services is handled through four types of EPSAs: private concessionaires (only in the case of La Paz and El Alto), mixed regional and community corporations (in the region of Chaco and in Bustillo in northern Potosí), cooperatives (fundamentally in the eastern part of the country) and autonomous municipal water companies clustered in the western region of Bolivia. In the rural areas, the administration, management, and maintenance of these services are carried out through Potable Water and Sanitation Committees (*Comités de Agua Potable y Saneamiento*—CAPYS) and small cooperatives. In indigenous zones or peasant areas, there are other forms of community management based on uses and custom.

For budget reasons, the regulatory activities of the SISAB have been concentrated in the EPSAs of the country's 29 largest cities, where 54 percent of the population resides. To date, no licenses or registrations have been granted, primarily because the regulations of Law 2066 on Potable Water and Sewage Systems,[3] which will determine the form and content of such activities for the smaller and rural EPSAs, have not been developed. The regulations will also establish whether the smaller and rural EPSAs will be exempt from paying the regulatory fee. Finally, they will determine the level of regulation with respect to rates, penalties, license revocations, and other aspects.

Quality control over water for human consumption suffers from a major gap, because neither the Ministry of Health nor the SISAB has sufficient funds to carry out that function. Moreover, their functions in this area are not clearly delineated. Control over the disposal of wastewater suffers from a similar problem. In fact, despite the existence of water pollution regulations for the Environment Act, Law 1333, the Ministry of Sustainable Development has not classified the bodies of water, nor has it delineated monitoring and protection functions for the disposal of wastewater.

There have been some initiatives to improve the situation described above, such as the creation of the Foundation in Support of Sustainability in Basic Sanitation (*Fundación de Apoyo a la Sostenibilidad en Saneamiento Básico*—FUNDASAB), and progress on a new financial policy for the sector, in addition to increased coordination between the SISAB and the Ministry of Health, to control the quality of potable water.

II. Diagnosis of the Principal Problems and Challenges

Coverage of the Services

In the past decade, the country's coverage in the provision of potable water and sanitation has grown considerably. In the period between the 1992 census and the 2001 census, access to better sources of water increased on a national scale by an average of 8 percent, while access to sanitation rose by 20 percent. Despite that, Bolivia's coverage of sewage systems, potable running water, and improved sanitation is below average for Latin America (Figure 1). However, these services' degree of coverage is similar to that of other countries with comparable per capita income. Only in the case of potable water coverage in urban zones does Bolivia rank higher than other countries with similar incomes.

Beyond this general panorama, there is an imbalance of coverage between relatively rich and other poorer departments, as well as inequalities between urban and rural areas.

Imbalance based on Poverty in Regions. Coverage of water services continues to vary depending upon departmental poverty: in 2001, all of the six departments with poverty rates above the national average (except for La Paz) had potable water coverage below the national average. It should also be noted that in some cases, progress in coverage for the services measured between censuses was slower in poor departments (Oruro, Beni, and La Paz with respect to water and Potosí, Beni, and Pando with respect to sanitation) than in the other departments, which further widened the gap (Table 1).

Imbalance between Urban and Rural Zones. Bolivia is one of the Latin American countries with the greatest discrepancy between urban and rural coverage. Table 2 shows that 86 percent of the water provided in cities is received through piped systems, compared with 28 percent in the rural areas, where the water consumed mainly comes from rivers, springs, or wells. There are also marked differences in san-

Figure 1. Coverage of Potable Water and Sanitation in Latin America

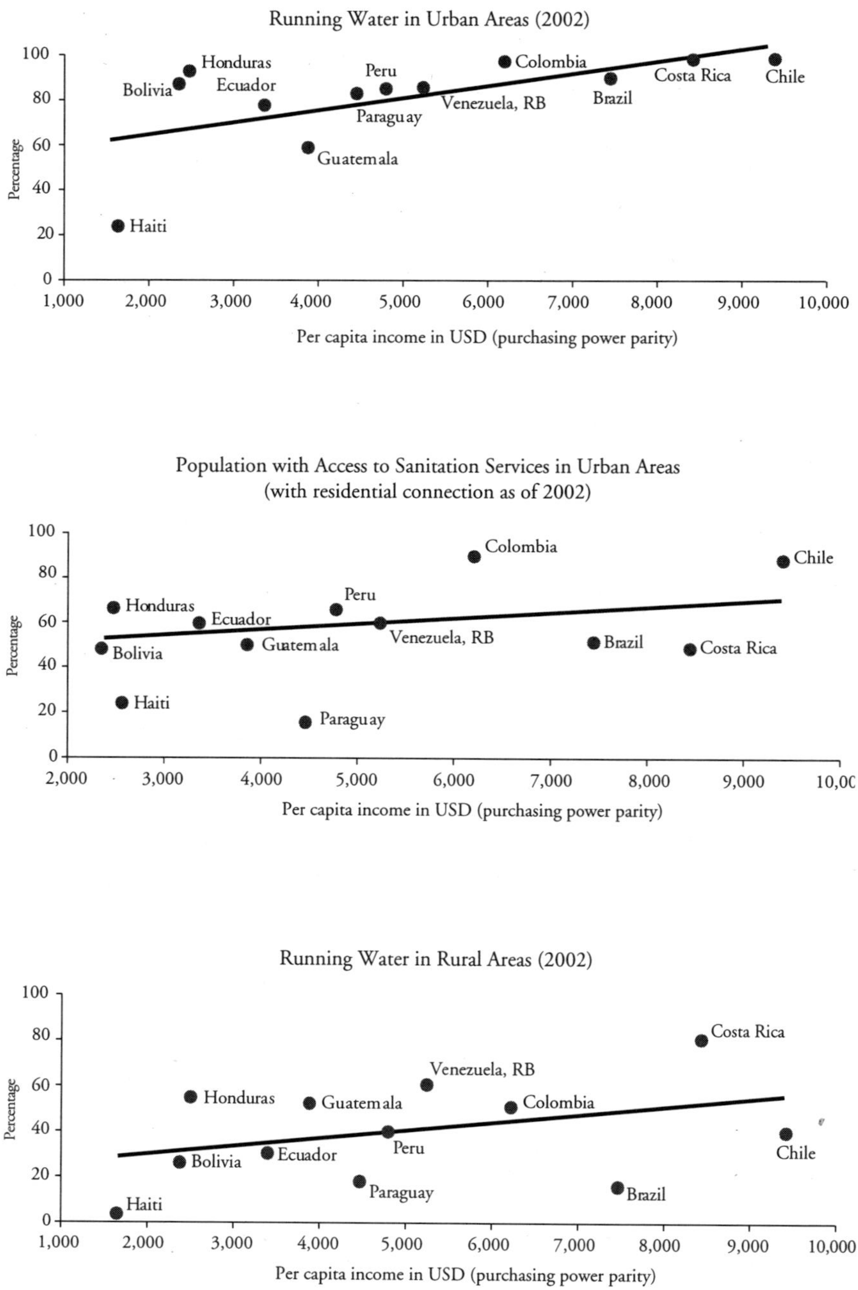

Figure 1. Coverage of Potable Water and Sanitation in Latin America (continued)

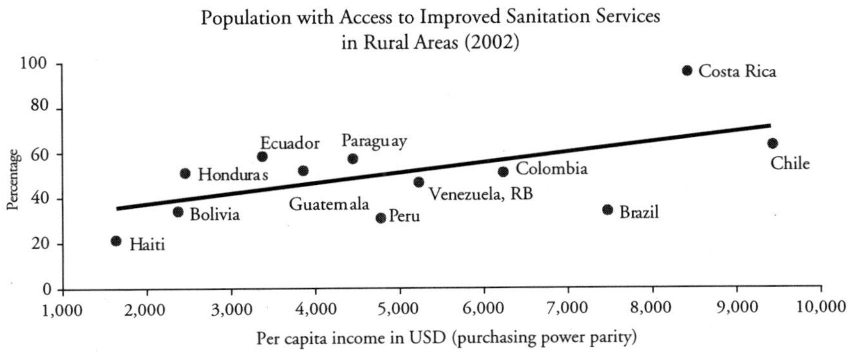

Source: Data published by the Pan American Health Organization (PAHO) based on information from United Nations Joint Monitoring Programme for Water Supply and Sanitation (JMP) and the National Statistics Institute (*Instituto Nacional de Estadística*—INE) for Bolivia.

Table 1. Improved Access to Water and Basic Sanitation
(Data by Department)

	Level of Poverty	*Access to Water (%)*			*Access to Sanitation (%)*		
Departments	*Census 2001*	*Census 1992*	*Census 2001*	*Variation*	*Census 1992*	*Census 2001*	*Variation*
Potosí	80	40	44	4	22	34	12
Beni	76	33	35	2	66	82	16
Pando	72	24	39	15	48	72	24
Chuquisaca	70	41	54	13	30	47	17
Oruro	68	63	58	−5	22	38	16
La Paz	66	58	66	8	37	57	20
Cochabamba	55	44	54	10	45	67	23
Tarija	51	60	76	16	50	74	24
Santa Cruz	38	69	78	9	68	87	19
National	**59**	**54**	**62**	**8**	**43**	**63**	**20**

Source: National Statistics Institute (INE) (access to water) and Economic Policy Analysis Unit (*Unidad de Análisis de Política Económica*—UDAPE) (access to basic sanitation).

Table 2. Water and Basic Sanitation Coverage
(% By Mode of Provision, Year 2003)

Coverage	*Urban*	*Rural*
Potable Water	**100.00**	**100.00**
Piped System	86	28
Public Water Tank	3	9
Well or Waterwheel with Pump	1	6
Well or Waterwheel without Pump	3	21
River, Spring or Canal	1	31
Lake, Pond, or Marsh	0.1	1
Cistern Truck	3	1
Other	3	3
Sanitation	**100.00**	**100.00**
Sewage System	48	2
Septic Tank	15	4
Dry Well	22	32
Surface (street/river)	1	1
No Service	14	61

Source: INE.

itation coverage. In 2003, 86 percent of urban residents had a bathroom in their homes as compared with only 39 percent in the rural area (61 percent had no sanitary installations).

Decrease in Public Investment

Public investments in potable water and sanitation are made through two sources. The Production and Social Investment Fund (*Fondo de Inversión Productiva y Social*—FPS) makes grants to finance the expansion of water and sanitation services in municipalities with fewer than 10,000 inhabitants. The Regional Development Fund (*Fondo Nacional de Desarrollo Regional*—FNDR) makes soft loans to finance the refurbishing or expansion of systems in municipalities with payment capacity, which are generally the larger municipalities. Funding for the sector from these two sources and from the international cooperation community is illustrated in Figure 2.

During 1997-1999, public investment in the sector grew due to the enactment of the Popular Participation Act and the Administrative Decentralization Act, which allowed municipalities to have more funds (average investments were US$69 million per year). In this period, several major projects were carried out, financed with funds from the international cooperation community.[4]

Since 2000, investment in the water and sanitation sector has diminished due to the high indebtedness of the municipalities. This situation was aggravated by the change in policy on the allocation of public investment funds that resulted from the National Compensation Policy and the Dialog Act of 2000.[5] Average public financ-

Figure 2. Public Investment in Water and Basic Sanitation (1997–2004)

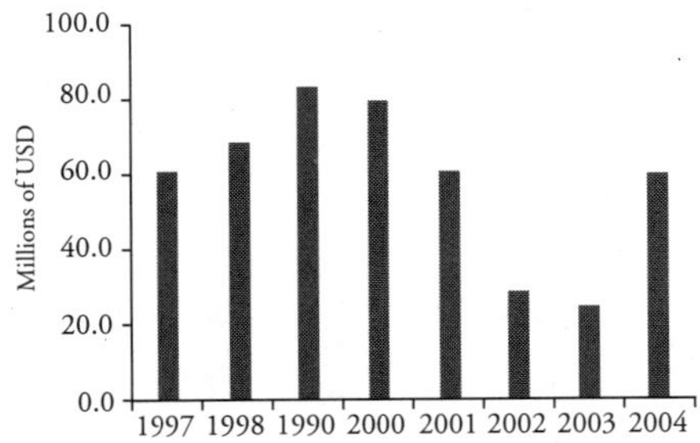

Source: Ministry of Finance, Vice Ministry of Public Investment and External Financing.

ing for water and basic sanitation between 2000 and 2004 fell to US$50 million a year, or a quarter of the annual investments made in the late 1990s.

Operating Inefficiency of the EPSAs

Another challenge for the potable water and sanitation sector in urban areas is low labor efficiency and the great quantity of water not accounted for by many EPSAs.

Labor Efficiency. Of the ten largest EPSAs in the country, only two (AISA/La Paz-El Alto and SAGUAPAC/Santa Cruz) have good labor productivity (1.7 employees for each thousand water connections in the case of AISA and 3.1 employees for each thousand connections in the case of SAGUAPAC), comparable with the best practices in Latin America (fewer than 3 employees per thousand connections) (Figure 3). Labor inefficiency diverts essential funds away from the other EPSAs, which could be used to improve coverage in areas that are not yet supplied and where the population (normally the most needy) has to get its water from sources of doubtful quality (wells, cistern trucks, rivers, springs, and channels). These sources, at times, have a higher cost per cubic meter than the basic consumption rate charged by the local EPSA. For example, in the outskirts of the area covered by Aguas del Illimani (AISA), a cistern truck sells a tank of 12 m^3 of water at a price of 200 bolivianos, which is equal to a rate of 16.7 bolivianos per m^3. The rate for piped water charged by AISA for the first 30 m^3 is 1.85 bolivianos per m^3—meaning the poor are paying nine times more than those who have piped water service.

Out of the eight EPSAs with low levels of labor productivity, four (COSAALT/Tarija, ELAPAS/Sucre, AAPOS/Potosí and EMAPYC/Yacuiba) provide water utility coverage to less than 90 percent of their concession area and two (SEMAPA/Cochabamba and COATRI/Trinidad) provide such coverage to less than 70 percent of their concession area. Among the same eight EPSAs, five provide sewage system coverage to less than 60 percent of their concession areas.

Figure 3. Labor Productivity
(Number of Employees per 1000 Water Connections, in Eight of the Ten largest EPSAs)

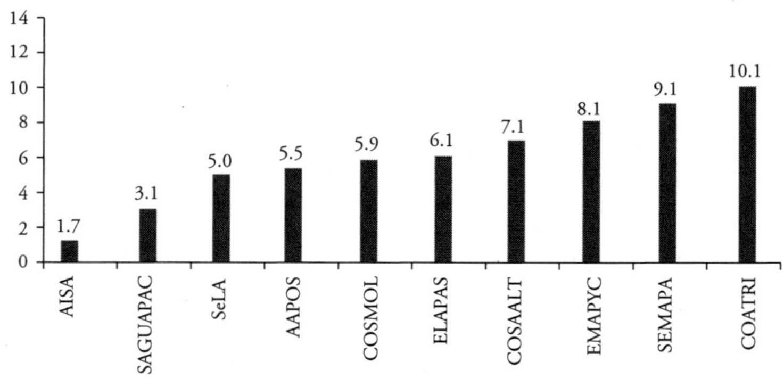

Source: Sector Regulation System (*Sistema de Regulación Sectorial*—SIRESE), based on information from SISAB.
Note: The number of employees was calculated by comparing the total personnel (the number of permanent and direct temporary employees of the company) with the number of potable water connections recorded at the company, with or without a water meter. All the data correspond to 2004, except for the data on the AAPOS (from 2001) and EMAPYC (from 2003).

Unaccounted Water. Four of the ten largest EPSAs in the country have levels of Unaccounted Water above 48 percent (SeLA/Oruro, SEMAPA/Cochabamba, COATRI/Trinidad, and AAPOS/Potosí (56 percent in 2002) (Figure 4). In the case of another four (COSAALT/Tarija, ELAPAS/Sucre, AISA/La Paz-El Alto, and EMAPYC/Yacuiba), 30-35 percent of the water they supply is not recorded through meters. Although there is standard level of Unaccounted Water (the most economic level depends on the marginal cost of production of water as compared with the cost of reducing the volume of Unaccounted Water), it is obvious that the four EPSAs with unaccounted water levels above 48 percent are far from optimal.

Continuity and Quality of the Service

Service continuity provided by the EPSAs has improved but has not yet reached optimal levels. Of 19 EPSAs registered with SISAB, five of them (SEMAPA/Cochabamba, COSAALT/Tarija, SeLA/Oruro, COATRI/Trinidad and EMAPYC/ Yacuiba) provide service on average fewer than twenty hours a day . These EPSAs include those in Bolivia's third and fourth largest cities in terms of population and economic development. Figure 5 provides comparative data, including slight changes, for ten EPSAs from 2003 and 2004.

Quality control of potable water supply is an even greater issue, since of 19

Figure 4. Percent of Unaccounted Water of the Ten Largest EPSAs

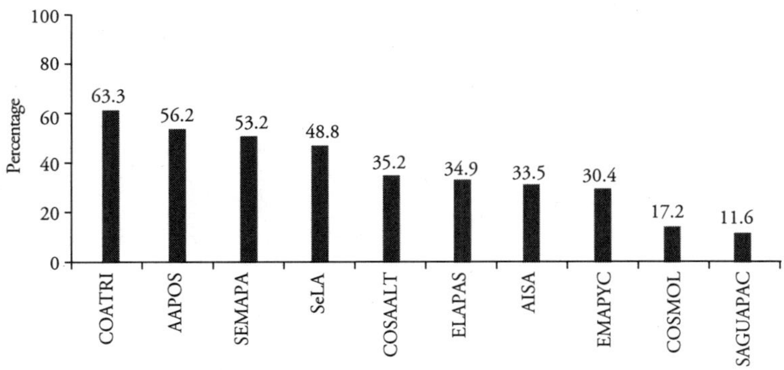

Source: SIRESE, based on information from SISAB, preliminary data for 2004. In the case of AAPOS, the data correspond to 2002.

Figure 5. Hours of Continuity in Select Regulated EPSAs

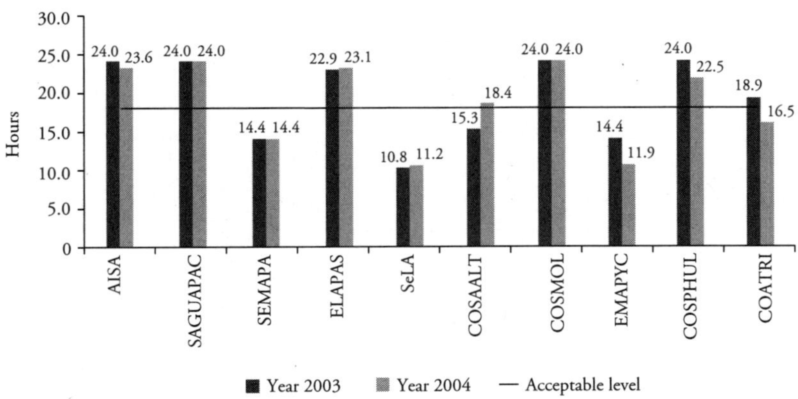

Source: SISAB.

EPSAs registered with the SISAB, 13 did not carry out their control and supervision activities as stipulated in their concession agreements. Although this situation improved in 2004, the percentages continue to be low for COSAALT/Tarija, EMAPYC/Yacuiba, and the cooperatives in the area surrounding Santa Cruz, with the exception of COSPHUL (Figure 6).

Independent of the control mechanisms, the quality standards for potable water are under review due to the level of the requirements, which contrasts with the financial capacity of the EPSAs.

Figure 6. Water Quality Control in Select Regulated EPSAs

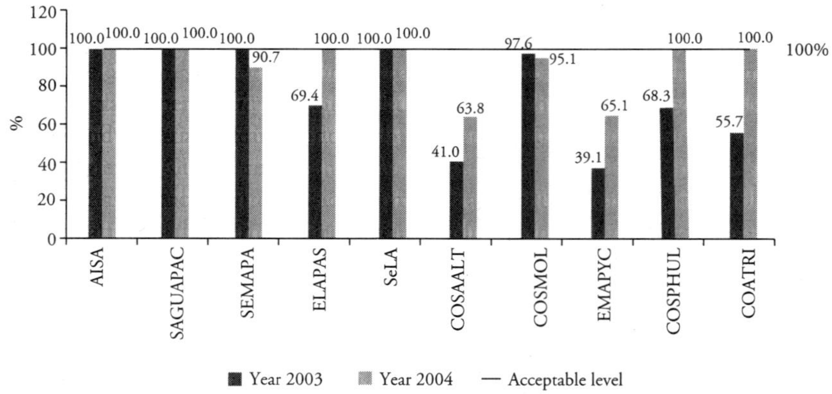

Source: SISAB.

Challenges in Rural Areas

There are no reports on service continuity or water quality in the rural areas. Not surprisingly, the rural areas are significantly behind the urban areas, despite the existence of continual financing programs.[6] Such programs form a part of the National Compensation Policy (*Política Nacional de Compensación*—PNC), which sets annual indicative allocations for each municipality based on five assessments of the poverty level in the municipalities. The allocations can be applied to productive, social, or environmental sectors. Potable water and sanitation services come under the social sector and should be part of the municipalities' multiyear programs. The PNC indicates maximum co-financing percentages from the national government, and social sector projects can receive between 80 percent and 85 percent,[7] with the remainder corresponding to the municipal and/or community counterpart. The management models promoted are generally the Potable Water and Sanitation Committees (*Comités de Agua Potable y Saneamiento*—CAPYS) or cooperatives, both of which come under community management.

A fundamental challenge for the sector is to increase the coverage of potable water and sanitation services until coverage is similar to the rural Latin American average. Also, as some of the rural water systems stopped operating after a certain number of years due to a lack of spare parts or maintenance as users did not pay the rates as agreed, the sector needs to more effectively incorporate community development into the pre-investment phase and afterwards, so that the rural water committees and cooperatives will be sustainable.

The Uncertain Future of the Service Provision Model in La Paz and El Alto

The sector is plagued by overall problems of coverage, quality/continuity, inefficiency in the provision of services, and a nationwide reduction of public investment in the sector. In addition, local coverage needs are still unsatisfied, particularly with respect to sewage in El Alto.[8] Yet the greatest concern at present is the uncertain future of the service provision model in the metropolitan areas of La Paz and El Alto.

Background of the Case

On July 24, 1997, the government signed a concession agreement for potable water and sewage services in the cities of El Alto and La Paz with the company named Aguas del Illimani, S.A. (AISA), whose operator is Suez.[9] The concession agreement established a "service area" within the limits of the urban development of the two cities as of the date of the contract (with defined objectives for the expansion of the two services). It also established a concession area defined as the municipalities of La Paz, El Alto, and the surrounding area. Between 1997 and 2004, water service expanded from 155,000 to 242,000 customers, while sewage service expanded from 96,000 to 165,000 customers. In addition, it was agreed that the concessionaire would be responsible for maintaining the pipes of the existing rainwater system of the city of La Paz but would not be responsible for the open canal rainwater system.

Despite the substantial increase in customers over the past eight years, the current concession agreement is facing several problems, including: (i) high connection fees (for both water and sewage), which hinder access to the system for poor users; and (ii) a large number of users (within the service area and a greater number outside that area) in outlying neighborhoods, who still lack access to water and/or sewage systems. In late 2004, 68,400 persons living in the area of the potable water system were not connected to it,[10] while approximately 170,000 inhabitants residing in Districts 7, 8, and 9, which have massive population growth—often not registered in the municipal land registry—did not have residential potable water services. These problems are increasing in urgency, especially in the city of El Alto, where the high population growth rate (more than 5 percent per year) has led to a rapid increase in demand.

Given these challenges, pressure from forces opposed to private sector participation in the provision of basic services, along with frictions between the government and AISA over issues related to the concession, led the government to issue Supreme Decree No. 27973 on January 12, 2005. It called on SISAB to "immediately take all necessary steps to terminate the concession agreement signed with Aguas del Illimani, S.A. (AISA), based on Bolivian law and the contracts signed with that company."

Achievements and Challenges of the Concession

Although the performance of the concessionaire and its compliance with the contract is the subject of a comprehensive audit recently contracted by the SISAB, it is worth noting certain achievements and challenges of the concession based on statistics available for the sector.

Water and Sanitation Coverage. With respect to the increase in coverage, the AISA concession underwent two stages: a *stage of rapid expansion* between mid 1997 and 2000, with an average of 17,400 new water connections and 11,300 new sewage connections per year, followed, in 2001-2004, by a *stage of more modest expansion*, with an average of 6,400 new water connections and 7,300 new sewage connections per year. It is important to stress that the rate of expansion during this first stage was far higher than the increase in new connections accomplished by SAMAPA in the 31 years prior to the concession, which, at the time the system was turned over to the concessionaire was 156,000 (5,000 per year). Comparing the two stages, there was a notable reduction in overall investment amounts, which fell from an average of US$12.9 million per year between 1997 and 2000 to an average of only US$3.3 million per year between 2001 and 2004. This fall in investments is explained by the five year rate review of 2001, when the SISAB accepted an increase equivalent to 12 percent, even though the concessionaire had originally requested a 24.6 percent increase in prices in US dollars, applicable immediately as of 2002. Based on the 12 percent rate, and given political and social problems for raising rates, a proposal was made to compensate the company by lowering AISA's monetary commitments and increasing associated charges (as opposed to rates *per se*). The SISAB agreed to reduce AISA's payment of the regulatory rate from 3 percent to 2 percent; to defer the SAMAPA leasing royalty, and to lower depreciation rates on the concessionaire's assets. SISAB also granted three other benefits to AISA: (i) an increase in the fixed business cost on its bill (from US$0.10 per bill per month to US$0.22 or US$0.34); (ii) an increase in connection charges paid by new users who wish to benefit from the concessionaire's water and sewage system;[11] and (iii) a limited expansion of connections with respect to the growing demand. Of these three measures, the high connection fees, without question, create an obstacle for new users, generally the poor, to connect to the basic services they need. Moreover, these fees were so high for the inhabitants of the city of El Alto that they provoked a serious social conflict in January 2005. Yet they did very little to improve the concessionaire's financial situation (in the case of AISA, water and sewage connection fees only represent 9 percent of their total revenue).

Connection Fees and Rates. In early 2005, in response to the social unrest that paralyzed the city of El Alto and affected the supply of goods to the city of La Paz, the SISAB issued a resolution that reduced the maximum water and sewage connection fees the concessionaire could charge.[12] Since then, AISA averages about the same as all the large EPSAs with respect to the absolute amount of their connection fees and the proportion of those fees to the EPSAs' total revenue. These connection fees (for water and sewage) are lower than those of COSMOL/Montero, SEMAPA/Cochabamba, and COATRI/Trinidad but are higher than those of other EPSAs (Figures 7 and 8). The proportion of connection fees in the total revenue of the EPSAs ranges from 0 to 9 percent for water (AISA: 5 percent) and from 0 to 5 percent for sewage systems (AISA: 3.8 percent).

Figure 7. Cost of Water Connections
(Value and as a Percentage of the EPSAs' Total Revenue)

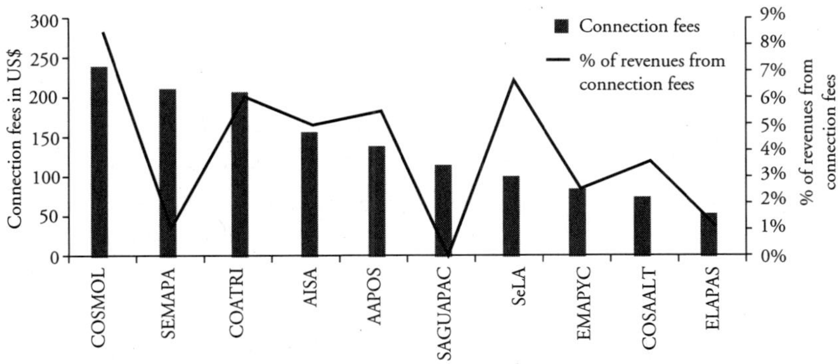

Source: SISAB.

Figure 8. Cost of Sewage System Connections
(Value and as a Percentage of the EPSAs' Total Revenue)

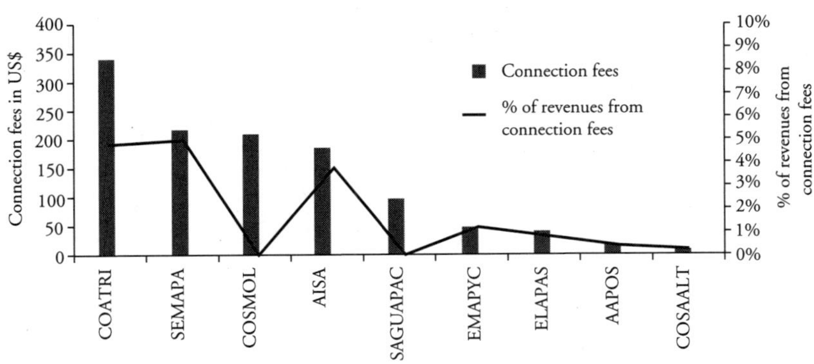

Source: SISAB.

Rates. Bolivia has two types of fee structures. One type, applied by AISA, SeLA, EMAPYC, and COSAALT, consists of a fixed charge for marketing and a variable charge depending upon consumption. The other, applied by the rest of the operators, establishes a payment associated with a basic or indispensable volume, whether or not the user consumes that amount; above that volume, a variable charge is applied on excess consumption. Each EPSA also has several categories of users. For instance, ELAPAS/Sucre has 12 categories, SeLA has 17, and SEMAPA/Cochabamba has nine. For its part, AISA contemplates three categories of users— residential, business, and industrial—and establishes various ranges of consumption for each of them.[13] In the residential category, the structure establishes four ranges: (i) low (1-30 m^3) with a rate of US$0.22 per m^3; (ii) medium (31-150 m^3) with a rate of US$0.44 per m^3; (iii) moderately high (151-300 m^3) with a rate of US$0.66 per m^3; and (iv) high (more than 300 m^3) with a rate of US$1.18 per m^3.

In the case of the other operators, a fixed charge is usually set on the first 10 m^3 or 15 m^3, that is, the user pays for that volume even if it is not consumed. A variable charge applies to the excess of that amount, with a fixed rate per cubic meter for each range. In general, the rate increases in intervals of 10 m^3 or 15m^3. Both the fixed and variable charges are set in the concession agreement for a five-year period.

It should be noted that the domestic rate billed by AISA on the first 20 m^3—the social service rate (a fixed rate of US$0.22 + US$0.22 per m^3)—is less expensive than the average of the ten largest EPSA, and is the lowest if it is considered that this covers potable water and sewage services,[14] while for the other EPSAs it covers only potable water services (Figure 9).

Principal Challenge. The considerations set forth above reveal a fundamental challenge: how to once again raise the level of investment in the metropolitan region in order to attain full coverage for water and sewage services (especially in El Alto). This needs to be achieved without losing the operating efficiency of the current concessionaire, while protecting low-income users (through reasonable rates and connection fees) and offering civil society and the municipalities of both urban areas a role in managing the services without having to politicize their technical provision.

Figure 9. Potable Water Rate of the Principal EPSAs—Residential Category

		Volume of Consumption: 20 m3		
	Operator	*2003 Bolivianos*	*2004 Bolivianos*	*Growth Rate (%)*
1	AISA	35.6	36.9	3.7
2	SELA	43.6	43.6	0.0
3	ELAPAS	34.2	35.4	3.7
4	AAPOS	27.4	27.4	0.0
5	EMAPYC	52.2	54.2	3.7
6	SEMAPA	24.5	24.5	0.0
7	SAGUAPAC	46.0	47.6	3.7
8	COSMOL	49.8	51.6	3.7
9	COATRI	79.6	82.6	3.7
10	COSAALT	30.7	31.9	3.7
	Average	42.4	43.6	2.6

Source: Calculated by the authors based on data from the SISAB.

III. Policy Options for the Sector

Increase public financing for the water and sanitation sector, and promote the modernization of the EPSAs at the urban level

In the urban areas, the estimated demand for investment over a five-year period is US$390 million, which would make it possible to extend potable water coverage from 80 percent to 87 percent and sanitation coverage from 41 percent to 65 percent.[15] This requires the proper use and allocation of loans and grants.

The government issued two Supreme Decrees in 2004[16] in order to achieve an efficient allocation of funds, increase financing and improve the sustainability of the EPSAs. One of these Decrees formulated a new financial policy for the sector. The other created the FUNDASAB.

The financial policy establishes a common fund into which the various cooperating agencies, multilateral and bilateral funds contribute financing, whether in the form of a grant or a loan. These funds, once integrated, are allocated to the EPSAs to cover multi-annual investment programs aimed at improving the coverage and quality of potable water and sanitation services. Through a financial allocation mechanism for the sector, the percentage of transfer or credit applicable to each EPSA is determined, with additional financial incentives for integration through joint efforts, which would also be subject to periodic evaluations of their performance. The financial policy seeks to create synergies for the financing provided by the cooperation entities as it establishes multi-annual investment schedules and efficiently links the infrastructure works with technical assistance measures.

For its part, the FUNDASAB is the technical assistance arm of the financial policy. Its task is to comprehensively diagnose the EPSAs that may be eligible to receive funds; establish goals and indicators for each EPSA in keeping with financial policy guidelines; and provide comprehensive technical assistance for the development of human resources, institutional strengthening, and community management. The instruments available to the EPSAs include medium term consulting on technical, social, business, and financial matters; training on several levels; and organizational consulting aimed at promoting better administrative management. For the government, FUNDASAB will have a technical arm that will develop proposals for technical standards and support for applied research on suitable technologies.

The FUNDASAB will have a high council composed of authorities from the Vice Ministry of Basic Services and the SISAB. Professional organizations such as the Bolivian Association of Sanitary and Environmental Engineering (*Asociación Boliviana de Ingeniería Sanitaria y Ambiental*—ABIS) will also participate, which will make it possible to supervise policies for the sector and have a board composed of persons recognized in this field. In the executive and operating phase, FUNDASAB will be an institution with a small number of officials capable of responding with flexibility to political, social, and institutional changes. In all events, it will seek to integrate and strengthen the local supply of technical assistance. For this purpose,

FUNDASAB uses a cascading organizational approach based on outsourcing with networks of non-governmental organizations (NGOs), training institutes, and companies specialized in technical assistance on basic sanitation. The outsourcers, in turn, will contract consultants based on their various specialties. FUNDASAB will also be able to provide technical assistance to the EPSAs, even without investment projects, if they wish to improve their performance and efficiency, for which they could obtain substantial co-financing.

To promote the work of FUNDASAB, the German Agency for Technical Cooperation (GTZ), the European Union, and the Canadian International Development Agency (CIDA) have committed funds in the amount of US$4 million. The Swedish International Development Agency (SIDA) is also interested in cooperating in this effort. The EPSA would contribute with a counterparty fund. As the financial policy is consolidated, the FUNDASAB would receive government grants, either from the international cooperation community or from the national budget.

Financing and Sustainability in Rural Areas

In rural areas, the demand for investment over a five-year period is US$110 million, targeted to increase potable water coverage from its current rate of 39 percent to 58 percent and sanitation coverage from 33 percent to 52 percent.[17] In this field, it is necessary to make rapid progress in order to meet one of the Millennium Development Goals, which sets an objective of 70 percent potable water coverage and 67 percent sanitation coverage in 2015.

Rural potable water and sanitation programs are soon to conclude, but new funds have yet to be designated beyond those committed by the European Union for rural and urban programs. Several non-governmental organizations are carrying out projects in rural areas, applying their own co-financing and community development criteria. These actions should be integrated to form basic criteria for a unified policy on the sector.

Based on the above, in order to meet the community development requirement for the sustainability of rural systems, FUNDASAB is expected to provide technical assistance to new investment projects and to existing systems that require a new stimulus. The challenge consists of effectively coordinating the many organizations and institutions working in the rural areas so that technical assistance and financial policies for the sector will be united and consistent.

Strengthen and Define the Regulation Scope of the SISAB

The SISAB has a very limited budget to effectively regulate the more than 1,500 EPSAs in the countryside and the cities.[18] Therefore, Law 2066 and its proposed regulations have defined regulatory activity that will focus more on the goals of expansion, quality, and efficiency of the concessionaires (private or public) and less on licensees subject to potential inspections. In the case of indigenous and peasant communities, the registrations will act as an inventory, so that once shortages are identified, strengthening and training can take place. If the goal is to regulate the universe of service providers with the same rigor applied to supervising the concessionaires, the result would discredit regulatory oversight and would be difficult to reverse. Therefore, the proposed regulations to Law 2066 should maintain such an approach and establish requirements and demands that are consistent with the possibilities of the providers and the technical and financial capacities of the SISAB.

Articulating a system of regulations without complimentary policies would amount to an incomplete reform of the sector. Therefore, progress needs to be made in formulating management models that integrate small, generally unsustainable systems with intermediate or larger systems, in keeping with economies of scale and scope. The financial policy for the sector indicated above is essential so that the EPSAs can obtain grants and loans, and thereby fulfill their development plans and the goals to which they have committed.

Finally, beyond the adjustments mentioned above, the SISAB has considerably fewer funds than other regulators of the Sector Regulation System (*Sistema de Regulación Sectorial*—SIRESE). Conscious of this situation, the SIRESE has created an compensation fund among the Superintendencies to even out the asymmetries. A more rigorous analysis should be made of the SISAB's financing needs to ensure that it can carry out its differentiated regulation functions for the universe of service providers.

Transform the AISA Concession into a Mixed Company for La Paz and El Alto

The Model. Considering the level of demand in the municipalities of El Alto and La Paz, these municipalities should play more of a leading role in defining the service's priorities. To ensure top quality technical, financial, and environmental management, the possibility could be considered in the short term of creating a **mixed public-private potable water and sanitation company** that would serve La Paz, El Alto, and possibly other municipalities in the metropolitan area. The idea is not new. Mixed potable water and sanitation companies operate successfully in countries as different as Colombia (in Cartagena, ACUACAR and in Barranquilla, AAA) and Cuba, where the state contracted Aguas de Barcelona as a strategic partner to form the mixed company named Aguas de la Habana. Although in all the mixed companies, the private partners have operating control of the company, the public partners have critical rights, such as the right to determine the annual investment plans. In the case of Cartagena, the municipality of Cartagena, which is the public partner, also has the right to veto the designation of the company general manager, who is nominated by the private partner. As a complement to structuring a mixed company, a **Consultation and Monitoring Council** could be designed. It would be composed of representatives of civic organizations, professional groups, and neighborhood boards, which would supervise the operations of the mixed company, make recommendations to improve the services and key investments, and also channel complaints and claims to the SISAB for subsequent action when the case so merits.

The Transition. The transition from the current concession (a completely private consortium led by Suez) to a mixed company with the participation of the municipal governments of La Paz and El Alto (and perhaps others) as well as the employees of the company, could be accomplished in one of two ways: (i) through a capital increase in the company, by the municipalities using resources earmarked for expansion works; or (ii) through a capital increase in the company, used for that same purpose, but that also reserves a part for the partial purchase of some of the shares currently in the hands of AISA's private investors. In either case, the capital increase (whether or not it is combined with a partial purchase of shares) could be financed with public funds that the national government has available for the municipalities (such as loans and/or grants), using the government's own funds or those of the multilateral and bilateral cooperating agencies. The capital increase would be used to significantly increase service coverage, particularly of sewage services in El Alto.

An Orderly Departure of AISA. In addition to designing the mixed company, a **progressive purchase option** could be structured that would allow the municipal governments to acquire blocks of shares from the concessionaire over preestablished periods of time at predetermined prices. Through the purchase option, the councils would have a tool to accomplish an orderly withdrawal of the private partners of the mixed company. They could be replaced, for example, by calling a new bidding competition to select a new private partner at a regional, local, or international level.

Additional Agreements. Together with the structuring of a mixed company, the existing **concession agreement** between the concessionaire and the government should be reviewed. This process should allow for the necessary changes to facilitate the connection of new users to potable water and sewage systems, expand the coverage of both services, and maintain the financial balance of the concession agreement. A reduced, stable fee for connecting to water and sanitation services (and the institution of a system of payment in installments over the course of several years) could be offset through: (i) the additional income that would be generated by the new connections financed with the capital increase subscribed by the municipalities; and/or (ii) making the first water consumption usage interval smaller. Currently, the first consumption interval (which should protect only the most vulnerable users with subsidized rates for basic, essential consumption) is so large (30 m^3 per month) that 91 percent of domestic users in La Paz and El Alto do not reach that amount. In fact, that interval amounts to 61 percent of domestic consumption.[19] Reducing the size of this interval would mean that the relatively large middle and upper class consumers would pay higher rates for surplus consumption over the first interval, making it possible to finance more investments with the service's increased revenue.

Conclusion: the current crisis, which affects the provision of potable water and sanitation services in La Paz and El Alto, demands a solution through an efficient, proven model that guarantees: (i) service continuity in a context of high population growth; (ii) maintenance of the current operator's operating efficiency; and (iii) a substantial increase in sewage coverage in El Alto. In the current context, this solution should also grant a more prominent role to the municipalities of El Alto and La Paz and allow civil society to participate through a Consultation and Monitoring Council. Finally, the solution adopted should send a signal that there is legal security in Bolivia, thereby facilitating private investments for social purposes as a complement to the efforts of the government and the users. In the current context, the creation of a **mixed potable water and sanitation company** to service La Paz, El Alto, and possibly other municipalities in the metropolitan area of La Paz, could be a viable solution.

Bibliography

Aguas del Illimani S.A. (AISA). 2004. Comunicado REG-313, December 23, 2004. SISAB. AISA.

Gobierno Nacional de Bolivia. 2004a. Supreme Decree 27486 "Constitución de la Fundación de Apoyo a la Sostenibilidad de los Servicios" (FUNDASAB).

———. 2004b. Supreme Decree 27487 "Política Financiera del Sector Agua Potable y Alcantarillado Sanitario" (PFS).

Instituto Nacional de Estadísticas (INE). 2003. Statistics "Bolivia: hogares, según área geográfica, procedencia y distribución de agua en la vivienda, 1996 – 2003". INE

———. Statistics "Bolivia: procedencia y distribución del agua para beber y cocinar en la vivienda de los hogares por departamento y censo, según área geográfica, censos de 1992 y 2001." INE.

Ministerio de Servicios y Obras Públicas. 2002. "Plan Bolivia para agua potable y saneamiento." Ministry of Public Works.

Organización Panamericana de la Salud. Data for potable water coverage. <http://www.cepis.ops-oms.org/>

Sistema de Regulación Sectorial (SIRESE). 2004a. Preliminary indicators SISAB –"Número de empleados por c/1000 conex. A.P." La Paz.

———. 2004b. Preliminary indicators. SISAB –"Agua no Contabilizada." La Paz

Endnotes

1. Pursuant to Law 2066, sewage systems include wastewater treatment. In this chapter, the term sanitation includes sewage systems, wastewater treatment, and sanitation solutions *in situ*.

2. The SISAB grants concessions to EPSAs that operate in population settlements with more than 10,000 inhabitants; operating licenses to EPSAs that operate in population settlements of 2,000 to 10,000 inhabitants; and registrations to organized indigenous and peasant communities.

3. More than ten versions of the seven draft regulations to Law 2066 were prepared between 1999 and 2005, but to date, the government and social organizations of Cochabamba and El Alto continue debating a possible modification to Law 2066.

4. PRODURSA, PROSUB, PROSABAR, PRODASUB-JICA, PROANDES, and PRAS Santa Cruz-Beni-Pando.

5. These measures attempt to establish clear mechanisms for grants and loans.

6. PROSABAR in the period of 1996-1999, PROAGUAS in 2000-2005, and PROHISABA in 2002-2006.

7. Initially the percentages ranged between 55 percent and 85 percent. The changes were implemented as of 2004.

8. According to data from SISAB for 2004, coverage of water services in the AISA service area was 98.7 percent (both in La Paz and in El Alto) and coverage of sewage systems was 91.1 percent (La Paz) and 60.5 percent (El Alto). In addition to the population without service in the concession area, there is a growing population in the metropolitan area (especially around El Alto) that does not form part of the concessionaire's current coverage area.

9. The shareholders of AISA are Suez (55.5 percent), local investors (37 percent), and the International Finance Corporation (IFC) of the World Bank (7.5 percent).

10. AISA Communiqué REG-313 of December 23, 2004, to the SISAB, based on data from the INE and census verification.

11. Connection fees in effect during the period of 2002-2004 rose from US$155 to US$196 for water and from US$180 to US$249 for sewage services.

12. In January 2005, the SISAB decided to restore connection fees to their original amounts, based on an analysis indicating that AISA's revenues would not be affected, because the connections made from 2002-2004 were more than as scheduled for that period, and the remaining connections to attain the five-year goals could be charged at the original connection fees. This was not accepted by AISA and is still an issue under appeal.

13. With the exception of the industrial sector.

14. AISA's rate structure does not separate potable water services from sewage services. In the other cases, sewage services are charged at an additional rate or a percentage is applied on the rate for potable water.

15. Ministry of Services and Public Works, 2002.

16. Supreme Decrees 27486 and 27487 of May 2004.

17. Ministry of Services and Public Works, 2002.

18. Estimate by the Water and Sanitation Information System (*Sistema de Información Sectorial en Agua y Saneamiento*—SIAS) based on a survey conducted in most of the municipalities.

19. AISA consumption histograms, provided to the SISAB.

18

Transportation Systems

Maria Marcela Silva

Summary

Over the past decade, Bolivia has promoted a series of political and institutional reforms to modernize its transportation systems. Transport conditions are starting to improve, although there is still a long pending agenda, particularly to substantially reduce operating costs and consolidate the progress achieved in terms of efficiency. The government is facing the challenge of providing its people with an appropriate transportation infrastructure to encourage economic growth and meet the unsatisfied needs of the poor.

On a national level, it is recommended that priority be placed on strengthening the Vice Ministry of Transportation and the National Roads Service; protecting them against political and partisan interests; and devoting more attention to tertiary roads in the rural areas, which comprise more than half of the road network. The government needs to prioritize its investments to ensure the highest economic and social yields. With that in mind, it is worthwhile to give priority to strengthening departmental governments and local communities, as well, because they can contribute the most to the transportation sector.

I. Background

Overview

Given the nature of Bolivia's economic activity, in which agriculture, mining, and the manufacturing industry generate around 30 percent of the GDP, the role of transportation is very relevant. Over the past decade, Bolivia has introduced institutional reforms and policies to modernize the transportation sector and increase the country's competitiveness. Although conditions and services are starting to improve, much remains to be done to substantially reduce the cost of transportation and consolidate gains in terms of efficiency.

In its effort to develop its potential as a continental transportation center, Bolivia needs to overcome a series of structural obstacles, such as its high transportation costs,[1] deficient infrastructure, and avoidable costs derived from a flawed institutional and regulatory framework.

The Bolivian government faces the challenge of providing an appropriate transportation infrastructure to promote economic growth and maximize its global competitiveness. To accomplish that, the country needs efficiency and cost effectiveness in its transportation infrastructure and services to optimize the balance between investments and maintenance. The reforms of the past decade, including capitalization of the railroads and the recentralization and strengthening of the national roads administration, are steps in the right direction, but more progress is needed.

This study is divided into three sections. First is a brief summary of the principal characteristics of Bolivia's transportation sector, the principal reforms implemented in each subsector, and the achievements of those reforms. Next is an analysis of the sector's principal challenges, with emphasis on the roads subsector.[2] The final section provides recommendations to improve results in the sector.

Principal Characteristics of the Sector

Transportation plays a key role in the country's economy. Between 1992 and 2004, the sector, including the road network, railways, airports, ports, rivers and canals, represented on average 9.2 percent of GDP and almost a third of public investments (principally roads). During that same period, activities related to transportation provided approximately 6.5 percent of the total jobs in urban areas.[3]

Infrastructure

The transportation sector consists of: (i) the national road network, with approximately 12,200 kilometers of highways, administered by the National Roads Service (*Servicio Nacional de Caminos*—SNC); (ii) 14,200 kilometers of secondary roads under the jurisdiction of nine Prefecture Roads Services (*Servicios Prefecturales de Caminos*—SEPCAMs); (iii) 34,500 kilometers of tertiary or rural roads, which fall under the jurisdiction of the municipalities; (iv) 37 airports, three of which were granted private sector concessions; (v) 3,700 kilometers of rail, in two separate rail line systems; and (vi) a series of major navigable waterways (two principal basins: the Amazon and La Plata) including the Paraná-Paraguay waterway and the Lake Titicaca basin.

In 2003, approximately 33 million passengers and 7 million tons of cargo were transported within the country using the various transportation systems (in 1992 the figures were 14.6 million and 3.3 million, respectively). Highways, the country's principal mode of travel, account for almost 91 percent of total passenger transportation and 59 percent of cargo in terms of volume. Tables 1 and 2 show historic

Table 1. Movement of Passengers
(thousands of persons per year)

	1992	*1993*	*1994*	*1995*	*1996*	*1997*	*1998*	*1999*	*2000*	*2001*	*2002*	*2003*
Air	1,195	1,490	1,876	1,972	1,930	2,739	2,720	2,396	2,270	1,993	1,993	2,189
Roads	12,505	13,911	13,366	16,436	19,452	22,617	25,014	24,796	21,769	21,223	23,998	30,449
Railways	870	740	730	650	520	599	706	684	667	705	726	730
Waterways		12	12	9	13	12	10	13	10	15	16	7
Total	**14,570**	**16,153**	**15,984**	**19,067**	**21,915**	**25,967**	**28,450**	**27,889**	**24,716**	**23,936**	**26,733**	**33,375**

Source: UDAPE (2005).

Table 2. Movement of Cargo
(thousands of tons per year)

	1992	*1993*	*1994*	*1995*	*1996*	*1997*	*1998*	*1999*	*2000*	*2001*	*2002*	*2003*
Air	9	12	16	12	15	13	18	17	15	12	14	17
Roads	1,901	2,217	2,417	2,553	2,653	3,009	3,565	3,588	3,876	4,061	4,765	4,114
Railways	1,409	1,343	1,393	1,345	1,379	1,590	1,757	1,573	1,595	1,321	1,516	1,595
Waterways		259	410	285	523	594	786	892	917	1,028	1,072	1,245
Total	**3,320**	**3,830**	**4,235**	**4,195**	**4,570**	**5,206**	**6,125**	**6,069**	**6,402**	**6,421**	**7,367**	**6,971**

Source: UDAPE (2005).

trends in the movement of passengers and cargo in Bolivia based on the mode of transportation.

Bolivia has five principal transportation corridors: one interior corridor, two to the Pacific and two to the Atlantic. The only fully internal route departs from La Paz and arrives in Santa Cruz through Oruro and Cochabamba. This connects the four largest cities, where the majority of the economy is concentrated, since the departments of La Paz, Oruro, Cochabamba, and Santa Cruz account for approximately 75 percent of the population and represent close to 80 percent of GDP. Such a physical concentration of economic activity justifies the existence of good services along that corridor but detracts attention from other peripheral areas and hinders regional integration.

The country's high dependency on a small quantity of exports from identified geographic zones (minerals from the western highlands, soybeans and other agricultural products from the east) has resulted in a very fragmented transportation system that is not interconnected. The best example of this is the fractured railroad system, composed of two independent networks, one of which covers the Andean region, and the other of which covers the eastern zone.

Institutional Conventions

Transportation policy is formulated by the Vice Ministry of Transportation (*Viceministerio de Transporte*—VMT), an agency of the Ministry of Public Works and Services. The VMT establishes rules and regulations for most transportation services and infrastructure. It drafts laws on transportation matters for the Congress as well as decrees and regulations for the executive branch. In addition, the VMT takes charge of highway bidding competitions, administration, and maintenance. Within the VMT is the semi-autonomous SNC. A second key agency is the General Directorate of Civil Aviation (*Dirección General de Aviación Civil*—DGAC), which administers, coordinates, and controls air transportation activities.

There are two other related government agencies: (i) the Airports and Air Navigation Services Administration (*Administración de Aeropuertos y Servicios a la Navegación Aérea*—AASANA), which provides meteorological services and air traffic control throughout the country, and (ii) the remnants of the government-owned railroad company, *Empresa Nacional de Ferrocarriles del Estado* (ENFE), which administers the real property of the ENFE, although the company's operations (and transportation vehicles) have been transferred to the private sector. Waterways and lakes, given their strategic importance along the Bolivian border, are under the control of the Armed Forces.

The Superintendency of Transportation (*Superintendencia de Transporte*—ST) regulates economic matters and the quality of transportation services. Among its functions, it must: (i) promote efficiency in transportation services and operations; (ii) supervise the capitalized companies and publicly managed airports with respect to quality control, unfair competition, and the fulfillment of their investment obligations; (iii) establish or review rates (where competition is not present); (iv) promote competition; and (v) provide grants and licenses for new services.

The Current Situation

After the stabilization efforts of the 1980s, the transportation sector formed an essential part of the following decade's structural reform program, which emphasized: (i) maintenance and refurbishing of the road network in order to integrate the different regions, improve the distribution of agricultural products, and reduce transportation costs for exports and imports, which would reverse one of Bolivia's principal competitive disadvantages; and (ii) the introduction of private partners, to reduce government expenditures and improve efficiencies.

In general terms, the reforms of the 1990s were relatively successful, because they improved results indicators, attracted private investment, and provided experience for a sector characterized by public administration. However, the impact of the reforms was limited. This was due in part to unrealistic expectations that profits from privatization would be distributed, and in part to a lack of institutional capacity to attend to the various sectors under the new rules of play. Despite the improvements, capitalization has a very bad reputation among the population. Foreign investments are frequently accused of having benefited foreigners at the expense of Bolivians. Public complaints on the performance of railroad and civil aviation operators are relatively common. In the latter case, the complaints have become widespread and accompany the potential bankruptcy of the country's airline.

Road Networks

The ***roads subsector*** has undergone major institutional reforms, having been decentralized and then recentralized in less than a decade. The administration of assets and social development associated with the roads subsector are the areas that require the most public sector participation on a financial and technical level. In 1995, the responsibilities of the SNC were decentralized and transferred to the recently created SEPCAMs, to bring planning and decision making on investments closer to local demand. The idea could have worked well, but too much authority was assigned at once to the SEPCAMs, accompanied by insufficient capacities and technical resources. The abrupt decentralization over stretched the sector's limited technical and administrative capacities. Without a broad vision of national needs, the SEPCAMs failed to pay attention in a timely fashion to maintaining national roads and instead focused their attention on the secondary and tertiary roads (Box 1). They also failed to take economic considerations into account in setting priorities. Road maintenance systems were transferred to the new entities. Basic information on road and traffic conditions was no longer available due to budget restrictions. Actual maintenance did not keep pace with planned maintenance and was particularly affected by deteriorating repair machinery. In 1998, almost half of the original machinery was no longer in operating condition. The quality of the roads diminished, transportation costs rose, and many rural roads became impassable during the rainy season.

The new administration, which came into office in 1997, corrected this trend by recentralizing the national system, returning all jurisdiction to the SNC, and allow-

Box 1. Bolivia's Road Network

The percentage of paved roads in Bolivia (7 percent) is much lower than the regional average (27 percent) or the average HIPC country (12 percent). Almost 63 percent of the road network are dirt roads. This substantially increases transportation costs per kilometer and travel times, affecting overall transportation costs and reducing traffic levels.

System	*Asphalt*	*Gravel*	*Dirt*	*Total*
Primary	4,032	4,738	3,485	12,255
Secondary	195	6,928	7,101	14,224
Tertiary	56	6,856	27,630	34,542
Total	4,283	18,522	38,216	61,021
(%)	7	30	63	100

Source: UDAPE (2005).

ing the SEPCAMs to take charge of the secondary system, while the municipalities were assigned the tertiary system. Nonetheless, institutional jurisdiction over urban routes was not as clear. Much institutional experience, as well as the human and physical assets of the SNC, were lost during the process. In January 2000, the government contracted consultants to propose a reorganization of the SNC. What was sought was an entity capable of fulfilling its new functions, that is, of administering contracts and managing results. The consultants designed an institution with only 350 employees, the same quantity of personnel that remained at the SNC after the failed decentralization. As part of the institutionalization, the SNC has been turned into an autonomous agency whose directors are chosen by the President from a list proposed by the Congress, while the professional personnel are selected based on technical merit through competitive processes.

Institutionalization of the SNC also included guaranteed funding allocations for road maintenance, part of which consisted of 70 percent of toll revenue earmarked for those works (the remaining 30 percent is turned over to the departmental government). More recently, a growing percentage has been allocated from the Special Tax on Hydrocarbons and their Derivatives (*Impuesto Especial sobre los Hidrocarburos y sus Derivados*—IEHD), managed by the National Roads Maintenance Fund (*Cuenta Nacional de Conservación Vial*—CNCV). This is derived from a type of charge for services paid by road users through fuel consumption. The SNC has designed a program to contract road maintenance with the private sector. A pilot program, initiated with funds from the second road maintenance project, has had success. Following many difficulties during a transition period, the routine maintenance program now has an estimated cost of US$2,233/km-year (within international parameters). The maintenance is conducted through: (i) contracts with private companies for activities that require specialized machinery (43 contracts covering a total length of 12,200 kilometers, for a price of US$20 million); and (ii) a maintenance program with an intensive labor routine, carried out using micro companies, which covers 10,200 kilometers and creates more than 2,291 jobs, with a total cost of US$5.4 million. Over recent years, the SNC has improved maintenance scheduling, contracting, and supervision. Obviously, much remains to be done, and, unfortunately, the expansion and refurbishing of the system depends in large measure on external financing. Counterpart funds in such cases come from the departments.

On a departmental level, maintenance policies are far from clear and the works are conducted with little enthusiasm. The departmental governments are still responsible for providing counterpart funds for externally financed projects on the primary road network, which hinders their capacity to attend to investment and maintenance for the secondary roads. This jeopardizes the works on account of delays in funding allocations. Moreover the SEPCAMs often use the machinery handed over by the SNC under decentralization to attend to the needs of the municipalities on their tertiary roads, because the municipalities, which have no municipal roads agency, do not have the funds or the capacity to carry out such tasks. All jurisdiction over infrastructure is concentrated in the Technical Office (*Oficialía Mayor Técnica*), which directly reports to each municipal council.

To conclude, strengthening institutional capacity at the different levels would enable Bolivia to more efficiently administer the roads through use of results-oriented frameworks. It is necessary to establish a correspondence between jurisdiction and the allocation of funds, determine effective investment and maintenance policies, and develop coordination mechanisms among the three levels of government in order to have an articulated framework for the sector.

Financing is still far below what is necessary to keep the road network in an acceptable state, even though public spending on the national road network between 1999 and 2004 increased from US$98 million to US$188 million (Table 3). Almost 80 percent of the total budget is financed externally.

Table 3. Public Spending on the National Road Network
(in US$ million)

	1999	*2000*	*2001*	*2002*	*2003*	*2004*
Treasury	7.3	4.8	7.4	1.7	4.1	2.6
Own Resources	10.7	19.5	3.8	8.9	2.8	8.7
Other	11.1	13.2	29.5	8.6	3.1	5.8
External Financing	69.0	85.7	67.6	95.7	126.5	171.1
Total	**98.2**	**123.3**	**108.3**	**114.9**	**136.5**	**188.2**

Source: Vice Ministry on Public Investment.

Despite the financing problems, following the reform of the SNC, the condition of the primary roads has notably improved; good road conditions increased from 26 percent to 31 percent between 2001 and 2004.

In June 1998, the passage of a new Public Works Concession Act aimed to promote private investment. This law contemplated the collection of tolls as the primary revenue for investors in roads. However, there has been a lack of investor interest due to low traffic levels,[4] high construction costs, uncertain financing for the subsidies, and unclear laws. The feasibility of a private participation approach in the road sector would also require better preparation by the SNC to properly supervise and control the concession agreements.

Rail Networks

Prior to the capitalization of the railroads in 1996, ENFE, the national government-owned railway, was facing deteriorating operating results and financing; moreover, it lacked the funds needed to continue supporting unprofitable activities or to improve its infrastructure and services. The government believed that the system could substantially increase its capacity and reduce costs by eliminating political interference, excess jobs, rate distortions, and dependency on the national budget. At the time, it was argued that capitalization would attract funds to refurbish and modernize the system and that private investors could improve efficiency and labor productivity and generate revenue for the Treasury. It was further argued that by offering better transportation alternatives for international trade, Bolivia would improve its competitiveness as a regional transportation center.

The capitalization strategy separated the Andean and Eastern systems. Accordingly, Ferrocarril Andina (FCA) and Ferrocarril Oriental (FCO) became totally private corporations, owned 50 percent by a firm named Cruz Blanca.[5] The Andean system is centered in Oruro, with services to La Paz, Cochabamba, Sucre, Potosí, and Villazón (on the Argentine border), and to Avaroa and Charaña (both on the Chilean border). The eastern system, centered in Santa Cruz, has eastbound lines to Quijarro and Puerto Suárez (on the Brazilian border), southbound lines to Yacuiba (on the Argentine border), and northbound lines to Montero. The eastern system, which crosses plains, has mild slopes and wide curves, with tropical temperatures and altitudes below 450 meters. On the other hand, the Andean system has slopes of up to 3 percent, sharp curves, and altitudes ranging from 2,000 to 4,500 meters.[6]

The new companies own the vehicles and are responsible for all necessary investments. The tracks are leased from ENFE. The government limits its role to supervising contractual performance and controlling prices in the corridors without market competition (in practice, only Santa Cruz-Puerto Suárez). In exchange for using the infrastructure and for the license to provide railway services, the capitalized company must pay a licensing fee of 2.2 percent and a regulatory fee of up to 0.5 percent of its gross annual revenue.

In 2003, seven years after the capitalization of ENFE, the majority of the operating, financial, and quality of service indicators have improved. According to the

ST: (i) average speeds of cargo trains have increased (by almost 10 percent on the Andean system and 25 percent on the Santa Cruz-Puerto Suárez line); (ii) derailments decreased by more than half in both systems during the period of 2000-2003 (from 0.8 derailments/ton-km. to 0.35 in FCA and from 0.38 to 0.11 in FCO); (iii) between 2000 and 2003, delays in service declined from 80 to less than 40 minutes in FCA and from 130 to 120 minutes in FCO; (iv) cargo rates per transported ton dropped significantly between 1998 and 2003 (from US$0.046 to US$0.037 in FCA and from US$0.054 to US$0.035 in FCO). On the other hand, FCA and FCO passenger ticket prices increased between 1998 and 2002 by 36.4 percent and 29.2 percent, respectively—this is a matter subject to constant criticism, even though it is due to the fact that the rates were formerly subsidized; and (vi) the movement of passengers and cargo has increased, by 40 percent and 15 percent respectively, which reflects an annual growth of 5.2 percent in terms of passenger movement and 2.5 percent in cargo movement.[7]

Both companies have fulfilled their investment commitments. The FCA had seven years to invest a total of US$13.2 million in improvements and maintenance, while the investment schedule approved for the FCO was US$25.9 million. Between 1996 and 2003, the total investments of FCA and FCO were US$91.2 million (133 percent more than expected). Nonetheless, the majority of this investment was earmarked to improve and maintain most of the profitable lines. Users complain that there is barely any new equipment, and ENFE, the owner of the infrastructure, argues that maintenance on the less profitable lines is inadequate. ENFE also criticizes the abandonment of passenger traffic, particularly in the areas of La Paz and Cochabamba. To ensure the provision of services to the poorer segments of the population, the concession agreements include Public Service Obligations (*Obligaciones de Servicios Públicos*—OSP), through which the railroad operators must provide the ST with specific justifications if they decide to progressively withdraw a service. If the Superintendency of Transportation deems that the service must be provided for social reasons, the appropriate budget allocations to cover the service will be provided. This clause is limiting, since the operators cannot unilaterally withdraw service.

Air Transport

With respect to air transportation, until 1995 the government owned and operated its banner airline, *Lloyd Aéreo Boliviano* (LAB), all the airports of the country, and, of course, the air navigation system. Reforms were introduced in the administration of the country's principal airports and in civil aviation through the capitalization of LAB, and three years later concessions were granted on the country's three main airports. Although both events led to some improvements, serious problems also arose.

In 1995, LAB was one of the first government-owned companies offered for capitalization. In October 1995, it was turned over to VASP, a private airline based in Sao Paulo.[8] After decades of losses, market growth and an improvement in results helped LAB turn a loss of US$6.5 million in 1995 (its last year as a government-owned company) into small earnings in three of the next four years. In 2001, LAB's financial viability was in jeopardy, with losses of more than US$53 million, principally due to the financial difficulties of its private partner, which was hard hit by the Brazilian economic crisis of 1999. In mid 2002, in the midst of a series of reports regarding serious irregularities committed by VASP, a Bolivian group acquired the ownership of its shares. Since its capitalization, LAB has experienced an increase in capacity and volumes for passengers and cargo encouraged by competition in rates, which included a price war in 1997. Since the introduction of the private company Aerosur in the market,[9] LAB's market share has been drastically reduced from 93 percent in 1993 to its current share of 59 percent of the passenger market and 54 percent of the cargo market. At present, the country has six national operators, though LAB and Aerosur continue to dominate the domestic market.

In February 2000, the ST established two standards to improve the service. Only 22.5 percent of flights could take off with a delay of more than 30 minutes, and only 5 percent of flights could be canceled without justified circumstances. Airlines are fined for violations in this regard. To better protect customers' rights, the ST accepts written complaints through its customer service offices in the three main airports. Companies must respond to the complaints within 15 working days. In addition, customers who are not satisfied with the response can file an administrative complaint with the Superintendency of Transportation.

In terms of infrastructure, the three principal airports, La Paz (El Alto), Cochabamba (J. Wilstermann), and Santa Cruz (Viru-Viru) were tendered at the same time for a 25-year concession (the bidders expressed no interest in the smaller airports). These are the only three profitable airports, and they represent more than 80 percent of the activity. The winning bidder was SABSA (a division of Airports Group International of the United States), which offered the highest payment to the Airports and Air Navigation Services Administration (*Administración de Aeropuertos y Servicios a la Navegación Aérea*—AASANA), that is, 21 percent of gross revenue. Almost from the start, the contract between AASANA and SABSA has been the subject of intense dispute because of the vagueness of the terms of the agreement, due in part to the country's lack of experience with these types of agreements and the absence of good models to follow. Both AASANA and the government considered the agreement too generous for SABSA and took firm positions in the negotiations. The dispute harmed the reputation of both parties and became a case in point for the critics of privatization. In July 1999, SABSA took its case to arbitration with the London Court of International Arbitration. Although the two parties signed a conciliation agreement in 2000, certain matters are still pending resolution between them. While the government has some objections to the master investment plan presented by SABSA, SABSA has complained of governmental delays in the study and in approving the investment proposals it has submitted.

The other airports are still administered by AASANA and are financed with the revenue generated by the concessions on the other three airports. In most of these airports, maintenance costs are low and unreliable conditions result in flight cancellations or delays. Although none of these airports is profitable, it may be possible to improve the agreement in Trinidad, Puerto Suárez, Tarija, and Sucre.

Given the importance of the roads subsector within the transportation system and the fact that it is the principal area of public sector investment and intervention, the rest of this study will focus on that subsector.

II. The Incomplete Agenda: Key Issues for the Road Sector

Even though many tasks have been identified that are needed to reform the sector, and progress has been made in their implementation, the pace of action continues to be slow, which is aggravated by the incidence of social conflicts. The following are some of the key issues on this incomplete agenda.

THE NEED TO STRENGTHEN STRATEGIC PLANNING CAPACITY AT THE MACRO LEVEL TO ENSURE LOW COST AND HIGH EFFICIENCY IN THE INVESTMENT PROGRAMS, IN ADDITION TO GREATER TRANSPARENCY IN DECISION MAKING

Due to the complexity of Bolivia's transportation system and the constant search for new, more efficient, safer routes for trade, there are several ambitious projects being considered by the government and private operators. The scope and size of these projects are such that they require meticulous studies, because they could potentially entail a great deal of indebtedness and/or harm the environment. To overcome the funding shortage, the government needs to prioritize investments to ensure the best possible economic and social yields.

For example, there is a recent trend to reclassify secondary and tertiary roads and deem them to be primary roads, based on political considerations or social pressure, without a solid technical or economic justification. This is a means to promote investments in certain local routes. This practice weakens the capacity of the SNC to carry out vital works on the essential primary system and ensure proper maintenance. For that reason, it is necessary to clearly define the *measurable* characteristics and conditions that each type of road (primary, secondary, and tertiary) must have and strictly follow those considerations when reclassifying. It is fundamental for the sector's development to see the feeder (departmental) roads and capillary (tertiary) roads as integral elements of the ground transportation system (rather than try to turn them into primary roads).

The absence of a governmental policy to coordinate road development among jurisdictions, based on strategic planning principles to ensure that scarce funds are assigned efficiently and equitability, undermines all possibilities for improvement in the performance of the roads. This is perhaps a consequence of the fact that there is no planning office at the VMT, as exists in most other countries. The role of the VMT as the master planner of the sector needs to be strengthened, which requires expanding its jurisdiction and limiting its participation in other activities, such as the administration of road concessions.

THE NEED TO STRENGTHEN THE INSTITUTIONAL FRAMEWORK AND IMPROVE ADMINISTRATIVE CAPACITY IN THE ROAD SECTOR IN ORDER TO REDUCE THE HIGH COST OF GROUND TRANSPORTATION IN THE COUNTRY

Due to its high transportation costs, Bolivia cannot afford to be inefficient in the administration of its roads. Decentralization of the primary road system has caused the country to lose time, resources and knowledge rather than catch up with the sector's pressing needs. On a national level, the government must continue supporting the institutionalization of the SNC to consolidate the progress achieved to date and continue reinforcing its technical and implementation capacities. The SNC needs to continue improving in areas such as the planning and design of projects, the administration and supervision of contracts, as well as procurement and financial management.

To a large extent, the size and scope of the SNC's operations have given SNC a monopoly on the technical capacity it has been granted. For this reason, with a view toward efficiency and equity, a basic goal is to transfer that knowledge to the local level. So far, the local level's smaller size and major obligations have prevented it from gaining this technical capacity. The design and implementation of a system to accomplish this transfer is a key challenge for the sector.

The administration of roads at the departmental and municipal level is far behind. These governments are ill-prepared to maintain and manage the secondary and rural roads, whose neglect increases isolation and reduces income for the poorer segments of the population. Two important points are: (i) jurisdiction over and ownership of secondary and rural roads is not clearly defined, which creates overlaps in the administration of tertiary roads; and (ii) institutional agreements at these two levels are not always the most efficient. In terms of institutional capacity, deficiencies due to a lack of funds and modern technical tools undermine the development of annual road programs to care for the entire system under their jurisdiction. For that reason, the interventions are not prioritized based on either solid economic criteria or the need to attain results.

THE POOR IN RURAL ZONES LACK ACCESS TO MARKETS AND BASIC SERVICES

More attention needs to be paid to tertiary rural roads, which comprise about 56 percent of the road network. Their poor condition seriously affects the capillarity of the systems, limits economic efficiency, and diminishes the potential income of the poorest segment of the economy. Of the 34,500 kilometers of rural roads, 71 percent are dirt roads. More than half of the system can be traveled only using nonmotorized, animal-driven transportation, which is how most of the agricultural production is transported. The rest of the system is closed to transit during the rainy season due to poor drainage. There is substantial evidence that isolation on account of poor roads helps perpetuate poverty. The rural population's lack of access to markets generates monopolies. Attending to the problems of the rural road network will require active community participation with strategies that could include job opportunities for local community members and an improvement of local capacity to administer the roads. It has been shown in other countries that these tasks can influence a series of variables, such as a decrease in transportation costs, improved access to public services, an increase in the number of jobs, diversification of sources of income, increased local productivity, and, eventually, a gradual reduction in levels of poverty in the areas where community projects are implemented.

UNCERTAINTIES REGARDING FINANCIAL SUSTAINABILITY IN THE ROAD SECTOR INCREASE COSTS AND DELAY PROGRESS

With the creation of and continued support to the CNCV, the government has firmly committed to adequately financing this effort. Nonetheless, the initial commitments appear to be insufficient and an institutional and legal framework is needed to ensure appropriate financing for maintenance of the road network. The CNCV is nothing more than a bank account and does not incorporate mechanisms to increase the funds when the road network needs them. Revenue projected in 2002 through the CNCV is not being reached, even though the collection of tolls has exceeded original projections. The principal reason for this is low revenue from the IEHD, due above all to tax reductions, from 1.1 bolivianos per liter in 2003 to 0.8 bolivianos in 2005. For example, between 2002-2004, collections from the primary system were US$61 million (66 percent of original projections) of which US$28 million were from the IEHD (46 percent of original projections). As a result, only part of the SNC's maintenance program can be financed through this account.

In addition, to partly recoup the costs of the rehabilitation/resurfacing works, tolls need to be updated to reflect savings in operating costs (in some countries, a calculation is made on the savings in operating costs and tolls are increased as a percentage—up to 30 percent—of those estimated savings)..

To summarize, it appears necessary to expand the universe of roads that can benefit from the CNCV funds. Priority should continue to be given to routine maintenance activities and to emergency works, but alternative, stable financing sources need to be identified for periodic repaving tasks. The existing gap is financed through external loans. The strong dependency on external funding sources for maintenance works should be gradually reduced as the road network attains a stable situation.

It is necessary to clarify the role of the departments in the financing of roads. If departmental funds are going to continue playing an important role in co-financing projects of the primary road network, the expected allocations must be accounted for prior to engaging in the works. This is needed to ensure a continual flow of funds to the contractors and thereby avoid future complaints, delays, and increases in the cost of the works.

HIGH COSTS OF TRANSPORTATION, ASSOCIATED WITH WEAK LEGAL AND REGULATORY SYSTEMS, AND A PERCEPTION OF HIGH RISKS

A serious problem is the absence of a general transportation act that strengthens the government's regulatory and legal capacity, which would lend order to the government's various activities within the sector. The legal and regulatory framework for the sector has been only marginally adapted to the new structure. Currently, existing regulations sometimes contradict one another, which creates confusion and considerable risks. The current legal deficiencies are in the following areas: (i) the rights of public transportation users; (ii) legal security for the operators; (iii) responsibilities of the public agencies; (iv) anti-monopoly provisions; (v) the right to use public transportation and its relation to subsidies; (vi) the process for selecting and removing members of the regulatory entities; and (vii) enforcement of existing legislation regarding the performance of the sector. It is advisable that the proposed transportation act be reviewed and enacted. Even without this law, appropriate adaptations made by the various ministries, the regulatory agency, and the Armed Forces would to improve the sector's operation and customer satisfaction. We also recommend that the number of agencies be optimized, and once their functions are clarified, existing gray areas be eliminated regarding the authority of the ministers, the regulators, and the concessionaires.

III. Policy Options

Based on the preceding diagnosis, the government could orient its transportation policy as follows.

- ***Establish a solid planning system with strict scrutiny over the principal public and private investments in the sector to avoid future liabilities for the government.*** This would be achieved through an integrated vision of the road network, based on objective strategic planning criteria, which implies that Bolivia would: (i) strengthen the system by allocating funds on the basis of cost effective policies in accordance with agreed upon, coherent priorities; and (ii) establish incentives to improve performance and results-oriented programs. A proper balance is needed between maintaining the current amount of capital in the regions with different levels of development and expanding the system to support growth in economic activity. The coordination function of the VMT in this regard is essential but will require additional financial and technical support.
- ***Strengthen institutional coordination to integrate the road networks of all the jurisdictions.*** This would make it possible to reduce transportation costs and increase the productivity and competitiveness of local products on international markets. Given the nature of the country's economic activity, there is a structural need to integrate the key transportation systems of the different jurisdictions in order to connect the principal production and consumption centers. With this in mind, it is essential to devote time and effort to prepare coordinated road development plans. This work should be managed under the umbrella of the VMT, which would require the creation of a planning office for the sector.

  The organization of the VMT should be revised by better defining its functions in relation to policies for the sector, standards, rates, and overall planning, while reassigning other implementation activities to the sector's implementation agencies. One idea along these lines, for example, is to transfer the roads concession unit to the SNC. The contracting of suitable personnel is essential to ensure the required experience and technical skills.

- ***Continue the institutionalization of the SNC, with emphasis on professional development and contract management.*** On a national level, priority should continue to be placed on strengthening the SNC and protecting it from political and partisan interests. This institutionalization requires clear definitions and conventions regarding the "customer-provider" relationship that clearly specify the regulatory and supervision functions of the VMT and the implementation task of the SNC. Special emphasis must be placed on improving institutional capacity to optimize design functions, administration of contracts, and supervision of works while strengthening the procurement and administrative functions.
- ***Support rationalized spending on roads and work programs at the department and municipal levels, based on appropriate design and maintenance standards.*** This can be accomplished by adopting technical and economic criteria and emphasizing the need to ensure maintenance and an improved recovery of costs. It would be useful to create incentives for increasing the efficiency of the expenditures. It is also advisable to rely more on the private sector for routine maintenance works. In addition, regardless of the management approach adopted, suitable maintenance programs need to be prepared and developed systematically in each department. In that way, their effectiveness could be measured based on specific results.
- ***Design and implement a program to improve the roads of rural communities, oriented toward improving access and income generation.*** The local and municipal gap in road services needs to be overcome. Accordingly, the strengthening of subnational governments and local communities should be a priority on the policy agenda.
- ***Apply sound financing strategies to guarantee the sustainability of the road sector in a given fiscal framework.*** One of the most urgent needs is to design and implement a sound system to finance the road network, in which the allocation of funds is based on cost-efficient policies. Predictable, reliable sources of financing should be earmarked for maintaining the road network. These financing sources should be sustained through charges to the user. One option could be to establish: (i) guiding principles for allocation of available funds among the different jurisdictions for each type of intervention on the road network; (ii) the role of the departments in financing the system; (iii) the mechanisms by which a proper allocation of local funds can be achieved to ensure continual cash flows for the contracts (the long-expected implementation of the Local Contribution Trusts—*Fideicomisos de Aportes Locales*—would be a step in this direction); and (iv) a gradual phase-out of external financing for road maintenance.
- ***Strengthen the legal and regulatory system.*** It is worth reviewing the proposed transportation act and then proceeding to enact it. This law will clearly define the jurisdiction of the ministers and regulators in the transportation

sector. The institutional strengthening of the sector's agencies are equally deserving of support, as is the improved professional performance of the regulators to maintain their independence.

Bibliography

Sheperd, Jorge. 2005. *Condiciones para descentralización y otras opciones para la administración de caminos en Bolivia,* preliminary version, July 6, 2005.

Sector Regulation System (*Sistema de Regulación Sectorial*—SIRESE). *Informe de Fiscalización 2004,* Superintendency of Transportation, La Paz.

UDAPE. 2005. *Diagnósticos Sectoriales, Sector Transporte* 1992-2003, Economic Policy Analysis Unit (*Unidad de Análisis de Política Económica*—UDAPE). La Paz.

World Bank. 2002. "Road Rehabilitation and Maintenance Project. Project Appraisal Document," Report No. 23625-BO, World Bank, Washington, DC.

Endnotes

1. Bolivia does not have intense economic activity, which results in low traffic densities and hence high unit transportation costs. Further complications are created by the irregular terrain of the highlands and valleys, where floods and landslides are common.
2. This chapter does not cover urban transportation.
3. UDAPE, 2005.
4. Except for urban roads, traffic, even on national roads, is relatively light; it averages some 200 vehicles a day on unpaved roads and 1,000 vehicles a day on paved roads. Cars and light vehicles account for almost 44 percent of the kilometers traveled, trucks account for 30 percent and buses account for 22 percent.
5. Almost all the remaining equity interest is held in equal parts by the two pension funds, AFP Futuro de Bolivia and AFP Previsión BBV, except for a modest percentage acquired by the employees (0.072 percent of FCA and 0.089 percent of FCO).
6. For this reason, it has been estimated that the operational costs of the Andean system are 50 percent higher than those of the eastern system.
7. Although the movement of cargo in general has increased, this increase has not been homogeneous in the two systems. The cargo traffic of the Andean system increased marginally from 1996 to 1998, but then fell 14 percent in terms of tonnage and 23 percent in terms of revenue in 1999, due to a decline in exports of minerals (approximately 50 percent of total cargo by volume) and a general decrease in the mining sector's participation in the economy.
8. The Administrative Contract granted LAB exclusive rights to be Bolivia's airline on international routes under the bilateral and multilateral agreements for a period of six years. VASP bid US$47 million for its 49.99 percent stake in LAB, almost double the company's accounting value.
9. A private line based in Santa Cruz that entered the market in 1993.

19

Environmental Degradation

Ernesto Sánchez-Triana, Carolina Urrutia Vásquez, and Abel Mejía

Summary

Environmental management in Bolivia has made progress, principally in conserving biodiversity and decreasing deforestation. Nonetheless, the poverty in which more than 60 percent of the Bolivian population lives is being aggravated by environmental problems such as air pollution, waterborne diseases, and natural disasters. This is harming the health of the population, especially of children. Furthermore, its cost amounts to an estimated 6.2 percent of GDP per year, a higher percentage than in the majority of countries in the region. Measures that would effectively contribute to improving Bolivia's environmental problems and their relationship with poverty include: (i) safe water and hygiene campaigns; (ii) the design and implementation of a policy for controlling urban and indoor air pollution; and (iii) resettlement of the population and installation of prevention and early warning systems to address natural disasters.

I. Background

Bolivia[1] has abundant renewable and non-renewable natural resources as well as diverse ecosystems and ancestral cultures (including approximately 35 ethnic groups[2]). Despite this wealth of natural resources and of cultural and biological

This chapter has benefited from the contributions of Gabriela Arcos and Maria Donoso-Clark. The authors also thank Dan Biller, Jorge Muñoz, and Fernando Loayza for their comments on the drafts of this work. This chapter has made use of the reports prepared by consultants Juan Carlos Enríquez and Elena Strukova.

diversity, Bolivia is one of the poorest countries in Latin America. Environmental degradation exacerbates the poverty that approximately 65 percent of the Bolivian population suffers. Poverty is aggravated by serious environmental problems associated with urban and indoor air pollution, waterborne diseases linked to the quality of water consumed, natural disasters (particularly floods and landslides) and the degradation of natural resources.

With an infant mortality rate twice the average for Latin America, Bolivia ranks next to last in the region in terms of health indicators. Environmental conditions are at the root of this problem. Waterborne diseases are especially prevalent, particularly in the poorer rural zones (SNIS 2003). Between 2001 and 2003 more than 1.9 million cases of acute diarrheic disease were identified, 80 percent of which were in children age five or younger. In relation to cardiovascular and respiratory diseases, the principal urban centers of Bolivia have a concentration of air particles similar to that of cities such as Santiago, Chile, or Mexico City, with the resulting health consequences for their inhabitants. Natural disasters are another obstacle to eradicating poverty in the country: between 1970 and 1999 Bolivia lost 1 percent of its annual GDP and more than 2,780 lives as the result of 51 disasters (IADB 2001).

Bolivia is starting to apply environmental protection and conservation policies based on the commitments assumed at the 1992 Earth Summit under Agenda 21. By adopting these policies, the country has demonstrated its political will to make changes that enable a more harmonic and integral planning of the country's development. At the same time, it is addressing major challenges such as economic growth compatible with conservation, the sustainable exploitation of natural resources, social equity, institutional efficiency, and social participation (Ministry of Sustainable Development and Planning, 2002).

Over the past five years, the government has adopted measures ranging from restructuring the legal framework to strengthening institutional capacity for exploiting natural resources and improving the environment. Based on international

Table 1. Instruments for Sustainable Development

Environment Act, 1992
Popular Participation Act, 1995
Decentralization Act, 1995
Dialogue Act, 2001.
National Report on Water Resources; 2000
National Strategy for the Clean Development Mechanism; 2001
Environmental Action Plan for the Hydrocarbons Sector; 2001
Report on Mining, Minerals and Sustainable Development (MMSD); 2002
National Forestry Policy, 2002
National Biodiversity Conservation Strategy, 2002

Source: Ministry of Sustainable Development (2002).

donors' funding allocations over recent years, Bolivia has focused on two priorities: forestry resource management and biodiversity conservation (Figure 1). The government has made great progress in establishing a national parks system that covers 20 percent of the country's territory (SERNAP 2005), which is a far larger area than is covered by countries with similar incomes or the Latin America and Caribbean countries. Nonetheless, priority issues, such as greater costs from environmental degradation—which affects human health and directly contributes to accentuating poverty—have received little attention.

The cost of environmental degradation in Bolivia amounts to 6.2 percent of GDP (Strukova, 2005). The categories that contribute the most to the cost of environmental degradation in the country are waterborne diseases, urban and indoor air pollution, natural disasters,[3] and soil erosion and salinization. The health and quality of life issues associated with these environmental problems mainly falls on the poor, particularly on children under the age of five. This chapter examines the environmental problems most closely associated with poverty in Bolivia and proposes a series of public options and strategies aimed at consolidating the government's environmental policy efforts and alternatives to eradicate poverty.

This chapter is divided into eight sections. The second, third, and fourth sections identify Bolivia's most significant environmental problems, which are those associated with the morbidity and mortality of the population, particularly waterborne diseases and urban and indoor air pollution. The fifth section examines the effect of natural disasters on the economy and poverty. The sixth section examines the potential for turning the management of natural resources into a tool for poverty reduction. The seventh section analyzes the institutions responsible for environmental

Figure 1. Natural Protected Areas
(Percentage of Territory)

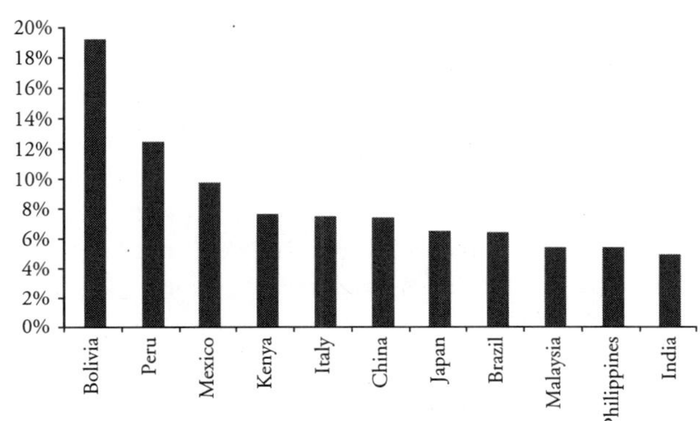

Source: National Protected Areas Service (*Servicio Nacional de Áreas Protegidas*—SERNAP) (2005), World Bank (2005).

Figure 2. Cost of Environmental Degradation

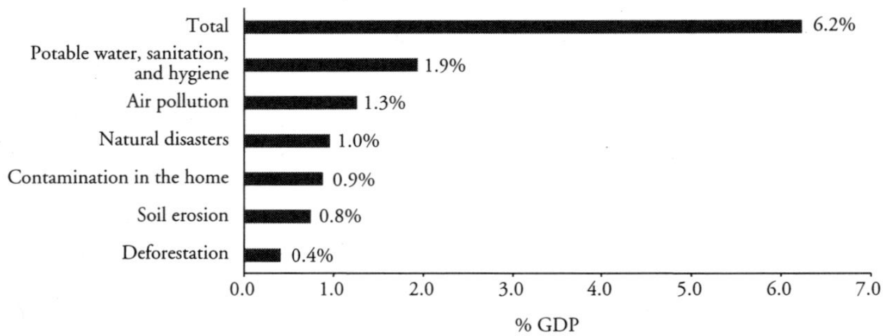

Source: Strukova (2005).

management in Bolivia. Finally, the eighth section provides a series of conclusions and suggests environmental policy alternatives to reduce poverty in Bolivia.

II. Waterborne Diseases

The poorest groups in Bolivia lack potable water and basic sanitation. The infant mortality rate is 75/1000 among children under the age of five, twice the average for Latin America. A good part of this mortality rate is caused by diarrheic diseases, particularly in the poorer rural zones. In 2003, 22 percent of children under the age of five had had an episode of diarrhea in the last two weeks, compared with 19 percent in 1998 (PAHO/WHO, citing ENDSA, 2003). Between 2001 and 2003 more than 1.9 million cases of acute diarrheic disease were recorded. In those three years, 80 percent of the cases occurred in children under the age of five.

Other diseases related to management of the natural environment and basic sanitation include malaria, dengue fever, and Chagas disease. The incidence of these diseases is closely linked to stagnant water and cultural animal-handling practices. In relation to vector-transmitted diseases, during 2000 to 2002, there were more than 62,000 cases of malaria transmitted by the *Plasmodium Vivax*, with an annual rate ranging between 8.8 per thousand in 2000 and 4.3 in 2002. The epidemic in infection by the *P. Falciparum* declined from 11,414 cases in 1998 to 2,536 cases in 2000, and 702 in 2002. Sixty percent of Bolivian territory is considered endemic for Chagas disease due to the presence of the *Triatoma infestans* vector, which affects 700,000 homes located in 169 municipalities and 13,776 communities; it is estimated that 4,000,000 inhabitants are at risk of contracting the disease. According to several studies, 40 percent of this population is probably infected, and 4 percent of the population presents some electrocardiographic alteration, possibly due to Chagas disease (PAHO/WHO, 2004: 3-4, citing SNIS).

According to the Vice Ministry of Basic Sanitation, in 2004 more than 30 percent of the population lacked access to potable water, particularly in the rural areas. In addition, more than 52 percent of the urban population and close to 100 percent of the rural population had no sewage systems. Programs such as the Basic Rural Sanitation Program (*Programa de Saneamiento Básico Rural*—PROSABAR) have made considerable progress in expanding the coverage of water and sanitation services. Nonetheless, water quality and service continuity are still deficient, particularly in the outskirts of the cities and rural areas. There are especially serious problems in cities such as Cochabamba (Departmental Government of Cochabamba, 2000).

At present, there is no policy for the prevention of waterborne diseases. One of the actions promoted by the government in past decades has been the development of potable water systems and sanitation. But this intervention provides only a partial solution. According to a study by the World Bank, actions to provide potable water and sanitation can help prevent 30 percent of diarrheic diseases (Fewtrell et al. 2004). This study concluded that interventions for improved hygiene, such as the hand washing, contribute to reducing diarrheic diseases by an average of 45 percent. These results urge the acceleration of aggressive environmental education campaigns to improve personal hygiene practices.

An analysis of alternatives for preventing waterborne diseases in Bolivia suggests the importance of designing and implementing a safe water program aimed at improving hygiene habits through educational campaigns on hand washing. In addition, this safe water program could include actions to promote disinfection of water for consumption through the use of water disinfectants at the household level. Other actions that should be promoted include the construction of systems to handle sewage and evacuate excrements.

III. Air Pollution

Air pollution is associated with cardiovascular diseases, lung cancer in adults, and acute respiratory diseases (particularly in children), as well as with mortality from diseases such as pneumonia. The most significant sources of particles are motor vehicles, industry (especially the production of bricks, metal foundries, and oil refineries), the burning of agricultural waste (especially from crops such as sugar cane), the burning of trash, and bonfires for certain festivities. Burnt waste from sugar cane harvests creates a high concentration of particles, which causes health problems. This process also notably affects activities in the areas surrounding the plantations. The Bolivian sugar industry is a major economic force, particularly in the department of Santa Cruz, with a cultivated area of 75,000 hectares.

Air pollution is a particularly serious problem in cities whose altitude is more than 2000 meters above sea level, such as La Paz, El Alto, and Cochabamba. In these urban centers, the principal air pollution problems are caused by particles with diameters less than 10 and 2.5 microns (Institute of Ecology/Universidad Mayor de San Andrés, 2000).[4] Concentrations of particles smaller than 10 microns amount to 106 micrograms per cubic meter, which is 2.5 times higher than average for Latin America and the Caribbean, and similar to very polluted cities such as Santiago, Chile, or Mexico City.

The most significant intervention to control air pollution in recent years has been the elimination of lead in motor vehicle gasoline, which has made it possible to reduce the concentration of lead in the air of the principal urban centers. However, few funds or human resources have been allocated for air pollution control. The need to design and implement interventions to reduce particle concentration levels in the air is urgent. Among the possible interventions, the most promising are the substitution of gasoline, diesel, and other liquid fuels with natural gas, improvements in fuel quality, the establishment of vehicle inspection programs, and control of emissions from stationery and diffuse sources, including emissions produced by the burning of agricultural waste. In the future, the possibility of replacing old vehicles with new ones can also be considered, along with the development of transportation infrastructure that promotes high-density urban development models.

IV. Indoor Pollution

The consumption of firewood and other solid and liquid fossil fuels inside homes is associated with chronic obstructive respiratory diseases and acute respiratory infections, particularly in children under the age of five (Harding and Staton, 2002). This type of pollution results from the incomplete combustion of firewood and other fossil fuels inside homes and occurs in both rural and urban areas (Smith, 2005; Ahmed et al., 2005).

Currently, 17 percent of total energy in Bolivia is generated by traditional fuels such as firewood (World Bank, 2005). The consumption of these fuels is higher than average for Latin America and the Caribbean (14.6 percent) or for low-to-moderate income countries (12.3 percent). Almost 80 percent of the rural population uses firewood and other solid fuels for cooking and heating. The burning of fuels inside homes particularly affects the most vulnerable groups, that is, the low-income population, particularly low-income children.

Among the measures to reduce indoor pollution is an improvement of stoves and of systems for cooking food, substitution of solid and liquid fuels by gas, and improvements in home ventilation systems. An analysis conducted in Peru (Strukova and Larsen, 2005) demonstrates a benefit-to-cost ratio higher than four from interventions to improve stove technologies.

V. Natural Disasters

Between 1970 and 1999, total accrued losses to the Bolivian economy from natural disasters amounted to 1 percent of the annual GDP, and more than 2,780 lives were lost on account of 51 disasters during that period (IDB, 2001; Mora, 2001). Bolivia's losses from natural disasters are among the highest in the region. Between 1980 and 2004, five El Niño phenomena affected Bolivia, principally in the form of floods, droughts, frost, and hail.[5] The El Niño of 1982-1983 was particularly severe and resulted in economic losses to the agricultural sector in terms of damage to genetic material in potato seeds (Muñoz, 2005). These phenomena have demonstrated Bolivia's vulnerability to a variety of risks. It is estimated that in this period, losses caused by El Niño were US$527 million (Strukova, 2005).

Landslides in the rainy season mainly affect the roads system and the outlying zones of the country's principal urban areas. The places most affected over the past ten years were the outskirts of La Paz and the municipality of Camargo in the department of Chuquisaca. In 1992, a landslide in the mining town of Llipi caused 209 deaths. The more recent landslides in 1997 and 1998 in the communities of Cotahuma, Mokotoro, and the Kupini area, in the department of La Paz, caused 24 deaths, destroyed 264 homes, and affected 523 families. An unprecedented hailstorm on February 19, 2002, in the city of La Paz caused 70 deaths and damages estimated at more than US$70 million (European Commission, 2005). In February 2006, natural disasters in the department of La Paz alone affected 40 percent of the secondary roads; eight bridges will have to be reconstructed; some 18,000 families were affected; 220 homes were totally destroyed; and 34 thousand hectares of crops were lost. Losses amounted to US$40 million, and another US$10 million will be required for repairs (*La Razón*, 2006).

Floods and droughts are not associated exclusively with the El Niño phenomenon. Relatively frequent during the rainy season, floods cause small and moderate disasters in a good part of the country. Droughts often recur, their area of incidence is quite large, and they are a major cause of migration from the countryside to the cities. Ecosystems such as the highlands are very vulnerable to droughts (given their predominant semi-arid conditions), hail (given the natural hydrometeorological conditions), and frost (given the prevailing temperatures).

Disasters have been a recurring reality in Bolivia. They directly affect the country's development, because they hurt its economic results, weaken its social well-being, cause capital losses, and damage the roads and energy infrastructure. Such losses, in turn, influence economic indicators such as inflation and production, which in turn increase poverty.

Investment in structural and non-structural measures would help to reduce vulnerability to natural disasters,. Structural measures include the resettlement of populations residing in floodplains, flood control works, use of wetlands as a buffer against rising waters, and erosion control/slope stability works. Certain very low cost non-structural measures include zoning of land usage, the design of emergency response and service programs, and the preparation and equipping of the citizenry for such events.

VI. Exploitation of Natural Resources

Historically, natural resources have played a very important role in the national economy. The extraction and exportation of natural resources (silver, tin, gold, gas, rubber, hydrocarbons, soybeans, and other resources) have been key for Bolivia's development and have had a major influence on the country's political life, population settlement, economic structure, and social organization. Environmental degradation and the over-exploitation of resources is leading to the impoverishment of the country's natural wealth. This situation is closely linked to poverty, since it reduces the possibility that present and future generations can benefit from the sustainable use of natural resources. Below, the principal phenomena involving degradation of the environment and of natural resources are described, along with their relationship to poverty.

Forestry Resources

Bolivia's forested area comprises nearly 54 million hectares, of which more than eight million are under legal forestry management. The forestry sector contributes approximately 2 percent to the economy. In 2003, forestry product exports amounted to 11 percent of total exports. Bolivia ranks first in the world in formal, voluntary certified tropical forests. Sustainable production of lumber surpasses 20 million cubic meters per year. Forestry production companies have been granted concessions to 5.4 million hectares, which corresponds to 64 percent of the country's total forestry production area (Ministry of Sustainable Development and Planning 2003). As compared with other countries, Bolivia does not yet fully exploit its lumber potential. In Chile, for example, forestry production amounts to almost 4 percent of GDP and creates approximately 130,000 jobs (Instituto Forestal, 2005).

Deforestation is estimated to be taking place at a rate of 160,000 hectares a year, corresponding to an annual rate of 0.3 percent, significantly less than the rate for countries such as Ecuador or Mexico and similar to the rate for Colombia or Peru. Despite the structural adjustment reforms that Bolivia has undertaken since 1985, recent studies (Kishor et al., forthcoming) indicate that no more than 2 percent of total deforestation can be attributed to increased logging associated with macroeconomic reforms. It would be worthwhile to assess the damage associated with deforestation in Bolivia. It would seem that the damage corresponds to a loss of biodiversity in the Amazon region; however, there are no studies that identify the groups that benefit from or are harmed by deforestation.

Protected Areas

Since its creation in 1992, the National Protected Areas System (SERNAP) has experienced exponential growth. In December 2005, national protected areas covered approximately 15 percent of the country's territory, while departmental and municipal protected areas covered an additional 7 percent. The SERNAP encompasses most of the country's biodiversity, the majority of its representative ecosystems, approximately 80 percent of its species of higher plants and ferns, and in the taxa of vertebrates, between 65 percent and 80 percent of its species (SERNAP, 2005).

Results of pilot production projects in three national protected areas have demonstrated that the sustainable management of natural resources in these areas can provide economic and social benefits. As of 2005, with an approximate investment of US$500,000 in technical assistance, minor works and inputs, approximately 10 percent of the population that inhabits the national protected areas has already received direct benefits from these projects (Arcos, 2006). In Pilón Lajas, the production of honey and its derivatives increased by at least 75 percent (from 1,600 Kg. to 2,800 Kg.), which benefited 35 settler producers and 27 indigenous Chiman–Mosetene producers. In El Palmar, the Quechua inhabitants' income from the marketing of agricultural products has increased by 30 percent, and production has been substantially diversified. In Pilón Lajas, income from the sale of coffee increased by 50 percent. In Manuripi, diversification of agricultural products and forestry species has improved the quality of food and provided new marketing alternatives (Arcos, 2006).

Mining

Mining is an activity of great economic importance. Between 1980 and 2000, it contributed an annual average of 5.1 percent of GDP. Cooperative and small-scale mining, in which more than 70,000 families work, is particularly polluting. The environmental impact of mining is principally due to: (i) the age of the mines (creation of environmental liabilities) and their size; (ii) the treatment of liquid wastes (tailings); (iii) mercury pollution; and (iv) environmental problems created by small-scale and artesanal mining (McMahon et al. 1999; World Bank, 1997).

Only one study has been conducted in Bolivia, to assess the effects in economic terms of traditional mining on premature mortality and morbidity (*Fundación Medio Ambiente y Minería*, MEDMIN 2000). The study made a cost-benefit analysis of the construction of a tailings dike in San Antonio, Potosí, whose benefits were calculated at US$28.4 million/year. Most of the benefits correspond to reducing mortality associated with the tailings (Escobari, 2003.).

Mining is an activity that can promote economic development in the west of the country, which has the highest levels of poverty. The market situation in 2005 and early 2006 has been favorable to mining. Taking proper advantage of these circumstances could contribute to reducing poverty. One alternative in the fight against poverty that needs to be examined is to strengthen cooperative and small-scale mining.

Soil Erosion and Salinization

Nearly 41 percent of Bolivia's national territory has lost its production capacity due to erosion and desertification (Ministry of Sustainable Development and Planning 2002). For example, in western Bolivia, in the zones of Oruro, Potosí, and Tarija, close to 45,000 square kilometers have low soil productivity on account of erosion. The highland *minifundios* accelerate soil degradation processes. In the northern highlands, the production area of family agricultural units is one to three hectares. In the central and southern highlands, the area of agricultural production units is three to five hectares. Demographic pressure has lead to more intensive use of the soil, which increases vulnerability to wind and water erosion. Excess grazing and other agricultural activities have contributed to soil compression and salinization. It is important to quantify the magnitude and rate of soil erosion and salinization and analyze alternatives for intervening cost-efficiently to counteract soil degradation. Such a study would make it possible to identify the population groups most affected by this problem and strategies adopted to address it.

Water Resources

In relation to its water resources, Bolivia can be divided into three areas or basins, which correspond to the eastern area (a tropical and subtropical region), the western area (the arid, semi-arid, and sub-humid dry region), and the Titicaca basin. The hydrographic system consists of three large basins: the Amazon basin, which measures approximately 724,000 km^2 and covers 66 percent of Bolivia's territory; the closed ("endorreic") basin, which measures 145,081 km^2 (13 percent); and the Río de la Plata basin, which covers 229,500 km^2 (21 percent) of the nation's territory (Mattos and Crespo, 2000). The Amazon basin has a good flow of water, but there are flooding problems. The Paraná basin represents approximately 42 percent of the total area of Bolivia and has desertification problems (Ministry of Sustainable Development and Planning, 1997). The quantity and quality of hydrological information is very poor. Despite isolated efforts to manage water resources, the sectors involved in their use continue to act separately, in accordance with the different laws for each sector. In fact, the Electricity Act, the Hydrocarbons Act, the Mining Code, and the Environmental Act each regulate water resources in their own way and set rules for their use without developing common usage criteria or priorities.

The contamination of surface water and aquifers results from domestic municipal wastewater dumping, dumping by industry and mines, runoffs, and non-specific sources. The greatest percentage of the pollution load is due to diffuse dumping from agricultural and fishing activities and runoffs in urban areas. There are no regulations or controls over major dumping from non-specific sources, despite its volume and, in some cases, its toxicity—due to concentrations of organochlorinated compounds such as aldrin and endrin. Rivers that cross the principal urban cores of the country suffer from high levels of organic contamination and in some cases anaerobic situations. Examples include the Choqueyapu River in La Paz, the Río Rocha in Cochabamba, and the Pirai in Santa Cruz. These rivers and other surface waters receive solid domestic municipal waste and hazardous industrial or hospital wastes (Mattos and Crespo, 2000).

With respect to municipal wastewater, some cities have wastewater treatment plants, particularly anaerobic and facultative stabilization ponds. Such is the case in Santa Cruz, Cochabamba, Tarija, Oruro, Trinidad, and El Alto. With respect to industrial dumping, the number of establishments that comply with industrial discharge standards is very low. In Santa Cruz, for example, out of the 600 largest industries, which include tanneries, battery factories, sugar refineries, and the production of vegetable oils, only a few pretreat their wastes (JICA, 2003).

Mining is one of the major sources of water pollution. In some mining areas, such as Potosí, acid mine drainage occurs. In others, such as the mining area of Oruro, wastewater discharge has a high concentration of heavy metals, such as arsenic, lead, and zinc. In Chuquisaca, there are high concentrations of nickel and copper sulfates in discharged wastewater. Mining discharges in Oruro dumped into the Poopó and Uru Uru lakes have reduced fishing production and have altered the trophic chains. These environmental impacts have caused social problems in population centers surrounding these lakes, which have traditionally used these water resources for human consumption and irrigation. The mining of gold in the Amazon causes a discharge of mercury, in addition to health problems provoked by toxic pollutants such as methyl-mercury (JICA, 2003).

VII. Institutional Analysis

Historically, the environmental management priorities in Bolivia has focused on three actions: (i) establishment of a system of protected areas to guarantee the conservation of biodiversity; (ii) control of deforestation; and (iii) mitigation of environmental impacts from mining and hydrocarbons activities and the construction of infrastructure. The definition of these priorities was a response to recommendations from international organizations, including bilateral, multilateral, and non-governmental organizations. Also, for historic reasons, the identification of environmental problems associated with the poverty suffered by the majority of the population has been relegated to a second rung. Issues regarding environmental health and vulnerability to natural disasters have received little attention, which is reflected in the great regulatory gaps and low levels of policy development and compliance.

Emphasis on the rational exploitation of renewable natural resources has significant precedents, such as the Waters Act of 1906, which institutionalized the assignment of tradable water rights, based on shifts (strictly controlled by time) and on the payment of monthly or annual quotas for the maintenance of channels and irrigation infrastructure. In many valleys, the right to irrigation water is more valuable than land (Escobar and Muñoz Escobar, 1997:16.).

The Environment Act (LMA 1333/92), enacted in April 1992, established a general framework for environmental planning and management and rational exploitation of natural resources. This general framework was complemented in 1995 with the Popular Participation Act and the Administrative Decentralization Act, and in 1996 with the Agrarian Reform Act (INRA) and the Forestry Act.

Regulations for the exploitation of forestry resources and conservation of biodiversity have been developed and implemented with greater enthusiasm than for other areas. Emphasis on the conservation of forestry resources and biodiversity is due in large measure to the establishment of funds such as the National Fund for the Environment (*Fondo Nacional para el Medio Ambiente*—FONAMA) or the Foundation for the Development of Natural Protected Area Systems (*Fundación para el Desarrollo de Sistema Áreas Naturales Protegidas*—FUNDESNAP), both of which have focused their activities on financing the SERNAP. The SERNAP, created in 1992, now has 22 protected areas that cover almost 20 percent of Bolivian territory. Out of these, the National Protected Areas Service (*Servicio Nacional de Áreas Naturales Protegidas*—SERNAP) implements management plans in 16 parks that cover 12 percent of the nation's territory.

Emphasis on the conservation of forestry resources and biodiversity is also demonstrated by the establishment of a Vice Ministry for Natural Resources and Forestry Development within the Ministry of Sustainable Development and Planning. The Ministry also uses environmental impact assessments and environmental impact statements as a central planning and management instrument. Elimination of the Ministry of Sustainable Development at the start of 2006 and the partial incorporation of its functions into a new Ministry of Planning mark a turning point in environmental management (Enríquez, 2006).

The environmental planning and management system contemplated in the regulations to the Environment Act follows the environmental impact assessment principle, which was incorporated into models developed in the United States in 1969 (NEPA, 1969) and then extended to more than 100 countries, including most Latin American countries. Licenses or permits demand an environmental impact statement for new activities and an environmental update for those already commenced. These licenses set mandatory conditions, actions, and specific environmental control measures for investment projects. Licensing requires the submission of environmental fact sheets to determine the category of the environmental impact assessment studies needed, such as the preparation of statements assessing the environmental impacts produced. To mitigate environmental impacts, the legislation demands the design of Prevention and Mitigation Plans and Environmental Implementation and Monitoring Plans.

The government's enormous limitations for guaranteeing compliance with environmental standards result in minimally adequate monitoring and supervision. A reconsideration of the country's environmental priorities is also needed to effectively address the aspects that most affect economic growth, poverty reduction, and the welfare and health of the population.

The regulations to the Environment Act issued in the second half of the 1990s emphasized the use of command and control instruments, as well as administrative procedures. The regulations establish procedures for granting environmental licenses or permits (General Regulations on Environmental Management and Environmental Prevention and Control) and set requirements for the control of water and air pollution, including, for example, the management of hazardous materials and solid waste (Table 2).

Regulations to control water and air pollution, such as for the management of hazardous materials and solid waste, were modeled on environmental regulations and quality standards from developed countries, whose environmental problems are completely different from those of Bolivia (Escobar and Muñoz, 1997). For example, the principal atmospheric pollutant in Bolivia is particles that measure less than 2.5 microns in diameter. Bolivia has standards to control other pollutants larger in size than 2.5 microns. In addition to the inevitable inefficiencies of establishing environmental quality standards that respond to the problems of developed countries, these standards are clearly regressive (Escobar and Muñoz, 1997).

VIII. Policy Options

To reduce the environmental impact on poverty in Bolivia, environmental policy could primarily focus on the control of air and indoor air pollution, the reduction of waterborne diseases, and the reduction of vulnerability to natural disasters (Table 3). One measure to reduce air pollution is to substitute liquid and solid fuels with natural gas. The most effective mechanism to guarantee the fuel substitution is based on the fuel pricing policy. Fuels could be taxed depending upon their capacity to create pollutants such as particles that measure less than 2.5 microns in diameter. Accordingly, it would be advisable to minimize taxes on cleaner fuels such as natural gas and, eventually, to consider programs to substitute solid and liquid fuels with natural gas.

Table 2. Bolivian Environmental Legislation: Environmental Quality

Law or Regulation	*Series and Number*	*Date*
Environment Act	Law 1333	April 1992
Regulations to the Environment Act	DS 24176	December 1995
Environmental Regulations for the Hydrocarbons Sector	DS 24335	July 1996
Environmental Regulations for the Mining Sector	DS 24782	July 1997
Expansion of terms for the submission of environmental impact statements in the mining sector	DS 25419	June 1999

Source: Escobari (2003).

In the future, based on cost-benefit studies and in keeping with the actual response capacity of different social groups, other pollution control measures could be introduced. For example, reform of the Environment Act's regulations could help control emissions of particles that measure less than 2.5 microns in diameter. This could be accomplished through a series of measures regarding contamination rates, environmental quality standards, and standards for emission of precursors to particles with a diameter of less than 2.5 microns (for example, control of these types of atmospheric emissions from industry, motor vehicles, and the burning of agricultural waste). Measures to control indoor pollution, in addition to the substitution of fuels by gas, include the use of efficient stoves and improved ventilation in homes.

To reduce the incidence of waterborne diseases, the interventions proven to be most effective are educational campaigns on hygiene (for example, hand washing), home disinfection of water for consumption, and the development of sewage systems and systems for the evacuation of feces. At a policy level, it is important to reform quality standards for potable water to make them more efficient and effective in controlling pathogens, measured in terms of probability of coliforms.

In order to reduce vulnerability to natural disasters, it is urgent to invest in structural and non-structural measures. Structural measures include the resettlement of populations that reside in floodplains, flood control works, use of wetlands as a buffer against rising waters, and erosion control/slope stability works. Non-structural measures include zoning of land usage, the design of emergency response and service programs, and the preparation and equipping of the citizenry for such events.

On an institutional level, it would be important to reconsider environmental management priorities as a basis for adjusting the respective legal, regulatory, and institutional framework. These adjustments should seek to generalize environmental management, with an emphasis on results-based management. In that way, they would concretely contribute to reducing waterborne and respiratory/cardiovascular diseases, alleviating poverty, and encouraging economic growth. The assignment of specialized human resources to achieve these objectives is a priority task in the short term.

With respect to the exploitation and conservation of natural resources, it is important to continue reinforcing the protected areas system, particularly by obtaining international grants for this purpose. One measure to consider is increased citizen participation in the management and exploitation of forestry and biodiversity resources. Their management could also be decentralized by assigning jurisdiction to communities that have traditionally inhabited these lands. Another measure, which might work to reduce deforestation rates, is to reform how property rights are awarded over idle and national lands. Finally, it is important to consolidate formal and informal rules for managing water resources. Decentralizing the assignment of usage rights and control over discharges would grant jurisdiction to users' associations established at the basin level. The structure of the new Ministry of Water includes a General Directorate of Basins. That entity could promote actions to strengthen decentralization processes for the management of water resources (Enríquez, 2006).

Table 3. Actions Recommended in the Short Term

Objective	*Actions Recommended in the Short Term*
Control of Air Pollution	• Substitute liquid and solid fuels with natural gas, based on a fuel pricing policy. • Reduce taxes on cleaner fuels. • Reform the regulations to the Environment Act to control emissions of particles with a diameter of less than 2.5 microns.
Control of Indoor Air Pollution	• Substitute fuels with gas. • Promote use of efficient stoves and improvements in the ventilation of homes.
Reduction of Waterborne Diseases	• Educational campaigns to promote hygiene (for example, the washing of hands). • Household disinfection of water for consumption. • Develop sewage systems and systems for the evacuation of excrement. • Reform quality standards for potable water.
Reduction of Vulnerability to Natural Disasters	*Structural:* • Resettlement of populations residing in floodplains. • Flood control, erosion control, and slope stability works. • Use of wetlands to buffer rising waters. *Non-structural:* • Zoning of land usage. • Design emergency response and service programs. • Equip and prepare the citizenry.
Institutions	• Reconsider environmental management priorities. • More widespread application of environmental management. • Results-based management. • Assign specialized human resources. • Create a Vice Ministry on Environmental Health within the Ministry of Health. • Create a Vice Ministry on Reduction of Vulnerability to Disasters within the Ministry of Water.
Exploitation and Conservation of Natural Resources	• Greater participation of the citizenry. • Reform the manner of awarding property rights over idle and national lands. • Decentralize the assignment of usage rights and control over discharges and grant jurisdiction to users' associations established at the basin level.

Bibliography

Arcos, Gabriela. 2006. "Notes for a Policy on Exploitation and Conservation of Natural Resources in Bolivia." World Bank. Washington, DC.

Britton, Barbara. 2000. "Comparative Risk Assessment. Setting Priorities for Urban Environmental Management in Developing Countries." Environmental Health Project.

Bruce, Nigel, Pérez-Padilla, Rogelio, and Albalak, Rachel. 2000. "Indoor Air Pollution in Developing Countries: A Major Environmental and Public Health Challenge." World Health Organization. Washington, DC.

Enríquez, Juan Carlos. 2006. *Bolivia: Notas para una Política sobre Medio Ambiente y Pobreza en Bolivia*. Consultant Report for the World Bank. La Paz, Bolivia.

European Commission. 2005. *Propuesta País "Reducción de Riesgos y Desastres Naturales en Bolivia."* For the New DIPECHO Plan of Action in the Andean Community. April 2005. La Paz, Bolivia.

Escobar, J., and Muñoz, J. 1997. "Marco regulatorio e instrumentos de mercado de la política ambiental en Bolivia," Working Paper 55/97. *Unidad de Análisis de Políticas Sociales* - UDAPSO. La Paz, Bolivia.

Escobari, Jorge. 2003. "Problemática Ambiental en Bolivia", *Unidad de Análisis de Políticas Sociales y Económicas (UDAPE)*." La Paz, Bolivia.

Harding, M.H., and Staton, D.M. 2002. "Health and Environmental Effects of Cooking Stove Use in Developing Countries." Harvard University www.med.harvard.edu/chge/textbook/papers/staton.pdf. December 8.

Henninger, N., and Hammond, A. 2002. "Environmental Indicators Relevant to Poverty Reduction." World Bank. Washington, DC.

Instituto de Ecología/Universidad Mayor de San Andrés, Karl Franzens University (Austria), and Municipality of Cochabamba. 2000. *Evaluación de la contaminación atmosférica en Cochabamba*. Bolivia.

Instituto Forestal (INFOR), 2005, *El Sector Forestal Chileno en una Mirada*, Ministry of Agriculture, Chile.

International Institute for Environment and Development. 2002. "Mining and Minerals of South America in Transition towards Sustainable Development." London, United Kingdom.

Japan International Cooperation Agency. 2003. "Environmental Analysis." La Paz, Bolivia.

Kishor, N, Mani M., and Constantino, L. Publication pending. "Does Stabilization Harm the Environment? The Case of the Bolivian Forest Sector," World Bank, Washington, DC.

La Razón, Digital Edition. 2006. February 16, 2006. La Paz, Bolivia.

Mattos, Roger, and Crespo, Alberto. 2000. *Informe de la gestión del agua en Bolivia*. La Paz, Bolivia.

Ministry of Sustainable Development and Planning. 1997. *Programa nacional de lucha contra la desertificación*. La Paz, Bolivia.

———. 2001. *Informe del estado de los recursos hídricos*. La Paz, Bolivia.

———. 2001. *Informe de calidad ambiental en Bolivia*. La Paz, Bolivia.

———. 2002. *Informe Río + 10*. La Paz, Bolivia.

Municipal Council of La Paz, Ministry of Sustainable Development and Planning, Prefecture of La Paz. *"Control de la calidad del aire en la ciudad de La Paz en la fiesta de San Juan."* La Paz, Bolivia.

National Information Health System, (*Sistema Nacional de Información en Salud—*

SNIS); Ministry of Health and Sports, Republic of Bolivia, (2000, 2001, 2002, 2003). *Estadísticas de Salud.* La Paz, Bolivia.
National Protected Areas Service (*Servicio Nacional de Áreas Protegidas*—SERNAP). 2005. "*Plan Estratégico para el Desarrollo de Áreas Naturales Protegidas,*" www.sernap.gov.bo. In preparation. La Paz, Bolivia.
PAHO/WHO Representation Bolivia. 2004. "General Situation and Trends. Specific Health Problems. Response of the Health System." La Paz, Bolivia.
Regional System for Basic Health Data (*Sistema Regional de Datos Básicos en Salud*). 2004. *"Bolivia. Perfil de País. Resumen del Análisis de Situación y Tendencias de Salud."* Version updated as of November 9, 2004. La Paz, Bolivia.
Smith, Kirk R. 1986. "Biomass Combustion and Indoor Air Pollution." *Environmental Management* 10.
Strukova, Elena. 2005. "Benefit-Cost Analysis of Alternative Interventions for Environmental Policy in Bolivia." Consultant Report. Washington DC.
Strukova, Elena, and Larsen, Bjorn. 2005. "Benefit-Cost Analysis of Alternative Interventions for Environmental Policy in Peru." Consultant Report. Washington, DC.
UNDP. 1998. "Human Development in Bolivia." La Paz, Bolivia.
World Bank. 2005. "The Little Green Data Book." From the World Development Indicators. World Bank. Washington, DC.
World Resources Institute. 2000. "World Resources 2000-2001: People and Ecosystems: The Fraying Web of Life." Washington, DC.

Endnotes

1. Bolivia measures approximately 1,098,580 km^2. The country has three major geographic regions: the tropical plains, the Andean mountain range, and the Sub-Andean region.
2. In 2001, almost 56 percent of Bolivians identified themselves as Quechuas or Aymaras, and 6 percent as Guaranís or as one of the 32 minority ethnic groups of the Bolivian Amazon. Sixty percent of the population is under the age of 25 and 7 percent is over the age of 65 (INE, 2001 Census).
3. Despite the magnitude of the impact of natural disasters in Bolivia, there is a clear need to improve information with regard to the topic. There is no source of data that includes all categories of infrastructure and productivity losses, which normally account for 80 percent of direct losses from natural disasters. The statistics cited in this chapter come from the existing literature, cited in the bibliography, which in many cases varies significantly.
4. There is no supervision network for air quality in Bolivia; therefore, we do not have a timeline of data on the concentration of atmospheric pollutants in the country's principal urban centers. Measurements have been taken of pollutants in La Paz, El Alto, Cochabamba, and Santa Cruz through a project promoted by Swiss Contact.
5. The periods are the following: (i) 1982-1983 (very strong); (ii) 1987 (weak); (iii) 1991-1992 (weak); (iv) 1993-1996 (no presence); and (v) 1997-1998 (weak).

20

Land Policy

Malcolm Childress

Summary

This chapter notes five main challenges for Bolivia as it strives to reduce poverty and promote growth, gain social stability, and achieve environmental sustainability. These five challenges are to: (i) complete land regularization and restore confidence in the institutions charged with this task; (ii) adopt land distribution mechanisms that are driven by objectives and employ multiple instruments; (iii) improve land taxation; (iv) regularize land ownership for indigenous peoples; and (v) maintain the integrity of protected areas and forest reserves. This policy note argues that land regularization must be completed quickly, by reviewing the status of the largest agricultural properties, in order to restore credibility to the National Agrarian Reform Institute. It advises establishing land redistribution targets and reaching those goals via a pragmatic approach that includes mechanisms such as land purchase programs. Under this approach, land taxation reform would focus on updating the property lists and their corresponding valuations as the cornerstone for fiscal decentralization. Indigenous land claims would be accelerated through procedural improvements, and the basis for indigenous land administration would be improved. Finally, this chapter proposes strengthening the Protected Areas System and forest management by increasing management professionalization and investing in communities in and around these areas.

I. The Challenge: Land Policy Implementation that Addresses Rural Poverty, Inequality, and Insecurity

This chapter describes the main challenges Bolivia faces regarding land issues and specifies goals related to growth and poverty reduction. It advocates dealing directly with the problems of the unequal distribution of land, tenure insecurity, and financial incentives to sustainable land use. These problems directly contribute to an increase in poverty, slow growth, social conflict, and political instability.

Land policies need to support a model of growth and poverty reduction that generates jobs, improves living standards, promotes social inclusion and a positive investment climate, and maintains environmental sustainability. The unequal distribution of land and capital; segmented and exclusive land markets; forest and indigenous land management challenges; the scarcity of arable lands; and poor connections to markets in the densely populated highlands tend to keep employment levels down in the rural areas and perpetuate rural poverty. This chain of factors drives migration toward urban centers, which not only fails to provide quality employment but accelerates ecological deterioration and social conflict.

About 38 percent of the Bolivian population lives in rural areas whose economy is based primarily on the land and its resources. Unless more attention is paid on a concerted and sustained basis to the conversion of natural resources (in other words, forests and lands) as a means for reducing poverty rather than as sources of conflict, Bolivia will likely continue down a path of slow, unequal, unstable growth. This situation could last for another generation, until the urban areas are able to generate significant improvements in the quality of employment. This chapter contends that it is possible to begin reversing the inequitable and poverty-perpetuating model of the past with a new model that combines redistributive and progressive justice (meaning justice that respects the rule of law, generates greater equality, and is impartial) with job creation policies to improve agricultural productivity and the service provision in rural areas. This land policy is completely compatible with market incentives. It is also likely to improve existing land use, wherein the forest is largely protected and cleared areas in the eastern plains are subjected to intensive farming. An improved land policy framework could help rationalize land usage.

Between 1996 and 2006, the land policy framework pointed in the right direction of making land ownership more equitable, secure, and sustainable. Yet it was inconsistently and often ineffectively implemented. Law 1715, better known as INRA, has not met social expectations, particularly in reducing underutilized lands and in achieving equitable land distribution. Land taxation is failing to create incentives that improve land usage and open land markets. The granting of title on indigenous lands has progressed, but the process has been characterized by conflicts and unresolved claims. A system of protected areas and forestry management is in place, but some areas are illegally exploited or cleared for raising livestock, soy cultivation or small agriculture. New approaches are need to achieve the same goals, but with better tools and more effective institutional solutions. In place of past approaches, which have been legalistic, procedure-driven, and shown to be neither sufficient nor effective, the new approach and institutions could gain credibility by being guided by specific objectives.

Where the policy framework between 1996 and 2006 failed, new approaches are needed to improve the use of natural resources and promote inclusive agricultural development and fulfill the promises of indigenous autonomy, forest preservation, and decentralization of local services. All this needs to be closely linked to a justice system that works in favor of the poor. Land is one of the flashpoints of conflict and has a key role in contributing to growth and equality in Bolivia. The way in which land access, land use, and land administration are handled will have a major impact on productivity, employment, and equality. Four key facts regarding land tenure in Bolivia underscore this point and hint at why these issues will continue to play an essential role in the social and economic development of the country for the foreseeable future.

- **Although Bolivia is a large country (almost three times the size of Germany), arable land is relatively scarce.** Out of a total of 1,098,580 square kilometers, almost half is covered by forests and a third is semi-desert or arid. Only some eight million hectares can be classified as potentially productive for agricultural purposes; and of these, almost 2.2 million have never been farmed. In recent years, the average area cultivated has been approximately 2.5 million hectares.
- **Land distribution is highly unequal.** About 10 percent of the farm units (or approximately 60,000 property units) control 90 percent of the farmland. The distribution is also very different on the plains as compared to in the highlands and valleys. On the plains, medium-sized and large estates predominate, whereas in the highlands and valleys, small farms are the norm. It is estimated that there are close to 550,000 smallholder families and approximately 50,000 commercial agricultural companies. Close to 450,000 smallholder families work the land in the altiplano and approximately 100,000 do so in the plains.
- **A large area of forest and agricultural frontier remains in the east and north of the country, in areas where local and federal government agencies have a limited presence.** Considerable pressures promote deforestation and settlement on lands that are not suitable for permanent agriculture, including lands that are situated within the protected areas and forest reserves. One of the main challenges for land policy is to help channel the existing demand for rural land into areas better suited for agricultural development.
- **The rural sector is extremely poor, with more than 80 percent of the population living below the poverty line.** Poverty in Bolivia is mostly rural, more than anywhere else, and income in these areas comes from the land. This is the main reason why land policies are essential for reducing poverty.

On the basis of these facts, the Bolivian Poverty Reduction Strategy Paper (PRSP) of March 2001 and the World Bank Country Assistance Strategy of February 2004 recommend redirecting a portion of public expenditures toward high visibility programs that respond to underlying factors of the social conflict over land, especially in sensitive regions. The PRSP prioritizes the need to address the problem of land, not only as a legal security issue, but also from the point of view of land redistribution. To this end, the PRSP outlined the following strategic measures: (i) expanding and improving productive infrastructure; (ii) broadening and strengthening access to land as a resource; (iii) increasing competitiveness; and (iv) diversifying non-agricultural employment opportunities.

While there has been significant progress, numerous issues remain unresolved. A redirection of policy, a stronger emphasis on **implementation driven by objectives** and a better system of transparency and accountability would allow for more visible progress. The following sections analyze how the current policies could be modified to achieve strategic goals, with an approach aimed at accomplishing the following five objectives:

1. Complete land regularization and restore public confidence in the institutions charged with this task;
2. Adopt land distribution mechanisms that are driven by objectives, not process, and that employ multiple instruments;
3. Improve land taxation;
4. Regularize land ownership for indigenous peoples; and
5. Maintain the integrity of protected areas and forest reserves.

II. Complete Land Regularization and Restore Confidence in Land Institutions

Land regularization or title clearance is the main objective of the current land policy based on the INRA Act. This law defines the regularization of agricultural property as an interim technical-legal procedure that allows for the provision of property titles through property awards. It also provides for the resolution of land tenancy conflicts, the annulment of spurious titles, certification of agricultural property regularization, and the creation of an official rural land cadastre. Agricultural property regularization consists of two major sequential stages: (i) review and clarification of the land tenure, under the responsibility of INRA; and (ii) issuance of resolutions to confirm, authenticate, amend, or annul existing property titles, which comes under the jurisdiction of the office of the President of the Republic. Since 1996, INRA has succeeded in clarifying the land tenure situation of 15.4 million hectares, and the work continues for 31.7 million additional hectares, out of a total of 107.5 million hectares that need to be regularized.

Despite these achievements, many challenges remain, and the institutions in charge of land issues, particularly the INRA and the Agrarian Tribunals, have suffered the erosion of public confidence. They have been accused of regularizing and granting titles of large land parcels of dubious legality. Moreover, the judges of the Agrarian Tribunals have made questionable decisions, complaints regarding contractors abound, and an enormous backlog of unissued titles remains. Resolving these issues and completing the title clearance process will take time; therefore, an extension of Law 1715 is needed. By working to complete the title clearance process, the country can provide security to the property owners. But this process must be complete in a way that is fair to all.

Title clearance activities beyond the current ones should be implemented on the basis of a larger demand (i.e., demand from a municipality or a group of municipalities) and linked to other development interventions such as the extension of rural financing and technology or marketing improvements. Community participation would help make the title clearance process more transparent and improve its acceptance. With regard to the enormous volume of titles that need to be processed, simply eliminating the requirement that the President personally sign off each title would ease the backlog. Perhaps most important, the title clearance process must carefully examine large properties (over 10,000 hectares) and Original Community Lands (*Tierras Comunitarias de Origen*—TCO) to ensure that they fulfill their economic and social functions and thus merit being titled. Failing to do so undermines the credibility of the process and the spirit of the law.

A new approach to land regularization should seek to complete the title clearance process in areas where the process has started and emphasize a demand-driven approach in the remaining areas. Greater public confidence for the institutions that implement the law can be gained by inviting public participation and reviewing the status of very large and underutilized properties. However, this course of action will require a renewed commitment by INRA to address the ownership of large and underutilized lands.

III. Adopt Land Distribution Mechanisms Prioritized by Objectives, Employing Multiple Methods

The great promise of the INRA Act was to achieve land tenure security and identify land legally available for redistribution. But while improved land tenure security has slowly progressed, land redistribution has failed. As of 2005, the INRA had identified only 30,000 hectares of public lands suitable for distribution, many of which are situated in high-cost, remote areas. A recent report on properties larger than 10,000 hectares suggests that many of them are substantially underutilized. Moreover, negligible advances in the reverting ill-acquired lands and the virtually stagnate settlement policy (only five settlements in nine years) has led to increased frustration of indigenous and peasant groups and seen the rise of increasingly militant tactics for land squatting and confrontation by some landless groups.

While land management is making steady progress, its impact on growth and poverty reduction continues to be minimal because of the highly unequal land tenure structure, exclusionary land markets, ineffective property tax system, and a lack of access to input and output markets, which places smallholders at a disadvantage that prevents them from expanding their land area through rental or purchase. The objective of evaluating large parcels of presumably underutilized land was meant to identify fertile land for redistribution through new human settlements. The reality of almost 10 years of implementing the INRA Law has been unsuccessful on both counts.

Access to agricultural land is a long-standing historical problem in Bolivia. It was addressed for the first time in 1953 with the Agrarian Reform. But the same problems that existed at that time have now resurfaced due to a highly unequal distribution of land resources. The Agrarian Reform Act of 1953 mainly affected the properties in the altiplano and valleys, where the majority of the large *latifundia* estates were located, and which has the highest density peasant population. As a result of this agrarian reform, the large estates were practically abolished and the lands broken up and distributed among the peasants and their communities. The reform in a massive land distributed in the altiplano and highlands (about 600,000 farms covering some 25 to 30 million hectares).

The settlement programs of the last five decades (mainly between 1958 and 1985) distributed between three and five million hectares of land in northern Santa Cruz, the Chapare region of Cochabamba, and the region of the Alto Beni to settlers, most of whom came from the highland areas. Today, almost 500,000 people live in these settled areas. Some of these households are relatively well-off, while others are very poor.

Despite the achievements in breaking up the traditional haciendas, land concentration and lack of access to it for new generations of the landless was reconstituted in the eastern part of the country during the 1960s-1990s. A new version of the large landholding system has surfaced there in a pronounced fashion. During this period, successive governments made large land grants, primarily in Santa Cruz, Beni, and Pando, often as a reward for loyalty and political support. These land grants amount to nearly 30 million hectares. This area has been the land base for the expansion of the livestock sector (between five and six million head of cattle) and for the boom in soybeans, wheat, sugarcane, and rice in Santa Cruz, making it the wealthiest area of Bolivia, but also the most unequal. The INRA Act was meant to address the popular outrage generated by this inequality, and the results are well known.

Land-related Inequality

Bolivia continues to face two main issues of land-related inequality. The first is the great inter-regional difference between the western highlands and the eastern plains. The western valleys represent 60 percent of the landowners in the country but account for only 10 percent of the agricultural land (1.1 million hectares). In contrast, the eastern plains are home to only 18 percent of the landowners but represent 75 percent of the surface area exploited (8.5 million hectares). This migration from west to east dates back five decades, but it is constrained by legal and logistical difficulties in accessing undeveloped forest lands in the east and by the difficulty for poor landless families have in buying or renting land from the large landowners.

The second issue is the intraregional inequality of land distribution. In certain regions, especially those of northern Santa Cruz, east of the Río Grande, along the Santa Cruz-Chapare corridor, and to the south of El Chaco, there are impoverished rural populations of recent migrants residing in areas where there is plenty of underutilized land belonging to large landowners. For example, more than 108,000 hectares of agricultural land in foreclosure and awaiting sale by the banks in Santa Cruz.

In the short term, land redistribution is needed in Bolivia as a response to the increasingly acute social demands; in the medium term, it can serve to structurally relieve rural poverty through increases in land-based income. In addition, the economy would benefit from improved equity in landholding through the secondary effects of increased productivity and employment, which could be achieved via effectively implemented land distribution. As Bolivia enters a new period, it should view the land distribution problem programmatically—as a social demand and as a rural employment problem. As Bolivia becomes increasingly urban, the land issue is not a long-term problem, but how it is handled now will make a difference over the next twenty years in terms of rural poverty, environmental sustainability, governability and, eventually, the composition of the economy and quality of the workforce.

Limited Effectiveness of INRA

For these reasons, it is important that Bolivia does not view agrarian reform through an ideological and excessively legalistic lens. Despite the good intentions of the INRA Act, after ten years of implementation, it is of limited effectiveness in land redistribution. The key problem is that the INRA Law has suffered from a legalistic approach, making title clearance its centerpiece and relegating the objective of actual redistribution to the margins. Confronting large landowners with such legislation and potential expropriation creates incentives for skirting, subverting, and defying the law. This leads to an interminable, process-focused policy with few results. While the INRA Law should not be abandoned, it needs to be strengthened and streamlined to have an impact. A more pragmatic approach to land redistribution would diversify the instruments used and focus on the objectives of obtaining good agricultural lands under the control of the most productive landless peasants. It is advisable that this be accomplished as part of a more inclusive view of rural development that embraces job creation and non-farm activities as solutions to poverty reduction. What matters is the actual distribution of land to those who most need and value it. This pragmatic approach requires the implementation of multiple mechanisms, including reversion of lands to the public domain, land purchase and leasing programs, improved private markets, social pacts, negotiated settlements for arable areas potentially subject to expropriation, contract farming, and joint ventures. Locally targeting these types of programs to achieve specific quantitative objectives at the regional level could reduce social tension over the land, increase productivity, and create new jobs.

Current Proposals

The government is currently preparing a complementary and more expedient mechanism for redistributing underutilized lands for the benefit of organized rural farmers through a land purchase fund and matching grants for productive investments. The proposed project (Pro-Tierras-DA) aims to reduce asset inequality, improve income-generating opportunities for the rural poor, and accelerate land redistribution. This project must be carefully monitored and evaluated and should be scaled up if it shows promise. At the same time, other innovative strategies should also be tested.

IV. Improve Land Taxation

The third pillar of this policy is land taxation. This is where the promise of fiscal decentralization meets the policy of redistributing land to the poor. Immense areas of underutilized land, held for speculative purposes, continue to make land markets exclusionary, inhibit intensification of agriculture, and prevent local governments from collecting much needed revenue to provide public services. Currently, about half of municipal taxes are property taxes, but 90 percent of this revenue is collected in only ten municipalities (out of 327). Improving the property tax system, especially in rural municipalities, could increase local government revenue and create a better system of incentives for landowners to use their properties in the most productive way or release it onto the market.

Improving the usefulness of the property tax is a political as well as technical matter. The tax has to be managed in such a way that its benefits are highly visible, especially through public works in the municipalities. In technical terms, the absence of a comprehensive register of real estate, low tax rates, undervaluations, and non-collection renders the tax system on rural properties ineffective. The current land registries lack the necessary mechanisms to maintain and update physical information on each property, in accordance with the land registry standards issued by INRA. Especially in the rural areas, municipalities lack the necessary physical and legal information on the properties, and their capacity to appraise property is virtually nil. But these limitations can easily be overcome. For a start, municipalities can simply create their own land registers for taxation purposes, using the self-assessed value statements of the landowners. This list could be upgraded if municipalities had access to the real estate information system of the official land registry under the responsibility of INRA and the Registry of Real Estate Rights. With this in mind, it is imperative to interconnect the municipal cadastre information systems with the official cadastre; this will facilitate having updated physical and legal data that can be supplemented with property appraisals. For rural areas, property appraisals should be based on the agro-ecological characteristics of the area in question and on market prices, although the self-assessment by the landowners are a good approximation.

The municipalities do not have the political will to alienate the large landholders by enforcing the tax provisions. Linking the tax effort by the municipalities with federal funds transfers could make the land tax more effective. Effectiveness could also be improved by opening the tax records to increased public scrutiny.

V. Regularize Land Ownership for Indigenous Peoples

A fourth pillar of a pro-poor land redistribution policy is acknowledging the claims of indigenous peoples. This acknowledgement should satisfy the social demands of the indigenous population and create a secure tenancy over the enormous areas subject to ancestral claims. Since the promulgation of Law 1715, TCOs have been created with a total land area of 5.2 million hectares. Currently, 124 additional claims are being processed on more than 16.1 million hectares and 50 new claims are pending on 4.5 million hectares in the highlands. Even though the plan has been successful, since it has created a large area of legally protected indigenous lands, the process has been characterized by many conflicts and confusions. Some of these conflicts stem from third party claims, forest and property concessions, disputes regarding the extent of the claims, tensions between individual holdings and collective title granted to TCOs, and the sluggish pace of the bureaucratic processing of the claims. One of the fundamental problems is that the TCO is a form of private land title that is, of necessity, being used by the indigenous communities as an instrument for territorial administrative control, which has other political implications.

The TCO claims must be processed and completed. At the policy level, it is necessary to reexamine the relationship between local land administration and the tools of land tenure. An area's designation as a TCO relates only to property rights, not to land administration. In addressing potential legal or constitutional changes, it might be preferable to expand the scope of indigenous land administration to allow for a wider range of land tenure designations within the indigenous territories (such as individual family use rights and common use rights), which would improve the current administration of the indigenous communities and simplify the fieldwork and technical-legal evaluation needed to establish the TCOs.

On a more technical level, the procedure titling TCOs could improve by making the fieldwork, technical-juridical evaluations and resolutions (all conducted by the INRA) more transparent and participatory. The resolution of third party claims could be improved if all claims and transactions were suspended when the field study begins. There is also a need for increased community participation in the INRA process (especially in terms of public outreach and legal/technical evaluation); greater coordination with the forestry sector before initiating the fieldwork; and more indigenous representation in the consulting and monitoring entities to cooperate with INRA on fieldwork, evaluations, and the issuance of resolutions. Linkage to land purchase programs may be the best way to consolidate lands titled to third parties into properties within the nucleus of the TCOs.

VI. Maintain the Integrity of Protected Areas and Forest Reserves

The fifth pillar of the land policy should be the sustainable management of protected areas and forest reserves, which comprise a significant area, particularly in the foothills and in the plains of the eastern section of Bolivia. If these areas are managed well, they have considerable potential to contribute to the Millennium Development Goals on environmental sustainability and poverty eradication. However, if they are neglected or opened up to inappropriate uses, their potential contribution to sustainable development could be irreversibly lost.

Bolivia's national system of protected areas (including national parks, national reserves, and natural integrated management areas) encompasses almost 22 areas with nearly 22 million hectares (almost 20 percent of the land area). These areas include a wide variety of forests, wetlands, and other natural ecosystems, with a great number of endemic plant and animal species. The extraordinary global biodiversity and the significant carbon storage within the protected areas have drawn considerable international interest and grant financing. These areas also generate important local and national benefits, including environmental services such as erosion control and improved water sources for family consumption, irrigation, and a variety of industries. Several innovative efforts are underway to link local governments with the national government in better managing the protected areas. One such example is the agreement between the Municipal Council of Tarija and the National Protected Areas Service (*Servicio Nacional de Áreas Protegidas*—SERNAP) to manage the Sama Biological Reserve, which is a primary water source for the capital city of that department. Protected areas can also generate significant income from tourism, an underutilized source but one that shows significant potential for local development. For example, the number of visitors to the Eduardo Avaroa National Reserve, the most visited in the country, rose from 13,000 in 1999 to 43,000 in 2003, and the trend continues to rise. This tourism generates more than US$160,000 per year in admissions fees in addition to the general impact on the economy. The challenge is to manage this economic activity sustainably and to ensure a broader and more equitable participation in its benefits.

Bolivia's tropical forest is the sixth largest in the world, with nearly half the country (approximately 54 million hectares) still covered by natural forests. Proper management of the forests is important for the general development of the country and to reduce poverty in specific localities. Currently, 8.5 million hectares of forest are under legal management; this includes the designated forest reserves. Bolivia is the world leader in voluntary forest certification, with 2.2 million hectares accredited as sustainably managed forests. The country's lumber reserves are 317 million cubic meters, and sustainable lumber production is more than 20 million cubic meters per year. The forest sector, which already includes almost 1,000 registered companies, generates 50,000 jobs directly and contributes more than US$5 million in tax revenue per year to the government. Forest products represented 11 percent of legal Bolivian exports (US$117 million) in 2003. Bolivia is also the world leader in exports of almonds, which are gathered in the forests. These benefits could increase with better forest management.

Most of Bolivia's forests have soil that is not suited for agriculture or any nonforestry uses. Therefore, the protected areas, forest reserves, and other forest lands will contribute to economic development only if they are managed as forests instead of being clear-cut for agricultural development. Land distribution efforts need to ensure a rational process for selecting agricultural development areas, consistent with official Land Use Plans (*Planes de Uso del Suelo*—PLUS) at the municipal, department, and/or national level. It is also important to reduce land clearing pressures on many forested areas by broadening the access of local residents to their benefits. This implies supporting the local social groupings (forest cooperatives established under the Forest Act of 1996) so that small producers can legalize their operations and manage forests according to their potential. It also encompasses increasing the benefits that flow from the protected areas and ensuring their equitable distribution.

The successful implementation of this project depends on the effectiveness of its institutions. In order to guarantee broad benefits to the country, public institutions must be able to resist powerful special interests. Many institutions in charge of land management enjoy certain advantages that allow them to do this. For example, the Superintendency of Forests is led by a professional whose term of office is longer than the country's political cycle and whose selection procedure reduces the possibilities of political patronage. SERNAP's personnel are selected on the basis of their abilities and not their political affiliation. It is important to maintain (and, where possible, strengthen) the professional capacity of these and other institutions to manage the land and its natural resources to achieve sustainable benefits.

VII. Conclusion

This study emphasizes five aspects of land policy considered to be of vital importance for achieving the objectives of the Bolivian Poverty Reduction Strategy Paper: security of land rights, land distribution, land taxation, indigenous land regularization, and forest conservation. These areas are singled out due to their important links to a comprehensive rural development strategy focused on improving employment opportunities and productivity.

The land situation must be regarded as a serious social and economic problem that is contributing to a distorted, exclusionary growth pattern and social conflict. However, this study concludes with an optimistic message: with sustained attention and a renewed commitment to the goals set forth in the law and the current policy, Bolivia's enormous land resources can become a driving force of sustainable development for its population.

Bibliography

CEJIS. 2003. *50 años de Reforma Agraria: TCO y tierras campesinas*. La Paz: CEJIS.

Fundación Tierra. 2004. *Twelve years promoting rural Development: Fundación Tierra in Bolivia. 1991-2003*. La Paz: Fundación Tierra.

Griffiths, T. 2002. "Indigenous peoples, land tenure and land policy in Latin America." *Land Reform: 2002*. United Nations Food and Agriculture Organization.

Instituto Nacional de Reforma Agraria. 2003. Ley No. 1715 y su Reglamento (Cuarta edición-Octubre de 2003).

———. 2002. "Estadísticas Agrarias: Tenencia de la tierra en Bolivia (1953-2002)."

Ministerio de Desarrollo Sostenible y Planificación, Viceministerio de Planificación Estratégica y Participación Popular. 2002. "Municipios, Distritos Municipales, Indígenas y Tierras Comunitarias de Origen en las tierras altas de Bolivia."

Muñoz, J. 1999. "Los mercados de tierras rurales en Bolivia." CEPAL/ECLAC Serie Desarrollo Productivo.

Plant, R. and S. Hvalkof. 2001. *Land Titling and Indigenous Peoples in Latin America*. Washington, DC: Inter-American Development Bank.

Roldán, R. 2004. "Models for Recognizing Indigenous Land Rights in Latin America." World Bank Working Paper 30886. World Bank, Washington, DC.

Vargas Vega, J. 2004. *La Reforma Agraria desde las regiones: Tierra y Territorio.* La Paz: CIDES/Pluras Editores.

Zoomers, A. 2003. "Land liberalisation and sustainable development in Latin America: Unravelling the Land Sales Market of Santa Cruz, Bolivia." *International Development Planning Review* 25 (3) 2003.

Part III

Without Corruption and with Civic Participation

21

Toward Better Governance

Edgardo Mosqueira and Azul del Villar

Summary

Since the enactment of the Financial Administration and Governmental Control Act, and particularly since the late 1990s, Bolivia has promoted a series of public administration reforms. Notable among them are reform of the civil service, reforms to key collection entities, expenditure reforms, and the fight against corruption. Yet given the political and social instability experienced by the country as of the late 1990s, these reforms were modest.

Reform of the civil service has contributed to building the legal and regulatory framework. Competitive selection processes have been implemented, together with a biometric registration of government personnel. The modernization of the National Tax Service and the National Customs Service have improved the administration of those entities and reduced corruption. Initiatives such as a strengthening of the Comptroller General and a requirement for government employees to submit affidavits of assets also contribute to reducing corruption. Despite all this, the reform process has not been extended to the entire public sector. Policies involving wages and the administrative career system are pending tasks. Slow progress is reflected in the citizenry's continuing lack of confidence in the political system and in government institutions.

The country's political and social instability could reverse with the political process that started in 2006. New authorities have been elected to the executive branch and the Congress. Prefects have been elected, and the upcoming constitutional reform will include decentralization at a regional level. All this creates a new opportunity to promote pending reforms and apply lessons learned. This chapter describes the lessons learned and proposes reforms to increase efficiency, transparency, and accountability in the planning and execution of public expenditures and in the management of government assets. Such measures will make it possible to improve the provision of public services, increase revenue collection, and increase citizens' access to government services and public information.

I. Background: The Functionality of Public institutions

Introduction

Since 2000, Bolivia has undergone some of the most serious periods of political instability in its history. Over the past five years, the country has been led by five different government administrations. Despite this turbulence, 25 percent of the central government's employees, or 3,500 out of a total of 14,000, were hired through the competitive and special selection processes set forth in the Civil Service Rules (*Estatuto del Funcionario Público*), and almost all of them remain in their positions. This illustrates the need to preserve the achievements gained in building a professional, stable government. Today, the threat is growing that these changes could be reversed, and that improvisation could grow, along with a partisan designation of public employees. Along these lines, the state's reforms have achieved important goals, but their sustainability is still fragile. Today, more than ever, the advances must be sustained and the reforms must be extended. One of the most important lessons from this stage is that all institutional reforms are consolidated provided that they result in better performance and higher revenue for the government. When and where the changes became routine, it was because their fruits were almost immediately visible. Governmental reform is far from concluded, but already it has made concrete achievements.

The economic reforms of the 1990s contributed to growth, poverty reduction, and the expansion of public services; they also opened the way to reform of the state. However, toward the end of that decade some of the progress was reversed, which affected job creation and poverty reduction. This situation created social discontent and political instability, expressed in the resignations of two presidents over the past three years in response to social pressure. In addition, public demonstrations, some of which were violent, were turning into a recurrent tool to pressure the government. In this context, the opportunity for significant progress in reform of the state has been closing. Certain strategies and lessons learned now make it possible to continue this important reform.

The Reform of the 1990s Created Growth and Opened the Way to Reform the State

The positive economic conditions of 1993 to 1998[1] facilitated political and social stability and opened the way for state reform. Macroeconomic reform was accompanied by changes in the structure of the State, led by municipal decentralization (through the Popular Participation Act) and the transfer to private shareholders of 50 percent of the shares of government-owned companies. Public administration reforms began with the enactment of the Financial Administration and Government Control Act (*Ley del Sistema de Administración Financiera y Control Gubernamental*—SAFCO), whose objective was to create order in and regulate the operations of eight administrative, financial, and control systems. The Institutional Reform Project (*Proyecto de

Reforma Institucional—PRI) started in 1999 with the aim of promoting a series of complementary reforms in public administration. This included staff issues, results-based management, combating corruption, and reform of key entities.

In this context, the study on institutionality and governance conducted by the World Bank[2] demonstrated that the principal cause of the problems in Bolivia was its informal mode of operation. Inefficiency, lack of transparency, and a lack of accountability were attributed to the fact that the results expected through the application of formal instruments (laws, regulations, and standards of organization) failed to match actual conduct, which was characterized by noncompliance with those formal frameworks. One of the most notorious examples has been a lack of implementation of many of the provisions of the SAFCO Act. The management tools of that act, such as the approval of Annual Operating Programs (*Programas Operativos Anuales*—POAs), which were meant to guide allocations during the preparation of the budget, turned into simple rituals. Under the guise of the formal preparation of those instruments, the activities and funding allocations of the agencies went ahead with no regard for the POAs. On the other hand, government agencies were unable to offer competitive wages in order to recruit quality personnel. This led to an indiscriminate contracting of "consultants" who, rather than engage in temporary, complementary, specific activities, as should be the case for a consultant, took on essential functions.

During 2000 to 2005, lack of growth affected job creation and poverty; this in turn struck a blow against social and political stability.[3] Institutional weakness was dramatically reflected in: (i) a lack of consensus among parties and leaders to modernize institutions and make them efficient; (ii) an inabiity to maintain the rule of law and order and to provide efficient, effective public services; (iii) an inability to maintain a coherent public policy in the medium and long term.

Political and social instability could turn around with the government that took office in 2006. New authorities have been elected in the executive branch and the Congress, along with nine prefects. A constitutional reform process is also about to take place, which will include decentralization with a regional emphasis. This creates a new opportunity to promote the pending reforms.

II. Progress toward a Transparent, Efficient State

Progress toward Modernizing Financial Management4

The fundamental instrument of Bolivian public administration is Law 1178, which created the Financial Administration and Government Control System (SAFCO Act).[4] This law's principal objectives were to:

- Establish management systems that cover all aspects of public expenditures, from the programming of objectives and the activities needed to achieve them, through the development of indicators to evaluate them.

- Underscore the importance of accountability and an individual rendering of accounts by government employees.
- Eliminate *ex ante* control of expenditures and create a results-based management culture that would allow the Comptroller General to audit public expenditures from the perspective of results obtained, replacing the custom of auditing only the performance of processes.

The key principle of the systems established by the SAFCO Act was "centralization of regulations and decentralization of operations." This meant that each public entity would be responsible for implementing the policies established by this act, while the central entities would certify the consistency of each entity's processes with the act's principles and evaluate results. Under the philosophy of the SAFCO Act, the role of the ministries would be to formulate policies, establish standards, and provide coordination.

Given that implementation of the SAFCO Act depended upon the approval of complementary regulations by the public entities, its implementation was delayed for a long time and the effectiveness of its principles was reduced on account of inadequate regulations.

Together with the SAFCO Act, the Integrated Administrative Management and Modernization System (*Sistema Integrado de Gestión y Modernización Administrativa*—SIGMA) was implemented, with the aim of creating a unified mechanism to administer, manage, and report on public sector expenditures. So far, SIGMA has been installed in all the ministries; the three development funds (the Unified Funding Board [*Direction Única de Fondos*—FPS], the Production and Social Investment Fund [*Fondo de Inversión Productiva y Social*—FPS], and the National Regional Development Fund [*Fondo Nacional de Desarrollo Regional*—FNDR]); the National Tax Service; and the Pension Service. The system covers disbursements made by the Treasury, including planned and actual disbursements, with a highly detailed breakdown. This information is available in real time and is important for financial control.

Despite achievements in terms of the quality and availability of information on the budget's implementation, SIGMA still has certain limitations. For example, it covers only the municipalities of La Paz, Santa Cruz, Cochabamba, and Sucre and the departmental government of La Paz. Accordingly, it is expected to extend its operation to another three councils, as established in the Multi-Donor Budget Support Program. Currently, the Fiscal Programming Unit (*Unidad de Programación Fiscal*—UPF) of the Ministry of Finance is the only entity that provides reliable information on municipal expenditures. The Fiscal Programming Unit gathers data on the largest municipalities, which represent 84 percent of the population, but is not sufficiently sophisticated to produce regular information on the budget's implementation. In addition, formal reports on the latest municipal expenditures are available with a delay of several months at the end of each year. The information is not available in user-friendly formats and is difficult to understand for civil society groups, which does not improve transparency of budget implementation.[5]

Progress in Professionalizing the Civil Service

The civil service is one of the areas most affected by the "informality" described above. In 2001, Law 2027 (better known as the Civil Service Rules) was enacted and the Superintendency of Civil Service was placed in operation. One of the law's main objectives was to professionalize government workers through the competitive selection and hiring of government employees. The law establishes mechanisms for supervising and evaluating government employees while creating an administrative career system and a new salary policy.

Despite political and social instability and a high turnover in administrations, the results of this reform have been significant. About 25 percent of the employees of the central government (ministries and decentralized entities), that is, 3,500 out of a total of 14,000,[6] have been incorporated into the administrative career system through the competitive and special selection mechanisms in the Civil Service Rules. Close to 100 percent of these professionals remain in their positions despite the constant turnovers in the administration.

These results show that one of the principal problems described in the "Institutionality and Governance Review" (2000) is already being resolved: the arbitrary selection and hiring of government employees and their high rotation due to the making and breaking of political connections with whomever is in office has been replaced by competitive hiring and functional stability. This change has contributed to the professionalization of public entities, which has been reflected in an improved performance of the principal entities that implemented civil service reform.

In addition, important steps have been taken to correct the payroll records. The government has started to apply the Biometric Registration of Government Employees, Retirees and Awardees, which will make it possible to have a single list of all persons with a right to collect wages, pensions, and other government benefits. This registration program makes it possible to collect reliable identification information on government employees in each institution, their time in service, or the functions over which they are in charge.

In the short term, the objective is to create a biometric identification system to make the payment of government employee wages easier and more secure. This also allows public payroll lists to be corrected by identifying workers who serve in actual positions and eliminating "phantom positions" (that is, positions that represent spending on wages but that are not actually filled or whose wages are collected by different persons than those appearing in the records). It will also be possible to detect government employees irregularly placed on the public payroll.

In the medium term, the information collected, together with the service record of each government employee, will make it possible to have: (i) a detailed description of the distribution of positions in each entity, available for review to improve their organization and distribution; (ii) information on salary ranges by position to correct differences and standardize the payroll; and (iii) details on the characteristics of government personnel and their remunerations. The registration process is one of the fundamental tools for developing new policies regarding salaries and administrative careers.

To date more than 100,000 persons have been registered out of an estimated total of 360,000 (200,000 government employees, and 160,000 retired persons, special pension beneficiaries, and rightful claimants) throughout the central administration (including the central government and the health and education sectors, with the exception of the Armed Forces and the Police).

Although civil service reform has made progress, it is also evident that political instability has not allowed all the original objectives to be attained. Many objectives are still pending, such as the introduction of administrative career systems and performance evaluations, in addition to the salary structuring policy throughout the public sector.

Anecdotal evidence exists that salary austerity measures, particularly the establishment of caps on public salaries, have increased the risk of resignation of skilled personnel, principally those incorporated into the administrative career system in specialized technical areas. This could reduce the quality of human resources and, in the short term, affect the sustainability of the achievements of civil service reform.

Functional Improvements in Key Public Administration Areas

Other successful reforms have taken place in specific agencies of the central administration: the National Tax Service (*Servicio de Impuestos Nacionales*—SIN), the Customs Service, and the National Roads Service (*Servicio Nacional de Caminos*—SNC).

Reform of the SIN has been one of the most significant successes of the institutional reforms. The old Internal Revenue Service (*Servicio Nacional de Impuestos Internos*—SNII) was notorious for its inefficiency, corruption, and lack of transparency. Creation of the SIN allowed for the establishment of a new legal framework, competitive selection and hiring of human resources (more than a thousand registered employees), and the modernization of its information systems. As a result, the collection of taxes and the tax service has substantially improved (see Figures 1 and 2).

In the late 1990s, the Customs Service was one of the least efficient, least effective public institutions. Under the old Customs Act, the existence of a large group of unsalaried government workers (*ad honorem*), lack of adequate procedures and systems and, above all, few results in the fight against contraband were some of the most visible symptoms of the institution's inefficiencies.

The reform showed progress until 2003. The main elements of this accomplishment can be summed up as follows:

- The incorporation of customs employees under the Civil Service Rules (*Estatuto del Funcionario Público*—EFP);
- the creation of an administrative career system and performance evaluation system (more than 800 government employees incorporated into the civil service);

Figure 1. National Tax Service: Tax Collections 2000–2005
(in millions of bolivianos)

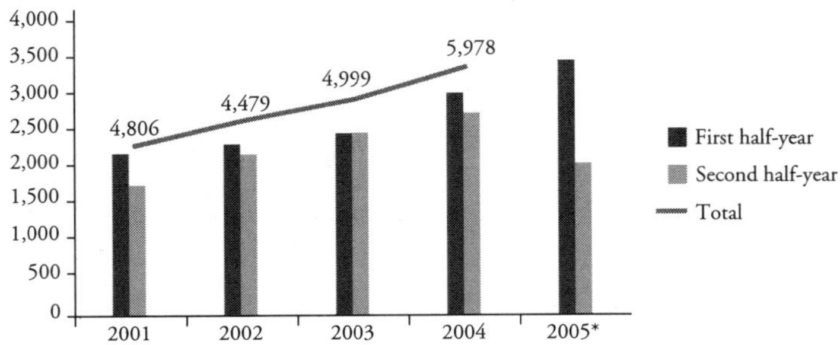

Source: SIN
Note: Does not include collections of Special Tax on Hydrocarbons and their Derivatives (IEHD), the Financial Transactions Tax (ITF), the Direct Tax on Hydrocarbons (IDH), duties, or the Interim Program.
*The second half of 2005 considers data as of the month of September.

Figure 2. Trends in VAT Tax Evasion

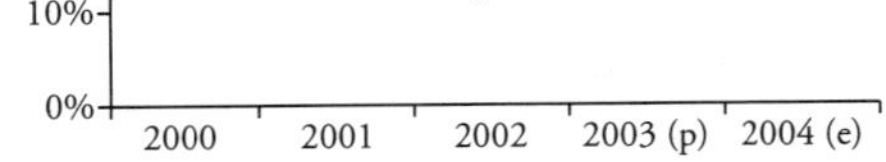

Source: SIN.

- The creation of an office of ethics to control corruption;
- Improved information management thanks to the implementation of the Automated Customs System (*Sistema Aduanero Automatizado*—SIDUNEA); and
- Good use of information technology to improve efficiency by expediting the processing of user operations.

However, since 2003, backtracking has occurred for several reasons. First, in 2002, the change in administration led to greater political interference. The congressional practice of designating interim—as opposed to permanent—managers has made it harder for the Customs Service to overcome this. Second, many customs employees who joined the civil service through competitive processes have hit the wage ceiling for their position. This undermines incentives and can result in an increased turnover. Third, the reform has not yet permeated the institution to the point of creating a new organizational and management culture.

Though customs collections have improved (Figure 3), many improvements are still pending and others need to be consolidated, especially in terms of administrative efficiency. Finally, the ineffectiveness of actions to reduce contraband undermines the Customs Service's reputation, though this problem needs to also involve other government entities for its solution.

Similarly, the reforms of the SNC restored that agency's performance and reputation. The SNC's past had been marked by irregularities in the management of road investment funds. By late 2005, the SNC had notably improved its performance, above all in highway maintenance programs, improved quality in and expansion of the roads system (Figure 4), efficiency in investment (reflected by lower road construction costs), and the competitive selection and hiring of employees.

Despite this, certain institutional problems continue to affect the entity's management. Failure to designate a board of directors using the legal mechanisms harms decision making. In addition, judicial intervention in the designation of directors harms the entity's management and results.

The Fight against Corruption

Progress in the fight against corruption entrenched in public functions has been modest. After taking important steps, such as creation of the Assets Affidavits System (mandatory for all government employees) and modernization measures to the Comptroller General, in recent years the fight has been limited to approval of the

Figure 3. The Bolivian Customs Service: Collections 2000–2005
(in millions of bolivianos)

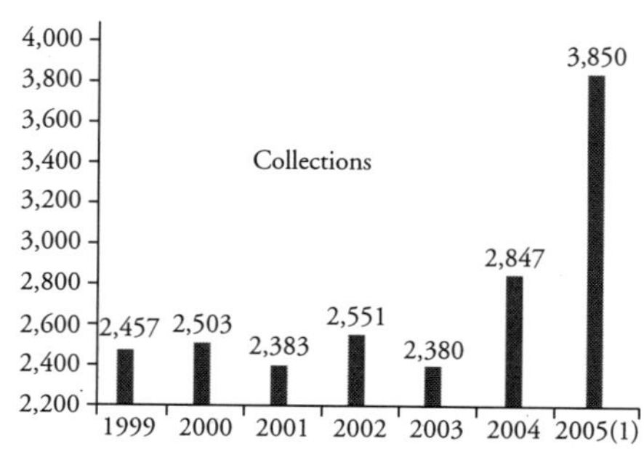

Source: Bolivian Customs Service (Data as of December 30, 2005).

Figure 4. Improvement and Expansion of the Roads System

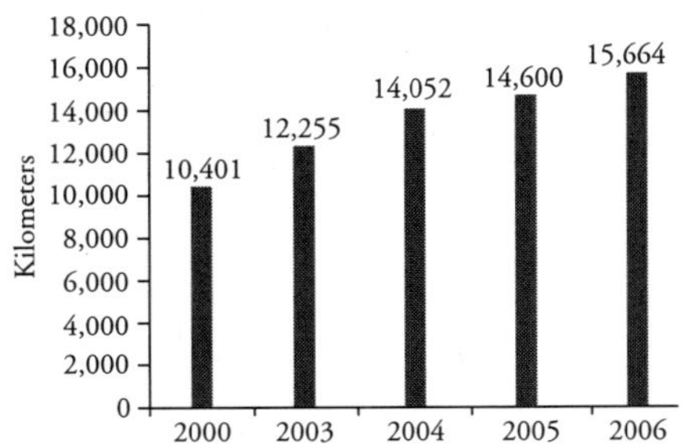

Source: National Roads Service.

2005-2009 Integral Anticorruption Plan (*Plan Integral Anticorrupción*—PIA), which seeks to combine the efforts of the Government Attorneys' Office, the Comptroller General, the Financial Investigations Unit, and the Presidential Delegation for Transparency and Public Integrity in Democracy (previously the Anticorruption Delegation).

The Anticorruption Delegation developed a plan of action principally aimed at promoting transparency, access to information, accountability (in terms of allocations and results), and support to the institutions of competent jurisdiction to investigate or penalize mismanagement of public funds. It also seeks to strengthen government integrity and citizen awareness through management based on principles and public ethics. Another measure, Decree 28168 of May 16, 2005, established mechanisms to guarantee the citizens' right to access information from the Executive Branch; but so far, its implementation remains in the preliminary stage.

III. Diagnosis of the Public Administration Reform

The Governance Climate Affected the Continuity of the Reforms

The reforms of the civil service, the SIN, the Customs Service, and the SNC were sustainable in part thanks to the positive fiscal impact implicit in each of these reforms, which were needed in order to increase tax collections and improve public expenditures. Reforms to the SIN and the Customs Service were based on a need to efficiently collect more tax revenue. The reforms to the SNC and the civil service, on the other hand, were driven by a need to make public expenditures more efficient, given that the operations of the SNC represent 4 percent of the national budget and expenditures on civil service amount to 10 percent of GDP.

The reforms did not succeed in expanding across the board to the entire central public sector, composed of the ministries and departmental administrations. Neither was it possible to overcome the problems diagnosed. Unlike the entities that did benefit from the reform, the rest of the public sector did not have similar incentives.

As explained above, the economic slowdown affected investment and job creation. Coupled with the country's extreme inequality, this fanned social discontent and the widespread belief that the distribution of income is unfair. This social discontent contributed to reducing governance, which made it difficult to extend reforms to new areas of the public administration.

For several years the World Bank has compiled indicators to measure perceptions of governance in six dimensions: (i) voice and accountability; (ii) political stability and the absence of violence; (iii) government effectiveness; (iv) regulatory quality; (v) the rule of law; and (vi) control of corruption[7] (Annex I). These studies cover 209 countries and territories in the years 1996, 1998, 2000, 2002, and 2004, and are based on hundreds of individual variables extracted from 37 separate data sources, assembled by 32 different organizations.

Currently, lack of confidence in the political system and in governmental institutions in Bolivia is high. The Corruption Perceptions Index (CPI) of 2004, compiled by Transparency International—an index that reflects the perception of businessmen as well as national and international analysts—ranks Bolivia as 122 out of 145 countries, with a score of 2.2 on a scale of 0 to 10 (the lower the score, the greater the corruption perceived).[8] The index places Bolivia at the same level as Zimbabwe, Venezuela, Guatemala, Kazakhstan, Uzbekistan, Kyrgyzstan, and Niger. It ranks lower than most Latin American countries, with the exception of Paraguay and Haiti.

Bolivia also faces a problem of overregulation.[9] Starting a company requires 15 procedures and takes 50 days. Furthermore, labor regulations are restrictive and costly. Labor benefits represent around 50 percent of the cost of labor and unlimited layoff payments mean that labor termination costs are two to three times higher than in other Andean countries. For indicators of regulatory quality, the complexity of bureaucratic procedures, the effectiveness of bankruptcy laws, and the cost of hiring and firing, Bolivian regulations are among the least efficient in the world, which affects investment and job creation (Figure 5).

In addition, basic institutions for ensuring market functionality and attracting investment to create jobs require many changes. Among the most severe problems are a lack of judicial independence, inefficiency of the legal framework, and the poor protection for and limited scope of property and intellectual property rights. Figure 6 illustrates the low quality of these institutions in Bolivia as compared with the rest of Latin America and the world, which explains the extremely high transaction costs with which investors must cope.

Finally, the perception that corruption substantially affects investment is very high (Figure 7).

Figure 5. Regulatory Quality

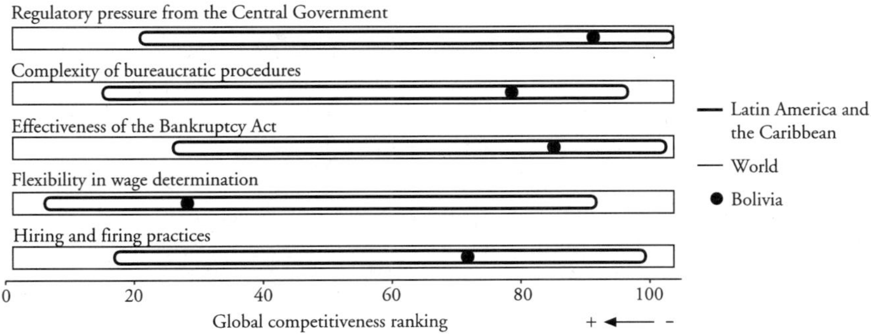

Source: World Economic Forum, 2004.

Figure 6. The Rule of Law

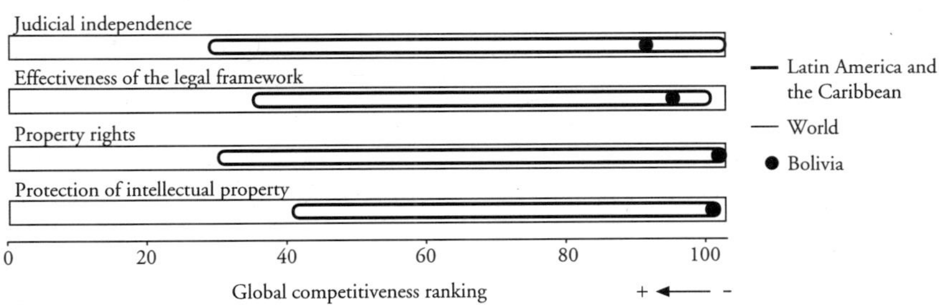

Source: World Economic Forum, 2004.

Lack of Transparency and Accountability in Public Expenditures

Several studies on processes related to the allocation and management of public funds in Bolivia have identified recurring problems that affect the quality of public expenditures in the country. One of the principal difficulties is a weak integration between the various phases of the budget process (planning – programming – formulation – legislative approval – implementation – follow-up and evaluation).

The financial management, administrative, and control systems created under the SAFCO Act have the following deficiencies: (i) lack of a logical system that was originally intended in the law; (ii) existence of numerous and complex regulations hindering compliance; (iii) lack of transparency and accountability; (iv) lack of timely response; and (v) lack of coordination of the control systems, which fail to

Figure 7. Corruption

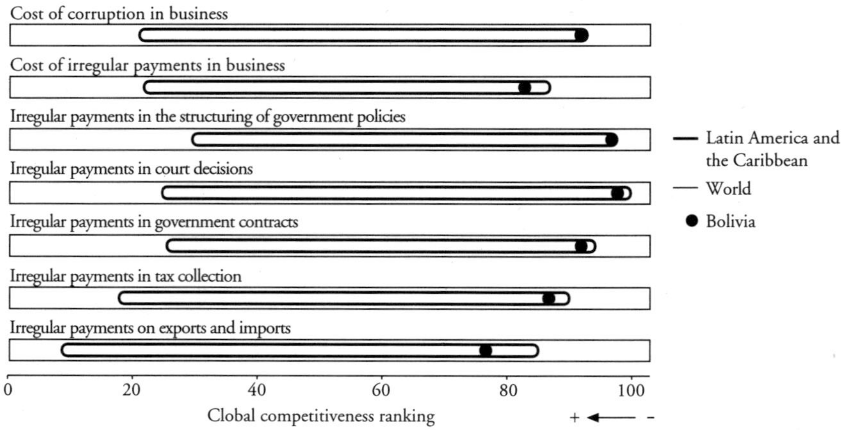

Source: World Economic Forum, 2004.

include the impact evaluations or preventive activities set forth in their mandate. The planning-budget-treasury systems do not provide adequate support to improve funding allocations and usage.

Planning. The SAFCO Act states that investment priorities in the budget have the National Planning System (*Sistema Nacional de Planificación*—SISPLAN) as their reference, but there are no instruments and/or methodologies to support that process. In fact, the Economic and Social Development Plan is not a strategic input, and pressures generated by the political situation of the moment take precedence over any medium- or long-term vision.

Programming. In general, the POAs of the institutions exceed budget limits and do not develop their programming based on identifying products, beneficiaries, goals, or results. This prevents them from being used as management instruments to prioritize funds and later formulate the budget.

Budget. The budget is not generally approved within the term set by law and tends to overestimate revenue. In addition, the budget is legally amended on many occasions in the course of the fiscal year, which causes problems in terms of expenditures and limits on indebtedness. Pressures for increased spending have been contained in part through administrative resolutions of the Minister of Finance and through legal provisions that limit expenditures as a function of the funds available in the Treasury. However, as indicated in a number of reports,[10] the budget submitted to Congress is a very poor guide for policy objectives. The budget systematically overestimates projected revenue; as a result spending limits are unrealistic. The Treasury confirmed that approximately 85 percent of budget limits were able to be spent in recent years, given the liquidity limitations that the administration has been facing. The Treasury could have enforced those limits by using SIGMA.[11] Overestimation also affects the lowest government tiers. The absence of a system to record commitments, even in the municipalities that have a subnational version of the SIGMA, makes the information on the floating debt sporadic and prevents it from being available in a timely fashion.

Although restrictions on expenditures have helped prevent a greater deterioration of the macroeconomic situation, they have also had negative consequences. First, they introduce arbitrary, *ad hoc* decisions on expenditures. Second, they make the formal budget process irrelevant. In the case of the subnational governments, several of them complain that they are not given the information they need on the funds they will be receiving until the start of the fiscal year. In addition, their budgets have to be submitted to the local councils prior to November 15, which creates a schedule clash. As such, there is no guarantee that the funds projected in their budgets will materialize.[12] As a result, no level of government takes the budget process seriously, and subnational demands are generally introduced as additional expenditures, without factoring whether they were included in the original budgets.

Treasury. The Treasury responds to pressures by adapting the cash flow, thus creating a vicious circle of overestimated budgets, poor budget implementation, repeated Treasury adjustments, and lack of transparency throughout the cycle in order to meet day-to-day needs. This situation does not lead to public policies in which accountability is customary. Neither does it lead to solid macroeconomic programming. Some of the consequences of this situation are: (i) budget planning and implementation are not consistent with projected revenue or with the cash flows of the Treasury; (ii) constant budget amendments cause delays in certain important programs, leave others without financing, and allocate funds inefficiently, which creates opportunity costs; and (iii) debts are created in the form of loans unaccounted for with providers or delays in payments, given the lack of a connection between the budget and the treasury.

Accounting. Budget and accounting items are not clearly and accurately applied. The budget classification of revenue and expenditures does not distinguish between recurring transactions and capital. Neither are financial versus non-financial transactions well defined, both with respect to their classification and their content. This can lead to confusion in the recording or payment of transactions in accordance with their current economic nature, and it can keep the budget's true impact on society from being measured.

SIGMA. Given the inherent weakness of budget planning, there are still numerous non-budget transactions that take place outside the system. This results in excessive expenditures in certain budget accounts and in the Treasury. While SIGMA does not permit non-budget transactions, it is possible to carefully alter the system and manually record accounting transactions. The institutions can justify the expenditure afterward through the issuance of an executive decree.

In addition to problems of coverage, there are other weaknesses:

- SIGMA was designed to operate as an administrative tool, but in practice it is used primarily as a payment system.
- SIGMA's original design did not incorporate the information needs of all the decentralized agencies.
- The recording of budget expenses is problematic, even for the capture of data. This is aggravated by frequent staff turnovers, which keeps the personnel from being familiar with the system.
- Lack of clarity over administrative requirements for capturing and managing budget data contributes to weakening the effectiveness of the system.
- Reforms in the budget's classification and structure have not been implemented.

Lack of Transparency and Efficiency in Public Tender Processes

Procurement. The decree that regulates the public tender framework in Bolivia has yet to attain the status of a law and has been modified five times during the past 18 months, almost always in response to pressures from local contractors, vendors, and consultants. The regulations and local tender documentation include practices and requirements that are not in line with international practices. This diminishes the transparency of the process, is conducive to agreements with the bidders, reduces the level of competition, and hinders the management of contract procurement. Changes in the rules and regulations hinder procedures and practices.

The legal and institutional framework for procurements requires a national entity that has the technical, legal, and financial capacity to supervise public contracting entities and ensure compliance with the decree on procurement regulations.

Regarding government electronic tender systems, in 2001 the Bolivian authorities implemented an information system named SICOES (*Sistema de Información de Contrataciones Estatales*—Government Procurements Information System). Among other information, that system announced business opportunities, procurements plans, and bidding documentation. Nonetheless, the service was interrupted after implementation of the SICOES web page. Later, Bolivia signed a bilateral cooperation agreement with the government of Brazil for the installation of COMPRASNET and the provision of technical assistance for its adaptation and adoption.

The limited progress regarding procurements includes:

- Basic standards for the procurements system.
- Purchase plans and rationalization systems to decentralize purchases, based on amounts.
- An information system on government contracting (SICOES).

Lack of Efficiency in the Management of Government Assets

The National Service for Government Property (*Servicio Nacional de Patrimonio del Estado*—SENAPE) is responsible for administering government property. The basic functions of this entity are: (i) registration and control of government property; (ii) monitoring of government assets; and (iii) promotion of title clearance. In addition to these functions, the SENAPE also manages the pending matters of what was formerly the Control Unit for Assets of Entities in Liquidation and/or Undergoing Restructuring (*Unidad de Control de Activos de Entidades en Liquidación y/o Reestructuración*—UCAELR) through the Interim Technical Office for Entities in Liquidation (*Dirección Técnica Transitoria de Entidades en Liquidación*). Following its initial creation, its jurisdiction was expanded to include receipt of the assets and liabilities of the Restructuring Unit (*Unidad de Reordenamiento*) for Funds in Liquidation (*Unidad Fondos en Liquidación*—UFL) and it was granted the necessary authority to ensure continuity of the liquidations.

If these functions were carried out efficiently, public revenue and savings could be generated that could be used for public or social programs. Nonetheless, the organization and functionality of the entity are plagued with serious weaknesses. The recording of assets is incomplete if one searches by information source (only 20 to 25 percent of potential counterparties are listed), by coverage (less than 10 percent of the assets are registered), by subject matter (intellectual property is not included; neither is the property of government-owned companies) or by geographic area. In addition, the obligation to "clear title" to or regularize the property is not carried out due to a lack of adequate procedures and technological resources. The Funds in Liquidation Unit (*Unidad Fondos en Liquidación*—UFL), which started in 2003, set an objective of liquidating three funds by December 31, 2005. So far, none has been liquidated due to, among other reasons, a lack of consolidated, valuated inventories of assets, lack of verified inventories of liabilities and litigation, and the absence of functional and accounting-administrative integration in the SENAPE.

In the case of the liquidation of entities, the SENAPE:

- Has not liquidated any entity of the 14 whose liquidation is underway and has held their assets for an average of five years.
- Has no method for carrying out (or has not carried out) the basic tasks of a "liquidating" unit, such as inventory taking and the asset valuation, verifications (physical, tenancy, or legal), and a plan of action for the liquidations.
- Has not verified the "collective" amount of assets on which it is acting.

Given this situation, the diagnostic on the SENAPE in late 2005 was as follows:

- The legal and regulatory framework is unclear and full of red tape.
- It has no strategic planning mechanisms.
- The functional and internal administrative-accounting organization does not respond to its institutional objectives.
- The information available (which is incomplete and unreliable) makes it difficult to develop strategies and plans of action and hinders management decision making.

- The organization, resources, methodologies, and tools of the area for the liquidation of entities are ineffective and inefficient.
- The historic performance of the UFL has been ineffective and inefficient. No concrete plans are seen to reverse this situation (only objectives without the corresponding plans of action).
- The "conceptual" distortions are reflected in an operating structure that is quantitatively oversized, but with a very limited "productive" capacity.

Improvements Pending for Reform of the Civil Service

The payroll cost of Bolivia's public sector is approximately 10 percent of GDP and represents almost 40 percent of the public sector's overall recurring expenditures. Since 1999, payroll expenses have increased in real terms, although the number of government employees has remained constant. At the same time, the cost of pensions from the old apportionment system has turned out to be double what was estimated when the pension system was reformed in 1996 because the number of beneficiaries increased by slightly more than 30 percent and the average benefit amount increased to more than twice the per capita GDP.

Payroll is a concern at the macroeconomic level, particularly with respect to teacher salaries. Bolivia has one of the best student/teacher ratios in Latin America, but the results do not justify the expense. Teachers comprise the largest group of employees of the central government. Previous attempts to decentralize the management of wages by transferring jurisdiction to the departments or the municipalities have been met with their fierce resistance.[13]

Teachers' wages are set based on the hours worked at each work site and therefore cannot be supervised by the central government. For their part, the subnational governments do not have incentives to restrict or supervise these contributions, because the teachers do not depend on them. In this state of "administrative limbo," it is not surprising that the payroll for teachers has grown so quickly and that neither the teachers nor low-level educational administrators have an incentive to change the status quo, which cannot be effectively monitored. This is an easy way for them to generate local revenue at the expense of the central government.

While the local governments are free to hire and set wages, subject to their portion in the revenue sharing (25 percent), the smaller municipalities are more likely to be the target of political pressure for wage demands. Political instability is accompanied by incessant appointments and firings of personnel situated in the high levels of the administration. Investment in skills and experience therefore is nil.

Efficiency and Transparency in Managing Revenue

The SIN and the Customs Service. Low levels of oversight and control keep the Customs Service from fulfilling its revenue collection function. Though there has been progress at the SIN, the system allows for proper supervision only of the formal sectors of the economy. At present, the modernization and administrative autonomy of these two institutions is in danger of being reversed, aggravated by the fact that the economy's high degree of corruption and informality create obstacles for monitoring its performance. The factors that add to inefficiency include:

- Failures in border controls and in the transit of merchandise, which allow for contraband and domestic sales without tax controls.
- The existence of many special regimens—free-trade zones, *maquiladoras* (export-oriented light assembly plants), temporary warehouses—with few controls.
- The low number of enrolled taxpayers who operate in the informal markets where the authorities cannot intervene.
- Little or no penalties, particularly judicial penalties, for failure to pay duties and taxes when detected by the institutions.
- Few judicial penalties against corrupt government employees and taxpayers, despite the high degree of detection and administrative penalties imposed by the Customs Service and the SIN.
- Little coordination between the institutions that monitor activities (the Customs Service, SIN, the Tax Superintendency, the Assistant Ministry on Tax Policy).
- Pressure from formal and informal groups could reverse or slow progress in the modernization of the tax collection institutions.
- Lack of instruments regarding human resources to consolidate good practices (such as vertical promotions, good performance evaluation processes, and, in particular, remunerations in keeping with market levels). Furthermore, the boards of directors of the two institutions, appointed by the political authorities, often intervene erroneously with respect to technical and operational aspects.

IV. Policies for an Efficient and Transparent Public Administration

Strategies to Continue the Reforms

The need to rationalize and/or reduce expenditures and increase tax revenue could be supported through institutional reforms as follows:

- Continuation of reforms in those areas in which they were being successfully implemented, in order to protect the progress made.
- Extension of reforms to selected new institutions on the basis of their likelihood of having a rapid fiscal return on a marginal investment of additional resources.

- Consolidation of reforms in the administrative, financial, and control processes regulated by the SAFCO Act (including planning, budget, treasury and procurements processes). Continued modernization of the SIGMA would serve as another tool for those administrative processes.

Policies for an Efficient and Transparent Management of Public Expenditures

Proposals to Improve Planning. Some of the key elements for pursuing this goal are:

- **Restrict the capacity of the government or Congress** to exceed appropriate limits in the absence of supplementary budgets. This is a fundamental principle, since there should not be any expenses without appropriations. Furthermore, Congress needs to respect the budget envelope and macroeconomic goals (which could be communicated to the congressional sub-commissions sufficiently in advance and prior to the submission of the complete budget) and not jeopardize the country's macroeconomic stability.
- **Ensure that the budget covers all government agencies** in order to have accurate information on the funds committed and the responsibilities of the government.
- **Tie expenditures to fluctuations in the prices of natural resources.** This is important to "save" revenue and avoid unsustainable expenditures when revenue collection levels fall.
- **Start to prepare estimates of the budget package for a progressive period of three years**, which will facilitate an assessment of existing responsibilities and provide a margin for new initiatives.
- **Provide estimates of transfers to the subnational governments in a timely fashion.** This will be facilitated by the medium term approach to the central budget and will allow the subnational governments to submit realistic, timely budgets to their councils or commissions. This is a fundamental element to consolidate fiscal accountability at the subnational level.

Strengthening of the National Planning System. There is a need to establish processes and methodologies to define priorities for investment and public expenditures for the general budget. This will make it possible to turn the Economic and Social Development Plan into a management tool to prioritize programs and projects, establish monitoring and evaluation indicators, respond more effectively to the development needs of the various sectors in the country, evaluate the results of those responses, and have an objective basis for decisions on the reallocation of public expenditures. Chile and Colombia, which have planning, follow-up, and evaluation entities and systems regarding public expenditures, offer alternatives that would be applicable and of great benefit to Bolivia. Introducing these mechanisms would also aid the implementation of an orderly decentralization process, since it would allow the central government to transfer jurisdiction and funds under specific requirements that would permit monitoring and evaluating the results of those transfers.

Functional Classification.[14] The budget does not include functional classifications. There is a classification of economic sectors (for example, energy, water, and waste), but that cannot be considered a functional classification *per se*. There needs to be a detailed classification of the activities and social and economic objectives pursued by the governmental entities through different types of expenditures.

The Classification of Functions of Governments (COFOG) provides an appropriate classification for public expenditures on functions, which has been proven to be of general interest and open to a wide variety of analytical applications. The statistics on health, education, and social and environmental protection, for example, can be used to study the effectiveness of government programs in these areas. The COFOG codes are somewhat different than the structure of other Government Finance Statistics (GFS) classification codes. The functions are divided into three levels. The COFOG classification makes it possible to track trends in government expenditures on particular functions or evaluate objectives over time. Conventional public accounting is not usually appropriate for this purpose because it reflects the organizational structure of the government. Not only can time series be distorted with organizational changes, but at any given time certain organizations could be responsible for more than one function. A given function could also be divided among several organizations. For example, if a government creates a new agency that takes over certain functions previously administered by another agency or by different levels of government (which happens constantly in Bolivia), it would not be possible to use conventional public accounting to compare such expenditures over time.

The items classified should mainly be individual transactions so that each purchase of goods and services, payment of wages, transfer, or other expenditure is assigned a COFOG code in accordance with the function that the transaction serves. For most expenditures, it will not be possible to use the transactions as classification items. On the other hand, COFOG codes could be assigned to all transactions of the agencies, program offices, and similar units within the ministries of the government.

A single classification cannot respond to every analytical objective. The selection of functions under the COFOG codes does not work that way. The scope of each function might be broader or more limited, and completely different functions might be grouped together. For example, expenses for medicines at schools are classified by COFOG under education, not health. Research and development could be a function in and of itself, but under the COFOG codes, research and development is classified according to the objective it serves. Therefore, COFOG statistics should be used with caution to ensure that the desired coverage is met for the specific analytical purposes in question.

The proposed classification respects the principles set forth in the Government Finance Statistics Manual of the IMF for 2001.[15] These classifications also include the COFOGs of the Organization for Economic Cooperation and Development (OECD) and of the United Nations. Nonetheless, it is important to stress that a complete implementation of these principles requires the preparation, among other items, of the balance sheet, a declaration of the operations of the government, and a declaration of all economic flows that require the adoption of the current accounting base.

SIGMA. Improvement of the financial management system will be facilitated by taking the following measures:

- Do not extend SIGMA to sub-national levels until their processing capacities permit.
- Take short-term measures to improve the system's functionality, transaction speeds, and report generation as requested by the principal users.
- Develop a web page that provides public access to SIGMA information, with user-friendly information.
- Establish a committee of SIGMA users whose principal objective is to discuss and define the desirable features of an information system. This conceptualization process is fundamental prior to making decisions regarding the system's future.
- Present budget information using the program-based classification in accordance with the strategic priorities articulated for the fight against poverty.
- Improve the monitoring of results for sectors that have solid program-based classifications; link key intermediate indicators to the respective areas of government intervention.
- Clarify information on the underlying budget rules and implement pilot projects to involve the general public in the basic elements of the budget process; use the examples of South Africa and Uganda.

Proposal for a Results-Based Budget.[16] To advance toward using the budget as an instrument for supporting results-based management, certain preliminary measures still need to be developed in public administration and the budget process. For public administration, strategically prioritizing funds and evaluating management are needed. This calls for establishing minimum references for priority action and investment areas in the medium and long term, in addition to reviewing the design and organization of program structures and identifying how they contribute to generating products, detecting duplications of functions with other public institutions, and determing whether the users and beneficiaries, as well as the objectives and goals they publicly address, have been clearly defined. Thus, migrating to a results-based budget (ascertaining the effects of the expenditures on the beneficiary population) always requires moving toward a budget and a programming approach based on the products that the entities provide. This requires the consolidation and efficient operation of the systems identified in the SAFCO Act.

For the budget process, it is necessary to develop a series of measures that consider the regulations and procedures, the players involved, and institutional capacities that affect overall results. This calls for systematization and consistency in budget regulations, greater complementarity among the various stages of the budget cycle and the agents involved, and the development and integration of mechanisms and instruments to improve public management.

In this context, it is fundamental for the instruments and methodologies developed to be articulated using a system-wide approach that integrates the phases and rationalizes the instruments of the budget process. This ranges from an objectives- or goals-based prioritizing of the funds to providing performance feedback in the evaluation phase on expenditure management and results achieved. In addition, it is necessary to continue current efforts to develop management conventions (currently in a pilot phase between the Ministry of Finance, the Customs Service, and the SIN) to allow for institutional learning and coordination by defining the objectives, goals, and performance indicators that will be monitored and evaluated.

Proposals for the Procurement System. The following are reform proposals for the procurement system: (i) establish its institutional framework through a Procurements Act; (ii) create a central office responsible for supervising the purchasing system, with specialized personnel; (iii) integrate the System for the Procurement of Goods and Services into SIGMA; (iv) start to install an electronic purchases system; (v) consolidate a database of providers; (vi) improve the information provided to the public regarding government purchases; (vii) establish and implement an auditing and special investigations plan that contemplates standards and results; and (viii) study the possibility of instituting corporate purchases to gain savings (see also Box 1).

Civil Service. In this area, the principal recommendations are the following:

- Update the registration of government employees to control, among other aspects, the hiring and termination of personnel, and extend the registration process to the entire public administration.
- Integrate the registration information with the individual service record of each government employee. This record should have all the information on the services provided to the state and, together with the registration, would constitute the information base for designing and implementing the salary and administrative career policy.
- Define penalties and incentives in the registration program to ensure compliance. The personnel and directors must have an incentive to ensure that the payroll roster and the personnel data and information are complete, correct, and included in the registration.
- Use competitive, transparent hiring for public employees and prepare and apply a new wage and human resources policy. These reforms should allow Bolivia to rationalize the body of government employees, reorder human resources, standardize public functions and wages, and establish performance-based promotion mechanisms. The current registration program for government employees is the ideal information tool for carrying out these pending reforms.

Box 1. International Experiences on Improving the Procurement System

In Peru, CONSUCODE is a specialized public procurements entity that enjoys technical, functional, administrative, economic, and financial independence. CONSUCODE: (i) plays a regulatory role and provides technical and legal assistance in matters related to compliance with regulations; (ii) administers the national vendor registration system, and (iii) resolves controversies related to compliance with regulations in the bidding competition phase. CONSUCODE has implemented a national conciliation and arbitration system but does not act as an arbitrator; it provides training and certification to independent professionals regarding local procurement and its practices so that they can act as arbitrators and resolve any disputes and conflicts that may arise during the contract implementation stage. The agency has made a commitment to develop and implement the Electronic Procurements and Contracting System (*Sistema Electrónico de Adquisiciones y Contrataciones del Estado*—SEACE).

In Brazil, COMPRASNET offers Internet services for government employees and vendors. COMPRASNET also contains information for the public in general, such as legislation and manuals. The service for government employees offers the following applications: a discussion forum, questions on government contract pricing, and the SIASG module, which is used to tender documents and also issues amendments, among other functions. This webpage allows government employees to download a catalog of goods and services, and search documents.

In Mexico, COMPRANET was established to ensure transparency and efficiency in the management of public procurement. The system allows purchasing agencies to announce tenders for goods and public works online; bids can also be submited online and in real time. COMPRANET has statistical information to supervise the performance of vendors of goods and services and allows online access using international communications for a secure electronic exchange open to the public in general and to individuals interested in specific information on the processes, providing coded applications and electronic signatures to ensure confidentiality. The system is recognized by a legal statute and all the transactions and electronic signatures are legally binding.

Policies to Improve Public Revenue

Tax Administration and Customs. These recommendations will facilitate reform:

- For the Customs Service, the pending tasks are: (i) determination of organizational redefinition, role, and titles for the board of directors; (ii) use of information to improve oversight; (iii) development of a comprehensive strategy to combat contraband; (iv) incorporation of management techniques and teamwork as well as coordination of other oversight entities; and (v) consolidation of the strategic plan throughout the institution.

- For SIN: (i) completion of the enrollment of taxpayers; (ii) improvement of the information technology control processes; (iii) continued reinforcing of oversight; and (iv) establishment of specialized units for the various economic sectors.
- Forging a political and social consensus that prevents appropriation of the tax administration and the customs service by special interest groups, and reinforcement of the technical capabilities of the SIN, the Customs Service, and the Tax Superintendency.
- Elimination of interim mandates. Particularly in the Customs Service, interim mandates prevent management from developing a long-term vision; this, coupled with the continual changes in directors and chairpersons, thwarts the institution's development.
- Establishment of a system of budget incentives to reduce tax evasion, tax fraud, and contraband as it moves to improve service for taxpayers and users.
- Evaluation of the financial sustainability of the institutions so that they will not have to depend on the international aid community.
- Technical evaluation of systems. For the Customs Service, the Automated Customs System (*Sistema Aduanero Automatizado*—SIDUNEA) could provide an alternative to developing a system of its own. For the SIN, the strategy of electronic procedures could be strengthened.
- Establishment of formal coordination mechanisms among the SIN, the Customs Service, and other entities of the Ministry of Finance, with the aim of strengthening oversight and the control of collections.
- Building a rapid, common government strategy that integrates the formal private sector and serves as a guide in the fight against contraband.
- Simplifying the SIN's procedures as well as the Customs Service's import procedures.
- Avoiding new contracts with pre-shipping clearance companies.

Asset Management. The institutional weakness of the SENAPE and a lack of management tools keeps it from efficiently fulfilling its functions. Redefining this entity could better enable it to fulfill an important role that would consist of:

- Regularizing, valuating, registering, and controlling government assets.
- Optimizing the management of government assets; generating income and fiscal savings through the optimal application of useful assets; and eliminating idle and/or unnecessary assets that cause unproductive expenditures.
- Acting as a specialized vehicle for the "departure" of assets when there is no justification to keep them in the property of the state.

The principal results expected would be: (i) assets would be "resolved" through their efficient allocation, generating income and fiscal savings; (ii) liabilities and litigations would be "reallocated"; (iii) resources would be released for reassignment and training purposes; (iv) a State Assets Management Program (*Programa de Gestión de Activos del Estado*—PROGAE) would be developed to optimize the management of government property; (v) Bolivia would have an instrument to execute PROGAE and to effectively and efficiently dispose of public sector assets; and (vi) fiscalization would be controlled effectively.

Policies to Improve Access to Government Services and Information

The complexity of government regulation and administrative procedures, along with a generalized perception of corrupt practices, are major problems for the government. To address these problems, based on international experience, the following can be implemented:

- A procedures simplification program.
- Appropriate e-government mechanisms.
- Citizens' evaluation mechanisms regarding public management.
- Approval of rules for access to public information.

Simplification of processes and e-government. Bolivia has had successful experiences with simplification of processes, which, together with international experience, form a basis for defining procedures to identify existing processes, evaluate whether or not they are advisable, and identify problems and unnecessary costs generated by those processes.

Participation of the citizenry in public management. Bolivia could introduce citizenry evaluation mechanisms for government services. Optional mechanisms could be similar to Argentina's Citizen Charters (*Cartas Compromiso*), which are governmental goals committed to by public entities to improve management of the service; Peru's feedback sheets (*fichas de evaluación*), through which users evaluate the efficiency of specific public services; or citizen control bulletin boards, through which the entities themselves evaluate the quality of the service.

Access to public information. A law on access to public information is a pressing need to increase the transparency of government activities. This would reduce the perception that corruption reigns.

Bibliography

Ahmad E., G. Brosio, A. Díaz, I. Fainboim, R. Villela, and C. Parente. 2004. Improving Budget and Decentralization Processes. IMF, Fiscal Affairs Department, November 2004.

Alborta, P., and M. Barg. 2005. *Evaluación de la Ley SAFCO*, World Bank. La Paz, Bolivia.

Fanta, E. 2005. *Evaluación Aduana Nacional de Bolivia, Su proceso de Modernización y Reforma Institucional 1999-2005 Recomendaciones para su fortalecimiento.* Institutional Reform Project (*Proyecto de Reforma Institucional*). La Paz, Bolivia.

Fizbein, Ariel. 2005. "Citizens, Politicians and Providers. The Latin American Experience with Service Delivery Reform." World Bank, Washington, DC, January.

Goméz, R. 2005. National Service for Government Property (*Servicio Nacional de Patrimonio del Estado*—SENAPE), *Proyecto de Reforma Institucional Consultoría # Utpri – 059/2005.*

Hashim, Ali, and Bill Allan. 2001. World Bank, Treasury Reference Model; Technical Paper No. 505; May.

Inter-American Development Bank. 2005. *Documento preliminar de concepto para un préstamo del BID a Bolivia.* April 18, 2005.

International Monetary Fund. 2001. Government Finance Statistics Manual.

Kaufmann, D., G. Mehrez, and T. Gurgur. World Bank Institute, Voice or Public Sector Management? An Empirical Investigation of Determinants of Public Sector Performance based on a Survey of Public Officials in Bolivia; June 2002.

Kaufmann, Daniel, Aart Kraay, and Massimo Mastruzzi. 2005. "Governance Matters IV, Governance Indicators for 1996-2004." World Bank Policy Research Paper No. 3630. May. Washington, DC.

Overseas Development Institute. 2002. Development Strategies, Center for Aid and Public Expenditure, Results-Based Public Management in Bolivia. Preliminary document. London, England, October 2002.

SAFCO. 1990. Act.

———. 2002. *Introducción: Bolivia y sus retos de Futuro;* Fundación Friedrich Ebert-ILDIS, La Paz, Bolivia, August.

———.1999. *Los desafíos de la representación política*, in *Opiniones y Análisis*. Fundemos, La Paz.

Shepherd. G., Waagstein, T. *et al.* 2005. *Bolivia Proyecto de Reforma Institucional Evaluación Independiente.*

Toranzo, Carlos. 2004. *Democracia Partidos y sus Desafíos.* La Paz, Bolivia. October.

World Bank. 1994. Bolivia: Economic Country Memorandum.

———. 1999. Public Expenditure Review.

———. 2000a. Bolivia: From Patronage to a Professional State: Bolivia Institutional and Governance Review.

———. 2000b. Country Procurement Assessment Report (CPAR). November.

———. 2004. Country Financial Accountability Assessment (CFAA). June.

———. 2005a. *Evaluación Independiente del Proyecto de Reforma Institucional (PRI) I*. April.

———. 2005b. *Evaluación Preliminar Ley SAFCO*. May.

———. 2005c. *Bolivia: Memorándum Económico del País: Políticas para Mejorar el Crecimiento y el Empleo*. July.

———. 2006. Institutional and Governance Review. First draft.

World Bank and International Finance Corporation. 2005. "Doing Business 2006. Creating Jobs." September.

World Bank, IDB, and Department for International Development of the United Kingdom (DFID). 2004. Bolivia: Public Expenditure Review. La Paz, Bolivia.

ANNEX I

Governance Indicators, World Bank Institute
(1996–2004)

Indicator	*2004*	*2002*	*2000*	*1998*	*1996*
Voice and Accountability					
Estimate (−2.5 to +2.5)	−0.01	0.01	0.23	0.35	0.1
Rank: Percentile (0–100)		50.0	56.5	60.2	56.5
Standard Deviation	0.15	0.18	0.22	0.23	0.20
Number of Studies/Surveys	10	9	6	5	5
Political Stability and Absence of Violence					
Estimate (−2.5 to +2.5)	−0.65	−0.06	−0.42	0.08	−0.23
Rank: Percentile (0–100)		36.8	35.8	46.7	31.7
Standard Deviation	0.22	0.21	0.27	0.27	0.34
Number of Studies/Surveys	9	8	7	5	4
Government Effectiveness					
Estimate (−2.5 to +2.5)	−0.63	−0.53	−0.40	−0.11	−0.44
Rank: Percentile (0–100)		34.5	39.7	55.2	33
Standard Deviation	0.17	0.16	0.20	0.22	0.24
Number of Studies/Surveys	10	8	7	6	4
Regulatory Quality					
Estimate (−2.5 to +2.5)	0.05	−0.12	0.65	0.90	0.82
Rank: Percentile (0–100)		50.5	75.1	82.1	81.2
Standard Deviation	0.19	0.18	0.29	0.33	0.27
Number of Studies/Surveys	9	8	6	5	5
Rule of Law					
Estimate (−2.5 to +2.5)	−0.55	−0.60	−0.51	−0.35	−0.66
Rank: Percentile (0–100)		32.5	40.0	46.5	29.5
Standard Deviation	0.13	0.14	0.16	0.20	0.18
Number of Studies/Surveys	12	12	11	9	7
Control of Corruption					
Estimate (−2.5 to +2.5)	−0.78	−0.82	−0.65	−0.41	−0.87
Rank: Percentile (0–100)		25.3	27.7	42.1	22.0
Standard Deviation	0.15	0.16	0.17	0.19	0.24
Number of Studies/Surveys	10	9	9	8	4

Source: Kaufmann, Kraay, and Mastruzzi, 2005.

Voice and Accountability /Latin America—2004/2000

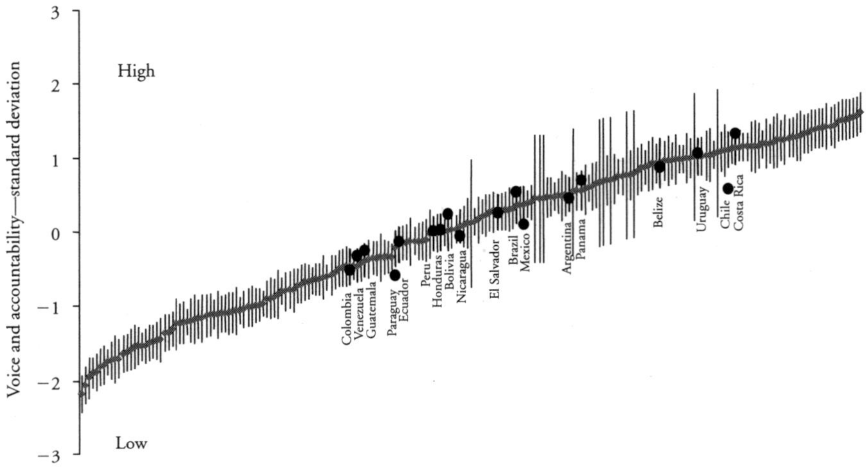

Note: The grey points represent estimated governance indicators for 2004. The vertical lines represent the standard deviation of estimates for each country in the global sample. The black points refer to the year 2002.

Political Stability/Latin America—2004/2000

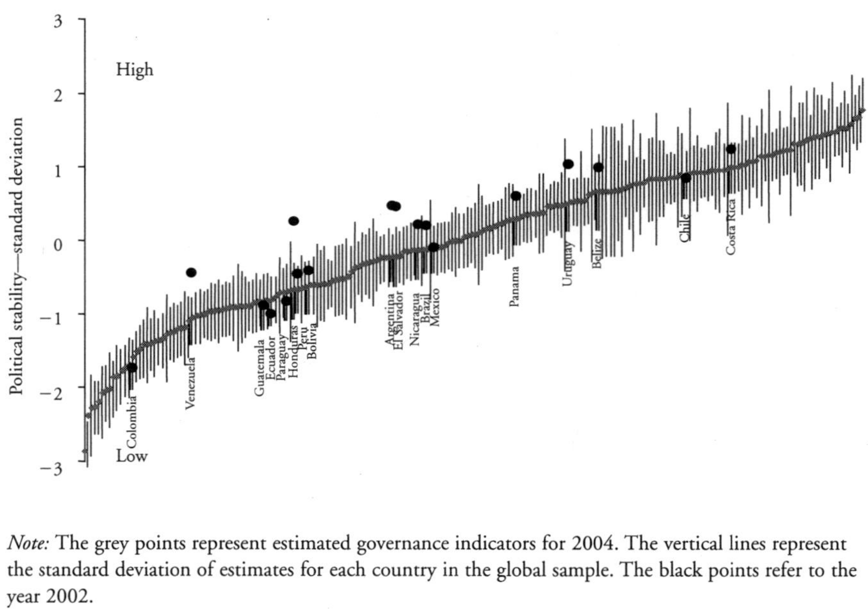

Note: The grey points represent estimated governance indicators for 2004. The vertical lines represent the standard deviation of estimates for each country in the global sample. The black points refer to the year 2002.

Regulatory Quality / Latin America 2004/2000

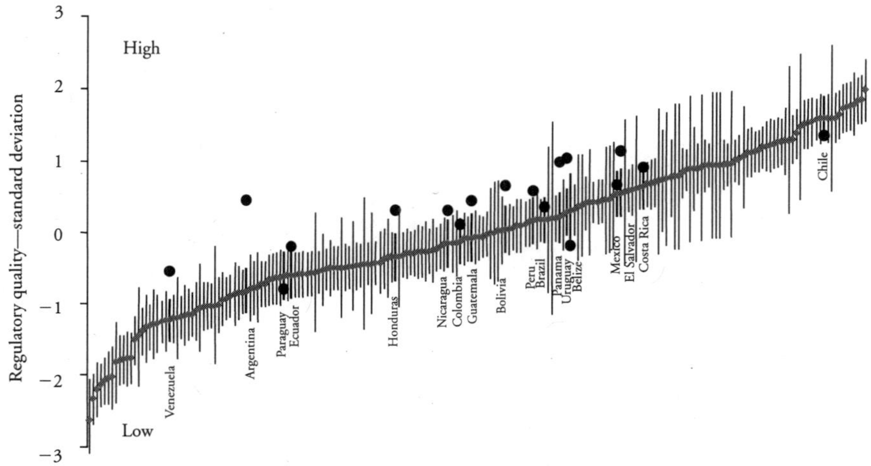

Note: The grey points represent estimated governance indicators for 2004. The vertical lines represent the standard deviation of estimates for each country in the global sample. The black points refer to the year 2002.

Rule of Law /Latin America- 2004/2000

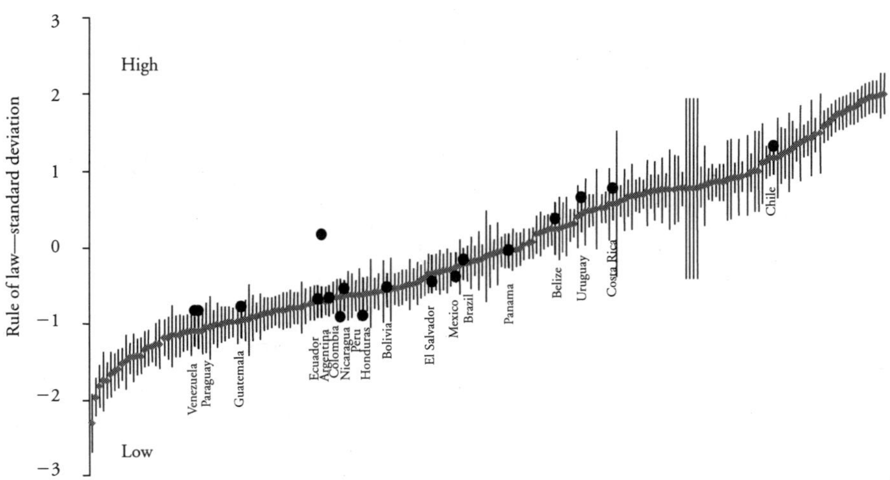

Note: The grey points represent estimated governance indicators for 2004. The vertical lines represent the standard deviation of estimates for each country in the global sample. The black points refer to the year 2002.

Control of Corruption/Latin America 2004/2000

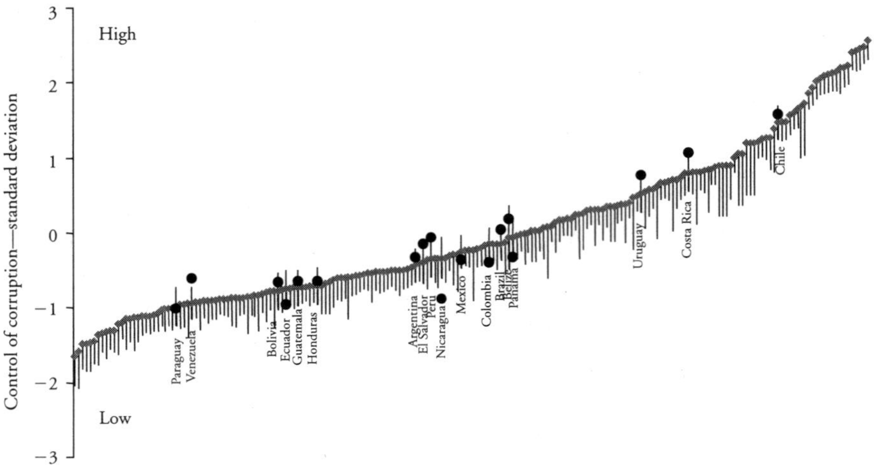

Note: The grey points represent estimated governance indicators for 2004. The vertical lines represent the standard deviation of estimates for each country in the global sample. The black points refer to the year 2002.

Government Effectiveness/Latin America- 2004/2000

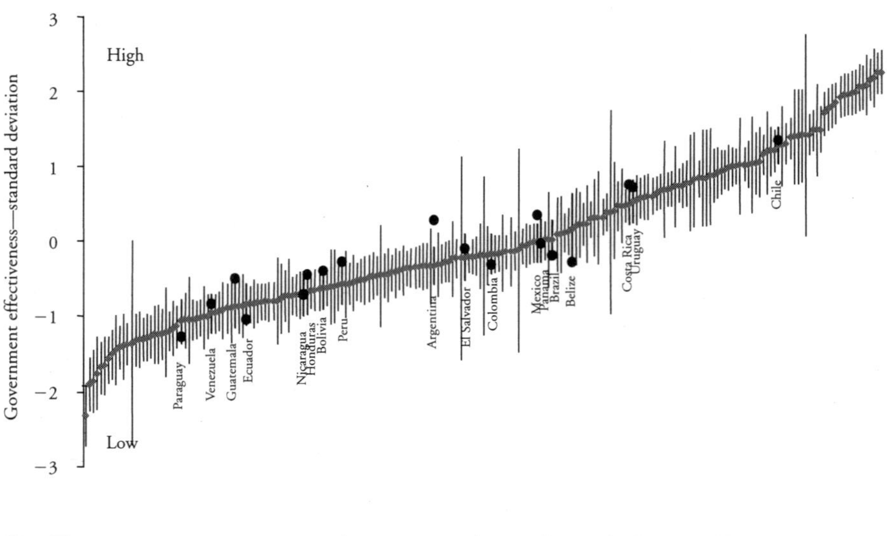

Note: The grey points represent estimated governance indicators for 2004. The vertical lines represent the standard deviation of estimates for each country in the global sample. The black points refer to the year 2002.

Endnotes

1. Between 1993-1999, Bolivia grew at an average rate of 4.7 percent, which surpassed that of other Andean countries. Investment reached 18 percent, higher than the average of the 1980s by 4 percentage points, and per capita income increased by 13 percent. The urban poor population decreased from 52 percent to 46 percent and infant mortality decreased by 30 percent. Enrollment in primary education almost reached full coverage (see World Bank, 2005c).
2. World Bank, 2000a.
3. The country returned to its previous levels of poverty, growth fell by half during 1999 to 2003 and unemployment grew from 6 percent to 9 percent. All of this, coupled with extreme inequality in the distribution of income, has made nine out of every 10 Bolivians state that the distribution of wealth in the country is unjust. These conditions have been feeding a high degree of social discontent.
4. This section is based on the analysis and results presented in World Bank (2005b).
5. See Ahmad, *et al.*, 2004; and World Bank, 2004.
6. Excluding the education and health sector and the Armed Forces and police, which have their own selection and hiring systems.
7. Aggregated indicators include data as of 1996. Available on the Internet at: http://www.worldbank.org/wbi/governance/pubs/govmatters4.html.
8. http://www.transparency.org.
9. World Bank and International Financial Corporation, 2005.
10. For example, World Bank, 1999 and 2004.
11. The central version of the SIGMA contains a commitments control module. However, due to difficulties with its functionality and coverage, some central agencies are not applying the controls and include unrecorded commitments, which must then be regularized at the end of the year (thereby placing pressure on the liquidity situation).
12. In 2004, this applied most prominently to the expected loans from the National Regional Development Fund (*Fondo Nacional de Desarrollo Regional*—FNDR) but also occurred with revenue sharing transfers to the departments. In addition, the central government has offered to make payments with 90-day notes (Fiscal Credit Certificates) that can be used to pay taxes.
13. Ahmad *et al.*, 2004.
14. IMF, 2001.
15. IMF, 2001.
16. This section is in line with the findings and proposals presented in IDB, 2005.

22

The Second Phase of Decentralization

Jonas Frank and Edgardo Mosqueira

Summary

After more than a decade of strengthening the municipal level of government, the second phase of decentralization in Bolivia will focus on the departmental level. The driving force behind this stage will, without question, be the redistribution of new revenue derived from the exploitation of natural resources and royalties. The priority challenges will be to reduce departmental inequality in the transfers, improve the provision of services, and ensure fiscal accountability. Bolivia could act in the short term to ensure the success of the second phase of decentralization by: (i) establishing minimum institutional capacities regarding the management of human resources, the purchase of goods, and follow-up and evaluation on the quality of public services; (ii) improving the system of fiscal transfers to attain greater departmental equity; and (iii) strengthening fiscal accountability. These strategies are essential to ensuring that, in the long term, the country will be able to grant the departmental governments greater autonomy to administer their funds, transfer other authority to them, allow the country to leverage the advantages of decentralization and improve services for all its citizens.

I. Introduction

In Bolivia, decentralization continues to be the greatest challenge in efforts to improve governability, strengthen fiscal accountability, and improve public services.

This chapter is based on "Bolivia. Institutional and Governance Review" (World Bank, 2006), under preparation.

Decentralization is key to rebuilding the country's shattered social contract and creating a more legitimate political system. Following the decentralization of the municipalities, which began in April 1994, the country is now moving into a second phase, oriented more toward departmental governments[1] and focused on the distribution of revenue from the exploitation of major natural resources. The first step in this new direction was the election by popular vote of nine departmental prefects in December 2005. The second step was the new Hydrocarbons Act, which defines the distribution of funds from the exploitation of oil and gas. This law will have a significant influence on the progress of this second phase of decentralization.

Given the experience of Bolivia and of other countries, it is clear that the benefits associated with decentralization cannot materialize unless the process is correctly planned and implemented. Fiscal accountability continues to be a challenge, particularly in the initial period of this new decentralized order, in which pressure to increase spending will be substantial. Furthermore, the quality of public services is still very low in all the departments and sectors. To improve this situation, new incentives are needed, along with a minimum of institutional capacities at the national and subnational levels.

This chapter makes proposals to strengthen fiscal accountability and obtain better public services in the decentralization process. It first reviews the background to these reforms. Next, it analyzes the principal problems faced by decentralization in light of recent events (particularly the election of prefects and the subnational revenue generated by the new Hydrocarbons Act). The final section proposes short- and long-term policy options aimed at resolving such problems.

II. Background

The **first phase** of decentralization was municipal in nature. The process commenced in 1994 with the Popular Participation Act, which created the current municipal governments. Although their functionality is far from perfect, the councils are playing an ever increasing economic and political role. As an indication of that, community spending now represents approximately 18 percent of total public expenditures and will further increase with the enactment of the new Hydrocarbons Act. As occurs in many countries, the municipal leaders are highly respected, much more so than the officials of other institutions in the country.

In 1995, shortly after municipal decentralization, reform was undertaken at the departmental level. Part of this reform consisted of establishing the prefectures as deconcentrated entities of the central government. Nonetheless, the prefectures were hybrid institutions. On the one hand, they were delegations of the central government, headed up by a prefect that the President designated. On the other hand, there were departmental councils, whose members were elected by the department's municipalities through indirect suffrage. The prefectures prepared the budgets, which were approved by the councils (Figure A.1 in the Annex). Prior to the enactment of the Hydrocarbons Act, the prefectures were disbursing 8.6 percent of total public expenditures.[2] But they are still very weak from an institutional point of view and have major limitations for providing services. In 1999, for example, in response to a deterioration in the quality of the roads service in the hands of the departmental entities, the roads system was recentralized and transferred from the prefectures to the central government.

In the initial round of the emerging process since 1994, Bolivia turned into a relatively decentralized country in terms of spending.[3] Prior to the enactment of the Hydrocarbons Act, the subnational governments were already managing 27 percent of total public expenditures. However, the subnational governments collect less than 6 percent of total taxes and royalties. This makes them highly dependent on transfers; the level of dependency of the prefectures (97 percent on the average) is far higher than that of the municipalities (68 percent).

Bolivia is now entering a **second phase** of decentralization that emphasizes the departmental level. While the driving force behind the first phase was democratization and popular participation, this phase is being driven by the fight for natural resources and, particularly, for revenue from the exploitation of hydrocarbons.[4] One of the major problems occasioned by these demands is that the departments are debating how to divvy up the funding pie, and not how to finance or improve public services.

For these reasons, two important decisions have been made regarding decentralization:

(i) *Election of the prefects.* This is a milestone in the process, because the departmental prefectures will have *de facto* autonomy, regardless of the decisions made by the Constitutional Reform Assembly in 2006. It should be remembered that the election of these departmental authorities had broad popular support (Figure 1). Political decentralization through the elections of the prefect means that there are now nine new negotiators or political players. It also means that corporate groups, above all from the private sector, have better possibilities of creating ties with the government under conditions more favorable than are present in most of the country's municipalities.

(ii) *The distribution of additional revenue from the hydrocarbons sector.* Close to two-thirds of the additional funds from collections under the Hydrocarbons Act[5] (estimated at US$240 million for the year 2006) will be available to the departments and municipalities without creating new jurisdiction over expenses for the municipalities[6] (Table 1). During the first year, the central government will retain 36 percent of the tax revenue from the Direct Tax on Hydrocarbons (*Impuesto Directo a los Hidrocarburos*—IDH), but this percentage will gradually diminish until it reaches 32.5 percent in 2007. The prefectures will receive 33 percent of the IDH revenue, while municipalities and decentralized institutions, such as the universities, will receive 24.8 percent and 6.2 percent, respectively, of that revenue in the first year; this will gradually increase to 27.6

Figure 1. Survey Results: Demand for Political Decentralization, March 2005

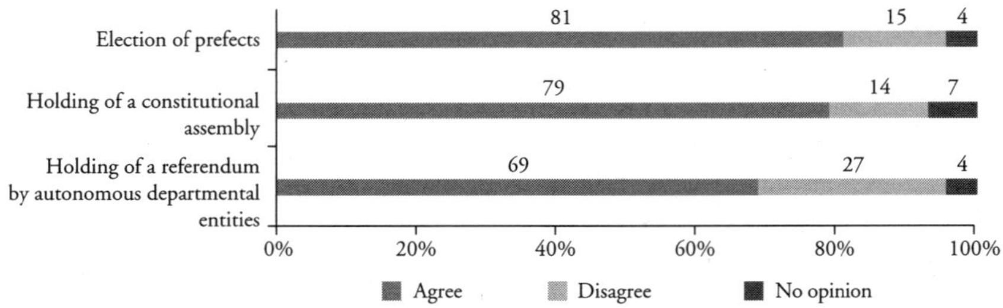

Source: Opinion and Market Survey (March to July 2005).

Table 1. Revenue from Royalties of the Oil and Gas Sector, by Level of Government, Hydrocarbons Act, 2006

Royalties and IDH (millions of dollars)	*Former Law*	*New Law (first year)*	*New Law (fourth year and later)*
Central government	132.0	225.7	208.9
Departmental government	203.1	326.5	326.5
Municipal government		119.5	132.9
Decentralized institutions		29.9	33.3
Total	**335.1**	**701.6**	**701.6**

Source: World Bank estimate, based on information from the Ministry of Finance (2005a).

percent and 6.9 percent, respectively. Following the enactment of the Hydrocarbons Act, 35 percent of public expenditures will be made by the subnational governments, as compared with 27 percent in 2004 (Table 2).

As will be discussed below, these two decisions will have significant effects on the form of the second phase of decentralization. Their application poses several problems that need to be resolved for the process to be successful.

III. Challenges of Decentralization

An Inadequate Decentralization Strategy

Bolivia still lacks a coherent decentralization strategy aimed at strengthening the subnational governments. In this regard, there are three challenges. The first involves the

Table 2. Ratio of Decentralization before and after the Hydrocarbons Act

	Before (percent, 2004)	*After (percent, 2006)*
Departments (prefectures)		
Ratio[a] of decentralization of expenditures	8.6	13.2
Ratio[b] of tax decentralization	0.5	0.4
Ratio[c] of dependency on transfers	96.6	99.3
Municipalities		
Ratio of decentralization of expenditures	18.3	21.5
Ratio of tax decentralization	5.4	4.5
Ratio of dependency on transfers	67.6	74.2
Subnational governments		
Ratio of decentralization of expenditures	26.9	34.7
Ratio of tax decentralization	5.8	4.9
Ratio of dependency on transfers	66.6	73.1

Source: World Bank

Notes: a. prefecture expenditures/total public sector expenditures; b. prefecture taxes/total public sector taxes; c. transfers/total revenue. Figures for the departmental prefectures exclude payroll.

starting points for the decentralization process and the chronology for their implementation. Experience in Latin America generally, including Bolivia particularly, suggests that for technical and political reasons, decisions adopted by a central government regarding decentralization end up being irreversible. It is therefore fundamental to choose the starting points for the process well, because afterward it becomes very difficult to reverse them. In Bolivia, the starting point for decentralization is political reform and reform of the representation system, through prefect elections at a departmental level. This starting point, though understandable in the current social context, is not so fortunate considering the experience of other countries in the region. Colombia, Peru, and Venezuela, among others, opted for this same starting point, which has created a new framework of incentives upon granting greater political autonomy to the departmental levels. They concerned themselves very little over first reorganizing fiscal relationships or expenditure allocations, which has created pressures to increase spending and has weakened fiscal accountability. In addition, this has had a political cost for the subnational governments elected by the population and now in charge of collecting their own taxes; in addition, it has often perpetuated a preference for transfers from the central government. Furthermore, the reforms have not eliminated duplication in service provision between municipalities and departments, since municipal and departmental politicians both seek electoral support (particularly in urban areas).

Political decentralization also brings in new negotiators at the local and departmental level who will work to control a greater share of public spending and national funds. Bolivia's departmental prefectures were already working with a certain degree of autonomy. But recent changes have formalized this trend, which will make it more difficult to agree on the size and nature of certain public goods and services. One area affected is macroeconomic stability. As seen in countries such as Brazil and Argentina, decentralization initiated at a political level can lead certain regions to overexploit and take advantage of the prudent fiscal policies of other regions as a public asset. Chile is one of the few Latin American countries that delayed political decentralization at the regional level. There, the starting point for decentralization was a carefully planned administrative reform. Improvements in the delivery of services and fiscal discipline are achievements that have lent credibility to decentralization.

The second challenge is related to the chronology of the reform, because decentralization does not progress in an integrated manner at the national, departmental, and municipal levels. The reforms tend to be considered and enacted separately. The best example of this is the municipal reform of 1994, which was unconnected to the prefectures. It would thus be essential for future decentralization to select another starting point and use a sector-based approach: this would facilitate the assignment of jurisdictions at the national, departmental, and municipal levels. This is a necessary condition to be able to reap some of the potential benefits of decentralization in the future, that is, greater efficiency in the delivery of services and more accountability to the citizens.

The third challenge refers to the nature of the prefectures. Unlike the municipalities, the departmental level faces certain structural restrictions for designing decentralization in each of the following aspects:

- Fiscal decentralization: departmental governments are more dependent on transfers, since they have no revenue of their own. This reality also places soft restrictions on the budget, which requires effective fiscal accountability rules.
- Administrative decentralization: the departmental level also is particularly susceptible to overlaps between its actions and those of other levels of government, due to its "intermediation" and coordination roles. This means that particular attention must be paid to clearly defining the jurisdiction of each level of government.
- Political decentralization: finally, the departmental level is not as "close to the people" as the municipalities, and its participation in defining public policies is more "corporate" in nature than "popular."

This means that some elements of Bolivia's decentralization strategy for the municipalities are not applicable or effective for the prefectures. A new decentralization strategy is therefore needed to address these challenges.

Challenges of Fiscal Decentralization

Intergovernmental Transfers

HORIZONTAL IMBALANCE: INEQUALITIES IN TRANSFERS AMONG DEPARTMENTS

One of the principal obstacles to improving services and distributing public expenditures more equitably among the departments is the current system of transfers to the prefectures, which is very unequal. As seen in Table 3, the transfers are not equitable. The department of La Paz receives only US$16 per capita, while Tarija receives US$246 and Pando receives US$407. The expenditures of the various departmental prefectures are also very unequal. These differences not only provoke confrontations among departments, but also keep the prefectures from being brought in line with one another in terms of public spending.

The new Hydrocarbons Act aggravates the situation (Table 3). Transfers to the departmental prefectures, which (in per capita terms) were already very unequal, are even more so with the new Hydrocarbons Act. This is because the distribution is now made in equal shares, after which another portion is added for the hydrocarbons "producer departments." In this regard, the transfers worked counter to redistribution prior to the new law and do so even more today. The same occurs with per capita spending.[7]

The municipal transfers system prior to the new Hydrocarbons Act did not create any horizontal inequality in municipal spending.[8] Transfers on a per capita basis have been quite equitable and do not vary much from one department to another. This situation is likely to continue in the future, because hydrocarbons revenue is allocated to the municipalities on a per capita basis.

It is also important to note that the flow of transfers to the non-producing departments is unstable, which further aggravates the problems described. Hydrocarbons revenue was pre-allocated to certain departments even before the enactment of the Hydrocarbons Act. This arrangement is prejudicial, because it increases fiscal pressures, since the non-producing departments must receive revenue offsets from the Treasury through other funds not derived from hydrocarbons. In addition, the pre-allocation of hydrocarbons revenue keeps these funds from being used for purposes other than as defined through the intergovernmental system, purposes that could have a greater economic and social impact.

Table 3. Impact of the Hydrocarbons Act on Interdepartmental Transfers, 2005 (Budget) and 2006 (Projections)
(dollars per capita)

	Before the Hydrocarbons Act (2005)	*After the Hydrocarbons Act (2006, projected)*
Chuquisaca	20.7	48.5
La Paz	9.5	15.8
Cochabamba	20.1	30.3
Oruro	22.2	60.0
Potosí	15.0	35.8
Tarija	199.2	246.0
Santa Cruz	18.4	25.7
Beni	31.0	71.8
Pando	125.5	407.2

Source: World Bank.

VERTICAL FISCAL IMBALANCE: THE SUBNATIONAL GOVERNMENTS' HIGH DEPENDENCY ON TRANSFERS

The councils depend on transfers for 68 percent of their budget, and this percentage is expected to increase in 2006 to 74 percent, following the enactment of the Hydrocarbons Act. There are enormous differences between urban and rural municipalities. The rural municipalities are even more dependent on transfers than are the urban ones. Unlike the prefectures, however, the municipalities have tax revenue of their own, from taxation on automobiles and real estate.

The departmental prefectures are even more dependent than the municipalities. Almost 97 percent of their revenue is from government transfers, and this will reach 99 percent in 2006, when additional hydrocarbons revenue becomes available. In the future, there may be additional transfers for decentralized expenditures, which would perpetuate this dependency on funds from the central government. Without question, this situation contributes to creating major vertical fiscal imbalance, because a greater portion of the expense would be financed through transfers. Worse yet, the volatility of revenue flows could increase as hydrocarbons revenue becomes greater in proportion to total public funds shared with the departments. This would expose the departmental prefectures to greater fiscal risk, which could be particularly prejudicial depending on how the new revenue from the Hydrocarbons Act are used: for rigid expenditures or, conversely, for investment, which in most cases can respond more flexibly if revenue falls.

For all the reasons indicated above, it is urgent to strengthen the various administrations' potential bases for their own revenue, which should have a broader variety of sources. This is the central issue in the debate on decentralization in Bolivia and other countries. Absence of a tax base of one's own as autonomy expands has created major obstacles for numerous regional governments in other countries. The experience of Peru, Colombia, Ecuador, and Venezuela demonstrates that if the regions do not have their own sources of revenue, fiscal dependency on the central government ends up determining the day-to-day management of the regional administration. As compared with these countries, departmental governments in Bolivia are highly dependent on transfers (Table 4).

Table 4. Transfers and Revenue of Regional Governments in Selected Countries
(as a percentage)

	Transfers	*Revenue Raised by the Regional Governments*
Bolivia (2005)	96.6	3.4
Venezuela (2000)	98.4	1.6
Colombia (2000)	59.9	40.1
Ecuador (1998)	92.8	8.8
Peru (2000)	93.8	6.2
Spain (2001)	76.7	23.3

Source: Venezuela (Del Rosario and Mascareño, 2002); Colombia (Ballesteros and Maldonado, 2002); Ecuador (Conam, 2000); Peru (Pollarolo, 2001); Spain (Monasterio-Escudero and Suárez-Pandiello, 2002).

TRANSFERS OF REVENUE BUT NOT EXPENDITURES

Under the Hydrocarbons Act, funds are transferred without assigning additional expenditures to their beneficiaries. This unconditional delivery of funds creates two types of problems. The first is that, between 2005 and 2006, the average increase in the amount transferred to the prefectures will be 55 percent (in small departments such as Pando, this increase will be much greater), although the prefectures' capacity to absorb and use these funds is very limited. This challenges the prefectures' implementation capacity. Such limitations were already clearly evidenced, even in the smaller municipalities when, following 2001, they received funds from the public debt relief plan for highly indebted poor countries (HIPC).

The second problem is that the flow of funds is likely to be volatile and unstable in the future, since it depends on unpredictable hydrocarbons production. This volatility could jeopardize fiscal adjustment at subnational levels, especially if the money is used to acquire long-term obligations, such as the hiring of new employees, whose wages must be paid for several years. The revenue's volatility also limits possibilities for new expenditures in sectors with a high level of recurring expenses. For example, in the education sector, close to 50 percent of the budget is for payroll. If revenue diminishes, the central government would be forced to provide additional financing in order to avoid a service interruption.

Fiscal Accountability

Ensuring subnational fiscal stability is very difficult. In fact, the country already went through a recent municipal debt crisis after 2000; it was later brought under control. It will be essential for the authorities to adopt mechanisms for defining the rules of municipal and departmental indebtedness in order to avoid future problems.

One question that requires immediate attention is the debt inherited by the newly elected administrations. Although departmental debt is moderate (approximately 0.5 percent of the GDP), it could increase rapidly if the departmental prefectures do not have a responsible fiscal policy. In addition, departmental and municipal debt (which represents 5 percent of the GDP) is undervalued, since it is not recorded in its entirety. In accordance with current indicators of debt capacity, the new funds provided by the Hydrocarbons Act automatically grant the departmental prefectures and municipal councils a greater margin of indebtedness.[9] Even so, there is poor supervision and, therefore, a lack of transparency. A large part of the municipal debt (particularly vendor accounts payable) is floating debt, which makes its supervision difficult.

Another problem is related to new spending pressures, which can be exerted, above all, during the initial period of decentralization. Most of the decentralized countries have had to struggle with fiscal pressures during the transition phases, that is, when the central government cannot reduce its size in proportion to the subnational entities and, at the same time, takes on new expenditures. For example, there can be great pressure on wages if the decentralization of human resources is not well organized or if public employees go through two rounds of wage negotiations, one at the central level and another at the departmental level. Although it would be theoretically possible to create new departmental taxes that could act as a counterweight to excessive subnational spending, it is likely that their magnitude would be limited.

Bolivia is not the only country facing these problems, although in its immediate future, it appears quite likely to repeat some of the pathologies that afflict recently decentralized countries. Obviously, if the subnational governments fail to apply a responsible fiscal policy, negative externalities could appear on several fronts, some of which were already seen during the country's recent municipal debt crisis. Such irresponsible fiscal policy threatens the sustainability of public services (for which the central government could bear the ultimate political responsibility) and jeopardizes the security of the financial system, the country's international credibility, and macroeconomic stability. The central government could find itself providing frequent financial bailouts, which could affect its fiscal sustainability and reward the irresponsible fiscal policies of the subnational governments.

Institutional Problems

In Bolivia, there are many unsatisfied basic needs. Although much progress has been made, much still remains to be done, particularly in certain departments (Table 5). Moreover, the need to close the fiscal gap has made it necessary to take recourse in volatile funds, which makes it difficult to maintain the quality of public services at the subnational level. The principal causes of this poor quality of service are: (i) lack of institutional capacity; (ii) poor efficiency in productive and allocative terms; and (iii) an inadequate distribution of jurisdiction.

Table 5. Unsatisfied Needs, by Department, 2001
(as a percentage)

Department	*Inadequate Housing*	*Inadequate Habitation Space*	*Inadequate Water and Sewage Services*	*Inadequate Supply of Energy*	*Insufficient Educational Services*	*Insufficient Healthcare Services*
National Average	39.1	70.8	58.0	43.7	52.5	37.9
Chuquisaca	53.7	72.1	62.2	62.5	70.7	40.4
La Paz	41.9	66.0	53.2	39.0	49.1	64.9
Cochabamba	37.3	68.2	55.1	42.2	52.6	28.3
Oruro	39.2	67.2	65.9	41.8	47.2	58.8
Potosí	60.3	67.1	71.5	65.0	72.4	59.6
Tarija	30.4	71.5	45.6	43.1	60.5	14.7
Santa Cruz	23.0	77.0	55.8	33.9	43.6	6.4
Beni	63.2	85.0	82.4	64.2	54.6	31.7
Pando	40.4	80.5	83.6	64.8	61.3	39.3

Source: National Statistics Institute (*Instituto Nacional de Estadística*—INE) and Economic Policy Analysis Unit (*Unidad de Análisis de Política Económica*—UDAPE) (www.ine.gov.bo).

Lack of Minimum Institutional Capabilities

Financial and budget management on the national and subnational level is deficient.[10] There are no financial or human resources management (payroll) systems, nor are there systems for public sector acquisitions. This could become a serious problem as decentralization advances and the subnational governments obtain access to more funds. Systems of these types are more transparent and facilitate supervision, which is crucial for strengthening confidence among levels of government, and, in turn, is needed for decentralization.

Furthermore, much basic information needed in the education, health, and roads sectors is not currently available. For example, payroll information on primary and secondary health care and quality-of-service coverage indicators are incomplete. Without this information, it is difficult to establish what service costs should be attributed to each level of government, which is a basic requirement to reassign jurisdictions. In a decentralized system, each level of government must know what part of the cost it is responsible for.

This implies that for future decentralization, greater capacity to manage the funds is needed, as is additional information to improve the services.

Low Productive and Allocative Efficiency of the Departmental Prefectures

The departmental prefectures at present have little autonomy to administer their funds. Therefore, they cannot benefit from a more efficient combination of inputs to produce services, which is just one of the advantages of decentralization (production efficiency). The multiple funds received by the municipalities are, in large measure, pre-allocated. Currently, the prefectures can spend only 8 percent of the funds (transfers and their own revenue)[11] in accordance with their own priorities (Figure 2). More than two-thirds of the funds (68 percent) are allocated to departmental prefectures that do not have decision-making autonomy, especially with respect to remunerations of health and educational personnel (Group 4, Figure 2). In recent years, new transfers have been added, but each is accompanied by limitations on the use of the funds. The result is a complex network of rules and regulations that are not properly supervised or enforced. The extensive pre-allocation of funds, explained by the role assigned to the departments and by the degree of centralization, implies that the departmental prefectures have but a marginal degree of control to combine various inputs and funds in order to produce public services. This also undermines allocative efficiency, since these entities face limitations for providing the services most needed by the population.

Distribution of Jurisdiction

One of the most prominent features of the Bolivian intergovernmental system is the inefficient distribution of jurisdiction to each level of government (Table 6). In the educational system, for example, the central government is responsible for paying teachers, the departments are in charge of managing them, the municipalities are responsible for monitoring labor matters, and the districts have the authority to hire

Figure 2. Estimate of the Departmental Prefectures' Autonomy in Decision Making on Budget Matters, 2004
(as a percentage)

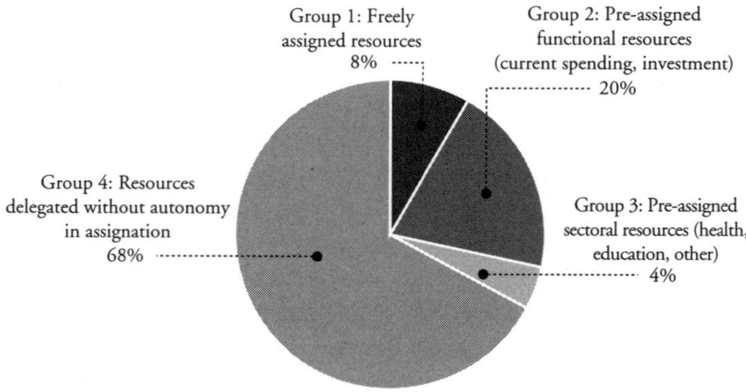

Source: World Bank based on executed budgets.

Table 6. Institutional Agreements in the Health, Education, and Roads Sectors

	Primary and Secondary Healthcare	*Primary and Secondary Education*	*Roads*
Central Government	Financing Planning	Financing Planning	National Roads Service: national roads system
Prefectures	Deconcentrated SEDES*: Payment of the health personnel (payroll). Administration of the health personnel. Control of standards. Infrastructure for secondary and tertiary services (if not transferred to the municipalities).	Deconcentrated SEDUCA**: payment of teachers (payroll) Management of the educational personnel. Control of standards. Issuance of certificates.	SEPCAM***: autonomous institution responsible for the departmental roads system.
Municipalities	Infrastructure (hospitals)	Infrastructure (schools)	Rural roads

*Departmental Health Services (*Servicio Departamental de Salud*—SEDES)
**Departmental Education Service (*Servicio Departamental de Educación*—SEDUCA)
***Prefecture Roads Services (*Servicios Prefecturales de Caminos*—SEPCAM)

and fire. When decision making is so fragmented, accountability becomes diluted. Accordingly, no individual level of government or service provider has sufficient control over inputs for the results to reflect their efforts. To eliminate this dispersion, an adjustment is needed in the complex existing institutional framework, particularly at the departmental level. The departmental directors for the various sectors (health, education, and others) often play two conflicting roles, because they depend both upon the prefect and upon their respective sector's national ministries.

One of the reasons for this inefficient distribution of jurisdiction is that the departmental budgets are not clearly delineated. The prefectures participate in preparing and implementing part of the ministerial budgets. Each sector follows its own logic and maintains relations of varying intensity with the departments. A substantial part of the departmental budgets is, in reality, a component of the national budget. The portfolio of the roads sector, for example, is agreed upon directly by each departmental SEPCAM with the Ministry of Finance and is not necessarily framed by the roads policies for the sector or the departmental budget policy. As autonomous institutions, the nine SEPCAMs set an example by way of their diffuse role in implementing the departmental budget. In this case, as in others, lack of a clear differentiation between accounting and budgeting on a national and departmental level leads to a confusion of roles and responsibilities.

Another factor that has contributed to this situation is the municipal decentralization strategy applied since 1994, under which the municipalities had the principal responsibility for infrastructure works in education and health, among others sectors, which created difficulties for coordinating provision of the service.

IV. Policy Options

Decentralization Strategy

A strategy for future decentralization should progress as follows. *In the short term,* it is essential to stabilize the intergovernmental system and make sure its basic elements are functioning. This requires an improvement in the transfer mechanism to reduce inequity on a departmental level in funding allocations. It also requires an improved exchange of information among the various levels of government to increase transparency and create basic institutional capacities. That would contribute to protecting and improving the quality of the services at subnational levels.

In the long term, the country could fine tune the intergovernmental system and take measures to expand the jurisdiction of the subnational governments. This needs to be done gradually; *only if* the conditions mentioned above are verified (a minimum level of capacities, information on the services and local budgets, and a more equitable fiscal system) could a new jurisdiction be transferred.

It would be appropriate to take a unique approach for each sector with the aim of decentralizing the health, education, and roads systems. This will facilitate the distribution of jurisdiction at the national, departmental, and municipal levels in an integrated manner. Such an approach is novel, because decentralization in Bolivia has always been conceived of as the strengthening of the departmental or municipal level, but not of both at the same time. To advance with a sector-based approach, it would be important to establish a framework of incentives based on an institutionalized negotiation between the departments and the ministries for each respective sector: the departmental and municipal governments would be able to receive new jurisdiction and funds only if they participate in this sector-based decentralization framework.

- Such negotiations should be formalized through a *framework agreement* between all the departments and the respective ministry (one agreement per sector).
- With the aim of limiting transaction costs, the municipalities should also sign a *collective framework agreement* with the ministries, though the municipalities should be grouped by department.

Given the limited institutional capacity at the national and subnational levels and the volatility of the transfers,[12] the following sequence should be followed:

- First: transfer of secondary roads;
- Second: transfer of jurisdiction over health;
- Third: transfer of jurisdiction over education.

Fiscal Decentralization

Intergovernmental Transfers

HORIZONTAL IMBALANCE: HOW TO IMPROVE THE DISTRIBUTION OF FUNDS AMONG DEPARTMENTS

In the short term, revenue from the Hydrocarbons Act could be used to offset spending needs. These funds would be transferred based on a per capita distribution formula to guarantee basic departmental equitability in terms of revenue. A per capita formula not only provides a sufficient approximation to measure spending needs at the departmental level, but also enjoys acceptance among the players (it has already been used for the municipalities) and is relatively transparent.

In the long term, it is advisable that two additional measures be taken.

- **Refine transfer methods and formulas in accordance with distribution objectives.** There are offsetting methods other than the per capita formula, but they require better information and are frequently less transparent. The alternatives are to use: (i) weighted indexes of relative needs; (ii) a sector-based formula (if the approach is to finance the various sectors and not opt to make a general transfer); (iii) per capita expenditure rules (per client); (iv) bottom-up or physical expenditure rules; and (v) a representative expenditure system. Once there are departmental taxes, the formula could change to one of offsetting lack of fiscal capacity (as is applied in Canada, for example), which makes it possible to use less complex methods than tend to be required to estimate expenditure needs. The idea of an equal quota per region with the aim of funding fixed costs is also acceptable, if it is limited to a small part of the total.

- **Eliminate revenue pre-allocations and group the different fundings.** The total amount of transfers from the central government to the departments and municipalities should be determined as a function of the central government's total funds. With respect to royalties, nothing indicates that they should be used as a source of intergovernmental transfers. Therefore, it is advisable that the pre-allocation of royalties be eliminated.

VERTICAL IMBALANCE: REDUCE DEPENDENCY ON TRANSFERS BY STRENGTHENING THE DEPARTMENTAL PREFECTURES' OWN REVENUE BASES

In the long term, it would be desirable to provide the departmental prefectures with access to their own revenue sources in order to reduce their dependency on transfers. Another advantage of this approach is that it allows local politicians to "feel" how much it costs to raise each boliviano spent. In this sense, taxes raised at a local level contribute to spending efficiency and more effective budget restrictions. Any subnational government that increases taxes and its own revenue lays the foundation for a successful decentralization.

Two possible sources of revenue for the departments could serve as a starting point for departmental taxation: (i) a tax on gasoline and diesel (not yet created); and (ii) a specific consumption tax (a transfer from the department quota, currently managed by the central government). With certain administrative features, explained below (Table 7), these two taxes could, in principle, reflect departmental fiscal capacity relatively accurately and would not have adverse effects on equity or efficiency in collections. Given the experience of other countries, such as Colombia, these two taxes are ideal for the departmental level, since the tax burden cannot be easily exported outside departmental jurisdiction (unlike taxes on foreign trade, for example). Furthermore, these taxes do not depend on where the taxpayer chooses to reside (unlike corporate income taxes). Finally, they are not very difficult to administer departmentally (unlike Value Added Tax) and are not used for purposes of inter-departmental redistribution (unlike personal income taxes).

It is essential to bear in mind that departmental taxation is not fiscally neutral for any level of government. This is obviously true for departmental governments, which could obtain more revenue; but it should also be borne in mind that the national level would experience a loss of income upon transferring a percentage of the specific consumption tax to the departments. These measures would also affect the municipalities, whose shared revenue would diminish due to changes at the

Table 7. Options for Departmental Taxation

	Tax Base	*Tax Rate*	*Tax Administration*	*Appropriation of Revenue*
Option 1: Departmental Quota of the Specific Consumption Tax (*Impuesto a los Consumos Específicos*—ICE)	Departmental	Different percentages depending upon the goods.	Alternatives: a) National, with a commission for the central government. b) Departmental, with revenue collected on retail sales. c) Departmental, collected at the producer level.	Departmental
Option 2: Tax on Gasoline and Diesel Sales	Departmental	Between 0 and 5 percent. The department can select the rate.	Departmental. Departmental: national, with a commission for the central government.	Departmental

national level. It is necessary to carefully assess these fiscal impacts before granting the departments new revenue sources (Table 8).

TRANSFER OF FUNDS AND EXPENDITURES

As noted above, the Hydrocarbons Act has transferred new funds to the departmental prefectures and to municipalities, yet those local governments have not assumed new responsibilities for expenditures, which violates the principles of decentralization. In addition, the possibility exists that part of these funds will be used to finance recurring expenditures of the departments. That is less than ideal, because some

Table 8. Departmental Taxation and Projected Net Gain in Revenue for the Prefectures, 2006–2010
(in millions of dollars)

	2006	*2007*	*2008*	*2009*	*2010*
Tax Collected through a Departmental Specific Consumption Tax	41.9	75.1	79.6	84.5	89.6
Tax on Gasoline and Diesel	31.4	33.6	35.6	37.8	40.1
Total Net Gain	73.3	108.7	115.2	122.3	129.7

Source: World Bank.

recurring expenditures are volatile owing to their link to hydrocarbons. This requires a response on several fronts, both in the short and in the long term.

In the short term, to prevent a deterioration of the fiscal situation, decentralization of new expenditures should be considered without additional financing, both for departmental prefectures and for municipalities, as part of a fiscal adjustment on a national level:

- The prefectures could assume expenditures related to secondary roads in the amount of US$70 million in 2006, in exchange for the hydrocarbons revenue (US$120 million in 2006), without additional financing.
- As compensation for the additional funds received from the municipalities (US$120 million), at least the nine department capitals could finance the provision of primary healthcare, if they have the minimum capacities to do so.

Strengthening Fiscal Accountability

To meet the challenge of fiscal accountability, some countries, such as Brazil, Colombia, Peru, Argentina, India, New Zealand, and South Africa, have enacted legislation with objectives that are also relevant for Bolivia. It is essential that the country adopt rules of fiscal accountability for the subnational governments as part of a series of national rules.

In the short term the following measures and rules could be important:

- Establish a different indicator of debt capacity, based on revenue that can be freely allocated,[13] not on total recurring revenue (as occurs at present).
- Continue servicing the departmental debt. In the process of transition, the departmental prefectures should be prohibited from further indebtedness until they fully meet the requirements of transparency.
- Introduce three new fiscal accountability rules for the subnational governments: (i) limit new hiring and wage increases; (ii) apply a freeze on wages and hiring in those subnational governments whose wages represents a certain percentage of revenue, until the moratorium on hiring, coupled with economic growth, reduces the ratio of wages/revenue to an acceptable level; and (iii) prohibit any new hiring or investment contracts in the final year of office of a departmental prefecture or a municipal council.
- Demand transparency through the publication of details regarding the programming and implementation of finances throughout the public sector.
- Link this final measure to the possibility of assuming external debt and to the regulations for the financial sector, by only recognizing loans as assets on the balance sheets of a bank if information regarding those loans is published.

For the long term, the following measures are important:

- Contain and prevent an increase in subnational deficits and/or apply special sanctions, more expeditious than the standard rules, to penalize excess indebtedness.

- Establish multiyear fiscal goals once the annual goals are working well. The fulfillment of these objectives could then be required by law, with revised fiscal accountability rules.

Institutional Strengthening

Ensuring Minimum Institutional Capacity

In the short term, the following reforms could be implemented prior to proceeding with decentralization. Among the recommendations is that all the departmental prefectures apply three basic management systems with a minimum standard of transparency and supervision:

- A financial management system linked to the national system;
- Procurement rules with common national standards;
- A human resources management system linked to the national system.

In addition, there are sector-specific conditions that must be present prior to transferring new jurisdiction over expenditures (Table 9).

Increase Productive and Allocative Efficiency

It is essential to grant more autonomy to the subnational governments, particularly to the prefectures, to manage their responsibilities. To accomplish that, it would be ideal to have the central government establish incentives for the subnational governments with the objective of improving efficiency both in productive and allocative terms. This means that the local levels would enjoy increasing autonomy to choose the most efficient combination of inputs in order to produce the services desired and demanded by the population.

In the short term, it is essential to implement three types of measures: (i) the adoption of a financing formula; (ii) the use of quality of service indicators that can be easily and regularly monitored; and (iii) changes in human resources management. *In the long term,* these measures should be accompanied by (iv) adjustments in the pre-allocation of funds.

(i) Financing formula for decentralized expenditures. One of the principal advantages of decentralization is that it creates incentives to improve the supply of services and to correct inequality. Current amounts of financing and conditioned budget allocations do not contribute to this goal. The following approach for financing is therefore recommended (Table 10).

(ii) Quality of Service Indicators. It would be important to establish quality of service indicators that can be easily and regularly monitored. The indicators will necessarily be different in each sector (Table 11).

At the same time, a sophisticated decentralization with a results-management orientation, as has been implemented in Canada, Spain, and other European countries,

Table 9. Preparatory Phase to Decentralization of Education, Health, and Roads

Education	*Health*	*Roads*
• Train the departments in human resources management. • Prepare inventories (of physical assets) for SEDUCA prior to its incorporation into the prefecture structure. • Provide full information on the number of teachers per educational level (primary/secondary) in each department, and their remunerations (including benefits). • Provide full information on the distribution of teachers *among* and *within* (urban/rural) the departments. • Agree upon supervision for each jurisdiction: select, discuss, and decide upon a basic set of indicators to measure quality of service; define the starting point for each department; and define jurisdiction over supervision; define penalties for failure to meet quality of service objectives.	• Train the prefectures in human resources management. • Prepare an inventory (of physical assets) for SEDES prior to its incorporation into the prefecture structure. • Provide full information on the quantity of healthcare personnel per level of service (primary/secondary healthcare) in each department, and their remunerations (including benefits). • Provide full information on healthcare personnel (physicians, nurses) *among* and *within* (urban/rural) the departments. • Agree upon supervision for each jurisdiction: select, discuss, and agree upon a basic set of indicators to measure quality of service; define the starting point for each department; define jurisdiction over supervision; and define penalties for failure to meet quality of service objectives. • Improve and make known the framework of incentives for the provision of services, especially the use of the SUMI*.	• Develop a national strategy for the roads sector that includes the three levels of government. • Define the primary, secondary, and tertiary roads system. • Completely open the accounts of SEPCAM. • Train the prefectures in human resources management. • Establish groups of public employees, one that would have to be trained and another that would gradually retire. • Prepare an inventory (of physical assets) for SEPCAM prior to its incorporation into the prefecture structure. • Outsource all maintenance activities. Train the prefectures on tender strategies and bidding competition instruments. • Agree upon supervision for each jurisdiction: select, discuss, and agree upon a basic set of indicators to measure quality of service; define the starting point for each department; define jurisdiction over supervision; and define penalties for failure to meet quality of service objectives.

*Universal Mother/Child Insurance (*Seguro Universal Materno-Infantil*—SUMI)

Table 10. Financing of Decentralized Expenditures

Type of Financing	*Explanation*	*Condition for Success*
Transfer the same amounts currently disbursed by the central government, but with a specific formula for each sector.	A formula would be used to establish a framework of incentives in each sector, which would be results oriented and not just consider inputs: • Education: formula per student. • Health: formula per capita. The prefectures would be responsible for correcting horizontal imbalance using their own funds.	The financing formula must be simple and clear. The financing formula must be introduced gradually to ensure that the various players accept the new framework of incentives, and to guarantee a stable flow of funds. There must be sufficient information to identify the financing levels. There must be sufficient information to calculate the new formula (number of students supervised from one year to another; population census, etc.).

would not be operative in Bolivia. Such a sophisticated approach requires a clear delineation of jurisdictions and a stable and continual flow of funds. Unless such conditions are present, intergovernmental results-based agreements would be impractical.

(iii) Management of Human Resources. A recent change in the departmental management of human resources allows the prefectures to hire personnel in the health sector with up to 10 percent of the funds received for investment expenditures. Although this might not be the ideal alternative, given the diffuse distribution of jurisdiction in these sectors, the decision has already been made. It is necessary to complete the framework of standards for human resources management. As a result, all the prefectures need to operate under the same set of national rules.

The measures would include:

- Establish wage and promotion policies for government workers at the subnational level. This calls for the development of standards on the payment of

Table 11. Quality of Service Indicators in Selected Sectors

	Education	*Health*	*Roads*
Quality of Service Indicators	Enrollment Rates	Health Coverage Indicators	Quality of primary, secondary, and tertiary roads (International Roughness Indicator—IRI).

wages, wage increases, the determination of expenditures, the management of promotions for professionals, and decisions on hiring, firing, and pensions.

- Train the prefectures and have technical assistance available to develop their new jurisdictional authority. The sector ministries would have to be more rigorous in their supervision, that is, they would need to strengthen all their units or areas related to the provision of services in a decentralized environment.

(iv) Destination of Expenditures. It is important to adjust the destination of the expenditures. The current system is too complex and adversely affects productive and allocative efficiency.

In the long term, the measures could include:

- Eliminating the functional classification (recurrent expenses/investment) and replacing it with the rules of fiscal accountability mentioned above, which limit expenses on personnel and the overall deficit.
- Establishing spending pre-allocations in accordance with national and departmental priorities (a specific percentage for health, education, and roads, for example).
- Gradually freeing spending allocations once the rules of fiscal accountability are functioning well. Start granting a margin of 10 percent in a given year, until reaching 30 percent, so that a maximum of 70 percent of the departmental funds are pre-allocated by sector.

Assignment of Responsibilities and Intergovernmental Coordination

In the long term, it is essential to strengthen intergovernmental coordination. The framework agreements to which we have made reference are only one possible form of clearly defining jurisdiction. Another consists of measures to improve human resources management. Both of these are interim measures, while the sectors' transfer process is underway. In the future, entities need to be created to ensure coordination of expenditures and policies in each of the sectors among the different levels of government. The example of Spain shows that such sector-based national/departmental coordination entities have useful results for strengthening intergovernmental coordination. Upon completion of the transfer of jurisdiction, they have continued to function as coordination entities in the various sectors.

Bibliography

Agosta, Roberto S. 2005. *Informe Final—Evaluación del funcionamiento del Servicio Nacional de Caminos como resultado de la reforma institucional aplicada desde 2002.* Republic of Bolivia, Institutional Reform Program, April 2005.

Aguilar Perales, Juan Carlos, coord. 2002. *Estudio de evaluación de capacidades institucionales y de gestión de los gobiernos municipales.* Ministry of Municipal Development – Assistant Ministry of Popular Participation and Strengthening, La Paz.

Akizuki, Kengo. 2002. "Controlled Decentralization:. Local Governments and the Ministry of Home Affairs in Japan." World Bank Institute, May 2001, Washington, DC.

Alonso-Biarge, José M., and Alexandra Ortiz. 2000. "Decentralization of Road Network Management: Lessons from Bolivia and Some Ibero-American Countries." Private Sector and Infrastructure Development, Transportation Division, Discussion Document TWU-37. World Bank, Washington, DC.

Ayo, Diego. 2002. "*Municipalismo-Participación popular. Apuntes de un proceso.*" Muela del Diablo, La Paz.

———. 2004a. *Municipalización: Diagnóstico de una década-30 investigaciones sobre participación popular y descentralización.* Two volumes. Friedrich Ebert Stiftung/USAID/Plural, La Paz.

———. 2004b. *Voces criticas de la descentralización-Una década de participación popular-14 entrevistas.* Friedrich Ebert Stiftung/Plural, La Paz.

Barrios Suvelza, Franz Xavier. 2002. *El Estado triterritorial.* Friedrich Ebert Stiftung/Plural, La Paz.

———, coord. 2002. *Estudio de evaluación de capacidades institucionales y de gestión prefectural.* Ministry of the Presidency/Embassy of the Netherlands, La Paz.

———. 2004a. *Dictamen especial sobre la descentralización en Bolivia: Visión sistémica, relaciones fiscales y reingeniería prefectural.* Interim Ministry on Popular Participation, Assistant Ministry for the Strengthening of Departmental Management. La Paz, Bolivia.

———. 2004b. *Dictamen especial sobre la descentralización en Bolivia.* USAID/Plural, La Paz.

———. 2004c. *La descentralización en la Constitución boliviana. Diagnóstico crítico.* Ministry of the Presidency of the Republic/Spanish International Cooperation Agency, La Paz.

Cárdenas, Marina. 2004. *Estudio de cuentas nacionales de financiamiento y gasto en salud.* Ministry of Health and Sports/Department for International Development of the United Kingdom (DFID), La Paz, Bolivia.

Czerniewicz, Nicole K. 2004. *Análisis exploratorio de la descentralización de los sectores agropecuario, salud, educación, saneamiento básico, medio ambiente, caminos y poder judicial.* Ministry of the Presidency, Coordination Unit for the Constitutional Assembly.

Frank, Jonas. 2002. *Competencias: ¿qué descentralizar?* GTZ-CONAM, Quito.
———. 2004a. *Descentralización del gobierno regional en América Latina.* World Bank, Washington DC, publication pending.
———. 2004b. "Decentralization in Ecuador: Actors, Institutions and Incentives." Doctoral Thesis, Potsdam University, Potsdam.
Gordo, Luis, and Pablo Hernández de Cos. 2000. *Los Acuerdos de financiamiento para gobiernos regionales (autónomos) en el período 1997-2001. Banco de España,* Study Service, Working Document No. 0003, Madrid.
GTZ-CONAM. 2002. *Los procesos de descentralización en Argentina, Bolivia, Brasil, Chile, Colombia, Ecuador, Perú, Venezuela.* Decentralization Project, GTZ-CONAM, Reference Line (Second edition), Quito.
Hans Seidel Stiftung, Fundemos. 2003. "Descentralización y autonomía regional." In: *Opiniones y Análisis.* La Paz.
———. 2005. "*Debate sobre las autonomías regionales.*" In: *Opiniones y Análisis.* La Paz.
Instituto Latinoamericano de Investigaciones Sociales (Latin American Social Research Institute - ILDIS). 2003. *La descentralización que se viene. Propuestas para la (re)constitución del nivel estatal intermedio,* Friedrich Ebert Stiftung/Plural, La Paz.
Instituto Nacional de Estadística (National Statistics Institute – INE). 2005. *Estadísticas de población,* La Paz, Bolivia (www.ine.gov.bo)
Inter-American Development Bank. 1994. "Bolivia. Road Administration Decentralization Plan." ATN/IF-4443-BO, Technical Assistance from the Italian Trust Fund of the Istituto per la Ricostruzione Industriale. Washington, DC.
———. 1998. "Bolivia. Plan of Operations: GIS-Based Decision Support System for Transportation Planning and Infrastructure Management." Technical Cooperation Project TC 9801053-BO, Finance and Basic Infrastructure Division 1. Washington, DC.
———. 2003. *Políticas y estrategias de administración vial prefectural—Sistema integrado de administración de mantenimiento (SIAM), Volumen I: Resumen ejecutivo.* Inter-American Development Bank, Strengthening Program for Subnational Roads and Transportation Entities, CAEM/Booz, Allen & Hamilton.
International Monetary Fund. 2004. *Mejorando los procesos de descentralización y presupuesto.* IMF, Washington, DC.
Leipzinger, Daniel. 2001. *Modelos y temas de descentralización en América Latina.* Mimeo. World Bank, Washington, DC.
Ministry of Finance. 2004. *Informe de la comisión revisión de gasto público.* La Paz.
———. 2005a. *Presupuesto general de la nación (proyecto), Titulo I: Resumen General, Dirección de Presupuesto y Contaduría.*
———. 2005b. *Marco estratégico 2005-2007 para el fortalecimiento de las finanzas públicas.* La Paz.
Prefecture of Santa Cruz. 2004. *Reglamento de desconcentración prefectural.* Santa Cruz de la Sierra.

Prud'homme, Rémy, Hervé Huntzinger, and Sonia Guelton. 2001."Decentralization in Bolivia," Report prepared for Inter-American Development Bank, Washington, DC, August.

Shepherd, Geoffrey, and Thorbjorn Waagstein. 2005a. *Bolivia: Proyecto de reforma institucional—Evaluación independiente*. La Paz, April 4.

———, coord. 2005b. *Bolivia: Proyecto de reforma institucional.* World Bank and Donors, La Paz.

Spahn, Paul Bernd. 2003. *Estrategias para descentralizar el Gobierno manteniendo la estabilidad macroeconómica*. In preparation.

Stevens, Andrew. 2004. "A Variety of Taxes Funds, Japan's Prefectures and Municipalities." In *City Mayors Government, Local Government in Japan.*

Urenda, Juan Carlos. 2003. *Autonomías departamentales, Academia Boliviana de Estudios Constitucionales* (ABEC). Santa Cruz de la Sierra.

Vargas, John D. 2004. *La reforma agraria desde las regiones. Centro Integral de Desarrollo Económico y Social* (CIDES). Plural Editores, La Paz.

World Bank. 2000. "Bolivia. Institutional and Governance Review: From Patronage to a Professional State." Washington, DC.

———. 2002. "Proposed Credit for the Road Rehabilitation and Maintenance Project." Report No. 23625-BO, March 15, 2002. Washington, DC.

———. 2004a. "Bolivia. Public Expenditure Review." Washington DC.

———. 2004b. "Implementation Completion Report for PSAC I." Washington, DC.

———. 2004c. "Implementation Completion Report for PSAC II." Washington, DC.

———. 2004d. "Health Sector Reform in Bolivia. A Decentralization Case Study." Washington, DC.

———. 2005a. *Bolivia. Nota de política: Manejo fiscal de la renta petrolera: Situación actual y opciones de política*. Washington, DC.

———. 2005b. "Program Document for a Social Sector Programmatic Credit II." Report 32066-BO. Washington, DC.

———. 2005c. "Protecting Households from the Impoverishing Effects of Health Shocks." Washington, DC. Publication pending.

———. 2005d. "Country Financial Accountability Assessment." Washington DC.

———. 2006. "Bolivia. Institutional and Governance Review." In preparation.

ANNEX

Figure A1. The Intergovernmental System and Political Representation Prior to the Prefect Elections in December 2005

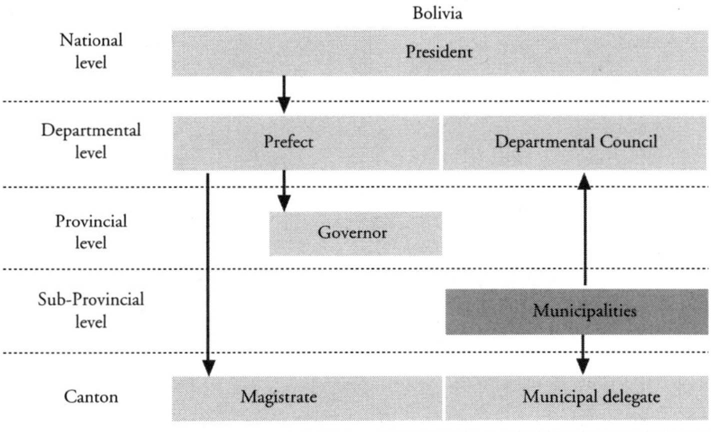

Note: The top-down arrows indicate delegation (designation of authority). The bottom-up arrow indicates elections. The shaded field (municipalities) enjoys constitutional autonomy.

Endnotes

1. The executive branch of the department is the prefecture, while the representational entity is the departmental council. The term "subnational government" refers to both the departmental prefectures and the municipalities.
2. This excludes the health and education payroll, for which the central government is responsible.
3. Bolivia does not compare with Colombia or Argentina, where approximately 45 percent of public spending is decentralized. On the other hand, the degree of spending decentralization is much higher than in Central America, where it averages no more than 7 percent.
4. One of the principal demands in Santa Cruz, for example, is to retain 50 percent of local tax collections. This proposal faces serious methodological problems in terms of quantification. It confuses taxes *collected* in a certain territory with those *generated* in that territory. The groups from these regions (particularly from Santa Cruz) also want more autonomy to protect themselves from national decisions (for example, regarding land) that they consider harmful.
5. Technically speaking, the Hydrocarbons Act eliminates what was called "*participations*," that is, a 31 percent tax on existing wells (which represented approximately one-fifth of hydrocarbons production), and introduces a 32 percent tax, the Direct Tax on Hydrocarbons (*Impuesto Directo sobre los Hidrocarburos*—IDH), on the entire production of hydrocarbons.
6. Decree 28421 of October 2005 reassigns part of the jurisdiction among the different levels of government. New jurisdiction for the prefectures includes public health (mobile brigades, prevention campaigns, and control of endemic diseases), rural development, and job creation.
7. Measured among the municipalities grouped in each department. The Law increases the transfers, but does so in an approximately proportional manner. Municipal per capita transfers, which were quite egalitarian, remain equal. The new Hydrocarbons Act also distributes funds on a per capita basis.
8. For this analysis, the municipalities were grouped within their respective departments. To confirm the above cited hypothesis, we would also need to know the fiscal capacity of the municipalities, which is unknown. Since the per capita municipal tax base (which is unknown) is probably a function of the per capita GDP, tax rates would probably vary considerably from one region to another. For example, the ratio between municipal taxes and the GDP—an approximate measure of municipal tax efforts—is twice as high in the department of La Paz as in the department of Santa Cruz.
9. Under the "20/200" rule, subnational governments cannot use more than 20 percent of their recurring revenue to service debt, and accrued debt cannot surpass 200 percent of their recurring revenue. In light of international standards and parameters, both rules appear to be too lax.
10. World Bank 2004a, 2005d.
11. The analysis in this section includes payroll. The decentralization ratios calculated in an earlier section of this chapter exclude payroll.
12. The proportion of recurring expenditures is higher in education than in health or roads.
13. The two most rigid elements of expenditures, above all, are the payment of debt and of wages. The margin (and capacity) of indebtedness would be calculated subtracting these types of expenditures from recurring income.

23

Justice and Public Security

Lisa Bhansali

Summary

Justice and public security are central factors for stabilization and preservation of democratic order, governance, and the rule of law. An important challenge for Bolivia is to expand access to justice so that it will be available to the majority of the population. Citizens must be able to enforce their rights through the courts and must have confidence in the judicial system. In that way, it will be possible to address criminal impunity. When the administration of state justice is slow, insufficient, and corrupt, the population avoids the courts and takes justice into its own hands. Land squatting and lynchings, among other measures, are expressions of popular discontent with the country's justice system. This chapter analyzes the situation of the justice sector and proposes alternative solutions to the problems identified.

I. The Justice Sector in Bolivia

The Bolivian state is composed of three branches (legislative, executive, and judicial), that are independent in their functions and attributes. However, when analyzing the scope of the justice sector, several institutions belong to each of those branches. In addition, there are other entities established by the Constitution, such as the Ombudsman's Office (*Defensoría del Pueblo*) and the Government Attorney's Office, that play a role in promoting justice, defending legality, and protecting the interests of the state and society. Indigenous or community justice, though barely recognized, also forms a part of this sector. In other words, when discussing justice in the country, it is a mistake to limit oneself to the formal judiciary.

With that understanding, the components of the justice sector are the following.

JUDICIARY

The Judiciary in Bolivia is composed of the Supreme Court of Justice (*Corte Suprema de Justicia*—CSJ),[1] the Constitutional Court (*Tribunal Constitucional*—TC),[2] the National Agrarian Court (*Tribunal Agrario Nacional*—TA),[3] the Judicial Council (*Consejo de la Judicatura*—CJ),[4] the District Appellate Courts (*Cortes Superiores de Distrito),* and the trial courts and their judges.

VICE MINISTRY OF JUSTICE

The Vice Ministry of Justice is the liaison between the executive branch and other branches of government in relation to the justice sector.

NATIONAL POLICE (WHICH REPORTS TO THE MINISTRY OF THE INTERIOR)

The National Police exercises police powers; its mission is to defend society, preserve law and order, and enforce the law.

GOVERNMENT ATTORNEY'S OFFICE

The Government Attorney's Office's mission is to bring court actions; defend legality, the interests of the state, and the interests of society; and represent them in accordance with the Constitution and the law. With the constitutional reform of 1994, the Government Attorney's Office took on a new structure as an independent entity of the executive branch. According to Organic Law 2175, the Government Attorney's Office has functional independence and is composed of the Attorney General of the Republic, the Departmental Government Attorneys, the Government Attorneys for Cassation Court Matters, the Government Attorneys for Criminal Matters, and their assistants.

OMBUDSMAN'S OFFICE

The Ombudsman's Office is an institution created through the constitutional reform of 1994. Its mandate is to receive, investigate, and report complaints of the population regarding human rights violations and abuses committed by any branch of government. The Ombudsman's Office drafts reports and makes recommendations so that the public authorities will fulfill their obligations and resolve the cases under investigation. It has an independent annual budget for its operations, incorporated into the budget of the legislative branch, and has funds provided through grants from national and international organizations.

COMMUNITY JUSTICE

Among the indigenous population, to a greater or lesser degree, community justice is applied as a conflict resolution mechanism. Under the community justice system, the community, through its elected assembly members, pronounces specific judgments in cases of theft, robbery, lack of respect to others, and violation of property rights or property limits. The community justice system resolves cases without recourse to the ordinary justice system. The Constitution grants conditional recognition to community justice[5] by indicating that community justice cannot contradict Bolivian legislation. The Code of Criminal Procedure incorporates the application of community justice when the crime is committed in an indigenous community by one of its members against another, provided that the traditional authorities have resolved the conflict in accordance with traditional indigenous law and its application does not violate constitutional guarantees and rights.[6]

II. The Justice Sector and Public Security

Background

Instability has become one of the most persistent characteristics in the Latin American region and has been manifested in political and social crises that have produced presidents' demise or premature replacement.[7] Public security[8] forms a mandatory part of public policy agendas, plans, and projects as a necessary condition to guarantee the quality of life of the population.

Foundations of Public Security in Bolivia

Public security in Bolivia is overseen by the General Directorate of Public Security and Crime Prevention, which reports to the Vice Ministry of Interior Affairs within the Ministry of the Interior. One of the mandates of this directorate is to implement the National Public Security Plan created under Law 2494 of August 2003. This law creates the National Public Security System, whose aim is to effectively and efficiently articulate policies, plans, projects, and programs emanating from the government and the community.[9] As its principal objective, the security plan seeks effective solutions to crime but also places special emphasis on the need for policies, plans, and programs to reflect the multiethnic, multicultural nature of the country.[10] The conflict-prone political and social situation in Bolivia has created obstacles and delays for the plan's implementation. In that framework, it comes as no surprise when the news reports that angry neighbors captured young robbers and tried to burn them alive as a punishment.[11]

The Security Situation in Bolivia

The figures presented below show trends in common crimes committed between 1989 to 2004. Figure 1 shows an increase in crime in the area of the country along its main highway (La Paz, Cochabamba, and Santa Cruz) as compared with the rest of the country between 1994 and 1999.

Figure 2 shows the high growth in the crime rate, above all during the year 1996, with a recent decrease, principally on account of the interim emergency plans carried out by the various governments in office.

Figure 1. Common Crimes Reported, by Geographic Area

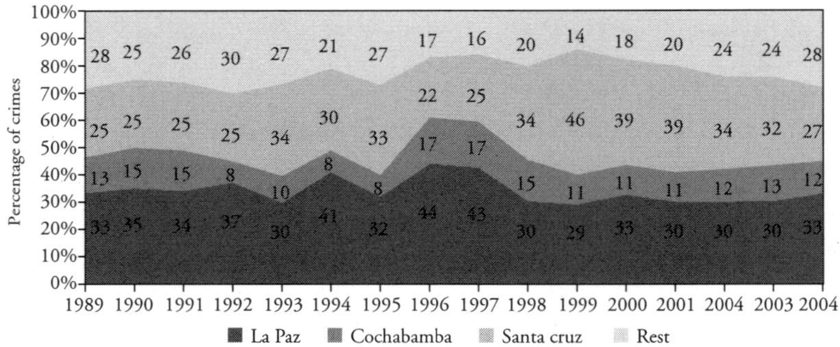

Source: National Police—National Statistics Institute (*Instituto Nacional de Estadística*—INE).

Figure 2. Trends in the Number of Crimes, 1989–2004

	1989	1990	1991	1992	1993	1994	1995	1996	1997	1998	1999	2000	2001	2002	2003	2004
La Paz	10,723	11,005	16,058	23,399	16,402	30,347	21,142	61,626	36,435	24,034	17,216	15,465	13,002	11,076	10,907	11,862

Source: National Police—INE.

Factors that Contribute to Insecurity

The majority of specialists argue that an increase in the crime rate cannot be attributed to a single cause. Rather, crime is caused by a series of contributing factors, such as inequality in the income distribution, family conflicts, loss of values, weak and corrupt institutions, or the more organized nature of crime and drug trafficking. Crime and violence affect everyone: the rich and, to a greater extent, the poor; women and men; young and old.[12]

ECONOMIC FACTORS

Poverty, unemployment, and inequality in the hemisphere are high tension elements that have created fertile ground for instability and public insecurity. The figures indicate that the number of poor is greater today than in 1980. The percentage of poor people has also increased to nearly half the total population. Similarly, unemployment rates have been high. It is important to clarify that generally, growth in urban poverty in the past decade has been associated with an increase in violence, crime, and insecurity. These problems result not only from poverty, but above all from inequality, together with other social, cultural, and psychological factors.[13] Table 1 presents the indicators of extreme poverty obtained by the Bolivian National Statistics Institute (*Instituto Nacional de Estadística* – INE), on a national level and in the urban and rural areas.

Among the causes of poverty in Bolivia are the country's demographic trends and profile, in addition to economic inequality.[14] The country has a very young population with low productivity. Population growth outpaces income-generating capacity. The high level of population growth is a major obstacle in the fight against poverty. The mean annual rate of demographic growth during the period of 1985-2001 for Bolivia was approximately 2.3 percent, higher than the rest of the countries in the Andean region or than the average for the region (1.55 percent). This population growth rate clearly highlights the enormous economic effort that the country must make to increase per capita income.

In addition, Bolivia is among the countries with the greatest inequality in its income distribution.[15] Unemployment is another factor that merits special consideration. According to the recent perception survey conducted by Latinobarómetro,[16] 77 percent of Bolivians believe that their jobs are in jeopardy. According to this source, this proportion has varied little since 2002. Fear of not having a job or becoming unemployed is higher than fear of crime, which makes it the region's most important problem (Figure 3).

POLITICAL AND INSTITUTIONAL FACTORS

- Lack of Coordination and Weakness of the State Security Institutions

Interinstitutional coordination is needed in order to undertake effective actions. Law No. 2494, which creates the public security councils, calls for intervention at several levels to reduce crime. To accomplish that, coordination is needed with local governments and private entities, the police, the courts, penitentiaries, educational institutions, and labor organizations.[17] However, implementation of the plan has been delayed due to social unrest. In recent years the state has used a good part of its economic and human resources to respond to the country's social conflicts. Between January and September 2005 alone, the police had to respond to 10,242 social protests, including marches, land squatting, and other protests.[18]

On the other hand, the state's security institutions do not easily accept the inclusion of civil society and of private entities in crime prevention programs, even though community participation has taken on a central role in public security policies in Latin America.[19]

Table 1. Indicators of Extreme Poverty by Year and Geographic Area, 1999–2002

Description	*Unit of Measurement*	*1999*	*2000*	*2001*	*2002*
Bolivia					
Incidence of extreme poverty	Percentage	36.78	39.85	37.04	36.55
Extreme poverty gap	Percentage	42.21	43.68	40.44	39.15
Intensity of extreme poverty	Percentage	23.83	25.69	22.62	21.22
Extreme poverty line	Bolivianos/person-month	159.46	160.72	157.41	157.48
Total population	Persons	8,000,798	8,274,803	8,248,404	8,547,091
Population in extreme poverty	Persons	2,942,514	3,297,508	3,054,884	3,124,064
Urban Area					
Incidence of extreme poverty	Percentage	23.63	28.42	25.93	25.46
Extreme poverty gap	Percentage	37.97	39.01	38.79	36.57
Intensity of extreme poverty	Percentage	21.25	21.97	22.68	19.92
Extreme poverty line	Bolivianos/person-month	174.04	176.22	172.99	172.24
Total population	Persons	5,035,535	5,268,526	3,099,633	5,330,045
Population in extreme poverty	Persons	1,189,659	1,497,125	1,335,210	1,357,177
Rural Area					
Incidence of extreme poverty	Percentage	59.11	59.89	55.48	54.92
Extreme poverty gap	Percentage	45.08	47.55	41.73	41.14
Intensity of extreme poverty	Percentage	25.58	28.78	22.57	22.22
Extreme poverty line	Bolivianos/person-month	134.70	133.57	131.53	133.03
Total population	Persons	2,965,263	3,006,277	5,148,771	3,217,046
Population in extreme poverty	Persons	1,752,855	1,800,383	1,719,674	1,766,887

Source: National Statistics Institute (*Instituto Nacional de Estadística* – INE),
Note: Corresponds to indicators obtained using the poverty-line method.

Figure 3. Most Important Problem—Latin America 2005

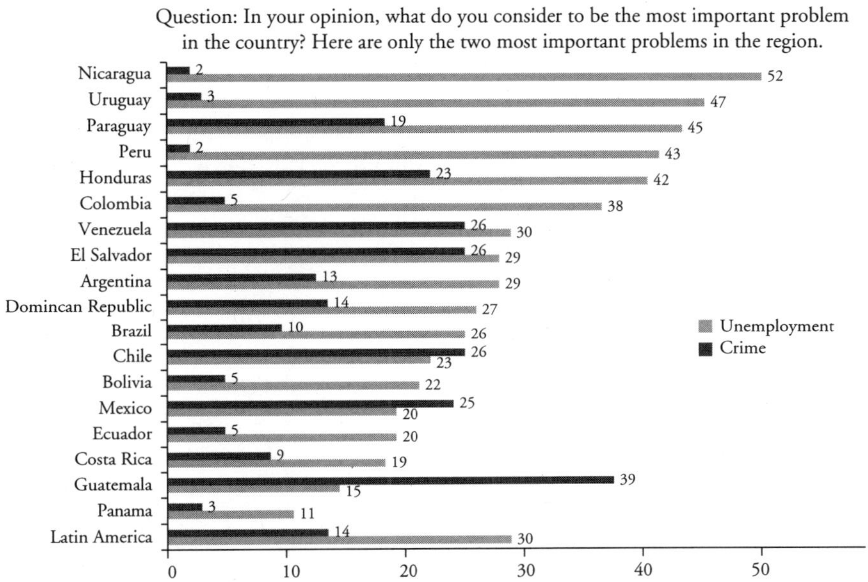

Source: Latinobarómetro 2003–2005.

- Weak Judiciary

One of the principal causes of frustration for the population related to the growing insecurity is the extreme crisis of the judiciary. Large sectors of the population have no access to judicial services: in 180 of the 314 municipalities there are no courts; judges are not distributed in a rational manner over the territory, and their performance and subject-matter distribution are not optimal.[20] There is also a certain amount of political interference, which affects the independence and performance of the judiciary, in addition to major administrative and procedural failings of the judicial system.

The consolidation of Bolivia's democratic institutions requires an accessible, credible judiciary that responds to precise indicators in terms of quality and quantity and guarantees due process in order to offer justice for all. Criminal impunity is a telling sign of inequality under the law and is one of the most pernicious signs of corruption.

- Administrative Corruption

Corruption favors the persistence of an institutional crisis and has undermined the credibility of leaders and political parties. From an economic point of view, it is costly, because it diverts public funds to private uses to the detriment of society as a whole. According to the Transparency International Index, on a scale of 1 to 10, Bolivia scores 2.2 and ranks 122 out of 145 countries.[21]

The perception of insecurity is related not only to an increase in violence and crime, but also to the citizenry's lack of confidence in government institutions. On a global level, the evidence shows a significant correlation between the weakness of the legal regimen and corruption. The protection of property rights, the valuation of the legal framework, the independence and impartiality of the judiciary, and the capacity of the courts to resolve conflicts are closely tied to corruption.[22]

SOCIAL FACTORS THAT CONTRIBUTE TO THE PERCEPTION OF PUBLIC INSECURITY

- Social Conflicts and Exclusion of Groups

Social conflicts are a manifestation of old problems. Colonialism introduced a class structure marked by a negation of indigenous identity and the rejection of indigenous cultures, values, and traditions. This structure became consolidated as the result of sustained social inequality, which led to the need to transform the state.

Inequality of classes in Bolivia has denied marginalized populations access to social rights as compared with privileged groups. All that aggravates the underlying social crisis, as protests and mobilizations erupt. On the other hand, the lack of job opportunities, coupled with the difficulties for rural emigrants to adapt to the new urban environment, creates groups of persons who are socially and economically impacted.

Table 2 illustrates the magnitude of the social conflicts generated not only along the country's main axis (Cochabamba, La Paz, Santa Cruz), but also in the rest of the country, which leads to an increase in public insecurity.

Table 3 shows the results of the survey conducted with the rural population on the reasons for their migration from the countryside to the city.

Institutions Responsible for Public Security

There are several institutions with a mandate to guarantee public security in Bolivia. According to the law, the system's control entities are the National Public Security Council; the departmental councils, which determine needs in each region; and the provincial councils, which determine specific aspects from a decentralized perspective. The National Public Security Council is composed, in turn, of several national administrative entities, including the Supreme Court of Justice.

By law, the National Public Security System does not exclude or discriminate against any person in the country or in the departments. This appears to respond to the idea that the control of crime is contemplated not as an exclusive task of public institutions, but rather as a task and agenda that is coordinated among several public institutions, non-governmental organizations, and the community in general.

Table 2. Civil Unrest, by Department (2000–2004)

Civil Unrest	*2000*	*2001*	*2002*	*2003*	*2004 (p)*
Bolivia	**2,193**	**2,356**	**2,161**	**3,896**	**3,907**
Demonstrations and marches	1,450	1,293	1,256	2,371	2,254
Strikes and work stoppages	359	501	450	944	1,086
Roadblocks and rioting	384	562	455	581	567
Chuquisaca	**76**	**114**	**85**	**406**	**432**
Demonstrations and marches	22	34	26	166	127
Strikes and work stoppages	40	59	42	91	183
Roadblocks and rioting	14	21	17	149	122
La Paz	**1,661**	**1,739**	**1,550**	**2,709**	**2,395**
Demonstrations and marches	1,216	1,101	1,000	1,853	1,712
Strikes and work stoppages	184	209	214	565	518
Roadblocks and rioting	261	429	336	291	165
Cochabamba	**188**	**177**	**175**	**282**	**362**
Demonstrations and marches	92	90	81	182	175
Strikes and work stoppages	44	41	48	49	126
Roadblocks and rioting	52	46	46	51	61
Oruro	**50**	**25**	**39**	**106**	**215**
Demonstrations and marches	17	15	16	66	78
Strikes and work stoppages	14	2	9	18	69
Roadblocks and rioting	19	8	14	22	68
Potosí	**50**	**38**	**44**	**64**	**251**
Demonstrations and marches	9	10	10	27	98
Strikes and work stoppages	28	19	23	22	83
Roadblocks and rioting	13	9	11	15	70
Tarija	**25**	**158**	**131**	**242**	**131**
Demonstrations and marches	11		59	52	12
Strikes and work stoppages	14	138	63	175	68
Roadblocks and rioting		20	9	15	51
Santa Cruz	**129**	**91**	**117**	**79**	**80**
Demonstrations and marches	79	41	60	20	30
Strikes and work stoppages	25	22	40	23	30
Roadblocks and rioting	25	28	17	36	20
Beni	**6**	**6**	**10**	**8**	**20**
Demonstrations and marches	2		2	5	10
Strikes and work stoppages	4	6	6	1	3
Roadblocks and rioting			2	2	7
Pando	**8**	**8**	**10**		**21**
Demonstrations and marches	2	2	2		12
Strikes and work stoppages	6	5	5		6
Roadblocks and rioting		1	3		3

Source: INE.
(p): preliminary data

Table 3. Reasons for Rural to Urban Migration

No.	*Reasons Established in the Survey*	*%*
1	Looking for work	18.2
2	Job transfer	3.9
3	Education	25.6
4	Health	2.2
5	Family reasons	50.1
	Total	**100.0**

Source: Calculated by the author based on the Survey on Improvement in Living Conditions (*Encuesta de Mejoramiento de Condiciones de Vida*—MECOVI), 1999.

However, out of nine departments in Bolivia, only two have assumed the challenge: La Paz recently created and approved the Departmental Public Security Council, and the departmental government of Cochabamba created the first Provincial Public Security Committee, formed by local institutions.[23]

In the past decades a notable change has been seen in the approach to crime prevention in the world. Today, this is not considered to be an exclusive task of the public institutions; it is seen as a task shared by several public institutions, non-governmental organizations, and the community in general. Accordingly, the responsibility has shifted from the governmental sphere to the public realm. Within the region, countries such as Brazil, Chile, and Argentina have modified their security policies to create preventive strategies that contemplate community participation. The concept of prevention is taking top priority in policy discussions.[24]

Public Security and its Financing

Until the recent Law 2494, there was no integral national security plan that incorporated the citizenry and established educational programs, such as effective measures in the fight against violence and crime. However, since 1990 the public security budget has been gradually increasing to the effect that between 1990 and 2004, expenditure on public order and security nearly tripled in real terms (Figure 4). The majority of these funds, according to the study of the "Observatory of Security and Democracy" (*Observatorio de Seguridad y Democracia*)[25] are earmarked for the payment of police wages and salaries (representing almost 85 percent of the funds spent on security). The rest is earmarked for other recurring expenditures, including materials and supplies, and, to a lesser extent, for personal needs such as scholarships.

The Judiciary and Public Security

The inclusion of the Supreme Court of Justice on the National Security Council is of vital importance, even for applying the new criminal prosecution system in

Figure 4. Nominal Per Capita Spending on Public Security, 1990–2004
(in bolivianos)

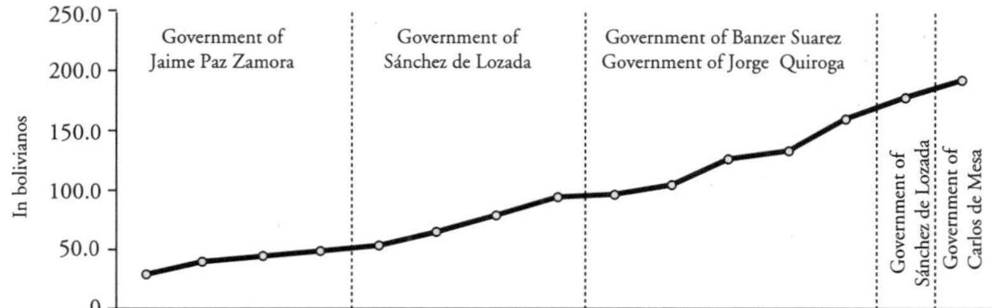

	1990	1991	1992	1993	1994	1995	1996	1997	1998	1999	2000	2001	2002	2003	2004
Per capita spending	29.4	39.0	46.5	50.0	54.3	65.5	79.8	96.3	96.9	106.4	128.2	135.3	162.3	181.8	195.8*

Source: INE.
*2004 preliminary data.

Bolivia, which is linked to the crime reporting system. Although the new criminal process improves the system, it has received criticism from the population and from the police forces. This is due to a lack a familiarity with the scope and application of the new process and the absence of intensive, systematic training to bring the operators of the system together in a single process (that is, the courts and Government Attorney's Office, as the entities in charge of guiding the procedure, and the police, who are in charge of fighting crime).

The new Code of Criminal Procedure grants the judicial and national police an auxiliary function not only in the arrest of suspects, but also in the investigation process. By law, the police must also identify and provide assistance to the victims and gather evidence. The connection between the judicial and police systems, as entities in charge of public security, brings them together in stopping crime.[26]

Reform of the ordinary justice system and the criminal prosecution system commenced with the introduction of new legal instruments and oral procedures (Supreme Court of Justice). For that reason, it is important that the entities of the judicial system, the Government Attorney's Office, and the police act in a coordinated fashion against crime.

Countries that have already reformed the justice system, such as Chile or Argentina, are incorporating mechanisms such as improvements in the quality of judicial services, the incorporation of the victim into the process, specialized investigations, the rationalization of criminal prosecutions, and the effective introduction of efficient negotiating mechanisms.[27]

Application of reform to the criminal system in Bolivia must be accompanied by measures to rapidly disseminate information on the scope, significance, and extent of the criminal process in effect.[28] An obstacle to appling the new law is the lack of correspondence between the auxiliary entities and the new process. According to the reform, it is up to the police to provide its officers with the corresponding procedural training so that they will become highly skilled in the investigation phase of the process. Furthermore, in the investigation phase, the prosecutor's office requires a great deal of knowledge on the management and orientation of the procedure in order to improve criminal justice and achieve public security. That is the only way to counteract the current lack of confidence and perception of insecurity originated by the large number of crime reports rejected by local prosecutors or the Government Attorney's Office.

Table 4 shows the number of reports of robbery, serious or minor injuries, fraud, contraband, theft, and homicide reported to the preliminary hearings courts (where criminal prosecutions commence) in the cities of La Paz and Sucre. Out of 3,163 cases submitted in La Paz, the prosecutor's office rejected or failed to file 3,066.

Diagnostic and Challenges for the Justice Sector

Justice reforms have been only partially successful and barriers to access persist. The following are some of the principal barriers.

Political Influence

Independence of the judiciary is essential to ensure the impartiality, effectiveness, and integrity of the Bolivian justice system. As in most Latin American countries, the judiciary in Bolivia is the weakest of the three branches of the state. In general, the justice sector is vulnerable to influences from the executive and legislative branches. The partisan interests of the governments in office result in delays in the designations of Bolivia's judicial authorities. The challenge lies in preventing the political class from using the administration of justice as an entity subordinated to the political elite.

Public security issues are not framed into a state policy that ties them to the administration of justice. Accordingly, it has not been possible to implement the National Public Security Plan approved in August 2003. Reform of the police and

Table 4. Preliminary Hearings Court: Most Frequent Crimes

Most Frequent Crimes	*Preliminary Hearings Court*							
	Submitted		*Rejected*		*Resolved*		*Pending*	
	La Paz	*Sucre*	*La Paz*	*Sucre*	*La Paz*	*Sucre*	*La Paz*	*Sucre*
Robbery	3,163	571	3,066	529	53	28	44	14
Serious and Minor Injuries	2,740	609	2,504	565	118	35	118	9
Fraud	1,582	512	1,470	485	44	16	68	11
Theft	1,579	426	1,507	403	40	20	32	3
Contraband	859		784		33		42	
Homicide	536		462		33		41	

Source: OCADEM-PE, 2005.

of public security is mentioned for electoral purposes, and each administration in office commences its own reform of the police, which is limited to replacing its upper echelon.

Due to political influence, the justice sector is considered partial, that is, inclined to act against the weak and in favor of the elite. The most recent survey conducted by Latinobarómetro ranked Bolivia among the Latin American countries with the lowest perception rating for law enforcement and the rule of law.[29]

The reforms undertaken to date have focused on guaranteeing judicial independence and on avoiding interference from other branches of government and individual interests. But these reforms have failed to pay attention to institutional strengthening and training for the operators of the justice system so that they can perform their task transparently and efficiently.

Unsatisfied Demands for Justice

Demands for access to justice go unsatisfied for several reasons, among them: (i) a shortage of courts and lack of an adequate geographic distribution, (ii) funding shortages for the justice sector, and (iii) congestion and delays in court cases.

(i) An insufficient number of courts and their inadequate geographic distribution. Although the number of courts has increased as the result of judicial reforms in years past, it continues to be insufficient for the vast territory of Bolivia, with only 60 percent of municipalities covered so far. Most of the agencies are located in the most heavily populated districts (La Paz, Cochabamba, and Santa Cruz), but those districts also have the greatest number of municipalities with no court (Table 5).[30] The average number of inhabitants per court is 12,405, one of the lowest figures in the region.

Table 5. Municipalities with or without a Court

Departments	*Municipalities with a court*	*Municipalities without a court*	*Total*
Chuquisaca	19	9	28
La Paz	24	51	75
Cochabamba	22	22	44
Oruro	11	23	34
Potosí	20	18	38
Tarija	8	3	11
Santa Cruz	18	32	50
Beni	9	10	19
Pando	3	12	15
Totals	134	180	314

Source: Ministry of Sustainable Development and Planning.

Similarly, the regional distribution of policemen is inadequate and unequal, and it does not bear in mind the crime rate in the assignment of personnel. For example, Santa Cruz, the department with the highest crime rate, is the one with the fewest policemen per inhabitant, even though it accounts for almost 50 percent of police revenue.

(ii) Lack of funds in the justice sector. The justice system needs to have a budget that allows it to carry out the tasks entrusted to it. Funding shortages make the administration of justice inefficient, complicate management of the case load, hinder infrastructure reforms, facilitate corruption, and, in general, lead to inefficiencies, which provokes dissatisfaction with the administration of justice among the population. This, in turn, contributes to increasing public insecurity.

In Bolivia, the Judiciary has traditionally received a smaller budget than the other branches of government. In 2004, the percentage of national public expenditures earmarked for the judiciary was 0.84 percent, compared with 63 percent for the executive branch (Table 6).

Even bearing in mind that comparisons of Andean judicial systems are only indicative (since they are not always comparable with one another),[31] according to data from the Andean Commission of Jurists, in 2004, the Bolivian judiciary had the lowest judicial budget in the region (Figure 5). Finally, the judicial budget per inhabitant in Bolivia was US$4.98, the lowest in the region (Figure 6).

To cope with the increased case load, the Constitutional Court has contracted more personnel. It has had to refer to the international cooperation community in order to do so, since the budget allocation is insufficient.[32] According to the evaluation made by the Canadian International Development Agency (CIDA), the Ombudsman's Office does not have sufficient funds to handle the cases filed with it. It therefore has to better manage the complaints system so that it can attend to special cases such as the defense of children, indigenous peoples, and detainees.[33]

Budget shortages also affect the National Police, which, as a result, cannot hire more officers, acquire state-of-the-art technology, or have sufficient means of transportation to carry out its task. According to figures provided by the Commander General of the Police, 81 percent of its budget was used for wages and the rest for basic services.[34] This has made it practically impossible to fully control the social unrest of recent years.[35]

(iii) Congestion and delays in court cases. According to the regulatory and institutional diagnosis provided in the document entitled "*Justicia para Todos*" (Justice for All), the modifications to the Code of Civil and Family Procedure decentralized certain processes that are currently assigned to the appellate courts and formerly went to the Supreme Court. In addition, recusals and self-recusals were limited—although cases continue to be delayed due to for-

Table 6. State Expenditures by Government Branch

Judicial Branch US$	*%*	*Legislative Branch US$*	*%*	*Executive Branch US$*	*%*	*Total (All 3 branches) US$*	*Other Public Institutions*	*%*	*TOTAL US$*	*%*
44,976,972	0.84	26,836,871	0.50	3,372,165,266	63.10	3,443,983,598	1,900,332,520	35.56	5,344,316,119	100

Source: Ciudadanos Trabajando por la Justicia ["Citizens Working for Justice"] (2005).
Note: Here, we are referring to the Bolivian judiciary in the strict sense, that is, the Supreme Court of Justice, the Constitutional Court, the National Agrarian Court, the Judicial Council, the District Appellate Courts, and the Trial Courts and their judges, and not to the Justice System.

Figure 5. Judicial Budgets (2004) in the Andean Region
(in millions of dollars)

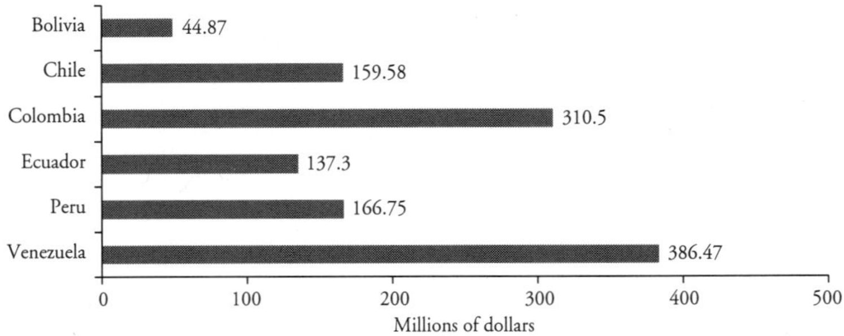

Source: Mendoza Cánepa, 2005.

Figure 6. Per Capita Judicial Budgets in the Andean Region, 2004
(dollars)

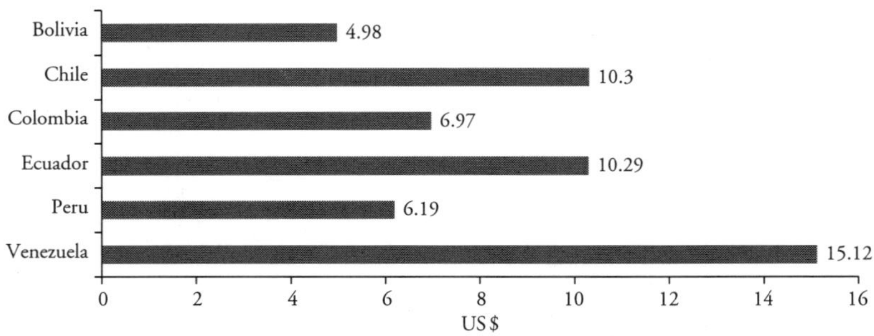

Source: Mendoza Cánepa, 2005.

malities and procedural invalidations.[36] These modifications have made it possible to ease the delay in judgments to some extent, although both delays and lack of transparency persist.

In terms of criminal justice, at the start of 2005 court year, the then-Presiding Justice of the Supreme Court of Justice, Eduardo Rodríguez Veltzé, indicated that the criminal courts handle 90 percent of the cases heard by the Judiciary and reported that at the start of 2005, out of a total of 3,077 criminal cases from the old system, 1,171 were still pending. According to this report, the incarcerated population in Bolivia is 6,768 persons (77 percent held without a sentence) in 89 penitentiaries.

Problems of Corruption

Bolivia is among the six countries with the highest rate of corruption in Latin America. According to the 2005 Transparency International Report, Bolivia ranks better than only Ecuador, Guatemala, Venezuela, Paraguay, and Haiti in the Latin American region. Corruption ranks as one of the major concerns of the citizens polled by Transparency International. The report also indicates that after political parties, the most corrupt entities are Congress, the police, and the judiciary.

The government has ratified the Inter-American Convention against Corruption (IACC) and for this purpose has appointed a Presidential Delegation (whose hierarchy recently changed), which formulated a proposal for the IACC's Implementation System. Furthermore, the Vice Ministry of Justice has introduced two legislative bills, one for a Conflict of Interests Act and another for a Law Modifying the Crimes Defined in the Penal Code and Including New Crimes regarding Corruption in the Exercise of Public Office.[37]

With respect to corruption in the judiciary, as shown in Table 7, between 1998 and November 2001, those who were the subject of the most denunciations were the judges (2,968), followed by court support personnel (1,547). Lack of training for the operators of the justice system also contributes to the generalized perception of corruption in the judiciary, while the personnel's low wages provide a motivation for corruption.

The population also perceives the National Police as a corrupt institution in terms of its internal organization (denunciations of embezzlement of accounts of the Police Insurance Union, the Police Housing Cooperative, and the Police Cooperative Union) and in terms of its relationship with the citizenry. That has provoked the designation in some areas of community police, neighborhood brigades, and public security councils as alternative mechanisms in defense of public security. Ninety-six percent of the police officers agree that the institution should be reformed to counter inefficiencies and fight corruption.[38]

Failure to Use Alternative Mechanisms for Conflict Resolution and Failure to Recognize Indigenous and Community Justice

Under the Arbitration and Conciliation Act (Law 1770), parties may submit disputes to arbitration or mediation at any time before or during the judicial process,

Table 7. Denunciations against Members of the Judiciary
(Period of 1998–2001)

Number of denunciations against judges	2,968
Number of denunciations against auxiliary personnel	1,547
Number of judiciary personnel sanctioned (judges and auxiliary personnel)	139

Source: Gaceta Transparencia (2002).

provided that the case does not affect the public interest. Arbitration is used infrequently due to its high costs for most of the population, and judges do little to promote arbitration during the litigation process. Both arbitration and mediation are generally handled by the chambers of commerce.

In more than half of the municipalities of Bolivia, there is no governmental justice unit. Accordingly, if official recognition were given to indigenous and community justice, more of the population would have access to this service. Community justice has as its foundation the existence of indigenous authorities elected in accordance with the custom and practice of the people, empowered by their respective communities to administer justice.[39]

The proposal to introduce community justice was taken into account by the executive branch in the legislative bill for a Law on Justice of the Indigenous Peoples and Peasants, whose enactment is still pending. The indigenous communities complain that the official authorities (judges, police, and prosecutors) fail to acknowledge the decisions and agreements adopted by the native communities. This is because the authorities consider that indigenous and community justice seeks autonomy, with which they are not always in agreement.[40]

Other Barriers to Access: Discrimination on the Basis of Race and Sex. The Language Barrier and Lack of Free Justice Services in Remote Areas

In Bolivia, many women and the majority of indigenous people suffer from discrimination for reasons of gender and ethnicity. This appears to be a widespread situation in the Andean area.[41]

United Nations studies denounce the marginalization and lack of access to justice suffered by the indigenous peoples in countries such as Bolivia, Guyana, and Mexico.[42] In Bolivia, more than 50 percent of the population identifies itself with an indigenous people.[43] However, barriers of marginalization and a marked inequality in access to funds, education, and sanitation create continual conflicts. The problem lies in the fact that, on the one hand, justice does not reach the indigenous communities, and on the other, traditional law is deficient and not formalized. In order to overcome the lack of access to justice, it is necessary to develop traditional indigenous justice to the point where Bolivia has a true body of Indigenous Law. To accomplish that, it will be necessary to deepen and formalize the legal instruments of indigenous or community justice and harmonize them with official law. Community justice embodies cultural values, institutions, and constructions that respond to the identity of the communities. Lack of information and understanding of this system has created problems of interpretation and has delayed its acceptance and application as part of the justice system, often equating indigenous justice to criminal acts, as in the case of lynchings.

Domestic violence in Bolivia is exacerbated by deep-rooted gender discrimination in the justice system. The rights of women go unprotected. As noted in the National Report issued by the Vice Ministry on Women: "...domestic violence continues to be a problem that affects women, since seven out of every 10 victims are women who suffer some type of violence in their households; in 75 percent of the cases, this tends to be repetitive and does not tend to be reported by the victims. Accordingly, out of the total number of women who state that they have suffered violence in their households, 53 percent took no action and only slightly more than 17 percent filed a report..."[44] The majority of cases of violence against women were not reported, due to the deficient protection offered by the judicial system. Discrimination on the basis of sex and gender bias in the administration of justice grant impunity to these practices, perpetuating violence. Moreover, Bolivia is one of the countries in the region[45] whose laws violate the human rights of women. An example of that is the law that allows a rapist to avoid punishment by marrying the victim.[46]

Finally, it should be indicated that the poverty of these two groups (indigenous peoples and women) ends up causing segregation and exclusion. Since there is no adequate counsel and no free representation, the poor feel that they are unable to enforce their rights through the courts.

III. Conclusions and Recommendations

Public Security and Financing

So far, much has been invested and little has been obtained. This means that funds need to be directed toward the creation of comprehensive measures that identify the risk factors behind public insecurity. A true crime prevention plan needs to be designed in order to equate the cost of defense and national security with the benefit obtained by the citizenry.

In order to implement the National Public Security Plan, it is necessary to comply with the terms of Law 2494:

- Creation of the Public Security Solidarity Fund;
- Redirection of funds derived from the monetization of seized drug-trafficker property to finance the implementation of prevention programs and the rehabilitation of the drug-dependent population, within the framework of the public security strategy;
- Coordination with and attraction of funds from the international community for the activities of the public security plan (see Annex).

Public Security and Justice

In order to guarantee the success of the reforms, it is necessary to strengthen the connection between the justice system and the Comprehensive National Public Security Plan.

With respect to criminal law, modifications need to be made to the Penal Code to bring it in line with the new Code of Criminal Procedure and the introduction of oral adversarial proceedings (the "accusatory system") by, for instance, including newly defined crimes. It is also important to promote the training and assignment of a greater number of prosecutors from the Government Attorney's Office to investigate crimes that affect public security, in order to avoid the high number of crime reports that are rejected or that fail to be prosecuted.

The creation of the departmental security councils should be promoted along with application and implementation of the strategies and policies of the public security plan. Compliance with the country's legal system must not be further delayed. In this regard, it is essential for the executive branch and Congress to draft and approve the resolutions, measures, and regulations needed to grant sustainability, transparency, competency, efficiency, and funding to the public security policy.

Public Security and Prevention

More knowledge and information on crime in Bolivia is needed in order to disseminate information over the communications media and create suitable response mechanisms that can prevent an increase in violence and public insecurity. Civil society should be included in control and social prevention programs aimed at preventing crime.

Strengthen the Capacities of the Justice Sector

Better allocation of funds and logistic resources to the operators of the justice sector will enable them to respond properly to the population's demands for justice. The justice sector's professional aspects and administration of personnel (training and human resources) must both be strengthened. The process of selecting and evaluating judges needs to be conducted using transparent, equitable processes, in order to ensure the independence of the judiciary and counteract its reputation for corruption and excessive subordination. New courts need to be created and adequately distributed to cover the more than 40 percent deficit at the local level and shape the justice system to meet the demands and needs of the population. The system must be designed to meet the justice needs of the different population groups in recognition of their differences and cultural particularities.

Strengthening Community Justice

It is necessary to recognize and consolidate community justice in Bolivia, where a large part of the population is self-defined as indigenous and wishes to be governed by community justice. Civil society will play a vital role in conducting studies on traditional law in order to identify and incorporate the justice needs of the peasant and indigenous communities and then shape them into national legislation.

Training of the operators in charge of imparting community justice requires application of a methodology that values cultural particularities as it provides useful information that is easy to understand and apply in such jurisdictions. Training the operators on gender issues and domestic violence would enable them to contribute to effectively protecting the rights of women and children.

Communication Channels and Monitoring

Improving channels of communication with the population would make the justice system more transparent. The perception of law enforcement and the rule of law in Bolivia must improve. To accomplish that, adequate statistics and updated indicators must be available, so that the campaigns and reforms will be correctly targeted.

Civil society needs to participate in its role as an external supervision agent and undertake an ongoing commitment to monitor anticorruption practices, universal access to justice, and follow-through in the management of the justice system (and the reform projects). Reform of the judicial and security system will be a complex process, to be achieved through the coordinated action of various entities, with financial backing, political support, and supervision by civil society. The reform needs to be implemented "from the bottom up" with participation of the people, who would determine their own needs. It is suggested to first satisfy the immediate security needs of the common citizen, so that the grassroots of society will become a staunch ally in promoting judicial reform through participatory mechanisms.

Bibliography

Andersen, Lykke E. 2002. *Migración rural-urbana en Bolivia: ventajas y desventajas.* Instituto de Investigaciones Socio-Económicas of the Universidad Católica Boliviana. La Paz.

Aramayo, David. 2005. *Políticas de seguridad ciudadana y reforma policial en América Latina.* Presentation at the International Seminar entitled: *Políticas de Seguridad Ciudadana y policía en América Latina. Oportunidades y Desafíos.* October 12 and 13, 2005. Santa Cruz, Bolivia.

Arriagada, Irma. 2001. *Seguridad Ciudadana y Violencia en América Latina.* Available at: http://www.flacso.org.ec/docs/sfsegarriagada.pdf.

Ayres, Robert. L. 1998. "Crime and Violence as Development Issues in Latin America and the Caribbean," Report No. 17408. World Bank Latin American and Caribbean Studies. Washington, DC.

Ciudadanos Trabajando por la Justicia. 2005. *Evaluación presupuestaria del sistema judicial en el área penal urbana de las Cortes Superiores de Distrito de la Paz y Chuquisaca.* Available at: www.participacionyjusticia.org/paginas/ac_p_reciente1.php?id=23.

Claudio and Álvarez. 2005.

Dammert, Lucía. *2003. Participación comunitaria en prevención del delito en América Latina. Estudios de Desarrollo, Santiago de Chile.* Available at: www.policiaysociedad.org.

El Deber (newspaper). Friday, October 14, 2005. http://www.eldeber.com.bo/anteriores/20051014/seguridad_3.html.

Fundación Paz Ciudadana. 2005. *Seguridad Ciudadana y la Reforma Procesal Penal.* http://colegioabogados.org/ensayos/seguridad_ciudadana_y_rpp.pdf#search='seguridad%20ciudadana%20y%20la%20reforma%20procesal%20penal%20fundacion%20la%20paz%20ciudadana.

Fuentes, Claudio and Álvarez, David. *2005. América Latina en la Encrucijada. Factores de Riesgo en Inseguridad.* www.nuevasoc.org.ve/upload/articulos/3272/1.pdf.

Gaceta Transparencia. 2002. *Sistemas judiciales. Reforma y modernización judicial. Órgano Informativo del Poder Judicial* [Information Agency of the Judiciary]. Year 4, Volume No. Gestión 2002.

Government of Chile. 2002. *Percepción social de la delincuencia y seguridad ciudadana.* Serie Análisis No. 2 (June 2002). Ministry of the Interior, Division of Public Security.

Hernández Valiente, René. 2004. *Justicia y seguridad ciudadana.* Supreme Court of Justice of El Salvador.

Kaufmann, Daniel. *2005. Corrupción y reforma institucional: El poder de la evidencia empírica.* World Bank Institute. http://www.worldbank.org/wbi/governance.

Klisberg, Bernardo. 2002. *El crecimiento de la criminalidad en América Latina: un tema urgente.* Desarrollo del BID. Available at: http://www.lawlatin.com/zll/LLMain.asp?LL=1&LeyID=956.

Latinobarómetro, Corporación. 2005. *Informe Latino Barómetro 2005.* Santiago de Chile. www.latinobarometro.org.

Law on the National Public Security System: Law 2494. 2003.

Lovatón, David. 2005. *Justicia de Paz en los Andes. Revista IDL* No. 169, April 2005. www.idl.org.pe/idlrev/revistas/169/justicia.pdf.

Los Tiempos (newspaper). January 4, 2005. http://www.lostiempos.com/noticias/04-01-05/04_01_05_nac4.php.

———. Saturday, September 3, 2005. http://www.lostiempos.com/noticias/03-09-05/03_09_05_nac14.php.

Macías-Aymar, Íñigo. 2003. *Orígenes y razones de la pobreza en Bolivia.* Instituto Internacional de Gobernabilidad. Available at: http://www.iigov.org/dhial/?p=44_03.

Mendoza Cánepa, Raúl. 2005. *Presupuesto e Independencia Judicial.* Comisión Andina de Juristas. www.cajpe.org.pe/banners/texto/articulosdeopinion/htm.

Ministry of Foreign Relations. 2005. *Informe de Bolivia Sobre el Cumplimiento del Plan de Acción de Québec de 2001.* Ministry of Foreign Affairs, Summit Coordination Service.

Ministry of Sustainable Development and Planning. 2004. *Informe para la XXXII Asamblea de Delegadas de la Comisión Interamericana de la Mujer.* Vice Ministry on Women. La Paz, Bolivia.

———. 2005. *Proyecto de Reforma Institucional. Justicia Para Todos, Consolidación del Sistema Judicial.*

Montaño, Edgar, 1997. *Seguridad Ciudadana y Neo Liberalismo.* http://www.monografias.com/trabajos12/segciubol/segciubol.shtml.

Mullucundo, Eugenio. 2004. *Experiencia de Campo.* Position Paper of the Instituto de Defensa Legal. www.idl.org.pe/publicaciones/boletines/bol09.htm#JUSTICIA%20DE%20%PAZ%20EN%20BOLIVIA.

OCADEM-PE. 2005. *Monitoreo de la calidad de la administración de justicia en el área penal.* May 2005.

Rodríguez Veltzé, Eduardo. 2004. *Consolidación Institucional del Sistema Judicial.* Document: *Justicia para Todos, enero de 2004.* http://suprema.poderjudicial.gov.bo/.

———. 2005. *Discurso ante el acto de Apertura Solemne del Año Judicial 2005.* http://suprema.poderjudicial.gov.bo/justicia.htm.

Spanish International Cooperation Agency. 2003. *Programa de Justicia para el período 2003 – 2007.* http://www.aeci.int.bo/programas_proyectos.htm.

Transparency International. 2004. Corruption Perceptions Index 2005. http://www.transparency.org./cpi/2005.10.18.cpi.es.html.

UNDP. 2004. *Democracy in Latin America: Towards a Citizens' Democracy.* http://democraciaparticipativa.net/documentos/Democracy_in_Latin_America_New.pdf.

———. 2005. *Índice de Desarrollo Humano* (IDH) *2005* (Human Development Index - HDI). http://www.pnud.org.ec/.

Unidad Coordinadora Pueblos Indígenas en América Latina y el Caribe Estudio. 2004. *Estudio sobre la cooperación alemana con nacionalidades y organizaciones indígenas en Bolivia, Ecuador y Guatemala.* http://www2.gtz.de/indigenas/download/Fallstudie_Tomo_2.pdf.

USAID. 2005. Bolivia Country Strategic Plan (2005-2009). Drafted on February 22, 2005. http://www.dec.org/pdf_docs/PDACD586.pdf.

World Bank. 2003. *Resource Guide for Municipalities. Community Based Crime and Violence Prevention in Urban Latin America.* Department of Finance, Private Sector, and Infrastructure, Latin American Region. Washington, DC.:World Bank.

———. 2005. *Bolivia: Poverty Assessment.* Washington, DC.: World Bank.

Annex: Reform Initiatives of the Justice Sector and International Cooperation

The reforms implemented following the restoration of democracy in Bolivia sought to strengthen the institutionalization of the judiciary through changes in the selection of judges, separation of the Government Attorney's Office from the Executive Branch, and the creation of new entities such as the Constitutional Court, the Judicial Council, and the Ombudsman's Office. As of May 2001, these reforms also included implementation of the New Code of Criminal Procedure; this instituted oral adversarial criminal proceedings (the "accusatory system"), which reduced prosecution time in accordance with the principles of judicial economy and swiftness.

As part of the Quebec Plan of Action, entered into in 2001, the judiciary defined the course of the judicial reform for the short, medium, and long term. This process seeks to universalize access to justice in Bolivia and promote public security.

Similarly, with the aid of the international cooperation community, several studies have been conducted and projects have been implemented for institutional strengthening and reform to strengthen the independence of the judiciary and counteract the popular perception of corruption and excessive delays in the administration of justice.

The Bolivia Strategic Plan developed by USAID for the period of 2005-2009 includes the strategic objective of increasing confidence in democratic institutions and processes (USAID, 2005). One of its components is conflict management and resolution. Furthermore, the program framework for fiscal year 2005 contemplates financing technical assistance programs on access to justice[47] and on the supervision and monitoring by civil society of the judicial reform process.[48]

For the period of 2003-2007, the Spanish International Cooperation Agency, through its *Programa de Justicia* (Justice Program) seeks to support consolidation of the justice sector reforms (judicial and prosecutorial realms), which commenced in Bolivia with the constitutional reform of 1994 (Spanish International Cooperation Agency, 2003).

For its part, the Government Attorney's Office has the support of the German Agency for Technical Cooperation—Center for International Migration and Development (CIM/GTZ) to provide distance learning to prosecutors who are advocating criminal prosecution reform.[49] This training is important, because the change from the inquisitive system to the accusatory system called for a rethinking of the role of state-appointed counsel as the guarantor of due process. This change also involved a migration from written proceedings to a system in which oral proceedings dominate. In addition, all actions are public, so as to ensure the proper defense of the accused.

The Ombudsman's Office has the support of the Canadian International Development Agency (CIDA).[50] This aid seeks to consolidate management of the system for handling complaints, investigation procedures, and special programs for the protection of children, indigenous populations, and detainees.

During the 2004 court year for the Supreme Court of Justice, the final document of the ***Justicia para Todos*** **(Justice for All)** program was issued; it was merged into the executive branch through its Institutional Reform Program (PRI). This sets the course for a government policy whose objective is to facilitate effective access to justice for all citizens under conditions of equality. This proposal seeks to undertake a judicial reform that encompasses not only high-level entities, but also the grassroots of the justice service, that is, the entire community, which is the principal beneficiary of the justice system.

With respect to police reform, at least four reform plans have been presented over the past ten years, the last of which was undertaken on November 17, 2004, by former President Carlos Mesa.[51]

Endnotes

1. The Supreme Court of Justice is the highest court of ordinary jurisdiction for judicial and administrative matters, and has jurisdiction over the entire Bolivian territory. It is organized into specialized divisions for civil, criminal, social, mining, and administrative functions.

2. The Constitutional Court is the highest authority for control of the constitutionality of laws. It is the defender of the Constitution and the guarantor of fundamental rights. It hears reviews of Constitutional Relief Actions (*Amparo Constitucional*) and Writs of Habeas Corpus: it also reviews the constitutionality of treaties and of procedures to reform the Constitution.

3. The National Agrarian Court has jurisdiction to hear disputes over agrarian property possession and rights and is comprised by the National Agrarian Court and the Local Agrarian Courts. The creation of the National Agrarian Court is due to the diversity of land ownership regimens derived from the Agrarian Reform Act of 1953.

4. The Judicial Council is the administrative and disciplinary body of the Judiciary. It prepares and implements the annual budget of the Judiciary; oversees compliance with the Judiciary's goals, plans, and objectives; proposes candidates for judges at the trial-court, appellate, and high-court levels, attorney-notaries, and registrars of real property rights; and exercises disciplinary powers over trial-court and appellate judges and court officers. It oversees the Judiciary Institute (*Instituto de la Judicatura*), which is in charge of the training and education of judicial personnel.

5. Constitution of Bolivia: Article 171. III

The traditional authorities of the indigenous and peasant communities may exercise administrative functions and apply their own system as an alternative for the resolution of conflicts, in accordance with their customs and procedures, provided that the same are not contradictory to this Constitution or the law. The law shall harmonize these functions with the attributes of the branches of government.

6. Code of Criminal Procedure of Bolivia, Article 28 (community justice):

Criminal prosecution shall be terminated when the crime is committed within an indigenous peasant community by one of its members against another and the community's traditional authorities have resolved the conflict in accordance with their traditional indigenous law, provided that said resolution does not contradict the fundamental rights and guarantees of persons established by the Constitution of Bolivia.

The law shall harmonize the application of indigenous traditional law.

7. Claudio and Álvarez, 2005.

8. Public security is the right every person has to be protected by the State, through entities and institutions regulated by law, against threats or risks to his physical integrity, property, the enjoyment of his rights, or the performance of his obligations.

9. Law No. 2494 of August 4, 2003. Available at: www.mingobierno.gov.bo.

10. See http://www.mingobierno.gov.bo/vmripsc/dir_seg_ciu_plan_.htm

11. See *Sociedad.* "*Detalle Noticias*" section. "*Vecinos amenazan con justicia por manos propias.*" www.bolivia.com/noticias/autonoticias/DetalleNoticia4832.asp.

12. World Bank, 2003.

13. Arraigada, 2001.
14. Macías-Aymar, 2003.
15. According to the United Nations (UNDP, 2005), poverty affects almost 63 percent of Bolivians, which makes Bolivia the poorest country in South America. Approximately 14 percent of the population lives on a dollar a day, while 34 percent lives on two dollars a day.
16. Latinobarómetro, 2005: 63.
17. Law on the National Public Security System: Law 2494 (2003).
18. Aramayo, 2005.
19. Dammert, 2003.
20. Rodríguez Veltzé, 2004.
21. Transparency International, 2004.
22. Kaufmann, 2005.
23. Prefecture of the Department of La Paz. Public Security: www.prefecturalpz.gov.bo/SeegCiudad.asp (last visited on November 30, 2005).
24. Government of Chile, 2002: 182 *et seq.*
25. The *Observatorio de Seguridad y Democracia Bolivia* is a non-governmental institution associated with the postgraduate unit in Development Sciences (*Ciencias del Desarrollo* - CIDES) of the *Universidad Mayor de San Andrés.* Its principal objective is to contribute to developing the rule of law and the institutionalization of democracy. www.observatoriodeseguridad.org.bo.
26. Code of Criminal Procedure of Bolivia (March 25, 1999), Articles 298 *et seq.*
27. *Fundación Paz Ciudadana, 2005*; Hernández Valiente, 2004.
28. OCADEM-PE, 2005.
29. Latinobarómetro, 2005.
30. DPK—ECYT Study, 2002, *Justicia para Todos,* Ministry of Sustainable Development and Planning, 2004.
31. There are differences with respect to institutional makeup, geographic distribution, the composition of divisions and personnel, etc.
32. Interview with the Presiding Judge of the Constitutional Court, Justice Durán Ribera, on the "Al Filo" radio show. Radio Fides, September 10, 2005. http://prensa.tc.gov.bo/?p=15. The annual budget of the Constitutional Court is 23 million bolivianos (i.e., US$ 2,867,830).
33. According to an evaluation made by CIDA for the period of 2000-2005.
34. Aramayo, 2005.
35. From January to September 2005, the police dealt with 10,242 social protests, including marches, land squatting, and other demonstrations (*El Deber,* 2005).
36. Ministry of Sustainable Development and Planning, 2004: 30.
37. Ministry of Foreign Relations, 2005.
38. Aramayo, 2005.
39. Mullucundo, 2004.
40. Lovatón, 2005.
41. World Bank, 2005.
42. UNDP, 2004.

43. *Unidad Coordinadora Pueblos Indígenas en América Latina y el Caribe*, 2004.
44. Ministry of Sustainable Development and Planning, 2004.
45. Others are Uruguay, Guatemala, Costa Rica, Venezuela, Nicaragua, and Panama.
46. Article 317 of the Criminal Code of Bolivia establishes an exemption from criminal liability through subsequent marriage to the victim, provided that there is free consent and that the marriage takes place prior to final judgment.
47. USAID FY2005 Human Rights and Equal Access to Justice, Development Assistance for fiscal year 2005: US$ 640,000.
48. USAID FY2005 Human Rights and Equal Access to Justice, Economic Support Fund for fiscal year 2005: US$ 1,450,000.
49. Integrated Experts Program of the *Centrum für internationale Migration und Entwicklung* (CIM/GTZ).
50. CIDA Project No. 030422 for US$5 million. The project includes a strategic five-year plan with collaboration from the governments of Holland, Belgium, Sweden, Denmark, and Great Britain. The Ombudsman's Office has CIDA cooperation until the end of 2005.
51. www.pieb.org/contenido/ver_foto.php?cod_foto=20&id=640.